The Fighting Cocks

43 (Fighter) Squadron

Royal Flying Corps   Royal Air Force

1916 – 2009

JIMMY BEEDLE

With forewords by
Marshal of the Royal Air Force
Lord Douglas of Kirtleside GCB MC DFC
and
Air Chief Marshal Sir Simon Bryant
KCB CBE ADC MA CDir FCIPD RAF

Pen & Sword
AVIATION

First published in Great Britain in 1966,
with a second revised edition in 1985,
by Beaumont Aviation Literature, London

Published in this third revised and updated edition in 2011 by
PEN & SWORD AVIATION
an imprint of
Pen & Sword Books Ltd
47 Church Street
Barnsley
South Yorkshire
S70 2AS

ISBN: 978 1 84884 385 1

A CIP catalogue record for this book is available from
the British Library

Printed and bound in India by
Replika Press Pvt Ltd

Pen & Sword Books Ltd incorporates the imprints of:
Pen & Sword Aviation, Pen & Sword Maritime, Pen & Sword Military,
Wharncliffe Local History, Pen & Sword Select, Pen & Sword Military Classics,
Leo Cooper, Remember When, Seaforth Publishing and Frontline Publishing.

For a complete list of Pen & Sword titles please contact:
Pen & Sword Books Limited
47 Church Street, Barnsley, South Yorkshire, S70 2AS, England
E-mail: enquiries@pen-and-sword.co.uk
Website: www.pen-and-sword.co.uk

Contents

Major W Sholto Douglas MC, Royal Flying Corps

Foreword to first and second editions

MARSHAL OF THE ROYAL AIR FORCE
LORD DOUGLAS of KIRTLESIDE GCB MC DFC

I am happy to commend this history of one of the best-known squadrons of the Royal Air Force, one moreover which has special associations for me because I formed it in 1916 and led it into action on the Western Front in France in the following year. Ever since those early days 43 Squadron's record has been outstanding both in war and peace. The first to undertake ground-attack as a deliberate act in 1917 it was also the first to perform squadron aerobatics in tied-together formation. In the Second World War it fully maintained its high reputation, first with Fighter Command at home and afterwards in the Mediterranean theatre.

The first squadron to equip with the Hawker Hunter, it became as well known for its formation aerobatics with this aircraft as it had been a quarter of a century earlier with the biplane Fury. This is essentially a story of succeeding generations of men for whom duty to their country has been of paramount importance, greater, if needs be than life itself. For such men the history of 43 Squadron will, it is hoped prove an acceptable tribute.

Third Edition Acknowledgements

Alan Carlaw, Norman Franks and Wing Commander Andy Moir OBE MVO for their considerable research, editorial and production roles in the preparation of this third edition.

The many former members of the Squadron for their cheerful responses to continuing requests for information and reminiscences.

Most photographs and illustrations are from the 43 Squadron collection.
Permission to print photographs is acknowledged as under,
Flight International, Topix, Imperial War Museum,
Press Association Photos Ltd, MOD (RAF) Crown Copyright Reserved,
D C Thompson & Co Ltd, Time-Life International,
Portsmouth & Sunderland Newspapers Ltd, The Sun (News Group Newspapers),
Dugald Cameron, Alan Carlaw, Chris Golds, Gill Howie, Paul Lightbody, Roger Lindsay,
Barry Mayner, Roy McIntyre, Andy Moir, Mike Pugh, Andrew Rennie,
Andy Saunders, Berry Vissers (Squadron Prints Ltd), Alan Winkles.

Bibliography

Lord Balfour of Inchrye PC MC – An Airman Marches, Hutchinson 1933
Bill Pegg OBE – Sent Flying, Macdonald 1959
Lord Douglas of Kirtleside GCB MC DFC – Years of Combat, Collins 1963
John Rawlings – Fighter Squadrons of the RAF, Macdonald & Jane's Publishers Ltd 1976
Francis Mason – Hawker Hunter, Patrick Stephens Ltd 1985
James Halley – The Squadrons of the RAF & Commonwealth 1918-1988, Air Britain 1988
Peter R Foster – RAF Phantom, Ian Allan Ltd 1989
Steve Hazell – Warpaint Series No 31 Phantom, Hall Park Books Ltd 1992
Ken Delve – The Source Book of the RAF, Airlife 1994
Andy Saunders – No 43 'Fighting Cocks' Squadron, Osprey 2003
Roger Lindsay – Cold War Shield, Roger Lindsay 2009

Air Chief Marshal Sir Simon Bryant KCB CBE ADC MA BA CDir FCIPD RAF
C-in-C Air Command

Foreword to the Third Edition

AIR CHIEF MARSHAL
SIR SIMON BRYANT KCB CBE ADC MA CDir FCIPD RAF

By 2009 almost 25 years had passed since the second edition of 43 Fighter Squadron's history had been published. Much had occurred during this period, not least the end of 43's operations with the Phantom and its completion of 40 years' continuous service at RAF Leuchars. Most significantly, the period spanned the entire in-service life of the Tornado F3 with The Fighting Cocks, active service in three wars and the award of two Battle Honours, the first since 1944. It was therefore clear that a further revision was due and the 43 (Fighter) Squadron Association undertook to co-ordinate this task, securing the support of the publisher, Pen and Sword. Sadly the original author, Jimmy Beedle, had by then died, and so in deciding to produce this third edition of the history assistance was sought from elsewhere. Experienced aviation historian and author Norman Franks was approached and agreed to help. A former Commanding Officer, Wing Commander Andy Moir, provided support to Norman in a research and editorial capacity, acting as his point of contact with the Association. Those who had served on 43 Squadron during the preceding 25 years were contacted and invited to contribute their recollections. Many answered the call, notably former Chief Technician Jim Campbell who had served on the squadron continuously from 1992 to 2006 and Flight Lieutenant Roy Macintyre who completed three periods of duty with the squadron between 1986 and 2009. Both proved to be committed supporters of the project. Another association member, Alan Carlaw, who had served during Hunter days and had subsequently pursued a career in aviation art and publishing, was a rich source of advice and endeavour. His contribution to the new presentation and illustrations speaks for itself. The results of this dedicated team provide a more contemporary view of fighter operations and complete 43 Squadron's record of service since the early days of the Royal Flying Corps.

It was my privilege to fly the Phantom, to operate the Tornado F3 in my capacity as Squadron Commander of the Fighting Cocks and later to command RAF Leuchars. It follows that I have very strong ties, not just with the Fighting Cocks but with their operational base and the era covered by these new chapters. I congratulate the editorial team on their excellent work and am honoured to be associated with this important piece of RAF history.

"Ready for the Battle"

CHAPTER 1

Not as Other Men Are

'A gamecock stripped and armed for fight
Doth the rising sun affright.'
(WILLIAM BLAKE)

THE gamecock, or Indian bush bird, was referred to in the writings of Aristotle. It was introduced to Britain by the Romans and is therefore more British than most things that lay claim to that title. When trained for the cockpit it is a formidable adversary. It shows the normal healthy interest in the female of the species. Its manner and bearing are such that the verb 'to cock' means to hold up the head or to strut with a haughty and proud demeanour. All in all it was a most appropriate symbol to emblazon the banner of 43 Squadron in the Summer of 1939.

43 Squadron, the Fighting Cocks. Cocky by name and by nature, though not offensively so, for the cockiness was not a form of arrogance but the manifestation of an inward self-assurance, the outward display of what it knew to be true of itself; that it could do all things as well as anybody and do a great deal of them better than most. It was intensely proud of itself. In the universal order of things it might have given precedence to the Almighty but would have placed itself second. Grudgingly it might have admitted that No 1 Squadron, for fourteen years at Tangmere its greatest friend and deadliest rival, could on one of its better days just about be its equal. But that was all. The rest of the field was nowhere.

The Squadron possessed a tribal war chant that was peculiar to itself:

We'll defend your blue skies, over land and sea,
Through shot and shell we'll fight like hell
And merry men are we...

It was known in the Unicorn and the Nag's Head in Chichester. In messes and canteens at Tangmere it was roared forth, most often short of musical refinement but never lacking in spirit.

So if you go to Sussex, whoever you may be,
You can tell them all that we'll fight or fall
In the Fighting Forty-Three.

If primarily a song to be sung when the ale was flowing it possessed more sober overtones for it was a declaration of the Squadron's confidence in itself to take on anything that might be thrown at it.

And in the Summer of 1939 there were few who were not convinced that very soon the blue skies would need defending, for if the politicians in public refused to admit the inevitability of war, not many were to be found to share their apparent optimism. The rape of the rump of Czechoslovakia in the Spring had swept away for ever the weak aspirations and feeble hopes, born of Munich, that it was possible to deal with Hitler using the normal standards of reason and decency. With Slovakia digested it was becoming only too plain for any that had eyes to see that the dark storm clouds building over the corridor at Danzig were due soon to burst and bring in their wake the drenching necessity of declaring that at last the point had been reached beyond which the demands of honour, and the requirements for self survival alike, necessitated that one dare not retreat. Come circumstances as they might, it was time to cry 'Enough'.

So, 43 Squadron girded its loins; which in post-biblical terms might be translated roughly as saying that it continued to belt up its ammunition, practised its Fighter Area Attacks, formated and aerobatted, and awaited the outcome of events which it could not control but which assuredly would affect its destiny. Its strength was triple based. It had men, it had machines, and it had its tradition. In the ultimate analysis those who did not understand such things might have failed to comprehend that the last of these three parts was of any great importance. Pilots and mechanics and Hawker Hurricanes could be seen and their worth assessed but it was less easy to give credence to the notion that 'tradition', so often misunderstood and misapplied in service life, too often made an excuse for the survival of anachronistic nonsense which had lost all meaning, had very much to offer. But to 43 Squadron, tradition meant precisely what it was supposed to mean; an inbred acceptance of custom, habit, and action handed on by other men who in other days had done things extraordinarily well. In September 1939 (as at every other period before or since) the men of 43 Squadron were not merely themselves, nor the Squadron the sum only of their individual strengths. For the men were also the descendants, in Service lineage, of those who in 1917 had turned their guns on to ground targets and inaugurated a new method of air support. They followed along after those who at Hendon and elsewhere during the twenties and thirties had made the black and white chequers on Gamecock, Siskin and Fury alike a sign of high endeavour and a mark of great achievement. They had tied their Siskins together and aero-batted in formation, which nobody had then ever done before, and on less formal occasions, and not always completely in accord with King's Regulations, they might for a diversion fly their Furies through the Arundel Gap, low down, off the clock at 260 mph! Except on Monday when the Flight Commander forbade it for fear that somebody would bring home the washing wrapped round the undercarriage!

And so a way of life had been evolved and to be posted to 43 Squadron was not merely to join a fighter squadron; but it was to become one of a company of men who did everything supremely well, just because it had been like that so long that nobody knew of any other way. It was habitual and customary to be like that in 43, it was the traditional way of getting on with the job.

Of the men who got on with the job and of the tools with which they did it, it might be said neither quite matched the popular image projected to the country at large by some sections of the national Press. For instance, the Hawker Hurricane, on the strength of a solitary flight from Edinburgh to London, had been hailed as a 400 mph fighter, and that such a conclusion quite disregarded the effect of an 80 mph north-easterly gale was not permitted by Fleet Street to spoil a good story. In a like manner, a Sunday paper had carried an article on a race of supermen which the RAF was allegedly nurturing, a breed of young, dedicated heroes, abstemious in all things and who, with faces turned firmly from the vices of alcohol and tobacco, could alone acquire the exceptional standards of physical perfection which would enable the human frame to withstand the enormous stress and strain to which the super fighters would subject them.

Odd pictures indeed, not truly reflecting reality. Of course, the Hurricane was basically an excellent aircraft. Compared with the Fury biplane with which 43 had stood to at the time of the Munich crisis it positively dazzled. A nominal maximum speed of 320 mph was 100 mph better and the eight gun armament outnumbered the Fury by four to one in numbers and six to one in weight of fire. It was immensely strong (the mainplanes were stressed for 14G) and though not as fast as a Spitfire or the Messerschmitt 109 yet it had advantages in manoeuvrability, steadiness as a gun platform and all round visibility that made it capable of holding its own in such company. It could not catch a 109 that had decided to run, but as one famous Hurricane pilot afterwards wrote, 'that was not the object of the exercise'. It was, initially, deficient in items that affected its efficiency as a weapon of war, some plain to see, others less so for what one had never had was never missed. Obvious shortcomings were an unheated pitot head and an absence of warm air supply to the gun bays in the wings, which meant that in certain unfavourable weather conditions the airspeed indicator was liable to malfunction and the guns would freeze and fail to fire after a short period in excess of 15,000 feet. Modifications to obviate these troubles were embodied soon after of the outbreak of war.

Because nobody had ever thought much about it, there was less awareness of the complete absence of armour plating protection for the pilots or the absence of self-sealing fuel tanks. Armour plating was fitted early in October by fitters from the Hawker factory and the self-sealing tank had become almost universal by the Spring of 1940, although not completely and more than one pilot suffered thereby.

Lastly there was the two-bladed wooden propeller (or airscrew, as official technical nomenclature insisted in those days, until, so the story goes, a request for twenty replacement air-screws resulted in the despatch of twenty aircrews whereupon the Air Ministry cast its references to 'airscrews' away forever and replaced them with 'propellers'!).

The need for a constant speed, or at least a two-pitch replacement, was recognised by higher authority but their provision had been prevented by lack of money forthcoming from the peace time Treasury.

The fixed-pitch wooden propellor gave a sluggish take-off and initial climb, and the effect on overall performance was such that in the first combat report from 43 a pilot went on to record that 'his rate of climb' (near sea level) 'was at all times inferior to the enemy aircraft'. And the e/a was a Heinkel 111 bomber!

But for all the failure to equal its potential performance the Hurricane was still a potent weapon in the hands of a resolute and competent pilot, and there were more than a few of these to be found in and around the Pilots' Room. A diverse assembly, they had come from far and from near; from Southampton and South Africa, Somerset and Saskatchewan. Commissioned and otherwise, of short or long service, regular and volunteer reserve, none was bad though some were better than others. Among them were a few destined to survive all the ill chances of war and to finish ranked high among the great and the famous, others whose names all too soon were to be rubbed off the Ops Board. Some of high skill and experience and wise in the ways of flying men, others as yet only reaching out for such heights, they were a goodly company.

Behind, or beneath, at any rate very much in support of them was the technical organisation. Administratively the Squadron had all but converted to a new system whereby the skilled tradesmen were grouped in a Maintenance Flight and carried out periodical inspection and repair, leaving simple routine servicing and refuelling to be done by semi-skilled Flight Mechanics in A and B Flights.

Joining the parts together, very much in command of everything and everybody, was Squadron Leader R E Bain. Dicky Bain was small in stature but loomed mighty big in most other things, ruling the Squadron with an authoritative fist, patrolling its precincts with eyes that swept in sixteen different directions at once, seeking for fools whom he might devour. If he were sighted walking the forty paces from the Squadron Admin block to the back door of the hangar, then the caveat of 'the old man's coming' resulted in a melting away of those on the hangar floor before he had reached the door, an action based on the sure principle that to be invisible was the only way of not incurring his wrath. Many of his idiosyncrasies, such as his method of dismissing the Squadron from parade, 'Officers and gentlemen, fall out, Other Ranks, to the left, DISMISS', would have provided copious ammunition for the Arnold Weskers of this world, but such apparent example of arrogance, browbeating subordinated serfs, could not have been farther removed from actuality. Too often those who enter (mostly at a profit to themselves) violent protest on behalf of an alleged down-trodden caste merely display their own failure to comprehend the real position. And indeed the barking and dictating produced no festering of mutinous thought, for 43 Squadron possessed no 'them' and 'us' but only the collective 'we' of a single team in which some gave orders and some took them: some midway up the ladder did both. That was the way things had to be if anarchy and resultant chaos were to be excluded. But essentially everybody mattered, for everybody was an equally important part of the machine without which it could not tick; and if anybody regardless of their greater or lesser superiority failed then the whole thing suffered. And in 43 Squadron that was not allowed to happen because it was 43's way of doing things that it did not. It was its custom and habit; it was in the tradition, and it had all begun a long long time ago.

CHAPTER 2

First Faltering Steps

'Raged the full contest far and wide
Then was the strength of Douglas tried'.
(Lord of the Isles – SCOTT)

43 **SQUADRON'S** beginning was on the ancient tilting ground at the foot of the castle at Stirling. The field is now covered by a housing estate and children chalk hopscotch boxes or dodge the police to play football in the street where once the primitive machines wobbled uncertainly into the air.

No doubt they know nothing of the little bit of history that surrounds them. Like many Scots their knowledge of that subject probably begins and ends with the battle that once was fought beside the winding Bannock Burn, two miles to the south of the castle, when at the crossroads of national destiny Scotland stood and broke the invading English army.

Captain W Sholto Douglas MC

Foremost among the lieutenants of Robert the Bruce on that fateful day was a Douglas; Sir James, baron from the south western borders, a 'will-o-the wisp who had harried the English for many years', of whom men said 'the maist coward, stouter he made than a leopard'.

Six hundred and two years on from the age of Scotland's triumph, another Douglas, not yet then as illustrious if destined to become so, arrived at the field beneath the castle walls, first Commanding Officer, first member of the as yet non-existent 43rd Squadron of the Royal Flying Corps.

Captain William Sholto Douglas, although

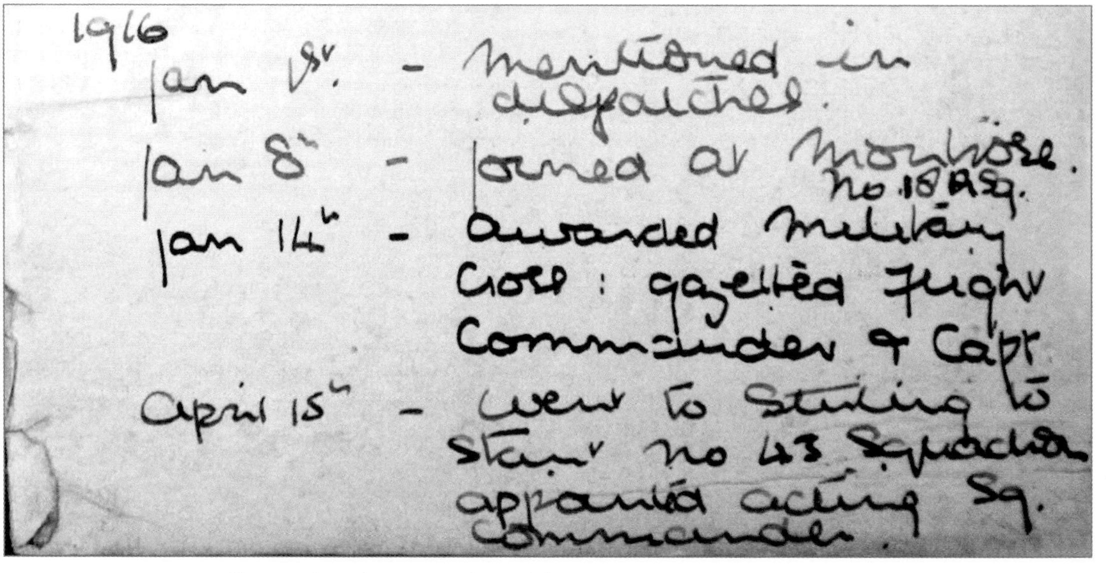

1916
Jan 1st. - mentioned in despatches.
Jan 8th - joined at Montrose. No 18 R.Sq.
Jan 14th - awarded Military Cross: gazetted Flight Commander & Capt
April 15th - went to Stirling to start No 43 Squadron appointed acting Sq. Commander.

Extract from lower section of the summary page for 1916 of Captain Sholto Douglas's Flying Log Book.
Of particular note is the entry for April 15th –
"went to Stirling to start No 43 Squadron, appointed acting Sq. Commander."

Falleninch Farm with Bristol BE 2s and the farmer's family (1)

only twenty-two, already had experience of combat in the air over the Western Front. Thereafter, posted to Home Establishment he was with No 18 (Reserve) Squadron at Montrose when ordered to proceed with a nucleus of mechanics and motor transport from this unit to Stirling. From the Stirling depot of the Argyll and Sutherland Highlanders there came an Adjutant, or as it was then called, Recording Officer, one Lt Tom Purdey. He remained in that position for two and a half years. 'An ebullient, noticeably cheerful character, universally popular, his short plump figure, invariably clad in a kilt' was to be a continuing welcome sight around the Squadron during its entire wartime life. 'The best comrade any man could wish for' was what Captain Balfour said of him, expressing a universal opinion in doing so. During the early stumbling, chaotic, days of its lifetime, during later days of great stress and heavy loss, Thomas Purdey presented to 43 an example of devoted service that was not easily bettered.

The first MT vehicle, a Leyland repair lorry, arrived on 22 April. Another month passed before the first aeroplane arrived, a BE 2c which Captain Douglas borrowed. Four days later an Armstrong Whitworth FK 3 arrived, the first machine allotted to the Squadron.

By the middle of June 43 had three flight commanders, Lieutenants A Lees, G M V Bidie, and C Liddle, eight aeroplanes and a bunch of raw pilots straight from elementary training school. And the CO had his orders to get the Squadron trained to a standard fit to take to France before the year is out.

At the end of August after training a nucleus of the newly formed No 63 Squadron, 43 left its collection of Avros, Armstrong Whitworth FK 3s and BEs to the rookies and went to Netheravon on Salisbury Plain. Here the intention was to equip it with the Sopwith 1½ Strutter before it left for France. In October Major Douglas went to France to gain experience with No 70 Squadron, the first to operate the 1½ Strutter. When he returned he found that all of his nine trained pilots had been posted and within another fortnight his three Flight Commanders, Captains A Lees, J C Russell and W V Strugnell were taken over by No 54 Squadron. The last named of the three later destroyed the first enemy machine claimed by No 54.

Many weeks of frustration and discontent for Douglas followed. As fast as his new pilots began to acquire some experience they were taken away to reinforce the squadrons in France. Nor was there any sign of the promised Sopwiths until one finally turned up on 4 December. Then things happened quickly. A move to Northolt on 8 December was followed at last by a steady stream of the 1½ Strutters and by the end of the first week in January, twenty-three were on charge. Major Douglas however was still entitled to complain that 'too much time

(1) This view was taken in 1916 by Mark Bennett, a local photographer, and shows the scene during the early days of the establishment of this military airfield. During the First World War the Stirling area was one giant military training camp. Many local buildings were requisitioned and hutted and tented accommodation was erected in many places throughout the district. Up to 11,000 servicemen were stationed here and this provided a vast pool of trainees for the fledging Royal Flying Corps. No 43 Squadron formed at Falleninch on 16 April 1916. (Source: 43 Squadron RFC Diary)

First known photograph of Major Douglas in a BE 2 at Stirling, 1915

was wasted in getting all our equipment and again and again he was robbed of his aircrews'.

Surviving all these impediments the Squadron finally readied itself to leave on 16 January. A hundred and more ground crews departed via the Metropolitan Line, Waterloo, Southampton, and Le Havre. The pilots took off on 17 January for a direct and (theoretically) a much quicker route to St Omer. None of them arrived that day. The deputy Commander of 'B' Flight stalled and crashed on take-off, killing himself and his observer as well as Captain Balfour's small dog which was stowed aboard in a sack. Captain Scott led this flight down the

A Sopwith 1½ Strutter

Thames, coming down below the cloudbase, which, that day, necessitated flying below the level of the windows of Adastral House on the Embankment. Lt Harold Ward who was flying in the rear cockpit of Major Douglas's machine, which landed and stayed overnight at Lympne, maintains that it took them a week before they arrived at the aerodrome at Treizennes, which was the ultimate destination for the Squadron. 'Lousy weather, engines conking out and just getting lost' were three reasons he gave. By the latter date, though, the whole unit was duly assembled and ready to begin work. It shared the aerodrome with No 40 Squadron. It formed part of the 10th Wing, which already included No 70 Squadron with aeroplanes similar to 43's, the idea being to minimise the chance of the Germans realising that a new unit had arrived.

The 1½ Strutter was so named by reason of the struts which, in addition to a central cabane structure ran outwards from the top longerons to the top wing spars. The first British aeroplane to have a gun (Vickers) synchronised to fire through the propeller, the first to have an adjustable incidence tailplane, and also fitted with flaps on the lower mainplane inboard trailing edge, the 1½ Strutter had been on its inception a very handy and effective weapon. It

Training with Bristol Scouts and BE 2s at Falleninch, Stirling 1916. The Scout 'D' was designed by Frank, one of the Barnwell brothers from Stirling, who became Bristol's chief engineer

(from a painting by Dugald Cameron)

gave the pilot a good view, the observer had a full field of fire for his Lewis gun, and with a 110 hp (later 130 hp) Clerget engine its performance up to 10,000 feet was good. Above that, as with all rotary engines it became rapidly less effective. It had structural weaknesses and some alleged that 140 mph was a sufficiently high terminal velocity; anything more would pull off the top wing. 'Rather fragile, broke up if clumsily handled' was the diplomatic way Major Douglas expressed it.

During the Summer and Autumn of 1916 the '1½' had given excellent service and played its part in establishing the complete supremacy then enjoyed by the RFC over the Western Front, but by the time 43 arrived it was past its prime and was out-performed by the new German Albatros and Halberstadt Scouts. Thus, in its capacity as a long-range strategical reconnaissance squadron, the outlook for 43 Squadron was not bright. It was as well that there were stout hearts to meet the dangers and hardships that were to come.

Foremost among them was that remarkable man, Captain Jack Scott. Old for a pilot by the standards of those times (he was in his middle thirties), he had survived a very bad crash early in the war which had broken both of his legs so that he still could walk only with the help of sticks. No disability however was allowed to stand in his way and though he had to be lifted into and out of the cockpit he cajoled and intimidated higher authority successfully to get himself posted to 43 before it went overseas. 'Always cheerful and imperturbable, and charming in his manner towards everybody . . . we all came to such a warm admiration of him, and his way of doing things,' said Major Douglas. Jack Scott was the first man in the Squadron to get involved with the enemy. After only a few days on operations he returned to Treizennes with his aeroplane completely riddled with bullets. The instruments and gun sight in front of him were wholly destroyed but he was himself untouched. It was, unfortunately for 43, not long before Scott was sent to command No 60 Squadron. His subsequent career remained on the same high plane. His premature death after the war, brought on by a bout of pneumonia contracted as a result of his insisting on returning to duty when not fully fit, robbed the young Air Force of a potential Chief of the Air Staff. At least that was the opinion of more than one person best qualified to judge. In a tribute to his memory, the late Lord Birkenhead wrote : 'a more constant heart never beat for those whom he loved, nor a more valiant one for England. May his brave spirit rest in peace'.

Of such calibre was one of the few who guided the first faltering steps of the infant 43 along the rough killing paths of war. It was as well that it had such men for the losses in the early weeks and months were appalling. With an initial establishment of thirty-two pilots and observers it sustained thirty-five casualties in April alone, and by the end of the month only six of the original crews remained. Inferior aircraft, inexperience and wrong tactics all contributed to the sad results.

'Nearly every day,' wrote Major Douglas, 'somebody was wounded or missing.' At first the Sopwiths had gone out singly or in pairs to make their reconnaissance flights. The Germans were very often to be seen before the lines were crossed, mostly in strength, for it was about this time that the Richthofen Circus became a feature of the air war pattern. If their practice of flying in large numbers meant that there was less likelihood of being intercepted it also ensured that one would be vastly outnumbered on the occasions when the enemy was met with.

Captain Harold Balfour in his book *An Airman Marches* has given, from first hand experience, as good a description of the life-and-death nature of the struggle as may ever be written. As the following long extract will show:

"Our usual work was offensive patrols somewhere about five or six miles over the

Captain Harold Harrington Balfour MC and Bar
OC 'B' Flight and later OC 'A' Flight

German lines and then up and down. Obsolete and structurally weak as our Sopwith two-seaters were for the requirements of aerial fighting against the D III and D V German Albatroses, our casualties were heavy. We used to cross the lines at 9,000 to 12,000 feet, but long before we got there we could see waiting for us these German scouts.

It only needed a few days of experience for us to know that we were up against Richthofen's famous circus. From afar off we would watch these gaily painted Albatroses gambolling around each other and about the sky as we crossed the lines. They would be over Lens, looping and rolling and spinning, just like puppies playing with each other; but directly we got near our objective away they would swoop into the sun only to wait for the propitious moment in which to come headlong down on top of our formation. Very often we used to follow above and behind the FEs, but it was always we whom they came down on first. After some weeks we learnt the best tactics. As soon as ever we saw them and before they could dive on us, we would go round and round in a circle, the whole formation of us, each one chasing the next machine in front, until we had formed a big revolving wheel. The wheel would then edge slowly towards the lines and woe betide any German who dared to come down on top of that circle. He would get the concentrated fire of six observers' guns, and, brave fighters as they were, no German could face that with impunity. But equally, woe betide any one of our machines who got out of the circle. I saw this happen twice. On the first occasion the wings were shot off a machine in front of me and one of my best young pilots, a South African named Charles Rimer, and his observer were pitched out into space as the machine disintegrated. I watched Rimer's bright leather coat as his body fell towards the earth. I could follow it for thousands of feet. The other occasion I think the pilot must have suffered from engine trouble and have been forced to leave the circle. His petrol tank must have been punctured and the aeroplane soaked with petrol, when an incendiary bullet struck it, for, one moment it was gliding away from the wheel and the next it was a mass of flames from wing tip to wing tip. At this time I received from America a photograph of von Richthofen's study, decorated with relics from his victims' aircraft. Prominent on the wall was the number A1108 on the rudder of little Green of 'A' Flight's Sopwith shot down a few weeks previously.

We had some thirty-two officers in our Squadron, pilots and officers. During February, March and April, we suffered heavy casualties and in one of those months we had thirty-five casualties out of our establishment of thirty-two officers. There are some moments and crises in life which are photographed on the mind clearly, and for always, from their shortness, their horror and their vividness. Such a photograph do I carry of one fight in March 1917. We had had to take some camera views of the Hindenburg line behind Lens, and, for the job, we had six Sopwith two-seaters and below us six FEs. All the time we had been over our objectives we had seen the Germans gathering above us between ourselves and the safety of the lines. Finally, putting our noses down, we streaked for home but were intercepted. It was almost at the beginning of the fight that I looked at the machine directly on my left and above me. As leader of the formation of Sopwiths I had put this machine close to me on my left in order that it could have some protection from myself from the front and by the other machine, above and behind it, from the rear. So heavy had been our casualties that the observer of this machine had only joined the Squadron from a Canadian Infantry unit the night before. He knew how to handle a machine-gun. He had only been up in the air once in his life, but eagerly he had volunteered for the first flight next morning. I knew how short-handed we were and that the alternative was one of our trained mechanics who would probably be wanted for some job on a machine being repaired at the aerodrome. I suppose that this Canadian lad did not realise the swiftness of aerial combat, perhaps his strange environment had robbed him of the power of swift action; perhaps he had been hit and rendered helpless, for as I looked to the left where his aeroplane was flying some twenty yards away and parallel to me, I saw that the fabric of the fuselage appeared to have become unlaced and was flapping in the air, while something which looked like yellow straw was gathered around the bottom of the petrol tank, the end of which was exposed to me, being placed between the pilot and the observer. As I looked the straw moved and I realised that what I saw was the fabric ripped up by a bullet which had entered the petrol tank, and that the fuel was on fire. All this can only have taken a fraction of a second, but I shall always see that observer standing up, motionless, looking back over the tail of his machine. And then he turned, looked down, and tapped the pilot on the shoulder. I suppose he was indicating to him what had happened. I saw no more for at that moment, where the ground had been, the sky appeared and where a second before had been bright blue was the scarred brown earth of the trenches; for an Albatros came down with a swoop on my tail, my observer fired and I heard the crack of the enemy bullets as I pulled the Sopwith two-seater over on to its back and kicked on full rudder in order to slip out of my unpleasant position. I had no time to see more except something which looked like a burning piece of paper very far below me, plunging down to earth. A few days later the Germans dropped a message saying that all they could find was a Toronto tailor's tab on the back of a charred coat. So perished a very gallant Canadian, a good pilot and an obsolete aeroplane.

This period was the one in which I first realised the full terror of aerial combat, but, at the same time, learnt in some way to cultivate a detachment of mind which enabled one, not to overcome fear but to separate oneself from it. Going into a fight, after some mental practice of attaining this state of mind, was something like going into a cold bath; but once in the fight one became impersonal: some secondary person did the right thing at the right moment; this secondary being took the initiative and would do some brave act or some clever manoeuvre; it was not oneself, for one's own self could watch this secondary being in operation. The trying and exhausting time was when at the end of the fight one's personality displaced once more this secondary being and took charge of one's body; then would be realised the full terror, then would hands and feet shake and mouth go dry with fear and the full reaction set in. This secondary being detachment was the only means that kept one going. I have often wondered if any of my fellow pilots felt the same, but in those days such thoughts were too sacred and too intimate to bring to light. Each of us had such secrets closely guarded and treasured. I do not think the way in which we were made to go to the same place at the same time every day, so that at this hour the German scouts could always expect our arrival, was worth the achievement of moral ascendancy, which was its object, when compared to its cost in life. General Trenchard himself came to the Squadron just when our losses were at their worst and told us to stick it and that we should have to continue to suffer casualties, but that at all costs we must maintain, if not an actual, at any rate the moral ascendancy by keeping our daily task of offensive patrols well over the enemy lines; even though these patrols had to be in aircraft inferior to those of the Germans. Looking back now, this policy was rather akin to that of aerial attrition and the survival of the side with the maximum airman power. Our air policy may have achieved what was desired, but I believe that it could have been done in a more cunning way, with more of an element of surprise, and so at a lighter cost.

We did have one attempt at originality by copying the French, who used to pursue the tactics of sending one lone aircraft over the German line at some unexpected hour and so high that it could only be caught up after a long climb by the German scouts, and by which time it could have reached its objective, made its reconnaissance, or taken photographs, and be safely on the way home. The only objection to our employing these tactics was that whereas the French were allowed to lighten their aeroplanes and throw away useless gear in order to achieve a higher ceiling, when we tried this, and I was the pilot selected for the first of these lone attempts, our aeroplanes were so laden with bomb racks, cameras and other paraphernalia that the height at which I could cross the line was well within an easy climb for the enemy scouts. I was detailed to go nearly to Douai, then take photographs of the German defensive back line up to Izel. I got there and got back thanks more to good luck than anything else, chased by about six Huns who would take turn and turn about to dive on my tail. My observer was officially confirmed to have shot down one of the enemy, and perhaps this held the others back, but I pursued firmly the policy that James McCudden, who brought down some seventy Germans and won the VC, DSO, MC and the Legion of Honour, once gave to me as good fighting advice:

He who fights and runs away
lives to fight another day.

But the next day we had to get those photographs, and this time with eight machines. We managed to carry out our orders and obtain a most successful set without any casualties by doing the job at dawn, and not at our regular patrol time. Our early unpunctuality surprised the Germans to such a degree that we were allowed to escape unattacked."

There are also some reports from 'the other side of the hill' about these early combats and the diaries of the great Richthofen record that the inexperience of the crews of the (43 Squadron) aircraft he attacked on 4 March was doubly evident. Not only was he on them before he was detected but even after firing several bursts the pilot of the machine he was attacking held a steady course. When it finally banked violently away a wing broke off and the machine disintegrated, 'only the Lewis guns Nos 17500 and 20024 were salvageable'. This last statement is rather typical of the spirit and outlook of Richthofen. Every victory that failed to yield some trophy for his collection was less than satisfying to him. Another aspect of his character, suggesting that the lust for the kill was the most important motivating factor in his mind was shown in another combat with 43 Squadron on 2 April. Six Sopwiths endeavouring to protect some BE 2cs, and much hindered by heavy clouds from so doing were themselves set upon by five enemy scouts, three of them piloted by Richthofen, his brother Lothar and Voss. One of the Germans attacking the Sopwith piloted by 2nd Lt de Berigny was shot down in flames by his observer Air Mechanic Second Class Bowen. He had previously emptied a drum from his Lewis gun at Richthofen who was himself concentrating on the aircraft at the end of the formation flown by 2nd Lt Warren, whose observer Sgt Dunn was mortally wounded by the first burst of fire from the German. Warren dived away towards cloud which proved to be too thin to be of help and a second and third burst smashed the instrument panel, stopped the engine, hit the fuel tank and cut the cartridge belt of the front firing Vickers gun. The elevator controls were damaged which made even gliding difficult but as the stricken Sopwith floated down towards the earth Richthofen continued to attack and ripped both the shoes and sleeves of the pilot without, miraculously, wounding him. Of such incidents, Capt Balfour wrote, "a wonder I have never solved in so many cases where it seems a Divine Providence allowed the bullets to go everywhere except in that small space that held the pilot's body".

2nd Lt Peter Warren

Providence or otherwise Lt Warren executed a crash-landing that caused little further damage to the aeroplane, and attempted to assist the badly wounded Sergeant Dunn. As he did so he was again fired on by Richthofen who subsequently excused himself by claiming that 'he had been hit by several shots fired from the enemy machine, as he flew low over it and returned the fire, killing one of the occupants. The truth was that 2nd Lt Warren was far too concerned with his injured observer, who died shortly afterwards, to have either the desire or the opportunity to fire at Richtofen. So much for the latter's 'gallantry'.

A third 1½ Strutter to fall to Richthofen went down only six days after this previous encounter. After an opening burst which disabled the observer the Sopwith went into a steep. and apparently uncontrolled dive. Richthofen continued to fire and finally saw the aircraft crash heavily into the ground. He was most amazed to find, later, that the pilot, Lt J S Heagerty had survived the crash although his observer Lt L H Cantle was killed, his body being found a week later when advancing British troops overran the site of the wrecked aeroplane.

The dangers which beset the airmen in these days did not all emanate from the enemy. Flying machines be it remembered were still incredibly unreliable at the best. Leaving aside extraordinary risks, like the seizure of twelve engines (out of fourteen) in two days after Headquarters Equipment Branch had insisted on the use of a pharmaceutical oil in lieu of the normal castor oil lubricants, a forced landing was no unusual occurrence. The log book of Lt Harold Ward for the first eight weeks of the Squadron's action is highly informative. After a first quiet week comes an entry 'Archie pretty good, some holes'. Four days later, 'brought down by AA; rudder controls shot away, crashed at Mearis, pilot (Lt T Edelston) wounded. Fini 1107.' After some days of gales, snowstorms, low cloud and rain, and one or two uneventful photographic flights there comes, '27 February; Patrol, crashed. 2 March; Patrol, crashed. 4 March; Patrol, two hours thirty minutes. 6 March; Patrol, Lens, Scrap. Lost four men.' And so until the 16th when, 'Patrol, Lens, two hours, fought nine Huns. Brought one down.' This was in fact a very fine effort on the part of Lt Ward, his pilot Lt Kitto and another crew Lts McClatchie and Burnand. These four men, all that was left after four accompanying 1½ Strutters went home with engine

Lieutenant John S Heagerty

trouble, joined the six FE 2bs of 25 Squadron for an offensive patrol. Attacked by first eight, then sixteen, enemy scouts the RFC crews destroyed four of their opponents for the loss of one man killed, three others wounded and three forced landings on the right side of the lines.

On the following day another mixed force from 43 and 25 Squadrons went out to escort a photographic flight of three FE 2bs. The entry in Lt Ward's log book, the last with 43 Squadron says, "met the 'Circus' twenty-one Huns, shot down two, wounded through wrist, leg and foot. Landed Treizenne OK. Went to 51 CCS." With such terseness and brevity were the brave deeds of those times modestly recorded.

In the battle that day three enemy machines were 'crashed', three others, in the terminology of the time, 'driven down'. One FE from 25 Squadron, and two Sopwiths from 43 were lost. The 43 crews, 2nd Lts Rimer, Lownds, Constable and Knox were all killed. The final sentence in the official history on this action reads: 'The hostile machines were all dispersed; our camera machines continued their photographing, the escort continued their patrol'.

'Bloody April' was the epithet given by the RFC to that month of 1917 but in fact the time during which they had to fight under such difficulties in inferior machines was not confined to that single four-week period. The Sopwith triplanes and Camels, the DH 4s and the SE 5s which were to redress the adverse balance were only just coming forth in quantity. Until they arrived there was nothing to be done except get on with the task allocated for the morrow.

Every night a sealed envelope came from Wing HQ carrying the orders for the next day. 'It usually managed to arrive halfway through dinner. Somehow food lost its attraction and spirits sank for an appreciable time after we knew the contents of that envelope.' So wrote Captain Balfour who, during a short period at the end of April in which 43 lost some of its finest crews, was himself put out of action. Flying north to south along the crest of the Vimy Ridge Captain Balfour became so interested in watching the shell bursts and the infantry crouching in the remains of their trenches that he quite failed to realise for a while that the wind had drifted him eastwards. When he turned to correct the error and to regain his patrol area he was fired at by machine-guns and rifles on the ground. Zig-zagging his machine he dodged most of the fire apart from a few holes that appeared in the wings until suddenly there was a harsh metallic clang and the engine and propeller stopped dead. There was nothing to do but glide for the front lines, hoping that he was not hit again en route, and trust that he would crash on the right side. As he approached the ground he recalled a discussion in the mess a few days earlier as to whether or not it was best to remain strapped in when crashing. Balfour had been of the opinion that it was best to stay strapped in but the majority had disagreed with him. As he dropped the last two hundred feet he decided to go with the majority and released his straps. Whereby he certainly saved his own life. As the aircraft stalled in from twenty feet and tipped over the edge of a mine crater Balfour was thrown through the narrow triangle formed by the centre section struts, and head first into the mud, quite uninjured. As he was ejected thus from the front seat the engine smashed back into the space his legs had just cleared. Balfour was laid out by the impact, his observer who flew in an even higher arc was likewise rendered unconscious. Gradually Balfour recovered his senses and staggered around the wreck before being rescued by some Canadians from a nearby dug-out. Evacuated under shell fire that night he next saw his observer in an Isle of Wight hospital four months later.

Two days after Balfour's crash 2nd Lt Reece and 2/AM Moult failed to return from a reconnaissance and were taken prisoner, and on the next day the outstanding 2nd Lt de Berigny and his faithful gunner 2/AM Bowen who had several times given an outstanding account of themselves in the face of the heaviest opposition, died as their machine stalled on take-off after landing at No 16 Squadron's aerodrome at Bruay to refuel. On the first of May 2nd Lts O'Brien and Edwards were shot down and taken prisoner. During this patrol Captain Rutter lost the greater part of his tail, shot away by a hostile scout. The latter was itself destroyed by his observer, Air Mechanic Cant and Captain Keen of 40 Squadron in a Nieuport. On that same day after a jammed camera had rendered an attempted recce patrol abortive, 2nd Lt S H D'Arcy with Lt Pickering as his observer flew out alone with no pre-arranged escort from friendly scouts and brought back the required photographs.

2nd Lt Thomas S Edelston

CHAPTER 3

And History was Made

IT is recorded in the official History of World War I that No 43 Squadron, during the Third Battle of the Scarpe, on 3 May 1917 "can be said to have definitely established the novel development in the employment of aeroplanes directly to assist troops on the ground, operating in fact as 'tanks of the air'." If it was the first 'first' in the Squadron's (then) brief history it was certainly not destined to be the last.

Actually as far back as 10 April attacks had been made on ground targets during line patrols but 3 May was the first occasion when the Squadron set off with the avowed intention of attacking ground forces. Following a mid-morning report that the troops who had forced their way into Fresnoy were threatened by a counterattack, five Sopwiths set off post-haste to play hell with the enemy's plans.

Two days before the attack began 43 had been ordered to prepare to undertake 'counterattack patrols', from dawn to dusk, low down behind the captured positions and to report at speed any signs of preparation by the enemy for counterattack. On 3 May aerial reconnaissance had been much hampered by the fog of war. Heavy bombardments by both sides had made much of the area hard to recognize and visibility was poor in the clouds of dust and smoke. Definite information was lacking except, vide the Official History, 'in the morning when observers of No 43 Squadron reported enemy troops massing in the trenches'. On receipt of this report at Brigade HQ 43 Squadron was ordered into the attack.

Major Dore and 2nd Lt E H Jones went at 1115 hrs; within minutes 2nd Lts Collier and F S Jones, Potter and Giles, McClatchie and Gorringe, and Hon D'Arcy and Pickering followed them. The first crew came back with engine trouble (and some unused ammunition) after attacking a densely packed enemy trench and the village of Neuvireuil. The remaining pilots and observers had better behaved motors that day and came back without a solitary round between them for either front or rear guns. 'Considerable casualties among a group of battalion strength around a farm', 'shot up trenches in face of heavy fire, fired at by several machine-guns so dived to 200 feet and attacked them, together with groups of men in vicinity', 'wrought execution among troops on Mauville Farm and the Fresnes Road', 'successful attack on motor-car, twelve lorries, ten horsemen and other troops', 'every trench around Oppy was packed with men into which we fired from heights down to fifty feet'.

2nd Lt Eric H Jones

2nd Lt Samuel Collier

2nd Lt Bertie Giles

2nd Lt Frank Gorringe

Thus ran the reports of those ten pioneer ground-strafers. The official history also records that no counterattack was launched that day by the enemy in this area.

In the afternoon four more machines attacked trenches full of troops until their ammunition was exhausted. Lt Woolliams completely immobilised a field gun battery, killing some of the crews and sending the rest to cover. The day's flying also recorded three flights, of six machines each, on two-hour patrols Avion – Gavrelle. All in all, a busy day, marred only by the death of 2nd Lt M J Morris whilst on a practice flight. The Commanding Officer's opinion of the day was that: "Our success appeared to be due mainly to the enemy being so startled by the audacity of our attacks and bombardment that they could not bring themselves to throw at us any very heavy fire. The 1½ Strutter came into its own in this work, its performance and manoeuvrability near the ground being good; and the chief danger that we had to face was from our artillery barrage. When we shut off our engines for a moment we could clearly hear our own shells rumbling past our ears with a noise that sounded like a succession of trains passing through a tunnel. But we suffered no casualties and that boosted enormously the morale of my pilots and observers. The results that we achieved brought congratulations from both the Wing and the Brigade Commanders." (*Years of Combat – 1963*).

Following a quiet day on 4 May the 5th opened well, for 2nd Lt Richmond and his observer 2nd Lt Pritchard shot down an enemy two-seater. Twenty-four hours later Lts Libby and Dickson used only twenty rounds in disposing of another hostile machine, but on the 9th ill fortune again came to the Squadron.

Lt Frederick Libby MC

Taking off on patrol, with Lt Dickson in the rear cockpit, Major Douglas suffered engine failure and in the subsequent forced-landing his machine came off worse in a collision with the substantial rear quarters of a sturdy white farm horse. After two days Major Douglas was forced to retire to hospital. Dickson, more badly injured, had been admitted already. Thus 43 Squadron lost its first Commander; one who "had formed and commanded the Squadron through a most difficult period. With out-of-date machines, and confronted when newly arrived in France with the most recent and formidable fighters manned by the cream of the German Air Force, 43 had under the able guidance of Major Douglas maintained the offensive spirit which was the characteristic spirit of the Royal Flying Corps, and maintained it with success".

Major Alan S W Dore

Fortunately a worthy successor to Douglas was immediately to hand, Major Alan Dore, former front line soldier with the Worcestershire Regiment and Observer for nine months with 13 Squadron, had joined 43 at Northolt after completion of his pilots course. Promoted to Command 'C' Flight when Jack Scott left, he now found himself commanding the Squadron. It was a task he fulfilled with distinction until November.

On 9 May five hostile scouts found the two Sopwiths of 2nd Lts Richmond and Pritchard, Richards and CSM Nava, too much of a handful and some spirited shooting by the two observers sent the Huns away more quickly than they had arrived. Less fortunate was 2nd Lt Frank Woolliams and his Canadian observer, Lt J B de M Harvey. Volunteering to make up a shortage in another Flight their machine was hit by German AA almost as soon as they crossed the lines. The engine was damaged and all control was lost. The Sopwith went into a semi-flat spin and crashed in no-man's-land only a few yards from the German front line trench. Thrown clear of the crash Woolliams found himself lying in a shell hole. Deciding to get back home he stood up to get his bearings but rapidly dived flat again as machine-guns opened fire from both sides. Two bullets hit his coat without touching him; 'Lucky you will say – so do I, there were several shell splinters from the Archie burst as well'. After a while a German patrol appeared and both airmen (Harvey was severely wounded in one arm) were taken back to the trench. During the next three days Woolliams was subjected to intensive questioning by the Germans about the low flying attack made by Kitto, Libby and himself on 3 May. They seemed especially annoyed about it but Woolliams stoutly and successfully lied away that he had no idea at all of what they were referring to. Finally his captors gave up and sent him off to a POW cage.

As with the Royal Flying Corps generally, 43 Squadron was now finding a welcome decrease in the losses which it sustained together with an increasing rate of destruction of the enemy. For many squadrons this improvement was to a large extent hastened by the arrival of better machines. For 43, who had to soldier on with their old 1½ Strutters (it was the last squadron to exchange them for something better), the improvement was due to better tactics, larger formations and a general all round increase in cunning and skill, the outcome of dearly bought experience for which there was no substitute.

Though figures alone cannot be the sole criterion they may not be wholly disregarded and it is significant that, whereas from February to April thirty-five men were killed, wounded or missing while ten enemy machines were being shot down, between May and August exactly twice as many of the enemy were destroyed against Squadron casualties by enemy action of twenty-three. All the same, numbers are but part of the story and essentially the history of 43 during these days is a tale of young men, in machines they knew to be mainly inferior to the enemy's, going bravely and resolutely into action. And if their deeds are not as fully documented as they might be, sufficient remains to show how well they performed. Like this for instance . . . .

"On 28 May Second Lieutenants C S Richmond, pilot, and E W Pritchard, observer, whilst on photographic patrol ran into three hostile scouts to the south-west of Esquerchin. They were first attacked by one which was ahead of the other two. This machine got right on their tail but Pritchard despatched it in a flat spin, decidedly crippled and out of control. Another came up instantly and also attempted to get under the tail of the Sopwith and, taking advantage of the pause while a new drum was being fitted, the hostile machine crept up to about thirty yards, whereupon the Sopwith dived vertically and 'S' turned. Pritchard now got his gun into action but the enemy would not be shaken off. One of his bullets hit Pritchard's magazine, exploding some rounds, whilst another smashed his goggles, temporarily incapacitating him. The enemy persisted in his pursuit of the Sopwith until the lines were reached, when two Nieuports appeared from the west. The enemy aircraft then turned east, immediately accompanied by the third hostile scout who had seemingly taken no part in the fight. During the whole action the Sopwith's engine was missing and this considerably impaired its performance."

2nd Lt Samuel D'Arcy

There is something in that last sentence which possesses a Homeric quality. One can almost hear those two lieutenants, neither of whom had reached their twenty-first birthday, complaining sadly that if only that damned engine had run smoothly they would have, as a matter of course, shot all their opponents to pieces.

Again, on 24 May: "The first line patrol had to return after a short flight owing to bad visibility but the second patrol which started at 0720 hrs met nine hostile scouts in the neighbourhood of Neuvireuil. Captain K L Gopsill, pilot, with Second Lieutenant E H Jones as observer, engaged one, driving it off, but in the meantime two other scouts attacked them and Jones was wounded in the leg. Despite his wound, however, Jones opened fire at the nearest enemy machine and after twenty rounds it was seen to turn on its back, burst into flames, and go down vertically. Second Lieutenant C H Harriman's Sopwith was marked down by two of the hostile machines, but his observer, 2/AM O'Shea, opened fire on one at close range, with the result that the enemy went down in a spin, cartwheeling over as it fell. Another hostile scout was engaged by Second Lieutenant S V L Gedge who was piloting CSM L M Nava. It fell out of control. By this time Flight Commander C D Booker of No 8 (Naval) Squadron in a Sopwith Triplane had climbed up from his aerodrome and joined in the combat. He attacked one scout which was driven down in flames and crashed. The remainder then fled east and the Sopwiths continued their patrol. In the course of the combat one of the Sopwiths (Lieutenant S M Goode, pilot; Second Lieutenant J Gagne, observer) was seen to go down in flames."

Then there was another great character, 2nd Lt the Hon S H A D'Arcy who, in his few weeks with 43, again and again displayed outstanding gallantry and skill. Sam D'Arcy, invariably referred to as *The Honourable* in the Squadron records could not, strictly, lay claim to the prefix, for his father's title, Count D'Arcy had been bestowed on an ancestor by the King of France in 1746. The ancestor, as it happens, was an Irishman who was a supporter of Bonnie Prince Charlie and forced to flee with him after the collapse of the 1745 uprising. D'Arcy, whose elder brother fought the war with the French Army, was commissioned soon after his eighteenth birthday and had been a qualified pilot for just seven days when he joined 43 as one of the early replacements in March 1917. Thrown into the cauldron of 'Bloody April' his undaunted cheerfulness was expressed in a letter home in the middle of that month, ". . . I'm happy and well although we've all been put through it in the last few days. We average about five hours flying over the enemy lines every day. Still it's damn interesting work'. Two weeks later in another letter, 'Yes I am quite well, just a wee trifle tired . . . just off on another patrol, that's five hours again today.

'A popular, ebullient extrovert, gifted with intelligence, charm and musical talent', (he played the violincello with some skill) he was also 'something of a dashing rake'. If the official Squadron records are anything to go by Sam D'Arcy was equally outstanding as an aggressive fighter and during his all too-short sojourn with 43 his name constantly appears in the lists. His long lone flight to bring back some badly needed pictures on 1 May has already been mentioned. For this he and his observer, Lt Pickering, were mentioned in the RFC communiqué. On the 11th of the same month the same pair were robbed of a certain victory over a hostile artillery machine when their guns jammed at the crucial moment. The following morning, before breakfast, this same pair, on a front-line patrol encountered six enemy aircraft. Two Albatros scouts closed up behind the Sopwith; D'Arcy stall-turned and Pickering fired a whole drum at the nearest Albatros. It spun away, apparently out of control. Opening fire on the second scout Pickering saw his bullets hitting the enemy which dived away and left the flight. An enormous loop, then successfully left the remaining four enemy machines out of range and apparently fearful to close after seeing with what accurate fire the first two Albatroses had been met, they turned and left the solitary Sopwith to continue its patrol.

Only a week later D'Arcy dived away from a patrol formation to engage a solitary single-seater Fokker which was dogging their route. He opened fire with his front gun and the enemy went into a spinning nose dive from which it failed to recover.

Again on 2 June they received the highest commendation from Brigade HQ for a 'brilliant photographic mission', bringing back from an unescorted and unaccompanied flight seventeen photographs which were urgently required by Army HQ.

D'Arcy's last flight with 43, only a few days later, ended with his admittance to a Casualty Clearing Station. The details will follow in due place. It is enough to conclude here that in the few weeks he was with 43, his deeds earned him admittance to the Distinguished Service Order, rare honour indeed for one so young and of such lowly rank. He was in fact the youngest man in the British Army to be so honoured.

Throughout 1917 it fell to the British and Empire soldiers to sustain alone the burden of battle on the Western Front. The French Armies, thoroughly disorganised and mutinous after their Spring offensive had collapsed in bloody ruin within four days and were a non-effective force for most of the Summer and Autumn.

The first attack launched by the British was at Arras in April. A limited attack at Messines in June was followed by the terrible Third Battle of Ypres, more commonly remembered as Passchendaele. This began on 31 July. With all these battles 43 Squadron was involved. Its part at Arras has already been described. Messines, a limited operation to improve the positions at the south end of the Ypres Salient was laid on when it became imperative to attack after the French army had folded up. Described as 'a classic of preparation' it was preceded by a seventeen-day bombardment. Shrapnel, high explosive and gas shells alike were employed together with another end product of western civilisation – drums of boiling oil! 43 Squadron joined in just sixty minutes after the zero hour of 0310 on 7 June. 'Their experience of ground-strafing was put to good use and the effect of the attacks from the air were little less marked than those which followed the underground explosions.'

Which says a lot because the attack by the infantry was preceded by the simultaneous explosion of nineteen enormous mines tunnelled beneath the enemy's defences. The largest left a crater 140 yards in diameter. The German front lines vanished, and such defenders as still lived were too shattered to fight. Before the dust-clouds had settled the infantry assault went in behind a creeping barrage. One hour later, in the first glimmers of dawn, 43 Squadron sent off the first of six Sopwiths. Their orders were, working in pairs, to strike the enemy on the ground wherever he might be found.

Captain D C Rutter MC

It was an order duly carried out, but it cost the Squadron dearly. Captain Rutter, first away at 0410 hours, with his observer 2nd Lt Jackson was never seen again. Almost certainly their aircraft must have received a direct hit from a heavy shell as they flew low towards their targets. Captain Rutter, who had seen service in the front line trenches of the Royal Sussex Regiment and the back cockpits of No 8 Squadron's BE 2s, was the only surviving Flight Commander, the sole surviving pilot in fact excepting Major Dore, of the original Northolt contingent. He had been in the forefront from the beginning. His aircraft was riddled and his observer was killed in the first engagement with the enemy in far off February and through all the trial and tribulation of the heavy casualties that followed he had proved a tower of strength. 'A fearless leader with a most gallant and distinguished record; the thoroughness with which he did his work was beyond praise.' Thus spoke the official history.

Lt Richards and CSM Nava, second away and failing to find Rutter, crossed the lines alone. Descending to carry out a low flying attack they came under heavy machine-gun fire which shot away an incidence wire and forced them to return.

Lts Veitch and Bettinson in number three went down to harass a small body of troops. Soon after opening fire they were themselves hit, the engine almost stopped, and they too had to return to base. The next crew, 2nd Lts Harriman and Dixon, shot up an enemy dump with good results before anti-aircraft fire dislodged the fuel tank. Flying home through the barrage more machine-gun fire damaged the aircraft so badly that they were forced to crash-land. Both were unhurt. Sgt Webb and Lt Gaunt played havoc with an enemy battery and shot up some transport before more engine trouble sent them home prematurely too. Last, but by no means least, at 0450, came the Hon S H D'Arcy with his faithful Lt Pickering behind. "Crossing the lines at 200 feet they shot up troops in a farm and more along the road. Next D'Arcy turned his attention to a hostile kite balloon near Comines which he attacked. The balloon seemed to crumple up and go down, but not on fire. Another balloon was attacked near Mai-Comet, but it was hauled down.

2nd Lt John Jackson

Lt Lionel Bettinson

2nd Lt Charlie Harriman

2nd Lt George Dixon

Reserve trenches near Ploegsteert Wood were shot up, but here D'Arcy was wounded in the right leg. Refusing to return until he had finished his ammunition, he carried on and made a second attempt on the balloon at Mai-Comet which he caused to break loose. D'Arcy was then forced by loss of blood to return. He forced-landed and although almost fainting insisted on passing on the valuable information he had gathered to W Group, 2nd Anzac Heavy Artillery. As a direct result of this information good work was done by the artillery during the afternoon." That was No 43 Squadron's contribution to the opening of the Messines offensive.

Six more Sopwiths set out at 0930 hrs on special reconnaissance. They brought back news of German concentrations and reported much transport and troop movement. Second Lieutenants F Libby (pilot) and E W Pritchard (observer) came down to 900 feet and fired several bursts at a long convoy which was going towards Warneton. The leading lorry was hit and forced to stop across the road, thus holding up the convoy for some time. Next 250 rounds from the front gun and two drums from the observer's gun were pumped into troops massing at Warneton, with marked effect.

The Messines offensive lasted only seven days. When it ended the indentation in the British line south of the Ypres Salient had been removed and the area thus made very slightly less unattractive as a springboard for the next 'great push'. This was planned to be an overwhelming thrust to burst out from Ypres and sweep northwards to the Belgian coast. The necessity for the attack was urged upon the Generals by the Admirals of the Royal Navy who successfully convinced everybody, including themselves, that unless the German U-boat bases at Ostend and Zebrugge were captured the war would be lost inside six weeks. In the meantime they rigidly refused to consider any system of convoys for merchant shipping.

As far as 43 Squadron was concerned all that this implied was that in June, following Messines, when it returned to its familiar home ground around Arras and Lens, nothing very much happened at all apart from two enemy aircraft being destroyed on the 16th.

Activity quickened in July. On the first of the month six 1½ Strutters under the leadership of Captain W A McClatchie fought off no less than sixteen enemy Albatros scouts with Lt Gaunt, wounded, the only casualty. On the next day another patrol of six came under Archie fire. Captain Wynn, the pilot of one of them, was wounded in the head and during temporary unconsciousness his aeroplane dropped below the rest of the formation. It was then attacked by five enemy single seaters who doubtlessly thought this was easy meat. Corporal Moultrie, the observer had other ideas. At 100 yards range he fired a complete drum into the leading Hun, changed the drum and reopened fire. Before the second drum was half used the enemy aircraft turned over out of control and subsequently crashed. This dampened the ardour of Moutrie's four remaining adversaries and they departed. Captain Wynn, recovering full consciousness, was now able to climb and rejoin the rest of the Squadron. Soon afterwards six more enemy Albatros scouts attacked. A lot of ammunition was used by both sides with no visible damage to anybody. 'The patrol returned', says the official history, 'with sixty excellent photographs, and with Captain Wynn wounded in the head.'

Captain W A McClatchie MC

Lt William Cattell

Lt William A Cox

Captain Kenneth L Gopsill

The manner in which the Squadron was now capable of defending itself against attacks by greater numbers of theoretically superior enemy machines was now becoming a regular and happy feature of the daily round. "Twice, on the 7th, hostile formations were driven off and, on the 8th, four Sopwiths definitely won the honours in a fight with seven enemy Albatros single seaters. Captain Gopsill, leading the formation, got underneath an enemy that was going for 2nd Lt Thompson's machine and thus enabled his observer, Captain Cranstoun, to shoot it down; subsequently attacked by two other machines Gopsill was wounded in the foot, the petrol tank was holed, and Cranstoun's gun jammed all at the same time, but the wounded pilot, with some brilliant flying, evaded his attackers and brought his machine back to Treizennes. 2nd Lt Thompson had his rudder control shot away, but with his observer 2nd Lt Buschmann, himself wounded, continuing to fire away, the attacker was forced to break off. Meantime Lt Cattell, with Lt Cox piloting, was sending one enemy machine down in flames and frightening off another whilst the fourth crew 2nd Lt McPherson and Lt Bell also attacked by two of the enemy sent one down in a spin to crash and caused the axle and one wheel to fall off the other."

Presumably this last battle was enough for the time being, for the Germans, because the official report says that 'for the next month there was relative quiet on this front'.

A little behind the front, unofficial reports suggest, life still had its moments. A letter written by Captain Cranstoun, one of the senior observers to Sam D'Arcy, recuperating from his wounds at home, gives some details of this unreported part of the war.

43 Squadron, RFC
BEF
22/6/17

My dear D'Arcy,
Purdey gave me your message the other day and I was very pleased to get it. First of all I must congratulate you on your DSO which you jolly well deserved. I was very pleased to hear about it only I should have put you in for a VC. We were all naturally very depressed at losing Alf and I still miss him – we can only hope that he is safe although I fear he will suffer bitter pangs from 'sexual starvation'. We miss you too but our loss is probably your gain if you have succeeded in getting back to Blighty – the gramophone in your absence has to do double work and is threatening to go dead from overstrain. The flight commanders are now Gopsill, Collier and McClatchie and we have various new pilots and observers, some fair to mod and others mod to ruddy. Potter has gone to home establishment and Mackay has left for the American Flying Corps; Forrest has also gone to the Australian Flying Corps and I can only say that in neither case is the loss felt. Mackay put up a splendid performance the other day – he took off across wind, swinging round downwind, whistled round again crosswind in the other direction – thereby covering some 300 yards without once getting up wind and gaining speed all the time – and then shed his undercarriage and wrapped himself up in what was left of the machine: neither he nor his observer (Lizzie) were hurt but the machine was a write-off. Libby did not improve his temper by telling him that it was rather near the ground to try looping. Purdey has gone on home leave with a Ferry pilot but he left with fearful wind up. He was sent to Omer with a driver who was completely new to tenders, 'meteor' had prophesied dud weather for several days and so he expected to spend most of his leave at Omer. He was told he would be sure to get an RE 8 which was bound to spin and catch fire and lastly he expected to be recalled as soon as he reached England. We have been having beautiful weather (for all but the RFC) but at last it has gone dud and looks like remaining so for a bit. I am rather glad though flying has not been excessive since you left, I get a very fair quantity of 'flips' but have broken three more tail-skids which is rather trying: they are now trying to design a stronger one for me. I went over to 23 Squadron the other day and saw Buchanan again – he asked after you and I told him you had got a blighty and (probably) a DSO and he sent you his best wishes. Unfortunately 23 have left B. now. Well cheeri-oh and the best of luck. Yrs ever,

Craniebun.

Sadly, it must be related that D'Arcy did not enjoy the wished-for good luck. When he recovered from his wounds he went to the Aeroplane Experimental Squadron at Martlesham Heath. There in June 1918 he was killed in a crash. The Assistant Commandant in a letter to D'Arcy's parents diplomatically reported that 'he lost control of his machine when flying very low and crashed into the ground'. A close relative has since said he understood that the cause was a misjudged low-level loop or some similarly dangerous manoeuvre, 'the element of exhibitionism and high risk involved both seemed to appeal to him'. So ended the brief life of a remarkable man and if he died to no apparent end perhaps his death was inevitable. The spirit that accepts the challenge of starting a loop on a Camel fractionally too low for assured safety is in no wise different from the one that sends a man off to have another (and successful) crack at an elusive enemy balloon when his flying suit is becoming progressively more sodden with his own blood. The less bold that would have added another 100 feet to the altimeter reading before looping would, with the same caution, have set course for the Medical Officer at base.

Preparations were going forward for the Third Battle of Ypres, the main blow of which fell to the Fifth Army. The offensive was launched on 31 July 1917, a day of very threatening weather which rendered the work of the aeroplanes very difficult. During the afternoon, while fighting was in progress, rain began and fell steadily all night. Thereafter for four days the rain continued without cessation, and for several days afterwards the weather remained stormy and unsettled. The low-lying, clayey soil, torn by shells and sodden with rain, turned to a succession of vast, muddy pools. The valleys of the choked and overflowing streams were speedily transformed into long stretches of bog, impassable except by a few well-defined tracks,

Sopwiths of 'B' Flight at Treizennes in June 1917, with early style flight letters and numbers

drowning, and in the course of the subsequent fighting on several occasions both men and pack animals were lost in this way.

These were the conditions on the ground during those four months of fierce fighting which it was hoped would result in the rolling up of the enemy's right flank, but any such hopes were shattered, not by the enemy, but by the weather, and we had to rest content with the gain of the Passchendaele Ridge.

Towards the middle of August a slight improvement took place in the weather, and advantage was taken of this to launch a second attack east of Ypres. Thereafter unsettled weather again set in and the month closed as the wettest August that has been known for many years.

No 43 Squadron took no direct part in the launching of this offensive. But it was essential that the enemy should be prevented from reinforcing his line in the north by depleting his divisions in the south. So it was arranged that the Canadian Corps should attack in the region of Lens, the strongly fortified hill known as Hill 70, which had been very useful to the enemy ever since we failed to hold it during the battle of Loos on 25 September 1915.

In the course of the preparation for this operation No 43 Squadron reconnoitred the area to be fought over with a view to co-operating with the Canadian Corps during the attack.

On 15 August 1917, the day of the attack on Hill 70, No 43 Squadron was ordered to send twelve machines to be ready to operate from the advanced landing ground at Mazingarbe at 0600 hrs. Their chief purpose was the engagement with machine-gun fire of bodies of hostile infantry, particularly at points of congestion, and to report indications of hostile counter attacks. Captain S Collier, the first off, proceeded over the lines at 0600 hrs at 2,000 feet, dived down to 800 feet and fired 100 rounds into trenches at Loison. His observer, Second Lieutenant E W Pritchard, also fired about one and a half drums. Although the latter was hit in the foot Collier continued to patrol and fire on roads until his petrol tank was shot through. He recrossed the lines at 100 feet and landed safely.

Captain T S Wynn with Second Lieutenant S M Peterkin, his observer, flew low over Cite St Auguste and spotted troops moving along Eastern Railway embankment. He saw a large number of troops in the Drocourt trenches and strafed them from 200 feet.

Second Lieutenant R P Hood (pilot) with Lieutenant H G S de Carteret (observer) dived on a party of about 150 men causing them to scatter, and fired on three guns nearby bringing them to a halt by accurate shooting. Captain A T Richards with Lieutenant W G Bell dived to attack transport near Fouquines, and some troops.

Lieutenant C L Veitch (pilot) with Second Lieutenant F Marshall-Lewis dived on a body of about twenty men who were carrying boxes, and fired about ninety rounds into them and shot up about 1,600 men marching in extended order. Many casualties were inflicted and the troops were seen to scatter. Then they dived and silenced a battery from which large clouds of black smoke were seen to rise. Finally 100 men were shot up near Wingles.

2/AM E P Croll, the observer to Second Lieutenant S Thompson observed a massing of troops at the Bois de Dixhuit into which a drum and a half was fired. Second Lieutenant S V L Gedge with 2/AM C A Blatherwick as observer scattered some troops, shot up motor transport and cyclists. Their remaining ammunition was expended on Highgate Trench, which was full of troops.

2nd Lt C A Hargreaves

Second Lieutenant F M Kitto with 1/AM A W Cant sighting large bodies of troops massing, dived and opened fire. Before returning they fired many rounds into the Bois de Dixhuit. Captains W A McClatchie and A E Pickering fired into the Bois de Dixhuit where they observed a general concentration of troops. While flying over the trenches their Sopwith was attacked by six enemy machines which they drove off. One appeared to go down out of control.

Second Lieutenant A N Maplestone and Private J Watson were shooting some trenches when they were attacked by three hostile machines, one of which Maplestone crashed. Watson drove off the other two. During this combat Maplestone was wounded in the ankle.

This sort of work was kept up

at frequent intervals the whole day, often 5,000 rounds being fired.

Great credit is due to 2/AM Croll who was the first person to observe the massing at the Bois de Dixhuit. He reported to the Canadian Corps who successfully dealt with this attempted counterattack with artillery. As an immediate result of Croll's information three Sopwiths were sent out at once to harass these massing troops, and many casualties were inflicted. One pilot, Second Lieutenant C A Hargreaves, died of wounds received in action. Two Sopwiths, one manned by Second Lieutenants C G Moore and] B Smith, the other by Second Lieutenant H D B Snelgrove and 2/AM W Addison were lost. The next day the Squadron was detailed for similar work, but on a small scale. The flight which went out found matters exceedingly quiet, enemy activity being almost nil, and a patrol which left in the evening likewise had little to report.

"The Squadron was highly complimented by both the GOC RFC in the field and the First Army Commander for its splendid work. Their disruption of the enemy's back areas helped to ensure that the whole of our objectives were gained rapidly at light cost and in accordance with the plan for the day of the assault."

On the morning of the 17th no fewer than thirteen enemy machines approached a formation of the 1½ Strutters. For some reason only four of the thirteen actually attacked and one was last seen spurting flame and diving away from the fight. On the evening patrol more enemy machines were seen. 1/AM Cant, piloted by Lt Kitto, one of the Squadron's original Northolt crews, now returned after a period *hors de combat*, fired 100 rounds at one adversary, an Albatros scout, and forced it to crash-land. As three other Albatroses came in to avenge this loss 1/AM Cant fired away until gun stoppage silenced him. Whereupon, Lt Kitto took over the attacking role and sent one of his three opponents down out of control. Four other enemy aircraft now appeared, making the odds for the gallant Sopwith pair rather heavy, but fortunately for them at this juncture six Nieuports of No 40 Squadron arrived and the hostile scouts immediately made off eastwards.

A less happy ending was in evidence three days later. 2nd Lts Winser and Young, last seen in action with four enemy scouts near Vitry, failed to return and were subsequently known to have been killed.

September was a month of great change. On the 3rd, the first Sopwith Camel arrived. On the 15th the first patrol by Camels was carried out. 2nd Lts Gedge and Womersley and Sgt Webb 'set out on a special mission in pursuit of enemy aircraft but owing to the great altitude of the enemy failed to get within striking range'. On the 25th Captain C Y McDonald led the last patrol with the two seater 1½ Strutters.

For most of the pilots the 'conversion' meant merely a few short trips in a Camel, although for one, Captain Bill McClatchie, one of the few surviving stalwarts from the distant days of March, it resulted in a nasty accident which deprived the Squadron of a very fine fighter. Thereafter there was nothing to do but bid a sad farewell to the half of the crews for whom there was no longer a place. Captains and Lieutenants, Sergeants, Corporals, Air Mechanics, and Privates, they could all be proud of a job well done as the pilots in their front seats knew better than any. Many of the pilot and observer teams had fought together for several months and a great deal of genuine heartbreak at the rupture of such close comradeship was inevitable. As one of them said: 'Up there you had to trust your life to the other chap; the great thing about it was that you knew you could.'

By September's end the last two-seater had gone, the last farewell carousal was over, the last observer had packed his kit and left. Some went to train as pilots in the UK, others left for squadrons where there was still a place for them. For 43 it was the end of a short era, the start of another. Henceforth for fifty years the single seater fighter would remain the weapon with which it armed itself.

2nd Lt Frank E Winser

CHAPTER 4

Camel Captains

THE Sopwith Camel, 'that popping firecracker', was an aeroplane that never failed to arouse passionately held opinions of like or dislike among the pilots of its day. There were some who would go to any length to avoid being sent to a squadron or training school where the Camel was flown; others by contrast would never for preference have gone into action against the enemy in anything else.

The Camel, so named because of its humped cowling over the twin Vickers in front of the cockpit, was as fierce as its predecessor, the Pup, had been gentle. Henry Woollett, who latterly never flew anything else in battle and destroyed thirty-five Huns as well as a near record number of observation balloons, said it was about the most sensitive machine ever built. Perhaps that was why so many pilots abhorred it, for the Camel was unforgiving in its reactions to the heavy-handed or the careless. Normally tail heavy in flight it was necessary to apply a constant forward pressure on the stick, which made control in the pitching plane even more difficult, while the gyroscopic effect of the great flywheel of a Clerget rotary engine up front required precise and copious compensatory use of the rudder in a turn. In a left turn the nose attempted to rise, in a right turn it tended to go down and, if not corrected almost before it had begun. the nose would drop so quickly that even subsequent full rudder could not prevent a powered spiral descent.

But to the man with the requisite skill and the lightness of touch the Camel provided the finest infighting machine of all. A right-handed bank, with the pilot remaining in charge, led to a turn so tight and quick that no other aeroplane in the sky could stay with it. 'Not even the Fokker triplane', Henry Woollett says. The protagonists of the contemporary SE 5 or Spad claimed that their superior speed, climb and better altitude performance allowed their pilots to do battle at the time and place of their own choosing. The Camel pilot by comparison had not this advantage. In fact it was said that he 'had to shoot down all the Huns to get home himself for there was no chance to run for it.'

The Camel pilot could retort that, if that were so, he had a machine that enabled him to easily regain the initiative after the enemy had pounced. Properly handled by a pilot who knew his stuff, would outfly anything and, if at a push a bit of evasive action were needed, it was easy to induce his machine to spin and thus present a nearly unhittable target. Norman MacMillan, the author, once saw a Camel pilot, a pupil, spin right, overcorrect and spin left, overcorrect again and spin right and still pull out unhurt. 'What other aeroplane ever built,' he asked 'could do all that in under 1,000 feet?'

The published words of the champions and detractors of the Camel suggest that none of their opinions for good or ill have changed with the passing of time. But if proof were required that, for all its trickiness and its unforgiving reactions to the ham-handed it was, when skilfully flown, a potent weapon, its record of destroying more of the enemy, 1,294 (908 by the RFC and RAF on the Western Front alone) must speak convincingly in its favour.

It was 43 Squadron's good fortune that some of the best exponents of the art of subduing the Camel were on its books during the last year of the war. And if 43 could never lay claim to any of the most famous and most publicised heroes of those days, the men whose score went up to and beyond the half century mark, it could show a corporate record that lagged little if at all behind anybody else. In Captain Henry Woollett and

A Sopwith Camel

A Camel cockpit

Captain John Trollope it possessed the only two men ever to destroy six of the enemy in one day. With Captain Harold Balfour, who returned in November 1917 for a second tour, and Cecil King these made up a quartet of Camel Captains as good as any to be found in the Flying Corps. Add the consistent solid backing up of others like Lingham, Daniel, Banks, Bailey or Keary and the end product was a highly efficient team, one in which personal glory was less important than the continuance of the Squadron's high reputation and good name.

An early photograph of Harold Balfour

And this task moreover concerned not only the pilots. Though the surviving records relate mainly to what occurred in the high blue sky and there is record of neither name nor deeds of the groundcrew, the importance of the latter was never lost on the pilots nor their part in the overall squadron performance forgotten. As witness the opinion of the great Henry Woollett himself.

"One day I noticed, a row of small brass tacks in one of my struts. I quickly called my rigger and asked him what they were doing there. He calmly replied, 'We put one in every time you bring down a Hun, sir.'"

"God bless him and all other riggers, fitters and armourers. We owed them everything for what they did for us. We were entirely in their hands and what reward did they get out of the war? In my own case just my appreciation for what they did for me and the knowledge that our war in the air was won through their absolute help in looking after my safety and my guns. 'No praise is too great for them. They were true friends and I loved them.'"

Henry Winslow Woollett was born, and spent his boyhood, at Southwold in Suffolk, where his father, who subsequently became the Senior Medical Officer of the hospital ship Dover Castle in the 1914-18 war, was a doctor. In August 1914 Woollett was in his second year as a medical student at the London Hospital but was commissioned in the 6th Battalion of the Lincolnshire Regiment before the month was up. Twelve months later he led his platoon ashore at the Suvla Bay landing in the Dardanelles to find that war was all discomfort and little glory. 'For six nights,' he wrote, 'I slept back to back with my corporal for warmth. We had no cover overhead, no blankets and as two weeks passed before our packs were landed I often had to hand my one and only shirt over to my batman so that he could clear the lice out of the seams.'

Lt George Lingham in his Camel B3839 'W' showing his personal marking below the cockpit. January 1918

During the subsequent campaign Woollett, like all infantrymen, had to endure a great deal of intense artillery bombardment. He survived it all unscathed but the experience left him with a marked dislike for all enemy gunners and their observation posts – especially balloons. His record as a destroyer of these stems to some extent from the poundings he was forced to endure in the Dardanelles.

Transferring to the RFC in 1916 Lieutenant Woollett gained his wings after three and a half hours dual on Maurice Farman Longhorns and Shorthorns. He was soon afterwards involved in a crash caused by a faulty ignition switch in an Avro. Visited in hospital by the CO of his training squadron Woollett was berated for 'his clumsiness' and told that he would be posted to Scouts. 'It was the only thing,' said H W 'I could really thank him for.' Posted in November 1916 to 24 Squadron, flying DH 2s (later DH 5s), Woollett remained until the following August, finishing up as a Flight Commander with seven Huns to his credit and the Military Cross. Following a spell instructing in England Woollett was posted to 43 in March 1918 to command 'C' Flight. Before he returned to England in August, to take command of three training squadrons at Eastbourne, his total of officially confirmed kills had risen to thirty-five (six of them on 12 April) plus eleven balloons shot down in flames and he had earned the DSO ('For considerable skill and gallantry in attacking and destroying enemy aircraft'), a bar to his MC, the French Legion of Honour and Croix de Guerre. His fame and name were known along the entire front. Equally so his flying gear

Captain Henry Winslow Woollett DSO MC and Bar,
Chevalier de la Légion d'Honneur, Croix de Guerre avec palme, who shot down twenty-eight enemy aircraft (out of his total of thirty-five) and eleven balloons while serving with 43 Squadron between March and August 1918

and his machine. The latter had a special prop boss nose cap superbly decorated with the war painted and much-befeathered head of a Red Indian. Woollett himself was still more outstanding in helmet and flying gloves made from a leopard skin. 'They took my fancy once when on leave in the West End of London and being young I could not resist the temptation of being different from others in the air. They caused quite a sensation.'

'Mick' Mannock, the great Irish ace who was always trying to poach the best pilots from other squadrons, tried several times without success to tempt Woollett away from 43. Woollett was more than content with his 'wonderful lot of young and full-out pilots, lively and enthusiastic', and in turn the youngsters were all the better for the leadership of the 'old man' (he was twenty-two!) for Woollett 'was no glory bagger who flew without regard for his flight'. 'Quite often on these patrols', wrote Lt John Milner who came to 43 in June 1918, 'Captain Woollett would wave his deputy in, then fall away from the patrol, and when he did he invariably had a combat report when he got back to base. For he seemed to anticipate, or spot, the Hun movements and would leave the patrol to be in a position for events ahead. Jerry at this time generally followed us at a safe height waiting for the novice to make an error on the turns, then one or two would dive on the stray. When this happened Henry Woollett would appear diving out of the blue with the Hun, and he was a very good shot.'

Woollett knew the Hun and his ways and the enemy knew of Woollett too. When John Trollope after his capture was interrogated by the German Senior Intelligence Officer at Lille– 'The Baron of Lille' as he was titled by the RFC – he was told 'By the way Captain Trollope you have a fellow in your Squadron named Woollett and we are out to get him.'

They never did; their huntsmen were no match for the quarry. Often it was the other way about, indeed one great action which Woollett conceived a short while before he left in August may fairly classify him not so much as a hunter as fisherman-in-chief. In his own words:

"The lines in front of our aerodrome formed a great salient from the enemy's point of view, and I discussed with my CO the possibility of leading a large formation of fighters over the lines to the south of the salient, then do a big sweep so as to drive into the salient as many Hun machines as possible. From experience I knew that the Hun would sooner try to escape being netted by flying straight home rather than make a detour over our lines. A week later I was given three squadrons – sixty machines – and arranged that they would be stepped-up from 43 Squadron at 8,000 feet to the top squadron at 18,000 feet. It was a fine morning with little wind when we formed up at the exact minute and at the exact heights, and I led the massed formation about twenty-five miles inside the enemy lines before turning to drive into the salient. Below and ahead I soon picked out enemy aircraft in three squadron formations, with another big formation above me. The enemy reacted as I thought they would. Their squadrons broke formation and headed for home as I gave the signal to our chaps to break and attack individually. The Hun was in the net. The air became thick with machines – I had never seen so many at once – and I was after the enemy leader. He was quite a good match in his Fokker D VII but after about four minutes I got the inner circle and held my sight and both guns on his cockpit. Within seconds the D VII burst into flames, and within more seconds I had switched to assist one of my men who was in trouble, something which always disturbed me. My action so surprised the Hun that he broke off his engagement and I had him on his own. He was no leader but a good fighter and, after my fourth burst, a piece of one wing fell away and I left him spinning down to earth .... In this action we were credited with fifteen enemy aircraft destroyed for the loss of two."

The only time Woollett might be found in a lone-wolf *rôle* was when he was after the enemy's artillery observation balloons. Even then he had on occasion an escort of Camels above him. Woollett's score of eleven balloons destroyed was bettered only by one British pilot, Beauchamp-Proctor VC. Nor was his success merely a matter of luck, he said:

"Balloon strafing was not child's play by any means, for they were well protected by a variety of ground defences all lined up and waiting for you at the end of your dive. The balloons were usually up at dawn at a height of about 4,000 feet, height principally governed by the cloud, and the best amount of cloud from the pilot's point of view was about eight-tenths near the balloon line which was 6 to 8 miles behind their lines.

The night before I set out on one of these trips I used to arrange for the Armoury to fill the belts of my Vickers guns mainly with incendiary bullets, but with a sprinkling of ordinary and armour-piercing ones for any aircraft I met by chance. On the way to the lines one could see – visibility permitting – where the balloons were, and it was a case of climbing just above the cloud layer before crossing the lines and so take them by surprise in the initial dive through a gap in the cloud. A good approach was half the battle. The first sign of success was a small red patch in the balloon which quickly spread and soon it looked like a big 'flaming onion' floating down to earth."

Woollett once destroyed three balloons in the course of a single early morning patrol above the Somme. His final words in the report: 'Owing to lack of ammunition I was compelled to terminate the mission', sounds almost like a complaint. At one period he had his Camel camouflaged to look like a Hun, reasoning that since English machines were, without exception, painted a drab brown his oddly coloured machine would lead the German ground defences into mistaking him for one of theirs and so hold their fire. Unfortunately in a dogfight his own pilots mistook him for a Hun and bowing to their request he had his Camel repainted in standard colours.

Captain Woollett's Camel specially camouflaged for balloon busting

None of Woollett's contemporaries in the Squadron appear to have possessed his burning desire to destroy the enemy's balloons but there were several who were very close if not equal with him in other aspects of the air war.

Among them the longest service to 43 was given by Cecil Frederick King. His first victory as a Second Lieutenant was recorded in November 1917. A year later Captain King MC DFC, leading his Flight in the Squadron's last combat of the war recorded his twentieth victory. Soon after the war he returned to England and joined Major Harold Balfour at his training unit in Norfolk. On 24 January 1919, when flying in formation with another ex-43 stalwart, Captain 'Daisy' Daniel MC, the wing-tips of their machines touched and King was killed in the ensuing crash. He was still but barely twenty years old. Although his youth was not so very exceptional in the company of his fellows it was that aspect of him that is still remembered by one of them. "He seemed so young I could imagine him sporting his new school tie. Always exuberant and gay, and in the air very much on the ball. One day I recall he landed with a machine-gun bullet through one of the humps on his tail. He made quite a joke of the disgrace of being wounded in such a place but we told him that though it might not be a wound to boast of in an olden-time pistol duel, it rated under the circumstances of a dogfight or ground-strafing as an honourable wound. Anyway, typical of him, he went to the Doc, got plastered with horse liniment and tape and was off on the very next show. He laughed at any suggestion of discomfort and just said he would sit on the other hump. I noticed he did that in the mess for some time afterwards but he still flew and during the next week shot down two of the enemy that I know of. Cecil was a great morale builder, at least for me. How much I would like to meet him again."

These words, written forty-five years afterwards by the American Lieutenant George Whiting, known inevitably in the Squadron, as 'Fishy', were echoed in similar vein by Harold Balfour in his book, *An Airman Marches*. Even in their imperfect tributes one can sense just how great was the loss to their country in after years of the Cecil Kings of the 'lost generation'.

George Whiting was one of the Americans who came to 43 in the Spring of 1918. Henry R Clay and Earl Zistell were two others. Whiting had been at Harvard and joined the newly formed University Aero Corps when it was formed in 1916. The project, at first forbidden by the College Authorities because of 'great risk of death and accident to the pupils', was finally permitted to proceed and when the United States entered the war the twenty-two Harvard-trained aviators were a fair proportion of the total number of qualified flyers in the country. Although he had a ticket from the Aero Club of America Whiting was sent with many of his compatriots to England. Via Queens College, Oxford, Stamford, Croydon, Dyce and Turnberry, he finally reached CFS Upavon and received the RFC Pilots Certificate No. 9696. And so to 43 Squadron to become their first American. Arriving at St Omer, Whiting received a cordial greeting from the CO Major Miles, and all the officers, although he felt that at first he was closely watched to see if he ate peas with his knife or perhaps had a bow and arrow secreted on his person. 'This was,' he said, 'soon resolved and I never hope to find myself in better company.' He was attached at first to Captain

Trollope's flight and his observations of his early days threw much light on the character of that great fighter ace.

"I still remember him with admiration and affection; he was a truly great man. On my first Offensive Patrol, after he had lectured me about keeping tight formation, we took off and soon ran into what seemed to me to be deadly bursts of Archie. I followed orders and kept just off crash position on his wing tip – like a scared child holding mother's apron strings in the dark, if you know what I mean. When we landed he congratulated me for keeping such fine formation. The fact was that our Flight got a number of Huns on that show but nobody knew less about it than I!

I got used to Archie though I never really enjoyed it. Although I never saw anybody shot down by it, I think it served a purpose for newly-arrived pilots frequently followed the natural urge to dodge these ugly and often close bursts, only to wander off by themselves and provide easy picking for the Huns who always seemed to be higher than us."

Whiting, and the other Americans all left 43 Squadron in July and went to the newly formed 148th US Squadron, which was under overall RAF Command and armed, like 43, with Camels. Henry Clay, 'a quiet unassuming charming fellow', whose first victory was won with 43, rapidly made his mark with the 148th and had destroyed eight enemy machines when he was killed in August 1918.

Captain John Trollope, in whose company the rookie Whiting had felt so assured, was the third of the great triumvirate that served so brilliantly with 43 in the Spring of 1918. He had joined the Army as a Dispatch Rider at seventeen, was invalided home at eighteen and joined the RFC. He had flown 1½ Strutters with 70 Squadron in 1916-17 and, following a spell of home duty, joined 43 on 17 January 1918. It was not long before he had established himself as a brilliant pilot, an excellent shot and game to take on any odds at any time. Woollett said of him, 'He was a very good shot with a wonderful personality. A most likeable young fellow - I could never speak too highly of him. His leadership was perfect.' In his first combat two days after arriving Trollope destroyed an enemy DFW reconnaissance machine, then, attacked by nine escorting enemy Albatros scouts he fought his way out and home. Ten weeks later after sixteen victories, including a record-breaking six on the same day, he was finally vanquished in a fight with eight of the enemy. This battle and its aftermath were a classic of personal courage. Henry Woollett has said that what he hated above all was to see, when engaged with an enemy, one of his machines with a Hun on its tail. It made him feel inwardly sick and all the more determined to finish off his opponent so that he could go to the aid of his friend. This was the way of Trollope's last combat. Outnumbered in the initial clash he saw his pilots shot down one by one, 19 year old Harold Adams and Charles Maasdorp and the more experienced Prior and Owen, until he was all alone. He did not know just how many of the enemy there were, he did not know that Cecil King had climbed up to help him, he was too busy using all his superb skill and trying every trick the Camel possessed to avoid one constant attack after another. Finally he was hit, once, then several times in the leg, arm, head and back, one bullet lodging so near to his spine that during the next forty years no surgeon was ever prepared to remove it. A bullet passed through the windscreen, leaving a neat round hole and then, faint with the loss of blood from his many wounds Trollope passed out. He was still out when his spinning Camel hit the ground and the control column was pushed into his stomach and his left hand was mangled by the collapsing airframe.

His machine crashed just on the wrong side of the lines. In after years Trollope said that if there had been just one good puff of wind in the right direction as his Camel spun down he would have been safe. Removed to a German hospital it was found that his mangled hand would have to be amputated. There were no anaesthetics available – by 1918 the Allied blockade was very effective. He was visited after the operation by Hermann Goering who had been involved in the air battle. Trollope gave him a gold identity disc which he possessed. Goering in return, and full of admiration for the great fight Trollope had put up, smuggled eggs into the hospital in direct contravention of an order that he was not to do so. Trollope said those eggs saved his life for there was virtually nothing else he could eat.

Three months after his capture Trollope was repatriated. Of course he never flew again and his injuries continued to plague him for the rest of his life. As a result of delay in treating his arm a gangrenous condition developed and thirty-nine more operations became necessary during the years after the war. Eventually the arm was removed up to the shoulder, which 'stopped him playing golf'. In World War II he rejoined the RAF and rose to the rank of Wing Commander. His home at Purley was destroyed by a bomb, a

Captain Harold Balfour MC in Camel, 'A' Flight, 43 Squadron, Royal Flying Corps
Lens, March 1918
from a painting by Bertram Sandy, 1919

married quarter evacuated by his wife and daughter at 1800 hours received a direct hit at 2130 the same night. It seemed the Germans had not forgotten what he did to them twenty-two years before. To the last of his days he was at times in great pain because of his multiple wounds – 'but I never *once* heard a word of complaint', his widow will tell you with pride. Whatever else John Trollope may have lost in the crash that ended his ten weeks of glory in 1918, his courage was not among it.

Lieutenant 'Daisy' Daniel, a South African, 'my right hand man' Woollett called him, was another breezy character generally to be found there or thereabouts when the Hun was around. He shot down nine enemy machines between February and May, was awarded the Military Cross and promoted to Captain. In World War II he was a Colonel in the South African Air Force. He died a few years afterwards in a Pretoria hospital.

Lieutenant George Lingham, an Englishman, who was another to fly with 43 for almost the entire year in 1918, made up with Daniel what Woollett swore was the finest pair of pilots that any Flight Commander was ever fortunate enough to find on either side of him. 'Even had I wished I could never have shaken them off in any manoeuvre; always they were in their exact position until, of course, the formation broke up to attack an enemy formation. I owed my life to them on many occasions and without them I would not have been able to accomplish half of what I managed to do in the air.'

Captain C C Banks, ten months with 43, ten enemy machines destroyed, had the unique distinction of being the first British pilot to shoot an enemy machine down at night in France. It happened on the last day of May. Following the failure of their Spring offensive the Germans started a bombing campaign on a hitherto unparalleled scale, aerodromes being singled out for special attention. No. 58 Squadron at Fauquembergues was particularly troubled and appealed to 43 to help deal with the menace. Accordingly, on the night of 31 May, Lieutenant Banks was on patrol at 2350 hours. Seeing an enemy bomber held in a searchlight beam he dived to within twenty-five yards range and opened fire. The bomber, a Friedrichshafen, burst into flames and exploded as it hit the ground. Captain Banks had had experience with 44 (Home Defence) Squadron in England before joining 43 and had a half share in the shooting down of a Gotha, by night, in January 1918. Like C F King, Banks remained with 43 until the Armistice and was engaged in the last reported clash with the enemy on 30 October. He gained both the Military and Distinguished Flying Crosses. Lieutenants' George Lingham, Military Cross and G G Bailey, Distinguished Flying Cross were two others decorated while serving with the Squadron at this time.

But the story of 43 and its Sopwith Camels, as the next chapter will show, is not just a story of a few brilliant men, important though their leadership may have been. There is more to it than that. There were forty men who were killed or wounded in battle or in the accidents to which their early, unreliable machines were always prone. There are as many again who survived but of whose name there is now no record in official lists, except it appears briefly as a victor or near-victor in the summary of the Squadron's history that was written after the war. Of the host of lesser men who swung the engines into life during the cold dawn starts, the armourers who cared for the guns and fixed the bombs (Woollett once landed with one caught up by the cross-bracing wires of the undercarriage – when an armourer was quickly called to cope with it!) the riggers who patched the ripped fabric and glued the broken wood, there is hardly one that has left sign or name. Tom Purdey, imperturbable, still wearing his kilt and still 'playing the piano well', and his henchman 'Bert' Hull, Recording and Engineer officer, are two whose names have not vanished, and on a faded sheet of paper headed 'Routine Orders, In the Field, 24 August 1917', you may read that Corporal Gates was Orderly Sergeant with Corporal Lamb next for duty and 2/AM Stenberg S, Rigger, was admitted to hospital (sick). Nearly all the rest will be sought in vain.

So you will just need to take the word of the very few who still live to remember the great and grand company that was 43 Squadron then. 'No praise is too great for them. They were true friends and I loved them. We were all young and happy together. Fear may have been present inwardly but strength of character won every time. Our pilots were second to none and I had the best of the best – or I would not now be here saying so.' Or from the first American to come as a stranger into their midst, 'I never hope to find myself in better company'.

CHAPTER 5

'Our Airmen have Established ...... A Superiority'

BY the standards of earlier years 1918 was one of unprecedented movement on the Western Front. From the time that the German break-through on the Somme in March had stormed their way forward twenty plus miles in five days, until November when the Allies were racing even faster towards the German frontier, there was a fluidity in the fighting that had not existed before.

For 43 Squadron this naturally brought a change in the pattern of their life and, whereas in 1917 their fighting had been conducted almost entirely in the Lille – Arras area, they now found themselves in action from Ypres to the outskirts of Paris; in so doing, the Squadron engaged in just about every activity open to a Sopwith Camel. Offensive patrols, bomber escorts, ground-strafing, low-level bombing, reconnaissance and interception of enemy machines engaged in the same task, plus a bit of night-fighter work thrown in for good measure.

During the entire year the Squadron was commanded by Major C C Miles who replaced Major Dore in November 1917. An experienced active service campaigner, Major Miles had been flying since 1915 and while serving as a Flight Commander with No 3 Squadron in 1916 had been wounded in action. The only reference to him in the official record for the Squadron during his command is that he destroyed two enemy machines during a single patrol in February and in fact he did not fly very often at all. Yet, though keeping himself apart from his pilots and not sharing much in their activities (the comment, 'he seemed so very much older than we young pilots', may provide the clue to the reason why) he seemed to have had sufficient knowledge of what went on to apply the firm steadying influence that was necessary at times without in any way stultifying the offensive spirit of the hour. 'Height tests', defined by Trollope, were 'the name given to the excuse for going out (on one's own) by a pilot who felt pugnacious' are often evident in the log books of those times, while on the other hand Woollett remembers how a dawn attack with guns and bombs that he had planned to make on an enemy squadron's hangar was called off in the middle of the night after Miles had sent for him and insisted firmly but pleasantly that 'it was too dangerous – I do not want you to go'.

2Lt George P Bradley

The early months with the Camel were not marked with a lot of violent action. The first recorded blow and counterblow was on 28 September 1917 when 2nd Lieutenant Hood was killed by a Fokker triplane, which was in turn sent down in flames by Hood's Flight Commander Captain T W Wynn. Before he despatched his opponent Captain Wynn's machine was itself damaged and he subsequently had to make a forced-landing far from base.

Almost a month later a carbon copy of this action occurred when Captain Fellowes, who had already destroyed a DFW reconnaissance two-seater, fell like an avenging angel on a Fokker scout which was following down its victim, a Camel flown by Second Lieutenant George Bradley.

To complete this same busy morning, Second Lieutenant Harris shot down another DFW, Second Lieutenant George pulled off a successful forced landing after being badly wounded by an incendiary bullet and Second Lieutenant Parkes of the 7th Battalion, Worcestershire Regiment, displaying great gallantry, left the comparative safety of his front line trench to go out 250 yards under heavy fire to rescue a dazed and injured Second Lieutenant Wickendon after his Camel had been shot down and crashed in no-man's-land. Lt Parkes was awarded the Military Cross for this selfless act.

The very last day of October recorded that six Camels went on a special low flying mission, firing into the enemy 'until their guns jammed', a remark which could suggest the armourers were having one of their off days, but apparently not for the action which brought a special letter of congratulations from the GOC of V Corps.

November, which saw the Third Battle of Ypres drag out to its muddy and inconclusive end also, by contrast, saw at Cambrai the first attack to be spearheaded by a force of massed tanks. As part of the widespread diversions laid on in support of this battle 43 spent three days in concentrated ground attack missions, work which again brought a pat on the back from the Corps Commander.

December was apparently a month of extended goodwill to all men, neither loss nor damage to friend or foe being reported. January was equally quiet until the 19th, when the newly arrived Captain Trollope and 2nd Lieutenant Madeley found themselves up against nine enemy Albatros scouts. Trollope had both his guns jam after a short burst but was able to escape by virtue of the Camel's ability to spin down to within a 100 feet of the ground and still pull out. George Madeley apparently tried to use the same tactics for he was last seen low down in a spin, failed to return and was killed.

The first bombing raid made by 43's Camels was recorded on 4 February. Two machines dropped a total of seven 20 lb bombs on three enemy-held villages. Some enemy troops who appeared to resent this action to the extent of firing at the Camels were themselves 'shot up by machine-gun fire'.

On 16 February Major Miles, leading the Squadron on Offensive Patrol attacked an enemy scout and sent it spinning to earth, thus providing a curtain raiser to an eight week period of continuing success. In that time fifty-four enemy machines either went down in flames or were seen to crash and another twenty-four were last seen, in the language of the time, 'to go down out of control'. On 24 March the record for the number of enemy machines destroyed in one day was broken and on 12 April, the day on which Haig issued his famous 'backs to the wall' message, the Squadron responded by breaking it yet again. In addition they took a full part in the intensive ground-strafing that went on against the advancing enemy's ground troops, urged on by the order 'very low flying essential . . . all risks to be taken'.

And this considerable damage was wrought upon the opposing air force for the loss of sixteen pilots, seven of whom were killed and two but slightly wounded.

Harold Balfour, who personally had three confirmed victories in three days, and five in a fortnight, modestly states in his book that during this time 'the best German airmen seemed to have moved away from the areas where 43 was operating', yet even if there is some truth in this the positive virtues of Trollope, Woollett, King, Balfour, Bailey, Lingham, Daniel and their fellow pilots ought surely to be given most of the credit. The more so because a lot of the victories were claimed in battles, where the odds were very much against the Camels. A few excerpts from the combat reports are typical :

17 February. Trollope's patrol of five Camels encountered an enemy formation of eight machines. As a result of the combat which ensued, three enemy machines were driven down out of control.

18 February. Captain Trollope while on a special mission (alone) saw three Arrnstrong-Whitworths under attack by six enemy machines. He at once attacked the enemy who were then joined by six more. Trollope fought the twelve for ten minutes until all his ammunition was exhausted, by which time the enemy machines had all flown away to the east.

19 February. Second Lieutenant R J Owen while on patrol on his own was attacked by five enemy scouts in the vicinity of the Bois de Biez. He fought the five, one of which according to the testimony of anti-aircraft gunners was seen to fall in flames.

26 February. Captain Trollope leading a patrol of nine Camels saw four DFWs escorted by fifteen enemy scouts. He led the patrol into the attack. Although gun trouble prevented him from joining in, he stayed in the middle of the fight to see two enemy machines crash and a third fall out of control.

On 13 March a pair of photographic machines of No 2 Squadron set out under the care and protection of seven Camels of 43. Midway through the mission a mixed force of fifteen Albatros and Pfalz scouts appeared and in spite of the odds the Camels immediately attacked them. The first one that Henry Woollett fired at 'fell to pieces' in the air; the second spun erratically out of control and crashed. Two more went down before the guns of Second Lieutenant Peiler and, with four of the remaining pilots, Second Lieutenants Lingham, Lomax, King and Dean, each adding one, more than half the enemy force was destroyed with no loss to the Camels. Just to ram the victory really home a ninth enemy machine was shot down by one of the 2 Squadron observers.

On 17 March Captain Trollope, while flying alone on a 'Height Test', saw six enemy scouts. He climbed above them and attacked. One immediately 'fluttered down like a falling leaf',

Captain John Trollope MC in the Camel in which he shot down six German aircraft on 24 March 1918

the other five dived away. Returning to base after this action Trollope then sighted four more enemy machines and attacked one at close range. It caught fire and broke up in the air, as 'Trollope finished up chasing the other machines away east'. Although the odds facing Trollope in these actions were not truly representative of those which the Squadron generally met during these times his willingness to do battle, even in unfavourable circumstances, certainly was. It was an attitude that brought the Squadron forty-four victims in thirty days and its solitary casualty in that whole period was one pilot wounded.

The increased activity which gave rise to this scale of success was interwoven with the preparations by the Germans on land as well as in the air for their great Spring offensive. Reinforced by the armies released in the East after the collapse of Russia, and urged on by the need to gain victory in the West before American manpower could reach the battlefields in decisive strength, the enemy began his attack on 21 March.

The first gains were spectacular. The British Fifth Army, guarding a forty-two mile front with only ten divisions, folded up. Contact between the Fifth and Third Armies was lost and as each wheeled back to south and north respectively to guard the open flank, the Germans poured through the gap. After only five days the lynchpin of rearward communications and transport, Amiens, was in danger. Although outside this town the onrush was at last stemmed the situation on the ground remained critical and, as the armies struggled to re-establish a firm front, the Air Force threw in everything to their aid.

The German airmen were out patrolling the battlefield in strength in a bid to establish control of the airspace and so permit their reconnaissance and spotter machines to operate at will. Against them the RFC went with every machine it could muster but in addition it went to aid the hard-pressed soldiers in a more direct manner.

Every aeroplane in the vicinity of the main onslaught took to the air loaded with every kind of bomb which was dropped on the first hostile troops sighted. Machine-guns were fired at close range, often into concentrated bodies of troops, and then it was home again for fresh supplies to repeat the attack.

How well the airmen met the call for 'all risks to be taken' and just how much their incessant efforts influenced the ultimate course of the battle were shown in Field Marshal Sir Douglas Haig's dispatch:

"Throughout the period of active operations our airmen have established and maintained a superiority over the German airmen without parallel since the days of the first Somme battle. Not content with destroying the enemy in the air, they have vigorously attacked his infantry, guns and transport with bombs and machine-gun fire, and in the fighting south of the Somme, in particular, gave invaluable assistance to the infantry by these means on numerous occasions. In addition the usual work of reconnaissance, photography, artillery co-operation and bombing has been carried out vigorously and with remarkable results."

For two days after the attack began 43, which was then operating from La Gorgue, near Merville (fifteen miles west of Lille), was rather far removed from the battle but on 23 March 1918 moved twenty-five miles nearer by transferring to Avesnes-le-Comte near Arras. Detailed next morning to provide day-long protection to other machines of the Brigade engaged in low flying attacks on ground targets, 43 responded so well that before sunset it had set up a record by destroying twelve enemy machines, a result gained with no loss to the Squadron. Captain John Trollope had himself shot down half the Squadron's total and bettered the recorded feat of Captain Albert Ball VC DSO** MC who had five of the enemy fall to him in one day's fighting. Writing home to his mother that evening Trollope exuberantly began 'This has been the most wonderful day of my life'; as well he might.

On the first patrol of the day three DFW reconnaissance two-seaters were seen. Trollope leading the Flight worked round to the east to prevent them escaping and then led in to attack. His guns jammed as he fired at the first but he cleared the stoppage and firing 100 rounds at the second saw it break up in the air. After firing even fewer rounds at the third it went on fire. The first DFW having escaped from Trollope's jammed guns was attacked by Cecil King, who with the aid from the third member of Trollope's flight, 2nd Lt Owen, caused it to break up in the air. Trollope meantime was adding an Albatros scout to his brace of DFWs, while Henry Woollett whose flight was lower than Trollope, had hit the fourth DFW of the morning out of play, his victim too going down in flames. Finally Lt Daniel, losing Woollett during this attack, joined up with No 3 (Naval) Squadron and, seeing five Pfalz D III scouts, shot one to pieces at point-blank range.

Seven before lunch was a good score but more were yet to come. During the afternoon the cloudbase lowered considerably but patrols went on and Trollope espied four enemy two-seaters attacking a formation of RE 8s. Some enemy scouts were also around and battle was soon joined. Trollope diving onto one of the RE's tormentors opened fire from short range. Pieces fell away from the target and then the whole wing structure folded up and the wreckage exploded and fell apart. Breaking downwards from the fight Trollope saw two pink-painted two-seaters below and flying very close to the ground. Closing swiftly by using his height advantage Trollope fired at one and then the other and in quick succession the two enemy machines dived into the ground and disintegrated. 'I then saw one of our fellows attacked by twelve Huns', Trollope said, 'so I climbed up to him and let him get away but then I ran out of ammunition and turned for home but not before being able to confirm that two enemy scouts, attacked by Second Lieutenants Owen and Highton, respectively, had crashed.'

The last named of these two was killed the next day, the Squadron's first fatal casualty since far off 12 January. The loss was evened out by Captain Woollett who, flying near the altitude limit for a Camel around 20,000 feet, fired rounds at fifty feet into one of two enemy machines. 'Going down like a falling leaf it was ultimately seen to crash.'

Five thousand eight hundred rounds were fired at hostile troops by nine Camels which went off during the afternoon. Henry Woollett leading this patrol also had sufficient ammunition to dispose of two enemy balloons in flames. Some days later the same pilot went even one better. Flying along the Somme from Bray to Méricourt he sent down three balloons in quick succession before his ammunition was all spent.

On 28 March luck finally ran out. Nine Camels went out on an Offensive Patrol to provide cover for the ground attack machines operating below; five failed to return. Two pilots, Second Lieutenants Adams and Maasdorp were dead; three others Owen, Prior and, worst of all for the Squadron, Captain Trollope, became prisoners-of-war. Cecil King had seen Trollope fighting a lone battle with eight enemy scouts. Climbing up to assist him King succeeded in drawing off two and shot one down. But then he was himself wounded by an enemy bullet and forced to return.

Trollope had fought his way out against similar odds before but this day fortune deserted him and, wounded in several places, he passed out from loss of blood and spun in.

Cecil King was promoted from Second Lieutenant directly to Captain to fill the vacant post in Trollope's flight and, although still suffering from the wound sustained in going to his predecessor's assistance, it was he who was first to avenge the loss by destroying one of two enemy triplanes on 3 April. Later four Albatros scouts attacked, and King and his companions, Captain Loudon and Second Lieutenant O'Neill all returned with badly riddled machines.

Following two days of poor weather, 43 was sent on 6 April deep into the Salient made by the German advance and during the afternoon some desperate fighting, mainly with the crack JG 1 unit ensued. During the day this German unit claimed five of 43's Camels in their total of ten British aeroplanes listed but 43 in return had five of the triplanes' scalps and an Albatros as well.

An early afternoon ground-strafing mission to Abancourt was attacked as it arrived over the target by a number of Fokker triplanes. Two were shot down, one in flames, by Lt Daniel.

Captain C F King, Lt C G Bailey, Lt A C Dean, April 1918

2nd Lt George Lingham killed the pilot of another that overshot him and 2nd Lt Henry Lewis, who crashed a fourth, failed to return and was later found dead. The next patrol was disastrous, three out of six Camels failing to return (two dead, one prisoner), but before nightfall Cecil King, still not fully recovered from his wounded seat, helped to make the overall picture a better one.

Leading his flight into six triplanes, he destroyed one of them after a head-on attack. Lt C C Banks caught an Albatros which joined in the mêlée later and saw it crash before returning to attack the ground target which, as with all the flights that day, had been the prime reason for the mission. Heavily engaged by ground fire Banks had his petrol tank holed and elevator cables shot away but succeeded in getting about two miles on the right side of the lines before crash landing.

Four days of fog and drizzle followed. On the third of these the Germans attacked westwards from Lille along both sides of the River Lys. 43's former stable mates at La Gorgue, Naval 8 Squadron (renumbered to 208 nine days earlier following the merger of the RFC and RNAS to form the RAF) had to abandon the aerodrome at speed, burning sixteen Camels that they could not fly off in the prevailing zero visibility.

It was forty-eight hours before the fog began to clear enough to allow 43 to get up a patrol above the new battleground or for the Army staffs to obtain a clear picture of the fighting. What the latter did see was frightening enough. Aided by the complete collapse of two Portuguese divisions the Germans were heading swiftly toward the road and rail centre of Hazebrouck with little apparently in front to stop them. Moreover, as was pointed out by the faint-hearted, an advance as great as that achieved on the Somme would put the Germans on the Channel Coast and result in the total isolation of the large forces stationed in Flanders. On the next day, 12 April, with nothing but black reports continuing to pour in and the situation seemingly beyond all hope, Haig issued his famous 'backs to the wall' message. It was addressed to his Army as it happened but 43 Squadron responded with its most successful day of the war. The record set up in March was broken as fourteen enemy machines went down during the course of the day. If John Trollope was no longer there it still possessed a Henry Woollett, able to hit a six, and most of the now familiar names also appeared in the successful combat reports.

Fittingly it was Cecil King, leading Trollope's former Flight who opened the score. Fifteen Camels, every serviceable aeroplane that the Squadron could muster, were on patrol when King sighted another friendly squadron and a force of enemy scouts about to clash. Signalling to the remainder of his own Flight, King led them into the battle and both he and Lt Banks caused an enemy machine to fold up in the air. On the way home Banks also shot down a second, one of a formation he sighted below him.

In the meantime Woollett had spotted eight Huns just south-east of the overrun aerodrome at La Gorgue. Three of them fell to his guns, the last falling on fire and exploding. A fourth machine, an Albatros, was destroyed at short range by Lt Daniel who then set off after a Pfalz which he had just seen shoot down a friendly Camel. This enemy too went down to crash whereupon Daniel found himself set upon by five of his foes. Kicking his Camel into a spin Daniel went down, apparently in great trouble but at 1,000 feet he pulled out and with the enemy successfully shaken off made for home.

The last pilot of the Squadron to return, Second Lieutenant Bailey, added another Albatros to the pre-lunch scorecard. It was one that had tried to stop him as he went to attack an enemy balloon and was itself destroyed for its effrontery.

Only thirteen Camels were ready for the afternoon patrol but, in spite of the loss of Second Lieutenant Kissell (killed) and Dean (prisoner) the outcome was far from unlucky. Daniel and Lingham, Woollett's two trusted aides, each destroyed an Albatros and with the maestro himself, again equalling his score of the morning with three confirmed victims the day's bag went up to fourteen. Major-General John Salmond, C-in-C RFC in France, turned up in time to share a congratulatory cup of tea.

Lt G A Lingham, Lt Tom Purdey, Lt H Daniel, Capt C F King and Lt G D Daly, May 1918

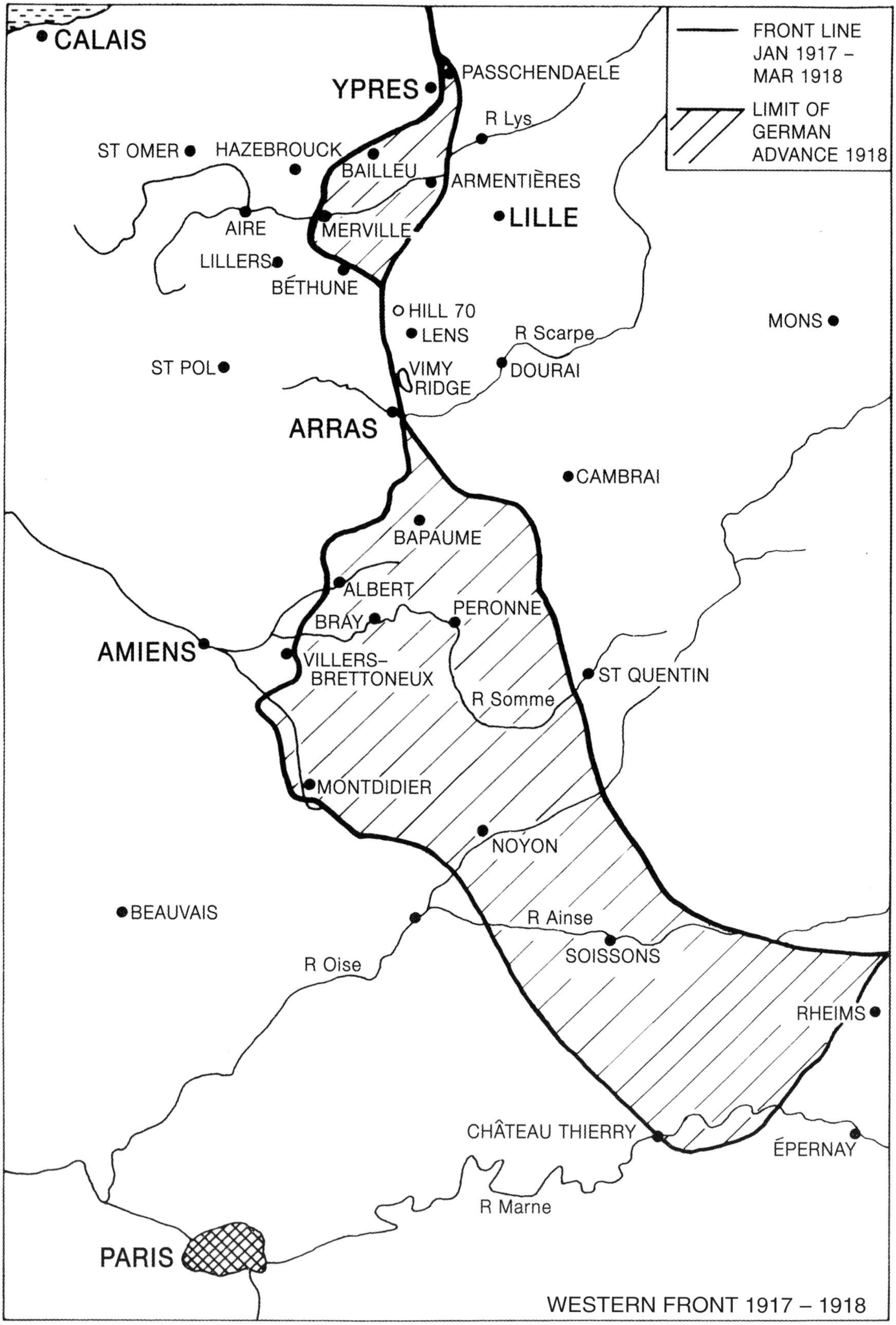
CALAIS
YPRES
PASSCHENDAELE
FRONT LINE JAN 1917 – MAR 1918
LIMIT OF GERMAN ADVANCE 1918
R Lys
ST OMER
HAZEBROUCK
BAILLEU
ARMENTIÈRES
LILLE
AIRE
MERVILLE
LILLERS
BÉTHUNE
HILL 70
LENS
R Scarpe
MONS
ST POL
VIMY RIDGE
DOURAI
ARRAS
CAMBRAI
BAPAUME
ALBERT
BRAY
PERONNE
AMIENS
VILLERS-BRETTONEUX
ST QUENTIN
R Somme
MONTDIDIER
NOYON
BEAUVAIS
R Ainse
SOISSONS
R Oise
RHEIMS
CHÂTEAU THIERRY
ÉPERNAY
R Marne
PARIS
WESTERN FRONT 1917 – 1918

Lt G A Lingham, Lt G D Daly, Capt C F King at Avesnes-le-Compte, May 1918

At such a rate of attrition the German airmen must have considered it a great relief that during the remaining eighteen days of April bad weather kept 43 grounded for all but two of them. Not so the sorely tried and weary soldiers on the ground for whom the continued absence of the Camels in the ground-strafing role was but an additional burden. Nevertheless, by the end of the month the undiminished doggedness of Tommy Atkins and the peculiar British trait of never knowing when they are defeated had finally removed all cause for anxiety on this front and the Germans, now twice foiled by the British, were heading for Champagne and the shortest route to Paris. As a result of this southward switch by the enemy May was a comparatively quiet month on the British-held sectors. Four pilots were lost but fifteen enemy machines were destroyed. Seven of these, Albatroses, went down on the 30th during a great fight in which two of the newly arrived Americans, Lieutenants Whiting and Clay, recorded their first victories.

At the end of May the expected attack for the capture of Paris began and was temporarily halted on the River Marne. Meantime, anticipating another German move southwards from the newly won Somme Salient, the 9th and 51st Wings (43 made up the latter, with Nos 80 and 2 (Australian) Squadrons) were sent to this area. This was the first of several such moves.

'These moves to wherever the fighting was hottest both in the air and on the ground was a good thing,' says Henry Woollett. 'It gave us the Huns to attack, but it was very inconvenient where comfort was concerned since the packing up and moving always took place at night and without any notice at all of course. It often happened after retiring for the night, when an orderly would come down the village High Street banging on the doors of our billets and telling us to report to the CO at once. The transport was packed and left before dawn and we would take off at the first glimmer of light.'

In such a manner 43 arrived in the Beauvais area on 4 June. On the 7th the expected attack began. An immediate increase in the size of the enemy air formations was reported, up to forty machines at a time being encountered by our bombers, whereas previously, according to the French, more than six at a time was rare. Cecil King and his Flight took on one group of the enemy Albatros scouts, and destroyed three of them.

Massed counter-attack patrols were ordered for 9 and 10 June, a far cry from the first tentative pioneering efforts of 43 a year before. Over a hundred machines from the 51st Wing were employed on a non-stop all-out attack on the enemy ground forces. 43 Squadron alone in these two days dropped over one hundred and sixty 20 lb bombs and fired more than 13,000 rounds of ammunition, playing havoc with transport, guns, horses, troops and other targets. One ammunition cart blew up to a height of several hundred feet. Six enemy aeroplanes trying to protect their unhappy troops were shot down as well, three by the old firm of King, Lingham and Banks, one of the remainder by another American, Lt Earl Zistell. Two more Fokker triplanes were bagged on the 12th, two Pfalz scouts the next day. By the 21st 'the danger in (this) area was past'. The Camels had done their work well. Forty-eight hours later they were back among the slag-heap countryside at Aire.

Here it was that Henry Woollett conceived the idea of using the great salient carved out by the Germans during April into a trap for the unsuspecting Hun. 'Woollett's Circus', they called it, of a size 'that put Richthofen's in the

'C' Flight sheds at Le Touquin, July 1918

Ridley, Cecil King, Bloomfield, Keary, Lingham relax at Lietiers, July 1918

shade and caused complete consternation in the German air service'. The success that attended this venture has been told. Unfortunately, the idea could not be operated for very long because the Wing was temporarily detached to the Somme area for a few days early in July to help clean up the air while the Australians were making a limited attack to clear the Villers-Bretonneux plateau and secure the approaches to Amiens. There wasn't much work for 43 in those parts. Nor much in the way of home comforts either for the temporary hosts, 5th Air Brigade, were primitively provided already. However Lt Coghill raised some good cheer with one enemy scalp and on the next day the official report said that 'only one enemy machine was seen and this fled east on sighting No 43's Camels'. Obviously another pilot who agreed with the great James McCudden's dictum about 'living to fight another day'.

Returning to the Ypres area there was hardly time to settle into the regular billets before another round of early morning knocking-up heralded a further rough journey over the low-class French roads; this time all the way south to the area south of the River Marne and ten miles from Paris. The aerodrome was a former allotment in the grounds of the Chateau Mumm. The Squadron's Camels, part of a force of 162 machines of the 10th Brigade, flew in to reinforce their French allies on, of all days, the 14th of July, Bastille Day. Next day at dawn the Germans attacked. By midday three bridges were across the Marne and the enemy was rapidly building

Camels at Le Touquin, July 1918

Kitto, Roy Royston, Henry Woollett & Geach Le Touquin, July 1918

up his strength on the southern side before proceeding to Paris. But then, the Air Forces arrived.

43 Squadron alone dropped thirty-nine bombs and fired 4,710 rounds in its first twenty-one strong squadron sortie. Among other reports was one of a column of horse transport stampeded, the subsequent confusion being unimproved by our attacks which caused casualties. By the 17th, less than forty-eight hours after the first assault, a squadron OP reported that 'all the bridges across the river were completely destroyed'. A subsequent German document spoke of the havoc wrought on the ground troops and the incessant bombing of the Marne bridges which prevented the transport of supplies across the river.

The aerial assault continued for a fortnight. When it was over, the Germans, broken on the Marne, taken in flank by a counter-attacking French Army, had started on the retreat that was not to stop until the cease-fire in November. 43's part in the victory had cost it four dead and two missing but it could claim, besides the damage wrought among the enemy's ground forces, six enemy aeroplanes confirmed as destroyed and three balloons in flames. It hardly needs to be said that Henry Woollett, one of five Squadron pilots to receive the Croix de Guerre from the French Government for their share in the battle, was responsible for this last item. Shortly afterwards he left for England. Captain A H Orlebar replaced him.

By 4 August 43 was back in the British sector again and for the next month continued very much as before. On the opening day of the Battle of Amiens (8 August) the Camels, now carrying an increased bomb load (four 25 lb), attacked two bridges near Peronne. In heavy rain and poor visibility the Camels, which went off in

Sopwith Snipes

pairs at twenty-minute intervals, played hide-and-seek in the low clouds with the German airmen, who were as keen to protect these particularly important bridges as the RAF were to knock them out. In the course of some heavy fighting the RAF lost sixty machines. One of them was that of 2nd Lt Arundel who was killed, another belonged to Lt Ben Lefroy who lived to tell his story:

"I had done my work for the day, two sorties, and was reading my mail in the mess. An orderly came haring in and asked for volunteers, as a pilot in 'A' had gone sick. As the only person in the mess – it was me! The only machine I could get was 'R', the target practice aircraft, a slow and bad machine. My own Camel was being repaired, having collected some Hun bullets on my previous sortie. Soon after coming out of cloud we ran into fifteen Huns. My engine was not good and, trying to get more out of it, I 'choked' it. At this time I saw Cecil King with a couple of Huns on his tail and so pulled up to give 'em a squirt and down they came on me. The universal joint was shot off the joystick, my rudder wires cut and petrol was squirting all over the cockpit. With the throttle I kept pulling the nose up until, at 300 feet, I went into a spin and went in. I came to four hours later, on the ground, in our barrage, with a Hun by my side. I had three bullet holes in me, both knees out of joint fractured skull and fractured wrist and of course a POW."

Cecil King on this flight himself destroyed a Fokker. So did Lieutenant Forbes, who attacked by six triplanes, crashed one and dodged the others. On the following day twenty-two enemy machines attacked an early morning patrol, which was taking some DH 9s to Cambrai and it lost three of their number as a result.

On 12 August a Sopwith Snipe arrived, the first of twenty-four which were to re-equip the Squadron. The last one did not come until mid-September and since, initially, the new machines were only permitted to be flown on defensive patrols on our own side of the line, the Camel remained in service concurrently with the Snipes. Most of September was given up to practising with the new machines. With 230 hp available from a very reliable Bentley rotary engine, the Snipe was a powerful weapon for its period, although like the Camel it was not particularly docile.

By the time the Squadron got back to a full resumption of operations the outcome of the war seemed settled beyond doubt. All the same the enemy continued meanwhile to resist stubbornly, giving nothing away, so there was

2 Lt Reg Houlding and Aero-Mechanic Gagnor with Snipe E8032 'Q' of B Flight at Canada Camp, Fienvillers in September 1918

'C' Flight's Lieutenant George G Wakeman in Snipe 'Y' at Bickendorf, Cologne - April 1919

plenty of work for the airmen. Mostly, for 43, it consisted of escorting, or flying patrols in conjunction with the increasing numbers of bombers daily setting out to hammer the Hun. In the six days following the resumption of active flying on 26 September, ten enemy machines were shot down in various stages of unserviceability for no loss to the Squadron.

October was a month of continued protective patrols, mostly for the DH 9s of 98 and 107 Squadrons. On occasions 43 would join in a bombing party themselves, as on the 23rd when they obtained six or seven direct hits on the station at Hirson.

On the 30th of the month, 43, again flying an Offensive Patrol to cover the retirement after a raid of 98 and 107, by now becoming old pals and for whom they were getting quite an attachment, found 'a formation of at least six Fokkers over Aulnoye' and against them fought the Squadron's last battle of the war.

Perhaps these German airmen were demoralised in the face of impending defeat, perhaps they were just not as good or experienced as some earlier opponents had proved. Whatever the reason, the flight ended with all six of the enemy down and never a scratch to man or machine. Captain Cecil King, celebrating that very week the anniversary of his posting to 43, recorded in this fight his twentieth victory, Captain Banks his tenth. The other four machines fell to Lieutenants Mulcair, Murray, Mitchell and Howsam. For the last three it was their first success. That was the Squadron's last battle. Its last casualty, caused by engine failure, was Lieutenant A C Macauley who spent just seven days as a prisoner after a forced landing on the 4th of the month. The last protective patrol, recorded as 'wholly uneventful' was flown on the 10th.

At 1100 hrs the following morning there began, as men thought, the age of eternal peace. The war to end all wars was won. It had cost 43, during twenty-two months in France, Belgium and Germany, at least sixty-six dead and as many again grievously wounded or prisoners of war. 'Officially' there were 110 enemy aeroplanes and twelve balloons to the Squadron's credit, a figure which incidentally is less than the sum of accredited individual victories. Not that that matters now, nor ever did. For the thing that is still remembered by the survivors of those days is not what the scoreboard read but the way in which that team of young men were prepared to sling their bats at everything, however sticky the wicket, however professionally hostile the bowling. When they got hurt there were no complaints, and in between times there were some pretty lively high jinks around the place. A collection of habits that has characterised 43 Squadron ever since.

In December 1919, after some months with the Army of Occupation at Cologne and elsewhere, 43 Squadron was disbanded at Spitalgate, near Grantham. Apart from the fact that it had three Commanding Officers in the last seven months and that one of its pilots was killed in a collision with a 70 Squadron machine at Cologne there is no trace at all of anything that happened during these months.

Captain G A 'Titch' Giles with members of 'C' Flight
Lt Gilbert, Lt Fowles, Lt Hodgson, Lt Murray, Lt Thomas
Lt Wakeman - September 1918 – August 1919

43 Squadron RAF, British Army of the Rhine, May 1919

7 Flt Lt Thomas (Commanding Officer)
succeeded by Major A W C Parr in June 1919

1 Lt Kemp (Admin)
2 Unknown
3 Lt Stewart
4 Lt Davidson
5 Capt Colyer
6 Capt G A Giles, OC 'C' Flt
8 Capt Anderson MC, OC 'A' Flt
9 Capt Burgher MC, OC 'B' Flt
10 Lt Murray
11 Lt Wakeman
12 2nd Lt Fowles
13 Lt Lovell
14 2nd Lt Gilbert
15 Lt Crowe (Stores)
16 Unknown

CHAPTER 6

Mother Meyrick's Own

IF, as the Duke of Wellington avowed from his experience, 'There are no bad soldiers, only bad officers', it follows that an exceptionally good squadron is an indication of an exceptionally good Squadron Commander. Therefore, since 43 was, by 1930, acknowledged to be one of the outstanding squadrons in the Royal Air Force (in that year it was noted that nearly all the cadets passing out from Cranwell opted for 43 as their first choice), the credit must go in the first place to Sqn Ldrs A F Brooke and C N Lowe, the two men who commanded it, in turn, during the first five formative years after it re-formed. By the time the last named of this pair handed over control at the end of 1930 to Sqn Ldr Lionel Slatter (a Schneider trophy pilot of 1928, CO of the High Speed Flight and no mean leader himself) the custom and habit that 43 Squadron performed all things at the highest possible pitch of perfection was well and truly established. Coming into such an atmosphere of accepting nothing but the best it was not surprising that later arrivals did not fail to maintain the standard.

Sqn Ldr Brooke began the task of building up his Squadron at Henlow in 1925. In that year the Command called the Air Defence of Great Britain, ADGB for short, was formed as a result of the recommendations of the committee, appointed by the Government in 1923, under the Chairmanship of the Marquess of Salisbury. The fighter squadrons reactivated from 1923 onwards, as a start to the task of rebuilding the Royal Air Force at home after the post 1918 decline (at the beginning of 1923 there was one fighter squadron in the UK), were put under the command of ADGB and were grouped into the subordinate command of ADGB known as 'Fighting Area'.

Squadron Leader Arthur Brooke, an Ulsterman, was never known by any other name than 'Pongo'. This was long before this word came into general use by the RAF as a descriptive term for the Army. In fact it was bestowed on him in boyhood by his elder brother Sir Basil Brooke (later Lord Brookeborough), who was the Prime Minister of Northern Ireland from 1943-63. Squadron Leader Brooke served in the 10th Hussars before transferring to the RFC. He graduated with RFC Flying Certificate 670 on 21 October 1915 and then served with Nos 6 and 18 Squadrons in France. On one occasion when setting out for a bombing attack on Zeppelin sheds at Bruges he was promised the Military Cross if he got a direct hit. Alas, two near misses were the best he could manage. He was later wounded in action and lost the top of a finger.

In 1922 he was commanding a squadron in the Boys' Wing at Cranwell where by his keenness and enthusiasm – 'above all he was fair' – he gained the confidence of the boys and a reputation for watching after their interests like a hawk. Neither he nor his wife Lola were ever known to miss any match or other event in which his squadron was participating.

In 1923 he became Personal Secretary to 'Boom' Trenchard and was sent by that great man to Henlow in 1925 to re-form No 43.

Air Chief Marshal Sir Leslie Hollinghurst GBE KCB DFC, who was the Wing Adjutant at Cranwell when Brooke was there, believes that Brooke's service with 43 was the highlight of his career. 'He gave all that he had got to it. No one was allowed to say a word against 43, and he instilled all his chaps with the same enthusiasm. At that time I was on the Staff of Inland Area and can safely say that 43 had the highest morale of any of the new squadrons. His wife was even more of a '43' fanatic than he was, were that possible, and both their lives revolved around 43.'

Squadron Leader A F Brooke

Sopwith Snipe E7724 at Henlow in 1925. The aircraft is being prepared for flight using a Hucks Starter

The results of such devoted leadership were soon visible, some of them for the world to see when the Gamecocks arrived at the Hendon Pageant one year and two days after the Squadron reformed. But firstly a word about the Gamecock's forerunner in the Squadron, the Sopwith Snipe.

The Snipe, first flown by 43 on the Western Front in 1918, was again used for the first ten months at Henlow, nothing more modern being immediately available. As it turned out 43 was the last Squadron in the RAF to fly the Snipe, before it was relegated from front-line service.

In its loaded state the Snipe weighed less than one ton, had a top speed in level flight of 125 mph, and climbed to ten thousand feet in just under ten minutes. Its handling characteristics are well described by the world-famous former Chief Test Pilot of the Bristol Aircraft Company, A J 'Bill' Pegg, who was sent to 43 at Henlow in 1925 as an LAC under training as a pilot (with subsequent promotion to Sergeant), a system adopted to help the overloading of the Flying Training Schools following the decision to increase the size of the RAF.

Bill Pegg's opinion was that the Snipe was quite tricky to fly. It had a very sensitive elevator control and the usual bungee-rubber type of undercarriage shock absorber with, of course, no damping at all. Consequently what was put into the undercarriage was returned in full measure, which really meant that if the landing was heavy then the rebound sent the Snipe up about five or six feet. It was, therefore, usually the 'second' landing that caused the damage.

"Another difficulty, one which I found disconcerting and which I never really mastered during the short time I was flying the Snipe, was the gyroscopic effect of the large rotary engine. This effect was most marked during steep turns and particularly in a loop, when, as the loop progressed the gyroscopic effect would turn the aircraft to the right. This could be corrected fairly easily by rudder during the first part of the loop but at the top with very little airspeed and the controls becoming relatively ineffective the tendency became very difficult to control. In my own case I invariably 'fell off the top' into a spin, much to the amusement of the more experienced pilots who were usually watching my attempts. In those days no instruction was given in aeroplanes, the pupils being expected to go away to a quiet spot and get on with it as best they might. In fact,' says Pegg, 'some of the more experienced pilots were very loath to give away their self-taught secrets and I am sure that many lives were lost during these experiments."

In those days with the aircraft fitted with very few instruments the weather had to be 'pretty good', to quote Pegg, for anybody to fly at all and 'exceptionally good' for the less experienced. A certain amount of ground training in such subjects as Airmanship, Signals or Navigation was undertaken but neither planned system nor specialist instructors existed and generally it was a case of getting hold of the Air Publication relevant to the subject and getting on with it alone. Saturday morning was always the time for the weekly wash, when with copious supplies of water, soft soap and a scrubbing brush the week's dirt was removed. The rotary engines were still lubricated with castor oil which stuck particularly hard to everything. Nor did many ever suffer from constipation.

The days of castor oil lubrication were, however, numbered. On 26 March 1926 Squadron Leader Brooke flew 43's first Gamecock in to Henlow – and so arrived the title *The Fighting Cocks* which has stuck to the Squadron ever since. Precisely why it should have been 43 that snaffled the name is not clear. No 23 Squadron equipped with the Gamecock just before 43 and Nos 3, 17, and 32 soon afterwards. Fg Off Cubitt, who came later to 43 but at this time was with 19 Squadron, recalls that they were 'terribly fond of the Gamecock and swanked no end'. Presumably it was just this swank which resulted in 43 getting in the first claim to the title when, as happened around this time, the Air Ministry called on its squadrons to choose a badge and a motto for themselves (official crests approved by the College of Heralds did not arrive for another ten years). The motto *Gloria Finis* had been the family motto of the Brookes for centuries and its literal translation, *The Glory the End*, having been understood to mean true to the last gasp or game to the end was singularly appropriate to the Gamecock insignia. The Cock itself which subsequently appeared on the Squadron's badge was not any old cock either. One of Squadron Leader Brooke's first actions after the Ministry had approved his suggestion was to order for his wife a diamond studded cockerel brooch. This was made by Carringtons, the London jewellers, who used as their pattern an etching, dating back to 1760 of the champion Gamecock of All England. It is in fact this Gamecock which has appeared on the Squadron's crest ever since. Matching their CO's enthusiasm the officers all kitted themselves out with special Fighting Cock cuff-links, at least one pair of which were still being worn forty years later. It was also at this time that the black and white chequered markings appeared for the first time although in this instance there is no recorded reason for this particular choice nor any who remember the reason why.

The Gloster Gamecock was a development of the earlier Gloster Grebe. Powered with an unsupercharged Bristol Jupiter VI, nine cylinder radial of 450 hp, it had a top speed of 155 mph (a specially cleaned up model reached 275 mph in a dive!) climbed to 10,000 feet in seven and a half minutes and was armed with twin Vickers Mk I machine-guns synchronised to fire through the propeller. Of these guns W E P Johnson said that 'it was extremely rare for the two guns to fire. In one firing camp lasting two weeks at Sutton Bridge, I got *four* rounds off. And these were supposed to be the last word in fighters!' Provision for oxygen equipment as well as wireless receiver and transmitter units existed but these were rarely fitted. Apart from the fact that anything which detracted however slightly from the aerobatic qualities of the aircraft was unpopular, the Gamecock reacted badly to the fitting of wireless for it put the C of G back so far that, to quote Tommy Rose, 'recovery from a spin was not an even money bet'. The poor spin-recovery characteristic was probably due to the already small rudder being made even less effective by the blanketing effect of the deep fuselage but the subject of spinning Gamecocks appears to be a very fishy one. W E P Johnson, a rare bird inasmuch as he was a trained engineer as well as a pilot, tells that "whereas one was not supposed to spin Gamecocks to the right (it was absolute nonsense) my particular aircraft J8421 uniquely hated spinning left. When I left the Squadron I handed her over to a new boy from Cranwell who spun left on her on his second trip, failed to recover, and that was it."

Another thing said about the first batch of Gamecocks was that they suffered from wing flutter, inherited from the earlier Grebe. During the early days of familiarisation there were visits from the manufacturers' representatives, one at least of whom spent some time lying on his back on the ground with a telescope watching the aircraft flying overhead. On another occasion after a Gloster Test Pilot had failed to induce

Gamecocks at Henlow in 1925 carrying the newly applied black and white chequers

flutter on a particular aeroplane and expressed his doubts as to the fact that it did so, he was silenced by the famous Dick Atcherley, then a Plt Off with 23 Squadron, also at Henlow, 'who dived to within twenty-five feet of the tarmac, pulled out and disappeared upwards in a frightening Blurr-r-r of flutter.' In the opinion of H W Woollett, who at one time was Atcherley's Flight Commander, he was the greatest aerobatic pilot in the RAF. 'He was always up in the air and most of it on his back.' The flutter problem allegedly disappeared after the fitting of inter-aileron struts but W E P Johnson says 'They still fluttered – and no harm came of it, except that the stick bashed your knuckles'. The same man said that 'for its purpose the Gamecock was the best aeroplane of its generation', and Tommy Rose is not alone in his opinion that 'it was a real gentleman's aeroplane', and that the performance of the Gamecock at the Hendon Air Pageants was never quite equalled by its later and heavier successors.

Re-formed four days after the 1925 Pageant, 43 got stuck into preparing for the 1926 show. To quote Mrs Brooke, 'they really worked like blacks that Summer, day after day after day'. Using a reservoir near Biggleswade as the target they spent all their time practising formation bomb-dives. The particular part allotted to 43 was to attack the set-piece 'hostile aerodrome' with bombs and then make another attack with machine-guns before retiring and allowing the 'heavies', Vickers Vimys to finish off the job. This part of their job 43 did to perfection at the actual display but more, they followed by doing what nobody else had then done at Hendon and landed in Squadron formation. 'Actually,' said Tommy Rose, 'it was a close run thing for we never succeeded during the rehearsals but on the great day itself everything was spot on.' A

Squadron Leader Brooke in front of his Gamecock

subsequent signal sending 'My hearty congratulations on the magnificent display given by your Squadron in the set piece. Give my personal congratulations to all your pilots and mechanics' was received from Air Chief Marshal Sir Hugh Trenchard, indicating that 43 had succeeded in impressing the knowledgeable as well as the great mass of spectators.

In February 1927 43 moved from Henlow to Tangmere in Sussex. Here it was joined soon afterwards by No 1 Squadron, lately stationed in Iraq, and so began a period of intense but friendly rivalry that lasted for more than thirteen years. Tangmere had been used during the latter part of the war but it was 43 who became its first peacetime permanent inhabitants. Before long the camp had a reputation as a highly desirable posting and its 'Summer Routine', which from May to August compressed the working day into an extended morning session and so allowed every afternoon free was a perk not available on any other Home Station. Superimpose on this leisurely routine the proximity of facilities for bathing or sailing, the Goodwood races, the Whit Monday cricket match at Goodwood

Gamecock J7904, the Squadron Leader's aircraft, with chequered spine

Gamecock J7907 from which Sgt Freestone emerged unhurt

House – 'Duke of Richmond's XI v The Duchess's XI and a wonderful salmon and wine lunch with the estate staff', the rugger, cricket, squash, and all the comradeship of team games, throwing in the fortnight when one of the London Auxiliary Squadrons joined in the fun and the flying, and the whole adds up to a way of living that was not to be bettered in any day or age. Could it be more than a coincidence that in those times the Medical Branch required no psychiatric department?

Even when flying there was time to spare. Ian Brodie wrote how, "Being by nature a quizzy type, I once summoned up enough courage to nip up through a ten mile hole in the clouds that was sometimes found at Tangmere in dicy weather, and fly away towards London: I don't think I have ever experienced such a moment of a reverence for creation – such as one gets on a still day on top of a mountain or at sea; a moment in which one can listen to the 'still small voice' that Elijah heard, the sound of tender silence. After that first break through I went up through the hole whenever the opportunity came; with radar and ground control I doubt

Groundcrew in front of a Gamecock

Gamecocks attack the set-piece at the 1926 Hendon Air Pageant

whether one could experience such a beautiful moment, alone with The Almighty." W E P Johnson in a similar vein wrote how he found himself hypnotised by the beauty of the night when flying at 16,000 feet near to cloud 'so dense I could almost touch it'.

Night flying was an activity of which, to quote "we did very little and for good reason; it was impossible to pick up an enemy at night with no radar, ground control or searchlights – and no landing strip guiding lights either, when it was time to return, except four or five goose-necks laid out in a tee, headed, with luck, into wind – and the red lamp at the end was known to have been hung on the second strand of a wire fence which was small encouragement especially as the tendency to undershoot at night was common. We were reluctant to use a pair of pyrotechnic wing-tip flares because if the aeroplane tipped over the risk of catching fire was considerable." The first time Johnson went flying at night in a Gamecock he thought that the generator mounted on the starboard lower wing was on fire when he throttled back for his first landing. Carrying out the correct drill for such an emergency he turned off the petrol and opened the throttle whereupon the fire went out. Switching on the petrol with some trepidation he landed and taxied in, expecting meantime that

Gamecocks at Tangmere

the whole lot would go up in flames at any moment. "Nobody had told me", he concluded "that the 'fire' was the normal exhaust flame of a throttled-back Jupiter."

So much for the hazards of night flying in these primitive times. The use of single seater fighters as bombers which had proved so successful in 1918 had not, by 1927, fallen into disuse and in the course of a normal summer many 20 lb smoke bombs were aimed at the circular target on the aerodrome. A Fighter Command competition to find who could most quickly drop sixteen bombs was held and another variation was a simultaneous converging attack by four aircraft from four points of the compass. The usual technique for these practice attacks was to dive at 45° from 1,000 feet and leave the rest very much to luck. 'The more experienced', according to Bill Pegg, 'got 10 per cent hits.' To improve on this poor result Sergeant Freestone proposed a method of 'no deflection' bombing, which involved a vertical dive above the target and thereby, so the theory went, ensuring a direct hit. Putting his idea to the test Freestone made four successive attempts, overshooting the target each time and therefore not releasing his bombs. On the fifth attempt he went over the vertical and to quote W E P Johnson, "it was the first time I ever saw a real 'mush-stall'– he went in doing about 130, nose *up*, rolled like a ball for about 100 yards, with the rear fuselage wrapped over his head, he crawled out and push-biked back to the tarmac". Bill Pegg said he greeted him with 'My God, Freestone, your bomb missed the target but you certainly hit it fair and square'.

There seems to have been a high rate of attrition to the Squadron's machines about this time for Fg Off Hare got lost in heavy mist en route to Sealand and, vide the local press, 'narrowly missed colliding with the hillside but immediately afterwards his propeller struck and demolished a wall, causing the machine to turn turtle. The pilot managed to escape and the machine was only slightly damaged'. That's what the paper said but you should have seen the accompanying photograph!

Fg Off Jimmy Addams had two lucky escapes. His first crash, again caused by demon mist when coming home from Upavon, deposited him and his machine in the wood on Trundle Hill, overlooking Goodwood racecourse. The pilot had to be sawn out of the wreckage but was unhurt. Shortly afterwards this same pilot 'returned to the aerodrome calmly smoking a cigarette' after 'somersaulting and crashing from 1,000 feet into a field near Chichester.'

Gamecocks in formation at the 1927 Birmingham Air Display
Flight International

Lest the story of 1927 should be construed as one of unrelieved disaster the credit side of the Squadron's life must be related. Or some of it. The Hampshire Air Pageant in May saw Sqn Ldr Brooke, Flt Lts Collier and Smythe, Sgt Pilot Wells and a naval refugee, Lt Byas, provide 'the finest displays of stunting in formation we have ever seen'. This show was twice repeated over Whitsuntide at Bournemouth; 'as perfect an exhibition of close formation flying as could be desired'. During the Air Manoeuvres in July No 12 Squadron was decimated on at least one occasion and in the same month the Sports Cup was duly lifted at the Station Sports. An even more famous victory was won at Uxbridge in September when 43 and 19 contested the Final of the Fighting Area Cricket Cup. 19 Squadron, batting first, scored 75 and 43 replied with 71. The rules of the contest were that first innings would decide the match if no decision on the second innings was forthcoming. So, with all to gain by closing up the game 19 Squadron batted in a manner appropriate to a timeless Test and, at tea, with ninety minutes to go and nine wickets standing they appeared home and dry. 43 had other ideas; LAC Halewood (4 for 7) and Flt Lt Smythe (5 for 10) bowled with all the fury of the gamecock rampant – 19 Squadron was skittled for 38, leaving 43 to get 43 runs in twenty-one minutes. It got them with sixty seconds to spare, the fourth ball of the last over being clouted for the winning run. Fg Off Hare, who scored 27 including one massive heave for six over long on, was the particular hero of the innings. The Cup was presented to the winning team by Lady Salmond, wife of the AOC-in-C 'Fighting Area'.

In January 1928 the Squadron lost Squadron Leader Brooke, who was posted, with only ten days notice, to fill a vacancy caused by the death of the Commanding Officer No 28 Squadron at Ambala, India. It was during his service with this unit that he contracted an illness which led to his premature retirement from the RAF in 1932 and his all too early death in 1949. His memorial may truly be said to be No 43 Squadron. Not only in the Gamecock and the family motto which it carries to the present day but in the outstanding spirit that has been a feature of 43 throughout its entire active life. That spirit can be traced back to Arthur Brooke, who reformed it out of nothing and filled it with his own brand of dedicated enthusiasm, of whom on his retirement C G Grey said 'more than an ordinarily good pilot he always regarded the mere art of flying as a very minor part of the work of an officer or man in the Royal Air Force. His energies were concentrated on teaching those under him to live for the Service . . . He had a peculiar gift for handling both officers and men . . . all have recognised his sense of justice as a Commanding Officer, and his value as a friend. Few officers have had as much influence for good as he has had'.

After little more than two years the Gamecock gave way to the Armstrong-Whitworth Siskin. The Siskin, the first all-metal, aeroplane was no faster than the Gamecock and the change was, at first, unpopular. Compared with the stubby, compact Gamecock the Siskin was an ungainly looking design. Its top plane provided three quarters of the total wing area and it had an unusual and clumsy-looking undercarriage. Pilots said that when taxiing it gave one the feeling it would tip on its nose. Once in the air however the story was quite different. 'A real fine aeroplane, immensely strong, very easy to fly, extremely light on the controls and really wonderful for stunt flying in spite of its rather limited speed rang',' was the opinion of one Squadron pilot of those days. For three years with the Siskin, and for the three years under the command of Sqn Ldr C N Lowe, two periods that almost though not quite coincided, 43 Squadron went from strength to strength and its fame multiplied.

Sqn Ldr C N Lowe came to command 43 in December 1927. In the Great War he had destroyed ten enemy machines and gained the MC and DFC and, in the next five years, more English International Rugby caps than any three-quarter had ever won before. He had retired from big games before he came to 43, but his reputation lingered; 'A little giant, strong and beautifully built, a track sprinter for speed, a dancer for balance. He could be baulked but that was merely a challenge. He would check, perform what he called his hesitation waltz, double inside and likely as not drop a goal.' In 1921 when the RAF beat the Army by 26 points to 3, Lowe scored four of the five tries, each good enough in the ordinary way to bring down the house, one of them scored after a run that began two yards from his own goal line.

Squadron Leader C N Lowe MC DFC

The prowess he had displayed on the rugby field was now to be matched as a Squadron Commander and by 1930, when he took 43 to Hendon to astound the aviation world with the first ever display of tied-together aerobatics, he had established 43 as the greatest Squadron of its day. Nor was the result achieved at the cost of grinding down the Squadron's morale with an excess of effort so that all else was sacrificed in pursuit of perfection. All reports point to the contrary. Plt Off J Heber-Percy, coming to the Squadron from Cranwell, remembers those days with 43 as one of the happiest and best in his service life 'when he was not flying himself', he says of Sqn Ldr Lowe, 'he used to sit on a stick on the edge of the tarmac . . . so good flying was of supreme importance'.

Another who came to 43 during Sqn Ldr Lowe's reign was Flt Lt Ian Brodie. Just back from India where he had been flying DH 9s ('which one just did not throw about') he arrived at Uxbridge to await posting. While there he saw in the *Daily Graphic* some sensational photographs of 43 doing its 'tied-together' stuff and duly prayed he would be posted somewhere else. ('In those days there were no dual aircraft in which pilots could be shown how to aerobat – we just had to teach ourselves.') Within a week, prayer unanswered, Brodie was reporting to the Adjutant, Fg Off Elsmie (one of two Cranwell Swords of Honour serving with 43 at that time, the other was Plt Off Coote). Elsmie suggested 'go to the tarmac, the CO is never in his office, he's either in the air or on the tarmac'. Lowe's words of welcome to the newcomer were short and frightening. 'See those chaps up there,' (they were practising aerobatics) 'I expect to see you up among them in ten days' time.' The last two words to this story are, 'I was!'

Armstrong-Whitworth Siskins in tied-together formation, 1930

Such was the manner of compulsive persuasion that produced the best flying team of 1930. And withal in a service where, reflecting the class pattern of the social structure of the day, there were officers who were classed as gentlemen and other ranks who were classified as nothing much at all except numbers on parade, 43 Squadron achieved a different kind of relationship.

'We had', said Brodie, 'ten officers, six sergeant pilots, and fifty-eight NCOs and airmen. We were happily self-contained for maintenance. I write happily because the Squadron spirit was wonderful. There was no stuffiness as between the officers and the airmen; indeed one of the things which to some people these days would be remarkable was the respectful chiacking which used to go on within the Flights. 'We were a very happy Squadron, worked hard and played hard and the relationship between all ranks was unusually close.'

The origin of the tied-together aerobatics, like the black and white chequers, is not known. The suggestion that it probably began with two types at the bar seems as good a one as any. The tied-together flying began with two aircraft, increased as confidence and practice built up to three and then to three flights of three. At first the cords were tied after taxiing out to the take-off point but with practice this was abandoned and the cords, which were of cotton decorated with cotton streamers, were attached on the tarmac.

On 28 June 1930 43 duly laid on their display at Hendon. The reports in the aviation press are sufficient to show the effect that they had "The only absolutely new and original event in this years' show . . . The Squadron took off and did aerobatics with three flights of three aircraft tied together . . . they looped as a squadron, did a succession of loops with flights in line astern . . . firmly looped and did a Prince of Wales feathers at the top, thus deliberately breaking the cords. It would have been a very skilful and effective display, even without the cords. The teamwork and the handling of the machines was quite perfect . . . . The most spectacular event and the most perfect formations of the day . . . even when the first loop went slightly off line every machine deviated by exactly the same amount showing striking proof of accurate station-keeping."

This display by 43 was all the more remarkable inasmuch as it came in a display where the general standard of formation was poor, with the inevitable conclusions being drawn from such a performance. C G Grey, stormy petrel of the inter-war aviation scene and then editor of *The Aeroplane* was, as usual, not silent.

Part of the Siskin Aerobatic Team, 1930.
Standing - Fg Off R F Fletcher, Plt Off Heber-Percy, Plt Off R Elsmie.
Seated - Fg Off E R Simmonds, Flt Lt I E Brodie, Flt Lt E Thornton, Sqn Ldr C N Lowe, MC, DFC, Flt Lt C T Walkington, Fg Off R Barrett, Fg Off E Esmonde
(Flight International)

'. . . Some hold that formation flying is unnecessary, serves no useful purpose in war, is merely a trick. In fact formation flying is an outward and visible sign of the inward and invisible grace of a squadron. It is like march-discipline in the Army and sloppy formation in the air is first hand evidence that the CO is unfit for his job, or at any rate has just taken over from one that was. 'One or two squadron formations would have disgraced the third-line of a Continental Power. Only two or three regular squadrons were as good as the Auxiliary Bombers of 600 Squadron . . . some of the regular squadrons should be ashamed of themselves . . .'

Following this attack Grey went on to pinpoint his reasons for the poor showing.

"Too many men were made Squadron Leaders because they were good in the war, or at staff duties, or at engineering or some other thing without possessing the natural ability to command and lead a squadron. Such a post called for some sacrifice of home life, if married, in order to keep in close touch with his junior officers. He must make himself the father of his men, as too many at present do not. Until this close touch with the men is established, until Squadron Leaders are chosen deliberately for their ability to command, the average level of squadrons in the RAF will not reach the point at present reached by certain crack formations."

There were times, especially when Communism was mentioned, when the judgement of C G Grey was not all it might have been. There were many other times when he was so very, very right. In this particular instance, the spirit of 43 Squadron under Sqn Ldr Lowe set alongside its outstanding display at the 1930 Show suggests that this was one time he was right.

Following their success at Hendon, three Siskins were sent to perform at a meeting organised by the Aero Club Royale de Belgique, at Brussels on 21 September. Two demonstrations by Belgium and Netherlands aeroplanes were described as good, then . . . "The Flight of 43's Siskins tied together was magnificent . . . their show one of the very few to rouse the huge crowd to enthusiastic cheering. Their formation seemed closer than ever before and their loops came right down to the ground. A French military formation down on the programme to follow 43 did not materialise!"

Some few weeks later during the Empire Prime Ministers Conference in London a further display was provided for these VIPs at Croydon. This last act was considered by the knowledgeable, including the prime actors, as the most difficult of the lot. Some of the Hendon pilots had left and been replaced by less long-practised types. The weather was very blustery with a lot of low broken cloud scurrying along at only 800 feet. Such was the confidence of the CO in his men that he refused to cancel any part of the programme. After the second of two

Armstrong-Whitworth Siskin IIIA, J8822

successive Squadron loops the Siskins came out just below the level of the top of the control tower on which the Prime Ministers and the Chief of the Air Staff, Sir John Salmond, were standing. It was reported that some of the great ones ducked. Commenting on this display *The Aeroplane* said :

"Unjustly known by the jealous members of rival squadrons as 'Mother Meyrick's Own', Forty-Three then gave its world famous display, amazingly tight and accurate in spite of the bumpy weather. With their usual modesty the Americans claim to have first thought of stunting tied together but the Royal Air Force certainly do it best. After their display at Hendon the majority of the RAF cadets at Cranwell applied to be posted to 43. This popular Squadron therefore got the two cadets with the highest qualifications." Pilot Officers Paddy Coote and Reggie Elsmie, both Sword of Honour cadets at Cranwell, came to 43 around this time. Another, Robert V Ralph, who came at the end of 1932, was unfortunately killed soon afterwards in a mid-air collision.

The reference to Mother Meyrick's Own was to a title which far from being bestowed by jealous competitors was one that 43 had already claimed for itself. 'Ma' Meyrick from County Cork, the mother of three 'smashing' daughters, also owned the famous (the 'unco guid' would say infamous) 43 Club in the West End which was 'roughly our headquarters when we were in town on the loose'. Fighting Cocks and Mother Meyrick's Chickens were wholly synonymous terms.

The Croydon display was the last event in a memorable year. Apart from its aerobatic displays the Squadron was second in the Command Air to Ground firing, 'B' Flight won the Chalmers Trophy and 'C' Flight was second

Siskins on the flight line

The Squadron Commander leads a starboard echelon of Siskins

in the Sassoon Cup navigation competition. When, in the last days before Christmas, Squadron Leader Lowe relinquished his command he might truthfully have said that there were no more worlds left to conquer. Significant of the calibre required to lead such a crack outfit, his successor, Squadron Leader Lionel H Slatter, came from no less an important and illustrious unit than the High Speed Flight, twice winners in three years of the Schneider trophy. The 'High Speed' was not without interest too, for, rescinding an earlier announcement of intent to re-equip 32 Squadron with the new Hawker Fury, the Air Ministry selected 43 to be the first to receive this keenly awaited aeroplane, then by a wide margin the fastest fighter in the world.

One very unfortunate incident marred the closing weeks of the Siskin age. Air Vice-Marshal Vesey-Holt, the newly appointed Air Officer Commanding Fighter Area visited Tangmere and when the time came for him to leave in a Tiger Moth piloted by Flt Lt Moody, 43 Squadron went aloft at full strength to present an airborne salute. Unknown to Squadron Leader Slatter, a second Moth flown by the AOC's Personal Assistant took off soon after the first. Sighting this second Moth and mistaking it for the AOC Squadron Leader Slatter led the Siskins into a shallow dive. Almost immediately Flt Lt Brodie leading 'C' Flight was furious to see his wingman, Sergeant Wareham, drop out of formation and turn for home.

On landing Brodie at once sensed a marked air of tension; then he saw Wareham's Siskin, with its tail unit so badly damaged that to have landed it safely was itself a highly commendable feat. The unsighted AOC's Moth with which it had collided was found in a wood near Bury Hill. Both the Air Vice-Marshal and Flt Lt Henry Moody had been killed in the crash.

A dual-control Siskin III, J7173, at Tangmere

CHAPTER 7

Fastest in the World

THE arrival of its new aeroplanes was awaited with desire by more than the Squadron. An *Aeroplane* photo of the Squadron's Siskins in the autumn of 1930 carried the inscription, 'How long O Lord, how long'. 'A bit longer than it would have been if a 43 Squadron Siskin had not collided with our prototype (then called the Hornet) last April', the Hawker Aircraft Company might, with justice, have replied . . . A tale that had ended with George Bulman, chief test pilot to Hawkers walking into the Officers' Mess, holding a small bit of aluminium and saying sadly, 'Well they told me to come down and salvage what I could.'

However by April 1931 the first production Fury was photographed flying over Brooklands; in the same week the Air Ministry weekly orders proclaimed that 'The Hawker Fury will replace the AW Siskin in 43 Squadron etc.' Production was so good that by 27 May another order announced that 43 had been completely re-equipped, and less than two weeks after that *The Aeroplane,* producing some photos of the Squadron, commented that 'the accuracy of the formation is particularly creditable considering that the Squadron had received its new machines only a few days before this photo was taken'.

The Hawker Fury Mk I fighter was such an advance on any comparable aeroplane as to be in a class entirely on its own. The first 200 mph fighter (207 max at 14,000 feet) it showed an advance of more than 50 mph over the Siskin IIIA and more than thirty over the Bristol Bulldog which slightly preceded it into Squadron use. More significant still, it was, until the arrival *five years later* of the Gloster Gauntlet, the only fighter faster than its companion Hawker Hart day bomber. It was classified as an 'interceptor-fighter', being endowed with an exceptional rate of climb (10,000 feet in four and a half minutes, 20,000 in nine minutes), which theoretically allowed it to stay on the ground until enemy bombers were sighted on crossing the coast and still be able to climb and intercept them before they reached their target – London.

The other feature which for a fighter was a breakaway from the customary design of those times was the use of an in-line liquid cooled engine in place of the familiar radial. Although, according to the purists this detracted from manoeuvrability, it made for good streamlining and excellent forward visibility. It likewise provided initially a fair amount of twitch to one pilot and probably more. Ian Brodie recounts how he was sent to the maker's works at Brooklands to collect the second or third Fury. In those days there was no nonsense with Maintenance Units, Ferry Units or such like

Hawker Fury Mk I, K1933 in 43 Squadron markings

An aerial photograph of Royal Air Force Station Tangmere in the early 1930s

intermediaries. The pipeline went direct from makers to squadron and if, as with the Fury, the type was new and the squadron pilot had no experience of it so much harder the luck, operational conversion and delivery flight being thus achieved at the same time. In Brodie's case, having taken off from what he thought was a very small aerodrome at Brooklands he set course for the short flip to Tangmere. Before very long a feather of steam from the cooling system vent, just in front of his face brought visions of forced landings with a seized engine. Hoping that his worst fears might be all for naught Brodie kept on and duly landed normally at Tangmere. Then only did some kind soul inform him that the nerve-wracking plume of steam was quite normal to the liquid cooled Kestrel engine.

Although the pilots had been very fond of their Siskins it did not take long to transfer affection to the Fury, with its high speed, excellent vision and beautifully balanced controls. By the middle of June, only weeks after equipping, three Furies (Flt Lt E T Carpenter, Sgts S F King and A F Underhill) were showing off to the taxpayer at the Hendon Air Display the latest piece of value for his money. "Their flight aerobatics were just as good as the Siskins the year before . . . the formation was very tight and very accurate as it had to be when manoeuvring at that speed. The Fury is as tractable as it is beautiful, its evolutions must be seen to be believed . . . with its amazing speed though the manoeuvres are performed at only half throttle!" (*The Aeroplane*).

Amazing speed forsooth! That was not the opinion of one of the noisier band of critics of the Royal Air Force in those days who were forever proclaiming that fighters were a waste of time, that they were far too slow to catch enemy bombers and that the only way to shoot the latter down was with anti-aircraft guns. The interceptor was the least useful aeroplane ever built; its use was a policy of defeatism because static defence was the first stage of defeat. *The Aeroplane* produced the following gem a few months before the first Hurricane and Spitfire flew, '300 mph monoplanes are a waste of time and money. Turn them into high speed scouts. Sit underneath with plenty of guns and shoot (enemy aircraft) up so that they keep at heights where they can hurt nobody.'

'We hope the forthcoming rearrangement of the Air Council will result in new types selected according to the experience of fighting men and not to the vision of theorists.' For sheer unmitigated balderdash such opinion is hard to beat. It was as well for England that others took a contrary view.

43 Squadron anyway, full of theoretical visionaries took to their 'useless' Furies with the greatest enthusiasm. In the Air Defence exercises of July 1931 they drew especial praise for their keenness and efficiency which enabled them, in spite of all obstacles, to intercept more enemy raids than all other Squadrons put together!

The Air Exercises held by ADGB were an annual feature in the training routine. Lasting from four to fourteen days they were based as a rule on the splitting of the forces employed into two sides with fanciful names like Redland and Blueland or Southland and Northland and divided by a mythical boundary which varied according to the disposition of the two sides but might be for instance, as in 1933, along the line Liverpool-Reading-Croydon. The targets that were to be attacked were known to both sides in advance. Thus was battle joined, though much of it had an unrealistic air. The use of cloud for tactical purposes was forbidden, not more than one fighter was permitted to attack a bomber at any one time; when attacked, bombers could not take evasive action. Nobody must ever get closer than 100 yards to an opponent. It hardly needs to be said that the carrying of bombs and ammunition was forbidden, or that pilots were forbidden to go beyond gliding distance of the coast! No nonsense requiring a lifeboat naturally.

However both sides managed, if the weather stayed fine, to enjoy themselves. Those in a position to know also claim that the experience and practice gained by the Air Staffs justified the effort. Even the embryonic organisation of the Observer Corps, absent in most places, thin and full of inexperience where it did exist found an annual justification for its being in the grandiosely named Air Defence Exercises of the Air Defence of Great Britain Command of the Royal Air Force. Four nights under the stars with a thermos and a telephone, if it did nothing else, helped to show up the faults in the system.

The sight of apparently unopposed formations of bombers crossing London during these exercises invariably brought wholesale condemnation of the efficiency of the Air Defence organisation from many quarters, the loudest wails coming most generally from those whose opposition to the spending of any money on the Services was the heaviest. The fact that the bomber formation serenely crossing Trafalgar Square had already been twice intercepted by fighters, duly coming in to 100 yards before going home was of course unknown to the 'unprotected' public below. On the other hand of course the bombers might well not have been attacked during their flight. In 1931, with their new Furies, 10,000 feet in four and a half minutes – and a bit less minus guns and ammunition – 43 Squadron in spite of getting into the air in under a minute, thereby drawing much praise upon themselves, found that they were unable in many cases to catch the 'enemy' bombers before they reached their target (which said even less for the hopes of a Bulldog). Stationed, as they were this year, at Tangmere (in other years they operated from North Weald or Hornchurch) the warning they

Some 'A' Flight pilots in front of a new Fury

received, for instance when the Hawker Harts of 12 Squadron were first spotted at Bognor, was quite inadequate for them to intercept before Northolt was duly 'bombed'.

Pointed remarks were pushed in the direction of 604 (Auxiliary) Squadron for one act of infamy. These visitors from Hendon, actually formed part of the enemy air force and by inadvertently taxiing across the line of 43's Furies at precisely the wrong moment caused them to take four and a half minutes in getting airborne.

One report on the Squadron's efforts that year carried almost prophetic descriptions of the Summer of 1940. 'None can deny that the organisation is sound, the quality excellent, but the quantity is pitifully small.' Another remarked on their 'taking off in untidy formations, upwind, downwind, crosswind, all at the same time', a habit that was to reach perfection ten years later at Drem.

Another regular feature of the annual routine was the Squadron's visit to an air-firing practice camp. This was almost certainly the only time during the year when all the aircraft were fitted with guns. Some avowed it was also the only time that anybody ever saw an armourer outside of the Station Workshops. Which, if it were true, was not without good reason, for an Air Force existing on a total Air Estimate of around seventeen million pounds had no money to waste on tradesmen for whom there was no useful employment. Time enough to train such when war was approaching.

Sutton Bridge, on the Wash, was the usual

Flt Lt McEvoy in K1934 at 7,000 feet

The Fury Aerobatic Team, 1933. Fg Off R C Reynell, Flt Lt J G Hawtrey, Fg Off H W Mermagen

milieu for 43's annual visit. Invariably the camp was a period of hard work and hard play within a general holiday atmosphere generated by the absence of normal home station duties, routine and 'bull'. 'We knocked back so much Scotch and ale into the small hours I marvel we ever managed to fire at all', quotes one pilot. Air-to-air and air-to-ground firing was carried out. The drogue for the latter was towed by a Bristol Fighter. The guns having singularly unreliable stoppages were legion and more often than not could not be cleared in the air. No scientific equipment was required to sight the guns when fitted into the aircraft, the usual method being to 'squint up the barrel at a target, such as an aircraft wheel held up by a bored airman, placed about 200 yards away'.

In the last year before 43 collected its Furies it set up an indisputable if wholly unofficial and unacknowledged high speed record for a Siskin formation flight when en route to Sutton Bridge from Tangmere. The appointed start at 0900 was delayed by a full south westerly gale, but at 1130 following a 'Signs of gale moderating' report from Met, the Siskins took off, taxiing into wind with four airmen to each wingtip. They had scarcely formed into loose formation above the aerodrome when the Adjutant appeared holding a signal correcting to 'NO SIGNS of gale moderating' in one hand, a red-loaded Very pistol in the other. None of his warning lights were seen by the pilots however (of course there was no RT) and the Squadron flew off, covering the 145 miles in forty minutes. Sqn Ldr Lowe made a perfect landing and some other pilots who knew the trick from former visits landed close to some old wartime canvas hangars which gave them a little lee, but three machines landing rather far out finished upside down, in spite of the efforts of over fifty airmen who valiantly dodged among the descending aeroplanes to assist the pilots in keep the aircraft under firm taxiing control.

Sqn Ldr Slatter left the Squadron in January 1932 and was followed by Sqn Ldr R H Hanmer, who in turn was succeeded by Sqn Ldr F Wright in October 1934. Sqn Ldr A M Wray came seven months after that date for a special purpose connected with aircraft carriers of which more later. At a period when the turnover of Squadron personnel was accelerated by the Abyssinian upheaval it was the more remarkable that R I G MacDougall, who came to 43 as a Pilot Officer newly passed through Flying Training School in

1931, should have set up a record for pilot longevity by remaining with 43 for six continuous years.

In general the first half of the thirties brought years of continuing success and better than average achievement. In 1932 at the Hendon Air Display 43 tied their Furies together and provided 'ten different formations without making a mistake or losing a moment'. They took off, performed and landed, still tied together in Squadron formation. To quote a contemporary report the crowd was 'staggered by the wonderful formation flying of 43'.

In 1933 the Squadron contented itself with 'a very fine show' in the form of an Audax (4 Squadron) versus Furies (43) battle and permitted No 25 Squadron to try their 'prentice hands at roped together aerobatics, following, as one Squadron pilot put it, 'where better men had led before them.' Just to let it be seen however that there was no diminution in perfection, Flt Lt John Hawtrey went, with Fg Offs Mermagen and Reynell, to the International Air Meeting at Brussels on 11 June. At 1630 hours rain was falling heavily and visibility was reduced to 1 kilometre when, to everyone's amazement three Furies of 43 leapt into the air. The enthusiasm of the crowd knew no bounds at their display. With low cloud base, no horizon and restricted visibility the closeness of their formation showed the supremacy and thoroughness of their training. One can only class their show as superb.

It was rather gratifying to hear all the eulogistic remarks from Belgian Air Force pilots and members of the public . . . impeccable, *épatant, une pure merveille, etc,* on all sides.

Not for the first time across the Channel the Squadron's effect on its rivals was shattering. The French squadron, down on the programme to follow 43, called off and sent only a solitary Dewoitine into the sky, the pilot of which contented himself with a few stall turns. A little later after an improvement in the weather three Swiss Dewoitines took to the air. They had scarcely begun their display when one of them hit the roof of a hangar. The ensuing forced crash-landing was highly spectacular but not quite to be compared with 43 Squadron as a controlled display of brilliance.

There were many occasions in subsequent years when aerobatic displays of this kind were given. At the opening of Portsmouth airport squadron air drill was in evidence and shortly afterwards Flt Lt T N McEvoy and Fg Off R I G MacDougall gave the loyal Irish an opportunity to crick their necks skywards and to wonder at a similar opening ceremony at Newtonards. The RAF Flying Club display at Hatfield in 1935 gave 43 the top spot in the day's programme. Also in this year there took place at Mildenhall the first ever Royal Review of the RAF. This was part of the Silver Jubilee commemoration ceremonies and for this royal occasion 43 Squadron, with Nos 1 and 25, formed with their Furies, No 3 (Fighter) Wing. Also round these times it was noted with pleasure that a Flt Lt Tommy Rose had won the King's Cup Air Race flying a Miles Falcon. In the following March, using the same aeroplane, he captured the London to Cape Town record with a time of 3 days, 17 hours 38 minutes. His return home took 6 days and 7 hours but this included twenty-four hours under arrest by the Italians in Tripoli.

This was of course the period when Mussolini, in quest of a second Roman Empire was succeeding, with the aid of poison gas and vast quantities of high explosive, in overrunning the tribesmen of Abyssinia. One result of this act of aggression was a build-up of British Forces in the Mediterranean and Middle East areas, and this had more than one effect on 43 Squadron. The first was unique and 43 became bell-bottomed. This tale is related by Air Chief Marshal Sir Brian V Reynolds KCB, CBE, who was intimately connected with the events.

"The background to this was the outcome of a continual war between the Air Ministry and Admiralty as to the 'ownership' of the Fleet Air Arm. Having lost the old Royal Naval Air Service as the result of the merger in 1918 the Admiralty from the early twenties had been pressing for the FAA to be returned fully to their control. The position over the years had been

Ready for the AOC's inspection in 1934

An unfortunate collision!

Fg Off W J Hickey, Fury K1928 outside the Squadron hangar on a wintery day

that from 1918-24 the FAA was under direct control of Coastal Command and the Air Ministry. The operational control afloat in the carriers was exercised by the Naval C-in-C through the Captain of the ship and an RAF Wing Commander and Staff embarked.

From 1924 onwards (following strong pressure by the Admiralty which nearly broke the RAF into two services as before 1918) a compromise in the FAA was reached whereby the flying personnel were established in the proportion two thirds RN and one third RAF: observers and Air Gunners to be entirely RN but ground personnel to remain RAF. Operational control to remain as before, ie under RN C-in-C afloat but under RAF ashore. The naval pilots were given RAF ranks and provision was made that they could be promoted as they gained experience.

The pressure by the Admiralty continued however and in the early thirties came to a head. With the big expansion of the RAF the Air Ministry tended to neglect the FAA both in the quality of the RAF personnel and the aircraft. This led to the Navy saying that the FAA would be inefficient unless it was entirely manned by RN personnel. The Air Ministry countered by saying that an RAF squadron could easily (with a reasonable work up period) take on the job at sea.

In 1935 the Government of the day directed that an experiment should be made as a first step in the interchange in role of a FAA and an RAF Fighter Squadron. 43 Squadron was selected and arrangements were made for its conversion to the Nimrod, the Naval version of the Fury aircraft with which the FAA was equipped. 800 Squadron of the FAA took over the Furies.

The Squadron Commander, Sqn Ldr A M Wray, Flight Commanders and several of the pilots had FAA experience and were specially posted in for the experiment, a fact that did not pass unnoticed by the Admiralty! The Squadron pilots were all given deck landing training and 43 stood by to effect the exchange.

However just as this was to take place Mussolini invaded Abyssinia and threatened to throw the British out of Egypt, so Fighter Command had to hastily improvise a large force to go to the Middle East. This involved postponement of the experiment and the breaking up of 43 Squadron which was put on a cadre basis for some months.

Sqn Ldr Reynolds, as an experienced FAA pilot, was then (February 1936) posted in to command 43 Squadron with a view to later carrying out the project but finally the experiment was abandoned and 43 reverted to its normal role in Fighter Command."

Sir Brian ends this tale with the comment: "Who knows, 43 Squadron, the crack squadron of Fighter Command might have satisfied the politicians and prevented the Fleet Air Arm being absorbed by the Navy two years later?" A further result of this rundown in Squadron strength was that by the end of 1935 the pilots could be numbered on the fingers of one hand.

When the build-up began early in 1936

A nine-ship Fury formation
(Flight International)

things could never be quite the same again.

The after effects of the Italian success in Abyssinia lingered on and together with the distant rumble of a resurgent German Air Force brought an urgency to life that had not existed in those more carefree years when 43 had first sported the Fury around the sky, cocking a friendly snoot at the outpaced radial-engined Bulldogs. Now even that superiority had gone; the Gloster Gauntlet, first in service with 19 Squadron in March 1935, had stolen the blue riband for speed from the *corps d'élite* of 43, 1 and 25.

But while it lasted it had been a little golden age, a glistening period that reflected the brightness of the men who made it so. And in the sterner days that were to come their names would be found among the foremost in battle. Many were killed before the victory was won. Bill Hickey and 'Paddy' Coote, 'Paddy' Slocum and Reggie Elsmie, Lt Cdr Eugene Esmonde VC DSO, leader of the Swordfish strike force when the *Scharnhorst* and *Gneiseneau* broke through the Channel, Badger, Reynell and 'Popsy' Polglase among them. Many more happily survived and, if one knew where to look, could later be found from the Highlands of Kenya to the lush pastures of Ireland. With hair greyer than once it was and lacking the ease as of yore to fit comfortably into the cockpit of a Fury it might have been hard to imagine that they were once the young men who brought a noble Lord Hutchinson to his feet in debate. He proposed that 'five to seven hundred young officers from the Army and the Royal Navy (were required) to secure for the air service a personnel with military training and a sense of discipline'.

Yet such was the case. No doubt to the hereditary peerage a sense of discipline implies the ability to strut up and down outside a Royal Palace, dressed up like a chocolate soldier.

For men like McEvoy and Mermagen, Finlay and Fairclough, Lewis and Loxton and too many more to name, discipline meant something different. Such as sticking your wingtip twelve inches away from your leader's and keeping it there while moving in three dimensions at 250 mph. And, since the kind of spirit to which such things appeal is not likely to be constrained by archaic ideas of 'military training and sense of discipline', it inevitably meant that life was generally more than hectic so that thirty years on one of them could write 'Remember me to – we were together involved in most of the wilder parties . . . nearly wrote me off in his racing Austin, returning to Tangmere, from a night out in Chichester. A head-on smash, can't think how we survived. We had gone in for a haircut which we never got round to. The accident occurred at 2230 hrs.'

And, whatever the Establishment may think to the contrary, of such untamed spirits are great Squadrons composed. It was 43's good fortune that it always possessed in these times an abundance of such men.

CHAPTER 8

The Stiffening of the Sinews

When the blast of war blows in our ears . . .
Stiffen the sinews, summon up the blood .... (Henry V)

THE beginning of the end of the small but highly professional peacetime Royal Air Force was signalled on 19 July 1934. On that day the Government announced its intentions, in the face of what the Foreign Secretary euphemistically described as Germany's 'very marked' interest in air development, to create forty-one new squadrons during the following five years. As is well known, in the face of subsequent evidence of the rapid resurgence of the German Luftwaffe, this programme was further increased the following year and the Royal Air Force continued to expand at an increasing rate up to and after the outbreak of war in 1939.

Inevitably the expansion of the Service and the changes which were made in organisation during this period affected 43 Squadron but, as with the Royal Air Force as a whole, the rapid increase in quantity was not bought by lowering the quality for which it had been justly famous. Notwithstanding the chops and changes the Squadron continued to be, as it had been at Tangmere for more than a decade, an exceptional band of dedicated young men.

'Morning, noon and night', wrote Sergeant Pilot Jim Hallowes, who came to 43 in August 1936 (and stayed with it for more than four years), 'on the ground and in the air, on the sports field or playing fields, *ésprit de corps* was drummed into all ranks. It was a great honour to be a member of such a squadron. If there was a hint that somebody would have to come down to the hangars after tea and get this or that plane serviceable there was never any lack of volunteers, rather the reverse. Always it was 43 above all.'

Two men of widely differing manner, Squadron Leaders Wray and Bain are officially recorded as commanding the Squadron from 1935 to 1939. In fact there were four, Sqn Ldr Reynolds following Sqn Ldr Wray and, during a long interregnum at the end of 1936 and start of 1937, Flt Lt R I G MacDougall, now in his sixth year with the Squadron, was OC. Squadron Leader Wray, affectionately known as 'Father', arrived in 1935 and remained until the run down brought about by the Abyssinian trouble.

Flt Lt R I G MacDougall after displaying at the Empire Air Day in May 1936

'Well liked by all for his charm and absent-mindedness alike' was the opinion of one of his young officers. This did not imply any 'softness'. The MC, DFC (Afghanistan 1923) and the AFC in 1926 well showed his worth. He added a Bar to the DFC in 1942 and two years later at the age of 48 was awarded the DSO for leadership in bomber operations over Germany.

His ultimate successor was far from mild in manner. Squadron Leader R E Bain was not very tall but there was never any doubt as to who was in command when he was around. He possessed a bark and a bite and both were to be avoided if possible. Nor, in the role of God, did he lack for a pair of Archangels in Flight Sergeants, Bill Blaney in 'A' Flight and Frankie Watts in 'B' Flight, and their various successors. In the peacetime Air Force, with never a penny to spare, there was no money to be wasted on Squadron Engineer Officers and in this fighter squadron the technical side was the entire responsibility of these two warriors. Pre-war Flight Sergeants are a vanished race. The modern Air Force possesses nothing like them. The product of a Darwinian 'survival of the fittest' process whereby most tradesmen were axed after twelve years service, their very presence midway through the 'second twelve' was proof enough of their ability. Nor was there then the modern kind of man who slips quickly up a technical ladder without assuming responsibility for discipline. These men were Flight *Sergeants* – when they bawled 'jump' the whole Flight jumped and when it came to technical problems they possessed as much knowledge as, and infinitely more applied cunning, than any of their underlings. Sgt Hallowes arriving on the Squadron was told 'You're not here merely to fly those Furies and then sit back and take things easy; there are other jobs to do. Like getting stuck in every week helping the fitters and riggers to scrub down and polish your aeroplane'.

Fg Off J V C Badger, Flt Lt R E Bain, Fg Off J D Miller

Thus did the Squadron prosper, for, if the hands at the top were firm they were no more so than was necessary to direct and control the high spirited and highly intelligent men who made up the bulk of the pilots and groundcrew. In those days before the pace of expansion resulted, as it had to, in some dilution, the men of the Royal Air Force were the *élite* of His Majesty's forces. Nor should this sound surprising remembering that four out of every ten recruits were rejected for lack of physical fitness, and half of the remainder for lack of brains.

From 1936 onwards the Squadron began to assume a little more permanence in its make up than had been apparent during the extreme fluidity of the Abyssinian panic period. One major internal change at this time, the reduction of flights from three to two, was aimed at making subsequent expansion easier by the simple process of hiving off one flight to form a new squadron, an operation which in fact took place at Tangmere in 1938 when Nos 43 and 1 Squadrons gave birth to Nos 72 and 85. Another change which had no immediate effect at Squadron level was the formation of Fighter Command following the reorganisation of the old Air Defence of Great Britain Command.

Though it was always to be hoped that war with Germany might somehow be avoided the increasing probability of it happening brought a sharpening of attitudes to all aspects of training in these days. The carefree times of the 'finest flying club in the world' had gone forever.

As far back as 1935 an Air Fighting Development Flight had been formed at Northolt for 'the study and practice of air fighting' and in 1936 one of 43's Flight Commanders attended the first Air-Firing Instructors' Course at Sutton Bridge. Although the Annual Air Defences of 1936 were on a greatly reduced scale (eight squadrons only and some, including 43, not at full strength) there was no letup in the training at squadron level. Following one of the Ten Commandments on the wall of the Pilots' Room, 'A flight without an objective is like a kiss from one's sister – it lacketh a kick', everything was done with a purpose. One log book of the period lists in rapid succession, camera-gun attacks on other aircraft, instrument flying, formation, cross-country flights, pinpointing, slow flying and spinning, battle climbs with full war load. These Battle Climbs to 25,000 feet or so, in the unheated cockpit of a Fury with the thermometer on the inter-plane strut registering minus 40 Centigrade were very, very cold indeed. The breeches of the Vickers guns in the cockpits were often concealed under a layer of frost. Even with inner silks, then woollen and finally leather flying gloves, it was very hard on the hands while the feet in two pairs of woollen socks and encased in sheepskin-lined flying boots felt as if they were frozen solid.

Before the Air Officer Commanding's Annual Inspection, Air Drill and more Air Drill became the repeated order of the day.

Flt Lt 'Hank' More, 'B' Flight's Commander, had a special way of ensuring that his pilots kept it close when formation flying. His technique was to take the Flight around the Isle of Wight, below the level of the cliff tops. Gradually getting nearer to the cliff face he would tell his men to come in closer or hit the chalk. 'There was plenty of room really but the optical illusion was there, and it worked. And heaven help the man who got the wind up and broke formation.' Thus speaks one who in those days flew with those formations – one eye on the cliff, one on the leader's wing tip.

'Hank' More was one of the outstanding characters who graced the Squadron in those times. RAF squash champion, he was 'unequalled as a morale builder and practical joker'. After leaving 43 he went to the Fleet Air Arm but by 1940 was in command of 73 Squadron in France when they performed some heroic deeds in the face of great odds. In much the same position two years later, at Singapore, he fell captive to the Japanese. Sent by boat to Japan because he had made himself such a nuisance to his captors he was killed when the prison-ship was torpedoed by an Allied submarine.

The vacancy left by More's departure was filled by Pilot Officer Fred Rosier. Two years as a Flight Commander and a further eight months as Squadron Adjutant meant that he was ideally placed to observe the changing facets of squadron life in these times and his observations make interesting reading. He was highly critical of some aspects of the training curriculum, considering them unduly restrictive and stereotyped, based as they were on the assumption that in the event of war with Germany only their bombers would have the range to reach the United Kingdom. Thus there was undue concentration on close formation flying and practice attacks against bombers. Dog fighting, fighter v fighter combat was officially frowned upon by higher authority because it was considered not to be of great importance and by the Squadron Commander because the

K1936 flying over Arundel Castle
(Andrew Rennie)

violent manoeuvres and aerobatics involved in such exercises resulted in oil-splattered aeroplanes incompatible with peacetime standards of cleanliness. Nevertheless it was practised surreptitiously by all pilots with the full knowledge of their Flight Commanders whose judgement was to be proved better than that of their seniors by the flocks of escorting fighters that came with the bombers in 1940.

Because of the rapid expansion of the fighter arm (there were four new fighter squadrons formed in 1935, six in 1936, and eight in 1937), the majority of pilots coming to the Squadron were either very new and mostly very young Pilot Officers or ex-apprentice Sergeant Pilots. The latter were all skilled tradesmen who had subsequently been selected for pilot training and since the competition for selection was fierce those finally chosen were almost all of a very high standard. Three of those in this category who came to 43 in 1936/37 had outstanding records in World War II. Sergeant Berry, posted to No 1 Squadron before they went to France, had a most distinguished record before his death in action in September 1940. Sergeant Jim Hallowes became 43's highest scoring pilot with more than twenty confirmed victories in the first twelve months of the war and Sergeant Frank Carey (Chota to his friends because he was short of stature), who incidentally had served with 43 in his ground trade before his Flying Training School days, had by 1945 an official score of 28·5 victories, a score almost certainly less than it should have been since in France, and afterwards in Burma, many of the relevant Squadron records were lost. Carey had the unusual record of 1,000 hours on Furies and the same number on Hurricanes, the type in which all his combat victories were won.

Nor only among the NCO pilots was there talent aplenty in the Squadron. Fred Rosier, 'B'

Flight Commander for two years before Flt Lt Peter Townsend took over, subsequently had a distinguished career in the Desert Air Force and elsewhere during the war and afterwards before finally retiring as an Air Chief Marshal. Flying Officer A M Bentley went on to fill the post of Chief of Staff of the Rhodesian Air Force. Flying Officer Joe Sullivan, who like Flying Officer Pat Christie hailed from Canada, earned for himself the title of 'Chopper' after chewing up his Flight Commander's Fury with his prop in a taxiing accident. He alas was among the first to die when he went to France with a mainly Canadian squadron in the desperate days that led up to the Dunkirk evacuation.

Pilot Officer Philip A N Cox, from New Zealand, died in the Battle of Britain when with No 501 Squadron and his fellow countryman, Malcolm 'Crackers' Carswell, was twice shot down, burned and wounded by September 1940. E R Bitmead commanded three different squadrons during the summer of 1940 and T E J Fitton, an engineer as well as a pilot, lived to retire as an Air Commodore in 1966. Others there were among this little band of warriors whose names, Simpson, Kilmartin, Folkes, Ottewill and Woods-Scawen, will occur in the next few chapters where the good or ill fortune that befell them will be told.

Yet without doubt among the many great characters in the Squadron in the last years of peace none could stand comparison with the one and only Caesar Hull. Rhodesian by birth, South African by upbringing, Caesar came to 43 on 8 August 1936 as the newest of Pilot Officers. By 1939 he was commanding 'A' Flight. All the superlatives have already been written about Caesar. Hector Bolitho in his book *Combat Report* comes nearest perhaps to a successful exposition of his character, although the ones who knew Caesar best would hesitate to affirm that even this does full justice to the man. In this history there is space only to say that Caesar Hull was so outstanding as a man and a pilot that the story of 43 Squadron when he was there cannot be told without his name coming again and again to the fore. His was a star that shone brighter and higher than his fellows, and in the reflection of his twinkling light 43 was a better and a stronger Squadron because of it. Twinkling indeed was not a bad description for Caesar. 'Bubbling unquenchable gaiety . . . 'possessed of a magic power of creating happiness in others; making them belittle their cares, of inspiring them with confidence, not simply in him but in themselves. Of imbuing them with his own abounding love of life. Where Caesar was, laughter was.'

John Simpson, another of the young Pilot Officers who arrived only two months after Caesar, relates how he 'found a confidence when flying with Caesar that was wholly lacking otherwise' . . . and another pilot said that 'I have never seen anyone who could throw a fighter aircraft about with so much confidence as old Caesar. Nobody gave me so much confidence to have a lead from, nobody gave me so much exhilaration and fun. Following Caesar you found yourself getting more out of your machine than you had ever imagined was possible, doing things that done by yourself would have made your hair stand on end. '

This is not the place to write a book about Caesar Hull, though it is a job that should have been done. Enough has surely been said however to indicate just how much the morale, the high standard of flying and the outstanding squadron spirit – 'which was more than an *ésprit de corps* as well as a bond of true affection between all the men of 43' – owed to one most remarkable man, Caesar Barraud Hull, of the crinkly hair and the croaky voice, the laughing warrior whose idea of a lark was to change seats in the air in a two seater Audax, repeating the performance above the aerodrome a second time after he and his partner, 'Prosser' Hanks of 1 Squadron had been accused of landing somewhere on the first occasion. The Caesar who had a phobia about worms or slugs, who would look under the bed 'in case there were any feenies about', then kneel beside it and say his prayers. The man of whom it was said, 'Nobody ever heard him say a nasty or unkind word about anybody' . . . . because of whom, 43 Squadron prospered so much.

The 1937 Hendon Air Display was the last of the line. The stated reason given for the discontinuation of this hardy annual was that modern aircraft could no longer manoeuvre within the confines of a single aerodrome. Unstated but probably more potent was the interference with the training schedule of the squadrons which could no longer be tolerated in the face of the dangers that threatened abroad.

A month before the display Caesar Hull, having come out on top of the Squadron's eliminating contest for individual aerobatics, finished in the same position when he competed in the finals to find the star performer for Hendon on 26 June. Caesar himself was of the opinion that the height limits set by authority were over-cautious and detracted from the spectacular effect of the show but in spite of that the reports from the informed sources were first class 'We had seen it all before but this was better than ever . . . spectacular in the true sense, Pilot Officer Hull always placed his machine and organised the sequence so that there was no pause in interest . . . etc. etc.' *Flight*. *The Aeroplane* said much the same thing, speaking of 'perfect timing of the display . . . altogether a most polished performance'.

Another pilot to appear at the display was Sgt Carey who came very near to winning the landing competition, which involved piloting a Hawker Hart over a wire and touching down as close as possible to a given point. The result was announced only after several protests had been considered, and although Carey was not adjudged the official winner 43 Squadron adamantly refused to admit that in a world of perfection of judgement he would not have been.

Following the demise of Hendon the *Daily Express* organised a display of similar magnitude at Gatwick Airport in 1938 and 43 Squadron was given pride of place for the formation flying and aerobatics.

The Empire Air Day Display a month before Gatwick gave an excellent opportunity for a dress rehearsal, the show additionally providing a fine opportunity to beat hell out of some Ansons of 217 (GR) Squadron who had recently established themselves at Tangmere and of course being Coastal Command types were looked upon as not quite the thing apart from getting in the way of the constant 43 versus 1 Squadron battles which were a long-standing feature of normal Tangmere life.

By 43's own standard the actual Gatwick display was distinctly patchy. In bumpy and windy conditions the Squadron formation, so the pilots thought, was ragged, the line abreast flypast being described as 'pure hell' especially by the extreme wing men. However, the reports the following day were full of praise and the enthusiasm expressed by some professional aerobatic flyers from Germany, France and the USA was all genuine and unreserved. Following the Squadron formation three Furies gave some formation aerobatics and Caesar finished with a solo display, which one report said 'sent the Germans and Marcel Doret, a former world champion at aerobatics, into ecstasies.'

Gatwick was to prove the swan song of the aerobatic Fury. In the summer of 1938 things of greater import than aerial pageants were pressing their way onto the stage. Throughout the spring and summer of that year Hitler, by expressing his determination to reunite the Sudeten Germans in Czechoslovakia, with the Fatherland, was daily increasing the chances of another European war. While the diplomatic messengers with their sealed bags, even Foreign Secretaries and Prime Ministers as the crisis drew to a head, hurried between the capitals of Europe, other signs of the danger were visible nearer home.

Between the barrack blocks and around the messes at Tangmere air-raid shelters were carved into the earth and the yellow gas-detecting posts sprouted around the camp roads like grotesque cubist flowers. The summer routine (0800-1300 and the afternoon off) which had made Tangmere such a desirable posting over the years went, never to return.

Although the first two weeks of August were spent at the long-arranged air-firing practice camp at Aldergrove the Squadron was all the while prepared to return at speed if so required. There was special urgency on this occasion for getting the maximum benefit from this training session, but such did not prevent the frolics normal to the occasion and one Sergeant Pilot soon to become famous in action still remembers with horror a quantity of eels which were placed in his bed after a long dissertation in the mess on his fearlessness of snakes. It is also worth mentioning that en route to Aldergrove a few Salopian rustics were given a post-Gatwick aerobatic display by Caesar and two others after the three had made a preventative forced landing in a field when bad weather caused the flight to get lost and split up en route to their refuelling point at Sealand.

Home to Tangmere on the 16th, many personnel went off on summer leave. Before its expiry recall telegrams were being sent out.

Now as the tension heightened 43, as with all the Royal Air Force, took guard and prepared as best it might for the oncoming crunch. Surveying the general picture of its strength there was little enough to give cause for confidence. The Fury, once the fastest fighter in the world, was now the slowest in the Royal Air Force. The 1937 Air Defence exercises had shown up its limitations, along with all the other biplane fighters, only too well. Faced by the high speed Blenheim monoplanes the only possible means of interception had been to get sufficient height at a hoped-for point of interception, then, if the bombers were seen, to dive nearly vertically upon them and get in a shot before the faster bomber pulled away out of range. There was no reason to think that the Dorniers and Heinkels would prove any easier to deal with, and the pilots were briefed that in view of the hopelessness of a tail-chase the enemy aircraft were to be intercepted with head-on attacks as

Final flight of the Squadron's camouflaged Furies in line abreast
Flight International

they approached the coast. If the guns did not bring down the bombers, and two notoriously stoppage-prone Vickers were hardly likely to, the pilots were, as a last resort, to fly straight on and collide with the enemy, baling out just before the impact!

Nor was this yet all, for now it was discovered that there were, on the station, just two belts of ammunition for each of the two guns in 43 and 1 Squadron's aeroplanes. This situation was rectified by the process of sending everybody, airmen, NCOs and officers, pilots and groundcrew alike to work round-the-clock shifts in the Station Armoury. Belt positioning machines were non-existent, thus the act required that each round should be tapped into place with a double-ended spanner. Pilots went off shift at 2300 hours, to get some sleep, just in case the coming dawn sent them into the air on a death or glory head-on charge into eternity. 'Had we gone into action', quotes one of the pilots 'heaven only knows what stoppages would have occurred.' 'As many', adds a second, 'as there were rounds in a belt.'

Etymologists biased towards the slangier side of the subject may wish to take note that the expression 'Belt-up', with a meaning synonymous with Cromwell's wishing an enemy 'to Hell or Connaught' almost certainly had its origin at this time. Definitely the expression became common and the unending monotony of making up an infinite number of ammunition belts from a never-diminishing supply of boxed rounds was such that to consign one's foe 'to go and belt up' was to wish him into the ultimate depths of drudgery and despair.

Finally here came the one thing for which 43 Squadron could never forgive Adolf Hitler, the order to camouflage their aircraft. In one long night, for the job went on indeed through the small hours, the end result of seven and a half years of loving devotion to polished cowlings, gleaming silver, and black and white chequerboards was swamped in a flood of dark green, dark earth and black. Before the pilots on dawn standby came into the hangar the empty dope-drums were being cleared away; the foul deed was done. But on the fin of each aeroplane, carefully untouched during the operation, there still flared out the *fighting cock* insignia within its surrounding spearhead background. The more things change, the more they stay the same.

By a stroke of the pen at HQ Fighter Command the Fury was now made night, as well as day, operational. Most of the pilots had recent experience of night flying of course. The Squadron had had its own Hawker Demon two-seater allocated since the previous January and, within the limitations of the serviceability of one aircraft and the English weather, as much use as was possible had been made of it. But the Demon, at least, was designed to fly by night. Not so the Fury. In a masterpiece of understatement Frank Carey says that "in the night-fighter role even we felt we were rather badly placed. For a start the Fury had no navigation lights, no signalling lights (vital as it was the only way to request permission to land from the flare path) and no illumination at all in the cockpit. Neither were the instruments fitted with luminous dials.

With the short stub exhaust pipes even dusk flying could produce some blinding light when throttling back."

Not for nothing though did 43 claim *glory to the end*. Undaunted, they acquired some downward signalling lamps which were fitted forthwith. The cockpit lighting was a bit more difficult but was overcome by lashing a torch to the top port longeron, so that the airspeed indicator and altimeter might be readable if nothing else.

"Had this ever been used," concludes Frank Carey, "with the very restricted early wartime flarepath layout, the effect would have been quite dramatic, to say the least!"

As everybody knows it never was used. Chamberlain came back clutching his piece of paper in one hand, umbrella in the other, and bringing *Peace in Our Time* for everybody. The Royal Air Force with its four squadrons of Hurricanes (with guns that froze above 15,000 feet), and its great host of antiquated biplanes heaved a massive sigh of relief and pressed on with an intensified training schedule, certain in its belief that the story of Ethelred and the Danegeld was due for a repeat performance with Adolf soon demanding more and more, whatever paper-waving Prime Ministers might assert to the contrary.

There was even a rumour that a genuine Hawker Hurricane might be coming to Tangmere in the foreseeable future. It did, though for some inexplicable reason it was allotted to No 1 Squadron. In but a few weeks, however, 'that lot' had been equipped and 43 came to the top of the list. On the last day but one of November Hurricanes L1725 and L1727 were delivered direct from the factory at Brooklands. There was no time to waste and before long the pilots, having duly signed a sevenfold affirmation as to their undoubted understanding of all that was needful in respect of, fuel system, retracting undercarriage, flaps, brakes, oxygen,

After the final Fury flight the crews gathered for a photograph. The pilots are, left to right, Hallowes, Christie, Carey, Kilmartin, Rotheram, Hull, Megh, Sullivan, Carswell, Bain (CO), Rosier, Simpson, Folkes, Cox and Berry

headlamps and sliding roof were permitted a short half hour 'High Drag' flight. This latter implied that the undercarriage should stay down and the hood remain open. Then came another hour or so of more experience, after which some went to Brooklands to ferry down more machines. On most of the ten days following the arrival of the first Hurricanes more machines arrived. Invariably, like the animals into the ark they seemed to arrive in pairs. By mid-December the full initial establishment of sixteen Hurricanes was on strength. The displaced Fury, for so long the Squadron's pride, lingered on for a few weeks before the last six departed to Kemble on 2 February 1939. Before they left, a final Squadron formation was laid on and John Yoxall, masterful air photographer from *Flight* who 'looked on 43 as his spiritual home', came to Tangmere to do his stuff.

If those who had long delighted in the magnificent handling qualities of the Fury felt any pang at the parting they had little time to indulge their sorrow for with the new aeroplanes training became more intensive than ever. 'At last we had an up-to-date aircraft capable of having a go at any German bomber', said Jim Hallowes and in like vein Frank Carey, who had just over 1,000 hours on the Fury (a total he equalled almost to the exact minute in subsequent flying in Hurricanes) 'felt that the Hurricane would be quite a lot more useful in a fight than its predecessor'.

The performance of the Hurricane is well enough known to require no great elaboration here. With the two bladed fixed-pitch wooden airscrews (all that the country could afford in peacetime!) its top speed was nominally 318 mph a 50 per cent improvement of the Fury but not as high as popular reports, which spoke too often and too easily of 400 mph being achieved. In time to climb with full load to 20,000 feet the Hurricane at 11·7 minutes was not much quicker than the Fury, although of course its potential for knocking holes in the opposition when it finally arrived was immensely superior. Eight Browning ·303 machine-guns firing twenty rounds each per second was a different conception of fire power altogether from the previous pair of synchronised and rather erratic Vickers Mk V.

And so through the spring and summer of this year the Squadron trained harder than it had ever done before. It was all the old old routine, practised again and again in a search for perfection. Formation, air-firing, interceptions, instrument flying, aerobatics, sector recces, cross country flights and practise attacks. 'No 1, attack from above and to the quarter with aircraft in line ahead. . .' etc etc, a series of 'set piece' attacks designed for use against unescorted bombers and destined to prove highly unusable when Messerschmitt escorts were around.

A modified Fairey Battle arrived for dual-control purposes, and proved as a trainer as unlovely and horrible as the bomber versions decimated in France in 1940. The faithful old Hawker Demon followed the Furies into retirement. With the Hurricane being fully equipped for night flying it was no longer required.

And when the moon was up, 43 was found more and more in search of flying hours. The Hurricane was not a difficult aeroplane to fly by night. Not that all the civilians in their beds below thought highly of them or their pilots, as witness a letter in the *Worthing Herald* from an irate resident.

'Twinkle Twinkle aeroplane
How I wonder what we gain
By your infernal noise on high
a B. . . . . nuisance in the sky.'

"I am stung into this sort of thing by the apathy of the authorities who ought to protect us from the sky pest who is making a quiet life impossible even at night. I don't care if his parents do live at Broadwater, I don't care if he is teaching others to follow his own foul example; I don't care if there are air pockets in other directions than Worthing. He ought to be suppressed. It may be very meritorious to spread the skill necessary to kill and maim the women and children of some future enemy but why should he practise on us?"

There is no evidence available to show whether or not the first German bomb to fall on Worthing went straight down that writer's chimney pot, although it would not have been unjust had it done so. Nevertheless, such cries of encouragement from the natives merely served to spur on the men of 43, although in their ignorance they continued to think that their main purpose was to prevent the foul enemy from killing and maiming their own women and children. For this privilege one of them paid with his life when, on the night of 22 April, Flying Officer Charles Rotheram's Hurricane crashed and burst into flames while landing. The fire was not visible as far away as Broadwater.

In the Spring of 1939 Flight Sergeant Hayden was posted in to take charge of the Wireless Section. Before long he had imbued the Sergeant Pilots with his own enthusiasm for practising R/T controlled approaches, or ZZ landings as they were then called, on every available occasion. Although there was little or no support for this venture from the topmost levels the pilot/wireless section co-operation continued with improving results. Jim Hallowes avers that one Hurricane for sure, not to mention himself, was saved as a result of the experience gained by these experiments. Flying a Hurricane to Acklington from Tangmere in January 1940 Hallowes ran into very bad weather and when he turned back discovered that the storm had closed in all round him. At 18,000 feet, as high as he dared to climb without oxygen, visibility was nil and although he knew he was more than a hundred miles from Acklington, Hallowes called on his RT for an emergency homing. In his own words:

"Doug Hayden guided me back the last hundred miles through snow and cloud, to a successful landing. It was all very much to the astonishment of those who had said that the range of R/T was very limited and there was no point in training fighter pilots on ZZ landings. It was a tribute to the Squadron's wireless section, the tuning of the radio sets and Doug Hayden in particular for introducing this type of controlled landing that both the pilot and the aeroplane were not lost that day."

Empire Air Day on 20 May 1939 was the last peacetime occasion for the great British public to survey their Air Force and if the thousands of people who came to Tangmere that day found the war-painted Hurricanes less attractive to the eye than the Furies, they at least must have gone home feeling a little more secure than in 1938. The Tangmere Squadrons anyway did their best that day to provide a host of satisfied customers and indeed found the occasion a welcome change from the customary intensive training schedule which left no spare time to entertain the masses at pageants or displays.

Already, in fact, before that last Empire Air Day the indications were everywhere suggesting a crisis of greater magnitude than that of the previous year. For Hitler had broken every promise given at Munich and occupied the whole of Czechoslovakia. Now he was implacably determined to re-claim the Baltic city of Danzig, which had been incorporated in the new state of Poland by the Treaty of Versailles. Although the Government in London still placed a wholly indefensible faith in the goodwill of the

German dictator a more realistic appreciation of events existed elsewhere and as week succeeded week during that fateful summer it became increasingly difficult to refute those who asserted that this time the crisis could end only by a further act of appeasement or an all-out war. There could be no middle way. Long before 3 September the mood of the country was that another Munich, another retreat, was something not to be endured and there was nothing left but to fight. In company with its fellows, 43 Squadron had, when the war finally started, already accepted its inevitability and the declaration was more a relief than anything else. It was a relief because the fear that its leaders would run away yet again was dispelled and with that doubt removed the task ahead was simple and plain. It was to put itself to the test. The past months and years of prolonged graft and intensive training had been directed solely towards preparedness for this hour. Soon it would be known whether the preparation had been in vain or otherwise. It was a measure of 43 Squadron's strength that everybody from Squadron Leader Bain down to the latest arrived AC2 was wholly confident in its competence and ability to do anything. Nor was the attitude vain glory or idle boast. For most of the groundcrew and pilots alike, squadron service was measured in years rather than months. Between everybody of every rank and trade and calling there existed a camaraderie which had to be experienced to be fully understood. 43 Squadron was a little exclusive club where men of vastly differing background, class, temperament and education found common cause, a world where you gave your everything yet seemed to draw out more than you put in.

To such a confident company the final onrush to war could cause no major alarm whatever private fears might linger in the breast. Mobilization on 5 August caused the Adjutant John Simpson a great deal of work, calling up reservists, recalling others from leave. One of these reservists, Sgt Plenderleith, a Volunteer Reserve pilot, was already with the Squadron for his annual training when the call-up came and on the orders of Squadron Leader Bain remained there. Three weeks later the local police were still trying to arrest him for failing to report to his calling-up station. The Air Exercises in early August held in conjunction with the French were short and sharp; 1,300 bombers attacked, and the Tangmere Hurricanes claimed to have intercepted (and of course shot down) a large proportion of those that came into their area.

Patrols for the benefit of the newly called-up Observer Corps, anti-aircraft guns, and searchlight companies were made but in general very little flying was done after 24 August. The Hurricanes were dispersed out of the hangar and away to the aerodrome boundaries. Oddly enough more than twelve Command Reserve Hurricanes which the Squadron held for weekly maintenance were left jammed in half the Squadron's hangar, a fine compact target for a single bomb. At ten minutes to eleven on 3 September after two days of great tension John Simpson walked into the hangar from his Adjutant's office and said to Warrant Officer Bill Chitty, then currently in charge of Maintenance Flight, 'The balloon goes up at 11 o'clock, that's official.' According to Hector Bolitho he was in the Officers' Mess ten minutes later, when Caesar Hull jumped from one foot to the other saying, 'Wizard, Wizard'.

43 Squadron was at war.

Hurricane L1734 'NQ-G' was taken on charge in early December 1938 and is seen here carrying the original 'NQ' code. This was later changed to 'FT-G'.
(Andy Saunders collection)

CHAPTER 9

Unglamorous Beginning

IT was symbolic of the unprepared state for waging war of the whole nation that only on the last day of August did somebody at Tangmere awake to the realisation that the aerodrome with all its aircraft and all its buildings was wide open on the north-east boundary for the whole world to enter. Looking around for men to plug the gap the searching eyes of Station Headquarters alighted on 43 Squadron. There was nobody else, for 1 Squadron was packing for France and 217 had taken its Ansons to war stations at St Eval, while 605 (Auxiliary) Squadron was scarcely fully mobilised. It had to be 43 or nobody. With the forced urgency that characterised everything in those last hectic and apprehensive days of peace Sqn Ldr Bain ordered every man in the Squadron to get cracking and to stay on the job until it was completed. He departed himself after two hours. By tea the pilots had gone. On the second day most of the Maintenance Flight crews had been called to dispersal for standby duties. A few men from the Flight (the most highly skilled tradesmen naturally!) remained. During the next six weeks, forgotten by all, they erected an impregnable wire fence, a barrier that crawled across the fields to the Arundel road, where they met with an admiring audience of small evacuees who were despatched regularly for chocolate and pop. Finally relieved by an influx of Class E reservists, they returned reluctantly to the task of servicing aeroplanes.

Meantime the Squadron had been called to readiness at 1115 hours on 3 September. The aircraft were dispersed on the east side of the aerodrome where a few old tents provided such shelter as there was. Pilots ate at dispersal and awaited the fleets of hostile bombers, which H G Wells and others had predicted would of a surety precede or at least accompany the outbreak of hostilities. They were still waiting when at 2130 hours the Squadron was released.

At 1300 hours on 8 September Fg Off Kilmartin became the first to fire his guns in World War II. Not in anger, 1,200 rounds were required to despatch a balloon which had broken free from the Portsmouth barrage and had drifted as far as Farnborough before being intercepted. The equinoctial gales gave several similar targets and between 17th and 23rd Flt Lt Townsend, Fg Off Sullivan, Flt Lt Hull, Fg Off Wilkinson and Sgt Hallowes all qualified as balloon busters. Caesar Hull had the most spectacular – a flamer – and Sgt Hallowes expended fewer rounds, 200, than anybody else.

Captain Harold Balfour MC, Under Secretary of State for Air, who in 1916 had been one of the first ever Flight Commanders, visited the Squadron and left with the impression that only the aircraft had changed. As September gave way to the worsening weather of October the Squadron continued its periods of readiness (now much reduced) and did a great deal of training. Practice attacks, local flying and formation figured highest in the programme as the old hands endeavoured to pass on their skill and the younger ones discovered just how much they had to learn. There was some night flying, co-operating with searchlight batteries, and on 7 October Fg Off Sullivan wrecked the undercarriage of Hurricane L1825, the first aircraft to be damaged 'on active service'.

On the 27th, Sqn Ldr Bain, promoted Wing Commander, departed to France. His almost last act before leaving was typical of the man. Out of his office at ten minutes' notice went his Discip NCO so that it might accommodate a WAAF officer. She was in fact the first of the species ever

Three Hurricanes, canopies covered, at Tangmere in 1939

to invade Tangmere. SHQ had treated her with coldness and quite failed to help her in any way. To this day she recalls her gratefulness to a Squadron and its Commanding Officer who demonstrated that the age of chivalry was not quite dead. To command, from 11 Group Intelligence, came Sqn Ldr C G Lott, whilst almost at the same time Plt Off S H Cary arrived as Adjutant. Two experienced pilots went on 3 November, for Fg Off Sullivan went as a Flight Commander to 242 Squadron with whom he was subsequently killed in France, and Fg Off Kilmartin departed also to France to join No 1 Squadron.

On 16 November the Squadron was ordered to reinforce 13 Group forthwith. On the 18th twelve Hurricanes flew to Acklington, accompanied by two Armstrong Whitworth Ensigns and one DH 86, which carried between them a great deal of essential equipment and a large number of men.

Acklington, twenty miles north of Newcastle-on-Tyne, was a peacetime Summer practice camp, pressed of necessity into service as a wartime operational aerodrome. There were no runways, a scarcity of hangar accommodation and living space was tight, for 111 Squadron was already installed and when it subsequently left, 152 Squadron arrived. Yet none of these inconveniences were as troublesome as the weather and the most abiding memory of Acklington is that it was always cold. The Northumbrian climate, superimposed upon the basic severity of the Winter of 1939-40, added up to utter discomfort. Coldest of all was the last dark hour before the dawn, when the eternal east wind that blew in from the dull grey sea a mile away sharpened its cutting edge of iciness to an extra keenness. Just at that hour on most days the Squadron prepared to come to readiness. For the mechanic, 'warming up' his engine, life held some promise, for he could shut tight the sliding hood and receive the full benefit of the main coolant pipes which ran between and beside his feet to the radiator amidships and below and produced a heat that rose rapidly to subtropical levels so that all life was lost in desire to stay forever in that one small space, insulated from the frozen world outside and to drift back into the sleep from which he had been so recently, so rudely, awakened. For his unfortunate rigger, half a wing span removed in distance and half a world away in comfort, there was no such redeeming pleasure. Hunched over the starter trolley, swearing at the ineffectiveness of scarves and balaclavas at combating the refrigerated elements, and at the clumsiness of hands made awkward by gloves and mittens, there was little solace but to count the hours to breakfast, or weeks before his next leave and to wonder at the perverseness of fortune that ordained such inequality for those bearing the bracketed (Engine) rather than (Airframe), after the trade designation of Flight Mechanics. Not infrequently life was even more complicated and damnable, for the electric starter trolleys, notoriously unreliable beasts in the absence of good recharging facilities, were likely as not to produce only a useless clicking of the relays, and then the only way to stir the Merlin into life was by using the hand starting gear, an operation requiring positively hard physical effort and offering only partial chance of success, for some engines displayed a mule-like cussedness in refusing to fire at the speeds induced by hand cranking, and always of course there was the near certainty of skinned knuckles from handles that slipped, a fair possibility of a sore wrist from a backfire and at the very worst decapitation from the propeller if one's foothold failed in the mud! It was very little better for the pilots, for in order to be ready for dawn it was generally necessary to sleep at dispersal, and, probably because reliefs were not readily come by, breakfast was sent from the mess by van. Cold bacon or kippers were no great delicacy and on one historic occasion Sqn

Squadron Leader C G Lott DSO DFC
(Andy Saunders collection)

Ldr Lott, scrambled to 30,000 feet when the kipper was but half consumed, remarked on landing that assuredly no kipper had ever flown so high before, and what a surprise its mother would have if only she knew.

Hurricane L1849 'FT-E' at Tangmere being protected by sandbags on 1 September 1939

For a Squadron accustomed to the luxury and the fleshpots of Tangmere there was not much at all about Acklington to make the heart rejoice, yet never a crack was apparent in its morale. It helped that the suffering was completely communal and everybody was in it without exception. Likely as not, the chap beside you debogging a mired Hurricane was the Flight Commander or one of his pilots. Hell could never be unbearably bad if it were known for a certainty that Heaven was empty. And sometimes at night when there was no moon and the Hurricanes were picketed down there were pubs at Red Row or Broomhill, perhaps even a theatre in Newcastle, where frozen blood might be thawed, or the intellectual wilderness escaped from for a brief spell.

Moreover, and this was at the heart of the matter as everybody knew, though in nearly all things domestic and technical Acklington was a foul place, there was no doubt that operationally it was far more promising than Tangmere could hope to be, and was it not the primary purpose of a fighter squadron to engage the enemy? Yet though there was always a hope of action, there was but slight glamour in the waiting for it to begin. Convoy patrols and shipping protection were described variously as 'dull and cold', 'monotonous', 'deadly boring' and 'not much fun'. Since enemy activity was evident only when low cloud cover was available, patrols were flown either at mast height or perhaps just below the cloud base, at not many hundreds of feet. The little ships which the Hurricanes watched over were the coastal convoys, the colliers from Blyth or Newcastle, the minesweepers and the inshore fishing boats, and if the attacks were never on a scale that suggested they might become a serious menace to traffic, they were irritating and dangerous for the seamen subjected to them. More to the point for Fighter Command was that only here was there any chance of direct contact with the enemy, only around these northern coasts was there opportunity to test itself against its adversary, and just for this reason 111 and 43 Squadrons had been moved, on the principle that if only a few squadrons were to be actively engaged they might as well be the best and the most experienced.

When not patrolling, or waiting at readiness, there was as much practice flying as weather and serviceability allowed, the latter not being improved by the necessity of having to leave the Maintenance Flight behind at Tangmere so that routine inspections required a ferry trip both ways. A Hurricane was lost early in December when Sgt Arbuthnot baled out after spinning in cloud. The aircraft crashed on a peat moorland and the salvage party reported finding one large hole with very little sign of an aeroplane at the bottom.

Four days before Christmas the Squadron was brought to readiness at 1500 hours and at 1505 was scrambled to intercept nine hostile mine laying aircraft at a great height. At 1525 seven Hampdens were intercepted over Alnwick at 1,000 feet! While landing at Acklington one Hampden crashed and destroyed the church at Broomhill. On Christmas Day, readiness from 0700 hours was ordered and Sqn Ldr Lott flew a one hour defensive patrol at 1500 hours. There was none who could not recall former Christmases spent in more congenial surroundings, but the day did not end without a certain amount of rejoicing and festivity. A week later when the old year died, the Squadron helped it on its way in lively fashion. Of the New Year only one thing was sure. It could scarcely be as unproductive and featureless for a fighter squadron as its predecessor.

Groundcrew with a Hurricane, its wooden prop protected from rain

CHAPTER 10

Bomber Harvest

NINETEEN-FORTY brought an initial double stroke of ill fortune when Sgt Henry Steeley and Sgt Edwin Mullinger, close companions on the ground, died together after their aircraft collided at 800 feet while carrying out practice attacks. Within the next week or so two or three other aircraft were damaged, and with Group showing signs of displeasure Sqn Ldr Lott issued a stern warning as to the probable fate of the next offender. Later that same day Caesar Hull, returning from a post-inspection air test caused a mighty disturbance, for his aircraft made its final approach flaps down, undercarriage UP, but just before the inevitable belly flop, engine power came on and the Hurricane flew past the assembled group, which included the Squadron Commander, with the pilot paying his respects to them by means of a sign that later became associated with Victory and Winston Churchill, but which in those earlier days had a less respectful connotation.

After several days of aerodrome unserviceability caused by heavy snow, Caesar Hull, Plt Off North and Sgt Carey were, on 29 January, vectored on to a Heinkel 111 bomber ten miles south-south-east of Hartlepool. After an exchange of shots it escaped in low cloud. L1744 (Flt Lt Hull) was hit by one bullet which passed through the fuselage behind the pilot, and that night the German radio claimed the destruction of one English fighter. Thus it was no more than justice that on the next day the same aeroplane with the same pilot, with Sgt Carey again in attendance, intercepted a Heinkel 111 five miles east of Coquet Island. The combat report was a model of how it ought to be done. 'Sighted two e/a, flying south, apparently attacking a small fishing vessel . . . I attacked one using beam to astern six times . . . number two synchronised his attacks with me . . . e/a seen to dive into sea and break up . . . no sign of other e/a after this combat . . . C B Hull.' The crew of five were rescued by one of the boats they had been trying to destroy.

On 3 February Sqn Ldr Lott, on leave in the south of England, received a telegram telling him to listen to the 6 o'clock news that evening,

The first enemy aircraft shot down in England in World War II was this well peppered Heinkel 111. It crash-landed at Sneaton Castle Farm, near Whitby, Yorkshire on 3 February 1940 after it had been attacked by Flt Lt Townsend, Sgt Hallowes and Fg Off Folkes (Imperial War Museum)

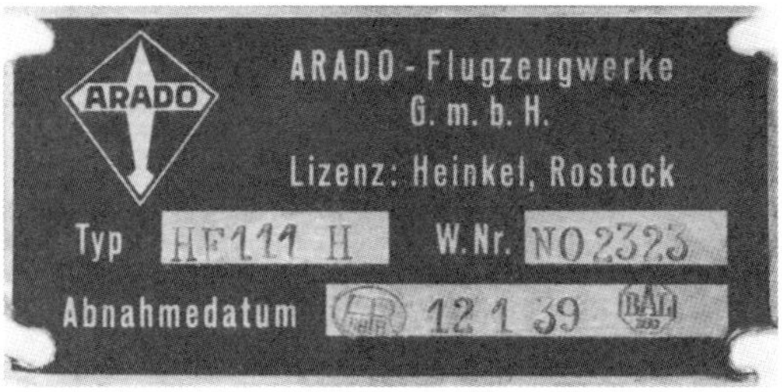

The maker's plate from the Heinkel was kept as a souvenir.

having done so he returned at once to the Squadron, fuming at missing the day's events. Three sections were scrambled at 0900 hours, one to South Shields, one to Tynemouth, one to Farne Island. At 0935 Fg Off Simpson and Fg Off Edmonds were circling a small convoy when bomb splashes were seen in the water and a Heinkel 111 was spotted just below the cloud base at 900 feet. Number one subsequently reported: 'I climbed up and attacked . . . hit him squarely in the wings and fuselage . . . a bit flew off . . . he disappeared in cloud. Number two called and said, "I can see the bastard" and fired. I caught up again flying towards English coast and fired all my ammo. He was well alight as he disappeared in the mist.'

They returned to base to find that Black Section (Flt Lt Townsend, Fg Off Folkes, Sgt Hallowes), already landed, had at 0940, three miles east of Whitby, intercepted a Heinkel 111. Townsend made a deflection attack, Folkes attacked from dead astern and Hallowes positioned himself to head off the e/a from taking cover in cloud. The Heinkel had turned towards land and crashed near Sneaton Castle Farm, Whitby, the first enemy aircraft to be brought down on English soil in World War II.

The raiders were out in force that morning and at 1030 Red Section (Hull, Carswell and North) damaged another Heinkel. Then at 1115, Sgts Carey and Ottewill, fifteen miles east of Tynemouth, intercepted a fourth in the act of bombing ships. The e/a was engaged with simultaneous beam attacks, both engines stopped and it crashed in the sea. The crew climbed on to the main plane until Caesar Hull arrived and beat them up, when they all dived back into the sea.

The badly-injured survivors of the Whitby Heinkel were visited in hospital by Caesar, Townsend and Simpson, the Germans expressing both their thanks for the fruit and cigarettes which were given to them and their surprise at such treatment as they had been led to expect nothing but the worst at the hands of the British.

Following this opening spate of action the remainder of February had plenty more in store. On the 9th, a day of very poor visibility and spasmodic enemy anti-shipping activity, Blue Section, (Flt Lt Townsend, Fg Off Carswell and Sgt Hallowes) attacked two Heinkel 111s near Coquet Island. Townsend, apparently failing to spot both bombers, went in to attack one and was himself fired upon by the other whereupon Hallowes gave this aggressive enemy a long full-deflection burst and saw bits fall from it before it jettisoned all its bombs and made off into cloud. Hallowes then saw a Hurricane gliding towards the sea and followed it. It sank as soon as it hit the water leaving Carswell supported by his Mae West. After some difficulty in attracting the attention of the crew of a nearby Swedish ship Hallowes finally succeeded in leading them to the rescue and little the worse for wear Carswell returned to the Squadron the next day. The Heinkel was claimed as 'Damaged' and allowed as such but more than a year later additional evidence found in the diary of an air-gunner shot down during a night raid on London showed that the badly-crippled machine had crashed 150 miles from the German coast and the Squadron was permitted to adjust its records although for some unexplained reason Hallowes was not allowed to add it to his official personal score.

John Simpson was the next to make news in the records when he experienced engine failure during a night take-off, bounced off the top of a haystack and swathed down thirty-six larch trees before coming to rest. The slight injuries suffered by the pilot were a tribute to the inbuilt strength of the Hurricane. On the 21st Sgt Frank Carey was awarded the DFM for 'determination and skill'.

The last victory at Acklington came on 22nd when Blue Section, (Flt Lt Townsend, Fg Off Christie and Sgt Ayling), patrolling the Farne Islands at 2,500 feet, saw contrails at 20,000 feet. They immediately climbed at full boost. Christie soon retired, his overheating engine a victim of the ubiquitous Acklington mud blown into the radiator during taxiing prior to take off. Townsend and Ayling continued to climb, lost the enemy aircraft in cloud at 19,000 feet but refound it soon afterwards. Townsend attacked from astern, positioned so that the top rear gunner dared not fire for fear of shooting his own rudder and the lower rear gunner was 'quite ineffective'. After a five second burst the e/a went into a dive; a second squirt brought smoke from both engines, which temporarily blinded the Hurricane pilot. At 10,000 feet and 400 IAS the e/a lurched violently forward and

Sgt Gough, Plt Off Oelofse, Flt Lt Hull, Plt Off Woods-Scawen and Sgt Ottewill relax 'at Readiness' in April 1940 at a rather muddy WIck

both ailerons broke away; the dive steepened and the Heinkel crashed into the sea. There were no survivors.

On 26 February Sqn Ldr Lott and nine other pilots flew to Wick, to help protect the Home Fleet in Scapa Flow. The rest of the Squadron followed by train. Wick was like Acklington, but '400 miles nearer the North Pole'; a small airfield into which three Hurricane and one Coastal Command Squadrons were jammed. The squadron personnel were billeted in the town and not the least besetting of their sorrows was the discovery that in Scotland the Burghers could vote to turn the town into a teetotal wilderness, and Wick was one such place!

On 10 March it was recorded: 'Since arriving at Wick the Squadron has endured most miserable and atrocious weather. Everywhere is mud. In spite of all hardships the operational efficiency has not suffered and the spirit and keenness of the Squadron is as high as ever before.' It might also have added 'in spite of the lack of appreciation by Station HQ that it primarily existed for the benefit of the squadrons operating there, and not the reverse'.

The three months at Wick each had a distinctive character arising from the events that happened within them. In March there was little but discomfort and boredom. In April the ennui was swept away by a flood tide of action as the assaults of the Luftwaffe on Scapa Flow were met and countered, and in May, as the threats receded and the events in the Low Countries and France became of primary importance, the Squadron found itself being drained of many of its best who went to help plug the gaps which appeared in those fighter squadrons who more and more were being drawn into battle in a hopeless attempt to stabilise the confused shambles across the Channel. In fact the weakening of the Squadron was but a reduced scale image of the draining away of Fighter Command which caused so much concern to its Commander-in-Chief and which was halted only after his intervention at Cabinet level. On the very last day of May, the day on which the Squadron returned to Tangmere, its diary recorded: '. . . a steady drain of good pilots who have not been replaced so that the strength is now fourteen. 43 Squadron cannot be considered

'A' Flight at Wick in April
Sgt Buck, Plt Off Woods-Scawen, Flt Lt Hull, Plt Off Wilkinson and Sgt Garton
(Andy Saunders collection)

to possess the same destructive possibilities as when the month opened'.

Both Flight Commanders had gone. Peter Townsend who had, on 4 May, been decorated with a DFC, to command 85 Squadron; Caesar Hull to Norway with the Gladiators of 263 and one of the very few bright stories of this dismal campaign was the tale of how at one moment of crisis he appeared to take on alone the might of the Luftwaffe and was recommended for the Victoria Cross. Frank Carey, commissioned, had departed to 3 Squadron, Fg Off Christie to help pioneer the first Spitfire PRU Flight, and on 16 May Fg Off Thom, only ten days with 43, and Sgts Plenderleith, Arbuthnot and Garton were called to London for onward transmission to an unknown destination; more plugs for the holes across the Channel. Fg Off Patrick 'Tiger' Folkes was dead, killed when his Hurricane crashed into the sea on convoy patrol leaving only a map, a piece of wood and a patch of oil for the destroyer that raced to the scene to find. 'The Squadron isn't what it was', said the old hands, forgetting that it never is! But though some faces had changed and its strength was reduced, the spirit was in no way shaken and the decrease in destructive possibilities was essentially one of magnitude and not quality. The great days of April were not so far away that there had been time to forget.

The month of March had three days yet to run, when a reconnoitring He 111, its mission violently terminated, dived with fuselage enveloped in flame, into the sea fifteen miles east of base after Sgt Ottewill had attacked it.

On 8 April, in the evening, as four hundred miles eastward the German invasion fleet set off for Norway, a determined effort was made by the Luftwaffe to disable or confound the naval forces at Scapa Flow, which patently were more able than any other body to interfere decisively with the German plans. Made by the largest force of bombers which up to that time had been launched at Britain, it failed completely and not a single ship was damaged in any way. Detected by radar when far offshore, Nos 43, 605 and 111 Squadrons were scrambled to intercept. At 2035 hours Green Section (Fg Off Edmonds and Sgt Arbuthnot) were the first to engage. Forty miles east of Copinsay lighthouse the two Hurricanes came upon six bombers flying in loose formation. Fg Off Edmonds dived head on into the Heinkels which scattered and broke in random directions. Selecting one of the e/a, Edmonds opened fire at 600 yards, closing rapidly. 'Lumps of perspex flew off the nose', the port engine burst into flame, and as Edmonds banked tightly to come into position to attack again the bomber dived into the sea and broke up. Meantime Sgt Arbuthnot was firing all his ammunition at another, which poured out white smoke and dived into a layer of cloud which covered the area at 2,000 feet.

Blue Section (Flt Lt Townsend and Sgt Hallowes) thirty miles or so east of Duncansby Head were patrolling with Townsend just below the cloud and Hallowes just above when the former sighted two Heinkel 111 bombers and went in to attack. He saw his bullets striking home, and flame began to flicker in the starboard engine nacelle. Then, strange things, the undercarriage was lowered, the navigation lights came on (possibly as a sign of surrender) and the aircraft gently hit the water, capsized and sank. Hallowes having missed out on this particular bit of excitement was feeling rather disconsolate, even more so when soon afterwards he was ordered to return to base. While complying with this order however he saw ack-ack bursts at 8,000 feet west of Pentland Firth and on going to investigate saw two more Heinkel 111s. At 400 yards he opened fire; after a little more than a second and 200 rounds his guns stopped firing (due to a fractured pneumatic line) and the two Heinkels both dived away into a rain cloud and were lost to view. Hallowes returned and landed along the flarepath. He was followed almost immediately by one of the Heinkels, which had been so badly damaged by his very short but extremely accurate burst of fire that the pilot was not prepared to attempt the return passage home. As it was, both of the rear gunners were dead. The pilot was misled by the poor dusk visibility into thinking that he was landing on the water and the first thing he did on coming to a stop was to let go the aircraft dinghy and also take off his boots. As for Hallowes he was met by the

The Heinkel 111 of 6/Kg 26 brought down by Sgt Hallowes on 8 April 1940.
It crashed on Wick airfield, both rear gunners dead, after a 1 second burst from 8 ·303 machine guns
(Andy Saunders collection)

Intelligence Officer and told to report at once to the Station Commander who was furious because he had shot down a friendly Hudson. When the Intelligence officer was finally prevailed upon to come and see for himself they found one very small private of a Scottish Regiment with fixed bayonet holding it about one inch from the stomach of the German pilot (finding the snow rather cold on his bare feet) and reiterating over and over again, "Move an' inch y' bastarrrd an' a'll stick ye."

Two days later, when the Squadron was low down in the order of sector availability, the sirens' wail brought a rush of pilots to dispersal. Six aircraft, led by the CO, found a lone raider some five miles east of Ronaldsay. (Although nobody knew it at the time the bomber was carrying a Luftwaffe Lt Col who had come to survey the area where his unit had lost so heavily on the 8th.) After several attacks it was badly damaged and Caesar and Peter Townsend formated on it in an attempt to bring another one back alive. "It was a ghastly sight," wrote Townsend, "tail unit vibrating, the fuselage and wings torn and tattered. The rear gun positions were a dreadful looking sight. The pilot's fair hair was streaming in the wind through the broken nose, he was leaning forward as if trying to urge the machine to fly, but it was all to no avail. It hit the water and the rear end fell off and sank at once. . . Then we saw three of the crew get into the water and start swimming, backstroke, in that icy water, towards the land. We didn't feel sorry for them any longer . . . "

There was one more victory for 43 at Wick. Flt Lt John Simpson newly promoted to 'A' Flight Commander, in place of Caesar Hull, was in company with Sgt Ottewill when they together destroyed a Do 17 on 9 May. It brought the Squadron's score up to twelve destroyed and two damaged.

The following day the Panzers burst into Holland and Belgium and the war had really begun. For three weeks the Squadron lingered at Wick, feeling very much out in the wings while the action was all on-stage. It heard of the mighty deeds of No 1 in France. 'I wish we could go there; I'm sure we should do well', wrote John Simpson to a friend. No 605 Squadron was

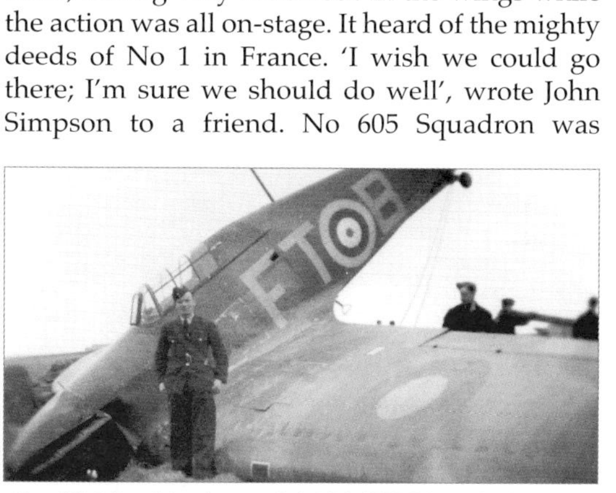

On 13 May Hurricane L1728 'FT-B' ended up on its nose after a minor accident at Wick
(Andy Saunders collection)

Pilots from 'B' Flight discuss a sortie at Wick - Sgt Arbuthnot, Sgt Plenderleith, Sgt James Hallowes, Flt Lt John Simpson, Flt Lt Peter Townsend and Fg Off H C Upton

pulled out of Wick for France which served to increase the frustrated desire to get into the battle for there was nothing now to do at Wick; the raids on Scapa had long since ceased as the Luftwaffe busily engaged themselves elsewhere. The news that 605 Squadron, in a matter of days had been decimated caused some alarm, and the sense of impending danger was little asuaged as the armies fell back continuously before the Panzer flood. But not until Dunkirk had become the first word on every lip did the Squadron receive its orders to move. On the last day of May it was ordered to move immediately back to Tangmere. Fourteen aircraft and pilots took off at 1130. Sqn Ldr Lott landed at Grangemouth (to which the Squadron Maintenance Flight had been moved in April) with fuel trouble and proceeded later by Magister to Tangmere. The other thirteen pilots in their Hurricanes had already arrived.

That evening the sun went down in a clear red sky. It was obvious that the morrow would be a busy day.

Flt Lt Townsend and his crew at Wick

Two of the Squadron try out the Heinkel's dinghy

CHAPTER 11

The Glorious First of June

FOR those who waited on the beaches Dunkirk was the end point of three weeks of continuous confusion, of a battle fought always on the retreat as one attempt after another to stabilise a crumbling front collapsed in the face of the thrusting Panzer divisions; until at last there was only the beach and the sea beyond. On that sea, as any Englishman would have expected, was the Royal Navy under whose guidance the little ships shuttled back and forth to snatch from under the very noses of the enemy the bulk of the trained manpower of the British Army.

To the nation as a whole, Dunkirk was more than a 'miraculous deliverance.' It was the alarm at the eleventh hour that aroused the quiescent energies of the people, and swept away the false optimism regarding the outcome of the war. The 'cardboard' tanks had proved to be steel plated, the washing that was so easily to have been hung up on the Siegfried line had been lost, abandoned on the beaches or along the line of retreat with all the tanks and guns and transport of an Army. It is history how, in realising the magnitude of the dangers that threatened it, the nation found a new strength and resolve, and rededicated itself to meeting the task that lay ahead.

But to 43 Squadron Dunkirk is not primarily any of these things. Emblazoned for all time upon its Standard, 'Dunkirk' is a commemoration of the events of a single engagement on a day when, outnumbered by more than six to one, it gave the Luftwaffe a very bloody nose. One hundred and forty-six years earlier, on the first day of June, Admiral the Earl Howe sailed into action off the coast of France to win a victory which, coming as it did at the end of a year of war that had been an unrelieved disaster, caused all Britain to rejoice. For 43 Squadron their action on the anniversary of that battle was equally glorious, and if it received no publicity and the nation knew not of it yet it was a cause for the greatest satisfaction to all the Squadron. Though it had already destroyed, up to the beginning of May, more enemy aircraft than any other home-based unit, all those victories had been against unescorted bombers, but at Dunkirk their opponents were entirely enemy fighters, Me 109s and 110s, both in many ways better aircraft than the Hurricane. However when the battle was over, 'the first game in the top division' as somebody called it, 43 Squadron could show, for the loss of Sgt Terence Gough, killed, and Fg Off Carswell, baled out burned but safe over a British destroyer, nine enemy aircraft positively and undoubtedly destroyed, three more probably and another three damaged. All this by a Squadron of whom the CO had reported the previous day 'had had its destructive possibilities sadly reduced during the preceding months'.

It was a salutory thought to imagine what the Squadron might have done had it gone into action in all its majestic strength of six months earlier. Hull, Townsend, Carey, Kilmartin, Christie and Sullivan would have made in any permutation two sections guaranteed to keep the German Quartermasters' aircraft replacement clerks very busy. Yet even with such stalwarts gone, to be the leaven in the rising lump of an expanding air force, with its original might and glory diluted by the needs of others, the Fighting Cocks that remained (and let it be made plain that not all the brightest stars had gone) still possessed sharp spurs and deadly dangerous claws; 43 could still do most things better than most others.

The story started the previous night. 11 Group Operational Order dated 31/5/40 detailed 43 Squadron together with 245, 145 and a French Squadron 'to patrol in company and protect shipping coming out of Dunkirk'. Rendezvous was over Hawkinge at 0600 hours and 145 and 43 were ordered to return to Manston to refuel at 0730. The order was carried out, and apart from the failure of the French to appear was without incident. At 1100 hours a second patrol was flown. At 1125 hours 145 Squadron detached itself to attack enemy bombers approaching shipping. 43 Squadron remained on the patrol line Calais-Dunkirk. Approaching Dunkirk, Me 109s were seen coming in head on 'in large numbers'. At the same time Me 110s broke through the cloud away to the west. There was a total of about sixty enemy aircraft in all. 43 Squadron had nine

Hurricanes, dispersed in three sections. They were:

Blue

1 Sqn Ldr Lott, 2 Fg Off Woods-Scawen,
3 Fg Off Wilkinson

Red

1 Flt Lt Simpson, 2 Fg Off Edmonds, 3 Sgt Ottewill

Black

1 Fg Off Carswell, 2 Sgt Hallowes, 3 Sgt Gough

Thereafter the story can be told only through the reports of the individual pilots, for the fight was essentially one of individual battles with no time or opportunity for cohesive action.

'For five to ten minutes', wrote Sqn Ldr Lott, 'I found myself concentrating on avoiding action as one 109 after another appeared in the rear of me. Eventually two 110s approached from the starboard bow and I turned in towards them hard and got a forty-five degree deflection burst at one at under 100 yards. This a/c now went into a steep dive which enabled me to give a five seconds steady burst from dead astern. Heavy black smoke appeared from both engines as soon as the burst was begun. I did not follow as I considered I had followed a straight course for long enough and being on my own I set course for home when I picked up Blue 3 en route.'

Blue 3 (Fg Off Wilkinson) had been involved with two 109s which he had fired on and hit. One had disappeared diving vertically into cloud at 3,000 feet, the other attacked head on, had disappeared. The other member of Blue Section, Tony Woods-Scawen, was 'returning to Tangmere alone, having left earlier than the rest of our pilots'. Having engaged one of several attacking 109s he had 'knocked pieces off his port wing trailing edge during two bursts of five seconds' when a hit in the radiator followed by a 'deluge of Glycol inside the cockpit' compelled him to retire.

Red 1, flying at fifty feet, had a more eventful crossing of the Channel. Pursued for fifteen miles by a 109 which 'I was unable to attack as my windscreen was covered in oil; I evaded his attack and fire by turning and skidding' reported John Simpson. He had had marked success. One 109 had been shot into the sea in flames after a single three second burst, after which, following a dog fight, he had got onto the tail of another and seen it dive, one wing aflame, into the ground three miles east of Dunkirk.

Fg Off Edmonds (Red 2) had been equally successful. Two short bursts at two 109s had no observed effect, both aircraft half rolling and diving vertically away and an attack on a third was frustrated by a 110 which attacked from the port quarter, hit the Hurricane and compelled it to break away. He then sighted a 109 attacking another Hurricane. Turning, he successfully got behind the enemy and a five second burst caused it to break up completely. Finally, a 110 diving away after an attack by another Hurricane received all his remaining ammunition and it went down completely on fire. This last contact, like those of the next two pilots, took place ten miles inland, for the German aircraft were tending to retire towards their own lines so that the area of combat drifted towards the east.

Sgt Peter Ottewill (Red 3) who had once in a jocular moment dubbed himself 'The Black Ace' (and was not allowed to forget it) now began to justify his title. His report is of interest not only for his achievements but for the pertinent comments made on the performance of the Hurricane relative to his opponents. 'In the dog fight that ensued I managed to get onto the tail of one of the 109s almost immediately. He had, I am sure, no suspicion of my presence for I closed to about 100 yards and fired two two-second bursts. The e/a exploded and descended like a ball of fire. I managed to get onto the tail of two other 109s who immediately half rolled, but I was able to follow and overhaul each of them easily. Although I fired two short bursts at each no damage was observed. On pulling out of the second dive another 109 passed me across my line of sight and I gave him a long burst of six seconds at about sixty degree deflection and the e/a spun into the sea with smoke pouring from the engine. By this time most of the e/a were flying fast towards the German lines over Dunkirk, and the fighting was taking place just over the land. I climbed up towards a large number of Me 110s who were sitting above the scene of the fighting and occasionally diving in when they saw a 'lame duck'. I singled out one of the 110s, farther back from the rest and alone. Unfortunately he saw me coming and climbed away from me easily although I was climbing at full throttle in 'fine' pitch, and with the automatic boost cut-out pulled. As it was obviously hopeless to follow him I dived away and very luckily found myself almost right on the tail of another 110 flying south-west over Dunkirk. I opened fire at 250 yards and gave a five second burst closing to 150 yards. The e/a dived violently with the starboard engine spurting black smoke and flames. I did not see it crash or make a landfall as I noticed another aircraft immediately behind me which I took to be an enemy (but was almost certainly Fg Off Edmonds) and on pressing my firing button to give the last of my ammunition to the 110 I discovered I was out of ammunition. I did a very tight right hand turn, half rolled and dived vertically from 8,000 feet to 1,500 feet at full throttle, when I pulled out and returned to base at sea level. There was no sign of the aircraft which had been on my tail after this manoeuvre which showed me as doing 450 mph on the ASI and broke the under panelling in pulling out. Although it caused me to "black out" it was by no means uncomfortable. My aircraft sustained no hits and showed marked superiority over the enemy in manoeuvrability.

Sergeant Jim Hallowes DFM
(Andy Saunders collection)

Of the remaining section Fg Off Carswell was in the sea, Sgt Gough had died, and Sgt Jim Hallowes, was collecting the best bag of the Squadron's day.

He got onto the tail of a 109 which was about to attack another Hurricane. The 109 looped and rolled off the top. 'This brought it into my line of sight, I closed to 150 yards and opened fire. The e/a burst into flames almost immediately and dived into the sea. I maintained height of approximately 10,000 feet and endeavoured to remain in cloud base. The mainplane of a 109 and several other pieces fell out of the cloud in front of my machine'. Two 109s, diving from cloud, were chased to 7,000 feet, and fire opened at 30°-45° deflection. One rolled but while on its back caught fire and one mainplane came off – it went into the sea or on the edge of the coast. A passing encounter with another 109 was inconclusive but soon after four Me 110s were seen diving through cloud. Selecting one a little behind the others, two short bursts were delivered from below and behind. 'The whole tail fell off this machine which dived into the sea. I then saw one Hurricane shot down in flames by another Hurricane . . . tried to get the attacker's number but broke to attack another 109 . . . e/a tried evasive tactics, half rolling as I opened fire and then fled inland. I followed for fifteen miles, getting in several short bursts. Pieces were falling off the e/a when my ammunition gave out and I last saw it diving steeply to the ground. I did not follow the machine down to see if it crashed but returned to Manston.'

43 was in high spirits for the remainder of that day. Seven Messerschmitt 109s and two 110s destroyed, six more damaged, three so heavily that their destruction was a possibility; and the debit side, two aircraft, one pilot lost, two other aircraft damaged but repairable, one pilot wounded but resilient and destined to return. And all achieved against odds of seven or eight to one. It had been a pretty good start to the month of June. That night 11 Group sent its congratulations, together with an ops order for the next day. 'Patrol Dunkirk 0630-0745 in company with 145, 245 and 17 Squadrons and destroy enemy aircraft attacking shipping or attacking Dunkirk.' It was an order which, to judge by the results of the day, would not present 43 with any difficulties.

In the event 2 June was completely without incident. Two patrols of nine aircraft saw nothing. On 3 and 4 June there was again no sign of the enemy during the Squadron's patrol times. At 0600 hours on the 5th Sqn Ldr Lott led a section of three aircraft on a reconnaissance to Calais. There was no activity on the ground or in the air. The Dunkirk story was finished, the last of the little ships was home. A quarter of a million soldiers scattered in reception centres across the country licked their wounded pride and asked where the RAF had been while they had seemingly been bombed at will by the omnipresent Luftwaffe. It took a Churchill to tell them that but for that reviled Royal Air Force not one of them would ever have left the Dunkirk beaches, and been carried safely across the intervening water. That a sheltering air umbrella must inevitably possess a few holes through which the occasional bombers will pass was a fact not as yet appreciated by the common soldiery (nor yet some of their leaders).

And in the shield which Fighter Command had provided and under which the Army had returned to fight again No 43 had provided a part that was not the least among the many. The Squadron diary recorded 'a very satisfactory début'. It was, and yet no better than 43 had expected from itself. Perhaps of greater importance, it had proved to itself that in the greater battles that must lie ahead the quality of its steel was such that there was no cause for despair but much for reasoned optimism. Though Dunkirk may be a symbol of defeat and disaster on the national tapestry, upon the banner of 43 it stood for a great victory against long odds, and as a promise of more yet to come.

CHAPTER 12

Ruin and Restoration

AT 1900 hours on 7 June, Sqn Ldr Lott and Flt Lt Simpson landed at Tangmere, the only two Hurricanes to return that day out of ten that had left to patrol Amiens-Abbeville at 1200 hours. The day's events had been an all too painful demonstration of how the lack of information and control that a radar-backed ground system could provide meant that squadrons were unlikely ever to be at the right altitude, in the right place, at the right time, and thus in a position to exert the maximum effect on the course of events. Instead there had ensued only confusion, chaos and disaster.

Ordered for a day to reinforce the dwindling and outnumbered fighter squadrons of the BAFF, they had given of their best, yet there had been little to show on the credit side and on the other half of the ledger was another squadron temporarily gone from Fighter Command. It was a process too often repeated in that period which, but for the intervention of the C-in-C at Cabinet level, could have led to the annihilation of the whole fighter force.

Flt Lt J W C Simpson DFC

After waiting all morning, ten Hurricanes from 43, with the same number from 601, had left Tangmere for their patrol line. There were seven of the victors of Dunkirk together with 'B' Flight's new Commander, Flt Lt Rowland, and Sgts Buck and Ayling. They flew in the usual vics of three plus one spare, the normal procedure though one poorly adapted for the needs of the hour, for too much concentration on formation gave too little time to watch out for hostile activity.

So it was that Sqn Ldr Lott's first indication of the enemy was when the port main tank of his number two (Fg Off John Edmonds) burst into flame and the Hurricane dropped away. Within minutes three more aircraft were lost. Fg Off Wilkinson was killed, Flt Lt Rowland injured, baled out, and Sgt Hallowes did the same, although first finding time, from the smoking cockpit that he was preparing to vacate, to fire at a 109 that suddenly overshot him, and which, so he was told a few minutes later when, with a dislocated ankle, he was assisted by a detachment of British soldiers, crashed as a result. Indeed his rescuers were in doubt as to whether he was the British or German pilot. The remaining six pilots landed, as ordered, at Rouen (Boos). Sgt Ottewill had destroyed the Me 109 which killed Fg Off William Wilkinson and Sqn Ldr Lott had damaged another, but it was not a very good balance sheet.

At 1800 hours five of the six survivors (Sgt Buck had burst a tyre) with three aircraft from 601 and six from No 1 took off to patrol the line of the River Somme. Sqn Ldr Lott was leading the whole formation, but as all three Squadrons were on different radio frequencies there was no cohesion. After twenty minutes No 1 Squadron left the patrol. Heavy, accurate flak required some quick evasive action and shortly afterwards twenty enemy bombers with an escort of five Squadrons of Me 109 and Me 110 were sighted. The Hurricanes turned and engaged.

At Tangmere that evening Lott and Simpson added up the score. Lott had destroyed a 109, Simpson, after an involved duel, had set fire to another 109, the pilot of which had baled out, and then attacked another which, hit in the tail, collided with a 110, the two falling locked together. That made four confirmed against which Fg Off Woods-Scawen, Sgt Ottewill and Sgt Ayling were missing, and only Sgt Buck, awaiting a new tyre at Rouen, was definitely known to be safe.

That evening an 11 Group Order detailed 43 and 601 to patrol Le Tréport-Aumale at first light next day. It was a commitment that could not be met. There were too few pilots and fewer aircraft. 43 Squadron, temporarily, was on the floor, and was therefore placed on a training basis.

But in war things are rarely as bad or as good as they seem. On the 8th Sgt Buck came back. On the morning of the 10th Sgt Ayling, who had had his plane badly damaged on the evening of the 7th but had succeeded in crash landing at Rouen, evacuated himself from Garnay airfield in a second-hand Hurricane with a punctured port wing tank, and the same night Tony Woods-Scawen appeared, his opened parachute gathered in untidy folds under his arm. 'Hello,' said Sqn Ldr Lott as he entered the mess at Tangmere. 'You've been a long time, why have you brought that all the way home?' 'Because I know this one works, so I am keeping it for the next time,' replied Woods-Scawen. Next, from No 4 Base Hospital at La Bause, came news that Rowland, Hallowes and Ottewill were all there, the last named terribly burned after his non-sealed gravity tank forward of the instrument panel had blown up. But Hallowes, it was clear, would not be long in rejoining, which made six out of the ten pilots saved to fight another day. Things had indeed not proved so bad as first they had appeared.

It took Sqn Ldr Lott, wielding carrot and whip as necessary, just fourteen days to repair his ruined Squadron and bring it to a condition where he could report, on 21 June, that it was once again fit to resume full day and night ops duties (though five days before this he with Fg Offs Upton and Haworth made a dawn reconnaissance of the Cherbourg Peninsula which brought a Special Signal of Appreciation from AOC 11 Group). During this time reinforcements arrived in numbers. Flt Lt Morgan left an Air Ministry desk to provide 'B' Flight with its third Commander in three weeks, Fg Off Haworth and Sgt Pratt exchanged the Blenheims of 25 Squadron for the Hurricane, and lastly from OTUs came Plt Offs Cruttenden, James, Brunner, Gorrie, De Mancha and Campbell and Sgts Mills and Crisp. These latter pilots from the OTUs possessed abundant courage, enthusiasm and willingness to learn, but naturally did not have the experience of those whom they replaced. Therefore the strengthening of that priceless commodity, which resulted from the return of Sgt Hallowes (ex hospital) and Plt Off Carey (fresh from his triumphs with No 3 Squadron in France but more than happy to be back with 43) was of immeasurable value.

By 7 July the Squadron strength in pilots had risen to twenty-one, of which one third were experienced and battle tested, and one third completely new from OTU with the rest somewhere between these two levels of operational effectiveness. On that day 43 fired at the enemy for the first time since 7 June when Yellow Section (Plt Off Brunner, Sgt Buck, Plt Off Cruttenden) intercepted a Do 17 near Beachy Head. Brunner lost contact with his numbers two and three as he dived at the bomber but pressed home his attack. The e/a retired southwards, using the available five-tenths cloud cover with great skill, so that Brunner continually lost his quarry in a cloud and saw it emerging in a different direction. Nevertheless he succeeded in firing some bursts at it though he admitted that 'it was rather an off day for gunnery because nothing seemed to happen for a long time until, as we neared the French coast, the port propeller stopped and the Dornier was losing height'. At this point, however, either by accident or in response to a call for aid, two Messerschmitt Me 110s appeared and with ammunition almost gone Brunner could only retire, making grateful use of the clouds which previously he had found so frustrating. Finally shaking off his pursuers he arrived back at base to discover that Plt Off Cruttenden had baled out unhurt after his engine (glycol leak) had burst into flames.

If this was a not too auspicious beginning worse was to come, for two days later, south of Littlehampton, a section comprised of Sqn Ldr Lott, Plt Off Carey and Sgt Mills met six Me 110s head on and Sqn Ldr Lott was wounded when a cannon shell exploded on his armoured windscreen. Blinded in one eye, suffering intense pain and with his aircraft on fire he attempted to return to base, but three miles short of Tangmere increasing flame forced him to abandon the Hurricane at 700 feet. It crashed on Fontwell racecourse and was completely burned out, only the tail wheel remaining at all recognisable. This the Engineer Officer gave to the local policeman who, accompanied by his young son, was standing guard over the wreck when the Maintenance Flight arrived, and who said it was just what he needed for his wheelbarrow. The forced removal of Sqn Ldr Lott was a great and grievous loss to the Squadron. Of exceptional attainments and character, he had been quite positively its leader through triumph and disaster. As no other he had been responsible for its rapid resurgence after the destruction and confusion of early June and for his presence and influence to be thus wrenched away on the very eve of the day on which historians would aver the Battle of Britain began was multiplied loss indeed.

It was assuredly good fortune and no little mitigation that Sqn Ldr J V C Badger, two weeks 'attached supernumerary for ops and admin', was a waiting understudy in the wings. Moreover, he was no stranger to 43, for their Flight Order Book of 1932 recorded that Plt Off Badger had been authorised to fly their chequered Furies. Now he returned, in days of greater moment, to lead the camouflaged successors to those Furies around the selfsame Sussex sky.

CHAPTER 13

Undaunted by Odds

What if our numbers barely could defy
The arithmetic of babes . . . ?
(Poems dedicated to National Independence and Liberty, XX I V – Wordsworth)

HISTORIANS have divided the Battle of Britain into five major phases. Throughout July and the first week of August, attacks on Channel ports and convoys were designed to draw the RAF fighters into combat under conditions least favourable to themselves. From 8 to 23 August coastal aerodromes (many of which had no connection with Fighter Command) and radar stations were attacked. Although the raids on the vital radar stations were fortunately assessed by Goering to be of little value, the importance of the fighter stations controlling the sectors was recognised and from 24 August to 6 September these stations became the target for continual attack; as did aircraft factories in the southern regions. These later raids were made by smaller bomber forces, twenty to thirty, escorted by larger, 100 plus, numbers of fighters. On 7 September, when Fighter Command, which during the preceding fortnight had lost 277 machines with 103 pilots killed and 128 seriously wounded, was beginning to lose the Battle, respite came from the Germans themselves who, partly for political reasons, partly because they were convinced that the RAF fighter force was finished, switched the assault onto London. It was on the first day of this attack that 43 Squadron, sorely tried for many weeks, at last reached a point where it had, of necessity, to be withdrawn northwards for refit. The last phase covering the attacks by fighter-bombers does not, therefore, come within the scope of this story. This action by the Luftwaffe was virtually an admission of its inability to carry out its initial aim of destroying Fighter Command and was the least important part of the Battle. In the most decisive days earlier, 43 Squadron had played a part not unworthy of itself, and had given all that might be expected from a squadron that had always been in the forefront of the ranks of Fighter Command.

When the story of those days is analysed it is seen that there was no equality of achievement. Some squadrons bore the brunt for long periods, others came and rapidly melted away in the heat of battle, eg 603 Squadron lost sixteen aircraft and twelve pilots in ten days and 235 Squadron, thirteen and nine in seven. Even in the best of the squadrons was to be found a solid nucleus of pilots who carried a heavier share than their less experienced comrades. All this is not to denigrate the less good pilots or the less good squadrons, for every one of them gave of their

"....... the broken metal of those who dared to come......."
43's first claim in the Battle of Britain was this He 111 of KG 55 on 12 July 1940 shot down by Sqn Ldr Badger, Flt Lt Dalton-Morgan, Plt Offs de Mancha, Gorrie and Upton and Sgt Ayling. It landed near The Horse and Jockey pub in Hipley, Hampshire where the four remaining crew were captured by Percy Tibble, landlord of the pub armed with a toy pistol!

best and no more than that could be asked. Nevertheless some, because they were longer trained and of greater experience, were better equipped to fight and to survive. Above all they were able to shoot accurately, by no means the least desirable attribute in the desperate decisive days of that summer.

Statistically, 43 Squadron during its involvement in the battle positively destroyed some sixty enemy aircraft, thirteen more were probably destroyed and another twenty-five damaged. The certain victories included more than twenty Junkers Ju 87 Stuka dive-bombers, thirteen twin-engine bombers and twenty-five fighters (eight twin, seventeen single-engine). Eleven pilots were killed in action during this time, and Sqn Ldr John V C Badger succumbed to his wounds in 1941. Ten other pilots were wounded (two of them twice), eight to such a degree that they were still non-effective on 7 September. There were twenty pilots on the strength at the start, eleven reinforcements arrived and on 8 September there were just eleven pilots capable of ferrying their aircraft to Usworth. Twenty-five Hurricanes were lost in action, and countless others damaged. Some of these departed to civilian repair units but most were made serviceable again by the Squadron's own ground crews whose efforts were always a match for the needs of the hour. If most of what they did, as throughout the service generally, was little known, that fact should surprise nobody. Much of it was routine, none of such unusual interest to be classified as newsworthy by an editor attempting to compress a world at war into a four-page newspaper.

The lack of knowledge and misunderstanding of the groundcrew role has extended into the post war era. In films or in books they are invariably misrepresented and caricatured as a little-worth briefly-mentioned collection of oafs, always speaking in thick bogus Clydeside or glottal-stopped Cockney accents and spending so much time saluting and yes-sirring the glamorous flying-men heroes that a discerning observer must justifiably wonder however they found time to use a spanner.

If such a state of affairs ever existed anywhere, and it is hard to believe that it did, it was certainly not true of 43 Squadron where no pilot ever looked upon himself as divinely appointed to fly, with the help of a retinue of low grade fellows, the ostlers and grooms of a mechanical age. If truth were told more than one would have admitted to the belief that the skill and expertise required to understand the workings of the masses of machinery and pipe work that interlaced the spaces behind the cowlings was as great if not more so than the skill that was necessary to execute a perfect half roll off the top or crumple the enemy with a sixty degree deflection shot. In the ultimate it was all a matter of proportion, there were no great ones and small ones, but each was a part of the whole, dependent on everything and everybody else.

In the posting of Flying Officer Sharman for Engineering Duties wef 1/4/40, 43 Squadron had been extremely fortunate. A product of the earliest apprentice entries he had survived the rigours of the twenties and the economic choppers of the thirties. He therefore possessed, in addition to a wide technical knowledge and experience, a monumentally unshakeable demeanour that nothing on earth at Tangmere, nor in the heavens above, ever appeared likely to ruffle. Never obviously in evidence until he was wanted he was then everywhere at once. His constant motto was 'Don't worry', advice that he brought to encourage harassed Flights and sections whenever enemy action and mechanical gremlins had combined to drop the serviceability state to a dangerously low level. 'Don't worry chaps, we'll soon have this little lot sorted out' . . . and, under his calm leadership and ability to draw from men twice what they thought was the limit of their capability, it was never long before the crisis was past and the magic S, for serviceability, multiplied on the Squadron's order of battle board.

Sharman was well served by most of his subordinates. 'A' Flight had Flt Sgt Parker, a lean and hungry Cassius who gobbled up alike both Flight Commanders who took aeroplanes without first ascertaining that they were ready and airmen whom he found doing nothing for more than ten seconds at a time. His only object in life was to ensure for his pilots the safety and fitness of the maximum number of Hurricanes, to which end he drove everybody with a terrifying ruthlessness and himself as much as anybody. God help the airman who came whining for a forty-eight hour pass because his wife was delivering a baby. He never returned to ask a second time.

Along the perimeter at the hangar was Flt Sgt Kay, a leathery-faced Scotsman who had won a Meritorious Service Medal at Archangel before the youngest airmen in his Maintenance Flight were born. Helping him was Sgt Arthur, six feet five, with a long mane of hair, a great roman nose and a blistering tongue that shrivelled and withered the incompetent and the idle while holding no threat to the honest toiler.

As for the airmen, they were individually no different, neither better nor worse than most of their kind before or since. Not averse to a little skive, feet up in the sun when things were quiet they could explode into action when the urgency arose. Let one example serve to illustrate the many.

On the evening of 15 August, four battle-damaged Hurricanes returned to Tangmere. One required a replacement cylinder block, a second had a shell-damaged mainplane and a third was short of half an elevator. The fourth had been hit by only one 7·92 mm bullet but this had bored through the oil tank, pierced the (officially unrepairable) centre-section front spar boom and finally lodged in the port main fuel tank. When these aircraft arrived in the hangar the Maintenance Flight was dispersed, with a few in the pubs at Chichester, most in the NAAFI or resting on their beds. By 0400 hrs next morning the last of the four Hurricanes was ready to taxi back to dispersal. Nine hours later the hangar went up in flames during the 'Tangmere blitz'. Two Hurricanes en route to a Maintenance Unit and a 'Queen Mary' transporter were lost when the roof and doors fell upon them. The four Hurricanes which might also have still been there were engaged in a running battle with the Stukas from Selsey to St Catherine's Point.

And after the hangar went, and all that was therein, so that nothing was left except for one tool box that an airman had luckily had in his car, and one Rolls Royce Merlin kit, which being of high grade materials remained unsoftened and still usable though the surrounding box had burned to a pile of ash, the Squadron just moved out to dispersal and carried on as before. There is an incident described in Douglas Bader's book *Reach for the Sky* telling how the squadron he commanded was unable to become operational because all of its tools had been lost weeks before in France. After a certain amount of acrimonious telephone conversations, Bader was hauled before the C-in-C Fighter Command and as a result the needed tools and equipment arrived. If the portrayal of their delivery in the film of the book is in any way near to reality then the amount of material sent must have taken a large part of the stock of an entire Stores Maintenance Unit.

43 Squadron indulged in no such dramatics. It was operational already, it just remained so. Everybody was too busy getting on with the battle to think of telephoning the AOC-in-C. Moreover it was not very long before its stocks of tools were replenished, though not by wholly official means, for the bomb that had shifted half the roof of the station store had also apparently blown away the common-sense of the store keepers. War or no war nobody was getting any tools without Form 674 in triplicate! There was however in Maintenance Flight a certain LAC alias Claud (who having since reached exalted rank must remain no better identified) and he obtained official blessing to assist with his ancient Austin 7 in the evacuation of the store to a dispersed site. In the circumstances it was no surprise that the quantity of tools available increased rapidly in the next few days and 43 was wholly back in business.

The first stage of the battle was an inconclusive period for the Squadron, as in the four weeks up to 8 August five enemy aircraft were destroyed and another damaged. These cost the lives of three pilots with another wounded. In addition Plt Off Kenneth Campbell was killed, crashing near Hawkinge on 29 July while operating from Northolt where the squadron had been briefly detached. First blood came on the 12th, a Heinkel 111 of KG 55, intercepted by six 'B' Flight aircraft crashed at Southwick with two crew dead. The next day Flt Lt Morgan with Plt Offs Gorrie and De Mancha pursued another 111 from Ventnor to the French coast. Losing it twice in cloud they found it again with the help of some brilliant ground control, which later brought forth a 'Most creditable to all concerned' signal from 11 Group. The Heinkel, port engine on fire, with 'bits falling off the starboard mainplane, finally hit the sea and burst up'.

After four days of bad weather fighting flared up anew on the 19th. Two sections of 'A' Flight, (Flt Lt Simpson, Plt Off Cruttenden, Sgt Crisp, Flt Lt Carey, Plt Off Woods-Scawen, Sgt Buck) were jumped by fifteen Me 109s as they patrolled the line Selsey Bill–Bognor. Simpson destroyed a 109 which he saw fall into the sea but was subsequently attacked by three more of the enemy, wounded, compelled to bale out and finished up in a cucumber frame in a back garden at Worthing. Carey got a good long burst at a 109, which dived vertically down through a thin cloud layer at 2,000 feet. On breaking cloud above the sea a large patch of foam and oil with a bit of smoke and wreckage were seen. Climbing up again Carey now saw the strange sight of Sgt Buck's Hurricane flying inverted, straight and level and with no one in the cockpit. Buck, wounded, had baled out and though normally a strong swimmer his drowned body was next day found in the sea, a result which brought some bitter comment from his fellow-pilots who not unnaturally felt that they were deserving of a much better air-sea rescue organisation than then existed. Certainly there was a lack of co-ordination between naval craft and the lifeboats and searching aircraft, whilst for the pilots themselves there were then no dinghies, nor fluorescence to show up their position in the water, and they had to rely entirely on their Mae West jackets for support. Such deficiencies however, should not be attributed to lack of concern or negligence in high places, but rather be viewed in the light of the desperate shortages of so much vital equipment which prevailed in the post-Dunkirk era. To criticise these weaknesses from a background of the infinitely better facilities that became available and were accepted as a matter of course only a few months later would be unfair. Indeed, by the end of July the AOC 11 Group had managed to borrow some Army Co-op Lysanders for use on search duties and by the end of January 1941 a well organised system was rapidly evolving.

Nevertheless, the Germans were then doing better in such matters, using seaplanes to search for and to rescue their lost crews and in fact it was on the very next day, 20th, that Fg Off Joseph Haworth of 'B' Flight, whilst on convoy patrol south of the Needles, dived to investigate one such seaplane, a Heinkel 115, marked with conspicuous red crosses. As he approached, his aircraft was hit by machine gun fire and he baled out. Although his companions obtained a fix on his position, he too was not rescued and died. Later that day Sgt Hallowes was uninjured after crashing beside the River Arun at Amberley with engine seizure.

On the 21st, 43 fought an action that was all too indicative of the conditions in which the *Few* too often found themselves.

Signal from 11 Group dated 22/7/40.

> 'To all Sector and Squadron Commanders. 43, 258 and 609 Squadrons to be informed immediately that Raid 27, at 1500 hours, on 21st was reported by HQFC as only 9 aircraft, so that Group Controller despatched three Flights to intercept a force that turned out to be 50 plus hostiles. Fighter Command has again been requested to improve accuracy of raid counting and height reporting.'

At least this helped to explain the events of the previous day, to dispel in part the clouds of bewilderment in the minds of men who found themselves outnumbered four to one while four-fifths of the sector strength was not even airborne. Perhaps too much magic was expected from a radar system which in spite of its ability to provide the early warning so vital to the defenders was still imperfect and unrefined. Although it could detect reliably at a distance, it lacked accuracy in determining numbers or altitude and thus the task of interpretation became a matter of chance and intuition rather than a straightforward numerical exercise.

So it had been that afternoon ten miles south-west of the Needles. Sqn Ldr Badger, Sgt Ayling and Plt Off De Mancha in the lead, Flt Lt Morgan, Plt Off Gorrie and Sgt Hurry above and behind, 11,000 feet below them a westbound coastal convoy. 'It was like looking

Sgt Hallowes made a skillful wheels-up landing in a meadow at Amberley after the engine seized due to lack of oil pressure on 20 July 1940. The Hurricane was P3784 'FT-U'
(Andy Saunders collection)

down Piccadilly Circus underground escalator', said Sqn Ldr Badger. "Forty plus Dorniers stepped up, with as many fighters rising still higher behind them. I called Morgan and told him to hold off the fighters while we took on the bombers. I attacked as they began to dive on the ships, fired a burst at one and had to break to avoid collision with a second. Then my starboard aileron jammed, damaged by a 20 mm shell, and control became very difficult so I had to return to base." In the meantime the top section manfully attempted to obey their Squadron Commander's order and the three Hurricanes were involved with a swirling mêlée of forty Me 109s. In such circumstances, it required all their skill merely to survive, as one enemy after another came into the attack. Eventually, however, Morgan slipped his adversaries long enough to take a shot at a 109 which, almost unbelievably in the circumstances of such favourable odds, was actually forming, with four others, into a defensive circle! Morgan's first burst caused the port aileron to break off and the Messerschmitt spun away down. The convoy later reported seeing a 109 hit the sea. Closing in behind a second 109 he opened fire and saw bullet strikes but a glimpse of two of the enemy bearing down on his tail compelled him to break hurriedly. As he did so a Dornier Do 17 flew across his line of sight. Turning into it he opened fire, saw his bullets striking an engine nacelle and then he lost all vision as oil from the stricken bomber spattered his windscreen. There was nothing for it but to return to base.

Pilot Officer R A De Mancha

Sergeant C A H Ayling

Pilot Officer J Cruttenden
(Andy Saunders collection)

Six against eighty. Plt Off De Mancha was missing to balance against Morgan's 109, and two other e/a damaged. It was not at all extraordinary by the standard of those days, yet in his book *Fighter Command* A B Austin, an experienced war reporter, wrote "that this was the fight that for the first time made the Americans, too many of whom had already written Britain off as lost, think that perhaps the Germans were not going to have things their own way after all, that perhaps numbers were not everything. Perhaps individual courage and the will to accept combat in the face of apparently suicidal odds was going to count, maybe there was an edge in training and equipment that yet might turn seemingly inevitable defeat into triumph."

It is well established that American opinion did become increasingly optimistic of Britain's chances of survival as the battle in the skies progressed. Whether, indeed, it was this particular action by 43 that first gave the Americans cause to revise their ideas is less easily ascertained, but assuredly Austin, mixing in the quarters where opinions were formed and much was known that remained unrevealed to the general public, was in a good position to judge.

One thing is certain. The men whose valour had allegedly made such an impact on the spectators in their secure transatlantic grandstand were not that night engaging in any flights of great optimism. Perhaps there was time to wonder if young De Mancha were alive or dead, and, if the former, whether the haphazard rescue arrangements then existing would save him or let him drown like Sgt Buck last week. Nor was there any comfort to be found in the daily Command Intelligence Summaries which (most accurately) detailed the strength of the enemy and reported no weakening of his morale. Tomorrow there would be six and the eighty all over again somewhere along the line, and the next day too, probably or the one after that. There was no hope to be found in statistics. Only from faith in oneself and in the will to endure did there come a sight of the possibility that one day the fleets of Heinkels and the swarms of escorts would cease to come because they no longer dared. But that day was not yet – tomorrow, undaunted by odds, unwearied by unceasing battle, the continuing challenge would be met.

CHAPTER 14

Forty-four for Three

ON 6 August Goering told his Luftflotte commanders that Sealion – the invasion of England – would be launched during the first fourteen days of September, but first it was necessary for the Luftwaffe to dispose of the RAF. Adlertag - Eagle Day - was designated for the start of the offensive, which Goering was convinced would in four days eliminate Fighter Command as an effective force. Thereafter Adlerangriff - the attack of the Eagles - would continue unopposed to clear the way for the invading armies. Eagle Day, because of bad weather, was postponed until 13 August, but the attacks intensified from the 8th.

43 Squadron, after a week of 'rest' at Northolt, during which time they had commuted daily to Hawkinge and patrolled the Dover Straits, had returned to Tangmere on the 1st of the month. On the 3rd they had received reinforcements, Sgts Noble, Deller and Montgomery and Plt Off Gray, all new and untried from No 6 OTU. Plt Off Le Roy du Vivier, of whom much will be heard in the ensuing pages, and Plt Off Van den Hove arrived two days later. This latter pair were Belgians who had fought for the few days in May before the capitulation of their country and then had escaped to England to carry on the battle. Like all the European expatriates they expressed an intense hatred of all things German. The war for them was a pitiless affair of revenge and retribution and life held nothing but a desire to find and destroy the enemy, an attitude that made them so much the more valuable to have fighting at one's side. Albert Van den Hove fought with distinction until 43 retired to Usworth, from where a week later he joined 501 Squadron but was killed on 15 September.

A victory within the greater victory, of the greatest significance and importance, and a measure of the quality of the fighter squadrons, was the decision forced upon Goering on the evening of 18 August to withdraw his Junkers Ju 87 dive bombers from the battle. At one stroke he lost the use of one-third of his bomber force, the moral significance was even greater. The Stuka, the airborne artillery of the German Army, had bombed and blasted a way across Europe through Poland and Norway, Belgium, Holland and France. In all of these countries the Stuka, ugly gull winged bird of ill omen, had been the spearhead bursting open the stubborn blocks of resistance. And although it retired in disgrace from Britain, the guts torn out of its élite squadrons so that they dared no longer come, it was still able, in easier circumstances, in the spring of the following year to terrorise and conquer in Greece and Yugoslavia before turning its attention to targets on the Russian plains. It was yet to come within an ace of causing Malta to surrender, it was destined to harass its enemies in the desert and the mountains of North Africa. But in England it retired in just ten days, with losses so grievous that to have continued must have resulted in ultimate annihilation, and in those days of high summer and high destiny the abolition of but one part of the outnumbering foe was relief indeed to the desperately hard pressed Few.

Some of the locals gather round the guarded weckage of a Ju 88 from 4/LG 1 brought down at Priors Leaze, Southbourne on 15 August 1940. It provided target practice for seven pilots although one of its gunners did score hits on Sqn Ldr Badger's Hurricane

The Ju 88's damaged wing and nose

And of all the squadrons that induced the downfall of this once invincible symbol of terror and destruction, none could claim that it had played a greater part than 43. Perhaps some of it was due to good fortune, just happening to be in the right place on the right day, but be that as it may, it in no way detracted from the value or glory of its achievement. At the time 43 Squadron claimed ten Junkers Ju 87s destroyed on 8 August, seventeen more on the 16th and two days later another eight. In the light of all the evidence now available from both sides, which shows beyond all argument that in those days of hard and incessant fighting all fighter squadrons appear to have overestimated enemy losses, this claim of 35 Ju 87's is overoptimistic. However, allowing for the impossibility of tying down each and every lost Stuka to a specific claim in a particular Combat Report it seems highly probable that 43 can claim four or five on the 9th, six or seven on the 16th and the eight claimed on the 18th still appears valid.

An example of the evidence comes from a report of the battle over Selsey Bill on the 16th by Sergeant Hallowes:

"In the first attack, delivered head on, I observed my target go down with smoke coming from it. After falling a few hundred feet the enemy aircraft exploded and fell in pieces. I then managed to get on the tail of another Ju 87 which fell into the sea in flames. Noticing another Junkers 87 attempting to get on my tail I did a steep stall turn and got in two or three short bursts after which the machine dived for the sea. Just before it crashed into the sea it jettisoned its bombs which exploded on impact." It should be noted that one of these Stukas 'exploded and fell in pieces', the second 'fell into the sea in flames' and the last 'crashed into the sea'. In each and every case the affirmation of destruction is positive. Hallowes does not say that the second e/a dived towards the sea in flames – had it done so it might have levelled out and the fire might have extinguished itself and thus it could have escaped undetected. But when an experienced pilot reports that his target 'crashed into the sea', or 'exploded and fell in pieces', then no possibility of doubt exists. The difference between such an affirmation and a claim that suggests that it is almost certain and therefore is being claimed is very important. This Combat Report by Sgt Hallowes is one of many which point to the positive destruction of enemy aircraft and generally the reports of such experienced and battle-wise pilots will stand critical scrutiny. Where caution is needed is in those compiled by men newer to the world of combat. This is in no way to suggest that anybody ever made untrue or exaggerated claims but the context in which the reports were written and by whom is a prime consideration. The critical position reached in the supply of replacement pilots which gave so much anxiety to Air Chief Marshal Sir Hugh Dowding meant that pilots came to the squadron with a total flying time of 180 hours or less, 30 of those on monoplanes with 15 or so on Hurricanes. Some had never fired the guns of a Hurricane at a towed target! Yet, within days these newcomers, whose courage and commitment in spite of their rawness was never in question, were flying on operations. Small wonder if at first they found themselves totally bewildered and in some cases, sadly, dead before they could adjust to the tempo of battle.

Like Sergeant Dennis Noble for instance – joined 43 on August 3rd, shot down and killed over Hove on the 30th. On the 19th he wrote to his sister . . . "We work more or less 24 hours a day so it is pretty tiring . . . The first day I went into battle I was shot down, I had seven holes in the machine but I was OK . . . one bullet in the cooling system so I came down covered in the stuff . . . anyway I learned more in those few minutes than ever before . . ."

Sergeant Alan Deller
(Andy Saunders collection)

Or Sergeant Alan Deller on his first op . . . 'We took forever to climb to 21,000 feet . . . somebody shouted, 'here come the bastards', there was a lot of noise of gunfire and I was in the middle of a lot of aircraft, then I was hit and glycol and oil were everywhere so I spun out and down, recognised Selsey Bill and coasted into Tangmere wheels up.'

Such examples give some idea of the tremendous mental stress which these raw, untried pilots encountered in the fierce and terrifying conditions of air combat, so if their reports written as a rule within minutes of landing, still in a very highly strung and emotive state of mind, did not always precisely mirror what had happened three miles up and half an hour before, it should not prove surprising.

Nevertheless, rejecting all claims of doubtful validity, 43 Squadron can still assert that theirs was a major role in the slaughter of the hitherto all-conquering Stukas. Nor was the Junkers 87 the only type to suffer from the power of the rampant Fighting Cocks at this time as the records between the 8th and 18th of August show. It was a truly successful eleven days. Forty-four of the enemy were claimed as destroyed, thirty-six more damaged, of which six probably never recrossed the Channel. Just how near the actual number of kills was to the number claimed will never be ascertained but sometimes the evidence was irrefutable. For instance, on August 15th (when the RAF shot down 75 but claimed 182) 43 claimed but two. A Junkers Ju 88, crippled near Southampton and then attacked by Red Section, led by Flt Lt Frank Carey, 'was such a sitting duck that it was used to give us some large deflection shooting practice before it eventually crashed north of Thorney Island.'

The second was a Heinkel 111 which Plt Off Woods-Scawen, witnessed by his No 2 (Plt Off Lane), sent 'trailing thick white smoke' crashing into the sea, while Sgt Hallowes last saw another Ju 88 'diving steeply towards the sea, the starboard engine on fire and the port side of the fuselage enveloped in smoke'.

There is much more in similar vein to the foregoing and though the relationship between claims and actual losses will never be finally resolved the evidence does strongly suggest that most of the 44 enemy claimed as destroyed positively went down. The Squadron's losses while gaining these victories were Plt Offs Johannes Oelofse and John Cruttenden missing on August 8th and Sergeant Herbert Montgomery lost on the 14th, plus four slightly wounded pilots and nine Hurricanes crashed, missing or damaged beyond repair.

Flt Lt Tom Rowland
(Andy Saunders collection)

'Forty-four enemy aircraft have been shot down, our losses were nine but the pilots of six are safe' . . . Such radio news announcements were commonplace in those days, and though the overall figures for Fighter Command have lost some of their glamour as the result of post-war findings, it is equally true that the 43 Squadron score sheet is not much different from what was claimed in 1940.

The first of the great days was 8 August. At 1540 hours twelve aircraft went off to the south of the Isle of Wight to patrol a westbound Channel convoy which, already twice attacked that day, was threatened by a detected build up of hostile forces in the Cherbourg area. Sqn Ldr Badger with Flt Lt Morgan and Plt Off Woods-Scawen led three sections at 15,000 feet, while three more Hurricanes were with Flt Lt Carey some way above. Then, to quote the last named, 'a most formidable and orderly array of enemy aircraft arrived to interfere with things. First of all, at the top level (around 15,000 to 20,000 feet) came formations of Me 110s executing roughly oval patrol flights and eventually stretching from the French coast to the Isle of Wight. About 5,000 feet below them, squadrons of Me 109s came out taking up station at intervals also stretching right across the Channel. Then underneath this 'umbrella' came a sizeable force of Ju 87s. We did nothing about the fighters to start with except that with my section of three above the rest of the convoy patrol I climbed up to gain height. When the 87s appeared on the scene, those in the squadron lower down went in to attack them while I was trying to keep the 109s from interfering. This I managed with only partial success, but in the fight that followed, I lost contact with my other two aircraft. On my own, I spotted a squadron of 109s in Vic formation which I took, at first, to be Hurricanes and I went off to join them. On discovering my mistake I was happy to note that I had not been seen by them and I continued until I had got behind one of the outside members of the 109 formation. I had just settled down to fire at this aircraft with some success, as bits started to fly off it, when a very large explosion nearly blew me upside down. A Me 110 had seen what was happening, had come down and was sitting about thirty yards behind me and his explosive 20 mm shots had blown up all the ammunition in my port wing, leaving a hole big enough for a man to crawl through. By the time I had righted the aircraft, all the 109s had disappeared so I laboriously climbed back up to get over the convoy again when I was once more jumped by some Me 110s. This time they blew one elevator and the rudder off. The aircraft did a half 'bunt' before I collected my senses. I had been hit in the arm on the first occasion and what with that and having only about three quarters of an aircraft to control, I thought discretion was the better part of valour and slowly brought the remains back to base. As if I hadn't had enough, the Tangmere ack-ack opened up on me as I entered the circuit – I suppose the silhouette must have looked a bit odd – fortunately they didn't hit me.

"I do recall the rest of the Squadron had somewhat better luck than my one damaged 109."

This last sentence was certainly true. Three Ju 87s, one Me 109, one Me 110 were confirmed (ie seen by pilots other than the claimant) and ten more, seven Ju 87s, three Me 109s, were 'unconfirmed' destroyed. The German Quartermaster's returns showed eight Ju 87s, five Me 109s and one Me 110 as lost. Additionally, four other e/a were damaged. Sgt Hallowes had got two 109s, one confirmed, one unconfirmed. The account of their destruction shows that, at any rate in his case, the difference was purely one of nomenclature.

"Four or five Me 109s detached themselves from the main formation as we engaged, and an Me 110 came in taking a deflection shot at myself. I turned sharply to avoid his fire and found myself about 300 yards astern and slightly to starboard of an Me 109. I gave a short burst of approximately two seconds and was gratified to see the 109 burst into flames and go into a vertical dive, the pilot baling out at about 15,000 feet. This was seen by my CO (Green 1).

I was then fired at by a Hurricane aircraft which came in from the beam but his shots appeared to pass about 100 yards behind me.

I gave another short burst at two Me 109s in fairly close formation, these two parted and turned back towards France, one diving steeply. A few minutes later I noticed two Me 109s going down in flames and a Hurricane going down in a spin – the pilot of this machine appearing to bale out before the aircraft hit the sea.

After this I climbed to rejoin what I took to be a formation of three of our machines at about 26,000 to 28,000 feet. These aircraft were circling round and were more or less in the sun, in line astern formation. On joining the circle I caught up with No 3 quite easily and noticing the tail struts under the tail plane and two radiators, realised I was in an enemy formation.

The top camouflage was similar to our own, and I do not think the pilot of the Me 109 saw me as I was able to take plenty of time sighting before opening fire. After a short burst at about 200 yards range the aircraft burst into flames and went into a vertical dive.

The pilot escaped by parachute at about 20,000 feet, he appeared to have been shot upwards out of the cockpit to a height of about 100 feet after releasing the hood and side panels – his seat must have in some way been spring-loaded to facilitate baling out.

I had pulled up the nose of my machine too steeply as I fired, causing the aircraft to stall and spin. The leader of the formation must have seen his number three go down in flames because he and his number two came at me as I stalled. Being well out to sea and knowing well that the 109s had the legs of the Hurricane, I kept in the spin and did everything I could to spoil the aim of the Jerries. Finally, I corrected the spin and went into a falling leaf, and I think I persuaded them that I had been hit and was out of control as they left me and turned south. I pulled out at about 5,000 feet and returned to Tangmere to learn that we had lost Pilot Officers Cruttenden and Oelofse in the dog fight." Besides these two officers killed, Flt Lt Carey and Plt Off Woods-Scawen were slightly wounded while Plt Off Upton had crash-landed on the Isle of Wight.

The four days following the 8th saw a great deal of activity with not much to show for it. The weather was unsuitable for large-scale raids but against constant intrusion by small numbers of the enemy 143 ops sorties were flown. Only on the 12th, when a raid was met mid-Channel to the south of Worthing (one Ju 88 probable, three He 111 damaged), was there any success to report.

By the 13th the weather had at last cleared sufficiently for the Germans to put into operation their plans to wipe out the Royal Air Force. This was their 'Eagle Day' and, while Tangmere still lay shrouded in early morning mist, a large formation from KG 54 came in for the first attack, their targets the aerodromes at Farnborough and Odiham.

Off the ground in good time to gain the necessary height, the Squadron was able to meet the bombers head on as they approached the coast. There were thirty Ju 88s in the lead of the formation, the same number of 88s and He 111s recognisable above and behind with Me 110s still further to the rear. The initial attack by the Hurricanes broke up the bombers' tight formation and with the Me 110s 'showing some reluctance to come in' there was time to turn back for a second bite at them. The pilots' reports spoke of burning and smoking bombers, of a Ju 88 which received bullets simultaneously from a Hurricane and a Me 109 which, aiming at the Hurricane, was firing too high and hitting the bomber. . . of Green 3 (Sgt Noble) going down with what appeared to be a glycol leak. . . three parachutes descending, either from my target or Blue Leader's (Flt Lt Morgan) . . . return fire by four guns from the top turrets of Junkers at 1,000 yards was wildly inaccurate . . . an 88 down in Arundel Park.

This particular 88 crashed into Swanbourne Lake close to the castle walls. Two of its crew went down with it, one, according to an eyewitness, being trapped around the tail by the cords of his prematurely opened parachute. The pilot, Hauptmann August Wilhelm Strauch, an experienced pilot of the kind that the Luftwaffe could ill-afford to lose, was rescued from the tree in which his descent ended but was very badly wounded in the stomach and died the following day. He was buried in Tangmere churchyard. The fourth member of the crew landed safely outside Poling radar station and was found to be wearing only his pyjamas underneath his flying suit. For him, apparently, the annihilation of the Royal Air Force required nothing more than a two-hour interruption in his normal daily ration of sleep. The pilots were back in time for a seven o'clock breakfast, a meal which the crews of three and maybe four bombers and a 109 pilot would not require while the occupants of some others had had their appetites spoilt by varying degrees. On the debit side were Flt Lt Morgan, ankle injury when baling out at Cocking Down, Sgt Noble's Hurricane requiring repairs and Plt Off Woods-Scawen's plane which went on fire seconds after he force-landed at Milland Farm. But the raid had failed completely, no part of it had reached either target area as the formation of bombers, shattered under the attacks of the Hurricanes, split and scattered. In fact it was very lucky for Tangmere that the protecting mist blanketed it from view, for some of the fighting took place immediately overhead, the pulsating drone of the bombers, the sound of diving fighters, Merlins at full power and the crackle of gunfire being heard very loudly in evidence. But for that friendly mist many of the raiders, concerned only with scrambling away as fast as they could, must have found it a convenient and inviting alternative target for their jettisoned bomb loads.

Although the early birds had found no easily surrendering worms and had gone back to their nests in great confusion, there were plenty more young eagles available for later in the day and, in the afternoon, with multiple attacks developing simultaneously on Portsmouth, Southampton, over Kent and into the Thames estuary, ten pilots of 43 found themselves just

This Me 109E of 1/JG 2 came down among the corn stooks at New Salts Farm near Shoreham Airport on 13 August following early morning combat with Sergeant Jack Mills

after 4 pm patrolling the Isle of Wight. A great pall of smoke hung over Southampton above which one pilot sighted anti-aircraft bursts. The Hurricanes turned to investigate, saw a few aircraft entering the clouds above Southampton Water and dived after them. Sgt Hallowes, with one other, made a head on attack at a Ju 88, 'a frightening experience as our closing speed was so great. I had time for only a two second burst and the e/a dived turning 180° to port. Suspecting he was diving to escape I followed him down and saw him crash in flames in the middle of a small wood at Thorness Bay on the north side of the Isle of Wight.

Sergeant Dennis Noble
(Andy Saunders collection)

"By this time I was on my own again and I climbed back through cloud to about 9,000 feet and, as I emerged, sighted a Dornier 17 flying south east. I closed to 300 yards before opening fire and after the first burst the aircraft dived sharply through the clouds. He was quite easy to follow and I remained behind him firing each time the pilot tried to straighten out. Over Ventnor the aircraft tried to pull up into the clouds but a further burst set him on fire on both sides of the fuselage whilst a thick trail of black smoke enveloped the machine. The aircraft then turned north east and glided down. I smelt something burning and as my cockpit was full of fumes I opened the hood and started climbing, hoping to reach land in case I should have to bale out. After a few minutes the smoke and fumes cleared and I realised that my machine was not on fire after all and the smoke I noticed must have come back from the enemy plane.

I climbed to 9,000 feet over the Isle of Wight, and noticed several ack-ack bursts over Portsmouth. On looking round I could only see one Ju 88 about fifteen to twenty miles south, so I gave chase. The machine must have been badly damaged as its speed was greatly reduced and I was able to catch up with ease. Having closed to about 300 yards I managed to get in a good burst from astern.

Pieces fell from the aircraft and the 88 dived into the clouds where it disappeared. The position last seen was some thirty-five miles south-east of Selsey Bill.

I returned to base at 1705 hours and it was subsequently agreed that a round of de Wilde ammunition that had exploded in the breach of one of the guns had possibly added to the smell of burning which I had noticed in the cockpit."

Pilot Officer Tony Woods-Scawen
(Andy Saunders collection)

All ten pilots engaged in this mission returned normally to base with all ten Hurricanes intact and so ended Hermann Goering's much vaunted 'Eagle Day'. For 43 Squadron it had resulted in their losing two Hurricanes against which they could with confidence claim to have decreased the strength of the Luftwaffe's trained aircrews by more than twenty. By no means an unlucky 13th.

Twenty-three hours later 'B' Flight, again patrolling the Isle of Wight, sighted a solitary Ju 88 away to the south. They closed in, firing in rotation, silenced the rear gunners, set the starboard engine on fire and finally witnessed the splash and plume of spray as the bomber smashed into the water not far south of the Needles. One of the pilots engaged in this action left prematurely when his cockpit suddenly filled with smoke, an unpleasant experience caused by the explosion of a round of de Wilde ammunition in the breach of a gun. This ammunition, classified as 'explosive incendiary', was alleged to have great destructive power. It probably did, but it also was a little touchy and eccentric and sometimes liable to go off in the wrong place.

There was little respite for the pilots this afternoon. Two sections of 'A' Flight landed at 1640 after a patrol and fifteen minutes later were again airborne for another which lasted ninety-five minutes. 'B' Flight, back from their victory, were on the ground for under an hour before going up again at 1805 hours. This time they went to Winchester via the Isle of Wight and were turning south again when Blue 2 (Sgt Hallowes) heard an RT conversation taking place in German. The signals became louder, Blue 2 asked for and was given permission to investigate above cloud. There he found a Heinkel, ten miles to the south. He notified Blue Leader and proceeded to chase it, when the Heinkel saw him it dived through cloud slap into the path of the remainder of the Flight. For some moments there was return fire from the upper rear gun and then something resembling a coil of wire was thrown at the pursuing Hurricanes. Bullets were entering the Heinkel's fuselage and pieces were falling from it when very heavy cloud and squalls enveloped the combatants and Sqn Ldr Badger called off the hunt. On returning to base Sgt Montgomery was missing.

On the 15th the Luftwaffe, flying around the clock and attempting to penetrate the defences around the coast from Portland Bill to Northumberland, flew 1,786 sorties. Against them the RAF put up 974 fighter sorties, thirty-six of them by 43 Squadron. Most of these thirty-six were flown between 1700 hours and dusk and apart from shooting down the two bombers mentioned earlier in the chapter, a Ju 88 and a He 111 were damaged. Operations were continued after dark and not until 0115 hours was the last Hurricane engine switched off, and pilots and crews retired wearily to their beds.

On the 16th, exactly on the stroke of 1300 hrs Tangmere was heavily attacked. The widespread damage which the enemy inflicted included the total destruction by blast and fire of the Squadron hangar and an adjacent air-raid shelter normally used by the men who worked in the hangar received a direct hit. Being lunch time it was fortunately almost unoccupied and the only Squadron casualty killed, was AC1 J Young, a nineteen year old flight mechanic. Bad as it was, the ordeal of those on the ground must have been far worse. This was particularly the case for 43 because most, if not all, of the bombers which they intercepted, scattered and forced to flee were heading for Tangmere. Once scrambled, as the first of the three squadrons in the sector, 43 had ample time to reach their designated 15,000 feet above Selsey, where they saw the incoming bombers, one hundred of them, mostly Stukas, flying in Vic formations stepped up from 12,000 to 15,000 feet. They met the raiders head on, a form of attack several times used with success at this time, and the Junkers broke wide open. Thereafter every one of the twelve pilots enjoyed some measure of success. Hallowes destroyed three (reported earlier in this chapter) Carey got two and two probables before, out of ammunition, he was chased most of the long way home by two Me 109s. Sqn Ldr Badger destroyed two more, and the other nine pilots involved, Plt Offs Woods-Scawen, Gray, Lane, Gorrie, Upton, Sgts Noble and Mills and the two unconquered Belgians, du Vivier and Van den Hove, struck with such venom and purpose that seventeen Ju 87s were claimed destroyed or probably destroyed with four more damaged. The old Fighting Cock, dangerous at any time, was doubly so in defence of his own roosting place. Mostly the Junkers, whose escorting fighters were nowhere in evidence when the Hurricanes attacked, jettisoned their bombs in the sea and fled, one pilot reporting 'that they were thoroughly demoralised', but one or two of the Germans showed more pluck, and amazement was expressed regarding their reaction when attacked of making a tight turn in an attempt to get behind the tail of their opponent. Such spirit and courage availed not at all and no amount of bravery or skill could endow the heavy Stuka with sufficient manoeuvrability to mix it with a Hurricane.

All except Upton and Woods-Scawen who force-landed at Selsey and Parkhurst (IOW) came back to touch down safely between the

The Squadron's hangar burns furiously after a direct hit on 16 August 1940
(Andy Saunders collection)

A group of pilots at Tangmere -
Sgt Mills, Plt Off Gray, Plt Off Woods-Scawen, Sgt Jefferys, Sgt Deller, Flt Lt Reynell

bomb craters on the airfield. 'B' Flight had five aircraft refuelled, rearmed and airborne again in under ten minutes and 'A' Flight sent another five away very soon afterwards. Thereafter, with increasing cloud, activity slackened but during a late patrol Sgt Crisp broke a thigh bone when parachuting to earth after his engine (probably over-boosted for over long during the Selsey battle) developed a glycol leak and caught fire.

The loss of its hangar did not decrease Squadron serviceability, it merely made it more difficult. Major maintenance was switched wholly to the Flight dispersals which had been untouched in the raid. The 'A' Flight telephone orderly, a large Irishman, became possessed of an unusual melancholy and daily forecast the inevitability of a return visit 'to finish off the dispersals this time', an outlook that did not endear him to those around him for, though the possibility of being blown up existed, it was no assuagement to be constantly reminded of it. In fact the aerodrome was never again seriously attacked during the Battle, perhaps because of the overoptimistic assessments of Luftwaffe intelligence of damage inflicted, and a failure to appreciate the near impossibility of rendering aerodromes unusable without constant repetitive attacks. Tangmere was never non-operational as a result of the raid and the bomb craters on the airfield were filled within twenty-four hours.

The cloud that came up on the 16th persisted for much of the next day and enemy activity was limited to reconnaissance. Four missions of twenty-two sorties during the afternoon brought no interceptions but at 1700 hours Blue Section, comprising Sqn Ldr Badger, Sgt Hallowes and Plt Off Gorrie, went after an unidentified plot over Winchester. At 15,000 feet Hallowes spotted an aircraft five miles northward, around 30,000 feet, informed Blue Leader and was told in return that he was seeing things but to take over the lead nevertheless. This latter remark of 'seeing things' was often made in good humour to Hallowes whose vision, much better than most, enabled him to sight far distant aircraft before anybody else, and indeed only a few days previously a report that

Pilots, August 1940 Standing - Sgt Noble, Plt Off Upton
Plt Off Gorrie, Plt Off Van den Hove, Sgt Hallowes,
Kneeling - Plt Off le Roy du Vivier,
Seated - Sqn Ldr Badger
(Andy Saunders collection)

One of the many Junkers Ju 87 Stukas destroyed

he could see, from the ground at Tangmere, five aircraft, heading north at 10,000 feet over Portsmouth caused an almighty flap in Operations Room, before the objects were identified by an observer post as five geese (or swans) at 2,000 feet above Thorney Island.

Losing the other two as he climbed into the sun, Hallowes finally caught up with the enemy aircraft, 'a strange looking Do 17'. Fire was opened at 300 yards, the Dornier went into a dive and the Hurricane followed. Though at full throttle the range did not shorten but Hallowes fired whenever the target was in his sights. After the third burst the rear gunners stopped firing and bullets were clearly seen entering the top of the fuselage. At 12,000 feet a terrific vibration, with the mainplanes fluttering violently at the wing tips and fabric tearing off the ailerons, suddenly occurred. Because of the thick haze there was no visible horizon but the instruments showed that the Hurricane was in a near vertical dive with the ASI off the clock at over 400 mph. An attempt to rectify this unhealthy state of affairs by first easing, then forcing back the control column was quite unsuccessful, the stick being solid, but happily the elevator trimming wheel gave a better response and the Hurricane came out on to an even keel around 5,000 feet. No further sight or sign of the Dornier was made although on return Hallowes rechecked the German aircraft silhouettes and was convinced that his target had been a Do 215. Moreover, he doubted if such a heavy aeroplane could have pulled out of such a dive although 'unfortunately I could not persuade the Intelligence Officer to submit a claim as when I contacted him he said it was too late to report the engagement to headquarters.'

The remarkable epilogue to this story is that the Hurricane was found to have been over stressed to such great degree that the mainplane root fittings had bent and some sweepback not incorporated in the original design had resulted. A subsequent investigation by highly interested Hawker technicians deduced a speed in the dive of 620-750 mph as being necessary to have caused the distortion.

If Saturday had been comparatively a rest day, Sunday the 18th was double time with a vengeance, and 43 was more heavily engaged than ever in an unending pattern of scramble, patrol, land, refuel and scramble again, while the enemy threw in a number of raids, cunningly mixed with feints designed to mislead the defence. Thus 'B' Flight sent off six pilots at 0930-1000. As they landed, 'A' Flight scrambled six more 1005-1020, land, scramble again 1045, joined by 'B' Flight's six at 1055 and all on patrol until 1135. And so, with no respite, 'A' Flight again, six aircraft 1235-1255, refuel, off 1310-1350, refuel and away again 1410-1500. During which time, 'B' Flight had sent off six at 1255-1355, and on landing, rapidly refuelled three which, up at 1410, joined with the six from 'A' Flight led by Flt Lt Carey in intercepting a heavy raid. This came in around Selsey Bill before splitting up and heading for the aerodromes at Gosport, Thorney Island and Ford, and the vital radar sector station at Poling, on the Arundel to Worthing Road.

Flt Lt Carey 'took the nine Hurricanes head on into a large formation of Ju 87s midway between Chichester and Selsey Bill. After turning round to get behind some of them I found myself in the middle of several Ju 87 formations. I fired at one ahead of me – it stood straight up on its nose, with flames coming out of it – when I was hit on the right knee by cross fire, or a stray burst from a Hurricane. Handing over the Squadron to someone else I had to drop out of the fight as my knee was locked and I was not feeling too well. I called Tangmere but they advised me to stay away as they expected more bombing. I did for a time, but eventually had to crash-land at Pulborough.'

Another remarkable bit of shooting came from the redoubtable Sgt Hallowes. His 'two

Flight Lieutenant Tom Dalton-Morgan DFC and Bar

Two airmen stand guard over a Ju 88

birds with one shot' must be quite unique and suggests that some of the Stuka crews were by this time in a highly nervous state.

"I followed Blue Leader in line astern but lost sight of him as we engaged the enemy. I caught up with one formation of five Ju 87s in line astern, opened fire at about 300 yards, two people baled out of number five aircraft and a further two from number four machine, both aircraft going into a vertical dive about three to four miles east of Thorney Island.

I then carried out a quarter attack on a third Ju 87 without any apparent result. Observing another 87 at about 200 feet which had released its bombs on Thorney Island, I came up into a position astern and gave it three short bursts. I was closing too fast and had to break away to the right, coming in again for a beam attack on the same machine which broke in two, just in front of the tail fin, and fell in the Solent about halfway between the mainland and the Isle of Wight.

I then spotted a Hurricane which was closing in astern of a Ju 87 with a Me 109 coming up in turn behind the Hurricane. The Hurricane turned left and I was in a good position for a beam attack on the Me 109.

I could clearly see my bullets entering the fuselage from the nose to the tail plane and could see the holes as the 109 flashed past me about 100 yards ahead, going south.

I heard the order to return to base and being almost out of ammunition I returned, landed and rearmed. I claimed the 109 as damaged but at a later date heard that an unclaimed Me 109 had crashed on the Isle of Wight that day with a row of bullet holes along the fuselage and assumed it was the one I had fired at."

Eight Ju 87s and one of the escorting Me 109s went down in this action, one which finally forced Goering into the decision to withdraw the Stuka from the fray (one or two furtive forays on the fringes excepted). Frank Carey's loss was the only one the Squadron suffered, and temporary though it was to prove, the loss of his especial skill and experience at this critical stage was nigh-catastrophic. With Morgan still in Station Sick Quarters, both Flight Commanders were now hors de combat.

Yet there was little time that afternoon to grieve. Five aircraft landed after their successful interception at 1435. Ten minutes later three of them were included in a formation of seven sent on patrol. In the evening sun, six aircraft from 'A' Flight rounded off the day with an unsuccessful hunt of a lone recce. And that was the end, for in one day, one squadron, thirteen pilots, sixty-four sorties, thirty-seven hours forty minutes, nine Huns were in the bag and one Flight Commander was in hospital. The last aircraft touched down at 2015. It was less than ten hours to first light when it would all start again. Actually it did not, for the next day was cloudy, and for the next four succeeding days generally overcast skies limited enemy activity. At Tangmere on the afternoon of the 23rd, a single Heinkel 111 flew across and machine-gunned the airfield. Fifty sorties were made during this time, three during the night 21st–22nd in which no casualties were sustained and none inflicted.

Goering met his commanders on the 19th. The Luftwaffe had lost 194 aircraft between 15th and 18th August. Fighter Command which, according to German Intelligence estimates of its original strength and reported losses, should have ceased to exist but was obviously still undefeated. Goering ordered as the main task of Luftflotte 2 and 3 the 'infliction of the utmost possible damage on the enemy fighter forces by constantly bringing them to battle, and attacks concentrating on fighter aerodromes and aircraft factories'. 24th August dawned fine and clear. Before 0900 hrs the first big raid was coming in.

CHAPTER 15

Fateful Fortnight

THE fortnight between 24 August and 6 September proved to be the most critical period of the whole battle for Fighter Command. Greatly concerned by their losses of the two previous weeks (over 400 aircraft, half of them bombers), the Luftwaffe altered its tactics, reducing the size of its bomber formations and stepping up the numbers of escorting fighters. Twenty bombers with one hundred Me 109s was not an uncommon ratio and the defending squadrons thereby found their task made that much more difficult and hazardous. So much, in fact, that by 5 September Fighter Command was facing a crisis. Vital sector stations around London were being damaged faster than they could be repaired, losses in pilots were of an order that made their replacement in sufficient numbers an impossibility, its sector control system was close to breakdown. Then, either convinced that the RAF was finished, or, as some aver, goaded by a Bomber Command raid on Berlin, the attack was switched to London. By so doing the Germans lost the battle.

All this is history and is important here only insofar as it concerns the story of 43 Squadron. On 24 August it had sixteen pilots, seven more were posted or returned from hospital in the period and losses during the same time were four killed and seven wounded. It destroyed seventeen enemy aircraft (of which sixteen were fighters). The figures indicate how the change in Luftwaffe tactics brought higher losses to the defence and just as these days saw Fighter Command brought almost to its knees, so it was also during this time that the Squadron fought itself to exhaustion. Fighter Command losses during this fortnight were 103 pilots killed, 128 wounded, 295 fighters destroyed and 171 badly damaged. Against which the Germans lost 378 aircraft. It was the nearest that the two sides ever came to parity of loss and the Squadron's effort stands comparison with the Command as a whole.

On the 24th and 25th the Squadron flew seventy-two sorties (eleven of them by night), totalling sixty-seven hours. Most of the raids were to the east, largely concentrated against aerodromes, while to one on Portsmouth during the 24th the Squadron was scrambled too late to be effective. On the 26th, after 'A' Flight had spent some time early on in abortive chases of individual plots, twelve aircraft were scrambled at 1600 hours. Sqn Ldr Badger, Hallowes, Gorrie, Van den Hove, Ayling, Brunner, Woods-Scawen, Lane, Deller, North, Mills and Gray were vectored against 150 aircraft of Luftlotte 3 approaching Portsmouth. All told, eight squadrons were despatched by Group and three of them attacked singly before the raid reached the target area. 'We felt rather insignificant as we deployed to make a head-on attack on a squadron of Heinkel 111s in the centre of the bombers', wrote Plt Off Brunner. 'I should think that, all told, there were at least a hundred bombers with a large number of fighters up above. We went slap into them, shooting time was short, but we succeeded in making them look pretty ragged, even if not completely broken up. I broke down from my target and remember the awe-inspiring sight of what seemed hundreds of slimy grey shapes sliding by overhead. I pulled up and turned behind another bomber which I apparently hit for it dropped out of formation, and I was then attacked by a 109. On turning to deal with him he dived away and I chased him down to sea level just off the coast and continued for a little way out to sea, but could not close enough to be effective. I returned, climbing, but by then there was no sign of another aircraft or any battle. (This was one of the amazing things, how quickly everybody disappeared after every melée). Returning to base, I heard the controller asking for anyone with ammo left to patrol Bognor as five plus had been plotted coming in from the south. I was (foolishly) stooging along the coast peering in search of targets, when there was an almighty noise, all the instrument panel fell to bits, the contents of the gravity tank sprayed all over me and I was hit in the ankle. I took the most violent evasive action, switching off the engine. I never saw what had hit me! I tried to see what was left working, the answer

Plt Off Geoff Brunner
(Andy Saunders collection)

being practically nothing except the controls. No engine, no RT, no hydraulics – and fortunately no fire, for I was soaked in petrol. Luckily I was near base and glided in wheels up to land safely'.

'I was despatched to the West Sussex hospital at Brighton. We had a complete 43 ward, Frank Carey (from the 18th), Roy Lane and 'Knockers' North from the same engagement as myself. Roy was badly burnt, but the rest of us were all pretty alive and noisy, and quite disorganised the hospital. And the nurses thoroughly spoiled us!'

Flt Lt Dick Reynell
(Andy Saunders collection)

During this battle Plt Offs Gray, Lane and North all baled out of fire-filled cockpits while besides Brunner's Cat 3 wreck, two other Hurricanes were badly damaged. In reply 43 had shot down a 109 and two, (possibly three) Heinkel 111s, one of which was initially attacked north of Havant by Sgt Hallowes and finally crashed beside the Arun at Littlehampton. En route it survived the aerodrome defence gunners at both Tangmere and Ford. Their ill-advised and ill-aimed shooting at the crippled bomber – one engine had stopped and the undercarriage had fallen down – greatly endangered the Hurricanes of Hallowes and Sqn Ldr Badger as, out of ammunition, they induced their enemy to surrender with a number of dummy attacks.

Good news was the arrival that evening of Flt Lt Reynell, Hawker test pilot on loan to the Air Ministry, to fill one of the two vacant Flight Commander berths: a position not entirely strange for eight years earlier he had been in command of 'C' Flight. 'Dick' Reynell was a remarkable exponent of the art of flying a Hurricane and in the few days he fought with 43 he displayed, in more than one air test, an incredible repertoire of low-level aerobatics. Nobody who saw him could remember anything that could stand comparison and it was not at all difficult to understand how in 1939 he had out-flown the best in Europe and stolen the show at the Brussels International Air Display. His presence did not come amiss. The triple loss sustained on the evening of the 26th left the Squadron with sixteen pilots, two of whom had been just twenty-four hours out of OTU and of the remainder, eight were comparatively new. The most precious commodity of all, experience, was becoming dangerously diluted and any strengthening of it was to be infinitely welcomed. The 27th was a day of comparatively poor weather. 'A' Flight spent a fruitless hour just after noon chasing a raider in the Portsmouth area, but otherwise there was little of note, and again on the next day no major calls were made on the Squadron. On the 29th attacks on airfields were interspersed by the Luftwaffe with massive fighter sweeps. Thirteen sorties totalling five hours fifty minutes were flown, but in adherence to orders not to engage if no bombers were involved, there was again nothing of note to report.

On the 30th, the Luftwaffe put in a maximum effort of 1,345 sorties to which the RAF replied with 1,054. In the morning, Kent and Surrey sector stations took another hammering and from 1330 to 1630 hrs continual raids up to twenty plus aimed at Biggin Hill,

Kenley, Shoreham and Tangmere among others, dodged about among a cloud layer at 7,000 feet. For half an hour either side of noon, twelve aircraft of the Squadron were in action over Kent and Sussex. During this time a 109 wrongly identified as the non-existent Heinkel 113 was claimed as probably destroyed and in the same engagement Sgt Dennis Noble was killed when his aircraft crashed at Hove.

Plt Off Roy Lane
(Andy Saunders collection)

During the late afternoon 'A' Flight sent off two single sections of three while at 1655 nine aircraft were vectored onto an X-plot over Kent. It was during this flight that Sqn Ldr Badger was hit and forced to bale out at Woodchurch, close to Tenterden. He was quickly picked up, and taken to hospital with dreadful internal wounds. There for nine months, enduring intense suffering, he fought against death with the same courage, the same tenacity of purpose and the same nobleness of spirit as he had shown in the fight against the enemy in the skies.

In the following June, uncomplaining to the end, he died, leaving an example of how a man might, without fear, look the Last Enemy squarely in the face. Just as in life, he had during eight weeks of high summer in 1940, matched himself against the demands of leadership of a great squadron and shown what might be achieved in the face of the greatest odds just so long as courage were sustained and not eroded by baser desires of self-survival.

The squadron diary for the last day of August records three main items. Firstly, that some of its pilots, notwithstanding their efforts of the day, proceeded to spend some of the night chasing some of the enemy bombers. Secondly it records several decorations (awarded actually on various dates preceding this, but summarised as under):

Sqn Ldr C G Lott
Distinguished Service Order
Sqn Ldr J V C Badger
Distinguished Flying Cross
Flt Lt T F D Morgan
Distinguished Flying Cross
Fg Off A Woods-Scawen
Distinguished Flying Cross
Sgt H J L Hallowes
Distinguished Flying Medal and Bar

A six fold recognition of illustrious deeds, no less nobly rewarded.

The third entry of note was that after a quiet day six aircraft of 'B' Flight scrambled at 1810 hours, vectored onto a raid on Beachy Head radar station, and leading them was Sqn Ldr C B Hull DFC.

There was no man living better fitted to take over 43, and to revive a spirit, sagging a little from the cruel loss of 'Tubby' Badger. A stranger may find it hard to understand, but for 43 Caesar 'seemed more than man could be'. Already a living legend when he left so suddenly in April for Norway, his fame had remained. Those who knew him remembered, those who never knew had heard. To a battle-weary, sadly tried squadron, Caesar, merely by his presence, brought a new surge of vitality. He was a *Hector* come to *Troy*, a *Drake* back from the mists of history to answer the drum at the hour of sorest trial.

It was also true that, just because of the God-like veneration in which he was held and the exceptional devotion that he inspired, when he died seven days later the collapse of morale was all the more complete. But this, as yet, was still to be and unaware of the future, the Squadron, reinvigorated by the return of the legendary Caesar, and additionally strengthened by the welcome return ex-Station Sick Quarters of the redoubtable Tom Morgan, awaited the next day with a renewed confidence. In the event, the Squadron was not called upon to any great degree on 1 September. On the 2nd came more bitter blows. The Germans continued to hammer away at airfields and four were bombed before 0800 hours. At 1235 two hundred and fifty bombers and fighters converged on Dover before splitting into smaller groups. Twelve aircraft of 43 Squadron, airborne at 1245, intercepted over north-east Kent. Only nine returned to Tangmere. Fg Off Carswell, nine days back on strength after three months in hospital was injured and baled out near Ashford. Du Vivier, wounded in the foot, also baled out at New Romney and Woods-Scawen, the seemingly indestructible Tony, was dead. Attempting to force land near Ivychurch until compelled by increasing smoke and flame to take to his parachute, he had enough height for safety but it must have been damaged in the fight and so it failed to fully deploy. It was the very same one that he had carried all the way back from France in June. Since then he had been once injured, twice wounded and survived three crash-landings in shattered aircraft. Small wonder that George Lott had said of him 'He was not a particularly good pilot, he was not a particularly good shot, but by ardour and all the stars he was a fighter'. And in truth he need never have remained in the firing line for there was latterly a secret, which he confided only to one person, a defect which would, had it been known, have brought to an end his operational career. Not long before his death he apologised to Flt Sgt Parker for the number of aircraft he lost or brought home damaged, admitted that his eyes were troubling him and that often he could not see much of what went on aloft. Hence the number of times he was shot up by the enemy aircraft he never saw. 'But for God's sake, Flight,' he said, 'don't breathe a word of this to anybody, or they'll whip me off ops.' So was lost one who might have retired to the safe backwaters of an OTU without disgrace or dishonour, but who stayed in the fight because that was where he wanted to be.

Plt Off Harold North
(Andy Saunders collection)

On the 4th the Squadron gained revenge for the losses of the 2nd. At lunchtime three hundred bombers and fighters poured in across the coast between Dover and Beachy Head before fanning out and 43, one of fourteen squadrons airborne, took on two formations of Messerschmitt 110s. The 110, twin-engined, heavily armed 'Destroyer' and Goering's especial pride, was a formidable aeroplane in some respects but had its shortcomings too, one of which was its lack of manoeuvrability compared with a Hurricane or Spitfire.

The 110 Squadrons had proved rather a disappointment to Goering – they had even on occasions called for an escort of Me 109s – and the particular adversaries that 43 met this day were especially out of luck. Caesar, leading the Squadron, found a large formation flying in a circle, line astern 200-300 yards apart and already engaged by other fighters. From out of the sun and above he led 43 into the fray. Tom Morgan drew first blood when a 110, spouting flame from the nose, dived vertically to explode on the ground inland from Worthing. Between this town and Shoreham a second formation of 110s of ZG 76 were encountered. One of these, damaged offshore by Morgan, flew back low over the coast, port prop windmilling to force-land in a field, as did another which Sgt Jefferys chased down from 8,000 feet. Caesar and Plt Off Upton each badly damaged two separate opponents while Van den Hove saw a 110 that he attacked fall into the sea seven miles out before his Hurricane was itself hit, 'shuddered and began to pour black smoke into the cockpit'. The Belgian prepared to bale out but the smoke stopped so he changed his mind and force-landed wheels down on Ford aerodrome. His was the only damage sustained by the whole of the Squadron in this highly successful encounter. Awaiting the return of the Squadron was a most welcome reinforcement for them in the person of Flt Lt Kilmartin. Since leaving the previous November he had joined in the triumphs of No 1 in France and now, following three months instructing at No 5 OTU was rested and ready, like any self-respecting Irishman, for another fight. His experience was greatly to be welcomed and that he was already attuned to the ways of the Fighting Cocks was cause for double thanksgiving.

On the 5th and 6th attacks came in unceasingly, ranging over Kent, Sussex and Surrey. The Flight order books are indicative of the response. Hull, Mills, Deller, Upton, Van den Hove and Ayling airborne 0800-0840. These six, together with Kilmartin, Reynell, Jefferys, Morgan, Hurry and Gorrie to intercept X-plot 1000-1100. The same twelve pilots to Thames estuary 1505-1630, when a 109, attacked by Sgt Hurry, caught fire and dived out of control to crash near Appledore railway station. Between 0900 and 1020 on the 6th, twelve pilots engaged an enemy force between Mayfield and Dungeness. Five 109s and a 110 were seen to crash, a Ju 88 and two 109s were damaged. Tom Morgan, having sent one 109 into the sea, was himself attacked while firing at another and the shell that smashed his Hurricane's hood also wounded him about the face.

Sergeant Hurry

The Squadron were back on patrol again, over Kent, before one o'clock and in some inconclusive action Sgt Deller

On 7 September 1940 Sqn Ldr Lott returned to Tangmere for the first time since being blinded in his right eye on 9 July. He is seen in this nostalgic photograph outside the Officers' Mess with (standing) Plt Off H C Upton, Plt Off A E A van den Hove d'Ertsenryck, Plt Off D G Gorrie (seated) Plt Off S Cary (Sqn Adjutant), Flt Lt J I Kilmartin, Sqn Ldr C G Lott, Flt Lt R C Reynell and Sqn Ldr C B Hull. Sadly, the last two named were killed in action some three hours after this photograph was taken.

left a 109 in some distress with black and white smoke pouring from the nose, but remembering what he had been taught he wisely did not follow down.

Sunday the 7th saw eleven aircraft airborne at 1155 but ordered to land half an hour later. The early afternoon was so quiet that Sgts Morrison and Palliser, both new arrivals from OTU, were able to fly an air-fighting practice mission. Then as 1600 hrs approached the radar plots received at Bentley Priory made it obvious that something extraordinary was building up across the Channel and soon the vanguard of the biggest raid to date was crossing the coast on a twenty mile front stepped up from 14,000 to 23,000 feet; 'a tidal wave a mile and a half high and covering 800 square miles' was one description of it. 11 Group scrambled eleven squadrons and called the other ten to readiness at the same time as they alerted the neighbouring 10 and 12 Groups.

The enemy force, 350 bombers and 600 plus fighters, came in two waves some 30 minutes or so apart. Initially the airborne squadrons, deployed to defend the airfields and aircraft factories which experience during the past two weeks pointed out as being the probable targets, were not best disposed to meet the main thrust which headed straight for London, so that part of it reached the capital unmolested.

During this stage 43 was still on the ground at Readiness. Earlier during the quiet of mid-afternoon the Sector Controller had indicated the possibility of releasing the Squadron before dusk – it was its turn for an evening off. But as the first part of the attacking aerial armada turned for home, harried all the way, the second wave showed up on the plotting tables and at 1635 nine aircraft of 43 were scrambled. Ordered to fly on varying vectors they finally sighted, crossing the coast near Folkestone at 18,000 feet, a formation of 25 Dornier Do 17 bombers with a ring of fighters circling 500 feet above and others behind stepped up to 25,000 feet. Following some miles behind were two similar groups of escorted Dorniers.

With no other friendly fighters in view, Caesar led his nine Hurricanes towards the front group, climbing until he was 1500 feet above the bombers with Kilmartin and his rearmost section of three another 2000 feet higher still. Telling Kilmartin to keep the fighters off, Caesar peeled off to the left and dived down. 'We heard his throaty chuckle as he told us to sail in and smash 'em' and those were the last words anybody ever heard from him. Sergeant Hurry, No 2 in his

Squadron Leader C B Hull DFC
(Andy Saunders collection)

section was the last to see him. 'He went in astern of a Dornier and I pulled out to make a synchronised beam attack. I raked the bomber from one end to the other and broke down and under. When I turned to come in again there was no sign of anybody else.'

At 1750, Flt Lt Kilmartin taxied into dispersal at Tangmere, took off his flying helmet, said just two words to Flt Sgt Parker, 'My God', turned and went into the dispersal hut. Van den Hove, Sgt Hurry and Sgt Barrow came back a little later and Sgts Mills and Jefferys phoned in from Detling where they had landed to refuel, but Caesar, Dick Reynell and Sgt Alan Deller were all missing. Deller had baled out unhurt near Ashford. Dick Reynell had baled out too, seconds before his Hurricane blew up in mid-air over Blackheath but something had gone wrong with his parachute and he had died on hitting the ground. Caesar was found ten miles away from his comrade at Purley, still in his aeroplane, itself so badly damaged by fire that it was identified only from the serial numbers on the guns.

His death shattered the Squadron for with him died the fresh hope and vitality that his return had brought to men grown weary with weeks of unrelieved battle. He had been their symbol of invincibility, an assurance that defeat was unthinkable. Now the doubts and tiredness flooded back and all was heaviness of mind.

Tom Morgan returned that night, still bearing his wounds of the previous day, to take command of what still was left. Of aircraft there was, as ever, no shortage but of the thirteen pilots available four were less than a week out of OTU, two others barely a month and with Hallowes suffering from a burst eardrum, only Kilmartin could claim any extensive pre-war flying experience. The Cockerel had taken a beating, though he was still far from dead. Too many of his finest feathers had been torn away, disappearing in the dust and heat of battle to be seen no more. But it had not all been unmitigated loss, and if he were wounded his adversary had been made to suffer more. Spread out across the green Downland and dark Weald of Sussex, or in the sea beyond the coast, beneath the blue skies of which once the Squadron had sung it would defend, there lay the shattered metal and broken bodies of those that had dared to come against it and, coming, had been clawed into the ground.

Now it was time to rest and refit. At Usworth, 607 Squadron the pride of Durham, recovered from the devastation it suffered in France, was eager to get back into the fight. Late on the evening of the 7th it was ordered to proceed at first light to Tangmere; 43 to take its place in the comparative quiet of the north.

CHAPTER 16

Thirteen Group

BLOODY and battered, wearied nigh to exhaustion, but by no means broken in spirit, 43 Squadron retired to Usworth on 8 September. Twelve operational pilots and twelve aircraft were all that was left. In the thirteen unlucky days since 26 August seven pilots had finished an operational trip in hospital or Station Sick Quarters and four more had died, yet there was no sense of failure, inferiority or disgrace for very few squadrons had lasted in action as long. Given a few weeks rest the battle would be resumed with the same zest and determination and success as before. Actually, had it been rested earlier than September it might well have returned for a second bite at the cherry, but coincidental with the move to Usworth on the 8th came a change in policy by the C-in-C Fighter Command.

Too many squadrons, newly drawn into the battle, were suffering grievous losses before they had had time to accustom themselves to the tempo at which it was fought. 607 Squadron who relieved 43 at Tangmere lost more aircraft and pilots in the first five days than 43 had lost in as many weeks. Reorganising his resources, Lord Dowding divided the squadrons into three categories A, B and C. Those in action were Class A, to receive priority in all things. Class B, few in number, were on the fringe of battle and at a strength where they were immediately available as replacements for Class A Squadrons irretrievably damaged in action. Class C, into which 43 now came, were stripped to a minimum of operational pilots. Tucked away in the quiet sectors of the north and west, in those parts where no German action could ever be decisive, they guarded against the lone intruder, such as the occasional reconnaissance or hit and run bomber, whilst concentrating their major energies on training the output of the OTUs up to a standard where they could be drafted as reinforcements to the squadrons bearing the brunt of the battle in the south. Such was the organisation, such was the role of 43. Not very stirring, not very glamorous, not the type of job calculated to encourage great achievement. Yet that is just what may be justifiably claimed for the twenty months following on from September 1940. Tired by battle, it welcomed for a few weeks the chance of a rest. Thereafter, as the desire to get back into the centre of things returned and the headlines were all of sweeps that probed forth daily across the Channel to carry the fight into the enemy camp, an achievement there was no hope of matching in the backwaters of Scotland, it humbly accepted the lesser role that it had been given, conceded that wars were not to be won only by the deeds that brought the bright publicity, but equally by the hard unremitting slog that never saw the light of a newspaper day and got on with it. And because in a rapidly changing world, in the midst of a rapidly moving war, the old long accustomed wont of 43 Squadron that it never did anything unless it did it better than most, remained, it proceeded to do just that. There were not many opportunities to attack the enemy but the fourteen aircraft which it positively destroyed during this period was just two fewer than the total number actually sighted and engaged.

Sergeant Josef Pipa buckles into his 'chute
(Andy Saunders collection)

Its primary task of training it fulfilled equally well. Although at Drem, and later at Acklington, it shared sector defence with only one other squadron so that for half the hours of daylight some of its aircraft were always

'Red section patrol Bass Rock, angels eight'. A pair of Hurricanes scramble at Drem, 1941

required for readiness or fifteen minute availability, yet the diary could record on 30 April 1941 that 'since 9 September last, eighty-seven pilots have been posted in for final training, many having done only a few hours on Hurricanes. Though ops or periods of readiness have restricted the time which could be utilised for practice flying and in spite of bad weather during what has been one of the hardest and worst winters for many years, the Squadron has been able to do a monthly average of 330 hours practice flying by day and twenty-six by night in addition to any operational flying. The Squadron has also had a larger number of operational and training pilots night trained than any other squadron in 13 Group.' This continuing ability to outmatch other squadrons that came and went through 13 Group during the period was an outstanding feature of the times. On 2 July a 13 Group report said: 'in spite of low camera availability 43 Squadron has used 2,287 feet of film, the highest figure ever recorded for a squadron in the Group. It also did well with regard to Air Firing training of which sixty practices were made with a large percentage of pilots getting hits.' This was a Group report on the Squadron for a month in which it had set up a record for 13 Group. Seven

'A' Flight at Drem, April 1941
Standing are Scorer, du Vivier, Ottewill, Kilmartin, Doll, "Chiefy" Parker, Lister and Flt Sgt (unknown)

'B' Flight, Drem, April 1941

43's 'League of Nations' at Drem
Plt Off Mize (USA), Plt Off Cotton (Australia), Fg Off Reid (Canada), Plt Off Mehta (India), Flt Lt du Vivier (Belgium), Plt Off West (Scotland), Flt Lt May (England), Sgt Pipa (Czechoslovakia)

hundred and fourteen hours by day, ninety-one by night in training, with another thirty-seven operational night hours, fifteen pilots from OTU, fifteen out to Squadrons. It was no little wonder that Air Vice-Marshal R E Saul, AOC 13 Group, regarded 43 as one of the brightest jewels in his crown, 'I well remember them,' he wrote in 1963, 'as an outstanding unit which we were fortunate enough to have with us for a period, all too short as far as I was concerned.'

Another 'record', one not quickly forgotten by the Royal Navy, was worthy of note. Late in February, heavy snow put both Drem and Turnhouse out of action, leaving the sector wide open to any marauding Hun. Herculean efforts throughout a bitter night by snow clearance parties, for whom a special rum ration was issued, cleared a narrow strip, enabling some pilots to take off between piled banks of snow, and to fly over the Forth to Crail where the captain and crew of HMS *Jackdaw* made them most welcome. Hospitality was there in abundance, knowledge of the ways of fighters was equally absent and the first 'scramble' from a room above the Duty Pilot's office swept a dozen naval ratings into the ground as pilots and mechanics poured in irresistible spate towards the readiness machines. A second shattering blow to the equanimity of the Senior Service followed at once, for the two Hurricanes proceeded to take off in formation, crosswind and without first asking for permission to do so! These customary, normal practices of fighter pilots were wholly foreign to the inhabitants of *Jackdaw*, and brought initially a reaction that such dangerous flying procedures were inadmissible and must cease.

The rapidity with which one or more sections could be got into the air was a feature of the times. Competition between crews became intense and improved ways were continually probed and sought whereby a few seconds might be chopped off the elapsed time. The all-time record was made by Sgts Scorer and Sims, forty-eight seconds from the first Tannoy words 'Operations Room calling . . .' to wheels up on take-off. This was exceptional, and generally sixty seconds minus was brilliant, ninety merely average and over two minutes unforgivable. Such results were the outcome of perfection in co-operation and timing between the pilots and their crews that required all the discipline and application of a well drilled *corps de ballet*. Each moved with speed, yet without haste or fumble, carrying out his allotted function at the precise moment co-ordinated with the movements of the remainder of the side. So, the mechanic having started the engine and switched the fuel cock to main tanks, vacated the cockpit as the pilot, parachute fitted after a sprint from dispersal, was ready to seat himself. Meantime the rigger who had, while the mechanic was pumping the primer, turned on the oxygen and refitted the starboard wireless panel which had to be removed to gain access to the oxygen. He proceeded, after starting up, to unplug the heavy lead and remove the trolley clear of the wing tip before arriving with a flying leap on the starboard side of the cockpit, there to assist the mechanic with Sutton harness, radio and oxygen plugs. Duty duly performed, the two groundcrew peeled off with a quick thumbs up and a grin that conveyed a wish of good luck and good hunting. The pilot, demonstrating his trust in his crew by making no further cockpit check, went at full power into the air. Crosswinds less than Force 9 were considered of no consequence – to get airborne in the shortest time by the quickest route was the sole aim.

Plt Off Freddie Lister holds up a suitably decorated trophy "borrowed" from an Edinburgh night-club. Looking on are Sgt Ball, Plt Off Daniels, Sqn Ldr du Vivier, Flt Lt Hutchinson and Flt Lt May

Two 'longest ever' records were set up at this time. 5 December 1940 to October 1941 was the longest stay on any one airfield during the war, while Sqn Ldr T F D Morgan (September 1940 - January 1942) recorded the longest spell of any as Commanding Officer. To him, more than any other, goes the credit for the performance of 43 during these days. Meeting all the operational commitments from Group and at the same time to achieve the maximum output of trained pilots necessitated a great deal of hard slogging and intensive application. The end products of which departed then to squadrons in the south! This was done, moreover, at a time when the training establishments were beginning to release a flood of both aircrew and tradesmen, resulting in a high throughput and constant change of personnel. The old, long-fostered Squadron spirit could easily have been lost in this welter of a shifting manpower whose conditions of service were not conducive to the generation of regard or affection for the Squadron. For these birds of passage were, if aircrews, mostly anxious to be off to more active theatres of war, and the groundcrews were still in the main bewildered and slightly resentful civilians, whose self-esteem had been crushed in the recruit training centres and subsequently powdered in the processing through the soulless cramming systems of wartime technical training. They had not yet had time to re-orientate themselves into a realisation that they were essential parts in the overall scheme and had yet to experience the boost to morale and self respect that such awakening to the fact that they were essential, brought in its train. Yet in spite of all these unfavourable factors, in spite of the fact that there was little in the basic routine of squadron duties to stimulate morale, it remained high and showed no traces of decline. There was always a nucleus of technicians sufficiently permeated by the old traditional way of doing things better than most to ensure that the ancient customary habits did not fade away, and Morgan had a marked perspicacity for selecting the best out of the considerable number of pilots who came and went quickly during this time, and these chosen few tarried a while, acted as instructors and flew on ops. They were the successors to the survivors from Tangmere who during the last months of 1940 drifted away to command squadrons or pass on their knowledge at OTUs.

Nor only as a chief conservator of 43's tradition must Morgan be remembered, for his other deeds were of an order that few could hope to equal. If the leadership that command implies is best to be achieved by example, then Morgan was a remarkably successful commander and outstanding in the matter of demonstrating the technique of destruction by single engined fighters of enemy night bombers.

Inherent in its design, the Hurricane as a night-fighter compared to its own disadvantage with the specialised Beaufighter or the more adaptable Defiant and Blenheim. Only in the Hurricane did the pilot have the dual task of flying and searching. For him there was no airborne radar, no radar operator to provide the solace of human company and to watch for the blip on the screen that located the distant unseen quarry. There was nothing but the lonely darkness, a darkness in which the enemy lay hidden and for whom the search was made even more difficult by the distortion of vision through the propeller blades and the restriction of the exhaust stub anti-dazzle plates forward of the cockpit. Moreover, condensation on hood or windscreen was never completely eliminated by anti-mist pastes and powders. Small wonder that under such conditions very few night bombers ever fell victim to single seater fighter pilots and all the greater glory that Tom Morgan, hunting quite alone, should have destroyed no fewer than six in just under as many months. Each one was a triumph of determination, extraordinary night vision and the essential ability, once in contact, to shoot straight first time before the quarry, alerted by the opening burst of gunfire, slipped as so easily it might, into the sheltering blackness of the night. Three of his victims went down in little over twenty-four hours, on the nights of 5 and 6 May 1941, when the Luftwaffe turned its major effort against Clydeside ports and shipyards, Glasgow, Clydebank, Greenock and Port Glasgow all suffering severely. Such losses as the RAF inflicted on the enemy, and it was little enough compared with the havoc that he wrought, was nearly all to the credit of 43. On the first night, while 'A' Flight sent five aircraft on a 'Fighter Night' (a patrol by individual aircraft each at a different height over the target area), which saw nothing except the fires beneath, 'B' Flight patrolled the approaches to the Firth of Forth, across the line of attack of bombers coming in from Norway. At 0001 hours, the Air Raid Wardens in the streets of the little Fife town of Anstruther heard, above the unbalanced drone of desynchronised engines, the unusual rattle of multiple Browning guns. There followed a flame in the sky, a flame which spread and fell away in an ever steepening arc, a flame in the light of which it was just possible to see the dim shape of a tapered fuselage. Falling ever faster the fire struck the waters, burst into a thousand parts which flickered, lingered for a moment, then were gone, leaving the night darker than before. Sqn Ldr Morgan was diving back to Drem to re-arm. Within minutes, refuelled, rearmed and refreshed, he was back on patrol and just ten minutes less than two hours after his first kill a second dark shape was sighted. Positive identification was not made, but it was too big for a Hurricane and no other friendly aircraft, large or small, were in those skies that night. Again there was no error in aim and a patrol boat off Fife Ness reported to shore that they had seen an aircraft crash into the sea. On the following night the Hun returned again to the still burning targets. Eleven Hurricanes of 43 climbed into the night, but again it was only Tom Morgan who found a target in the blackness. Plt Off Harries did make a sighting on a Heinkel but only at the very end of his patrol when shortage of fuel compelled him to return. The Ju 88 that received a six-second burst from the twelve guns of Morgan's Hurricane was less fortunate. At 0153 hours it gave the Observer Corps post at St Abbs Head the opportunity of reporting that an aircraft, on fire, had crashed into the sea. Fourteen hours later, as the kettle was steaming up for the mid-afternoon brew, the same Observer post reported another Ju 88 approaching from the north, flying in a weary and languid fashion and obviously in some distress. It was a recce Ju 88 that ten minutes earlier had been intercepted at the mouth of the Tay by Plt Off Cotton and Sgt Lister and had escaped into cloud 'with bits falling off it'. The observers at St Abbs saw it dive into the water. Even that was not quite the end of the story for the tin mugs were but recently washed up and back on the hooks when the same post was alerted to the presence of still another recce Ju 88, coming in to carry out the snoop in which its predecessor had failed. Du Vivier and Plt Off Mize, the latter an American who early on had strayed across the Canadian border, were on a

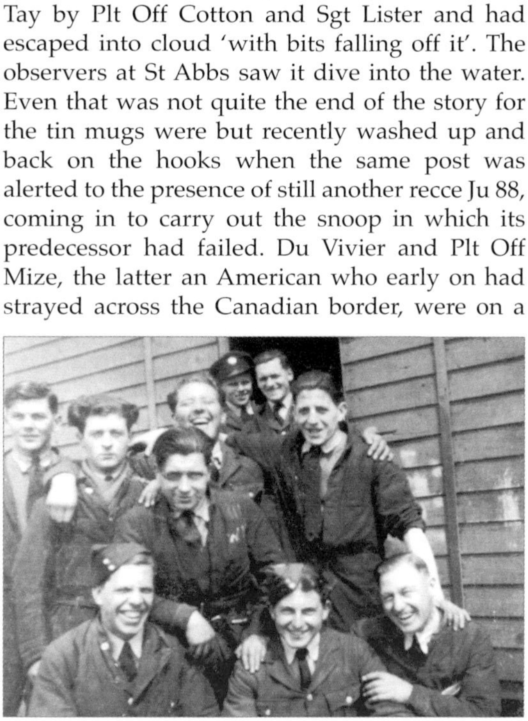

'A' Flight 'Erks' at Drem

training flight when ordered to intercept. This bomber was made of sterner stuff; the rear gunner scored hits on du Vivier's machine but to no avail, and like the two that had gone before, this Ju 88 went in flames into the sea. It made five in two days. Not very much but at least it was something to balance against the mountains of rubble and the thousands of victims on both banks of the Clyde. And if it was not much, it was still more than the rest of 13 Group combined had succeeded in doing. That night Group acknowledged 'Warmest congratulations on your good show these last two days'. Two days later came praise from yet higher spheres:

> 13 Group to 43 Squadron.
> The War Cabinet have expressed their appreciation of your Squadron's efforts on the night of the 7th.

There is a droll comicality in relating that the volume of the Official History of the War which covers the Air Defence of Great Britain does not include 43 Squadron in the list of night-fighter squadrons operating during this period. Nevertheless, the signal was acknowledged in the best possible way on the very next day when yet another Ju 88, having photographed the Clyde area, was intercepted on its way out. Sighted over the Pentland Hills it was chased by du Vivier and Plt Off Hutchinson, in and out of cloud, across the Border country to Berwick-upon-Tweed where at last, with smoke pouring from the starboard motor, it eluded them. The crew was later seen by land based witnesses to bale out and the aircraft to crash into the sea. It brought the total to six in five days.

Tom Morgan's bar to his DFC, and a Belgian Croix de Guerre for du Vivier, now 'A' Flight's Commander, both awarded at this time, were no more than was due to them.

The return of the damaged HMS *Prince of Wales* after the *Bismarck* incident was covered by the Squadron who had moved to Prestwick to carry out the commitment. From there du Vivier and Plt Off Czajkowski (Poland) were scrambled to intercept a Ju 88 at 24,000 feet. Climbing with boost overrider pulled, Czajkowski blew up his engine and was forced to land on an unoccupied aerodrome near Carlisle, but du Vivier pressed on and, though hit by return fire in the oil tank, saw his target crash in a field at Newcastleton. In it were two dead, two injured and an unscratched but very shaken pilot who on interrogation reported that 'every time the Hurricane fired large pieces (of the Junkers) fell off'. This victory brought Morgan and du Vivier level at three all in a contest in which the only loser was a third party, the Luftwaffe.

On 8 June Morgan regained the lead with another night victory that must be regarded as the most incredible and brilliant of all in one respect, for the initial contact was made not by sighting the aircraft (another Ju 88 at 100 feet) but its shadow on the moonlit sea. Morgan dived from 2,000 feet and opened fire at seventy-five yards, dead astern. After the first short burst nothing happened, after the second, during which he saw the bullets hitting the cupola, the target dived into the sea and broke up. Another month, the full moon period in July, and number five was clobbered. Two Heinkel 111s, two hundred feet above a north-bound convoy, east of Bell Rock, were sighted. As the unsuspecting bombers made their run up to the ships, Morgan attacked one from close range, with the inevitable subsequent report 'it dived into the sea – there was no return fire or evasive action, probably I had not been seen'. Probably not. Aware, as they were from their own intelligence reports, that the night fighter screen in these waters was most weak, that there was no GCI, no AI-equipped Blenheims or Beaufighters, the crews that flew the anti-shipping strikes or other night raids had little to fear, little danger of interception or destruction to face. It was a salutary comment on the exceptional and extraordinary ability and skill of Tom Morgan that at least five aircraft and twenty airmen had ventured just once too often into the allegedly safe areas of Scottish coastal waters. Nor was the story quite finished. Early in October a raid developed on Newcastle. Though not within the Sector boundaries, Morgan received permission to patrol the White patrol line south of the Forth, from where he deviated somewhat southward. Twenty miles south-east of the Farne Islands, not far from the place where John Simpson and Eddy Edmonds had claimed 43's second victim of the war, he saw a Junkers 88 at 8,000 feet. He was at 10,000. Diving below, he opened fire from astern. The top upper gunner replied to the first burst but not to the second. A third burst brought fire from the starboard wing, and comet-like the crippled bomber dived into the sea. It brought Morgan's score for the war to sixteen and a half, all with 43 – seven of them from Drem.

The tale of the six by night has been recounted. The story of the seventh is worth telling too. It brought from Wing Commander Eeles, Station Commander, the following :

> With reference to Sqn Ldr Morgan's accident on 24 July, I have no comments to make

other than that I consider this to be a classic example of how a first class pilot can attack an enemy aircraft while his engine is failing, shoot it down and force-land in the sea, and get away with it.

It had, as the foregoing shows, been no normal aircraft accident, and its finish was in keeping with the start, for the initial sighting of a Ju 88 east of May Island had also been entirely accidental. Blue Section (Morgan and Plt Off Bourne) was engaged in a practice interception with Ops at Turnhouse, when, unexpected, unannounced, but by no means unwelcomed, the e/a flew across their line of sight, at sea level. The chase at 300 mph plus, full boost, proved too much for Morgan's engine. The Merlin of that period had an inherent design weakness and high boost pressure at combat ratings often caused a distortion of the cylinder head sealing ring so that ethylene-glycol coolant got into the cylinders. Morgan's cockpit filled with the suffocating and irritant fumes now pouring from the exhaust, but he continued to engage the enemy more closely. At 600 yards return fire was experienced, it missed. Morgan did not waste his ammunition at this extreme range, but got closer and although visibility was now greatly restricted and the smoke was becoming worse throughout, made two attacks from rear and quarter. Blue 2 joined in after the second attack and Blue 1 saw bullets striking the wing and fuselage. After a third burst from Morgan the Ju 88 crashed into the sea. At almost the same time Morgan's engine stopped. At that low altitude there was no question of baling out. It was a measure of the deceleration forces involved when the Hurricane was masterfully belly flopped onto the water, that though correctly strapped into the seat, and in spite of shielding his face with his forearm, impact with the reflector sight was enough to loosen two front teeth. Du Vivier now arrived at the scene to relieve Plt Off Bourne, and he guided HMS *Ludlow* to the dinghy which Morgan had inflated, from where, transshipped to a trawler, his journey ended in hospital in Aberdeen.

When, late in July 1941, Lt Birksted and 2nd Lt Berg of the Free Norwegian Air Force arrived to join the Squadron, 43 was in the position of having, or of recently having had, on its strength pilots from fifteen different countries. England, Scotland, Ireland, Wales, Australia, New Zealand, South Africa, Canada and India from the Empire; Poland, Czechoslovakia, France, Belgium and Norway represented the down but by no means out countries of Europe, and finally let it be not forgotten that not all Americans were neutral before Pearl Harbor, and some had found their way to 43 Squadron. Occasionally they were there just because the chance of joining in a war offered a challenge to the adventurous spirits of youth. But more often there was another reason, and their presence in RAF uniform was the outcome of an unspoken but essential realisation that the neutrality of their country was a lie and that in a struggle becoming ever more world-wide, a man had to come down on one side or the other. And with hardly an exception they were good buddies to have beside you in a fight.

As early as May 1941 Plt Offs Reed, Scuddy and Mize had come, and gone to form the Second Eagle Squadron, No 121. Later there was Hank Helbock, a

Irishman Flt Lt John 'Killy' Kilmartin beside Hurricane 'FT-F' at Drem
(Andy Saunders collection)

great blond giant from a New York flour mill, whose grandfather and father were both German-born but who found that no cause to stay at home. He died in a high speed, low level stall while testing an anti-G suit at Acklington, to which the Squadron moved in October 1942.

The ten months at Drem ended abruptly and the move brought more sorrow than delight. Such is the inbred cussedness of men that even those who initially had most heartily abhorred the place and had hinted in a dark and confidential manner of the dreaded 'Drem-doom', a disease which allegedly drove to madness any who tarried there too long, were now ready to admit that lots of places were much worse. Indeed, survive and surmount the easterlies that funnelled up the Forth and the equal acerbity of Station Warrant Officer Copping there were few places better, never forgetting that only eighteen miles away Edinburgh was unequalled as an off duty centre for Servicemen.

At 1100 hours on 4 October a special train chuffed slowly away from the 'up' platform at Drem Junction. On the footbridge which spanned the track stood a lone piper, The Rev 'Jock' Sutherland, Minister of the Parish of Dirleton, Padre to the RAF Station of Drem and friend to all, played the Squadron out, lamenting 'Will ye no' come back again?' Ten years later he was asked if he recalled that day. 'I do,' he replied, and then added in his soft Highland voice, 'there was never a squadron at Drem in all its days that was quite the same as 43.'

Drawings by the war artist Cuthbert Orde

CHAPTER 17

Acklington Revisited

THE primary reason for the move to Acklington was to work up, in co-operation with No 1460 Flight, an experimental method of Night Interception. AI (Airborne Interception) equipment had at this time attained a standard of accuracy and reliability where, in the hands of skilled operators, it was a highly efficient weapon. The thirty-three enemy aircraft intercepted and attacked on a single night in May during a raid on London was proof of this. It was not insignificant, however, that this success had been registered on a night of brilliant moonlight and while radar could help enormously in getting a fighter to within range of the enemy bomber, final visual contact on a moonless night was very difficult to make except at the closest range. There were, indeed, at this time cases of pilots opening fire at unseen targets which their radar operators assured them were in front of them and successfully destroying them. One suggested method of overcoming this problem of sighting the enemy on non-moonlit nights, was to use a combination of Havoc and Hurricane, the first to seek, find and illuminate, the second to attack and destroy. The conception was sound, the practical difficulties were enormous. Perfect team work and co-ordination between pilot and radar-op and between pilot and pilot was required. Such perfection called for a greater length of time in practising and rehearsing than it was ever possible, for a variety of reasons, to find. The Havoc, a Boston light bomber converted by fitting a searchlight in place of the bomb aimer's nose position and loading the bomb bay with over 2,000 lbs of electrical batteries, was not free from technical teething troubles. The availability of Havocs and night-trained Hurricane pilots did not always coincide because 43 had still to meet its usual operational night commitments and to train the constant influx of new blood from OTUs. In addition there was never any great enthusiasm for the project at Squadron level, but some attempts were made to find the difficulties that were involved, and to experiment with ways and means of overcoming them. Not the least of the unfavourable factors, perhaps, was that during this period enemy night activity virtually ceased so that there was, to all intents and purposes, never any opportunity of trying it all out in action, when the spur of potential destruction of a night raider would have generated a keenness and an enthusiasm that, without such encouragement, was wholly lacking.

As far as 43 was concerned, the experiment virtually ended with it departing south in the spring of 1942. Subsequently the whole project lapsed and the business of night interception was left to the Beaufighter, which, like the Havoc, could seek and find, but which also carried in its formidable battery of cannon and machine-guns the ability to destroy.

But Havocs, or no Havocs, the move to Acklington brought no easing of the training schedule. In October eleven pilots came in, fourteen went out. There were two early tragedies soon after arrival – the loss of Sgt JohnTurner RCAF after a collision during a practice attack and the death of Plt Off Hukam Chand Mehta of India, who crashed into high ground at Peel Fell during a day of low cloud. Another incident that ended more happily occurred soon afterwards when Sgt Williams, an Australian, finished in the sea ten miles east of Blyth after engine failure during a convoy patrol. Sgt Joe Pipa, his section leader, proceeded to perform a feat that brought not only a commendation for a 'magnificent performance' from the AOC 13 Group, but additionally a bar to the Czech War Cross. Having seen that Williams, out of his aircraft, had no dinghy (it was lost when abandoning the Hurricane before it sank), Sgt Pipa obtained a fix to enable an air-sea rescue

Jack Reid, Wilf Webster, Morrie Smith, Ted Trenchard-Smith and Godfrey Le Gal

launch to be despatched and continued to orbit his No 2. Meanwhile in the confined space of a Hurricane cockpit he successfully removed his Sutton harness and parachute, extracted his own dinghy and inflated it, and threw it out with such accuracy that it landed within fifty yards of the floating human target. It was typical that, when finally relieved, he did not himself report this action. It was only later when Williams, fished from the water, had returned very wet nursing a cut and a bruised leg and somewhat shocked but otherwise quite sound, was the story told. It did not surprise those who knew Joe. Nor did a repeat performance, two years later, when he had tried again to do the same thing. By then a Flight Lieutenant with a Czech Squadron flying in a Spitfire, he succeeded only in wrapping the dinghy around his tailplane. In spite if this handicap he flew home and landed in one piece, notwithstanding that longitudinal control was virtually nil and the Spitfire was cavorting like a porpoise. But then it must be recalled that Sgt Joe Pipa was no ordinary pilot. His enlistment in the RAF had necessitated something more than a trip to the nearest aircrew recruiting centre. After the betrayal at Munich he went to Poland, thence via Romania to France, where after brief action in Potez fighters of L'Armée de l'Air in May 1940, the escape had had to start all over again. To Perpignan and thence Morocco in a little boat, back to Gibraltar and so at last to England, where he came to 43 during its days at Usworth. A pilot since 1935, he had naturally accumulated considerably more skill, and cunning, than his younger contemporaries and it was no odd chance that Tom Morgan invariably as first choice flew with Joe as his number two. He, of all men, was no fool at judging who best he should have behind him.

Sqn Ldr Danny Le Roy du Vivier

Together with his Flight Commander, Flt Lt Geoffrey May, Pipa had a share in the destruction of one of the two hostile aircraft destroyed whilst operating from Acklington. A solitary brace was not much of a bag but there were two good reasons why it went no higher. Firstly, the targets were few and far between. Additionally, when the Ju 88 reconnaissance bombers did come, they showed up only too well the limitations of the Hurricane as an interceptor fighter. It just had not the performance. Although its day as a ground attack fighter was far from over, a role for which its rugged construction and ability to withstand heavy punishment made it well suited, it no longer had the performance to climb and intercept high flying bombers within the time limits imposed on it by the range of the radar system and several times the Squadron's pilots had to endure the chagrin of sighting their enemy at the end of the vapour trail, only to watch him sweep eastwards and away before they could attain the necessary altitude to engage it. May and Pipa were lucky inasmuch as their victory came on a day when cloud base was at 7,500 feet and it was at this height that a Ju 88 was found ten miles east of Seaham Harbour, and duly despatched into the sea with one engine aflame and the rear gunners both dead.

Flt Sgt Josef Pipa

The second victory, achieved in spite of his aircraft's limitations, went to du Vivier in April and resulted from a combination of single-minded determination and an intelligent, indeed crafty, approach to the job. For du Vivier, destroying enemy aircraft and their occupants was his sole preoccupation, all other matters being wholly incidental. In January he had assumed command – the first Belgian ever to command a Royal Air Force Squadron – when Morgan had at last been posted to Group for a rest from operations and thereafter, leaving the routine details of training to the Flight Commanders, he spent almost

Sergeant Brodeur beside one of the all-black night intruder Hurricane IIcs

all his time waiting for the odd chance of combat. His outlook on administrative matters was one that sorely tried the patience and good nature of his Adjutants and only after a great deal of exhortation and urgent pleading did he vanish for a while to the Orderly Room, there to rush through the necessary chores before returning as soon as possible to the Flight. If during his absence from the dispersal site the slightest suspicion of an X-plot appeared on the board he was told immediately via his personal arrangement with sector. Then his return was most rapid, tyres screeching around the perimeter track, in a huge white coupé of great horsepower but not very great roadholding virtues. His approach to some things was quite unique. There was an occasion when a charged airman was dismissed from his presence with the warning that if it happened again 'I will put you on ze seven days wiz me', a saying that remained a Squadron classic long after its author had departed. Really it was not that du Vivier did not appreciate that wars were fought with administration as well as actions, but simply that he was essentially a warrior and the details applicable to the supply trains were to be left to lesser mortals. Let them get on with that, he would attend to the battle.

gt 'Hank' Wik beside the CO's Hurricane at Acklington. Note the crossed Belgian and RAF flags above 43's lack and white chequers - du Vivier's personal emblem (Andy Saunders collection)

Thus it was when not long after noon on 25 April a solitary Ju 88 came to photograph the shipyards of the Tyne. 43 was not at readiness and a section of Spitfires from 81 Squadron at Ouston was scrambled under sector control. At the same time du Vivier took off for what appeared in the Flight Order Book as an 'Air Test'. With his R/T tuned in to Channel B he listened to the orders given to the section of Spitfires and thus was able to get an idea of the position of the Ju 88. The only way, he decided, to intercept was to give himself the maximum time to climb to altitude. He therefore headed 090° at full boost! The Junkers came in from the sea, swept over the Newcastle area in a great arc and then, with its mission accomplished, headed back for home. Far below, two Spitfires in visual contact endeavoured both to climb and to stay in range, but all to no avail. At 32,000 feet, 300 mph, the Hun sped safely homeward. Fifty miles east, with the Spitfires long lost far below and behind, it was time to relax. At that moment a single Hurricane appeared half a mile away and dead astern. For several minutes a chase ensued, the Hurricane at maximum power holding the Ju 88 but quite failing to close the gap. Such a situation could not continue for very long and in near desperation, taking a no deflection aim, du Vivier fired a long burst, pulling up through the target as he did so. No strikes were seen but the range immediately shortened. As he closed in du Vivier realised that in the bustle of take off and preoccupation with the hunt he had left his goggles still up on his forehead. He pulled them over his eyes and as he did so the triangular panel to starboard of the armour plated windscreen shattered, cracking the right goggle glass, and badly lacerating his face with slivers of perspex. A second bullet passed through the shoulder of his Mae West and thumped against the armour plate behind the seat. As Wellington remarked about Waterloo – a damned close thing! Such defiance by the gunners merely served to increase the determination to destroy the quarry. The first burst of cannon must have caused some damage for the Junkers was definitely slowed. Closing to 300 yards a second burst set the starboard engine smoking. The Ju 88 dived away steeply and the smoke intensified and fanned into flame. One of the crew baled out successfully, the remainder were still aboard when the bomber dived vertically into the sea. Du Vivier went back to base, a bit more chopped off the debt.

A 'guinea pig' operation undertaken in the spring of 1942 was a trial of the anti-G suit, the product of Sqn Ldr Franks, a Canadian and specialist in aviation medicine. Not greatly different from the suits used successfully in post war flying, the initial tests were successful but frightening. No longer flying their aircraft through the seat of their pants, most found themselves in some difficulty for induced gravitational forces upon themselves were completely absent. Du Vivier reported that he found himself 'spinning wildly upwards' not knowing how he got there or what was happening. His comments in his particular brand of strong English were worth hearing. When Flt Sgt Harvey Helbock was killed at Belford after a low-level, high speed stall while flying with a suit the tests were temporarily suspended and before they restarted the Squadron had left Acklington.

First it went, for the last ten days of May, to Ford, to take part in 'Tiger' – a big Army exercise involving a great deal of low-level ground attacks – a task which caused mighty rejoicings in the hearts of the pilots, for nothing was more desirable than a good ration of *authorised* low-level stuff. During this period two of the Squadron Hurricanes were flown to Brooklands where the makers modified them to carry forty-five gallon wing tanks. It was a straw which unmistakably showed the direction in which the Squadron was heading and sure enough, after a few days back at Acklington the Squadron was sent again to Sussex, to Tangmere, where on 16 June it found itself occupying the same dispersals as those from which it had fought the Battle of Britain two years before. Its orders were to carry out intensive training in low-level strafing.

Sergeant Tony Snell was subsequently commissioned and served with 43 Sqn in North Africa
(Andy Saunders collection)

CHAPTER 18

Last Summer at Home

NUMBERS 1 and 43 Squadrons had been stable companions at Tangmere for fourteen years up to 1939. The only time during the war that they operated together was during three weeks in June and July 1942. No 1 Squadron had been back at Tangmere for more than a year when 43 arrived and had earned a deserved reputation at night intruding. Flying singly in long-range Hurricanes to Northern France, they disrupted the smooth pattern of night flying programmes, shot up any trains that might be found, generally made themselves an infernal nuisance to the German war effort at large and, by disturbing the peace of the sleeping inhabitants below brought, both discomfort to the enemy and encouragement and hope to the French.

43 took no part in this intruding work initially, concentrating all its efforts on repeated training sorties at Flight and Squadron strength, flying low and attacking targets around the aerodrome from every angle. When early in July the urgency died away (due to the fact, unbeknown at the time, of the postponement of the assault on Dieppe) and No 1 departed to Acklington to re-equip with Typhoons, 43 took over from them the role of night intruding.

The sole operational trip prior to this had been a dawn take off to attack trawlers off Le Havre. On approaching the target the 'trawlers' materialised as two large flak ships which immediately put up a fierce and heavy barrage of white and green projectiles. Surveying the scene from a safe distance du Vivier appreciated that an attack in such circumstances could lead only to loss with no hope of the Hurricane armament inflicting anything but the most superficial damage. Wisely but reluctantly he withdrew and the Squadron returned, disappointed, to base.

During July and August, unless the weather was impossible, five aircraft were made available for night intruding and five for searchlight or Havoc co-operation, while the remaining serviceable aircraft were used for intensive night training. There was very little of interest for the pilots who flew across the Channel. Caen, Carpiquet, Cabourg and Évreux, happy hunting grounds of 1 Squadron, were rarely found in use, a tribute to the effectiveness of the Hurricanes. Plt Off Wills on the night of the 24th, utterly bored by the whole business, used up all his 20 mm ammunition on a bridge and the solitary sentry upon it, a deed which drew from his Commanding Officer some acid remarks about pilots silly enough to risk his aeroplanes (not to mention their own necks) merely to knock down a few bricks and put the sh-- up a German soldier. A total during July of ten railway engines disabled was the sole result of the Squadron's efforts, balanced against which was the loss of Flt Sgt Ronald Whitten of New Zealand on the night of 26–27th.

An unusual casualty had been sustained earlier on the afternoon of the 11th. Flt Sgt Edwards, an eccentric but much liked character known as 'Yogi', (who wore a cat's head of grey cloth in the centre of his pilot's wings to show that he was a night-fighter!), took off from Tangmere in a Hurricane I for practice aerobatics. Plotted flying due south at 18,000 feet he was thrice instructed by the Sector Controller

A pair of Hurricanes fly over a line mainly all-black night intruder fighters at Tangmere
(Imperial War Museum)

to return, but failed either to acknowledge or conform to these orders, and continuing on this course was intercepted by twelve FW 190s over France. They scrambled to meet him and shot him down. In his kit was found a letter to his CO signed 'Yogi Edwards (deceased)'. It was a most strange incident indeed for he was an experienced pilot, perhaps possessed of some odd ways, but of no mean intelligence, while his knowledge of the books that gave would-be escapers details of entering, starting and flying away stolen German aircraft was exceptionally near to perfection, and one semi-serious explanation put forward was that he had gone to France in order to steal a Messerschmitt! A few of his closest acquaintances would not have been surprised if he had succeeded.

Reports on the night operations during August showed little more of interest than those of the month before. Sgt Alfred Lynds RCAF failed to return from Évreux and St André on the 5th, on a night when the weather deteriorated rapidly. The most outstanding thing that Sgt Ball could find to report after another sortie was that the blackout at Brighton was not very good, which about summed up the overall lack of incident during the three-hour long stooges across the Channel. Fortunately the month was redeemed by a single burst of action on the 19th, 'Dieppe Day'.

After the fade out of the previous build up and the departure of No 1 Squadron there had been a few days of uninspired normality, ending with further exhortation and orders to practise strafing intensively. The air was thick with rumour. A visit to Tangmere early in August by Air Chief Marshal Sir Sholto Douglas, the AOC-in-C Fighter Command, started a story that 'he had definitely said that when the invasion took place 43 should lead the way'. In the event this statement from the Squadron's first Commanding Officer came true at Algiers in November, but in the Sussex sunshine of August it was taken to mean, could indeed only mean, that the second front (long advocated as a pressing necessity in Trafalgar Square by left-wing politicians who were, naturally, not going to be in the forefront of the scramble up the beaches) was going to open up. Such reasoning was strengthened by the arrival at that time of the first US Army division to reach England and with Mr Churchill himself saying that direct help to our Russian ally would not long be delayed it was not difficult to see in everything a pointer to a sudden assault across the water, with 43 gallantly in the van. The wisdom of hindsight makes it dreadful to imagine what would have befallen it!

'Slim' Wills with John Daniels in the cockpit of a night intruder Hurricane

Accompanying the AOC on his visit was his former Flight Commander, now the Under Secretary of State for Air, Captain the Rt Hon Harold Balfour. Indicative of the continuity of tradition was a propeller from a German machine destroyed by Captain Balfour which then hung in the Tangmere Officers' Mess. Balfour said that he would like his propeller back some day; du Vivier offered to hand it over on the day that 43 got Spitfires. The remark on the return of the propeller was not meant seriously, unlike the reply which came from the heart and expressed the feelings of most of the Squadron, for sadly it now had to be admitted that the Hurricane was past its greatness. The memory of those unreachable high flying Ju 88s at Acklington lingered long and though the Hurricane might still prove useful in lesser roles, in the forefront of the battle which was the only place for a Squadron like 43 it just was not good enough. Yet, if past affection for the Hurricane was being lost, and the sprightly coquetry of the slimmer and more beautiful Spitfire had now become the centre of tempting desire, the Hurricane was to enjoy one more chance of showing that, if deficient in beauty of form it possessed compensatory qualities not lightly to be spurned and, for all its tendency to corpulent stoutness of outline had the invisible asset of another stoutness, a robust strength that enabled it to bring home its pilot long after a Spitfire equally afflicted would have broken up and deposited him in the sea.

More than one member of 43 Squadron had cause to discover that on the morning of 19 August. At ten minutes to five, twelve Hurricanes, cannons and machine-guns blazing, went in line abreast against gun positions on the beaches and in the buildings to the west of the harbour entrance at Dieppe. First into attack though they were, the Hurricanes found the

Sgt "Rigger" Hall & Sgt Wilf Webster (NZ)

defences alerted after a smoke-laying mission made a few minutes earlier by Boston medium bombers. Intense and accurate flak poured up and, during that initial run-in, seven of the Hurricanes were struck, of which only du Vivier's with a cannon shell through a non-vital part of his starboard wing could be classified as negligibly damaged. 'B' Flight especially suffered severely, five of their six aircraft being hard hit. 'Hank' Wik, a Flight Sergeant from Canada, his engine dead, could do no more than glide over the houses of the town to crash in the fields beyond. Plt Off Snell, a little more fortunate, managed to claw his way upward to 2,000 feet before rolling over and abandoning his burning aircraft above a tank-landing ship which picked him out of the water, dried his clothes and set him to earn his keep for the rest of the day by operating the machine-gun on the port side of the bridge (he claimed to have shot at two FW 190s but to have missed by a mile). Of four other sorely smitten Hurricanes that turned back for base one carried a pilot who had felt the whole aircraft shake at the same time as he heard a loud bang but did not discover the cause – a pram-sized hole in the fuselage behind the radio – until he reached Tangmere. Fg Off Turkington made a most creditable touch-down with the elevators partly missing and wholly shredded, and Plt Off Trenchard-Smith of Australia earned for himself the enduring name of 'Tail-less Ted' after returning to the owners a Hurricane on which the top half of the fin and the rudder had vanished and the remnants of the latter hung to the rudder post only by the bottom hinge and the control cables. But Flt Lt Lister outperformed the field and turned in the supreme exposition of all. Hit over the target twice his port wing was a shambles, the panels above the cannons blown off, a four foot square hole in the trailing edge took in the aileron up to its inboard hinge and the outermost cannon wrenched from its by no means slender mounting was askew, damaging the front spar and buckling the leading edge. But the Hurricane kept flying though cautious experiment on the way back established that 190 IAS was the minimum speed at which level flight could be maintained and the damage visible from the cockpit was patently sufficient to make Lister realise that he dare not lower the flaps.

So it was that those who at dispersal watched the return of the Squadron in ones and twos suddenly saw an all-black Hurricane come boring out of the mist, flying above the main runway so fast that it might have been an early morning beat-up, born of exuberance, except that the pilot was obviously trying to make contact with the ground by repeatedly jerking the nose downwards, losing a few feet each time he did so. The early morning mist had not fully dispersed so that the south-west areas of the 'drome were still lost to view and the Hurricane was still making its quick stabbing dabs at the ground when it vanished into the haze. A solitary voice, recognising the aircraft, said 'Christ, that's Freddie', but no one else spoke. There followed an anguished silence of waiting for the sickening 'whoomph' of exploding fuel tanks: but there came no sound save the drone of other airborne squadrons as, unseen in the distant haze, the Hurricane brought its pilot safely to rest.

Sensing rather than sighting the fast approaching boundary fence, Lister drove onto the deck with 210 on the clock, and the Hurricane took it. Most aeroplanes of that period, hitting the ground at such speeds, would simply have disintegrated. Others, dug in the nose, flipped over on to their backs and crushed the skulls of their unfortunate occupants. The Hurricane, possessed of no such venomous streak, just kept going straight and level, ripping open the green turf beside the runway and spewing out the brown clods to either side until, with the radiator wrenched away, it slid to a halt close to the boundary fence and the sunken road beyond. The air intake had gone, the propeller blades were all sheared at the roots, the spinner was stove in, the bottom cowlings torn. The wheel bay and cannon muzzles were packed with hard driven earth, and the port wing was a scarcely cohesive jumble of twisted metal and torn skin. But from out of it stepped, quite unhurt though a little stunned by his good fortune, one very valuable Flight Commander. Returning with du Vivier to dispersal he arrived with the flourish 'Freddy lives to fly again', which he did three more times that day, at the end of which he had won a DFC. No bad effort after that kind of landing, and no slight recommendation for the Hurricane either.

Pilots from 43 and 87 Squadrons gather round a Hurricane after the Dieppe Raid

Notwithstanding the loss of, or damage to, seven aircraft in the first attack, 43 flew three more missions, all at full strength, and the total of forty-eight sorties was the highest of all twenty-one squadrons that operated that day from the Tangmere sector.

A second mission at 0750 was directed against ten E-boats alleged to be approaching Dieppe from Boulogne, but none was seen, and the last two attacks, at 1115 and 1345, were both against gun positions on the east headland, a strongpoint from which there came all day a heavy and continuous fire on the luckless Canadians. Only minor damage was sustained in spite of the appearance of some FW 190s during the last attack. By 1505 it was all over except for the Spitfires covering the return of the ships.

Dieppe was virtually the end of the story in England. A few more nights of intruding and the Squadron went to Kirton-in-Lindsey. The 'second front' which had failed to materialise at Dieppe was about to begin on the shores of North Africa, and 43, unknown to itself, was, as had been promised, to lead the way. September was a month of upheaval as all was prepared for a journey to an unknown destination, Dakar in French West Africa being the favourite objective among the many possibles that conjecture and rumour cast up. Postings in both directions were manifold, those out including Sqn Ldr du Vivier, forcibly and unwillingly rested after two continuous years of ops. He finally departed carrying a Fighting Cock encrested silver tankard given to him at a ceremony that remained in Lincolnshire memories for a long time. His successor, Sqn Ldr Rook, had been to Russia with the Hurricane Wing in 1941 and consequently had had some acquaintance with the untidy state of affairs that existed when he came. The first hard lessons of inexperience were already being learned. Packing cases arriving in sections were nailed together incorrectly so that the bottom fell out when, once packed, they were hoisted away. Pilots, warned that they might require to operate for some days in advance of the arrival of their crews, were initiated into the mysteries of the rite of Daily Inspections, a performance that most found far too technical so that they contented themselves with ensuring they knew where the fuel and oil went and prepared to trust the rest of it to keep working until their 'plumbers' arrived.

Before long the strength of the Squadron had doubled to over three hundred all ranks, the great increase being brought about by the

Aussie Pilot Officer Ted Trenchard-Smith beside his Hurricane IIC Z5153 'FT-H' with its Australian emblem on the nose

Plt Off J Daniels, an American, in the cockpit of a night intruder Hurricane IIC - a 'Belgian Congo' presentation aircraft carrying the name 'R P DE DEKEN'

inclusion of those normally found only on Station Headquarters books; the cooks, batmen, MT drivers and fitters and others necessary to a Squadron designed to be self sufficient. Not the least of the newcomers was a sizeable detachment of the RAF Regiment under the command of Plt Off Steen. Alias 'Gremlin', a name not unassociated with his lack of inches, he was in other days an Entertainment Manager at a large seaside resort. He possessed a remarkable capability for making the whole business of ground defence of such absorbing interest that the technical grades who almost universally looked upon this business of playing at soldiers with a most jaundiced and disinterested eye, and as something to be dodged at all costs, now entered wholeheartedly into the training. As a result they became thoroughly absorbed with the task of improving their efficiency in the complicated arts of concealment, cover and fields of fire. They performed fifteen-mile marches with full pack before lunch, crawled on their stomachs through cabbage fields in mock assaults, blackened their faces and went out happily on night exercises and blazed away at the butts with Sten guns in a manner that threatened the greatest ill to any unfortunate marauding enemy! It is no exaggeration to say that the few months during which Plt Off Steen was with 43 was the only period in its whole wartime history that it would, in the event of a hostile ground assault, have given any sort of account of itself at all. It was a measure of his competence and inspiration that this was so, for neither before his coming nor after his departure would it have done anything but dissolve in disorder.

By September's end all was ready. Weeks of waiting, caused by the undisclosed postponement of Operation Torch, from October to early November, proved irksome though an eight-weeks advance of pay provided some amelioration. At last, on 19 October seventeen pilots departed to Greenock. The remainder of the Squadron went a week later, again to Greenock, to board the SS *Strathmore*, P and O luxury once, converted now and 'licensed to carry 4,750 souls'. After dark on 1 November the great grey ship passed the boom down river of the Cloch Light and nosed into the North Channel. At post-breakfast boat stations next day the hills of Donegal were sliding away below the horizon; the last pair of escorting Spitfires was turning for base. A thousand miles southward the SS *Ashland* was arriving with seventeen pilots at Gibraltar. One chapter was ended, the next already begun.

Pilots and groundcrew pose for a Press photograph at Tangmere

CHAPTER 19

43 Will Take Off Regardless

AT Gibraltar the Squadron's pilots, along with many others, were locked up in a compound, given lots of beer and told to have a good time but to be sober by the 7th. This last admonition was the only clue they possessed to their future. Life was spent mainly at the bar except for the time required to select from the hundreds of newly assembled fighters, some tropicalised Mk IIc (four-cannon) Hurricanes, and to air test them. The tropicalised version they found even slower than those they had left behind at Kirton-in-Lindsey.

Duly on the 7th all assembled for their briefing and at last the pattern for the immediate future was unfolded. The strategic aim was to take control of the entire North African coast from Suez to Morocco; thereby the Mediterranean would be opened to Allied shipping and the alleged 'soft underbelly' of *Fortress Europe* exposed in its entirety. The first step towards achieving these objectives was already under way in Libya where Montgomery and the Eighth Army were driving the Axis armies westward, the second would commence at 0100 hours on the morrow when combined Anglo-American task forces would land simultaneously at Casablanca, Oran and Algiers. From the last named, as soon as was practicable, the British First Army was to strike out swiftly towards Tunis, in the hope of capturing that place before the Germans could react in strength.

The Royal Air Force fighter squadrons involved in these plans would all be used in defence of the Algiers landings and in support of the subsequent advance of the First Army. Initially these squadrons, eight with Spitfires and three with Hurricanes, would proceed to Maison Blanche, the Algiers civil airport. This had an all-weather runway and its capture was a primary objective of the forces landing in that area. With one exception, no squadrons could proceed to Maison Blanche until it had been captured. The solitary exception was 43. 'We got a bit of a shock', wrote Flt Lt Lister, 'but I think we were all very proud of the honour at being selected'. 43 were to proceed from Gibraltar at first light, regardless of the progress made by the invaders, and were to fly to Algiers to give airborne cover to the landings. If at the limit of their endurance Maison Blanche was not in friendly hands the pilots were to bale out over the sea in the vicinity of the ships. 'This last bit brought forth much

Squadron Leader Michael Rook DFC

laughter from the Spit boys.' Additionally, a considerable force of Dewoitine 520 fighters was based at Maison Blanche, and as these aircraft were not inferior to a Hurricane (especially when the latter was fitted with two forty-five gallon long-range tanks) their opposition could not be altogether discounted, although 'it was not expected that they would intervene'. The meaning of this last cryptic encouragement was not understood until later.

Next morning, on time, the Hurricanes went roaring down the single runway, blue exhaust flame stabbing at the enveloping darkness. One by one they climbed away across the waters of the harbour until eighteen, together in loose but coherent company, turned and headed into the lightening eastern sky. For a short while their tail lights swung in a dancing constellation until to the watchers below they faded one by one and the silence returned again. The dawn rushed in to meet them as the pilots aloft settled down for their three hour stint. 421 miles, course 084 true, boost plus four, revs 1,800, check fuel, keep an eye on Mickey Rook up front, scan the sea below, listen out for news of capture of Maison Blanche, to jump or not to jump? Perchance to ditch? Across or along the swell . . . and all the time the steady hum of the faithful Merlin, bags of reassurance, never a miss, thank God for Rolls-Royce. Alone with themselves in an empty sky above an empty sea they pressed on, part of a great scheme, if temporarily removed from it so that they could know nothing of its progress for good or ill. At 0745 a signal was received at Gibraltar, reporting the capture of Maison Blanche – nobody remembered to relay the news to the eighteen men most concerned and they were still unaware of it when at 1000 hours they cruised in to a landfall above the Bay of Algiers. The Royal Navy had done their homework on aircraft identification that morning and no unwelcome shots were fired at them as they surveyed the scene beneath. All was apparently peaceful and the shuttling of the small ships between the beaches and the larger ships seemed to be proceeding without disturbance. The airfield likewise appeared quiet although there was no sign of the prearranged 'Captured' ground-signal. Leaving 'B' Flight on patrol, Sqn Ldr Rook led 'A' Flight down, took a long low-level look and landed, the rest followed quickly behind. Swiftly refuelled by a Servicing Commando newly arrived after a forced march from the coast, the Hurricanes resumed patrolling, permitting 'B' Flight, who had experienced nothing but a little inaccurate light flak, to land. For the rest of the day a standing patrol was maintained with the remainder of the aircraft on instant readiness. During the afternoon reinforcements arrived in the shape of Spitfires of 81 and 242 Squadrons, and those who yesterday had chuckled at 43's assignment were now themselves twitted for their tardiness in arriving.

Group Captain Edwardes Jones, commanding 323 Wing, assumed the post of Station Commander and organised a code of Very lights to scramble the squadrons on the ground. One or two enemy aircraft were reported but nothing was sighted and the landing of the ground forces continued without air opposition. At 2100 hrs the Americans reported that the city of Algiers had surrendered. The rising sun soon dissolved the early morning mist on the morning of the following day and the system of standing patrols with the remaining aircraft at readiness was resumed. All possible help was given to the invaders by the French Air Force Commandant, himself completely pro-Ally, and it was he who gave an explanation for the immobility of the Dewoitine fighters the previous day.

"Messieurs, we have no petrol in our tanks and we may put in enough for only twenty minutes of flying so that we do not get lost and land at Gibraltar. Yesterday the one man with a key to the petrol dump is given a day's leave and is in Algiers and cannot be found before the Americans reach the aerodrome." It was a story of initiative and some cunning repeated many times in the first few days following the landings as Frenchmen sympathetic to the Allies gave them all the help they were able to provide.

As the second day wore on it seemed that it would be as uneventful as its predecessor but at dusk, at the same time as General Mark Clark was arriving at the aerodrome in a B-17, a mixed force of some thirty Junkers Ju 88s and Heinkel He 111s came in to attack the shipping offshore. The General's escort of thirteen Spitfires broke away to attack the enemy and were joined by all available standby aircraft. Flt Lt Lister wrote: 'We were a bit late being scrambled. However, we managed to get among the tail-end-Charlies. I fastened on to a Ju 88 and chased it a long way. Everything was wide open but it was nearly as fast as me and finally I was hit in the oil tank and only just made base with a very hot engine.' Others were more successful, Flt Sgt Morris Smith destroyed a Heinkel 111 and Plt Off Trenchard-Smith claimed a probable Ju 88. Of the total enemy force half was destroyed.

On the following day no targets were offered until the evening when a solitary Ju 88 came into the area, probably on reconnaissance. Fg Off Robert Turkington, on patrol, was the first to spot it, and having some height advantage was able to dive and blow off the nose with a concentrated burst from four 20 mm cannon. It fell into the sea and the victor duly returned to report 'the first today for auld Ireland'. There was also certain personal satisfaction that the hole the Germans had blown in his aircraft on the early morning attack at Dieppe was now truly avenged. 'Paddy' Turkington was a large loveable character with the build of a second-row forward, a soft cultured Irish voice and all the charm so often associated with the Emerald Isle. He came to 43 at Acklington, one of a draft from an OTU, stayed when the others went because nobody would ever have seen *him* posted, and went for a rest finally in January 1944 with a fantastic first ops tour of 766 hours, and a DFC. After a short rest, he went back on ops, commanded No 601 Squadron, adding both a DSO and bar to his DFC but was killed flying in Italy on 29 July 1945.

At dusk on the 12th, at the same time as the *Strathmore*, which had arrived in convoy that morning, was docking in Algiers harbour, the pilots were coming to the end of a busy day. In the morning they had flown twelve Hurricanes as close escort to twenty-six Dakotas carrying two companies of paratroops to the airfield at Bone, 'a trip that caused many a twitch as the Hun was beginning to react quite strongly and this (270 miles east of Algiers) was the FW 190 country. All went well (thank Heaven) and we got a great thrill at seeing our first paradrop'. The day was rounded off with a dusk patrol to Bougie, a port 120 valuable miles nearer to Tunis than Algiers, where off-loading ships had been attacked the previous two evenings. On this third day 43 went off, with long-range tanks filled, to provide their adversaries with an unexpected and unwelcome interruption. 'The subsequent night landing that was necessitated presented no problem for we were all night operational', wrote Flt Lt Lister, 'except that the French had a happy twist of turning off the power for the flare path as you were on the approach, which didn't help.' Led by Wing Commander Flying 323 Wing, Wg Cdr Pedley, the Hurricanes were perfectly positioned to intercept a mixed force of unsuspecting bombers that flew in at last light. Wg Cdr Pedley himself bagged a brace, both Ju 88s, Plt Off Lea a Do 17 and Flt Lt Lister 'chased an 88 who got away in a cloud but made up for it by blowing up a Heinkel 111. Champers flowed in the evening.'

On the next morning, Friday 13th as some of the more lugubrious were not slow to note, the three hundred strong ship-borne party filed onto the quayside, and in the absence of all transport set off to march to Maison Blanche. The sixteen miles would have been covered comfortably in Lincolnshire three weeks before, but an abundance of rich living on a ship newly provisioned in unrationed Canada, and a near complete absence of exercise, had softened the toughened muscles and hardened feet and by the end of the third hour during which the Adjutant, misled by an out of date map, had missed the bypass at Maison Carrée and gone straight up a one in four hill, the solid ranks began to waver. Nevertheless, at 1600 hrs more than two thirds, sticking it to the end, swung through the gates of the aerodrome, lustily singing 'Tipperary' and feeling pleased with themselves. Before long, contact had been made with the pilots most of whom were located among the scattered Squadron aircraft, surrounded by a liberal stock of compo rations. The stragglers all arrived eventually, mostly rounded up by a shuttle service organised by the Engineer Officer. The Adjutant noted that 'these groups were supposed to be highly vulnerable', for the natives and French alike were allegedly liable to cause confusion and prove hostile if the opportunity offered. That night, in the shelter of the big Air France hangar, 43 sank wearily to rest. Never for a long time before or afterwards were so many people so pleased to remove their boots from their aching feet.

Flt Lt Freddie Lister

Plt Off Snell with Hurricane IIC HV407 'FT-S' at Maison Blanche

The 14th was all bustle and confusion, especially the latter. 43's and 253's Hurricanes were taken under control by the Squadron and before the day was half gone a swarm of Beaufighters belonging to 153 Squadron arrived from Gibraltar and were also thrust upon it. There was little time to stand and stare, yet it did not require more than a cursory survey of Maison Blanche to realise that nobody had ever before seen an aerodrome that looked quite like this. Three Hurricane and eight Spitfire squadrons with one Beaufighter squadron totalled over two hundred RAF aircraft and the Americans with sixty Dakotas, thirty plus Forts, Lightnings, Mitchell and Marauder bombers were not much fewer in number. All this, not to mention the half hundred immobilised Dewoitines and a Heinkel 111 and SM 79 which, filled with eggs and vino destined for Axis Sardinian airfields, had been the first prizes of the campaign. Now, looted and stripped by souvenir hunters, they stood pathetically out of place amongst the concentration of Allied power.

Whilst the technical side were beginning to wrestle with all their problems, the Adjutant and Engineer Officer set off for the harbour at Algiers, optimistically but quite erroneously expecting to collect the Squadron's transport and stores. Disillusionment came quickly, remarks such as 'feverish search all day, transport being stolen at quayside, went into Algiers and played hell with the Sqn Ldr i/c MT Park' abound in profusion in the Adjutant's diary of this period and many days elapsed before all was safely gathered in. Since every vehicle and every box of Squadron stores was duly marked before shipment with its code number A 9220 and the requisite pale blue diagonal band, such difficulties were certainly not expected and, looking back from afar, justice demands that the harassed and greatly maligned stores and transport unit officers were not responsible for the chaos and shambles into which the unloading and distribution of equipment deteriorated. Essentially the reason for it all was inexperience at all levels in planning an operation of such magnitude, an invasion on such a scale, and at such a distance from two starting points, themselves separated by 3,000 miles of ocean. The marvel was not that disorder was so great, but rather that it never became overwhelming. And fortunately there was time to learn the lessons which were henceforth applied and always thereafter units went ashore in their own vehicles, loaded with their own equipment.

Notwithstanding the lack of much equipment during these early days the flying hours continued to pile up. On the 15th, 43 escorted twenty Dakotas for a parachute drop on Tebessa airfield. The target was 100 miles inland, near the Tunisian frontier. 'This', wrote Flt Lt Lister, 'was a tricky one, as the Daks had to cross a mountain range and wanted to keep low-level. The result was that in trying to give them close escort we had to fly in and out of valleys, and as there was a lot of low stuff about we were all expecting to hit a hard-centred cloud at any moment. Luck was with us and the drop was successful – airfield captured. Airborne all told for four hours.'

On the night of the 17th the darkness was disturbed for the first time by a solitary intruder, which dropped four HE and some AP bombs and made a lot of noise before retiring out to sea, an event which gave cause for doubt as to the wisdom or desirability of packing all the Squadron's men into a hangar, which in the moonlight stood like some great lump of sugar icing, and on the next day some newly acquired tents were erected beside the Hurricanes on the far side of the airfield.

Three nights later, as darkness fell, a word-of-mouth warning was received of an impending air attack. One conversation at this time went, 'I don't want to frighten you chaps, but there are twenty plus coming in from the east.' 'Yes,' was the reply, 'I know, I'm heading west.' The ensuing raid was noisy and spectacular and if some bombs fell inaccurately those that landed within the confines of the aerodrome could scarcely fail to strike something. Two Fortresses, early hit, were burning brightly, and a few of the many small dumps of petrol cans were alight when the first Beaufighter, carving a swathe through the writhing clouds of oily smoke, thundered down the runway and climbed into the night. Two more followed quickly, then a fourth, all of them enabled to get airborne because the stout hearted men of 43's echelon had remained at the starting post even though some were bowled over by the blast of near misses. Unfortunately security reasons had precluded the Beaus from flying out from England with their Airborne Interception equipment fitted and all the determination and clear vision of their crews was no substitute for such a deficiency and they made no contact.

It is well known that exhortation or even direct orders are poor substitutes for high explosive in persuading men of the necessity of digging into cover and certainly nobody that night had made any provision for such an eventuality, but fortunately all managed to find shelter of a sort, even if in some cases it meant sharing a dry ditch with spare (unfused) American 500 lb bombs or sitting down behind 'earthworks' which in daylight proved to be constructed of boxed 0·5inch ammunition. Universal surprise was evident when the next day found the aerodrome looking very little different and it was discovered that the total destruction that the flares and flames of the raid had suggested was more apparent than real. For every aircraft (mostly American) destroyed there were fifty untouched and 43, in fact, had lost none at all. Nevertheless, further dispersal was ordered and, fitting in the move with their other multifarious daily duties, the Squadron had by evening repositioned itself half a mile from the aerodrome, building a bridge suitable for 3 ton vehicles in the process.

That night it began to rain, a portent of things to come, but not sufficiently to prevent six Hurricanes taking off to join the Beaufighters hunting the Hun who returned again to attack the airfield and harbour. Four hour patrols brought no reward and the Hurricanes landed at Blida, twenty-five miles away, as the flarepath was out of action and in addition a large number of anti-tyre spikes had been dropped. These

Sqn Ldr Michael Rook (right) and crew with Hurricane FT-Z (possibly HV560) at Maison Blanche. Note the 'Rook' emblem on the rudder

(Andy Saunders collection)

objects were designed so that they invariably rested on three spikes and pointed a fourth vertically upwards, a device that was easily spotted and scavenged up on a surface as bare of grass as Maison Blanche. Unexploded anti-personnel bombs were a greater menace but these were easily recognisable except by the itinerant Arabs who, wandering unchecked around the aerodrome selling oranges at an exorbitant 5 francs each, and pilfering any loose objects, suffered several losses. The difference between an AP canister and a tin of stew was not very marked until you picked it up.

After these two nights the raids tailed off, encouraged not a little by three Beaufighters of 89 Squadron which flew in from Cairo to hold the fort until 153 could get themselves properly equipped, and which in the course of the next few days claimed several successes, one of them a Ju 88 which was destroyed above the airfield only seconds after it had released its flares.

Some semblance of normality was now beginning to replace the first chaotic phases. Further convoys brought in the ground crews of 153 and 253 Squadrons and 43 returned technically to full strength, though still providing the station with a permanent duty crew who, on occasions, had found themselves called upon to filter 1,000 gallons of fuel through *one* chamois leather before pumping it by hand into the cavernous tanks of a Hudson en route to Malta. Or perhaps in the failing light, endeavouring to trace full forty Spitfires, reinforcements for the Tunisian front, which descending ex-Gibraltar, unexpected and unannounced, and had been dumped at the four corners of the airfield by ferry pilots who, mistakenly holding the impression that Algeria was synonymous with the mystic East, had rushed off to savour its delights!

Such matters the Squadron took in its stride as it did most of the problems arising on the domestic front, where all was rapidly becoming set fair. Enough tents existed to shelter all, cookhouses and messes were operating and a large number of camp beds had been 'won' so that the hours of sleep were tolerable. Then with every promise of further improvement nature intervened.

On 24 November it rained all day, eased during the evening and then rained all night. On the 25th it continued to rain and late afternoon blew up a gale. Throughout that wet and windy night tents collapsed at frequent if irregular intervals and the grey cold light of a still wet dawn lit up a scene of desolation. Two thirds of the tents were down, each a wet and silent witness to inexperience and the ignorance of men lifelong accustomed to bricks and mortar and tiles, the ten-foot-deep floodwater ditch alongside which had provided such useful cover during the little blitz a few days earlier was all but full, and the rough grass underfoot was tangled into a muddy quagmire. Bravely the cookhouse brigade rose above it all and provided breakfast while the troops, traipsing stolidly about their various business through carnivorous mud that sapped the very marrow from the bone, eyed awhile the collapsed mess marquee that flapped stupidly in the still fresh wind. In the midst of it all, the Adjutant received a signal 'Parachute troops reported to have landed in the vicinity – get dug in.'

Nevertheless, it was scarce light before the first four Hurricanes took off from the distant runway which seemed the only solid object left in the world – mission, patrol Bougie 1,000 feet or cloud base if lower. 43 was still coping. Later that morning even Wing HQ found itself driven to relent and to permit a search for billets to commence. The Adjutant and Engineer Officer departed at once, determinedly reached the main road a mile away and commenced to look for a better hole. They had no luck that day or the next, while ever the rain fell ceaselessly. Yet never a sign of despair was apparent and it could be written: 'Gales and rain unending, the earth is all mud, puddles and ponds. Tents down, blankets and kit awash and none have been dry for days. Everyone grumbles, but everybody can still grin; resilience and resolution abound. Uprooted and floundering in a strange land, food monotonous, bully beef and soya links, world without end. No booze and the first lot of mail has stopped – a torpedo in the *Strathallan* – bombs by night, rain by day, few tools and less equipment, oh what a lovely war! Still it could have been worse, we might have gone into France with this organisation . . . we will continue to plough and paddle on.'

On 26 November the Adjutant's diary recorded: 'Hectic search for billets – Wing HQ demand first pick of course'; the next day – 'Further mad search for billets. Mud everywhere.'

On the 28th came the first glimmer of success. 'Found wine factory, got half the airmen in, also found quarters for officers and sergeants.'

29th – 'Get quarters ready for officers and sergeants. All airmen now in billets.'

The next day triumphantly records: 'Officers and sergeants in their messes.'

The struggle was over, or almost so. Two days later the mobile cookhouse trailer was moved from the bog that once had been a camp. It took four hours to move it three hundred yards.

Ross Leeming in Hurricane HV406 'FT-E' was escorting Admiral Darlan (Vichy French) to Constantine in a Martin Maryland during December 1942. Leeming was ordered to shoot down Darlan's plane if he tried to double-cross the Allies and fly to German-held Tunisia

CHAPTER 20

Spitfires in the Spring

ALTHOUGH the various buildings into which the Squadron moved were not all 'highly desirable residences' they did at least provide weatherproof shelter and, thus released from the necessity of devoting all their energies to combating the unfriendly elements, the Squadron found time for happier pursuits. Rapidly all sections shook down into a routine that changed little during the remainder of the stay at Maison Blanche.

Operationally the Squadron put in an even greater effort during December than in November. Its Hurricanes provided patrols for all shipping in the three hundred miles of seaway between Oran in the west and Bougie to the east. Additionally, escorts were flown daily for the tireless American C-47s which took up supplies to forward bases and returned with battle casualties. The front line was stabilised by this time, roughly on an arc some twenty to thirty miles from Tunis and from behind this line the Luftwaffe, possessing several all-weather airfields, could operate freely, so that the FW 190 and Me 109G fighters virtually ruled the air in Tunisia in spite of the most valiant efforts of the advanced Spitfire squadrons whose out-performanced tropicalised Mk Vs were all too often bogged down on primitive landing grounds.

It was a constant source of amazement to the pilots on these missions that no reaction was ever experienced from the Hun who must have

Flt Lt 'Pip' Reading ('A' Flight Commander) with Sqn Ldr Rook at Jemappes, April 1943

been fully aware of what went on. Although they shrugged it all off with jocular remarks about 'being off to the Focke-Wulf country' there was no doubt that four (or at best, six) Hurricanes laden with long range tanks would have had a thin time against a mass enemy assault and the kind of massacre which occurred in reverse six months later when German transports were shot down at the rate of thirty or forty per day must surely have resulted. Be that as it may, the fact was that the Hurricanes continued unmolested and on one of the rare occasions (3 December) when enemy fighters were seen, Flt Lt Lister reported that 'three Me 109s were sighted but decided not to stay, so trip was uneventful'.

One interesting tale, arising from a Dakota escort, was related by Flt Lt Reading, 'A' Flight's Commander, who said he now knew why American claims for e/a destroyed were so high. Waiting at Biskra for the Dakotas to unload and return, he happened to be standing near an American Bofors gun when six Ju 88s attacked. The gun opened fire at the bombers and as one of the 88s pulled away after bombing, some black smoke (rich mixture) belched from both engines exhausts. The gunners danced with delight, 'We gottem boy, we gottem boy,' said one. 'Yeah, reckoned he stalled,' said another. Notwithstanding that the 88 flew off quite unscathed, 'reckon he stalled' put in a claim for one e/a destroyed.

Between 1st and 31st December the Squadron set up a record for the number of hours flown in a month by a single seater squadron; 1,400 hours were flown on Squadron aircraft and another 157.30 hours on aircraft borrowed from the replacement pool. As far as is known no other similarly equipped squadron has ever come within range of equalling this remarkable display of stamina and overall efficiency. Some of the pilots recorded over seventy hours during this month while for the ground crews the effort required of them to match such hours was additionally increased by the fact that the Maison Blanche runway was rapidly crumbling under the constant pounding it was getting from the swarms of heavy aircraft. It was being used at a rate for which it had never been designed and the change of runway surface from smooth concrete to something closely resembling Brighton beach caused recurring damage to centre section flaps, damage which was but slightly alleviated by the co-operation of pilots landing with the flaps only partially lowered. The replacement of this item was no minor task even if sufficient spares had been available – which they were not.

LAC 'Geordie' Boyd (FMA), Flt Lt 'Pip' Reading, LAC Jimmy Lawrenson (FME) at Jemappes
(Imperial War Museum)

Christmas Day did not pass unrecognised and the Arab chicken-vendors and the wine merchants in Algiers found a great deal of custom. Although there was no respite from ops there was plenty of time after they were done and on a day when news from up front was of land and air operations alike bogged hopelessly in mud there was cause to be thankful for the good fortune which the Squadron enjoyed as – at least temporary – 'base wallahs'. At this time, a

Fg Off Torrance, Fg Off Turkington, Fg Off Snell and Sgt Hermiston display their smiles of victory at Jemappes, March 1943

high class stage-show 'Revuedeville' was produced, almost from nothing by Sergeants Wooley and Fackrell. The former had a few scripts from pre-war Gang Shows and with the addition of some topical items, the 'company', never all together at once for rehearsals due to calls of duty, performed on a stage rigged up in the wine factory-cum-billet. The loan of some female clothing from French residents nearby which was required for some of the turns caused no little stir on the night and the Adjutant found himself restraining one who, heady with wine, was insisting on climbing on-stage to carry out a medical inspection on the ladies of the cast. The success of this concert led to the setting up of a cinema – the fame of which soon spread, and the Adjutant's diary for 1 February recorded: 'No wogs in cinema. Lice spread typhus'.

Regrouping by Command HQ led to the Squadron losing its RAF Regiment detachment early in the New Year. Before they went they played a combined officers and sergeants team at football. 'The result was a 3-3 draw in a game remarkable for its ferocity . . . it was fortunate there was only one casualty' Fg Off Steen, the 5 foot 5 inch 'Gremlin' was a major loss. His cheerfulness during the adverse conditions of the early weeks had been of immeasurable value and none saw him go without regret. Actually he was not lost altogether for during the next two years he was to keep appearing in the most improbable places, just as a true Gremlin should. There was a night when after dining with the Squadron he left somewhat merrier than on arrival, but failing to reach his Regiment camp, a search party set forth into a tempestuous and very wet night. Somewhere about the halfway mark there was heard in the black-out the sound of a revving engine accompanied by an occasional outburst of cussing. The Gremlin, having slid off the kerb-less and mud-smothered road into a ditch of no little depth was driving along it, looking for a place at which he might get out.

Sqn Ldr Rook was awarded a Bar to his DFC on 6 January and, as if to show their disapproval of this well merited gong, the enemy peevishly interrupted the party which was celebrating the occasion with a raid on the airfield followed by two more in the next nine days. In the first of these they set up something of a record, losing two Piaggio P 108 four engine bombers to defending Beaufighters on the way in, six others that reached the target failed to score a single hit inside the aerodrome perimeter, although the nearest miss unfortunately hit Station Sick Quarters, killing the Squadron's senior medical orderly, Corporal Thomas Lewsey, and wounding several other airmen. On the next occasion two days later when the bomb-aimers had a better night, the three Squadron aircraft damaged beyond repair included Sqn Ldr Rook's own Hurricane.

This upsurge of activity from the enemy by night was coupled with an increase in his daytime reconnaissance flights. These latter again highlighted the painfully obvious limitations of the Hurricane as a high level interceptor. '18 January, Ju 88 sighted but not caught', '20 January Me 210 seen, could not reach', '21 January Ju 88 seen but not caught', were reports all indicative of the frustration felt by the pilots. Matters brightened on the 24th however, when a solitary Spitfire was borrowed from the reinforcement pool and put onto permanent standby – after which no enemy plane appeared for a week! Brighter still was the rumour, which soon blossomed into confirmed fact that the Squadron was to re-equip with Spitfires. Thereafter, a move eastwards to relieve the Tactical Air Force of the necessity for providing cover to shipping east of Bone, an area in which the Coastal Air Force Hurricanes were no longer considered as suitable. The proposed change was welcomed with universal approval, the delight tempered for some with regret at the necessity of parting with a tried and worthy friend. Moreover, if the pilots of 43 no longer thought highly of the Hurricane there were two former ones who did. John Daniels and John Lewis who had been transferred (unwillingly) to the USAAF from Kirton-in-Lindsey passed through Maison Blanche, with their P-39 Bell Airacobras and called to renew, briefly, old acquaintances. Their blistering remarks on the performance of that all-electric ground attack wonder must have curled up a few ears if they had reached the manufacturers. John Lewis was prepared to trade his for a 'broken-down old Hurricane I', an opinion sadly confirmed all too soon for within days of reaching the front their Squadron was shot to pieces and these two of 43's pre-Pearl Harbor Americans were POWs.

The first six Spitfires came on strength on 14 February, and all eighteen had arrived by the 17th. On the 15th, Black Section ineffectively engaged a Ju 88 forty miles north of base and on the 22nd the first victory was recorded. It was one the Squadron would have preferred to do without. Eighty miles offshore, at 27,000 feet Plt Off John Wills of Canada engaged a Ju 88. On his R/T he reported: 'I've got him, the e/a is on fire; going down' . . . then there was silence, and he did not return. Grief is a commodity that fighting men must keep ruthlessly out of sight, but the Squadron Diary recorded 'the mess was very quiet this evening'. 'Slim' Wills had been that kind of a chap.

Before the month was out the Squadron was ordered to move to Jemappes, 250 miles East of Algiers, midway between Philippeville and Bone. It was to be ready to go as soon as the landing ground was completed. A small advance party departed on 7 March and others followed during the next ten days. Some proceeded by road, others flew by Dakota, the move by road being enlivened by one incident when the mobile Coles crane, negotiating a sharp and narrow bend in a mountain village, removed the top storey of a primitive house with its overhanging jib. The Adjutant, charged with the task of embarking those detailed to fly by air, found himself becoming more and more demented as his diary successively recorded:

12 March
Dakotas did not arrive.
13 March
Four Dakotas promised. Promised to do a double trip but didn't. Bombed reservoirs are beginning to flood billets.
14 March
Five Dakotas promised. Only three turned up.
15 March
Four Dakotas promised. Only got two.
16 March
Dakotas failed to materialise.
Floods now deep. Roads submerged.

But floodwater and phantom Dakotas notwithstanding, all were settled at Jemappes by the 18th. The landing ground was a bumpy, rough, wire-netting covered strip of sand 800 by 30 yards on which the Squadron's Spitfires landed for the first time on the 13th. They were followed by the Dakotas, whose pilots were compelled to land in a successively decreasing length, for the transports, unable to use the narrow taxi strips, had, of necessity, to park on the runway itself. It looked very dangerous especially when the last to land ground looped to avoid ramming the stationary number three. The Americans did not appear greatly perturbed, looking on it as all part of the day's work though being wise as well as extremely skilled at flying their transports into and out of impossible places, announced that their remaining ferry flights would terminate at Tingley.

The younger inhabitants at Jemappes were especially delighted at the arrival of the

Fg Off Jack Torrance (NZ), Sqn Ldr Mickey Rook (CO), Fg Off Paddy Turkington, Plt Off Tony Snell and Flt Sgt 'Hermy' Hermiston chat at Jemappes after shooting down four enemy SM 79s over a convoy near Philippeville

Squadron, for not only was the village school commandeered to provide billets for the majority of the men, but their pert and pretty schoolmistress was enlisted to assist as an interpreter so that she had no time to organise any alternative arrangements. Mademoiselle was generally to be found around the precincts of the Hotel Terminus in which the Officers' Mess had installed itself, where she struggled to understand the strange behaviour and customs of the English, her perplexity and bewilderment growing as the weeks passed. 'Mais le grand capitaine (the Adj) est tres fou', was said would be found engraved upon her heart.

Operationally March produced plenty of cause for celebration. As a farewell gesture to Algiers, Flt Lts Lister and Reading had on the 6th, chased a recce Ju 88 and got a flamer. On the 16th, Plt Off Barker destroyed another Ju 88, the first victory from Jemappes. Fg Off Deuntzer kept up the good work, the Messerschmitt 210 that he sent down into the sea took only twelve rounds from the starboard cannon and thirteen from the port before both engines blew up. Fg Off Lea attacked another and damaged it, afterwards receiving confirmation from a radio monitor that it had crashed on a beach in Sicily with two of the crew dead.

The high spot of the month however, occurred on the 27th when a convoy under the Squadron's care was attacked during the morning by some 13 e/a. Fg Offs Turkington and Torrance shared a Savoia-Marchetti 79 torpedo bomber, three survivors clambering onto the wing, there to wave hopefully until rescued by a naval escort. A relieving section of Fg Off Snell and Flt Sgt Hermiston were but newly arrived when the control ship reported two bandits to the east. The Spitfire's pilots turned and saw three 79s which immediately jettisoned their torpedoes and made off. The Savoia-Marchetti was built largely of wood, had a 12·7 mm rearward firing gun, but not much else, and very little armour. Hermiston engaged number two at 300 yards with cannon and machine-gun, it caught fire and crashed into the sea. Snell attacked number three with cannons only and after five bursts it too went down. He then turned on to the remaining enemy. His cannons ran out of ammo so he turned the selector to machine-guns and very soon the enemy's port wing and engine were ablaze. Helped on its way by a further attack from Hermiston, who had now joined up again with his leader, this aircraft also went in very much on fire. 'As we turned for base there were three palls of black smoke on the water, in a straight line, at half-mile intervals.' Before lunch, Turkington and Torrance, back again on patrol, added to their earlier success by damaging and chasing away from the convoy two Heinkel 111s. Not a ship in the convoy received any hurt whatsoever.

The following day Gp Cpt Edwardes Jones, OC 323 Wing, flew in to offer his congratulations. During the party which followed some of the more gay attempted to drive a Sherman tank which had stopped overnight in the square outside the Mess. Fortunately it failed to start.

Early in April the main road beside the aerodrome saw the passage of more than 200 tanks – Valentines, Crusaders, Churchills and Shermans – a portent that the now rapidly improving weather was going to bring a quickening of activity. Between 16 and 19 April the Squadron left Jemappes, to the sorrow of most, and spread themselves on the uninviting airfield at Tingley, which had been built as a satellite to Bone at a time when that base was taking a daily hammering from the Stukas, though all was now quite peaceful. Damp and unlovely, the campsite abounded in scorpions and snakes. Sgt Pendrick, a newly arrived Australian enlivened the evenings and entertained his friends by killing several of the latter, grasping the tail, swinging them rapidly in a circle and breaking their backs with a single snap. He had no imitators.

A frightening thunderstorm and cloudburst which inundated the camp one evening gave proof that the Squadron had learned much in cunning in five months for not a single tent collapsed. On 18 April, Flt Lt Lister was promoted Squadron Leader and left to command 152 Squadron at Souk-el-Khemis. 'It was a very sad day,' he wrote. The rest of the Squadron, many of whom had watched with admiration his meteoric rise from a sprog Sergeant-Pilot were equally sad. However, it was not quite the last time he was mentioned in the Squadron's history: on 21 April the following was noted :

"I visited the Squadron. All in good form. A hectic party was held during which Fg Off Lea threw a hand-grenade at a watchman's hut which served as the officer's lav. Unfortunately he did not know I was sitting in it. I was removed to an American Field Hospital where a charming nurse removed many wooden splinters from my behind . . . ."

Flt Lt Freddie Lister DFC

On 29 April the Squadron was ordered to move to Nefsa, near Djebel Abiod, twenty miles from Bizerta where, on a plain between the ruined town of Djebel Abiod and the hill from which it took its name, American engineers were constructing a fair-weather landing ground. The weather being not fair, the aircraft did not arrive until 2 May, from which time convoy patrolling continued as usual.

Djebel Abiod ('Bowler Hat hill' in Army parlance) had marked the limit of the advance made along the coastal hills by the Germans. It had been lost, retaken and lost again, being finally cleared by the Parachute and the Leicestershire Regiments a few brief days before arrival. At the top of it a W/T station was installed, the Squadron's only link with the outside world for several days, until a land line was laid. It was recorded that 'six horses, one mule and seven wogs were required to carry the equipment to the summit'.

That its months of sojourn in back areas had made it wholly ignorant of the ways of combat areas was illustrated by an entry in the Adjutant's diary:

"Bill Verney and I went forward to exploit an ASP (Air Stores Park) signposted large. We were surprised that one had arrived so soon. We got nearer and nearer the front, as we followed the signs, guns banging, and machine-guns rattling all around. We were in a valley so didn't worry too much, got to end of valley and met friendly pongoes who laughed merrily, to them ASP means 'ammunition supply point'. Our time was not wasted however as they put us on to some good things they had left behind in our area which we recovered for Squadron use, and regaled us with brandy."

The final stage of the African war lasted from 6 to 13 May. On the first day, after a carpet of bombs on the narrowest of fronts, the British armour and infantry went in an unstoppable thrust through to Tunis. That city was freed on the 7th and by the 13th the quarter of a million Axis troops had capitulated. Not involved directly in this, 43 was kept busy with its seaward patrols, in the course of which there were several skirmishes with Italian Macchi fighters operating from Sardinia, Fg Off John Newton being lost in one such engagement when the Walrus detailed to rescue him from his dinghy suffered engine failure. On the previous day Fg Off Richards, similarly placed after his engine blew its top during a chase of two Ju 88s was more fortunate and returned damp but happy.

There was much of a holiday flavour in the weeks at Nefsa. The war was going well and the springtime fields were lush and bright with flowers. At the base of the hill was a little river where, though the MO grunted dark warnings about water-flukes and bilharzia, bathing was free, and which, because Tunisia had not received the more advanced benefits of civilisation, ran unpolluted and was thick with fish. These, the purists angled for with hooks lovingly and carefully made with pin and soldering iron. The less refined fishermen went in for dams and sluices incorporating nets made by chopping off the meshed rear-ends of air-firing target drogues, while a few utter cads went after their quarry with grenades. These there were a-plenty. In the hills to the north and east, thick cork-forested and all but bare of humans, even the omnipresent scavenging Arab, were countless dumps of abandoned ammunition and grenades, and when there was nothing else to fill in an idle hour the hills resounded and re-echoed with crash and crump or the rattle of Sten guns for which copious supplies of Italian ammo were available. For a few days too, some possessed a great and wonderful collection of enemy vehicles, German reconnaissance sidecars, little fussy Fiats and even an eight-ton truck. The long arm of the Provost Major soon stretched out and took them all away but it was fun while it lasted.

The future of the Squadron was rather obscure during this period. Strong rumour, backed by those surveyors of top secret papers, the Orderly Room, was that it would return to UK where (it was said), the C-in-C Fighter Command pined for his own squadron! There is no evidence that any Orderly Room wallah ever risked sixpence of his own money on it but that was their story. The married and the lovelorn hoped that it was true. The heart-loose and fancy-free had less desire that it should be so for summer was coming and the Mediterranean area was very tempting.

The host of rumours were finally resolved when it became known that 43 Squadron would become part of the Tactical Air Force. Spinners were painted red and it duly arrived to join 324 Wing on the barren, dusty plain behind Bizerta, their own particular bit of dust being known as Protville II. It was dotted with the remains of several wrecked 109s. For a few days the Squadron became non-operational. Some pilots went on a few days' well-earned rest and most of the Squadron visited Tunis and the ruins at Carthage to find that the first had few attractions to offer and in places, especially around the docks, bore a close resemblance to the second. The best sight of the day was to see the mountains of wrecked and gutted aircraft at El Ouina, everything from giant Me 323 gliders to FW 190s. The future remained a mystery. That an invasion was on the cards was obvious, but the chances of it being Sardinia, Sicily or Greece appeared equally divided. There was nothing to do but wait. In the first days of June, the Squadron strength was drastically reduced and streamlined to assault scale. 120 NCOs and airmen were posted leaving, exclusive of pilots, 169 all ranks. Kitbags were handed in and anything that could not be carried on the person had to be left, an order which entailed the loss of the camp beds 'won' at Maison Blanche, and on the night after they disappeared the ground felt extraordinarily hard.

On 3 June the Squadron was ordered to move to Sfax. At 0600 hours on the 5th and all that day, and the next, the Adjutant spent scratching his head and wondering how he would move stores, petrol, oil and 160 men in the four 3-ton lorries which were all that was left to him. 'Here we are with damn all and very worried', he wrote.

However, by dawn on 5 June extra transport had materialised and the Squadron departed for Sfax, 200 miles south on the Gulf of Gabes. Arriving twenty-four hours later it found that the Embarkation Unit was by no means ready, so, after a pre-breakfast tour of Sfax, it retired to a more salubrious parking area in the country to the north. For the next forty-eight hours the Squadron lazed away the time beneath a grove of olive trees. Only the faithful cooks worked, for them there was never any rest as the Squadron was always ready to eat. An MT driver returning from a trip to the docks brought back a tale of strange ships that 'looked like baby aircraft carriers', a mystery that resolved itself on the morning of the 8th when, for the first time ever, the eye beheld a Landing Ship Tank.

At dusk on the 8th LST 303, with two others and an escorting corvette, passed the harbour bar and set course into the darkness creeping in from the east. All were in high spirits, though the destination still remained a mystery to all.

Fg Off Rayner explains to Flt Lt 'Doc' McNair and Flt Lt 'Spy' Eyles (Intell Off) how it got away. Jemappes, 1943

CHAPTER 21

Sicilian Summer, Autumnal Avalanche

LEAVING the LST in the Grand Harbour at Valletta, the compliment from its captain, 'The best behaved and cleanest Squadron it had been his pleasure to transport' ringing in its ears, 43 proceeded, swollen headed, to Hal Far. A primary target for the Italian and German bombers during the long months of siege, that place was in ruins. The hangars were flattened, most of the domestic buildings were heaps of rubble and bomb craters still pockmarked the earth wherever it had not been essential to fill them in.

Dispersal, several hundred yards from the south end of the airfield, was reached along rough stone-strewn roads up and down gradients that made plus-four boost essential uphill, and two men on the tailplane a wise precaution downhill. The aircraft shelters were massive affairs, built of sandstone blocks from blitzed buildings, with walls ten feet high and twelve feet thick and quite impervious to anything but a direct hit. The men that built them had humped all those great blocks on a daily ration of a dozen biscuits and a scrap of bully beef. 'Verily the modern counterparts of the slaves of the Egyptians', the corporate opinion summed it all up, adding, 'Thank God it wasn't us.'

The arrival of the aircraft, which flew into Hal Far on 11 June in company with the other squadrons in 324 Wing, Nos 72, 93, 111 and 243, also brought Hugh Dundas, Wing Commander (Flying) and his Spitfire to the Squadron, for he, the better no doubt to size up from within the capabilities of the Wing's newest arrivals, attached himself and his Spitfire to 43. As he was nicknamed 'Cocky', he had certainly come to the right place.

The degree of attention which he received from LAC Lawrenson and LAC Boyd most certainly impressed him. Detailed to the task, these two airmen, the first a solid imperturbable Lancastrian, the other a more ebullient Geordie, reacted with much remonstration and remarks about flogging willing horses, overwork and the unfairness of keeping two aircraft. Shortly afterwards they were heard to hold forth in the airmen's crew room to the effect that whilst any clot could look after Squadron Leaders or less, none but they were worthy of a Wing Commander. Following which, they devoted themselves to his interests in such a manner that Dundas was made to realise that 43 was indeed something out of the ordinary.

The 1943-44 vintage Flying Officer, who as a Squadron Leader in 1957 wrote: 'I must admit I have never had servicing like it since', was doing no more than justice to the Lawrensons and Boyds, the hundred or so men who, rain-soaked and sand-blasted alternately, were the very nexus of the Squadron's greatness. Possessed of all the inbred unmilitary-mindedness that characterises the English race they would have met sentimental expressions of patriotism with a loud raspberry, but have gone cheerfully to the stake for the honour of their Squadron. Too often forgotten, never enough honoured, the plans of the great ones and the valour of the flying men alike would without them have all been in vain.

Some hangovers from the days of blitz, the newcomers to the Island found irritating. It was as if the survivors of the siege had not yet recovered enough to realise that the hour of trial was over. Tankers now came at will into the Grand Harbour of Valletta, yet the siege restrictions on the use of petrol were unchanged; all MT was out of commission and the only means of transport for spares or long-range tanks were a few aged carts, pulled by decrepit horses. Another bane was the Aerodrome Marshal (a Flight Lieutenant in a jeep). This type, (whom 'Cocky' Dundas called, rather irreverently, the Marshal of the Royal Aerodrome) spent all his pompous life buzzing around the aerodrome and its precincts (no lack of petrol for him), grumbling and rumbling at the Squadron's dispersal methods. Two aircraft in one dispersal pen he equated with high treason, though since the Squadron had seventeen aircraft and only fourteen dispersal pens it was somewhat perplexed as to how to solve the problem. Moreover, one of these pens was a day's march from the Flight Offices. It was eventually found best to agree with all that he said and thereafter to forget it. Generally it could be compromised that things would be better tomorrow (it was always tomorrow) whereupon he would depart happily and the Squadron carried on as before.

43 Squadron, as part of 324 Wing, had now become incorporated into the Desert Air Force, which itself comprised the former Western

Desert Air Force (up from Alamein with the Eighth Army) and the British components of the North West African Tactical Air Force, ex Tunisia. Experience bought at high cost during the years in the desert had demonstrated the overriding and vital necessity of keeping Tactical Squadrons fully operational and fully mobile all the time. The heretofore haphazard methods of moving in driblets over indeterminate time were out, and henceforth a Squadron move was to be organised as follows.

1. 'A' Party (50% technical, admin, MT) to new base.
2. Aircraft fly in when 'A' Party arrive.
3. 'B' Party (50% technical, admin, MT) follow up as soon as aircraft have flown out *No* double banking of MT permitted – therefore dump *everything* but essentials.

If Sicily was never officially admitted to be the next Allied objective the operations of the Squadron after reaching Malta certainly pointed in this direction, rather than towards the alternatives of Sardinia or Greece. Escorts were repeatedly flown to bombers aiming at a variety of targets and in between there were fighter sweeps of three and four squadrons strength. After one of the latter on 18 June when some scrappy engagements with twelve Me 109s and a lot of flak at Comiso were reported, Flt Sgt M K Brown finished in his dinghy twenty miles from the enemy coast. An air-sea rescue patrol boat reached his reported position but found that the Italians had beaten them to it and Brown was a POW.

HM King George VI visited Malta in June and the Squadron joined in providing a standing patrol from dawn to dusk. During the afternoon, while making a tour of the airfields on the island, the Royal party approached Hal Far from the emergency landing strip at Safi, along the track which linked the two places. The first squadron on his route at Hal Far was No 43 which had but recently landed, with the result that the pilots and ground crews were largely dispersed. A frantic scramble ensued to get the Squadron on parade, though even this would have failed had not the royal cars halted temporarily a little way off. When finally His Majesty's car, leading the procession, came past, Sqn Ldr Rook, hustled from his cockpit to head the parade and still rather breathless, called for three rousing cheers for King George the *Fifth!*

At the beginning of July, as the invasion fleet began to load in the North African ports, the scale of the assault from the air on Sicily intensified. Lines of communication now gave place to enemy airfields as primary objectives for the bombers. With 126 Squadron for company, 43 escorted thirty-six Mitchell bombers to Gerbini on the 4th. Twelve Me 109s were seen at Augusta – they turned away. Above the target intense heavy flak was encountered, followed soon afterwards by a sighting of several more 109s. One of these was destroyed by Flt Lt G J Cox who, finding himself at the end of the action at medium altitude, decided to come home on the deck, and on the way, with his number two WO Hedderwick, who had faithfully stayed with him throughout, attacked a small train at Vizzini station and blew up the engine. This was Cox's last flight with 43, the following day he was promoted and left to command 229 Squadron. From this same escort to Gerbini, Flt Lt Peter Reading and Fg Off Ronald Barker failed to return. There was no explanation for their loss.

The two pilots had always flown together as a section since first meeting at Algiers, off duty they had been close friends, now 'in death were they not divided'. Two days later, a little man, unusually dressed for these areas in a blue tunic which bore both the DFC and the Polish insignia, came into the Flight office and announced, 'I am Flt Lt Horbaczewski, your new Flight Commander.' There was a something about his manner that suggested he was more than just another Flight Lieutenant – a first impression that the future was destined to confirm.

The 9th of July, D-Day minus one, was spent patrolling the convoys heading towards the beaches – 'not a sausage' reported. On the next day the Squadron, having taken off in the dark in order to arrive above the invasion beaches by first light, found two FW 190s attempting to interfere. Warrant Officer Webster, who three days before on a sweep had damaged an enemy fighter, improved on that performance and sent a Focke-Wulf spinning down in flames south of Syracuse. That was one up for New Zealand, Australia kept up the good work next day when the New South Wales pair, WOs Leeming and Hedderwick, sent a Messerschmitt 210 the same way after a fifty mile chase. Thereafter enemy opposition was slight, the next bit of excitement being a crash-landing on an empty but uncleared beach by Fg Off Lea after an internal glycol leak overheated his engine. He landed without exploding any mines, tiptoed very carefully to safer soil and after a day and night spent in a foxhole – 'frightened to death' he claimed – while the battle raged about, thumbed a lift back in a returning tank landing ship. Arriving at Hal Far on the morning of the 14th, he was just in

itfire Vc ES352 'FT-Y' *"ANN"* interestingly carrying red undercoat code letters. Comiso, Sicily - July 1943

Groundcrew lunch in the shade at Comiso

time to take off again on another patrol which terminated at Comiso airfield, from where henceforth the Squadron operated.

A small advance party had waded ashore and reached Comiso in time to receive the Spitfires, while the remainder, subjected to order and counter-order dutifully loaded its transport three times in four days. They thrice fitted and twice removed the waterproofing material fitted to the ignition systems of their vehicles, were routed, misrouted and finally re-routed on a Cook's tour of Malta. Eventually surmounting all that the nebulous *they* – from whom all chaos and disorder flow – could devise, they embarked and sailed from Valletta on the 19th.

At 0700 hours the following day the LST anchored offshore at Portopalo at the extreme south-eastern tip of Sicily. At 1000 it beached, the transport was hustled away for fear of air attack and a three mile march-stumble was called for until, in the assembly area, the footsore warriors climbed with relief over the tailboards and collapsed among the piled stores and equipment. 'A good job we ain't pongoes,' quoted the Adjutant. Comiso, reached before nightfall, had been a showpiece of the Italian Air Force, it was now badly shop-soiled, the hangars obliterated and the barrack blocks wrecked. At the end of the single concrete runway, close to the Squadron's aircraft, lay the wreckage of a Ju 87, whose pilot, mistakenly under the impression that the aerodrome was still friendly, had been blasted out of the approach. The Squadron pilots were in fine fettle; on the 18th six of them had tangled with seven Me 109s ending up with honours even; Fg Off Turkington badly damaged one of the enemy and WO Leeming in return had been slightly wounded by one of a number of cannon shells which had given his Spitfire a definitely ragged appearance.

The aircraft were dispersed between bomb craters: the domestic site was in a grove of olives, shared with an abandoned Luftwaffe bomb dump, some of which were 2,000 kg monsters ten feet long and four feet in diameter. Others of smaller size were impressed into use as tables. Much of the surrounding area was still mined and the skull and crossbones AGHTUNG MINEN notices still standing bore evidence to the haste with which the aerodrome had been evacuated. Further proof of this was shown by the abandoned equipment and clothing in the barrack area and before long the Squadron personnel, who had already rapidly absorbed the Desert Air Force tradition of wearing anything so long as it was not AM official clothing, blossomed forth in the livery of vanquished Hauptmanns and Unter-offiziers. The local Italians scratched their heads and wondered. July in Sicily is, of course, the month of ripened fruit – apples, pears, plums, peaches and greengages were all there for the collecting and many a strange brew of mixed fruit salad proved disappointing when the amateur cooks discovered that the recipe required sugar.

The stay at Comiso was comparatively short, concrete runways were luxuries reserved for bombers and soon the Wing went off to Pachino in the extreme south-east corner of the island where it found 900 yards of rolled dirt carved out of ripening vineyards. This was more than adequate for the Spitfires, if not for a solitary Liberator returning from the big Ploesti oil field raid which, with its fuel tanks all but dry, made grateful use of it. About this time the Americans carried out comparative tests on tail-wheel and nose-wheel aircraft and one of their findings was that a Liberator landing with no brakes would trundle for seven miles before stopping. Naturally, with brakes it stopped very much quicker, but its strongest protagonist would have had doubts about 900 yards. In fact, this particular lame duck, having swallowed all the available runway length, proceeded to gobble up a further quarter-mile of green fields before swathing a way through the jumble of

Sqn Ldr Rook has a briefing on the wing
(of an abandoned tank busting Me 109G of JG 53 'Pik As') in Sicily

tents that was Wing HQ and finally finishing up alongside the cookhouse. Whereupon, so an apocryphal story runs, one of the midship gunners leapt to the ground with the words: 'Hey fellers, chow, let's eat'.

More incident of an unusual nature followed some days afterwards as a captured, but wholly serviceable Messerschmitt Me 109 was taken up for an evaluation flight. Unfortunately for the pilot, neither he nor anybody else had informed the shipping offshore that the 109, which still carried black cross and swastika insignia, was friendly and immediately, on take off, it became the target for every gun on every one of the numerous ships. Assisted by a Spitfire, which dived through the flak to formate on the 109, thus identifying it as non-hostile, the Messerschmitt pilot made the tightest circuit and quickest landing witnessed for many a day.

On the 9th of August Horbaczewski was promoted Squadron Leader and took over from 'Mickey' Rook who went to a staff job in Egypt. It is no reflection on him and his undoubted quality that he had been for some time a desperately tired man, overdue for a rest, nor that there was something lacking in the Squadron morale and general performance. Horby's effect on things was immediate and electric, for shrewd as he was the prevailing state of affairs had not escaped his awareness. His first act was to take the solitary serviceable wireless set that the Squadron possessed from the Officers' Mess and place it where everybody could listen to the nightly news bulletins. The following day he shook his pilots up by taking every available aircraft on a Squadron formation! After some formal vics and echelons he called for a formation line-astern loop. Numbers two, three and four followed him, the remainder got a little mixed and fell out of the sky in all directions, a result which brought from Horby after he landed the observation that 'I think my pilots do not like me; I ask them to follow me and

Sqn Ldr Eugeniusz Horbaczewski DFC

they do not'. Nobody believed that he meant it – he would have been horrified to think that they had. It was significant, however, that on the next day a repeat of the loop with Squadron in line-astern was much better executed.

The arrival of six Mk IX Spitfires in mid-August was greeted enthusiastically by the pilots and not without reason, for gleeful entries in log books like 'reached 39,000 feet, aerobatics at 32,000 feet' were not lightly to be disregarded in the pre-jet era. Henceforward the normal Squadron formation consisted of two sections of four Mk Vs with a top cover of four Mk IXs. The increased performance of the Mk IXs came none too soon, for the tropicalised Mk Vs had long been outspeeded and outclimbed by Me 109 and FW 190 alike, while the latter could turn as rapidly too. The arrival of the Mk IX with its four-bladed propeller and two speed, two stage supercharged Merlin, restored a slight measure of superiority in all respects. It had not been without some significance that the only enemy fighter shot down in Sicily after the successes on D-Day had been a Messerschmitt 109 which Horbaczewski and Fg Offs Reid and Johnson caught just as it had taken off and future operations were to bring even greater confirmation. In November the Squadron's Mk IXs destroyed fourteen e/a, probably destroyed three and damaged another three in fifty-two sorties totalling sixty-five hours, while their accompanying Mk Vs logged one hundred and seventy hours on 142 flights and finished with a completely blank score sheet.

The pattern of battle in Sicily was never very complicated. The British-Canadian-American forces landed on the south and south-east coasts, the Germans withdrew from the western half of the island and, fighting a delaying battle, finally went out under a near-impenetrable curtain of massed flak, across the Straits of Messina to the Italian mainland. The Eighth Army on the eastern flank had a severe fight before they finally captured Catania, halfway up the east coast, and thereby the important Gerbini group of airfields. Thereafter, forcing their way around both sides of the mountain mass, in the centre of which Etna towered heavenwards for more than two miles, the advanced British troops finally reached Messina on the same day as the Americans coming along the north side of the island between Etna and the sea. By the 18th, the island was clear of the enemy.

The main tasks that befell the Squadron during these last days were to maintain control of the sky over the battle area, and to escort the formations of eighteen medium bombers which went, for several days at twenty minute intervals, to the key road junctions of Randazzo and Adrano, to the west of Etna. Once the enemy fighters withdrew from Gerbini their appearances became few and far between and the most noteworthy event of these days was the sight of Horby, with 'Your show is OFF' doped hastily, and large, along the fuselage of his Spitfire, formating on the leader of a bomber formation whose target had fallen into friendly hands since their take off from Tunisia. There was also some strafing of enemy transport undertaken, while a southerly flight to Malta, known as 'the gin run' helped to replenish the stocks at the bar.

On 29 August the first of four moves in ten days took the Squadron to Panebianco, one of the Gerbini landing grounds. Two hours after arrival it rained for the first time since May, making the runway unfit for landing, so 43 was sent to Catania Main to hold the fort on behalf of the Wing. Between the numerous craters made by the bombs of the Air Force and the big guns of the Navy, and around which were the remains of one hundred and thirty-two enemy aeroplanes, it operated for the next two days. On the second of these, Fg Off Snell leading a high altitude escort for a bombarding cruiser, was sent after a Ju 88 at 33,000 feet. At 29,000 feet his aircraft went into a dive and crashed into the sea after symptoms suggestive of oxygen failure. Tony Snell had trained on twins but came to 43 at Acklington after the Commanding Officer of the Beaufighter squadron at that place had considered him too short in the leg to properly control the vicious take-off swing that characterised the early marks of Beaufighter. More than usually popular with everybody he was of a calibre, had he lived, that could have designed a Coventry Cathedral.

From Catania the Spitfires flew back to Cassala, another Gerbini satellite. The motorised ground crews followed, passing, *en route*, mile upon mile of Army transports loaded and waiting to embark for the assault across the Messina Straits. Nothing bore greater testimony to the impotence of the enemy's air power than the complete absence of any attempt at concealment. It was hard to imagine it was only two years since a British Army had been chased out of Greece, harassed all the way by the Luftwaffe. Difficulties caused by a wrong map reference and the tracked vehicles of an entire Armoured Brigade deploying at speed and in no mood to give way to anybody, were both encountered and surmounted before arriving at Cassala. There followed four dusty days, during which time the invasion of the 'toe' of Italy was duly covered, several FW 190s were chased, and the Spitfire IXs developed an alarming, highly dangerous in fact, trait of engine cutting dead on take off. This trouble afflicted other Squadrons similarly and, until the cause was tracked down several days later by the engineer wizards at DAF HQ, caused a great deal of justifiable apprehension in the pilots' minds.

On 4 September 'A' party left for Falcone on the north coast of the island and by the 7th the whole Squadron was there. The move was routed over secondary roads, eminently suitable for mules in the first instance and indescribably worsened by the war that had recently flowed over them. A continual succession of hairpins, temporary bridges over bottomless chasms and heart-stopping lengths where the road, blown away into the valley below, had been hastily scraped back into place, gave cause to marvel at the Army that had traversed them first in the face of the enemy's fire.

Falcone was pleasant, near to a sandy beach, set among more vineyards and hedgerows flushed with ripening prickly pears. On the evening of the 8th the Squadron assembled in loose and recumbent style and heard its CO announce that the Italians had formally surrendered and tomorrow the Fifth Army would land at Salerno. Even while he spoke the sky was made bright with the navigation lights on the gliders and their tugs already on their way with parachute troops. So that, the Squadron felt, was that: *'Benito finito'* the last round was about to begin.

The following morning 'A' party set off for Milazzo, scheduled to embark in time to set out for Salerno on D plus 3. When they finally arrived on D plus 6 they mostly wished they had tarried a little longer – but more of that anon. Wishing the pioneering half of the Squadron well, the remaining 'B' party, firmly convinced they did all the work while the rest got all the glamour (and were not so far wrong in such thinking), buckled down to the job of keeping twice as many aircraft as usual airborne for three times the normal number of operational hours. The expected three days stretched into eight, and by the end of the octave three hundred and forty-one hours on one hundred and fifty-seven ops sorties had been totted up (plus a few air tests), and all with the ninety gallon overload tanks. 320 hours in six days over Sicily looked more impressive but that was achieved with the servicing side at full strength.

The ninety gallon tanks were absolutely essential to provide the endurance which the lengthy beachhead patrols necessitated, but they were nonetheless universally unwelcome for all that. The pilots disliked the ruinous effect that they had on the Spitfires' handling characteristics and the ground crews swore heartily at all the inconvenience that they caused. They were virtually undrainable through the drain plug, for that item was made of plastic and generally broke up on the application of a spanner. The standard RAF refuelling bowsers would not suck the fuel out of them after they had been dropped clear of the fuselage – though a captured Italian one did. So the only practicable method, bearing the manpower and time factors in mind, was to invert them and allow the petrol to run to waste into the soil. Wholly typical of the determined attitude of the ground crews during that extraordinary week was the emergency transfer of a full overload tank from one aircraft to another. It required more than combined muscle and will power to heave up and finally lock into position such an unwieldy, slippery and hard-to-handle object, for it took stout hearts of no little courage to dive under the half-raised tank and apply the shove that raised it the last vital inches, knowing that there was more than half a chance that the entire seven and a half hundredweight might come crashing and crippling down. But the tank went on, and five minutes later twelve instead of ten Spitfires of 43 were on course for Salerno.

On D-Day twelve aircraft, led by Wing Commander Dundas, went off at first light, arriving at the invasion scene to relieve the carrier-borne Seafires which, being nearer the scene of battle, were covering the dawn and dusk periods. After lunch twelve more Spitfires did a second patrol during which Flt Sgt Leighton turned back early with an overheating engine. He was not seen again, and when no news was forthcoming was presumed lost. In fact, he made a masterfully good job of ditching close to a northbound destroyer of the Royal Navy and became the first of the Squadron to set foot on the Italian mainland. When 'A' Party eventually arrived, they found him washing his shirt in a stream.

The fifty-two hours on D-Day were comfortably exceeded on the one that followed when twenty-eight sorties totalling sixty-seven hours were recorded. The pace slackened a little after that, but the next three days averaged forty hours each. The Germans had reacted powerfully on the ground to the invasion forces, but their daylight aerial effort was on a much smaller scale and none of it coincided with the

Spitfire Vc JK188 'FT-D' moves out while JK539 'FT-C' waits to follow at Salerno – very dry and dusty until it rained
(Imperial War Museum)

Squadron's patrols until the 15th, when two FW 190s came streaking in from the north just after 43 began its forty-minute patrol. The enemy aircraft turned and made off at speed, but Horbaczewski, with a long burst closing from 400 to 300 yards, damaged one of them before it finally escaped. On the following day another battle with a strong force of FW 190s developed. Horbaczewski set a fine example, personally destroying two, both of which crashed in flames. Flt Lt Rayner leading 'B' Flight got a third, Flt Sgt Webster, finding himself fifty yards dead astern of another that foolishly was keeping no watch on the sky behind, made it four, and Fg Off Deuntzer damaged a fifth, and all without damage or loss to themselves.

On the 16th, when at last the beachhead was considered to be finally established, the aircraft took off for the last time from Sicily. The weary ones at Falcone watched them go, pride in a good job well done mingling with a mighty sigh of relief that it was ended. Now there were forty-eight hours of blissful idleness while waiting to embark at nearby Milazzo. As for the tales that had come from the north, telling of the alleged dangers and hardships of the advance party, there would be time enough for that, if they were true, when they arrived themselves. Meantime, a good kip would not come amiss.

Those on the beachhead were, for their part, more than delighted when the Spitfires taxied in for the first time. During their initial twenty-four hours after landing, they had had good cause to wonder if all they would ever see was an Italian version of Dunkirk.

Delayed for three days in their embarkation from Milazzo because the allotted ships were switched to Tripoli, the manner of their arrival had been equally unpropitious. The beach was under sporadic shellfire as the LST ran in, and the first person to address them when the bow ramp went down was a harassed Staff Major inquiring if they were the 7th Armoured Division, whose reinforcing presence was at that hour both expected and necessary. His reaction on hearing the identity of the newcomers was a heartfelt invocation of the Almighty, an expression doubtlessly excused at the seat of the Recording Angel, for in all truth the arrival of half of 43 Squadron at that precise moment offered neither aid nor encouragement to those charged with ensuring that the entire Salerno landing operation did not finish up in the sea whence it had begun. 'Avalanche', in fact, was threatening to become a disastrous landslide.

To the south the solitary American Division, the 36th, was all but split in two by a German thrust coming down either side of the Sele river. The British 56th and 46th Divisions, who made up the greater part, at this stage, of the American Fifth Army, were being equally hard pressed. The former had been pushed out of the key junction of Battipaglia, the latter could make little headway in their attempt to get through the defiles in the hills that would lead them on to the flat land south of Naples. The landing area, semi-saucer shaped and ringed by hills, was under constant enemy surveillance and his artillery, checked only by the necessity of dodging the overwhelming counter-fire of the Royal Navy's big guns, ranged with accuracy on everything that moved. One of the three landing strips prepared by the engineers of the American Army, Tusciano, to which the advanced half of the Squadron proceeded, took its name from the small river that ran into the sea nearby, although for the benefit of control it was less tongue-twistingly called 'Roger'. Nobody required to be told to dig in when the landing strip was reached, although the excavating had not got very far when the arrival, on the far side of the road, beside the dispersal and little more than a hundred yards off, of the entire impedimenta, guns, limbers and quads of a battery of the Royal Horse Artillery (a unit of the longed-for 7th Armoured Division incidentally), provided a good excuse for leaning temporarily on the handle of the spade. The sight was also welcome inasmuch as, so argued the innocents, that if such a unit could be going into reserve, the situation must be well in hand.

This blind optimism vanished ten minutes later, blown away on the blast of the first cordite charge, smothered by the tearing, rushing sound of the first shell speeding overhead. The Gunners had gone, not into reserve, but into action. It was fully four hours later before they got the command to cease fire. There was nothing for the unhappy, unfortunate airmen to do but shelter as best they could from the continual shock and crash from the muzzles of the 25-pounders. Their position so close up was, as any old soldiers would have told them, the one for optimum discomfort and din.

Hot and dusty, Spitfire Vc 'FT-F' taxies out while groundcrew (tin hat at the ready) watches.

Fraternisation that evening with the now silent artillery men elucidated the information that one of the several targets of the afternoon had been a force of enemy infantry forming up for a counterattack at a mere 3,000 yards range. Double guards were posted at night and many an unsleeping eye kept apprehensive watch on the fields of waist-high tobacco plants that rolled away eastwards from the edge of the orchard of apple and walnut trees in which the Squadron was entrenched. All through the night there came, above the rumble and rattle of the battlefield, the better known sound of friendly Wellingtons, flying in from their North African bases, to keep up the bombardment of the Germans occupying Battipaglia. The breakfast time queue in the morning was interrupted by three formations of twelve Mustangs which began from out over the sea that looked suspiciously like a dive-bombing attack on the airstrip. Actually they were bang-on target and continued the dive inland before letting go their bombs. All the same, it required no involved calculation of height and speed and trajectory to conclude that the target was not so far away.

In point of fact though, this day marked the end of all doubts as to the outcome of the battle. Though it was not immediately obvious the Germans counterattacked strongly at two places at first light. On this day the mind of the German C-in-C was persuaded that he could no longer continue 'in the face of overwhelming naval gunfire which made all movement impossible within the coastal area' to withstand the assault. At far off Frascati, Field Marshal Kesselring granted permission for a systematic and fighting withdrawal to the line of the Volturno river, twenty miles north of Naples.

After their arrival at Tusciano, the main activity for the Spitfires continued to be beachhead area patrols. Little enemy activity was manifest, but an attack by four FW 190s on the airstrip one afternoon was followed the next day by one at breakfast time and a second in the late morning. This last attack coincided with the movement of the newly arrived 'B' Party from the beach to Tusciano. Misrouted to Montecorvino aerodrome, the convoy was doubling back when the whole sky was laced by Bofors fire. The leading dispatch rider, previously remarked upon as looking like a submarine, so immersed was he in dust, drove his motorcycle into a ditch before taking cover and several other rapid dismountings from the back of the transports were reported.

The latest arrivals noticed the great depths to which the earlier party had dug in, and knowing their inherent lack of desire for such hard work, concluded that perhaps there was some truth after all in the tales they had heard. Very soon afterwards they were digging themselves in. Yet another dive-bombing attack on the next morning scored two direct hits on 'B' Flight's dispersal and wounded LACs Thompson and Massie. The runway remained serviceable, a fact appreciated soon afterwards by a B-25 bomber of the USAAF which made use of it to bring urgent medical aid to a badly wounded air gunner. Although in much pain from a great gash ripped by flak fragments in the region of the groin, he could still remark, in the slow drawl of the Southern States, 'That it mighta' been a lot worse, it could have gone the other way and taken off ma John Thomas'.

On the first day of October it was reported that Naples was in Allied hands. The Commanding Officer of 43 Squadron, accompanied by 'Spy' Eyles, Intelligence Officer, therefore set out by jeep for what he euphemistically called a reconnaissance but which was not altogether unconnected with the recent demise of the only wireless set capable of receiving the BBC and the total absence of vino throughout the Squadron. Some way from the centre of the town he was halted by friendly but frantic Italians. Polish-Italian relationships being finally established via some peculiar English grammar, the point was taken that a German tank was covering Horby's intended line of advance. Never one to run from such a situation, he scouted around until he located a troop of Sherman tanks from the 7th Armoured Division engaged at that time in clearing the city. With their aid and the local inhabitants' knowledge of back alleyways and one-way streets, the German tank (a Mk VI Tiger, carrying an 88 mm gun) was successfully attacked and disabled. Horbaczewski returned to base, the back-seat filled with a walnut-cabinet radiogram and the observation that the next time he heard that Naples had fallen he would not be in such a hurry to believe it.

Among the plums that fell with the capture of Naples, and the subsequent advance northwards, were two all-weather aerodromes. To one of these, Capodichino, 324 Wing was ordered to move on 4 October. But on the 3rd it rained. By the 7th the Adjutant was entering in his book 'Floods 6 inches deep, help!' Not until the 11th, when twenty-four hours of dry weather offered a half chance of success, and a forecast of more rain approaching threatened a 100 per cent bog down until next spring, did the Spitfires move off. Even so, with the runway spotted with patches of very soft earth, it required a bit of luck, judicious use of the throttle and elevator trim hard back initially before, one by one, the pilots eased their wheels off the cloying gluepot and made for the friendlier turf at Capodichino.

The remainder of the Squadron followed apace by road, the entire forty miles of the journey being strewn with the wreckage and the uselessness of war. In one small field were grouped six Panzers, their slim-barrelled guns pointing uselessly skywards, looking for all the world like evil and obnoxious beetles that had huddled together for companionship in death. Already the red rust was bubbling through the blackened paint. The farms and little hamlets were all quite wholly wrecked. In some, the erstwhile inhabitants had already returned and, pausing in their grubbing among the ruins, gazed at the passing convoy with eyes stripped of all emotion. In them, there was neither love nor hate nor anything but the deep blankness of utter despair. The Bay of Naples had none of the poster-blue about it under the leaden sky that day, as heading northwards the lorries debouched from the hills at Nocera and pushed on past Pompeii and up the autostrada. Already the Liberty ships were unloading among the wreckage in the harbour. The Germans had considered that they had made it unusable for at least two months, the Royal Engineers and the Navy had it operable in a week. So at last to Capodichino, where the old familiar sight of hangars blasted to steel skeletons, buildings tumbled and wrecked, and the lumps of bent metal in which once men had flown were everywhere to be seen. But at least there was some grass and already the PSP was going down to make a runway.

Just two days after the Squadron got to Capodichino, Sqn Ldr Horbaczewski was posted away to the United Kingdom. 'We are all quite stunned,' the Adjutant wrote in the Squadron diary – "Dear little Horby, with the heart of a lion and the eyes of a hawk. In the short time he has been with us he has endeared himself to all, and is highly respected by all. His energy, zeal and quiet but firm grip on the Squadron have made him an ideal Commander." To which sentiments none would have hesitated to add a fortissimo 'Hear! Hear!'. By any standard Horby was a most remarkable man, possessed of that intangible characteristic that made disciples out of subordinates, turned obedience into devotion and evoked a response immeasurably greater than mere respect for his obvious quality. He rarely gave anybody orders. A request, approaching an apology at times, in his imperfect English, accomplished as much, for not to do what he asked was impossible. He was that sort of man. Once he said that when the Germans were finished he would take 43 with him to drive the Russians out of Poland, 'otherwise we shall never be free'. This, be it remembered, in the year when the bejewelled Sword of Stalingrad was being forged in Sheffield and blind adulation of all things Russian followed upon the success of the Red Army. It was a measure of Horby's mystique that the Squadron would have gone with him. Indeed, had he asked it to accompany him to storm the Gates of Hell there would have been none dragging their feet behind him in the assault, and few who would have given much for the Devil's chances of avoiding defeat.

His qualities of leadership were no less marked in the air. He had the uncanny eyesight of all great fighter pilots and could identify enemy aircraft at distances where to lesser mortals they were but indeterminate blobs, or just scratches on the perspex hood. If he hated the Germans and Russians as much as he did, it was because he loved Poland so much and, like so many of his fellow countrymen better versed in mid-European history than the more insular British, he was cast in the role of unhappy prophet. Perhaps that was why, though he smiled a lot, he seemed loaded down with sadness.

Anyway, he was destined neither to see his prophecies fulfilled, nor to witness the betrayal of his unhappy country by an American President convinced he could handle the Russians, for in August 1944, by which time, promoted again, he was Wing Commander Flying to a Polish Mustang Wing, he was killed in action above the battlefields of Northern France. On a flight not long before he died he landed to investigate one of his formation which he had seen crash and overturn. It necessitated side-slipping into a rough meadow that measured just 300 yards between the boundary hedges, and flying out again minus parachute with the concussed, semi-conscious pilot replacing the seat cushion. Not everybody would have been sufficiently concerned for one crashed pilot to contemplate such a manoeuvre in so confined a space – fewer would have attempted it, and had the skill to get away with it. But then, as ought by now to have been made abundantly clear, Wing Commander Eugeniusz Horbaczewski DSO DFC* VM KW***, the little Pole with the great heart and 16 enemy aircraft destroyed, sometime Commanding Officer of 43 Squadron, was no ordinary man.

Wing Commander Eugeniusz
Horbaczewski DSO DFC* VM KW***

CHAPTER 22

Rome via Anzio

ON arrival at Capodichino (invariably shortened, colloquially to Cappo) the Squadron stowed away its tents for the first time since the previous April and retreated into billets, a move which the autumnal weather made not unpopular. The officers went into an eight-roomed villa from which all glory had departed and the remainder of the Squadron were to be found in a school, both buildings forming part of a rather grubby but extremely friendly village, Casavatore, which lay about half a mile north of the aerodrome.

Liaison with the villagers proceeded apace. A small piece of soap handed over to one of the many, untidy looking 'lavarebints' who touted for customers outside the school gate was sufficient to ensure a high-class, same day laundry service. The soap of course was sold on the black-market and the clothes washed with nothing more than water and copious elbow grease; all the same they came back more khaki than khaki. Free issue cigarettes (unsmokable) and ration chocolate (uneatable) were exchanged for vino or bartered for fresh eggs, such business being often conducted in one of the many little smoky cafés that were disposed around the unpretentious village square, in which some rare parties were held. Among these unusually friendly surroundings then the last months of the year were spent, a period marked by much illness, successful combat, and postings. Replacing Horby came Flt Lt Parrott, christened Peter but obviously, never known as anything but Polly. He had flown with 145, alongside 43 at Tangmere in 1940, so was not a complete foreigner. Promoted to Sqn Ldr three days after arrival he promptly marked his elevation by going into hospital with malaria. Infective hepatitis, the clinical name for jaundice also smote the ranks of the Squadron heavily at this time and during late October nearly half the pilots, the NCOs i/c both flights, and the Adjutant were all absent.

Sqn Ldr Peter 'Polly' Parrott DFC

The airmen gleefully attributed the higher incidence of the disease among the NCOs and officers as due to the excess of spirits (one bottle per month!) which they received from NAAFI bulk supplies. Alas for the airmen's haloes, they were subsequently shattered by post-war research which showed the corporate use of cutlery and crockery to be the chief cause for the uneven spread of the disease. Equally scandalous was the suggestion made good-humouredly to Flt Lt McNair, who was posted back to UK around this time, that he was taking himself off before he became the first Medical Officer in history to have every one of his patients in hospital. 'Doc' McNair had served the Squadron well, in spite of a naturally wild temperament that at times made life difficult for the more serious minded.

November was a month of success the like of which had not been recorded for a long time, and by its end fourteen enemy aircraft (all bar one a single-engined fighter) had been destroyed, with three more probables and another three damaged; all for the loss of Fg Off Norman Craig of Australia who disappeared on a dawn patrol on the 15th and WO Smith who baled out two days earlier near Venafro and became a POW. There was some poignancy in this latter loss for Smith was more than tour-expired but had delayed his departure until some of the jaundice victims were wholly recovered.

The first victories came on the second day of the month. A Messerschmitt 109, attempting to interfere with escorted Baltimores, was disposed of in the morning, and after lunch two others were destroyed. Another one confirmed, one probable, one damaged followed on the 6th. A three day bonanza began on the 10th when a bomb-line patrol found twelve Me 109s orbiting Sessa Aurunci, and destroyed two with one probable and one damaged. Next day a Ju 88 at the end of a vapour trail at 25,000 feet was overhauled by 'Paddy' Turkington and sent down in flames. Yet another bomb-line patrol on the following morning, meeting a mixed force of 109s and 190s, sixteen strong, which were prepared to stay

Fg Off Bill Reid DFC

and contest the day, finished with three more 109s and a probable 190, those responsible, WO Hedderwick, Flt Sgts Booth, Leighton and Smith providing thereby quadruple excuse for livening up the Sergeants' Mess that night. Proof that the subsequent hangovers were not long protracted was provided by Hedderwick, a few days later joining Fg Off Reid in another double destruction of 109s.

It was typical of the way that luck came very much in cycles, that following this purple period when two hundred odd hours had produced fourteen victories (almost the total for the entire Wing during this time) that the next eight weeks recorded one solitary 109 as the total reward for nine hundred and sixty hours, the Squadron's patrols on several occasions being just too soon or too late to coincide with enemy activity. This last item was in any case becoming a decreasing quantity, since no squadrons at all saw much of the enemy anyway. Plenty of times nobody saw anything else either, as on the last day of 1943 when it was recorded that 'the weather ten-tenths over battle zone in morning spread to the aerodrome later in the day. Escort to Bostons attempted but all returned without bombing as cloud over target was ten-tenths at zero feet.' The next day the same record merely said, in capitals, NO FLYING. Boxing Day a week before had had a truly nautical ring, "We fear the worst, runway is u/s, rain all night and all today. Hourly we expect the hoisting of the black ball and the sounding of 'anchors down'." By 3 January it was fine enough, however, for the last remaining Spitfire Vs to be flown away to Bari where they were exchanged for the infinitely superior Mk IXs with which alone the Squadron henceforth operated.

Spitfire Vc (Tropicalised) of 'A' Flight raising the dust while taxying at 'Roger' airstrip, Tusciano, on the Salerno beach-head - September 1943

The inclement weather was in no way permitted to dampen the customary Saturnalian revelry, a feast that had additional significance on this occasion for it coincided with the departure of the last remaining pilots who had come overseas with the Squadron. By early January they had all left; Rayner, Reid, Smith, Deuntzer, Torrance, Turkington, Webster, and Hedderwick, the last three dating back to far-off Acklington had between them amassed over two thousand two hundred hours on ops, and the others were all around the same mark. Of the original twenty-six pilots, eight had died and one was a POW. The ground crews, many of whom had known these departing stalwarts since they were day-old chicks were sorry to see them go for together they had journeyed far and achieved much, but there was compensatory comfort to be found in the quality and outlook of their successors, among whom an increasing proportion of Australians and New Zealanders brought with them the freshness of outlook and sunshine of the south.

10 January brought the first rumblings of a move. On the 15th 'A' Party went, the aircraft followed at dawn next day, and by the same evening all were arrived at the new base, an area of scrub and tree-covered sand dunes half a mile from the sea and one mile north of the River Volturno. It was called Lago (Italian for 'lake') a name that was to prove not wholly inappropriate. It had a 1,100 yard PSP runway, with tight dispersal facilities and acres of woodland for the tents, in which a very high degree of comfort was soon achieved, draught-proofing, oil heating and electric lighting all being much in evidence to combat the Italian winter weather. Palpably the errors and ignorance of Algiers had long since been left behind.

The reason for the move became obvious five days after arrival when at 0300 hours on Friday 21 January one British and one American division went ashore at Anzio, thirty miles south of Rome and sixty miles in the rear of the main battle line. This landing, first envisaged and subsequently strongly urged by Winston Churchill, was an attempt to end the stalemate that had developed in the mountains at Cassino where, in the face of a determined enemy occupying superb defensive positions, the Allied

Group Captain Duncan Smith, Commander 324 Wing, briefs 43 Squadron pilots at Lago - April 1944

advance towards Rome had come to a definite halt. It is possible that if the Anzio operation had been pursued in a more determined fashion the threat to, if not the actual physical severance of Highways 6 and 7, the two major supply routes for the German Army at Cassino, might have compelled them to withdraw. In the event the whole landing, suffering from overcautious leadership, bogged down and was subsequently so heavily counterattacked that the entire beachhead was for a while in jeopardy. Eventually the position was stabilised but until May it remained as nothing more than a potential springboard for a breakout.

Nevertheless its protection from the air required all the attention and effort of two out of the three Spitfire Wings which were controlled by the 12th Tactical Air Command, and this overall demand set the pattern of operations for the next four months. Two days in three, Anzio patrols, eighty-minute, thirty-gallon long-range tank sorties were flown. On the odd day, two and a half hour bomber escort missions were interspersed with bomb-line patrols in the Casino area. There was little contact made with the enemy in the air during all this time and the only positive victory, an Me 109 which fell to the newly commissioned Plt Off Johnson, was offset by the loss in the same action of Fg Off P J Richards. Several other enemy aircraft were damaged on various occasions and a fair amount of damage was sustained from allegedly friendly flak above the beachhead. An unauthorised return from Anzio via Highway 6, instead of by the normal overwater route led to an attack on 'something resembling an ammunition dump'. Intense enemy fire was encountered; WO Cyril Luke was killed and Flt Sgt Henry Booth, staggering to the coast in his damaged aircraft baled out close to a cruiser of the Royal Navy but was dead when pulled out of the water.

A further hazard, a by-product of the very wet February weather (the aerodrome was unusable for four days, '100 per cent rum issue to all ranks, things must have been bad' was noted on one of them) was an outbreak of engine failure caused by water contamination in the fuel. Although every precaution was taken to obviate this danger several pilots had to force-land on the beachhead emergency strip at Nettuno. Fortunately no casualties resulted from it all, although one remarkable incident did when the Engineer Officer of an adjacent squadron, on hearing that five out of a patrol of eight had forced-landed at Anzio, took himself off to that place in an old Spitfire V. Although his sole flying experience was a few hours in a captured enemy biplane of Tiger Moth standards, he successfully reached and landed at Anzio, firing all the ammunition en route just to find out what it felt like. Remedying the trouble in four of the grounded aircraft he sent the fifth pilot back to Lago in the Spitfire V and was preparing to fly the remaining Mk IX back himself when the arm of the law intervened.

In spite of the continuing and heavy flying commitments, Lago was not all unrequited toil and the daily output of effort was matched by a correspondingly high outburst of conviviality at night. As few people considered a day or evening in Naples was worth the discomfort and roughness of the thirty-mile night return journey over semi-ruined roads, and sought their pleasure nearer home, Lago become the perfect forcing ground for the growth of the communal spirit. The concert party of a year earlier at Algiers came back with a passable show, presented in an open air theatre that boasted an orchestral pit, excavated in front of the stage; frequent visits by the Army Cinema Unit also began. Thereafter the evening often continued with a visit to the nearest mess where some very fine vermouth, obtained in large quantity from Naples, was in copious supply. This tipple was the basis for a great many long drawn-out evenings, two outstanding ones being linked with the departure of old friends. Flt Lt Taylor went home to Australia at the end of his third ops tour. Sqn Ldr Parrott handed over to Laing-Meason in March, the latter's post i/c 'A' Flight being occupied by another Aussie, Flt Lt Terry, who, all of twenty-eight years of age was promptly christened granddad. Wing Commander Dundas, another to bid the Squadron farewell in these days made his final exit from the Sergeants' Mess memorable by tripping, in the blackness of a moonless early morning, over an unsighted fire extinguisher and ending in a thicket of thorn. His successor, Wing Commander Loudon, having prior affiliations with 72 Squadron, did not fly with 43. Perhaps that was a mistake for three weeks after his arrival he suffered engine failure when on a long range escort many miles north of Rome and, baling out, was captured. In his shoes there arrived no less a personage than Wing Commander du Vivier and naturally there was no question where his affections lay. He too however, was unlucky at the start for on his first flight, in a very new Spitfire bearing in place of Squadron letters, his own initials, he finished with a broken undercarriage after misjudgement of the final approach. Wholly inconsolable at the time he eventually recovered and remained to lead the Wing with distinction in the busy weeks that followed his arrival.

Sqn Ldr P B Laing-Meason DFC

The merry month of May brought much with it. The sun shone more and the winds blew warmer. Nightingales sang in the trees that had not been cut down to fuel the cookhouse fires. Slit trenches dried out and flowers bloomed among the hedges. And as nature stirred so did the rumours of the big push that at last would take us through to Rome. Almost daily the heavies of the USAAF went formating northwards, and in the too short evening hour before the early dusk a cricket bat and ball, found one knew not where, were put to use. Australia has produced a countless host of great fast bowlers but never one who manifested a greater threat to life and limb than Warrant Officer 'Happy' Harris, seventy-five inches of sinew and muscle, who bowled mighty fast on a pitch cut and serrated by six inch deep tyre marks. If, perhaps, receiving an almighty bone crushing blow from one ball that flew from a bump like a cannon shell, the pained batsman withdrew a little from the threat of the next, Happy would throw back his mane of flowing hair, hurl the ball that much more venomously and ask how England ever hoped to win back the Ashes with chicken-livers like that. Perhaps it wasn't really cricket but it was a fine school for finding out the depth of a man's courage.

Then there was the incident that began with WO Prior, the Squadron's Discip, shooting with a 12-bore at flights of wild duck which nightly flew inland from the coast. Successive evenings brought a multiplicity of imitators until the sunset hour found fifty or more marksmen banging away with Sten guns and rifles. It did not take long for the racket to come, in the most literal sense, to the ears of Group Captain Duncan Smith who promptly intervened to order a cease fire.

Meantime Flying Officer Cunningham found himself shot at, one afternoon off Anzio. Two days earlier in the same place he had damaged a Messerschmitt 109. Now he found his own aeroplane damaged to such an extent that the elevators gave no response to stick movement. Fortunately the trimming tabs were still operating so he set course for an emergency landing at Nettuno but six hundred yards offshore these subsidiary control surfaces packed up too and he was compelled to ditch. He left the Spitfire's cockpit and, to quote an eyewitness, 'began to kick up a hell of a row and shout for rescue' until, suddenly, discovering that he could touch the bottom with his feet (being by good fortune at a place where the beach ran out flat for a long way) was able to wade unassisted ashore. At 2300 hours on 11 May, a two-thousand gun barrage started the offensive that was finally to break the Germans along the Cassino line. A week later, a hurried call to all Section NCOs sent them hot foot to the Adjutant's lorry-cum-office. The orders were brief and uncomplicated: the Squadron must be ready to move to the Anzio beachhead at dawn the following day. Before it was dark, a mere ninety minutes later, the Daily Inspections for the morrow were done and signed for, and the Flight's equipment stowed aboard the transport. Such a noble effort deserved a better requital than it got. The dawn departure was put back to 1030, then 1230 and finally 1530.

When the Squadron in convoy arrived at Naples neither British nor American Military Police knew of the 'Oklahoma' transit camp to which it had been told to report. Eventually somebody suggested a site five miles out of town. 'Sure bud', said an American inhabitant of the place when the Adjutant inquired there on arrival, 'this is Oklahoma transit camp OK but we ain't gonna start erecting it until next Monday'. Frustrated, and now in a steadily increasing downpour the weary warriors backtracked to Naples, finally holing up for the night with their vehicles packed, in the dry, beneath the arched cloisters of the one-time Ducal Palace. The following night was spent *en route* to Anzio, aboard Tank Landing Craft, blunt nosed square ships, smaller than the by now familiar Landing Ship Tank, which surprisingly behaved better in the medium swell than their aspect ratio might have suggested. Under a cloudy, starless sky the little group of ships went steadily on. The only sound to disturb the night, in which men tried to sleep as best they might in the cramped confines of the driving seats or sprawled among the loaded equipment, being the throb of the diesels in the stern and the constant splosh of the water as the waves smacked against the bow ramps and sent a continuing spray battering onto the steel roofs of the driving cabs.

The peaceful nature of the arrival the following day, between the lines of billowing smoke pots that kept the anchorage hidden from the enemy on either flank, was a surprise to most. The tales that had come from Anzio during the days of crisis in February had invested the beachhead from afar with the aura of something approaching Verdun or the Somme. Notwithstanding that two different detachments forming part of a Wing servicing party had both survived three weeks on the airstrip in earlier and more dangerous days, there were many surprised to find that the entire area was not under a constant rain of enemy shellfire.

It was true, of course, that no part of the beachhead was beyond the range of the enemy's guns; this being no doubt a major factor in producing the remarkable spirit of comradeship that existed there. Danger sat equally at every man's shoulder and there was no such thing as a safe cushy billet at base.

The LCTs docked in the harbour at Anzio at 1430 and before the Squadron could move its transport a great quantity of mailbags and stores had to be unloaded, which was done by a party of American jailbirds. The Squadron then moved to a marshalling area where they were met by an RAF camera team who requested them to return to the docks and do it all again while they took pictures (these films were shown in War in the Air, part 13 on BBC TV and were described as RAF going ashore in Greece!). Nettuno airstrip was soon reached and passed by, the Squadron going to a nearby beach where tents were soon erected – in most cases well below ground level for the soft sand was not difficult to shift and patently to dig deep was a wise precaution.

At sunset a nearby battery disturbed the evening air. Before midnight an enemy air raid had given rise to a most prodigious expenditure of Bofors shells in a barrage of unparalleled density and more unfamiliar noises began in the dark hour after midnight. A far off thump began the sequence, then after a short period of silence came the long drawn out sighing whine terminating in a crash which echoed and rumbled like coal pouring down a steel chute. Anzio Annie had delivered another calling card.

An aircraft blast protection pen at Anzio

"Anzio Annie"

Flt Lt Lowther with LACs Ashfield, Hayles, Torrance and Massie, Nettuno, 1944

This was a nightly occurrence though fortunately the length of time that Annie, a collective name that included a sister or two, was in action was short. They had to scuttle away to reach the safety of a tunnel before dawn where alone they could stay out of reach of the ever present threat of fighter-bombers.

The Squadron aircraft flew in soon after first light on 22 May. Their main duty was to provide dawn and dusk cover and during the remainder of the day to share patrols with the other more distant squadrons. 43 was in fact the only Squadron of the RAF ever to operate as such from Anzio for, before the remainder of the Wing came to join them two weeks later, the beachhead as such had ceased to exist, being joined to and integral with the main Allied Front.

On 23 May as the Germans at last prised from their long-held positions at Cassino were retiring northwards, the Anzio Army began to break out to cut their lines of retreat.

This brought out the Luftwaffe in greater strength than had been met with for some time. On the 23rd a recce 109 was damaged by Warrant Officer Carrick and three days later Fg Off Guest destroyed two FW 190s in two minutes. These same two pilots four days later claimed one destroyed and one probable respectively after eight Spitfires had jumped twelve 109s out of the sun. Less successfully, Fg Off Cassels and Warrant Officer Saville went missing without their respective number ones knowing they had been attacked. The first (who actually was the victim of another squadron's Spitfire!) was taken POW, the second was found burned and injured, in a Rome hospital, a fortnight later. By 31 May the Squadron had flown more ops hours than in any month since December 1942 at Algiers. 1,117 hours on 919 sorties were amassed in twenty-seven flying days. Five enemy aircraft had been destroyed and seven damaged for the loss of two pilots.

The arrival of two untidy looking 'Italian civilians' provided a surprise when they proved to be two Desert Air Force pilots, who baling out six months earlier had successfully evaded capture and had finally got clear in the general chaos then prevailing in the enemy's camp. A less welcome visitor was an American P-40 which, damaged, attempted to land but overshot by half a mile and ended in the domestic site. It came within a yard or less of decapitating an airman who, sitting with his back to its approach, was industriously reaffixing a shirt button. Half an hour later an electrical short circuit set all of its six 0·5 inch guns firing. Later on the same day a badly damaged B-24 Liberator bomber almost hit the Squadron's tents before crashing and going on fire with some casualties resulting amongst its crew.

On 29 May a final burst of hatred from the enemy's artillery sent more than six hundred shells into the harbour and surrounding areas – the airstrip was not greatly inconvenienced. By

More victory smiles at Naples, November 1943, Flt Sgt Booth, WO Hedderwick and Flt Sgt Leighton

2 June enemy shelling had ceased and on the 5th the Squadron moved to Tre Cancelli, four miles distant, where it joined with the remainder of the Wing. On 4 June, Rome was evacuated by the Germans and two days later the news of the Normandy landings brought forth a general response of 'high time those folks at home got off their backsides and into the war instead of leaving it all to us.' On the same day Sqn Ldr Patrick Laing-Meason was posted home to England (where he was killed, aged 25, on 28 October in a Tiger Moth on the slope of Box Hill in Surrey) and Sqn Ldr Jupp, came from 72 Squadron to post of Chief Cock.

Plt Off Reg Lamont

Tre Cancelli was a most unlovely spot - dusty, with treacherous soft spots of sand that caused much taxying trouble.

At night the camp site, on either side of a deep wadi, was lit by countless glow-worms. Fortunately the stay here was short. On the 11th 'A' Party departed to Tarquinia, forty miles north of Rome. 'B' Party, aircraft duly despatched, departed at 2200 hours on the 14th. The night move was ordered because of low priority for Air Force transport at this stage, ammunition for the front line being of much greater importance. In the early hours of the morning, en route through Rome, a kit bag fell onto the exhaust pipe of the Squadron fire tender and caught fire. Sten-gun magazines started to explode bringing a horde of white-capped American MPs on the scene. They got into a frightful state and wanted to blow the whole lot up, but saner counsels prevailed and soon all was well.

Shortly before the end of this move, while crossing a detour near a blown bridge at Civitavecchia, a booby trap exploded, wrecking a nearby house. LAC Derrick Tester was wounded by flying debris and died three days later. Two airmen were hurt when a second lorry overturned.

Tarquinia was a long slab of concrete surrounded by soil sun-baked to an equal hardness, just how much was discovered when the Group Captain, warned to expect enemy retaliatory raids ordered all ranks to dig slit-trenches, a command honoured more in the breach than the observance, for the ground was so very hard and there was no longer any shellfire. Anyway they were never required, for the amount of air opposition was almost nil. On land the Germans were still retreating, fighting their customary delaying actions while preparing another defence line in the Appennines north of Florence. The rate at which the Army swept forward made another move in the near future a certainty and with 232 Wing (Boston medium bombers) already sniffing around the concrete runway and casting envious eyes upon it, the Wing upped to Grosseto, fifty miles to the north, there to discover that if the ground was still as unyielding, at least there was a ditch or two nearby.

There was a great deal of coming and going among some key personnel at this time. Flt Lt de Pledge – adjutant since far off days at Acklington – interchanged with Flt Lt R J Fisher of 208 Squadron. 'Dippy's loss was much felt.'

His was a resilience more than sufficient to absorb the increasing shocks which constantly bombarded squadron adjutants, and an apparent cluelessness and tendency to dither in his demeanour belied an incisive and mature mind.

Few had ever moved so many airmen so far with so little transport, or been ordered on to six different landing craft in one day and finally sailed in a seventh, and still succeeded throughout, buffeted and bewildered by order, disorder, command and countermand, to display such a sane and reasonable exterior to the world. Amidst it all there was not one single man in 43 Squadron that could ever say he had not been fed in accordance with the ration scale then prevailing, nor complain that if there was any mail within fifty miles of the Squadron it had not been fetched as fast as the Post Corporal could be dispatched. Occasional insufficiency of tentage could scarcely be attributed to him for, if the truth were known, he had already got twice as much of that rare commodity as anybody else:robbing the squirrels of distant Stores Parks in a manner hardly likely to meet the

Plt Off Bruce Robertson

A spectacular Vesuvius eruption

approval of senior equipment officers. Before he left he had been Mentioned in Dispatches – a small token indeed for a mighty job carefully accomplished. More to the point he took with him the high regard of a Squadron, in whose close-knit corporate life the value of his selfless service had often been much greater than was readily apparent.

A second departure was Flt Lt Eyles, Intelligence Officer, though in his case the loss was not total since he went only to Wing HQ and contrived to remain with the Squadron much of the time. 'Spy' had become a fixture with all ranks. When the war was fluid there was a continual coming and going to his office tent in which the black wax-pencilled 'bomb lines' were on view, drawn on the perspex overlaying his large-scale maps of the fighting area. He had advanced them across the fields and mountains of Tunisia and Sicily and, latterly, the Italian mainland. Always he provided the admonition to the optimistic that 'Of course, that's only the bomb-line ahead of the troops; they haven't got all that way yet', which said in his manner suggested that inevitably it was only a matter of time before they did. Such occasions were a great uplift to one's morale. There was a solidity emanating from his ample frame as permanent as the University of Cambridge where in more peaceful times he had passed his days. To see him with his maps and crayons was to feel that all was well and there would always be an England, for neither God in his Heaven nor all being right with the world carried half the certainty of final victory than the fact that tomorrow 'Spy' would be presiding in his tent

A tropicalised Spitfire Vc sits on the rain-soaked airfield at Naples with a cloud-topped Vesuvius in the background.

and the bomb-line would have crept, inexorably, another half-inch northwards across the perspex. Out, too, at this time went Pilot Officers Robertson, Johnson and Leighton, all of whom had been commissioned while serving with the Squadron. As they went, others came, soon to absorb the spirit that made 43 the exceptional unit that it was. Flt Sgt Edwards from New South Wales, who early on earned himself fourteen days Duty Pilot as a result of forgetting his wheels, Harry Rendall from God knows where in Australia, a great figure of a man, half bushwhacker, complete rebel, rough, ready and crude with a heart and a laugh big enough for ten, whom nobody could help but like more than most. Harry Wilkinson from Newcastle, who kept calmer and thought quicker when it mattered, and others besides. And as had ever been, the more permanent members of the Squadron sized up the new faces, fearful that they would not be up to the standard of the old and things would change for the worse, a feeling that inevitably passed quickly when in a matter of days the new chaps fell into things as though to the manner born and it was hard to realise that they had not been in it since the beginning of time.

It was not long before the Wing was pushed out of Grosseto and nobody grieved at the move. Grossetto was a characterless, grubby uninviting spot, mostly railway yards, and they were a wreck. The only memory that survived was one of an American Army sergeant i/c a Bofors gun post located by the Squadron's tents. 'Gus' was a character from Buffalo, inordinately proud of the fact that his battery alone had been trained in North Africa by the British in the matter of aircraft identification, and his battery alone had never fired on a friendly aircraft. 'Those Goddamn stupid b's', he pronounced with the authority of one who really knew (the collective illegitimate noun covering every American AA gunner in the world except his battery) 'only have one rule – if it's got two bodies it's a Lightning, if it's got four engines it's a Fort – if it's anything else, open fire'. Those who recalled the day at Salerno when 93 Squadron's Spitfires, wheels and flaps down, were shot out of the sky, understood what he meant.

Out of Grosseto to Piombino, to where the Chianti grapes were ripening, to a runway that was dusty and soft, where the days were hot and the sky was blue and the setting sun went down in a ball of gold over the glistening balloons that hung above the ships outside of the port. They were halcyon days when the war was a matter of an occasional sweep and the enemy had quite vanished from the stage, and like all good things they could not last.

Suddenly there were conferences in the Adjutant's caravan and within three days 'A' Flight had packed, back tracked to Civitavecchia, sailed to Porto Vecchio in south-east Corsica, and motored to Calvi, on the north-west tip of the island. It had almost to be written that one of our vehicles was missing. Cpl James, auxiliary driver of a 3-tonner, had brake failure in the mountains west of Bastia. Pressing on undeterred, his gear box the sole means of retardation, he was more than a little flabbergasted when the gear lever came away in his hand while he was negotiating a steep decline. Full rudder to starboard into a providential wall averted further bloodshed.

On arrival at their destination the half Squadron (the rest had stayed in Italy for a direct trip to France via Naples) sorted itself out in an olive grove. Somebody, better versed in history than the majority, recalled that it was at Calvi that Nelson lost his eye way back in 1794. It was then 19 July 1944.

Spitfire LF IX, MK118 'FT-F' refuels from an ex-Italian Air Force bowser sharing the Calvi airfield with a USAAF P-51B Mustang - July 1944
(Andy Saunders collection)

CHAPTER 23

Vive la France

IT is now conceded by most that the decision to invade France along its Mediterranean coastline in the Summer of 1944 was a mistake, for the advance from the Normandy beachhead to the Rhine and the Swiss frontier would have compelled the Germans to evacuate the southern half of France in any case. Such advantages as may have accrued as a result of the invasion were wholly incommensurate with the repercussions following the inevitable weakening of the Italian front for thereby the Russians rather than the West were able first to reach Central Europe and the Balkans with far reaching results on post war politics too well known to require reiteration.

The French interlude for 43 Squadron, however, took place with no awareness of these vital future consequences. A period of first class attacking opportunities on operations, combined on the ground with a near-holiday atmosphere among an overwhelmingly friendly populace, was not to be quickly forgotten, though alas it was over all too quickly.

The pattern of events did not lack change or variety. While half of the ground crews sat out three extremely boring weeks ship-borne at Naples, from where they sailed to land at fashionable St Tropez on the evening of D-Day, the remainder of the Squadron, including the pilots, were producing a remarkable display of stamina at Calvi. The two halves were briefly reunited on French soil at Ramatuelle, just long enough for the Corsican contingent to pass fleeting remarks on D-Day heroes. But how easy it was to see who did all the work before racing off along the Route Napoleon to Sisteron. Very shortly even that was too far away for proper air support and by early September the Squadron came to Lyon, third city of France. An attempted move to Besançon, near the Swiss border, was foiled by the weather and eventually at the end of September the whole of 324 Wing were returned via Marseilles to Italy. Flt Lt Roland Griffiths, who disappeared during a sweep on 4 August, and Plt Off Maurice Simpson, killed two days later in a crash, were the only major casualties from Calvi. Flt Sgt Rendall, force-landed after engine failure, made a third aircraft lost there. These three apart, not a single aeroplane was bent at that place although it possessed as many hazards as a Ryder Cup course. Eight hundred yards of metal-covered runway laid across a prevailing onshore wind terminated at one end in a one-in-two descent, and at the other was a great pit of sufficiently capacious dimensions to accommodate comfortably a Flying Fortress, which at some earlier date had landed in distress, and deep enough to ensure that the tail fin offered no hazard to navigation. A wind which blew by no means rarely, originated in the Alps, rushed down to the coast and over the sea to create an uncomfortable grit-laden atmosphere that blasted man and machine alike. When the sun shone it was rather better.

Over and above the normal routine servicing already doubled by virtue of their being at half strength, the technical side of the Squadron during these days also brought completely to operational standard fourteen

Spitfires with 90-gallon underslung tanks at Ramatuelle in southern France - August 1944

Engine servicing in the open! Spitfire LF Mk VIII MT714 'FT-F' Ramatuelle (South France) August 1944

Mk VIII Spitfires which, arriving in the replacement pipeline in lieu of Mk IXs, were concentrated within 43 Squadron, the better to employ their superior range and speed. This task befell nobody else whose replacements were the operational Mk IXs passed on from 43, but in spite of this additional burden the Squadron, able as always to prove that it was anything but ordinary, still maintained the highest serviceability figures within the Wing. The effort produced by 'A' Flight and its supporting arms was in fact never bettered within the Squadron at any other period of the whole war.

For the aircrew life aloft was initially unexciting, for the overstretched Luftwaffe had little to spare for the Mediterranean fronts so that the bomber escorts and fighter sweeps brought no reaction. On 12 August everybody got particularly annoyed at being called on to undertake an abnormal number of quite pointless 'offensive sweeps', the sole purpose of which was to permit the 12th Tactical Air Force USAAF under whose operational control they were placed, to celebrate some Air Corps anniversary with a day of two thousand sorties: a target reached by an unenthusiastic Royal Air Force flying long into the evening. The three days preceding D-Day, however, brightened the contemporary scene. Eighty sorties to attack coastal gun positions and radar stations were made and if the results were problematical, a fine strafing time was had by all. The first days of the invasion necessitated a sobering up, the primary need being for high level defensive stooges along patrol lines carrying the fruity code names of Apples, Pears, Peaches and Grapes. The entire enemy reaction on D-Day consisted of one raid of two aircraft and the succeeding days were equally quiet, but when on D plus 5 the Spitfires flew in to Ramatuelle the pattern of operations underwent a radical change. Defensive matters were left entirely to others and the Wing went over to intensive close support.

The German troops facing the attacking armies, outnumbered, outclassed in equipment, possessing no air forces for either defence or attack and occupying indefensible positions on an overlong front, doing the only thing possible for them by withdrawing northwards, an operation which the Führer himself with all his obsession for never yielding an inch of territory could scarce forbid. The retreat was conducted, as such things invariably were by the Germans, in masterly fashion and although subjected to relentless and unceasing air attacks at no time was there anything resembling a headlong flight, nor ever did the forward progress of the Allies appear to go any faster than the pace the enemy was willing to allow. Wise to every trick that could delay, masters of demolition and mining or of the art of concealing a well sited 88 mm gun that could hold up for hours the opposing armour, until the air forces were called up to deal with it and when they came it was not infrequently to find their target had slipped

Fg Off 'Jimmy' James at Lyon - September 1944

away unseen. The discipline and fortitude of the German soldier, without which such retreats could never have been conducted, did not fail to draw from even the most ungracious a genuine respect for his quality. Among those who daily harried and discomforted him from the sky was not a little perplexity that he could endure so much, for all the conclusions drawn from experience in Norway and France, in Greece and Crete, had been of the impossibility of conducting operations on land in the face of overwhelming hostile air power.

The main axis of the American-French advance was up the Rhone Valley, the mopping up on either flank being left to a resurgent Maquis, and it was along the river that most of the efforts were concentrated. Daily in sections of four, the Spitfires set out on the hunt and only occasionally did they return without some kind of quarry having been found. Their most memorable day was one on which a mile-long convoy of armoured, motorised and horse-drawn vehicles was found near Valence. By setting on fire both ends of the column it was effectively immobilised and thereafter attacks were kept up throughout the day, before the end of which nothing remained except a blackened mile of shattered vehicles and slaughtered horses. Such a feast day was exceptional and though the targets were plentiful they required finding. Flt Lt Browne, leading four 'B' Flight aircraft came upon forty to fifty men on the march near St Symphorien, an unusual display of carelessness, and observed his 20 mm and machine-gun fire 'plough right through the column'. On occasions the attackers were themselves smitten by retaliatory flak. Fg Off James and Flt Sgt Hindson both had their aircraft badly damaged on 30 August and on the following day Fg Off Guest had to bale out when set on fire. He landed unhurt.

The move to Bron airfield, near Lyon, on 5 September, brought a temporary slowing of operations, for that place became the receiving end of a massive American airlift. The available motor transport being inadequate to maintain essential stores and supplies over the long haul from the Mediterranean ports, two hundred B-24 Liberators were thrown in to assist. Daily they arrived from bases in southern Italy, at one-minute intervals, streamed off the runway, unloaded bombs, pumped fuel from their tanks into empty drums and went away. As a display of the ability of the Americans to act in an elephantine and decisive manner when the need arose it was most impressive, but as the bombers hogged the runway for eight hours daily it

Spitfire IX MK445 'FT-H' seen at Bron (Lyon) in September 1944 carrying a 500 lb underslung bomb.
(Andy Saunders collection)

inevitably dampened all offensive inclinations. Just as soon as the airlift eased the old routine was quickly re-established and 8 September 'a busy and successful day' recorded six missions between 0640 and 1840, all in the area north and northwest of Dijon. The first patrol destroyed a locomotive, the second found low cloud but nothing else. The third, fourth and fifth concentrated on 'a column of 200 horse-drawn vehicles, double banked in places', and in face of 'intensive small arms fire' claimed one hundred and five vehicles as damaged, one of which blew up in a sheet of flame; another, full of ammunition, exploded. Additionally, two trains were attacked and damaged. The final mission for the day added 'five motor vehicles left in flames' to the score. On 12 September a section of 'A' Flight made history with an attack inside the German border, and in a subsequent strafe Fg Off Guest hit a house but returned – with tiles from the roof resting in the port radiator intake! Two days later targets were all out of range and operations were brought to a halt after a projected move northwards to Besançon was frustrated by continuous poor visibilty at that place. The final score on the French wicket came to one hundred and six motor vehicles, five locomotives, three wagons, one tracked howitzer, a hundred and twenty plus horse-drawn vehicles and two cyclists, in the total of which about half were destroyed and half damaged. The only aircraft totally lost was that from which Fg Off Guest baled out on 31 August. With flying at a standstill, there was abundant time for rumour and speculation on future movements to run riot. Ever since leaving Tunisia, the heading had been permanently northwards and with the English Channel now a mere 360 miles away the Golden Fleece of Blighty leave was tantalisingly close. The menacing or hopeful rumours were finally stilled by no less an authority than the Deputy C-in-C Mediterranean Allied Air Forces, Air Marshal Sir John Slessor. With all the *force majeure* that a visit of this eminence implied, 324 received its marching orders. It would return to Italy, where there was a job waiting to be done, assisting the men who were, while some enjoyed the joys of liberation in France, still fighting and dying among the mountains and in the mud. The war was yet to be won, and this object would be soonest accomplished with 324 Wing in Italy rather than the 2nd Tactical Air Force. So pack up, chaps, and go!

The justice of the decision was unarguable, the disappointment no less bitter for that, for in truth everybody had been utterly spoiled and softened by the remarkable welcome the people of France had given to them. Moreover, as the sole British representatives in an otherwise entirely American-French army area, they had especially received the whole flood of goodwill which the RAF had built up by its ceaseless support of the Maquis (which in these parts meant most of the male population) and by its unending reminder, by its presence above, that all was not yet lost. Moreover, among the older generations the memories of twenty-five years before still lingered and their major ally of those days still possessed a very special place in their affections. Over and above the attractiveness of France, there was the possibility in a foreseeable future, so long as one stayed there, of some hitherto undreamed of home leave. For some the loss of this was the hardest bit of all as the near hope of sweet reunion and the visions of the long unseen things of home were swept far off into an indeterminate distance in time. That reality must surely have confounded the dreams and that blackout, flying bombs, blue uniforms and bull would each and all have been concomitant with a return to UK was wholly overlooked and left unconsidered. Those of grosser leanings for whom the main attraction was the taste of a pint of ale in the special atmosphere of an English pub would have been saddened to find these places shut half the week and the specific gravity forever approaching unity.

All the same, in the ending of the dreams and the termination of the sweet life of a liberated land, there was sorrow and loss. Deep pillowed and scented down the pretty mademoiselles were left to sleep alone, and within days everybody was disposed upon a bleak terrain near La Jasse, westward of the Rhône delta, where for a week they endured the blast of the purgatorial Mistral winds which blew away the cobwebs and the hangover of Lyon and warned of Italian wintry weather yet to come. There too the Squadron received some new pilots from the disbanding 322 Wing, while sending others northward to help plug the holes which the German flak gunners were blowing in the ranks of the 2nd TAF Typhoon Squadrons. On 1 October most embarked at Marseilles for Leghorn while an advanced servicing party flew to Florence, where the Spitfires also went, via Corsica. The manner of their arrival was sorrowful and bloody, a story of loss and disaster caused by a multiplicity of ill judgements, all of which need never, and ought never to have happened.

In the first instance 43 could have flown direct to Florence, the increased range of the Mk VIII making their scheduled halfway refuelling stop at Bastia quite unnecessary. When the four squadrons of the Wing landed there it was soon evident that the progress made by the over-stretched refuelling parties was too slow to enable everybody to arrive at Florence in daylight. Because there was, anyway, no question of resuming operations before the main parties arrived a week later the sensible decision would have been to remain overnight and fly in the following day. But in the event 43, getting the worst of all possible worlds, were ordered off, without refuelling, at too late an hour. Arriving at Florence at dusk they were kept in the circuit while 111 Squadron (who had refuelled at Bastia) were brought in.

It was dark when eventually they were permitted to land. To assist the pilots (none of whom had very much, nor any recent, practice in night landing in Spitfires) two petrol tankers were disposed to illuminate the touch-down area. Like all British transport they had a solitary headlamp, masked by the standard blackout shields and the light obtained was the poorest imaginable. The Americans, who took a more realistic view of the enemy's night-time air potential and habitually drove with dazzling undipped beams, could have provided something far better, but nobody thought to ask for their help. Yet in spite of all the hazards ten aircraft came safely to earth. The eleventh, piloted by Lt Duchen of South Africa, hit the cab of one of the tankers with the port wing tip, and somersaulted onto its back. Close behind him, unaware of this incident, Flt Lt Lowther safely negotiated the gap between the tankers and smashed at speed into Duchen's upturned aircraft. The combined wreckage burst into flames. Lt Michael Duchen and Plt Off Hudson Ainslie RAAF of 111 Squadron from Queensland who was helping to extricate him from the cockpit, both died; Lowther got out, terribly burned about the head.

The wreckage of the two Spitfire VIIIs, MT786 'FT-P' and JF887 'FT-U', involved in the landing accident at Florence on 1 October 1944
(Andy Saunders collection)

Spitfire LF IX, PT530 'FT-A' allocated to the squadron commander. It is interesting to note that there is a dark band round the rear fuselage

Lt Dalton, another South African, saw this funeral pyre, but mistaking it for a flare deliberately lit to assist in landing came boring in, smote the same tanker as had been hit before, crashed and was badly hurt about the head by the gunsight. The triple wreckage now completely blocked the runway, and the pilots still orbiting above were told to stay there and subsequently to abandon their aircraft when the fuel was exhausted. A parachute jump in the dark, above unknown countryside, was a grim and unhappy prospect and for those on the ground anxiety was little less. The loss of another five aircraft and possible death or injury to five more pilots seemed almost certain, when out of the darkness there came an unexpected voice of hope. Control at the US base at Pisa, listening to the frantic R/T traffic quickly summed up the desperate position and in typical American style plunged in, unasked, to assist. 'If you boys have enough gas, come on over here, we'll turn on everything we've got.' The offer was accepted with speed and Flt Sgt Wilkinson, not the highest ranked among those still flying but first in speed of thought and action, immediately called the others to join up with his section and headed westwards through the night. There was no margin for errors in navigation over the trackless miles of mountain for everybody's tanks were perilously close to empty, but 'Wilky' did not err and bang-on course brought the anxious formation over the centre of the lit-up airfield. Quickly the Spitfires slipped in to land. One lost its engine on the runway, the fuel running out at the very moment of touchdown. WO Dauphin in another, turning quickly off to clear the runway for those that followed, made two hundred yards in the darkness before his fuel too ran out. In daylight the next day he discovered that he had taxied unscathed through the only gap in half a mile of fencing. At the very last it seemed the Fates had relented.

On his third 'ops' tour,
Flt Lt B H Thomas DFC ('A' Flight Commander July - December 1944)

CHAPTER 24

The Strife is O'er

There was no leaf upon the forest bare,
No flower upon the ground
And little motion in the air ....

PERCY BYSSHE SHELLEY, erratic unorthodox genius came, like 43 Squadron, from Sussex and his poems at times indicate that he shared with them the same dim view of winter weather in the Florence area. The 'Sunless sky heavy hung with cloud'; 'frozen winds', 'freezing streams' and 'tempests fleet' or his 'wind-swept Apennines' were all alike familiar to 43 as they had been to the poet over a century before. All this moreover in a city which Shelley would have found strangely uninviting. The great collections of art treasures were gone, all save one of the bridges spanning the Arno were down and desolation, ruin and dejection everywhere abounded.

Through seven cheerless weeks the Fighting Cocks, reunited on the arrival of the seaborne contingent, roosted, during which time its morale for several reasons sank consistently lower. Italy revisited held less attraction than before and compared entirely to its disfavour with the memories of Sisteron and Lyon. The apathy, even veiled hostility which was sometimes apparent, of a people bewildered and lost following the collapse of their political régime and individually concerned to the exclusion of almost all else with the basic problem of survival, contrasted sadly with the cameradie and good humour generated in France during the joyful days of liberation. The weather, unbelievably abominable, passed through various combinations and permutations of frost, rain, fog, sleet, hail and mist, with an occasional interlude of tepid sunshine that served merely to increase the humidity but not the temperature.

Yet, essentially the main affliction was boredom resulting from 'little motion in the air', a consequent complete absence of purpose, and a universal feeling of uselessness. Fighter squadrons, in the purest sense of the word, had in these parts become redundant for such was the complete air supremacy enjoyed here by the Allied Air Forces that the Germans, knowing full well that no decisive action was possible before the following Spring, preferred to denude this area the better to cover the more important fronts. Although the heavy bombers from the deep south around Foggia still met fighter opposition when they ventured north of the Alps the continual Allied flights of interdiction against lines and centres of communication stirred up no reaction, nor when the fighters alone trailed their coats on sweeps through skies quite emptied of winged adversaries was there anything at all to enthuse over.

Only the inevitable enemy flak remained to contest the day, and that sometimes gained encouragement through success as for example on 24 October when Flt Lt I G Thompson was engaged in 'sweeping the area Bergamo-Verona above continuous ten-tenths cloud interspersed with intermittent ten-tenths flak'. Some of the latter found a billet in the pilot's thigh, other fragments spread themselves liberally among the airframe to such an extent that approaching base 'both ailerons went up at the same time, following which the reflector sight fell off and jammed the rudder'. Whereupon Flt Lt Thompson, wisely, opted for a landing by parachute.

The heaviest daily loss sustained during these days however was inflicted on six of 'B' Flight's Spitfires by Mustangs of the USAAF. Flt Lt Cummings was shot down and killed as the 'friendly' fighters dived from above and behind; Flt Lt Creed saved himself with a rapid loop and roll after a cannon shell exploded in the cockpit. Alone after this manoeuvre he came home, assuaging his flaming anger and the nagging pain of an injured arm by attacking a German gun position, an action that brought a rocket from the AOC on the grounds that firing his guns weakened the case for complaint against the Americans (who in the event insisted that their own fighters had attacked Me 109s in this area).

An additional hazard that now arose was a decision to add to the already excellent runway a large acreage of all-weather taxi strips and hard standings, which meant that such parts of the airfield as were not already flooded were devastated by enormous earth moving monsters. Though the ultimate objective was entirely to be welcomed, the interim condition was one of confusion, confounded for the worse as such grassy parts as remained vanished under oceans of mud and mountainous piles of gravel.

Nevertheless all the mud and muck, combined even with the general purposelessness of the daily routine, would have been endurable if some foreseeable end had appeared probable but any such hopes were bedevilled by one indisputable fact. Up front the army was stuck, nor would it move either far or fast until winter was gone and until then there was little promise of any real work for the Squadron.

The situation on the ground which so entirely controlled the Squadron's actions and operations was briefly as follows :

Following the collapse of the German resistance at Cassino and Anzio and the consequent capture of Rome the Eighth and Fifth Armies both continued to advance northwards, though at a steadily decreasing pace as the German resistance stiffened and the Allies' lines of supply lengthened, in addition to which the withdrawal of the Divisions earmarked for the invasion of France had a gravely weakening effect. The Germans moved back slowly to their next prepared defensive position, the 'Gothic Line', which ran from Massa, south of Spezia on the west coast, through the mountains north of Florence to Pesaro on the Adriatic and not until August's end were preparations for an Allied assault on this line completed. For this attack the Eighth Army was switched to the Adriatic end of the front with the Fifth on its left flank. Attacking on 26 August the 8th made good initial progress in spite of being slowed up by rain and after a week, when the Germans had been compelled to reinforce this part of the front, the American Fifth Army set off along Routes 65 and 6524 into the mountains south of Bologna.

After two months it had become clear that the major breakout into the great valley of the Po would not materialise in 1944. In the foulest of weather, amid those 'windswept Apennines' which so greatly nullified the Allied superiority in armour and artillery, against the bravest of opponents unquestionably experienced in the ways of defensive warfare, the men of the Eighth and Fifth Armies gave all that they had but, lacking the strength which had been taken from them earlier in the summer, failed when victory was all but theirs. Only in the extreme east where the mountains gave way soonest to a coastal plain could the Eighth Army in part break through to the southern fringes of the plains of Lombardy and there it was to find one river barrier after another to thwart and delay its advance up the coast to Ravenna and north-west along the first miles of Highway 9, which pointed like an arrow straight into the heart of industrial Turin and Milan.

For the long-enduring soldiers, battling against such a combination of adversaries and adversity, it was not possible to offer too much assistance and so it was that 324 Wing were ordered to change their mode of life, and to become like every other fighter wing in these parts. Adapted to the dual fighter-bomber role, it was to turn its arm to tactical support of the armies in the field, a decision that was welcomed with a plenitude of enthusiasm. At long last the days of idleness were over, the empty pointless stooge no more and in their place was something of obvious and useful value.

So did the cockerel raise himself from his soporific state, dust down his feathers and prepare again for the main arena. It required but a few days before 43 Squadron was ready.

The damp environment that had all but washed away its soul at Florence was left, far behind and on the green grass at Rimini where the wind blew cold and sharp off the Adriatic, so

Fg Off Evans, Flt Lt Hedderwick and Fg Off Edwards at Rimini, January 1945

that a few of the elders had cause to remember another east wind and another sea at Acklington in the long ago of five years since, 43 Squadron bombed up. The wheel had turned full circle from those early Acklington days, through desperate defence and the subsequent long slogging years for mastery of the air until now. That aim at last achieved, every effort could be thrown into all-out attack.

At 1105 hours on 21 November a little bit more of history was marked up when Sqn Ldr Jupp led out six aircraft, each armed with one 500 lb HE bomb to attack an enemy-occupied house. All the bombs fell in the target area. Whereupon the weather immediately cocked a decisive snoot at further hopes of repeat performances and between the 23rd and 30th of the month ops were possible only on the 24th. An improvement arrived with December and the game was on again.

The bombing technique possessing the virtues of simplicity with acceptable accuracy was to locate the target visually, thence to dive at 60° from 8,000 to 4,000 feet keeping the target aligned along the top of the nose cowling. At 4,000 feet or thereabouts a gentle pull out of the dive was commenced and when the target had passed an estimated three times the width of the propellor spinner under the nose the bomb release button on the throttle lever was pressed. The odds against a direct hit using this method were three to one and since a section normally consisted of four aircraft this gave an even money chance of a direct hit. And, as many Algiers veterans would have agreed, even a near miss from a 500 lb bomb was not conducive to improvement of morale or appetite. The 25 per cent ratio of direct hits remained virtually constant as an overall figure, though on a daily basis the accuracy varied inversely to the density of flak.

Flt Sgt Leigh, who on 4 December was seen to crash after 'attacking through intense accurate flak' was the only major casualty in the last month of the year though many aircraft were damaged. Flt Lt Thomas, 'A' Flight's commander, approaching the end of a third operational tour was reported in the Squadron's diary on 4 December as 'having made three trips and missed his lunch', a noble example which deserved a better reward than a further entry of the 15th suggests; 'hit by accurate flak he recrossed the line and crashed piece by piece among some trees'. After which Group Captain Duncan Smith decreed he should tempt fate no further, removed him from ops and told him that after three years it was time to go home to his wife in far off New Zealand.

With reluctance the order, whereby was lost a remarkably popular Flight Commander, was obeyed though not before 25 December had come and gone, a day which was brightened by the arrival on Christmas Eve of a replacement 3-tonner which had, on its maiden trip from the MT Base Depot at Naples transported vermouth and the like to the value of 800,000 lire. Fg Off Butler, the Engineer Officer also succeeded in remaining over the festive period by the simple act of concealing from sight the DAFHQ signal ordering that he should, after eight years abroad, return to UK. When in January a second signal arrived requesting reasons for non-compliance with the first signal, only one person knew of what they spoke. One casualty of this feast was a cockerel of the feathered kind which, taken as a mascot by the Officers' Mess, displayed a lack of stamina and breeding and being not up to true Fighting Cock standard died, erratically, early on the 26th. A Squadron sweep of the Verona-Vicenza area made on the forenoon of Christmas Day (the sole operation carried out by the Wing on a day of ten-tenths at 1,500 feet), is best left undescribed, two pilots returned with spots (and it was not oil!) on their windscreens and a third mistook the customary thump of a supercharger changing from 'medium' to 'full' for flak. Just, however, to show that it was capable of obeying a call from the AOC for no diminution of effort over the holiday, the Squadron on Boxing Day sent twenty-eight aircraft on seven different missions and scored eleven direct hits and five near misses on gun positions. During the last mission Flt Lt Hedderwick and WO Dauphin both received unwelcome presents in the form of heavy flak damage.

The start of the new year found the Eighth Army still moving slowly forward, all the time

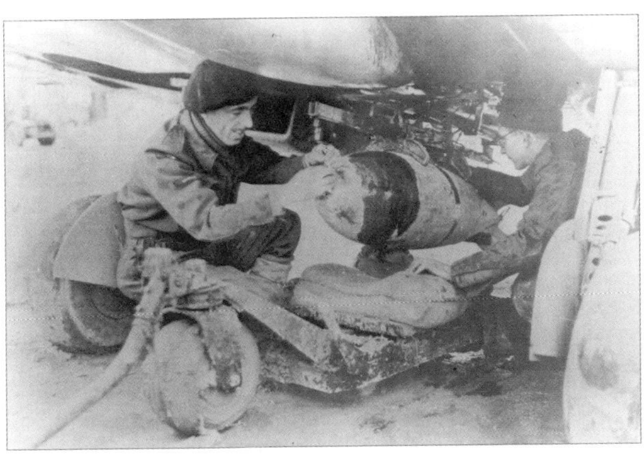

LAC Collis (Armourer) fitting a 500 lb GP bomb under a Spitfire at Ravenna LG – April 1945

expanding their small bridgehead on the plain and giving the Germans no chance to relax or to move any substantial numbers of men to other fronts, and always, weather permitting, the Air Forces were to be found in support. Generally with a fair amount of success although even the best have their off days and on one memorable occasion the greater part of the Desert Air Force attempted all afternoon to demolish a road bridge without success; just to pour salt into the wounded pride it was found next day at dawn that the Germans had themselves blown it up overnight. One thing that remained constant during all these days was the quality of the enemy's flak, and at some places, like Imola or Castel Bolognese where it came up particularly thick and black it was never considered wise to loiter longer than was necessary. Inevitably there were casualties.

On the very first day of the New Year WO Dauphin was killed in action; three days later Sgt Basso, a nineteen-year-old Rhodesian, whose record of 100 per cent direct hits in over twenty trips was quite exceptional, blew up over the target in an attack during which 'spirally white trails moving upwards' (later identified as a type of anti-aircraft rocket) were seen. The day following, WO Hollingsworth was very fortunate to reach Forli and crash-land before his Spitfire fell apart and so the story continued. Because the final victory when it came was both complete and mighty it should never be assumed that it was lightly won. The last casualty that the Squadron suffered came in fact only twelve hours before hostilities ceased when Sgt Crookes was shot down while strafing transport. Altogether the 1,800 bombs dropped in 1945 cost the lives of seven pilots, with eight others wounded and three lost as POWs (two more shot down on the wrong side of the line evaded capture). Twenty-eight Spitfires, almost twice the Squadrons' total strength of sixteen were destroyed or badly damaged. Both Flight Commanders were lost within eight days in February. Flt Lt Creed of 'B' Flight, shot down while strafing barges on the River Po ended in a POW camp after an unpleasant interlude with the Gestapo. His deputy Flt Lt Tom Allen, a survivor of the Florence/Pisa debacle the previous October thanks to the greater fuel capacity of the Spitfire Mk VIII he had been flying, stepped in to take over his duties. Eight days later 'A' Flight too lost its leader. Flt Lt Hedderwick was disabled near Portomaggiore, attempted to glide back to safety but when within half a mile from success, spun in from low altitude. His loss was more keenly felt than most, for so many had known him for so long. His war had been fought exclusively with 43. Night intruding, Dieppe, Algiers to Naples via Sicily and Salerno, 740 hours in one unbroken tour at the end of which he was described as 'not really clapped or in need of a rest'. Back within months at Corsica in time to join in the French frolics and survive the Florence debacle. A week before he died he led the Squadron on its first ninety-gallon overload mission into the heart of Yugoslavia. Many a dark hour he had enlightened with his cheerful nature that brought him the name of 'Happy', and for all in whose affection he held high place it was an especial cause for sorrow that his luck ran out just so soon.

On 22 February Sqn Ldr Jupp was awarded what most people considered a long overdue DFC, which led to a party of such extraordinary duration that it warranted an entry in the Squadron's diary. An earlier entry in the same book had recorded that 'in some countries they celebrate today as Burns Day. The general attitude in the mess towards this was that anyone who watches spiders in caves must be OTE (Operational Tour Expired), a statement that must surely remain for all time as a warning of what Italian vermouth can do to befuddle an Englishman's grasp of Scottish history – and that from an Adjutant of a squadron formed in Stirling!

In mid-February came the last move of the war to Ravenna LG, a single strip laid between the sea and the pinewoods of Marina di Ravenna, forty miles up the coast from Rimini. All the airmen of the entire Wing were accommodated in a great building originally constructed as a centre for Fascist youth and illicit love. Both were then absent but from the flat roof above the fourth floor it was possible in the early days to stand and watch the Spitfires take off, fly the five miles or so to their targets, bomb and return. The NCOs and officers went half a mile north of the airfield, into adjacent villas, with sea view, no mod cons – water strictly cold only from a bucket – but no rent payable either as the owners could not be traced! A suggestion that a reduction in the rates was called for was made during one seventy-two hour period when a 5·5 inch artillery piece dug its trail into the back garden and commenced providing intermittent 'support' to some far off infantry. To eat, to sleep, to drink were all thereby made less simple than usual. The Roman Catholic padre was moved by compassion to visit the mess and to assure Roman and heretic alike that they need have no fear of counter-battery fire as the Hun in those parts had no suitable weapons with which to reply, a gesture that bespoke a right interest in the mental contentment of the laity, but which though duly accepted with appreciation was really quite unnecessary for nobody had even thought of such a possibility. The idea, in those days, of any danger arising (flak always excepted) from the enemy never entered a single head. The last days were unquestionably near and not even the daily sight of fast-moving vapour trails that showed up the jet-propelled enemy recces caused any great concern for obviously they were too few and too late.

So during the lengthening days in March, while the Army, now at the east bank of the Senio river from Highway 9 to Lake Commachio prepared for the last thrust of all, the war of attrition from the air continued. Occasionally the medium bombers on a particularly deep and hazardous mission required an escort, but mostly it was bombs. Some days there would be a house or the corner of a field where the enemy had been located by his opposite numbers who called down on him from the heavens the wrath of a 4 x 500 lb Spitfire visitation. If there was nothing specific to hunt there was always plenty of employment in road and rail cuts, just for the hell of blowing a hole to make the enemy's movement even more difficult and slow. Never for long was there an absence of flak and losses continued to be suffered. Flt Sgt Howarth (Mess Treasurer) disappeared into a POW camp, and having failed to empty his pockets on a dawn mission after the night before caused a certain amount of difficulty in balancing the bar takings for that week.

Sqn Ldr J A 'Paddy' Hemingway DFC

Flt Lt Manson and WO Holliss both went down in flames and Australian WO 'Bluey' Mathers whose appellation belied a ruddy and carrot-haired appearance exploded while attempting, on fire, to crash land. Strangely, two members of his section affirmed that *after* they saw the explosion they heard his voice, 'I've had it chaps, cheerio . . . '

A near miss, attributable not to the enemy but to the triumph of the flesh over natural prudence came at the end of a first light sortie when a not unusual post-sunrise coastal mist made it necessary to divert a section of four Spitfires to Forli. Three went, the fourth, gaining through a funnel of clear vision in the fog a glimpse of home, and tempted it is said by the aroma of bacon frying in the mess below, succumbed to his stomach's urge. The end result was a landing that finished as an inverted tail first overshoot. The happily undamaged pilot found the hardest part of life for the next week or two was the total absence of mateyness from a formerly friendly groundcrew whose polished-to-perfection masterpiece he had so grossly laid in the dust.

At the beginning of April Sqn Ldr Jupp after ten months in command went home, OTE to Horsham, in 43's own county. Replacing him, Sqn Ldr Hemingway DFC, a Battle of Britain veteran, soon found more than a fair share of adventure which no doubt made him wish that he had not after his first sortie with 43 (an unusually quiet affair) made some derogatory remarks about flak. For having, on one day in April, destroyed a truck with his bomb, he returned to strafe and was hit by fire from the ground. Rudder useless he climbed to 2,000 feet and was hit again; engine and cockpit 'full of smoke' he made for friendly soil followed by his number two. A third direct hit stopped the engine but 'before I could make an orthodox exit another hit on the tail pitched the aircraft violently forward and threw me out. I landed safely and ran to a farmhouse but two Germans came after me so I ran off. They pursued me for several hours but I finally lost them by hiding in another farmhouse whose occupants hid me in a field and fed me with plenty of wine. Eventually, near dusk I met up with an armoured car of the 27th Lancers and so returned, not much the worse, to Ravenna.'

On the Eighth Army front D-Day for the last push was set originally for 7 April but because most Desert Air Force airfields were unserviceable through high winds was postponed for forty-eight hours. 'One more river to cross' would not have been an inappropriate theme song for an army that had been assaulting one river barrier after another ever since landing in Italy nineteen months before, and their final task promised to be another succession of them. Immediately before them was the Senio, with the Santerno and Sillaro both running across the first twelve miles of advance.

MEDITERRANEAN JOURNEY NOV 1942 – 1947

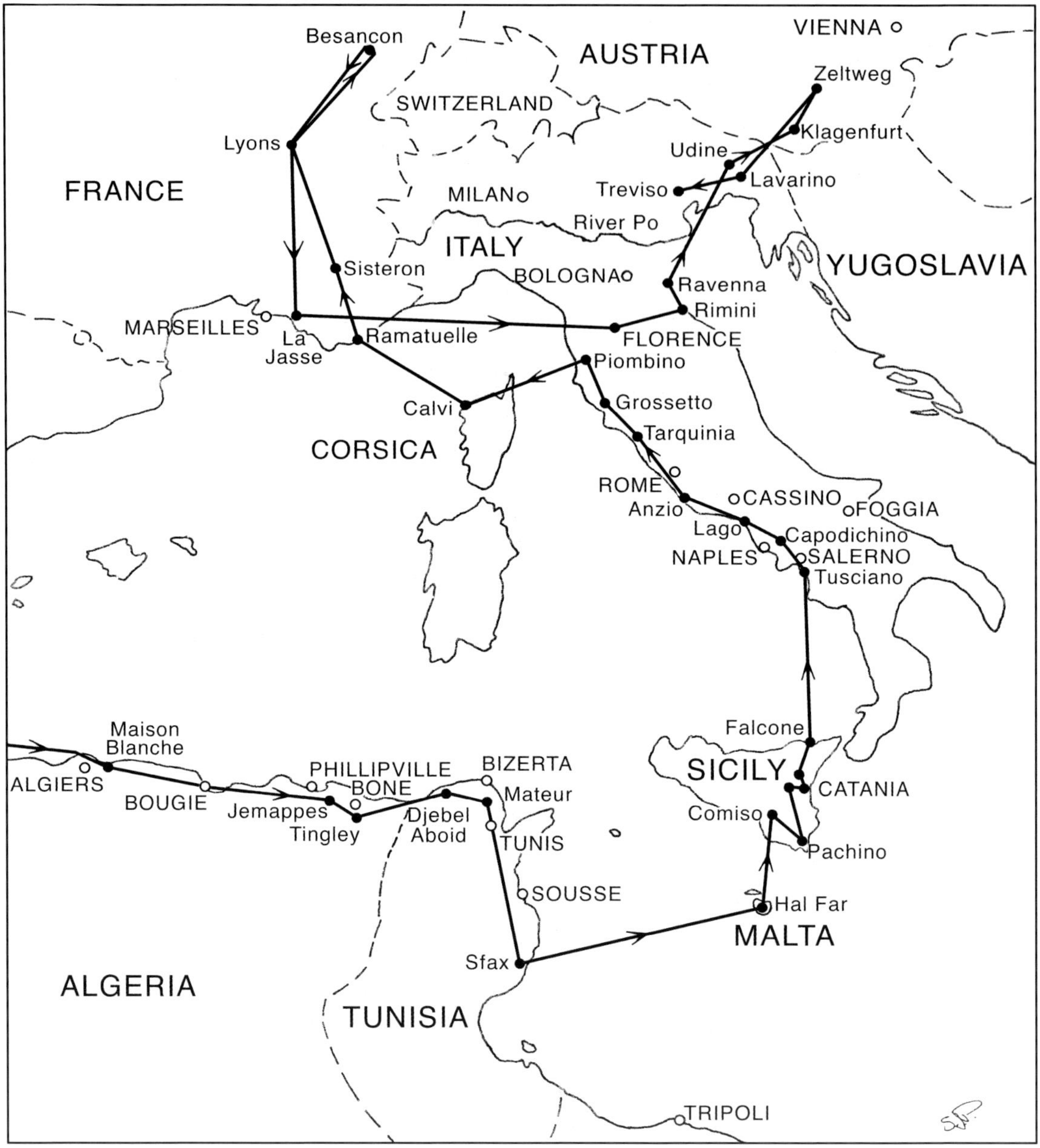

Ferrara's capture required fording the River Reno, then came the wide and mighty Po while beyond that the Adige was the deepest and fastest flowing of them all.

The morning of the 9th saw just enough flying to make the day appear normal to the enemy. Then at 1430 hours, with 43 Squadron and Group Captain Beresford in the lead, 324 Wing dropped 48 x 500 lb bombs on enemy positions in the steep flood bank on the western side of the River Senio. The Spitfires were soon back, nor hardly all landed before the first formations of medium bombers came winging in from the sea, high above the airfield, their bomb-doors already open so that nothing loose should fall on friendly heads.

The afternoon sun reflected off their silver wings and fuselages, making even more plain by contrast the dark recesses in which the bombs could be clearly seen, giving more than a suggestion of an irresistible, terrifying destructive power. If that in itself was a welcome assurance that this must surely be the beginning of the end, yet it could not be contemplated without a certain amount of sympathy for the men upon whose heads this mass of concentrated explosive was so soon to fall. For more than the hour, formation after formation, each as impeccable as the one before, streamed overhead, monopolising the air with the cumulative and continuing noise of their beating engines, until at last they were all gone and then it was time for the Spitfires to go off again, carrying for the first time napalm 'fire' bombs made up by filling Hurricane forty-five gallon long range tanks, and ignited by the comparatively crude method of an incendiary grenade fore and aft, though the end result was effective nevertheless. At H minus ten minutes these bombs went down on the forward German position so that 'the whole bank was a mass of flame and great pillars of smoke into which we repeatedly dived to strafe'. It says a great deal for the German Army that when at 1700 hours the first assault boats were dropped into and set off across the river they still met 'considerable small arms and mortar fire'. By nightfall crossings had been made at several points and advances of up to a mile on the western bank recorded.

At dusk there were reports of Ju 87s in the vicinity of the airfield but the only aircraft obviously in evidence were another great swarm of British, Polish and South African night bombers whose landfall was made right above the Sergeants' Mess and from which the Pathfinders' skymarkers could be seen plainly in the sky, shooting off a bright green coloured ball at ten second intervals. On the 12th the Army, preceded by another napalm bomb raid successfully stormed the Santerno and so as the days passed the Sillaro and the Reno yielded, Bologna and Ferrara fell and the Army came to the banks of the mighty Po. Here was one of the great river barriers of Europe, an obstacle so formidable that it had been considered possible the entire German forces might have retired to it when Italy collapsed in the Autumn of 1943. But now the Allies were to find that there was nothing left to bar their way.

'It was the River Po crossings that finished us,' wrote General Von Senger, commander of the German 14th Corps. 'We could have withdrawn successfully with normal rearguard action despite the heavy pressure but due to the destruction of the ferries and river crossings we lost all our equipment. North of the river we were no longer an army.' Von Vietinghoff, who commanded German Army Group C was even more definite in his views. 'The fighter-bomber pilots had a genuinely damaging effect. They hindered practically all essential movement at the focal points . . . even tanks could not move during the day because of the employment of fighter-bombers whose presence alone over the battlefield paralysed every movement. Especially in the region of Ferrara and Lake Comacchio the resistance of the troops was greatly reduced and communication and command were disrupted as never before . . . (so that) orders failed to come through at all or failed to come through at the right time . . . In any case the Command was not able to keep itself informed of the situation at the front, so that its own decisions and commands came, for the most part too late. The crossings of the Reno and Po rivers were decisively influenced by the employment of the Allied Air Forces . . . The morale effect upon the German troops of Allied Air Power must not be underestimated.'

Such a testimony from a document containing even more of a similar nature, written by the enemy Supreme Commander, not as an excuse for defeat but as an explanation thereof, eloquently shows how great a part of the final victory and the speed with which it was achieved was due to the efforts of the Air Forces.

For 43 Squadron, each day of the three weeks of which Von Vietinghoff wrote was not much dissimilar from any other so the details of one taken at random describe, in essence all of them.

23 April. Eight aircraft airborne on armed recce 0550 hours; one returned early, remainder bombed MT and staff car. Four a/c up at 0830, armed recce, bombed MT 1035, four a/c on Rover Paddy were called on to bomb four separate targets, hitting two houses, two lorries entering a farm, five motor cyclists and a gun position. 1300 hours, four a/c armed recce strafed barges on the Po. 1335, four a/c Rover Paddy, houses hit. 1645 four a/c armed recce bombed and strafed fifty box cars on a siding and thus on to last light when four a/c, (1900-2020 hours) on close support had three near misses on a road bridge and four more a/c on armed recce bombed and strafed a convoy of horse-drawn vehicles. That was the tally of one day and one squadron. Multiplied by fifty squadrons for three weeks the conclusions in Von Vietinghoff's report are better understood.

During the month of April alone 43 flew 675 sorties, dropped 591 HE bombs, 24 napalm bombs, scored 108 (20 per cent) direct hits and 160 (28 per cent) near misses.

The Germans continued in the face of everything to fight back and inflict casualties, although the Squadron's losses were happily less heavy than in the preceding month. Sqn Ldr Hemingway's little contretemps has already

Spitfire IX RR246 'FT-B' Ravenna on 12 April 1945. It was shot down the next day

been noted. Flt Sgt Williams, wounded by flak, flew home to safety on the 12th; Warrant Officer Edwards, an Australian, was captured when shot down before breakfast two days later. He never reached a POW camp for after fourteen days the train in which he was being transported was overtaken by American armoured forces, his captors having during those two weeks succeeded in moving him just one hundred miles. The reasons are made clear in another German report. 'Rail traffic was stuck in the most protracted fashion by the destruction of bridges . . . and with the increasing intensity of air attack especially on the stretch of the Brenner Pass the damaged sections were so great and so numerous that despite the best of repair organisation and employment of the most powerful rebuilding effort it became even worse and was only locally and temporarily usable.'

On the last day of April, when the German surrender delegation was already accepting conditions laid down by the Allies at GHQ Caserta, Sgt Crookes was shot down and on the following day when Flt Lt Evans and Lt Armstrong (South Africa), both of whom had been awarded a DFC two days before, led ten a/c to attack what turned out to be the last targets of the war (forty horse-drawn vehicles, two MT and one single-deck bus) they both reported 'accurate and intense 20 mm flak' which damaged two of the Spitfires engaged on the mission.

The very last op of all, and the only one recorded for 2 May on which day came the cease fire on the Italian front, was pure bathos.

'Spitfires PT487, MJ562; Pilots WO K F Hindson and Flt Sgt A A Cooper sent to investigate unidentified shipping, eight miles on 120° off Ravenna LG. One MTB and one LST seen going north. Reported to control and returned to base. Weather eight-tenths at 10,000ft.'

AND THAT WAS THE END.

Spitfire IX SM176 'FT-N' at Ravenna fully armed with a 500 lb bomb

CHAPTER 25

After the End

FOR forty-eight hours following the cease-fire all driving seats and cockpits were positively out of bounds: a wise precaution ordered by DAFHQ, to inhibit foolish accident and loss of life.

Because it took the Allied Forces in North-West Europe a few more days to tidy up their end of the battle front V-E Day was not celebrated until 8 May. Before then the Squadron had moved to Campoformido beside the road leading west from Udine. Here the 'official' victory came as an anti-climax, for the celebrations begun six days earlier had never quite stopped and for some at any rate the day was spent in unloading fuel from Liberator bombers acting as transports. Also on that day and the next, reconnaissance flights were made over the Austrian-Italian-Yugoslavian border areas where trouble was being experienced from an enemy SS Division which, showing reluctance to obey the 'unconditional' aspect of surrender, had blown some bridges in their area. The pilots reported that all roads were heavily loaded with transport and infantry on the march, all travelling towards the west away from the less considerate Russians and Yugoslavs.

It was the Yugoslavs who were mainly responsible for the Wing being ordered on 10 May to proceed at speed to Klagenfurt, the capital of the Austrian province of Carinthia. Pursuing the retiring Germans, the Yugoslavs had flooded across their borders into Italy and Austria, and there was good reason to suspect that with the permanent annexation of these border areas in mind the forces under Marshal Tito were acting on the doctrine of 'what we have we hold'.

To prevent any such *fait accompli* the 6th Armoured Division was despatched northwards to take over control of the threatened area of Austria; the veteran tank crews travelling all the more swiftly on hearing that the wanton destruction they were to stop included the pouring of thousands of gallons of wine down the gutters. Not far behind them, inevitably, came their supporting Spitfires.

So 43 went to Klagenfurt, and on the green grass of the airfield beside the tram terminus, with the distant strange broken peaks of the Karawanken range away to the south, it pitched its tents for the last time.

Early on it helped win a bloodless victory, when the Army, exasperated by unending delay and procrastination, reluctantly decided to wave a big stick. As part of the persuasion a four squadron, extra low-level, bombed-up beat-up was laid on. Whether the potential destruction they threatened or merely the noise they made had the greater effect was not determined: of the subsequent Yugoslav withdrawal there was no doubt at all.

From Klagenfurt the Squadron flew to take part in the final great flypast by the Desert Air Force; a few days afterwards twelve Spitfires flew escort to Field Marshal Sir Harold Alexander when he went to Vienna for the first meeting of the four occupying powers.

The rest of that Summer was mostly one long holiday, nor was there ever such more hardly earned, more richly deserved. Venice and the Adriatic were near enough for the asking but

Spitfire IXs at Klagenfurt in June 1945. The 43 Squadron aircraft are behind those of 72 Squadron

Squadron personnel relax beside the well-polished Spitfires at Klagenfurt, Austria, 1945
(Andy Saunders collection)

even nearer was the Wörthersee and beside this lake's clear deep waters the chalets and hotels became the base for round-the-clock swimming and all night carousals. There were tales of fish and boats that at times capsized, of fräuleins and fraternisation (at first forbidden though with slight effect).

There were unending parties, fuelled for many weeks by a great tipple – Verschnitt 38 per cent – a brandy of no little virtue, found by the Squadron in an abandoned SS Divisional Store during a hunt for billets. It was grabbed by Wing HQ on the grounds that they alone could ensure a fair distribution, but before the Sqn Ldr Admin got it within his grasp, a sensible proportion of it had been hidden, the reasoning being that fair shares meant 80 per cent for the Wing HQ and the remainder among the four squadrons.

A particularly strong fellowship sprang up with the locally billeted 3rd Battalion of the Grenadier Guards, who had come the selfsame road as the Squadron ever since Tunisia and were never slow to voice their appreciation of the support the Air Force had always provided. On one especial occasion the regimental Sergeant Major had stood up and, with all the terrible authority attached to his rank within the brigade of Guards, had ordered – yea, ordered his men to rise to attention and drink a toast to 'Our umbrella'. For a brief moment following the toast there was silence. The Air Force, whose discipline was of a different kind, coming largely from within, were quite awe-stricken by such a display of authority and obedience on what was essentially a social occasion. A reply in similar vein would have been wholly incongruous, but the night and honour were saved by the never-at-a-loss Sergeant Earthy, armourer and raconteur supreme, rising straight faced to his feet with the response 'Up Gamps, and drink to the Grenadier Guards'. There was only one thing to blight the joys and delight of those hot Summer days in the months after the war was won, and that paradoxically the very thing for which everybody had fought during the past five years; that now it was time to go home. As the weeks passed there were more and more handshakes of farewell as one old familiar face after another, some that seemed to have been part of the world since time began, went and was seen no more. The Aussies. New Zealanders and South Africans left first of all, followed before long by the Canadians. Soon the Squadron was what it had not been since the early nineteen-thirties, almost 100% British, and these, under the normal 'demob' procedure, were whittled slowly but continuously away. In September 1945 324 Wing moved into winter quarters on the undamaged airfield at Zeltweg, sixty miles north of Klagenfurt and a year later returned to Italy, there to spend a cold and lacklustre Christmas at Lavariano. Early in 1947 it moved to Treviso where 43 and 111, companions in the early days at Acklington

'A' Flight Spitfire HF IXs outside the hangar at Zeltweg, late 1945. RK853 'FT-C', nearest, while TB546 'FT-E' had just been taken on charge from 93 Squadron and the chequered tail strip had not been completely painted

chasing the trawler-hunting Heinkels became the last two squadrons in the last Wing of the once great Desert Air Force. And there on 16 May 1947, like the old soldier it was, faded away, destined to be dormant for twenty-one months before, at Tangmere, it burst again into active being.

The last days were different in many ways. In the dim long ago at Tangmere, there had been inscribed on the wall of the Pilots' Room, Ten Commandments. 'A Flight without an objective is like a kiss from one's sister; it lacketh a kick', one of them had pronounced. Now that appeared to sum up the whole of life, for it seemed, in the light of Hiroshima that the old pattern of air warfare into which the Squadron had fitted had gone; the close support at which it had excelled, and for which it continued to train, became as obsolete as the long bow or the muzzle loader. The term 'brush-fire wars' was, as then, yet uninvented.

On the technical side the first cold-blooded tentacles of planned servicing began to reach and envelop the Squadron, a process that may have been made necessary by the increased and increasing complexity of aeroplanes and their equipment but which was destined to wipe away forever the old conception of ground crews being an integral and all important part of a squadron's being. Soon, converted into soulless numbers of a servicing team they would never know, or perhaps even see, the men whose lives depended upon their skill and expertise.

In the face of all these unfavourable circumstances the old customs and spirit of the Squadron might well have shown signs of decay. In fact, though there may have been no stories about the last days to match the brightness of the war years, there was never any lack of spirit, nor was the Squadron roll full of nonentities.

Outstanding among many, Sqn Ldr Ambrose, Commanding Officer for the last year, was a great character, who came too late to 43; the wartime days would have been the better and the brighter for his earlier presence. As it was, the birth of a second daughter to his wife in England caused an upheaval in far off Styria, remarkable even by 43's standards. And there was Flt Lt Cox, who pining for the P-47 Thunderbolts in which he had stormed along the road to Rangoon, compared the Spitfire IX to its disadvantage while habitually flying it lower and faster than any other man who lived to tell the tale. Perhaps the most remarkable fact of all was that if any one of the pilots of the last year had been transposed six years back in time, he would not have failed to fit in with his predecessors, standing by in their Hurricane Is on the first day of the war or perhaps it was not remarkable at all, it just went to prove that some things about 43 never altered.

In 1946, Group Captain Beresford stirred things up with a competition for the best kept aircraft in 324 Wing. It surprised nobody in 43 Squadron that they finished first (with 98·1 per cent) and second. Possibly it was not really a fair competition and the Groupie should have cast back his memory to 14 April 1945, when he had stood, close to the Squadron's dispersal, with the Air Officer Commanding the Desert Air Force. They were awaiting the arrival of Field Marshal Alexander and, during the time before his aircraft came in, the AOC had said: 'I do not understand how 43 Squadron keep their aircraft so clean and still manage to fly.' What answer he received is not recorded. Perhaps in any case, if he wished for one he should have directed the question elsewhere. He might have asked one of the more than a hundred airmen who had soldiered with the Squadron all the way from Algiers; better still, the forty who knew it at Acklington, the twenty-five at Drem or the handful still left from Battle of Britain days. Best of all, the two survivors of the last months of peace in the summer of 1939.

They would have told him of pounds of beeswax and polish, applied on no directive from NCOs or Flight Commanders but voluntarily rubbed on through many an hour of hard work, because that was the way to make a Spitfire shine best on the ground, and best travel faster in the air. And they might have added that 43 Squadron always did things the best way because it was the natural order of things that they should. It was customary and habitual; it was the Squadron's tradition.

"Tailpiece or chequers restored"
This early post-war picture at Klagenfurt shows MH997 proudly carrying the newly restored black and white squadron markings on the fin with many abandoned Luftwaffe aircraft in the background

CHAPTER 26

Old Ways Refound

43 **SQUADRON** came back onto the active list on the morning of 11 February 1949. Under a blue winter sky with the air crisp and clear following a night frost No 266 Squadron was renumbered No 43. The Ceremony (which took place on the site of the 43 hangar destroyed in August 1940) was commendably brief but none the less impressive for that. In the presence of the High Commissioner for Northern Rhodesia Nos 245 (Northern Rhodesia) and 266 (Southern Rhodesia) Squadrons were combined to form 245 (Rhodesia) Squadron and the former 266 received 43 Squadron's cockerel badge from Air Marshal Sir William Elliot. In a short speech Marshal of the Royal Air Force Lord Douglas said that it was a source of wonder to him as it was to many other people that such a sense of tradition and continuity could grow up around a number. It was an opinion wholly shared by the many former members of the Squadron who were present that morning among whom not one could have explained, nor equally have denied, the particular characteristics of 43.

The parade and march past was followed by high speed formation flying and some solo aerobatics, after which all did justice in an adjacent hangar to a buffet spread, of a quality and variety rarely experienced in the austerity ridden world of those times.

Sqn Ldr D L Harvey receives the Official Squadron Badge from AOC-in-C Fighter Command, Air Marshal Sir William Elliot KBE CB DFC, at Tangmere on 11 February 1949

One could not expect that a Squadron used to thinking of itself as 266 could overnight absorb the history and mannerisms associated with 43 Squadron. Nevertheless before March was out the diary had already recorded that 'we were in the happy position with our good serviceability to offer the 2nd XI, in the shape of No 1 Squadron, help in the matter of aircraft. Obviously the new boys were learning fast. Within the course of the following few weeks further entries noted that the cleanliness of the aircraft was such that No 1 Squadron were shamed into action ". . . it is now possible to distinguish the type of their a/c and in some cases, the Mark".

The aircraft flown at this time was the Meteor F Mk 4, a development of the first operational jet fighter to enter RAF service. A hotted-up version had taken the world air speed record in November 1945 at 606 mph and though the normal version with armament, ventral tank and other drag-producing impediments was not up to this it nevertheless compared favourably with anything else then flying, and was capable of dealing with any potential opposition. Affiliation exercises with B-29 Superfortresses of the USAF showed no difficulty in intercepting them. A further claim was that films from the gunners of these formidable aircraft proved that *(a)* they could be shot down and *(b)* the best way of getting shot down yourself was to follow CFE (Central Fighter Establishment) theories and practice. This latter remark suggested that as in

Marshal of the Royal Air Force, The Lord Douglas of Kirtleside, inspects the 'new' 43 Squadron

the Battle of Britain a tendency to bind the pilot to set forms of attack might have undesirable results. Sqn Ldr P R W Wickham DSO DFC, who had taken over command of the Squadron very shortly after its reforming, must have been suitably pleased to be told by the AOC at his annual inspection in May, that 'As an ex-flight Commander of No 1 Squadron it was much against my will to say that No 43 looked better than No 1'; a remark subsequently rubbed in by a resounding victory in a 43 v 1 Squadron cricket match. The process of reverting to old ways was inevitably assisted by the arrival in August of one Flt Lt Fred W Lister. Last mentioned in Squadron records in the far off North African grenade-cum-latrine incident. 'Fred' came back to carry on where he had then left off. In between times he had commanded a squadron (2nd TAF) in NW Europe, added the DSO to his DFC, and then, after a spell in civvy street where he had found himself 'with lots of money and a good job, but no friends' he had returned to the RAF and not altogether by mere chance, found himself posted to 43. It was interesting that shortly after his arrival the posting in of Flt Lt S W F Daniel meant that for a brief period 43 had three out of its ten pilots holding both the DSO and the DFC (plus various bars). This unusual position did not last long however for before Christmas Sqn Ldr Wickham handed over to Sqn Ldr H R Allen, alias 'Dizzy'. The latter arrived from Holland and was viewed with suspicion for the first few days as he wore a No 1 Squadron tie in off duty hours. Sqn Ldr Wickham's almost last duty had been to take the Squadron to Acklington for air firing. A report of 'ice-age conditions, huddled in the bitter north, all hands down with pneumonia, 'flu, common cold and probably silicosis', suggests that the weather had not improved much since Sqn Ldr Lott and his men had made the same journey ten years earlier.

The last month of 1949 noted that 'Chequers', a bantam cock posted in during in August, the first of a succession of birds that have remained ever since with the Squadron, received two wives which settled well dispite one of them being chased onto the roof of the Officers' Mess by the mess cat. A rescue was effected by Flt Lt Lister. It also recorded that Flt Lt Eric Wingham had managed to land at Ford, the first aeroplane to do so for over a year, the runway being still under repair!

Three events marked the year 1950: the formation of a Squadron aerobatic team, re-equipment with the F Mk 8 Meteor and, in November, the Squadron left its traditional

The Meteor F4s in silver finish with 'SW' codes

Tangmere home for the Kingdom of Fife. The aerobatic team was formed on orders from Command to take part in a competition, the winners of which would perform at the RAF Flying Display at Farnborough in June. The team originally consisted of Flt Lt Farley (1), Plt Off Richardson (2) and Flt Lts Lister (3) and Dell (4) but the last named departed on a Fighter Leaders Course (which turned out to be the first step on a career that led to test-piloting Lightnings and the TSR 2), so Plt Off Wood was impressed into the side to make an equally competent number four. Thereafter the aerobatters, 'hogging the limited flying hours available' to the detriment of the rest, rapidly improved and had high hopes of success. However the days before the competition at Thorney Island on 3 May were interrupted by acting as bombers in exercise 'Stardust' and in another misnamed 'Morning Glory' which 'meant being blasted out of bed at 0400 hours' and on the day of the competition after two aircraft went u/s on taxiing out, the team 'apparently suffering from competition nerves' finished only second, very close behind 63 Squadron. However, though missing Farnborough, a display was given at White Waltham on Whit Monday. *The Times* reported that 'the most exciting event was a display of aerobatics by four Meteor jets of No 43 Squadron who, in spite of a gusty wind, maintained remarkable precision as they executed a series of complicated manoeuvres at about 500 mph.'

Aircraft taxy prior to flypast

Meteor F4s were not fitted with ejection seats

After comfortably winning the Station Sports at Tangmere the Squadron left for Acklington for its annual air firing and, returning from that place the richer by another 'real' fighting cock and three hens presented by that worthy Squadron honorary member Tom Nesbitt, coal-miner and breeder of fighting cocks, they found twelve 'beautiful new Meteor F8s waiting to be flown'. The change could hardly be called a stunning advance, the maximum power and thrust being virtually the same while an increase of 2,000 lb in the all up weight did little to improve the already soggy performance at altitude. The new aircraft were used in the autumn exercise 'Emperor' for which a move to Honiley was made, 'All aircraft arrived safely in spite of our being denied our normal navigational aid – a coastline.' Inexperienced controlling, dated equipment, lack of targets and long periods of readiness caused little joy.

The move to Leuchars when it came in November was, most naturally, highly unpopular. 43 had quickly re-established itself in the Chichester area and had small desire to move. The Squadron silver appeared in the Tangmere mess for the last of many occasions when the farewell dining-in night was held, the AOC-in-C of Fighter Command, Sir Basil Embry being present, following which came a few more nights of weeping and depression before the Squadron departed. 'The less said about our feelings on arrival at Leuchars the better' the Squadron diarist recorded. The next day the 'Cross Keys' was mentioned as a place where woe could be forgotten and with the aid of this medicine shop, and others like St Mike's or Kate's Bar, the Squadron soon found, as their predecessors on the south bank of the Firth had done exactly ten years earlier, that once you got used to the weather the east coast of Scotland was quite a passable place for a posting.

Anyway, January 1951 saw the 400 flying hour mark passed for the first time since reforming, a total again exceeded in sixteen flying days in February, when also the 'aerobatic team was dragged out of hibernation'. Nothing more of this lot appears in evidence until August when in the presence of HRH Princess Elizabeth,

The Squadron badge was painted on the nose flanked by black and white chequers

visiting the Station to present an Auxiliary Squadron with a trophy, the leading section of 43 in the station fly past looped out of it. In spite of this the team was then selected to represent the RAF at an international air show at Cannes. The Meteors were led by Flt Lt Eric Wingham with Fg Off Mike Beavis and (inevitably) 'Fred' Lister to port and starboard, and Sgt Pilots Alan Webster or Johnstone in the box. The subsequent reports indicate that the display was fully up to the highest 43 standard – beyond which one cannot go. The French had a word for it *'cinq puissants Gloster Météores Les Bireacteurs de L'armée britannique. Eus aussi sont supremants qu'on les admiraient et ils nous offrirent d'énormes loopings magnifiquement . . . .'* The non-flying part of the visit was up to the expected standard. Control broke down only once when the team unknowingly stood up and toasted itself at the dinner given by the Aero Club of Cannes.

This display was, sadly, the last important Squadron occasion for Flt Lt Lister, he departing to an OCU. 'A unique personality who will be missed a lot' was his epilogue in the Squadron records. It was no overstatement. In all its years there are very few who have given better service to 43 than 'Fred'.

Squadron Leader H R 'Dizzy' Allen DFC

Sqn Ldr Allen with the Squadron at Tangmere in 1949

By the time 1952 arrived the Squadron had quite become resigned to Leuchars and the placing of bets on the return to Tangmere was a thing of the past. Although it made little difference to the aircrew, the groundcrew, mostly National Service and therefore displaying a high turnover rate with comparatively short residence time, was soon composed almost entirely of Scotsmen so that the hangar floor was heavy with the glottal accents of Glasgow and the softer cadences of the east coast. Servicing at this time was, as throughout the Air Force as a whole, of a very mixed nature. The rundown of the skilled men after the war had not been arrested in time and the National Serviceman even if he was keen, and not all of them were, was generally just becoming sufficiently experienced to be useful when he became due for demobilisation. The few Senior NCOs available during these days carried a quite disproportionate burden of the load, mostly without due recognition, generally without thanks. 43 Squadron was probably better placed

The 1950 Team in line abreast

The F4 Formation Team in 1950 - 'SW' codes clearly seen

Groundcrew refuel a Mark 4
(Roger Lindsay)

Meteor F8 WA756/F carrying the Squadron's black and white chequers
(Roger Lindsay)

than most units in this respect. If the complete harmony and integration of effort between pilot and crew that characterised the pre-war and wartime Squadron was never so much in evidence under post war conditions, nevertheless the magic of 43 could still evoke a response in all but the most unfeeling National Service breast and though serviceability was not always as high as some eager young pilots would have wished, it was still better than most.

A lot of old faces went, a lot of new ones appeared in the first three months of 1952. Sqn Ldr Allen went to Fighter Command, clutching his presentation cigarette case presented, it is said, 'amid the thud of falling bodies and bottles' at a party which culminated in a tour led by trumpet-playing Flt Lt Lovell during which Sussex-by-the-Sea was sung to all and sundry. It can be inserted here that, eight years later, the only man ever to command Nos 1 and 43 wrote that he was 'still convinced that 43 was the best Squadron in the Air Force, and

Nine new Meteor F8s in arrowhead formation
(Flight International)

The F8 Aerobatic Team formed at Leuchars in 1950
with Flt Lt Lister, Flt Lt Dell, Plt Off Richardson, Plt 2 Wood and led by Flt Lt Farley

please send me a new tie.' Too much detail of the next two and a half years would tend to bore by repetition. By and large no changes of a fundamental character took place and everything went on in the usual 43 manner. This automatically implies that life was never dull or lacking in variety and every posting in, or out, every marriage and birth was an excuse for a party; when excuses were short the parties went on anyway.

Sqn Ldr Max Higson, who had originally arrived as a Flight Commander in place of Fred Lister was the CO for ten months in 1952. When he departed to the Korean War (where he destroyed at least one MiG-15 and won the US Air Medal) his place was taken by Sqn Ldr Roy Le Long, a New Zealander who had earlier himself been in that area and had won the American DFC, a medal which he added to the DFC won in 2nd TAF Spitfires, when among other things he had shot down the first enemy aircraft to be destroyed on D-Day above the Normandy beachhead. An exceptional leader, 43 was never a happier Squadron than under Roy Le Long.

Flying activities were those common to all Squadrons of this period, Wing and Command exercises, Royal Observer Corps co-op (invariably given the descriptive noun, nausea) battle formations at altitude, ciné, air firing and of course the inevitable annual visit to Acklington for air-to-air and air-to-ground firing. The 1953 visit recorded that Flt Lt Sid Walker had put up a score that made him the best shot in Fighter Command (35·9 per cent) for the year and also that one of the other twenty-nine Squadron pilots inadvertently sent a 20 mm cannon shell through the half-inch plating of the Seine net fishing boat *St Ebba* as it went about its lawful occasions in Alnmouth Bay. Contretemps with the nautical world seemed to flourish in these days for Flt Lt Lovell had removed part of a mast from a Dutch Navy minesweeper during a low-level practice attack (he afterwards won the US Air Medal and the American DFC while serving with the US Forces in Korea so perhaps it was worth it) and in the Summer of 1952 during Exercise 'Castanets' an attempt to sink two 'friendly' destroyers had drawn the wrath of Headquarters who were not at all mollified by the excuse that the ships were not showing black and white chequers.

A certain amount of aerobatics were laid on for special occasions such as 'Navy Days' at Lossiemouth and the Annual Battle of Britain open day at Leuchars and, on one occasion, at

Aircraft were camouflaged in 1953, WH293/Y with clear view canopy is seen in this scheme during a deployment to Cyprus.
(via Roger Lindsay)

the Edinburgh Military Tattoo. A flypast over Manchester in connection with the 35th Anniversary of the RAF in March 1953 was followed by another over Hampden Park, Glasgow two months later when Her Majesty Queen Elizabeth II visited Scotland after Her Coronation.

"In reasonable weather the flying was impeccable, the timing perfect; we were quite happy about the whole affair; in fact judging by the R/T patter one or two of the more excitable types were positively delirious." It subsequently transpired that the timing of Her Majesty's party had gone astray and there was some doubt as to whether anybody had seen anything at all. "However the following morning that wonderful *Forward with the People* paper printed the full story. Her Majesty, though late, had indeed seen the flypast between two adjacent chimney pots. Once again we emerge victorious."

A major characteristic of life during these days was the increasing frustration and discontent at the lack of a replacement for the Meteors. These machines, whatever virtue they may once have possessed were clearly inferior to the Russian MiG or the American Sabre, as Korea had shown only too well, and the Hunter and Swift replacements, which promised to restore the balance, continued to be nothing more than a desirable but unsatisfied dream. In fact the Swift, bedevilled by aerodynamic problems, never was to serve as a high-altitude fighter and the Hunter was delayed, partly by the small number of prototypes built for development and again, when on the point of entering RAF Service, by the necessity to fit an airbrake, a refinement originally proposed by the makers but initially considered unnecessary by the Air Ministry.

The Meteor, never outstanding at altitude, 'wallows like a sick cow above 30,000 feet when doing anything other than a Rate 1 turn', said a contemporary report, had coped satisfactorily enough when the target was nothing more lethal than a B-29 Washington or USAF B-36 but in the Autumn exercises of 1953 it met, for the first time in numbers Bomber Command's latest acquisition, the Canberra. 'It was most disconcerting', it was recorded, 'to find Canberras out-turning us at 40,000 feet and converting their mild-evasive-action-only tactics into perfect quarter attacks on our exposed bottoms. However we derived a considerable amount of valuable knowledge; for example the Meteor aircraft would make an efficient crop-sprayer – it certainly wouldn't make anything else.'

Again in October the heartache continued. "Tail chases and aerobatics are out; cases of severe wrinkling have occurred due to harsh braking after fast taxiing and a special order is being displayed reminding us that wings are liable to drop off during a heavy landing."

But all things come to those who wait and, following rumours that Hunters had actually been seen in the Spring of 1954 with the Central Fighter Establishment at West Raynham, the march of progress swept across the border on the afternoon of 29 July. Hunter F Mk 1, WW599, ex-5 MU Kemble rolled to a stop outside the Squadron's hangar and 43 at last were supersonic (anyway, in the dive). For the sake of posterity it must be recorded that as they were the first to receive a 200 plus mph fighter (the Hawker Fury) so were they the first in the RAF to receive the Mach 1 plus Hunter.

The first Hunter F1 WW599 arrives and is admired by all

CHAPTER 27

Supersonic

THE Hunter, F Mk 1, powered by the Rolls-Royce Avon RA 7 (7,550 lb thrust, Sea-Level Static) had a top speed of 617 mph (Mach 0·93) at 36,000 feet and 693 (Mach 0·9) at sea-level. It could climb to 45,000 feet in 9·8 minutes and had an absolute ceiling of 51,000 feet. Carrying no provision for wing stores, either armament or fuel, it was essentially a short range fighter with a range of action around 250 nautical miles. Its sole armament consisted of 4 x 30mm Aden guns firing at a combined rate of eighty rounds per second.

As the first squadron to fly the Hunter, 43 was to carry out intensive trials normal to a new aircraft entering the Service. After some concentrated lecturing, and a last burst of air-firing on the Meteors, the first Hunter entry in the Flight Authorisation Book at last appeared on 17 September. The next day was Battle of Britain Day and Sqn Ldr Le Long gave a demonstration producing, at his second attempt what the crowd were waiting for, a supersonic bang. This same bang was then still very much of a gimmick. Continued complaints from irate greenhouse owners or flashy Press articles reporting hundreds of tomato plants showered with glass had not, as yet, filtered through to top levels and the instruction to make all supersonic dives well out to sea had not been drafted. Consequently there was plenty of scope for varied, and not always very knowledgeable local comment. 'Along the Fife coast they are now quite accustomed to the bang of aircraft breaking through the sound barrier,' said one paper. But north of the River Tay the education of the people must have been more neglected. A year and a half after the first Hunter flight, under the large heading 'Mystery Bang' there appeared a most scarifying tale of an explosion which 'rattled windows and shook buildings in the Dundee area' so that 'one man rushed to his window thinking something had happened close at hand' while 'in the Sheriff Courthouse in central Dundee people felt the substantial stone building tremble'. A concluding paragraph both suggested and dismissed as the answer to the mystery, blasting in the local quarries of Cunmont or Longhaugh before leaving the papers' readers to fathom out the answer for themselves. Perhaps the scribe who penned in the Squadron's diary, beside this news article, the words 'ANSWER FOR THIS LAMPITT!' (and Co) was better equipped than the newspaper to come up with the solution.

The Squadron's first Hunter WW599 arrived on 29 July 1954

A second result of re-equipping with the Hunter was a spate of publicity quite unequalled at any other time before, or since, in the Squadron's life. It was not merely that comparatively minor incidents like an ejection brought great banners, 'Pilot of secret jet rescued from sea' – which was true but overdoing it a bit – as that the Air Ministry, long slated for the delay in bringing the Hunters into service and still rankling from the raspberries produced by the utter failure of the Swift, decided to strike back at last at their tormentors and to engulf and annihilate them with a torrent of publicity. The Hunter *was* in service, and the world should be told.

First in February 1955 came a great display at Wattisham. 43, who with the Hunters of 257 and 263 Squadrons provided the news claimed that they were sent as sixteen embryo film stars and returned to Leuchars a week later as shaken, hollow-eyed, twitch-ridden wrecks with chewed-up dinghies after several extremely dicey sorties in shocking weather . . . etc. Which suggests that either their spokesman had his tongue in his cheek or he was trying to get them each a commendation if not the AFC! The true facts of the case are of course that both Press and Parliament were greatly impressed (43 claimed that most impressed of all were 257 who borrowed two of their pilots to steady up their own formation), and for the

ne Hunter F1 Aerobatic Team initially flew three aircraft seen here over Crail airfield in Fife
(MoD (RAF) Crown Copyright)

The early Hunter F1 Aerobatic Team (1955)
Sgt Tom Lampitt, Flt Lt Alan Jenkins,
Sqn Ldr Roy Le Long,
Gp Capt P G O'Brien OBE DFC (Station Commander),
Plt Off Wally Forster (Reserve pilot and soloist)
and Sgt Norman Lamb
(MoD (RAF) Crown Copyright)

following few weeks every paper, periodical and news-film was avidly scanned. And if the weather had been half as bad as some made out there would have been no pictures to look at.

More pictorial fame was to follow; Sqn Ldr Le Long reformed an aerobatic team in March with himself, Sergeant Tom Lampitt and Sergeant Norman Lamb, and this innovation brought a visit from Air Ministry photographer Mike Chase whose quite remarkable air to air photographs of the three Hunters were very soon being displayed all over the world. More significantly, this move by Sqn Ldr Le Long began a series of aerobatic teams which in the course of the next few years became famous all over Europe. And not merely fame was acquired, but a reputation as *the* outstanding aerobatic team of their day, in exactly the same way as their predecessors in their Mach 0·2 biplanes had been a quarter of a century before. As has been said before in this history, doing most things better than the rest is a long established and continuing habit of 43 Fighter Squadron.

Since 43 Squadron began it, others with colourful names, like Black Arrows and Blue Diamonds have flown bigger and bigger though not better formations, but as nothing can ever replace the glory of Roger Bannister's first four-minute mile, so nothing can alter the fact that in the super as in the subsonic age it was 43 who first showed the rest of them the way to do it.

The Dutch, at Ypenburg, on Whit Monday, 30 May, were the first to see the team in action, following which the 21st French International Air Display at Le Bourget had a two day visit from them as the representatives of the RAF. On 7 July at Farnborough (in a show to celebrate fifty years of aviation) produced 'the finest and fastest exhibition of close formation ever seen at Farnborough' . . . a 'magnificent display, the three fighters performed a series of high speed aerobatics as though tied together' . . . Not that there would have been anything new in that if they had been. Formation flying had to take a back seat in July and August while extensive gun-firing trials were undertaken and when it restarted it was, in view of the impending departure of Sqn Ldr Le Long, led by Flt Lt Pete Bairsto with Fg Off Ron Smith at number two and the inevitable Lamb and Lampitt at three and four. This new team duly performed at Leuchars and Turnhouse on Battle of Britain Saturday, the display at the latter place being preceded by a low altitude run down Princes Street.

Following a special visit to Horsham for the benefit of the Prime Minister, September ended with the Annual Air Exercises, code-named 'Beware'. The remark that 'the Canberra looks quite different when seen from above' was indicative of the change brought about by the replacement of the Meteor. In the first ten 'scrambles' eight Canberras were claimed. As the local paper put it of one of them: 'The Canberra failed to "beware" and down it went, "destroyed" by the camera guns of the two flashing fighters. Aberdeen was saved!' (As it had held a flag day for the RAF Association the week before it was only fair it should be.)

At the end of October 43 visited the 18th Fighter Wing of the Swedish Air Force at Tullinge, near Stockholm. The Squadron was met on arrival by the Chief of the Air Staff, Major-General G A Westring, and at the end of the three day visit it was generally conceded by both sides that it had been a very good thing.

Sgt W Wilding, Flt Lt F Sankey,
Sqn Ldr R E Le Long, Flt Lt F U Holgate,
Flt Lt S Walker, Plt Off W Forster

A proposed display at West Raynham for the Italian CAS was foiled by unforeseen circumstances and that, apart from the expenditure of a great deal of 30mm ammo, to all intents and purposes brought 1955 to a close. In the New Year's Honours List Sqn Ldr Le Long received the Air Force Cross as a recognition of his three years' magnificent service in command of the Squadron.

He had been replaced late in 1955 by Major Ray O Roberts of the US Air Force, arrived on a two-year exchange posting and 'mighty proud to be leading such a famous Squadron'. Ray Roberts, from Georgia, had been a combat pilot in the Pacific and later flew in the Korean War. He had already flown the F-100 Super Sabre but if he found the Hunter slow by comparison was too polite to say so.

Major Ray O Roberts USAF

Hunter F1 WT585 'F' over St Andrews in 1955
(MoD (RAF) Crown Copyright)

Squadron pilots - late 1956
Standing: Fg Off Ian Aitchison, Fg Off Dickie Robertson, Flt Lt Jim Budd, Flt Lt Bob Shields, Flt Lt Ernie Powell, Major Ray Roberts (USAF), Flt Lt Pete Bairsto, Lt Alistair Campbell RN, Flt Lt Norman Maddock, Fg Off Ron Constable, Fg Off Ron Smith, Fg Off Mike Stabler
Kneeling: Fg Off 'Tommy' Thompson, Fg Off 'Mike' Tyrrell, Fg Off John Topping, Fg Off Johnny Pollock, Fg Off John Storey, Fg Off Sam Small, Fg Off 'Hank' Hancock, Fg Off John Merry, Fg Off 'Oscar' Wild

In February 1956 the Hunter F Mk 4 began to replace the F1. The F4 was to all intents and purposes equal in performance to the F1 but possessed an internal fuel capacity of 414 gallons against 334 on the earlier Mark and also had provision for the fitting of one fuel tank under each wing, which latter addition gave it a radius of action of 493 nautical miles.

An aerobatic display for the CAS Norwegian Air Force was 'clamped' off but more than enough consolation came in April when, during the visit of Marshal Bulganin and Mr Khruschev to Britain, a display by the RAF was laid on at Marham and 43 were brought in to do their stuff. The minimum height laid down for the Hunters was 500 feet. Some knowledgeable people present maintain that this was just ten times the true figure adhered to by Flt Lt Bairsto and his formation! A subsequent letter sent by the Air Minister said that he was 'most impressed'; even more to the point 'A N Tupolev, the aircraft designer, was beside me on the control tower balcony and his admiration of the accuracy exhibited, in particular by the formation aerobatic team, was quite spontaneous. It was a very fine performance'.

Four more displays in May at Yeadon, Hucknall, Scone and Linton-on-Ouse were

The Hunter F1 Aerobatic Team
(MoD (RAF) Crown Copyright)

The first Hunter Aerobatic Team in the Royal Air Force - Leuchars 1955
(MoD (RAF) Crown Copyright)

followed by the greatest challenge of all, a visit to Italy's Fiumicino (Rome) Airport to mark its official opening. Two cases of bird damage plus a cracked windscreen and 'a rudder that fell off at Istres' were hazards encountered en route to Rome but, came the day, all was well. There was a parachute drop from C-82s and the Italian Air Force P-8s set the centre of the airfield alight with napalm. Aerobatic teams from Belgian, French, Italian and United States Air Forces all added their share but it was left to 43 Squadron to provide the most spectacular and best appreciated eleven minutes of that whole day. Flt Lt Bairsto, with Fg Off Ron Smith, Fg Off Oscar Wild and inevitably Sgt Tom Lampitt (making a positively last appearance before departing to a test-pilot's job with Napiers) opened all the taps and demonstrated to the highly distinguished company beneath, including as it did the President of the Italian Republic, Signor Grouchi, the entire Italian Government, a fair sprinkling of high ranking NATO Air Force officers, and the AOC-in-C Fighter Command, that the reputation for formation aerobatics which 43 Squadron had established for itself thirty years before had not

In June 1956 the Leuchars runways were closed for resurfacing and 43 Squadron moved to RAF Turnhouse (Edinburgh Airport) for two months. By then the squadron was flying Hunter F4s plus a few of the earlier F1s as seen above.

diminished with the passage of time or the introduction of sweep-back. Just to conclude in a manner quite different from anybody else the four Hunters landed in two pairs, simultaneously from opposite ends of the runway. Of the innumerable compliments which 43 received subsequent to this display none sums them up better than the following report of a ceremony at Turnhouse in August.

"The aerobatic team of No 43 Squadron were yesterday presented with a silver bowl from the Italian Air Force in appreciation of their performance at the recent air display at Fiumicino, Rome. The presentation was made by Colonel G Pelosi, Italian Air Attaché, who praised the team's fine display, 'Everyone present,' he said, 'whether expert or layman, appreciated the outstanding qualities and professional skill showed by the pilots of the team. They made a brilliant contribution to the success of the display'."

In July, the team, with Fg Off Mike Stabler replacing Tom Lampitt, went off to the French National Air Display at Arras, hard by the spot where their forerunners had tried their 'prentice hands at ground strafing, but dirty weather proved too much even for 43. However at Horsham St Faith in the following week a display laid on for HRH Princess Margaret had more success and at Farnborough in September the team roused both the expense account and public day spectators to unqualified praise and approval. Following which the equally good shows at Turnhouse and Dyce for Battle of Britain Day were comparatively small beer.

In October the Warwick Film Company re-imported Ray Milland from Hollywood, tossed in one or two other stars and began to shoot their 'tribute to the RAF', *'HIGH FLIGHT'*. Fortunately they had the good sense to arrange for 43 to do

Fitting smoke canisters in Rome

By mid 1956 the Aerobatic Team was equipped with Hunter F4s
(MoD (RAF) Crown Copyright)

the flying sequences. The contingent from the Squadron invited to the World Première at the Empire, Leicester Square confirmed on their return the opinion held at the time of its making which was that this cinemascope-technicolour epic had everything except a plot and 'the only good point about it was the aerial photography'. Coincident with the premiere 'Fg Off 'Tommy' Thompson rose to stardom overnight, and produced some more pro-43 publicity on BBC TV Children's Hour. 'How we do our thrilling tricks' *(Radio Times)* or '17½, GCE and you're in.'

Then 'The Thrilling Story of the Fighting Cocks' appeared as a series in that peculiarly Scottish paper *The Sunday Post*. It is believed the reading public were suitably impressed. The 'crack supersonic pilots of No 43 Squadron at Leuchars' regarded it as an extension of the existing comic section *'Oor Wullie'* and *'The Broons'* for which the paper is quite justly noted. Although it would be fairer to say that the stories were rather a monumental reminder of the impossibility of translating the life of a fighter squadron into a language understood by the common people.

The last days of the old year coincided with the arrival of four brand new Hunter 6s (the first of many) and a firkin of beer (neither the first nor last of many) from Courage's brewery. The first day of the new one began with the award of the Air Force Cross to Flight Lieutenant Bairsto as a 'well done' token to his, and the Squadron's, aerobatic efforts of the previous twelve months, which necessitated another firkin of ale.

Fifteen point three per cent at air-firing was a good start for 1957. Less good news was a cut back of one third in pilot strength and a reduction in permitted monthly flying hours. However, matters brightened as the year progressed and in December the Squadron was

The 1956 Hunter Aerobatic Team – Standing: Fg Off 'Oscar' Wild, Flt Lt Peter Bairsto
Kneeling: Sgt Tom Lampitt (replaced by Fg Off Mike Stabler in July 1956), Lt Alistair Campbell RN and Fg Off Ron Smith

(MoD (RAF) Crown Copyright)

On 3 October 1956 Hunter XF705'P' suffered a bird strike on take off sliding into the River Eden estuary (fortunately at low tide). After a few total immersions the aircraft was hauled to the shore.

The steam traction engine from the Seven Dwarfs Garage at Guardbridge was used to drag the Hunter from the river. It had been used for similar tasks during World War II!

able to report that for the fourth consecutive month it had achieved its flying target, that it had flown more hours in 1957 than any other Fighter Command Squadron, and also had no avoidable accidents.

In between times it had seen the departure (in late summer) of Major Roberts to command an F-100 squadron in Europe and the arrival of his successor Sqn Ldr J F Langer. There was also the strange case of the arrival of the Air Officer Commanding upon his annual inspection in an Avro Anson and his subsequent departure in an Avro Anson bearing 43 Squadron's black and white chequered markings. Sadly too, this year had brought the winding up of the aerobatic team as the result of the decision to transform 111 Squadron into a special Fighter Command aerobatic outfit. Above all 1957 saw one of the greatest days in the history of the Squadron when, on 4 June, Her Majesty Queen Elizabeth II presented the Squadron Standard. This was the first time ever that a squadron of the RAF had received its Standard from the hands of a reigning monarch.

Naturally there was no lack of preparation for this ceremony, and the month of May was far from merry with flying virtually all off and a continuous round of cleaning, weeding, whitewashing, polishing and drill occupying most of the time. There was a course in sword-drill at Uxbridge for the officers, arranged not altogether by accident to coincide with the Annual Squadron Reunion in London. Though all these preparations were indeed a massive trial the foot-weary consoled themselves with the thought that it only happened to the best squadrons anyway. When the great day came the organisation of the ceremony went with the usual clockwork precision of such occasions. Her Majesty, accompanied by HRH the Duke of Edinburgh arrived by Transport Command Comet precisely on the stroke of the appointed hour. The Standard duly consecrated by the Chaplain-in-Chief of the Royal Air Force was then presented to the Squadron after which Her Majesty addressed the assembled ranks . . . .

Officers, Warrant Officers, Non-Commissioned Officers and Airmen of Number 43 Squadron:

This Squadron was first formed forty-one years ago, and although there have been two periods during which it has been disbanded it can boast of thirty-four years' flying, a record of which you may be justly proud and which few other Squadrons can equal.

Throughout its existence the Squadron has always been a fighter Squadron and has led the way in developing the technique and art of that branch of air warfare. It was among the first to be equipped with the famous Hurricane and the first to fly the Hunter.

In two world wars Number 43 Squadron has earned our country's gratitude. The Standard which I have just presented to you is emblazoned with battle honours, the names of which are enshrined in the hearts of my people, for they are names which speak of dauntless courage and endurance, of freedom saved and victory won.

I am sure that you who have inherited this great tradition will be true to it and that the spirit of service and devotion to duty upon which it was built will always be your inspiration. I am confident that it will be your guide in peace and that if the need to fight arose you would be worthy of the great deeds done by your predecessors. It is in that belief that I commit this Standard to your charge.

To which sentiments any comment would be superfluous.

A few weeks after the presentation Major Roberts, his two year stint with the RAF over, returned to the US Air Force in Germany where he took command of a F-100 Super Sabre squadron. He took with him a silver salver presented by the Squadron, the best wishes of all

Royal Air Force Leuchars - 4 June 1957
Fg Off Richard G Robertson receives the Squadron Standard from Her Majesty Queen Elizabeth II

who had known him, and in addition a high regard for the ways of Royal Air Force fighter men and 43 Squadron in particular. His first efforts to introduce a dining-in night routine to his parent air force resulted in the 'hospitalisation' of five officers and a request from the Commanding General not to ruin the USAF by introducing such disastrous Limey habits. Eventually settling for something quieter he went via Holloman Air Base to become Flight Chief of the TFX project.

The years at Leuchars following 1957 may justifiably be lumped together as an age when nothing extraordinary happened for all that the Squadron never lacked for either individual characters or corporate character. Not conducive to morale was the fact that the Hunter became progressively more useless for the task of defending the bases of the V-bombers, in whose retaliatory threat the real defence of the realm now resided. Even accepting that its primary purpose was ground attack the Hunter was falling rapidly behind the march of progress elsewhere. As witness a letter sent to the 'Commanding Officer of the 43rd Fighting Cocks' from the Fighting Red Cocks of Attack Squadron 63 US Navy, 'Our aircraft is now the FJ-4B Fury. Our primary interest in life is low-level penetration with a nuke but we can also join in most creditably with napalm, rockets, bombs, guns, or air-to-air with Sidewinders. We have no afterburner but with the Sidewinder feel that we can handle anything we can see. The plane also has a Buddy Tanker for air-to-air refuelling . . . .'

Perhaps because there was nothing new in this position to a Service too often badly equipped by the incompetence of politicians, and to a Squadron in particular, whose forebears had unflinchingly met the Richthofen Circus with 1½ Strutters, or prepared to do night battle with torches lashed to the longeron and a speed advantage over the enemy of minus 40 mph there was no obvious weakening of morale.

Squadron Leader John Langer, Commanding from 1957 to 1959, has always maintained that the AFC he received should have been a Unit Citation for the consistent good shows put up by the Squadron during his tour at the top, and in a letter to his successor, his comments that 'to have been CO of such a Squadron was honour enough for a lifetime' or that his tour had been 'two wonderful years with the best' scarcely suggests any diminution in Squadron performance or spirit. And although the times were in general nothing extraordinary and life consisted mostly of the routine jobs that were the warp and weft of the pattern of Fighter Command there were yet some events that stood out.

Vampire T11 XE897 'Z' at the 1957 Battle of Britain Airshow at Turnhouse

In April 1958 the 'impossible target' of 570 hours set up a new all time high for a Hunter squadron. It was modestly recorded that the previous record, twenty-two hours less than the 570, had also been set up only two months earlier by 43. In between these two scores an exchange of eight Hunters and pilots with 724 Squadron of the Danish Air Force had sent 43 to Aalborg. From that place they succeeded in sending to Leuchars 'as many picture postcards as there were bars in Aalborg', as well as bringing forth a protest to the British Embassy in Stockholm that 'two RAF Hawker Hunters had flown over Swedish Territory at a great height for twenty minutes.' To which complaint off-course Oscroft and Topping were heard to mutter mightily on radar controllers who located you somewhere other than where you really were, but how unusual it was to be intercepted by a SAAB 29.

A reinforcement exercise to Cyprus in July 1958 (see Appendix 7) was also the first of what was to become an annual visit. Two months of sunshine, battle flights, beer, air-to-ground, ciné, radar trips for the Navy, more beer, Army Co-op exercises, low flying, more beer, and scrambles ended with a final Squadron Formation to show the Middle East how it was done, before their return in September. Among the forty-nine different varieties of aircraft sighted or intercepted during these days were everything from the (then still secret) Lockheed U-2 spy-plane to 'a three engined Savoia Marchetti SM 79 from the Lebanon', carbon-copy of the type that the Squadron had hammered to destruction above the Phillippeville convoy in 1943. Detachments to Cyprus were repeated in 1960 and 1961, 1959 being an odd year out with a visit to El Adem in October. 'We pictured a water shortage, a burning sun, clear skies and all that, like in the *Desert Rats* or *Ice Cold in Alex*.' So much for conjecture. 'On the first day of our stay 1·75 inches of rain fell' – more than the

The Squadron pilots - late 1959
Standing: Fg Off Henry Ploszek, Fg Off Jock Heron, Fg Off Dave Malin, Fg Off Nigel Lane, Fg Off 'Thug' Thornton, Fg Off Neil MacIndoe, Fg Off Mike Kelson, Fg Off 'Ben' Sulaiman
Seated: Fg Off Chris Golds, Fg Off 'Kiwi' Williams, Flt Lt Bill Woods, Sqn Ldr Dave Scrimgeour, Sqn Ldr John Langer, Flt Lt John Harper, Capt George Wegman USAF, Flt Lt Eric Smith, Fg Off Dick Foster
(MoD (RAF) Crown Copyright)

whole of the previous winter – and subsequently three exercises were cancelled due to wind, low cloud and bucketing rain.

The death of Fg Off John Cleaver, returning home from Cyprus in a Hunter of 92 Squadron, ended a five and a half year period without a fatality. There had been some near misses however, bringing more excitement into the lives of some pilots than they might have wished and leading to reports such as 'Ernie Constable went roaring off the end of 23 into the Eden, engine spitting out bits of roasted seagull. Fortunately the tide was out and the helicopter snatched him off to sick quarters'. Compressors wrecked by birds remained an ever-present hazard but it was left to Fg Off 'Jock' Heron to enact in real life the old wartime line shoot 'There I was, on my back, fifty feet up and nothing on the clock except the makers name' during a solo aerobatic rehearsal for the 1959 Battle of Britain Day. Actually he had 1,500 feet to spare when his Avon flamed out while inverted, and was able to roll out, pull up and after failing to relight make a passable landing on the short (too short by a furlong) runway at Errol. 'An engine failure at 1,500 feet is a difficult thing to handle. This chap showed great judgement and airmanship in landing at Errol . . . it was a good show.' That was what the Wing Commander Flying at Leuchars thought of it.

Sqn Ldr Scrimgeour arrived in July 1959. Among the highlights of his two years in command were the arrival of the first interim Mk 9 Hunters. The Mk 9 was a Mk 6 converted to Ground Attack specification and with a capability for carrying a 230 gallon long range tank under each wing (in addition to the normal 100 gallons of the earlier Marks) brought forth the comment 'we shall soon have square backsides'. September 1960 found the Squadron on detachment at Stradishall where it operated for the first time for nine years, as part of a Wing with No 1 Squadron. A further detachment to

The T7 rests just short of the runway - November 1959

Coltishall produced the claim that the Squadron had entered every one of the 365 pubs in Norwich. Not only in the heat of battle it seems are fighter pilots given to miscalculated claim. Great jubilation greeted the demise of the Squadron's solitary Mk 7 (two-seater trainer) Hunter when it was laid on the approach lights by Flt Lt Woods after a flame-out. Although the pilot's notes claimed that it was light and pleasant to fly, the T7 appears to have been a constant bane to all men and hints of 'taking the chopper to the Mk 7' etc constantly appear in these days.

Sqn Ldr Bairsto's 66 Squadron at Acklington was bombed with 'seven rattlesnakes dropped by a formation of four' on New Year's Day 1960. One Hunter forced-landed and returned bearing the 'enemy' insignia. Two months later another squadron received a commander from a 43 Flight when John Howe went off to take over 74 before it began to re-equip as the very first English Electric Lightning unit. The arrival of this remarkable aeroplane in Fighter Command led to some radical changes. Squadrons not destined to receive it were in many cases marked for disbandment. No such hard fate befell 43 who, after a period of uncertainty found themselves earmarked to become the resident Fighter-Ground-Attack Squadron in the Near East Air Force, place of abode Cyprus. A two month detachment on this island ended in April 1961. Returning to Leuchars just in time to rush down to London for the Annual Squadron Reunion, they spent the month of May making merry with farewell parties to those who were leaving and consuming large quantities of liquid in welcoming those who came in. On the highest level Sqn Ldr Scrimgeour gave way, after two years, to Sqn Ldr Peacock. In between times they began to pack.

In June, the diary reported 'a highly successful take-over bid for the Squadron' – confusion took over. Every stage of the proposed move to the East has been struck by the old proverb . . . 'it's all been changed'. A 1942 veteran from Kirton-in-Lindsey surveying the scene might well have chuckled mightily in remarking that if the subject was confusion then nothing had changed very much at all. And for sure you could have traced an old ack-emma who had banged the nails into the crates at Ruislip before the 1½ Strutters flew off down the Thames – you would have found that the unchangingness of confusion in major Squadron moves went back to the very beginning of things. Right up to the very end the scene remained one of near comical chaos accepted with the inevitable good humour and resignation. Even the final plan which was to have a farewell parade on 16 June followed by the Squadron being dined out the same evening, the AOC being present at both functions, went awry for the AOC could not make the night of the 16th and the Army band could not arrive in time for parade on the 15th. So it all added up to a 'smashing' time on the 15th followed by a morning parade on the 16th. The remark in the squadron diary that 'this was as disastrous as it sounds' probably had a modicum of truth. But then Air Officers Commanding who were young Plt Offs when *Ma Meyrick's Own* was a byword in the Air Force understood these things. And as the diary concluded: 'Nobody actually fell over though D . . . M . . . had a 45° list to port.'

Hunters at Leuchars ready for departure to Cyprus - 20 June 1961

CHAPTER 28

Near East, Middle East

THIRTEEN Hunters, a total that included the repaired, though still unpopular, T Mk 7, provided the expected low-level farewell beat-up before heading off to Nicosia via Nice, Malta, and El Adem. The industrious groundcrew, whose sweat had provided this 100 per cent serviceability, and surplus pilots went non-stop by Britannia. Arriving twenty-four hours earlier than expected they found no accommodation available.

On reaching Nicosia, the Hunters went immediately into 'Battle Flight', a chore that kept everybody busy for the remainder of the month. Complaints from the Squadron that Command Operations had little knowledge of the requirements of Hunters were not wholly unfounded but in spite of 'being on ten minutes, stand-by, two minutes readiness, airborne patrol, armed and sterile, all in half a day' it was reported that 'morale remains high.'

It was still high when the Air Officer Commanding-in-Chief visited the newest arrivals in his Near East Command. That worthy arrived by Canberra. As other VIPs had done before, he departed with his aeroplane carrying on its fuselage, the black and white chequerboard of 43. In September the Squadron, in fair combat against all Akrotiri and Nicosia Squadrons, captured the MacDonald Swimming Trophy. Meanwhile, the *Scottish Daily Mail*, unaware of their prowess in eastern pools, was lauding their praises in an eve of Battle of Britain Day write-up. Three months out of date they proclaimed: '43 Squadron welcome you to meet them at Leuchars tomorrow' . . . 'televised for the first time on STV No 43 will be taking a prominent part in the display' . . . However, the sub-editor did manage to hit the jackpot of factual correctness with his last words, 'When 43 talk about formation aerobatics they know what they are talking about.'

Encouraged by such praise 43 pressed on with renewed vigour. So much in the case of Flt Lt Hay that he managed to overstress two aircraft during consecutive sorties. Less brutal, but officially described as 'impressive' was an aerobatic display laid on for a large party of visitors.

Early December brought promotion exams for the erudite and not so clever alike but once they were over life could be looked at in lighter vein. On the 14th six Hunters prepared to exercise the Olympus radar station, thereafter, 'four went u/s on start-up but undeterred the few got airborne – just then Olympus went u/s too. Apart from that it was a valuable exercise and we are glad we were asked to help.'

Pantomime, traditionally beginning on Boxing Day, got an earlier start this year. On the last working day before Christmas a 'fluid six' led by Flt Lt Chris Golds got airborne and their subsequent antics drew forth from the helicopter aces of 103 Squadron to 'The Officer in Command Entertainment, No 43 Squadron' the following letter:

Sir,
Pantomime.
I have the honour to have witnessed an excellent pantomime this morning, over Nicosia, at 0900 hours. I thought that the display of the six dwarfs was in keeping with the season, and I feel that the loss of Snow White was more than adequately made up for by the presence of Goldilocks whose instructions on the radio rounded off the whole show. I am sure a great deal of practice was put into the display which was well appreciated by the audience!
Yours faithfully . . . etc.

Having thus demonstrated their (inadvertent?) ability to behave like clowns the Squadron now proceeded to demonstrate that they were pretty good at other things too, and during an air-ground cannon and rocketing phase, (with Sqn Ldr Peacock struck by the lurgi and no less a person than Goldilocks taking over the whip), the dwarfs and their associates, in the course of flying their highest number of monthly hours since arriving in

The Hunters at Nicosia - July 1961

Nicosia, thumped up to a 42 per cent average on air-ground, which fact as they did not fail to mention 'BEAT ANY PREVIOUS RECORD BY ANY HUNTER SQUADRON'. In between times they 'intercepted and duly hacked' the Javelins of 23 Squadron when they arrived on detachment. The Javelin pilots denied this achievement, saying that they had seen no Hunters. 'This,' said the Squadron diarist, 'we are quite prepared to believe.'

'Winged Phoenix' took four aircraft and eight pilots to Kenya for an Army co-operation exercise. The ground forces were duly appreciative of the Squadron's efforts, particular admiration being shown for one Hunter 'approaching the floor of the Rift Valley with much vertical velocity', a manoeuvre less favoured by a wrathful Station Commander, an irate Squadron Commander, or even perhaps by the recipient of an extra week-end Battle Flight duty.

Cyprus weather being what it is, with each passing month the weather went from hot via very hot to too hot, and as the temperature went up so did the consumption of beer. Two cockerels and four hens, long delayed by a fowl pest outbreak in England, at last reached the Island, and another visitor was Air Vice-Marshal F E Rosier CB OBE DSO, 'A' Flight Commander in the years immediately prior to September 1939, and by then Air Officer Commanding Air Forces Middle East.

Flying had variety in abundance. Ciné, air to air, spring exercise 'Adex', exercises with the Army at El Adem and again to Kenya. Firepower demonstrations, formation on behalf of *Flight* photographers, interception of strikes by F-100 Super Sabres of the Turkish Air Force, a visit to Greece, a fly-past for Battle of Britain Day, and a detachment to Bahrain all fell to the Squadron's lot before the year was out. The last month of all brought another visit to Libya for 30 mm air gunnery and 3 inch rocket firing, during which course Fg Off Tim Robertson accidentally dropped a pair of 230-gallon overload tanks and obtained one of the few direct hits of the week. And so much less embarrassing than an earlier case (by another pilot) at Nicosia when the accidental depositing of four 100-gallon tanks on the tarmac produced no less than seven fire engines and one ambulance!

January 1963 was a time of 'all change'. After less than two years' residence in Cyprus the Squadron was ordered to prepare to move to Aden, there to form with two other long established Squadrons 8 and 208, the latter originally the famous 8 Squadron of the Royal Naval Air Service that had flown Camels with 43 in 1918 at La Gorgue, a tactical support and Ground Attack Wing. The farewell parade to march off the Squadron Standard on 22 February had to be held in a hangar because of heavy rain. The Air Officer Commanding-in-Chief, Air Chief Marshal Sir Dennis Barnett was present. A flypast during the parade by Flt Lt Bob Smith, one of several pilots scheduled to go to the UK instead of Aden, was low enough to give those inside the hangar the impression that the roof was meant to fly past as well. 'However', it was recorded, 'after long months of practice he just missed it'. The same pilot, the previous month had received the thanks of the AOC-in-C for 'a very polished display of low flying' for some high ranking visitors.

The parade on the 22nd was followed by a farewell party. After Flt Lt King had left as advance guard in the long lasting T7, there was another party on the 23rd continued on the 24th. When 29 Squadron arrived, as replacements for 43, on the 28th the Squadron had still not left. It was 2 March before they did. They arrived at Aden to be met by Air Vice-Marshal Rosier, their new C-in-C and the TV cameras of the BBC – 'seen by thirty-six million viewers on Eurovision – a genuine hero's welcome' the Squadron diary proclaimed.

Nor was it all quite idle boast and foolish word. A letter which followed to Aden, from Wing Commander Flying at Nicosia, Philip Thomas, showed that it was not themselves alone who had a good opinion of 43.

"Any station that has 43 resident should consider itself fortunate, for a more dedicated and professionally able assembly would be difficult to find. It was a delight to know and work with you all and any wistfulness I may experience at saying good-bye to you now is modified by the thought that I shall have the privilege to see you from time to time at Squadron reunions." Within weeks of its arrival 43 had improved the Wing averages for air-ground firing and on The Queen's Birthday fly-past provided five out of the nine aircraft after 8 Squadron, detailed for the job, had failed to supply enough. In May they led the fly-past to bid farewell to Air Vice-Marshal Rosier. After a dinner in June to celebrate their second year away from Leuchars, and a spate of nose-wheel trouble, they spent July and most of August at Bahrain, with detachments to Sharjah for weapons work. After that spell in those most blistering and unlovely places a two week detachment to Nairobi was doubly welcomed.

Camel Squadron 1963 style with Aden Levy Scouts
(MoD (RAF) Crown Copyright)

The main purpose of the visit was a display by eight aircraft at the Kenya Royal Show. This, the last show before that country was given its independence will no doubt be the last for all time. Following massed bands, grand parades of horses and cattle, the Molo hounds and more massed bands, the Squadron arrived, on cue at 1645 hrs. For the benefit of those who can understand the jargon the routine will be described in detail. It is the last occasion in this history, though surely not in all history, that 43 Squadron aerobatted in sizeable formation before a large and appreciative audience.

Sqn Ldr Peacock, Fg Off Law, Flt Lt Doggett, and Flt Lt Edwards made up a box of four. Stunt men Flt Lts Golds and Stoker initially formated with this box. Flt Lts Osborne and Chapman flew low and slow. The box plus two arrived, stuntmen turning and splitting off leaving the box doing dumb-bells. Halfway through this, two aircraft flew across low and slow with undercarriage down. The box then split in two and shortly afterwards returned at high speed from opposite directions. As the box reformed

The four man Aerobatic Team
Fg Off Derek Law (2), Sqn Ldr Peter Peacock (1), Flt Lt Jim Edwards (4) and Flt Lt Chris Doggett (3)

OC 'B' Flight, Flt Lt C C 'Chris' Golds on the left seen with Flt Lt W I C 'Bill' Stoker on 18 September, 1963 at RAF Khormaksar in Aden after a first synchro pair low level aerobatic sortie. A later 43 Flt Cdr in Aden, Bill Stoker would also command 8 Sqn at Muharraq and, on 19th July, 1972, lead the Sultan of Oman's Air Force Strikemasters in support of the SAS at the critical battle of Mirbat

the two stuntmen began some co-ordinated aerobatics, on completion of which the six threaded the needle and the show was over. The President and the Royal Show Committee gave thanks for 'a magnificent display, greatly enjoyed'. The RAF Station at Eastleigh, awarded a Silver Medal for its services, freely acknowledged that 43's contribution had been partly responsible.

Only one disturbing note appeared. A letter in the *Kenya Times*, signed by 'ex-Kerosene Cowboys' described the formation flying as 'not only noisy and disturbing but extremely tatty' ... 'same way same day'. There are some who believe that this letter had its origin with a certain coat-trailing, mickey-taking Fighting Cock. Be it so or not the response evoked by this letter was remarkable and 43's admirers leaped to its defence. 'A fabulous performance of precision flying', said one defender. Another, a 'former WAAF married to a pongo' quoted him as saying that 'the free falling parachutes were terribly impressive, but I really must take off my hat to your service, darling, they excelled themselves; by far the best thing in the show.'

On returning from Nairobi the Squadron bade farewell to Sqn Ldr Peacock and welcomed his successor Sqn Ldr P H Champniss whose first reported statement was alleged to be 'you play ball with me and I'll hit you over the head with the bat.' It was cannon and rocket however, not a bat, that the Squadron used to wallop the Wing averages again in October, following during the next month with a prolonged number of practice low-level strikes. 'Four aircraft racing through grey-gold wadis, across the undulating oceans of ochre sand, with occasional glimpses of a muddled village on a ragged outcrop, or a fort or mosque sticking up white and wart-like .... '

It was intensive practice soon to be put to the test, for the storm of civil war in neighbouring Yemen was already splashing in spasmodic warning droplets across the border. A lost Russian transport of the Republican Yemeni Air Force landed only eight miles north-east of Aden and deliberate penetrations by aircraft from north of the border became more frequent. These did not go unheeded and an increasing amount of time was spent at readiness though with nothing to show for it.

Several pilots left for the UK at the turn of the year. Among the group whose departure was made the more reluctant by the impending promise of action were two four-year Squadron men Flt Lts Golds and Malin. Those remaining went off to Bahrain for another detachment, got washed out by an ultra-high tide driven up by the Shamal wind at Sharjah, and finished by impressing the visiting detachment from the Day-Fighter Combat School with their 'matchless skill'. So back to Aden at the end of February, there to find that the unsettled situation on the northern borders of the Federation was now rapidly racing to explosion point.

Radfan and Harib are the kind of place names that mean absolutely nothing until, bursting from anonymity they thrust themselves upon the world in banner headlines and on television screens. There for a brief space they take pride of place until, overtaken by other names and other events, they sink back into the near-oblivion from which they sprang, unremembered by any save the few thousand who were for a space intimately associated with them. For 43 Squadron Harib and Radfan were two such places. Harib gave its name to a hill fort across the Yemen border, just one of several in those parts, of no special significance or tactical importance. The order to attack it was made entirely for political reasons after a year in which Yemeni Republican aircraft had on several occasions flown across the border to strafe property and people of the South Arabian Federation. Their place of incursion was seventeen Hunter minutes from Khormaksar and the raiders were able to recross the border unchecked. An aeroplane with a thirty mile radar and four times the endurance of a Hunter (like a Phantom) might have solved the problem. As it was there was no other course open but a retaliatory raid to demonstrate to the local inhabitants that the British had not only the ability but the desire to protect them. Therefore after a final warning to lay off had been followed

Aden Boys 1965
Standing: Flt Lt Peter Biddiscombe, Flt Lt Alan Pollock, Flt Lt Neil Hayward, Flt Lt Alasdair Liddle, Flt Lt Barney Lydiate, Sqn Ldr Philip Champniss (OC 43 Sqn), Flt Lt John Thomson, Flt Lt John Osborne, Flt Lt Roger Wilkins
Kneeling: Flt Lt Geoff Taylor, Fg Off Don Brown, Fg Off Tony McKeon. Fg Off Nigel Ashley, Fg Off Mike Fernee, Fg Off Rod Dean, Flt Lt John Batty, Fg Off Peter Skinner

by an enemy attack with helicopters firing machine-guns, eight Hunters, four from 43, followed by four from No 8 rocketed the Harib fort. 'It was a piece of pee,' was a speech of Pat Hill, the youngest pilot in the attacking force. 'We went in low and plastered it – got 92 per cent direct hits with 3 inch rockets.' There was a lot more that he said but the combination of a Squadron reunion and Pat's brogue made it difficult to remember.

Before the attack a leaflet raid gave warning to the locals to scatter and subsequently air reconnaissance showed no sign of casualties, but it inevitably produced a great deal of fury in certain quarters. The Afro-Asian bloc at UN viewing all things through coloured lenses, bellowed in anger. From far on the left, *Tribune* likened the Royal Air Force to 'hooligans breaking up cafés', a simile simply refuted by Peter Simple of the *Daily Telegraph* who queried whether 'hooligans normally sit with patience while café proprietors break up their homes, before retaliating'. The Labour Party 'regretted the action of the Conservative Government as not being the action of a great power'. (A few months later with the easy humbug of the professional politician, they gave their complete support to a similar but much greater retaliatory action in Vietnam by the American 7th Fleet). Lap-dogging faithfully along the party line, the *Daily Mirror* found enough space among its usual pattern of slush, sex and cheesecake to squeeze in some sneers about 'semi-illiterate staffs' in Whitehall and the 'anointed boys' piloting the Hunters at their command.

Not surprised at such vituperation, but perhaps a little dismayed that the case for making the raid, in honour of treaty obligations and to demonstrate to the Yemen that their attacks would no longer be tolerated, was not as forcibly stated as it might have been, the 'anointed boys' kept on with the job. The base at Aden, being in both British and American opinion of vital importance for at least the next ten years, there was little else to be done, except perhaps to recall Kipling's words and wonder how long it would be before 'blast your soul Tommy' would change again to 'Forward Mr Atkins'.

In any case the Harib fort raid was but the prelude to several weeks intensive operations which gave no time for introspection. The opening scene set in the Radfan area, found men of the Special Air Service moving in to clear the Aden-Dhala road which had been made near impassable by the hostility of the local tribesmen. Before long the soldiers, finding themselves opposed by three times the expected numbers of opponents and they, moreover, not merely gun-toting tribesmen, but a disciplined force armed with mortars and machine-guns and trained in company tactics, were in some trouble, lost two men killed and several wounded and so called on the Air Force for support.

The call was answered by the Hunters of 43 and 208 Squadrons. With 3 inch rockets and 30 mm cannon fire the immediate situation was relieved, so well that the SAS from less precarious positions reported that 'without their help we would have lost more men'. There was no letup after this initial action and during non-stop attacks that lasted throughout May and into June the Squadron flew more than 150 sorties, fired 1,000 rockets and 50,000 rounds of 30mm ammunition. Buildings which were, or were capable of, being used as enemy firing positions were attacked and 'airborne proscription' and 'close support of friendly troops' were also much in evidence in the order books. The latter was very close support indeed according to Mr Hugh Fraser, Minister of State for the RAF. After a visit to the area he was reported as saying 'that the skill and accuracy of the aircrew is such that the troops in forward areas are calling down RAF fighters to strike dissident strongholds only twenty-five yards from their own positions. Considering the nature of the terrain a twenty-five yard margin is incredible.'

Some veterans of other battles wondered just how credible a twenty-five yard margin could be in any sort of terrain and visualising the steep valleys and mountain peaks round which the Hunters flew, had the temerity to doubt it even more. Not that it mattered much; twenty-five or twenty-five hundred yards, the result was the same. By the end of May the road to Dhala was open, the Paramount Sheikhs of the large Ibdali tribe had denounced the struggle and come over to the British side, and the battle was won. It had been won by the individual courage and combined skills of the men whose victory it was. The soldier on the bare mountainside, the pilot above, weaving his way along the deep valleys to locate the near-invisible target below, and the groundcrew who back at base had sweated round the clock to provide all and more of the Hunters required for the fray. And if you checked on the facts and figures you would find that during it all No 43 Squadron had done all, and more than all, it had been called upon to do.

The opening of the Dhala road did not bring a halt to the fighting which was to continue for a long time. In June 1964 the Squadron was reduced to a skeleton of 18 pilots and one Orderly Room Corporal when 'in the interests of increased efficiency' a Technical Wing Pool was formed and the groundcrews' identity as proud members of 43 was dissolved in an amorphous soulless creation. The change was bitterly fought but it was decreed that it should go ahead for a six-month period. Within weeks it was noted that 'Out of a possible 23 Hunters we were lucky if a total of 6 was available. We got more than that when 43 had 11' . . . 'the lack of Squadron spirit became plain for all to see and pilots got increasingly frustrated at the many times they came out to fly only to find that no aeroplanes were available'. However a monthly thrash with the airmen ensured a continuing loyalty to 43 and a sense of belonging between the pilots and their forcibly separated groundcrews.

September 1964 found 'the enemy still tireless' so that the Hunters were often called in to support the ground forces or to provide standing patrols in the hope, never realised, of sighting the odd Egyptian/Yemeni MiG strafing on 'our' side of the border.

On August 10th, Flying Officer Ron Burrows, only weeks on the squadron had a flame out on take-off and made what was called a copybook ejection. Less happy was the tragic death of Flying Officer Ian Stephens in October when his aircraft crashed as he left Masirah to return to Khormaksar after a detachment. 'His loss was keenly felt, he had been very popular and had the makings of a good pilot'.

Surviving the annual visit from the 'Trappers' of CFS, who found small cause to complain, the 10th Anniversary of the Hunter on operations was celebrated at the Khormaksar Jungle Bar on November 20th and one guest summed up the success that it naturally was with a letter, 'I feel so ill this morning it must have been a wonderful party, – thank you'.

Two new Flight Commanders, Flight Lieutenants Pete Biddiscombe 'A' and Geoff Taylor 'B', along with five other new tourists arrived in February 1965. The two outgoing Flight Commanders, Flight Lieutenants Glyn Chapman and Bill Stoker, both received a Queen's Commendation in the Birthday Honours list for their service with the Squadron during the Radfan operations. The most important change in personnel this year was at the end of September when Squadron Leader Harry Davidson took over command of 43 from Squadron Leader Phil Champniss. Phil went home to Andover and Flight Safety duties having made his indelible mark on 43 and leaving it in the highest of spirits – in more ways than one.

In March the Royalist troops had recaptured Harib (shades of Fortbusting days), and with border infringements by UAR aircraft in support of the Republican troops expected, patrolling was stepped up. Generally however things had gone pretty quiet up country although in downtown Aden there were daily incidents of grenades and other noisy things which more often than not did harm only to innocent Arabs.

A crisis was declared in December when the stock of Black and White chequered material used for scarves and Cummerbunds ran out. As the last order had been placed in Cairo and 43 were currently very much out of favour with the UAR a search for alternative supplies was begun and sartorial correctness was restored by a supplier in far-off Birmingham, England.

The Labour Government elected in October 1964 produced in February 1966 a White Paper on Defence which announced among other things the complete withdrawal of all British Forces from Aden as soon as was practicable. Since there were no places in the world where any additional Hunter squadrons were likely to be usefully deployed this White Paper foreshadowed an end to 43 in its present shape in the not too far-off future. In fact the first plan set a date in July 1967 for 43 to disband, leaving No 8 Squadron to carry on to the end but early in 1967 the AOC decided that No 8 alone would not suffice so 43 were reprieved until November. Since, by the time this change was made most pilots had got their posting notices on the assumption that they would all go by July, nobody knew who would go and who would stay resulting, as the Squadron scribe said, 'in total chaos'.

However before November 1967 there were still to be eighteen months of life for 43, during which time it continued in its normal lively and superior way in cockpit and in bar, although with the grenade-loaded situation in Aden hangovers were now acquired in situ and got over in the same place rather than in a homeward bound jeep. In April Harry Davidson brought six pilots home to London for the 50th Anniversary Dinner where they discovered that, apart from having more hair and fewer ailments, they were not in any way different in spirit and outlook from their forerunners who in their day had gone ground strafing with Vickers guns or 20mm cannons. Harry Davidson said that as the 38th person to follow Lord Douglas of Kirtleside in command of 43 he hoped he might still become one day the Chairman of British European Airways and after everybody had agreed that the Tournedos Chasseur was the best thing they had ever had, the company, old and young, went home their various ways feeling that since 43 Squadron was still as good as ever, the world must not be so bad a place after all. So back to the Arabian sands and mountains where an eight-ship strike was called for at Wadi Bana while Flight Lieutenant Wally Willman took Dave Loveday, Bob Screen and Nick Kerr RN as companions to experience the delights of the Gulf in an exchange with 208 Squadron at Bahrain. By now Flight Lieutenant Dave Malin had escaped from his Instructor post at Chivenor and come back to 43 for a third tour as Commander of 'A' Flight. When he finally left, with a DFC one should add, he had been nearly seven years in total with 43, almost a record.

A 'Whistling Wheelbarrow', more generally known in official circles as an Argosy C1, took the ground support and surplus aircrews to Masirah in July and two months later, after they had come back again the whole might of the Fighting Cocks was seen when 144 hollow-charge HE rocket projectiles were expended in a 3 x 4-ship strike in Wadis Bana and Yahar, an operation to show 'How impressive we are and how good is our expertise at demolishing Wadis!'. Next month, October, Flight Lieutenant Al Pollock departed to England in order to 'ginger up a very inferior unit at West Raynham', (No 1 Squadron). Eighteen months later he went into the history books, and brought his service career to a premature end, when he flew a Hunter through Tower Bridge, a brave gesture to show that the RAF in its Diamond Jubilee year at least deserved a flypast over the capital, but like so many brave gestures it was lost in the philistine minds of politicians.

The year concluded with the two Flight Commanders, Geoff Taylor and Dave Malin, dropping leaflets (43 Xmas Card greetings) at Beihan, Mukeiras, Habilayn and Dhala and a flypast at the State capital of Qaiti on the accession of the new ruler, Amir Ghaleb bin Awadh al Qaiti, whereby anyone evilly disposed towards him would know that he had the best Wadi-busting squadron on his side.

1967 started with the AOC's Inspection prior to which enough paint was slapped onto walls to markedly reduce the cubic capacity of most rooms. In February Flying Officer Dave (Cid)

Sowler had the kind of experience he would have preferred to do without. One of four sent to the aid of a local friendly sheikh at Dhi Surrah, who was being troubled by somebody on top of a nearby hill, he had blasted away at all the right places when – calamity! Hydraulic failure, turret drive gone, no radio and ASI reading zero he headed for home. He got close, but eight miles out on finals, cockpit filling with smoke and the rear end burning like the proverbial torch, our hero mutters, 'I'll serve no more' and went for the handle. Everything worked and Cid, quickly picked up by helicopter, came back to ask where he wrote to collect his Martin-Baker Club tie. Less dodgy and quite funny was Flight Lieutenant Jack Jennings landing a T7 without the port undercarriage. The Trucial Oman Scouts' Captain flying with him wandered off to (ruefully) dhobi his underpants muttering 'That's my first and last time I fly in a Hunter' and 'Does everybody always laugh when things like this happen?'

Not long after this Jack Jennings, again, and Flying Officer Rod Harrison were scrambled to investigate an unidentified trace in the area. It proved to be a VIP Andover returning from Perim Island. Going in for a better visual identification, Rod Harrison was subsequently blasted for 'buzzing the Commander-in-Chief'. 'Sometimes', he said sadly, 'you just can't win'.

All Fools Day was aptly named. 2·6 inches of water, equal to Aden's normal annual rainfall, fell in six hours. Having spent most of March giving lots of help to No 45 Marine Commando, 43 went off to drier climes at Bahrain but came back to put in 109 Ops sorties before the end of May, mostly on border patrols and as top cover for convoys up the Dhala Road where escorting Wessex helicopters were being fired on.

In May also, the aircraft carriers, HMS *Hermes* on the way to the Far East and HMS *Victorious* on the way home, arrived at Aden. This gave 27 Hunters of Nos 8, 43 and 208 Squadrons the opportunity to join with 16 Sea Vixens and 12 Buccaneers from the carriers in a 55-ship formation. Led by Group Captain Browne, the Khormaksar Station Commander, it was the biggest formation ever seen in Arabian skies. After which came Air Defence exercises with the Hunters doing the attacking and the Navy claiming to shoot them all down.

By now the Squadron was on the last lap. Squadron Leader Davidson left in July, as planned with the original disbandment date and Squadron Leader Terry Thornton took over for the last few months. The Disbandment Parade and Farewell Dinner both took place on October 14th and from then until November 29th things happened so fast it was nearly impossible to keep track of them. Three pilots came from No 8 and stayed a while, three more from 38 Group came and hardly stayed at all. Some pilots and aircraft went back to the UK. Others went to Muharraq where they left the Hunters and went to the UK. Two pilots and aircraft went to Masirah with orders to stay there until somebody told them otherwise. Wally Willman leading four Hunters had everybody going berserk when he took a short-cut across Turkey without asking and then upset the Wing Commander Ops at Nicosia by parking on a spot reserved for VC10 transports.

On November 15th the Adjutant, Flight Lieutenant Tony Hughes-Lewis, had this to say. "We are now down to 6 aircraft and 7 pilots. We still have to maintain our dawn to dusk standby

An unusual early version of a dual-marked 43/8 Squadron Hunter FGA9, XJ684 'L', to denote the shared squadron usage of aircraft, with squadrons flying every alternate day from 1300hrs. The standard form of joint 8 Sqn markings in front of 43 markings, placed on either side of the rear fuselage roundels and seen in most Aden photos, quickly followed.

Last of the Huntermen, Khormaksar, 22 August 1967
Standing: Flt Lt A B 'Tony' Hughes-Lewis, Flt Lt D A Z 'Daz' James,
Gp Capt D F M Browne AFC* (Stn Cdr RAF Khormaksar), Flt Lt J K 'Jack' Jennings,
Wg Cdr R Ramirez (OC Strike Wing), Fg Off D V 'Bert' Loveday,
Admiral Sir Michael Le Fanu KCB DSC (C-in-C Middle East), Fg Off J J 'Joe' Whitfield,
Sqn Ldr Terry Thornton (OC 43 Sqn), Fg Off John V Loftus, Capt Leet (GLO), Flt Lt J B 'Jay' Norman
Kneeling: Flt Lt W T 'Wally' Willman, Fg Off T R C 'Tim' Smith, Fg Off D J 'Cid' Sowler, Fg Off R G L Gwyn Williams,
Fg Off A V B 'Tony' Hawken, Fg Off J G 'Ted' Heath

With 8 Squadron having departed to Masirah on 8 August, this Hunter has reverted to its full 43(F) Squadron chequer markings for the final weeks in Aden.
(MoD (RAF) Crown Copyright)

commitment of two aircraft which with only six of us doing it makes it a bit tedious. Of course with so few aircraft we cannot afford to fly except operationally, and so for the last week there has been no flying at all. This will continue to the end though now that the Navy is here with dozens of aircraft we feel slightly superfluous. Doubtless we shall sit here and twiddle our thumbs until the 29th. All the same, despite the fact that we all thought we'd be gone by the 22nd, morale remains surprisingly high, you can't get 43 down even if we do tend to swear a bit more than usual. However, we do all have the date Saturday 4 May 1968, (the date for the next annual reunion dinner) firmly printed upon our tiny underpowered brains, so have the doors open on the dot of 1730 or they may get broken in the rush!"

So, with the Squadron Standard and all the rest of the paraphernalia already sailing towards the Cape on the homeward run 43 finally switched off and went into the shades from which in due course, and after not too long a time, it would re-emerge to start again doing, as it had always done, most things better than the rest of the competition.

As for the Hunter, its days as a front line aeroplane were over, but for many who flew or serviced it in 43, the first to fly it and almost the last, it would not be quickly forgotten. They called it "The last real pilots' aeroplane" before the electronic age took over. It is a true and fitting epitaph to a great machine that was always the better for being decorated with Black and White chequers and a Fighting Cock in full boxing gear.

CHAPTER 29

Martin's Magnificent Men

43 **'OFFICIALLY'** reformed on the first of September 1969. Sadly, this was the middle of a 6-day late summer grant and nothing was done on that day to wet the head of the reborn infant. In any case, the prenatal embryo of 43 Phantom Squadron had been stirring and kicking for many weeks before its existence was formally and officially announced.

Two aircraft, XT874 and XV575, had arrived at Leuchars in June. Squadron Leader Pat Weatherilt, Senior Engineering Officer (SEngO), followed on July 2nd and to command, on the 7th, came Wing Commander I R (Hank) Martin AFC. Recalled to the UK from a ground posting in Singapore at a stage when he was near to joining Cathay Pacific as a 747 pilot it was for 43 very much a case of 'cometh the hour, cometh the man' as the next two years would show, for whatever you thought of him, he was of the kind of man you could not ignore. Off duty he dressed in fine fashion and could be described as a Beau Brummel who had been born two centuries too late and hardly it would seem the man to command a squadron forming to explore and develop a whole new world of Air Defence. To think thus was to be completely wrong. Beneath that outward veneer of foppishness there lay the strength and experience to meet the demands of the coming years. An exceptionally good pilot with a vast experience of Lightnings, a most astute and sagacious mind that could grasp, dissect and analyse a problem and more often than not come up with a viable solution. There would be no shortage of those. Most of all he had the indefinable touch that successful command must have, that which draws from subordinates loyalty, devotion and commitment. And he did not suffer fools or anybody who tried to interfere with what he thought was his field of decision. Before the 1st of September he received a call from an irate staff officer at Group, saying. . . "What's all this flying you are doing? Who gave you permission to fly the aeroplanes?' . . . so I told him 'I didn't need their permission to get on with the job thank you very much and I haven't heard from them since . . . "

Onwards and upwards!
The Boss in Phantom FG1, XT874
(MoD (RAF) Crown Copyright)

That 43 Squadron was reformed so soon after disbandment at Aden was a fortunate result of political decisions which in these times caused some major upsets in all three services. Following the cancellation of the supersonic VTOL Hawker 1154, the Fleet Air Arm was scheduled to equip with enough McDonnell-Douglas F-4K Phantoms (in British nomenclature FG1s) to form three squadrons. One was to be land-based for training purposes and the other two were to be embarked, one each, on HMS *Ark Royal* and HMS *Victorious*. However, before this plan could be put into operation more political trafficking and an alleged lack of funding for a refit for HMS *Victorious* led to a decision to scrap it. With one spare squadron of Phantoms therefore up for grabs the Royal Air Force, already committed to operating the Phantom FGR2, seized the opportunity to offer the Royal Navy the air defence cover that would no longer be available from *Victorious*. The reaction of the Royal Navy to this offer was classified under the normal 30-year rule, but whatever it may have been, the end

The first of the Phantoms – Leuchars, September 1969
(MoD (RAF) Crown Copyright)

result was that 43 Squadron was selected to take over the surplus naval aircraft and so become the first Phantom squadron in Strike Command (No 6 and No 54 Squadrons, formed earlier, were in the then Air Support Command), and to be integrated into the UK Air Defence force with a special responsibility for Maritime Air Defence.

For a number of reasons Leuchars was chosen as the best situated base from which the operational requirements could be met, and so 43 returned to the place from which they had left for Cyprus in 1961 and very welcome were they made too. The Station newspaper carried the story in bold typeface, and Hank Martin in a letter wrote that 'everyone up here is delighted to have us back. The barman tells me it was always his favourite squadron, my batman tells me the same and even the chap (a civilian carpenter) who is constructing various crew room coffee bars for us, served on 43 for a couple of years at Leuchars and Nicosia. They really are making us feel at home again.' So here for the second time, following the Hunter in 1954, the Squadron was to be the first to fly a type of aeroplane new to the Royal Air Force and to help develop its potential to the full. In the Phantom, they had something that in concept, performance and mode of operation was entirely different from anything that had ever before equipped 43. The progression from Sopwith Camel through eight types to the Hawker Hunter had been one of continually faster and more heavily armed fighters which nevertheless had all had one thing in common. They all relied on, as a weapon of war, a pilot using his eyeballs to position the machine and get it pointing at the target, whether in the air or on the ground, in such a way that when he used his armament he would hit it. The Phantom, apart from flying at twice the speed of anything previously encountered, was a massive jump into the world of electronics which left all that had gone before as obsolete as ring and bead gunsights. From now on the pilot would rely for initial target acquisition on his navigator in the rear seat, and he would have the capability of using the information supplied from behind to seek, track and destroy an enemy without it ever coming into visible range. Missiles effective up to more than twenty miles could make it so.

It all of course depended on teamwork. Pilot and navigator, neither inferior in any way to the other, forming a team which itself was linked through ground radar control and airborne early-warning aircraft into an overall pattern of defence. All this while flying faster, higher and further than heretofore. The demands it makes are not readily comprehended by the uninitiated. And when 43 formed in 1969 very few people in the Royal Air Force had had any experience in such matters. So the explorations into the problems that arose and the developments of methods and techniques to bring the systems as near as could be to perfection were first and foremost the job that faced Hank Martin in the Autumn of 1969.

He did start off with one advantage. The pilots and navs who arrived at RAF Leuchars after a course on the Phantom with the Royal Navy at Yeovilton were all of the highest calibre and all had been specially chosen as especially suitable for the task that 43 was facing. These, then, were the first of the many that were to follow, the trailblazers, the pioneers, who by trial and error but mostly by sheer hard work helped set the standards and smoothed the track for all those who have come since. It would not be unfitting to name them, for 43 Squadron from 1969 onwards owes them much. In order, more or less, of arrival at Leuchars they were Squadron Leader Alan Cushman, with long hours in Javelins, Squadron Leader Alan Walker, a former RN pilot, Flight Lieutenant Pat Richmond, Flight Lieutenant Nick Thurston, a jolly roly-poly type, Flight Lieutenant Brian Chappell, Squadron Leader John Owen, an early Phantom aerobatic exponent, Captain Jim Hoffman USAF, ex-Vietnam with much experience in dodging SAMs (you'd be surprised how easy you can turn your neck one-eighty degrees when that light comes on), Squadron Leader Phil Harris, another experienced nav, Flight Lieutenants Stu Miller, Mike Bettell and Will Roberts, the last being rather short but proving the old Scottish adage that 'Good gear comes wrapped aye in small parcels.'

All these aircrew had arrived by mid-October and the programme began to roll with a gradual quickening tempo, not too much affected by autumnal weather but sometimes by a shortage of aircraft, this latter the consequence of engineers and groundcrews all comparatively new to an untried type.

For the records, the very first flight by a 43 Squadron Phantom took place on August 5th 1969 when Wing Commander Martin flew XV575 for 90 minutes. His rear seat partner was the Station Commander, Group Captain J M Nicholls DFC AFC, the first of these decorations having been won in Korean War operations. August actually saw much more activity on the ground than in the air as all the administration connected with a 'new' squadron showered in. 'Squadron Property' – the records, diaries, silver, pictures etc, stored in far off Maintenance Units after shipping from Aden in 1967 once again saw the light of day and as appropriate were restored, hung up on walls in hangars, crewrooms and on stairways so the hangar slowly took on a 'lived-in' appearance.

"Cock of the North"
Fg Off Will Roberts, Flt Lt Stu Miller,
Wg Cdr 'Hank' Martin,
Flt Lt Pat Richmond, Sqn Ldr John Owen

The Command Accountant looked in to ensure that everybody knew how to fill in all the necessary (and unnecessary) forms ad infinitum. Air Commodore E W Wootten, SASO No 11 Group, who, as it happens, had flown briefly (as Wingco Flying, 324 Wing) with 43 at Florence in 1944 appeared, looked around, conversed and departed. Warrant Officer Tony Bell, appointed as Squadron Adjutant, a post he would hold until 1975, began his self appointed task of recording most things for posterity and so the wheels of admin began to grind, the piles of mortar and rubble on the hangar floor were swept away with the last of the contractors and the Squadron slowly began to take shape and form.

September 20th, Battle of Britain Open Day, gave 40,000 Scots who came to Leuchars the first opportunity to have their ears blasted by two re-heated Speys as Squadron Leader John Owen with Nick Thurston in the back demonstrated the aerobatic capability of the Phantom. But for 43 the next day, Sunday 21st was ***the*** day of the month. The Squadron Standard, presented first to 43 at Leuchars by Her Majesty The Queen in 1957, and since disbandment laid up at the RAF College at Cranwell was now to return to its rightful place. Escorted by a Colour Party of cadets from Cranwell, the Standard was marched-on. The Bishop of Croydon, also Bishop to the Armed Forces, the Rt Rev John Hughes blessed the Standard and gave a short address in which he related *'Gloria Finis'* to the famous prayer of Sir Francis Drake; 'That it is not the beginning but the continuing of the same until it be truly finished which rendereth the true glory'. Air Vice-Marshal George Lott, who reviewed the parade, spoke to the assembled troops; how he had known of its prowess and fame long before he came to command it, that his pride in having done so was undiminished with the passage of time, and that he was sure the future would match all the glories of the past. Thereafter, while the Leuchars Pipe Band blew into action, the Standard was marched past and 43 were once again fully back in business. Following this the

The Standard returns – Leuchars, 21 September 1969

Squadron marched to Leuchars Parish Church where the Standard was laid on the altar during the Battle of Britain Thanksgiving Service. It was, as it happened, the first time ever that a Royal Air Force Standard of any unit had been laid in the church.

And so to a formal lunch and thereafter to the crewroom in the hangar where the celebrations continued. Outside the rain which had started to fall before noon got heavier, the wind-strength increased to a point where the raindrops travelled near-horizontally, while some averred that the twin propellers of the Vickers Varsity which had carried the Standard and escort from Cranwell were turning in the wind though this last claim could have been the result of ale-induced hallucination.

As the afternoon wore on the temperature and humidity in the crewroom became progressively more uncomfortable. The windows, hermetically sealed during the hangar refurbishing, in spite of protest from Wing Commander Martin, were immovable. But not to 43 Squadron. Five windows, five former Squadron Commanders, one shooting stick and the windows were ceremoniously removed and all breathed again.

Wing Commander Phil Champniss, preferring his boot to the shooting stick perforce retired hurt needing six stitches to repair his self-inflicted wound. Next morning the Station Commander was not too disapproving and since that day the aviators of 43 had the benefit of God's good fresh air (perhaps at times polluted with AVTUR).

The only sour note in a great day, albeit a minor one, was a remark from the Station Engineering Officer, aggrieved that, in his opinion 43 were the spoiled darlings of Group and were taking all the available money which resulted in his men, or some of them, having to work in a hangar where the roof leaked. When it was suggested that this was good practice for the next war when, if the last one was anything to go by, his men would most likely have no hangar roof or hangar walls either, he was not amused.

Now finally established and with a slow build up of air and ground crews the Squadron buckled down to the serious business of reaching the state of Combat Readiness with all that that entailed in establishing, developing and improving operational procedures. Initially, these were interceptions at high, medium and low levels. On November 18th the first successful Air-to-Air Refuelling with a Victor tanker from Marham was accomplished. Sorties under the control of Buchan had begun in late September as did simulated Sparrow intercepts with head on attacks against Canberra targets. The flying time totals for November, 98·05 hours by day and 45·10 by night, were together comfortably in excess of the target 120·00 hrs. This excellent achievement was celebrated with a highly successful all-ranks party at Freuchie where the tipple included 144 large cans of beer received from the Courage (43's Own) Brewery.

A visit from the AOC No 11 Group, Air Vice-Marshal R I Jones, including a Phantom sortie by him, was scheduled for December. His first aircraft burst a tyre, the second went u/s at the end of the runway before he finally got airborne in a third one. This month also, Christmas leave and poor weather notwithstanding, saw another increase in flying hours, 165·40, up once more on the 156 planned as well as the first IAF (Interceptor Alert Force) scramble by a 43 Phantom although the crew drew a blank.

Christmas came early to Leuchars in 1969 and continued until the Burns Supper at the end of January. Perhaps the fact that the Station Commander was leaving had something to do with it. Group Captain Nicholls had been of inestimable help to 43 during their early days and on the morning after what was called 'a monumental party' it was 43 alone who took to the skies for a final farewell flypast to honour him. Of this, Hank Martin wrote; "Sad to say both Eleven and Twenty Three, (the two Lightning Squadrons) considered the weather far too bad to fly at all let alone a box-five, so we were on our own . . . there was no doubt that we impressed everyone, for I've had nothing but complaints from the locals threatening to enlist the support of the MP if it ever happens again. One chap complained that he saw four aircraft neatly framed in his bedroom bay-window, and couldn't understand how we missed the chimney at the end of the road. I can't think what he would have said had he known there was a number Five somewhere below the box-man. As one might imagine the other two Squadrons looked a little glum thereafter, and there were a number of very crinkly grins at the beer call in the evening."

January had seen the flying target again exceeded and also the first exercises with another unit when four Fairey Gannets of 849 Squadron from Brawdy arrived for 'Exercise Shinguard'. On February 5th, with ten pilots and eight navs available the Squadron was declared partly Operational and only a few days later came the first interception of a Russian reconnaissance plane. While exercising over the

Martin's Magnificent Men! – No 43 (Fighter) Squadron – 1970
(MoD (RAF) Crown Copyright)

North Sea with the cruisers HMS *Blake* and HMS *Fife*, one of two Phantoms was diverted to a CAP (Combat Air Patrol) and two Bears were successfully intercepted. This was the first of the hundreds that would be logged in the years to come.

The early months of 1970 are best summed up in two more statements from the Commanding Officer. In a letter he said, "... whatever else is happening, 43 continues to thrive and prosper both in the air and on the ground. Each month sees us 'clocking-up' more and more flying than the previous month, and the engineers really have been excelling themselves in producing the goods when most needed (like all the time) and I need not tell you that everyone, but everyone from C-in-C, AOC, and everyone else who comes here, invariably leaves with the impression that everything's 'swinging' on 43. One of my major difficulties is getting everyone to listen to our moans and groans about manpower and equipment backing – for they just shrug their shoulders and say 'What are you complaining about? Everything seems to be going far better than anyone, particularly the engineering planners, had ever imagined."

Again, at an Air Defence Symposium at Coltishall in March " .. with minor reservations due to shortfall in supply of equipment and armament, beyond our control or ability to affect, we are Combat Ready. It has not been an easy achievement nor will be the next three months to Full Combat Readiness but the stuff of which our Squadron is made will doubtless win through as it has done for so long and so often in the past."

Just three months after this symposium on May 31st 1970 the Squadron was declared Fully Operational and Combat Ready. As their Commanding Officer had forecast '. . . the stuff of which 43 is made will win through . . . as in the past.' It was precisely thirty years to the day that the Hurricanes of 43 had overflown Leuchars en route to Tangmere from Wick and twenty-four hours later had gone into action in the skies above Dunkirk, there to win through to a famous victory; thus does the past sometimes repeat itself.

With the initial reforming phase completed and the Squadron now playing a full part in the UK Air Defence things settled into the normal routine of a modern fighter squadron in the Royal Air Force which meant that nothing was ever routine, everything was changing all the time, most things were preferably required yesterday and the only sure thing was that tomorrow would provide the unexpected. One function which 43 were now required to undertake as part of the UK Air Defence was the duty related to the Interceptor Alert Force (IAF). This title, though not what it entailed was changed in 1978 to Quick Reaction Alert (Interceptor), QRA(I), which in turn was invariably shortened in everyday language to 'Q'. The Leuchars squadrons were classified as QRA (North), to differentiate them from other squadrons on similar duties based on English airfields, QRA (South), and they were concerned first and foremost with the wide open spaces above the sea northwards from the British Isles. The Leuchars squadrons sharing these duties with 43 were at first No 11 and No 23, both equipped with Lightning single-seat fighters. No 11 left for Binbrook in March 1972 and No 23 went southwards to re-equip with Phantoms in October 1975, their place being taken by No 111 Squadron who had been, by then, flying the

Phantom for twelve months. Since 1975 43 and 111 together shared the duties of QRA(I) North. Generally referred to as Treble One rather than One Hundred and Eleven they became, in Fighting Cock parlance, *The Tremblers*, regarded as inferior in every way to 43 although, having in later years had two Commanding Officers who had served previously with 43, their standards improved somewhat!

The reason for the necessity for the QRA requirement, together with a very well written and detailed narrative describing the mission by Fred Grundy, a pilot with much experience of Q, was supplied for the 1982 Yearbook of the RAF Association and is reproduced here in full as giving to those wholly or almost unacquainted with this subject a pilot's-eye view of it all, under the title 'Keeping the Bear at Bay.'

KEEPING THE BEAR AT BAY

"Mission 40, Vector 340 climb to flight level 350, to CAP Lima Echo Charlie, Call Buchan on fighter stud 44, Scramble! Scramble! Scramble!

The still night air is rent apart by the whine of two Rolls-Royce Spey jet engines starting up as the pilot, navigator and groundcrew work feverishly to get the Phantom fighter ready for take-off inside the 5-minute time limit.

40 scramble taxy?

40 clear taxy for runway 09, QFE 1008.

The Phantom taxies from its lair at the end of the runway, the pilot calls '40 take off?' and is cleared by the airfield controller one mile away in his glass-topped air traffic control tower. The pilot swings the aircraft onto the runway and, with all pre-fight checks complete, pushes the twin throttles 'through the gate' and up to the maximum reheat position. Any lingering idea that this is just a quiet agricultural stretch of the East Scottish coast is now shattered by the enormous roar of the Phantom at full combat power as it thrusts itself down the mile and a half of concrete on two thirty-foot streams of yellow flame.

As soon as the aircraft is safely airborne the pilot banks hard round onto the vector given during the scramble message and continues climbing to 35,000 feet.

Meanwhile the navigator is quickly bringing the radar into operation to search the sky ahead.

Buchan, this is Mission 40 heading 340, climbing to flight level 350, radar and weapons serviceable.

So, barely four minutes after receiving the order to scramble, a Royal Air Force Phantom of No 43(F) Squadron is beginning its long and lonely transit 500 miles (805km) north to the area known as the Iceland-Faroes Gap to intercept another unidentified intruder.

The Quick Reaction Alert (Interceptor) Force, in service abbreviation QRA(I), keeps four fully-armed aircraft at the highest peacetime readiness state, for 24 hours a day, 365 days a year. RAF Leuchars in Fife holds Northern QRA(I) with at least two Phantoms all the year round. In the south, QRA(I) is held alternately by RAF Binbrook (Lightnings), RAF Coningsby (Phantoms), both in Lincolnshire, and RAF Wattisham (Phantoms) in Suffolk. These three southern bases share the task of providing at least two fighters all the year round.

To support these fighters, Victor K2 air-to-air tankers are always available at a high readiness state, in order to keep the Phantoms or Lightnings airborne as long as required – sometimes up to seven or eight hours. These Victors are based at RAF Marham in Norfolk and will soon be supplemented by the VC10s modified from their civilian roles to serve as tankers, which will greatly extend the endurance of the United Kingdom's fighter force.

In the north of Scotland RAF Lossiemouth near Elgin is the home of the RAF's Airborne Early Warning (AEW) force of Shackleton AEW Mk.2s. These Shackletons are capable of travelling great distances and providing radar cover over large areas which are beyond the range of land-based radar sites and can control the fighters to intercept targets as an airborne radar-equipped operations centre. The Shackletons will be replaced in the coming years by AEW Nimrods, which will give a multi-fold increase in the UK's air defence capability.

Of course, Phantoms or Lightnings would never be scrambled if targets were not detected in time, so a chain of long-range radar sites exists from Iceland to Norway and down through Europe. On a typical QRA sortie, approaching aircraft will have been tracked for many miles before they are finally detected by UK mainland radar sites.

The role of QRA(I) is to protect the integrity of the piece of airspace allocated to the UK by NATO. As a result, any unidentified or potentially hostile track in what is known as the United Kingdom Air Defence Region (UKADR) is intercepted by an RAF Fighter, which will then escort the aircraft, known in Air Force jargon as 'trade' until it either leaves the UKADR or is no longer considered a threat.

To keep all these RAF resources permanently ready for action is no easy task, but it is considered to be essential to prove to any potential aggressor that the country intends to defend itself and is seen to be capable of doing so – yet another form of deterrence.

Mission 40 to Tanker 56, request join.

Our Phantom has now been joined on its transit north by a Victor tanker scrambled from RAF Marham.

40 clear join.

The Phantom pilot eases his 25 tons of aeroplane behind the huge Victor, from which dangles a 50 foot fuel hose. To make contact with this hose is like hitting 'double-tops' in darts every throw – only the board is bobbing up and down! Lights on the Victor illuminate to show that contact can be made and with tiny control movements the pilot nudges up into the refuelling basket on the end of the hose. With only an eerie glow from luminous cat's eye beads on the basket's rim, the navigator has talked the pilot in and now both can relax a little as the vital fuel exchange proceeds, between aircraft 15 feet apart, 35,000 feet up and travelling at 500 mph.

Once the refuelling is complete, the fighter gently drops back clear of its own airborne petrol station and then continues north to its pre-briefed combat air patrol (CAP) position. As many as six air-to-air refuels can be required on a long-range QRA sortie, making this one of the most demanding of all flying skills.

The Q-shed

RAF Leuchars sits on the northern shore of the Eden estuary in Fife. On the other bank a mile away the visiting golfers to St Andrews can hear Phantoms on routine training missions, but most will be unaware of the role of the grey hangar-like building at the end of the runway. This is the 'Q-shed', which houses the primary RAF Leuchars peace-time task, two menacing looking Phantoms fully fuelled and armed and waiting only for the word 'go'.

The Phantom is getting old now but is still better equipped to do the job of defending the UK from air attack than any other fighter, apart perhaps from the US Navy's F-14 Tomcat and, soon, our own Tornado Air Defence Variant. The Phantom's major advantages over other types are its pulse doppler radar associated with our Sparrow or Skyflash radar-guided air-to-air missiles, giving a look down, shoot down capability; four heat-seeking Sidewinder missiles; a highly accurate gun pod, and, most important of all, a two-man crew which spreads the workload and ensures greater mission success and survivability – very important when, as now, we are out-numbered.

The Q-shed is big enough for only two Phantoms and their paraphernalia to keep them 'gassed and oiled' at permanent readiness. The eight missiles on each aircraft are armed and safety locks removed, only the pilot's Master Arm switch and trigger press being required for a missile launch. Next to the shed, in a connected bungalow-type building, are the two crews and seven engineers waiting for the scramble order. Each crew of pilot and navigator shares a bedroom and the two crews share a small lounge with a TV and magazines. They all remain in the shed in their flying kit, minus life jacket and helmet, for a 24-hour period of duty, a third crew being nominated as reserve but waiting at home for a phone call that can have them rapidly airborne if needed. The six airman groundcrew and their Senior Non-Commissioned Officer are in the same building but have a separate lounge and two bedrooms where they spend a seven-day duty period; air and groundcrews share the same simple kitchen.

The flying kit the aircrews wear is hot, bulky,

Leuchars 'Q' Sheds at night
(MoD (RAF) Crown Copyright)

uncomfortable and very expensive, but all necessary to protect their lives in a rapid decompression at 40,000 feet, or in the event of an ejection into the icy waters of the North Atlantic.

The two resident squadrons at Leuchars, No 43(F) 'The Fighting Cocks' and No 111 Squadron, split the year into two or three week segments and alternate QRA duties over the whole year. Each squadron will hold either Christmas or New Year QRA but swop round the following year. Both squadrons, like all the other QRA(I) squadrons, have a distinguished history dating back to World War One and there is much friendly rivalry in the messes.

Shackleton 66 this is Mission 40 on CAP in Mike Lima Echo Charlie, flight level 350, looking 040°.

40 this is 66, your trade bears from you 050° at 150 miles.

40 roger.

One hour after take-off our Phantom has transited under a canopy of stars to a position of 500 miles north of Leuchars, half-way between Iceland and the Faroes. From the dark and cramped confines of the Shackleton AEW a radar operator gives the fighter crew the information they need to find the intruding Soviets.

40 your trade is now 050° at 120 miles, tracking 230°, height unknown.

A Pair of Bears

In the Phantom the navigator is searching the sky ahead with the electronic beam of radar hoping to catch an early 'pick-up' in order to give himself enough time to direct the pilot into a perfectly controlled intercept. A late radar pick-up often means a rushed intercept which puts more strain on the crew.

Mission 40, your trade has turned west and bears 040° at 100 miles.

This means that the intruders have altered course and now the Phantom navigator has to work out a different intercept pattern.

Roger Shackleton 56, 40 is now vectoring 020° for intercept.

The navigator has made his counter move and hopes that if the trade maintains its course he will pick up the tell-tale 'blips' on his radar scope in a few minutes. Still he searches the huge area of the sky ahead of the Phantom, from sea level to 60,000 feet. The crew together maintain an 'air picture' in their heads of what is going on around them: where the 'trade' is now; where the Shackleton and tanker are; what range it is to base, the nearest diversions and what their weather is like; how long before the fuel gets low and they have to air-refuel again, and a multitude of other considerations.

Cartoon by Chris Wren

40 in contact two targets bearing 035°.

Roger 40, you are clear to investigate. Check your weapon switches are safe.

Interpreting the information displayed to him on the radar scope, the navigator tells the pilot his own assessment of the intruders' heading, height and speed and then gives directions to fly that will bring the fighter up behind the target aircraft for an identification.

They're in five mile trail, which one do you want to go for first? the navigator asks the pilot.

We'll take a look at the leader first and then throw an orbit behind the trailer. We'll shadow them both from the rear man until told otherwise.

The pilot's reply is immediate whilst still concentrating on flying as accurately as possible the navigator's requested datums for the intercept and staring vainly out into the night blackness hoping for that glimpse of a flashing navigation light which would be the first visual sign of the unwelcome intruders.

We're getting close now and I still can't see any lights, we'll have to go for a VID (visual identification profile).

The navigator controls the intercept carefully to roll out two miles behind the lead aircraft and then the pilot and navigator together use the radar to control the VID which as they close below a mile requires very precise flying to the exact knot of speed and foot of height. A mistake now would mean a break off and set up again – five minutes and precious fuel wasted.

Through the reflected red glow of his instrument lights on the canopy the pilot makes out an area of even darker blackness in the night sky just ahead and above the Phantom. At the same time a gentle rumbling starts and noise can be heard from outside the fighter, both caused by resonance from the blades of eight huge propellers thrashing the cold night and driving the mighty bomber forward.

It's a Bear!

The intruders that QRA(I) are most regularly called on to intercept are the Tu-95 'Bears' and Tu-16 'Badgers' of the Soviet Long Range Air Force and Soviet Naval Air Force. Occasionally other types such as M-4 'Bisons' and Il-18 'Coots' come down far enough south to be intercepted by QRA fighters.

The Soviet aircraft are practising their war roles of maritime surveillance, anti-shipping, anti-submarine warfare, and simulated strike attack against the mainland UK. QRA intercepts provide valuable information on Soviet aircraft and equipment and any changes to the tactics they may employ in a future conflict.

The number of Soviet aircraft in a group requiring intercept varies from singletons to quite large groups at one time. If large numbers of 'trade' penetrate the UKADR (UK Air Defence Region) several QRA fighters with AEW Shackletons and Victor tankers in support can be involved all at once. Squadrons holding QRA therefore have to be able to generate extra armed aircraft if required. The Soviets are no respecters of Western culture and UKADR has been known to be full of 'trade' with many fighters airborne even on Christmas and Easter holidays.

Shackleton 66 this is 40, we are in company with the lead aircraft which is identified as a Bear Delta.

The pilot now has to hold the Phantom as steady as possible just underneath the Bear while the navigator looks through the magic green eye of the hand held image intensifier to discern any unusual features of this particular aircraft. This is a maritime surveillance aircraft and its number is recorded to be passed for intelligence analysis. If the intercept had taken place during daylight the navigator would have taken photographs of the Bear which again would have been forwarded to the intelligence services after landing.

40 is departing the lead aircraft and going to identify the rear.

After flying an orbit the Phantom rolls out two miles (3·2km) behind the rear aircraft of the Soviet pair and the same procedure for an identification is followed – again it's a Bear Delta maritime surveillance bomber.

40, this is Shackleton 66, you are to RTB (return to base).

Back to Base

The Phantom now leaves the Bears as they exit the UKADR and the crew decides whether any fuel is required from the Victor to get them safely home with enough to divert to another airfield if they cannot land back at Leuchars because of poor weather.

Leuchars tower, Mission 40 'Finals' gear down to land.

40 clear land, wind 080° eight knots.

As the dawn is beginning to break the Phantom screams in over the airfield fence and touches down on the runway with a flurry of grey smoke from the tyres. The pilot taxies back to the Q-shed as alarm clocks all over the country are beginning to wake others to a new day's work. As the weary crew unstrap from their rigid ejection seats after several trussed hours and climb down the aircraft ladders the engineers begin busily preparing the Phantom to be ready to go again to meet the next intruder.

After writing their reports, handing in any film used and checking their Phantom after turn-round, the pilot and navigator wait for the 0830 hours crew changeover. As others are normally on their way to work, Mission 40 is on its way home to bed after a normal 'day at the office' on the Quick Reaction Alert (Interceptor) force."

June 1970 began with a Flypast over Buckingham Palace for The Queen's Birthday after which came the first exchange with a NATO squadron. Six F-104's from No 427 Squadron of the Royal Canadian Air Force flew into Leuchars while the same number of Phantoms went off to Baden-Söllingen. As was invariably the established pattern for these exchanges the consumption of jet fuel was almost equalled by the input of ale and both home and away 43 were declared winners on all counts. Then came a number of AD exercises and weekend trips to Norway. This, it was said, 'wreaked irreparable damage to livers and wallets', the writer of this rather exaggerated judgement of 43's medical state then adding a little nearer the truth that 'we have in addition all the routine stuff and just to prove ourselves even more capable we have the AOC arriving tomorrow to spend three days flying with 43 including our Flypast for the opening of the Commonwealth Games. The Ops Room is taking one hell-of-a pasting and serious consideration is being given to raising the Ops Room ceiling to

The 8-ship formation over the Grand Harbour at Valletta in Malta – October 1970
(MoD (RAF) Crown Copyright)

accommodate an adequately sized chart.'

The Flypast at Edinburgh for the opening of the Commonwealth Games by the Queen went with the expected precision. Four Fighting Cock Phantoms with the Boss in the lead, followed by two four-ship formations of Lightnings arrived over the Games within one second of the appointed time. This led, it is said, to Edinburgh bookmakers laying odds of 100 to 1 that such precision would not be repeated when the Flypast took place at the ceremonial Closing of the Games. Well, the bookmakers were cleaned out, a happening all the more outstanding because the organisation in the Stadium went awry, the timing went to pot and when Hank Martin got the signal from the ground that he was due overhead in 120 seconds exactly he was, 'twelve miles away and pointing in the wrong direction!' Nevertheless as the last of the National Anthem died away twelve Leuchars fighter-planes in impeccable formation came sweeping over the throng below. It was, said the Chairman of the Games Committee, 'Worth two Gold Medals'.

Battle of Britain Day brought superb weather and the best day's flying seen for a long time. The individual aeros ace, John Owen, put on four displays around the country and 43 a four-ship formation at Leuchars and everybody enjoyed themselves.

Next came a seemingly never-ending stream of exercises with various ships and convoys of all nationalities, the biggest and best being in the Mediterranean. A whole month split between Malta and Cyprus, perfect weather, a tremendous amount of flying, absolutely no sleep which 'did nothing but good for the squadron's point of view'. The crew of a 13 Squadron Canberra provided enthusiastic co-operation in obtaining a highly impressive photograph of a 43 eight-ship formation over the Grand Harbour at Valletta. Perfectionists that they were, the Canberra crew required four flyovers before they were satisfied with the pictures by which time the inhabitants below were heartily sick of the 43-induced racket and wished nothing better than for them to return and frighten the grouse nearer home.

Back home the Squadron's masters seemed to realise how much they had enjoyed their Mediterranean 'holiday' and had them sitting on QRA thereafter up to and beyond Christmas.

The early months of 1971 were unusually mild which suited the Boss very well as it was perfect for golf, at which he was extremely good, but not so good for his ski-ing at which he was

Briefing for a Royal rear-seat passenger. HRH Prince Charles with Wg Cdr Martin – July 1971
(MoD (RAF) Crown Copyright)

even better. In between times, he went off to another symposium at Coningsby, there to explain to all the other Phantom squadrons just how it was that 43 managed to get nearly twice as much flying out of their Phantoms as any other Squadron in either Air Support Command or RAF Germany. In fact, at this time the engineers were performing what Hank Martin called 'miracles' as there were never less than seven of the ten aircraft on strength serviceable every morning and that he said 'for an aircraft like the F-4 is damned good'. Even more remarkable insomuch as many of 43's groundcrews, classed as 'experienced' were being posted to newly formed Phantom squadrons in Germany to leaven the lump.

A strong and lively contingent from Leuchars went off to the RAF Club for the Annual 43 Squadron Association Dinner, returning with three paintings, the work of 43's ex-Hunter pilot Chris Golds, showing aspects of 43 Squadron glories and presented, to cover some bare area of the crewroom walls, by past Fighting Cocks. The pictures duly got back to Leuchars along with some thick heads.

A visit to the Royal Norwegian Air Force at Sola (Stavanger) in July was followed only two weeks later by an exchange with the 32nd Tactical Fighter Squadron, USAF, at Soesterberg in Holland, this latter visit resulting in an account being presented to 43 on their return in respect of 'one inertial Nav platform, damaged when left switched on' – cost 84,115 Dollars and 65 Cents (US) or, as a preferred alternative 420,577 beers.

Although it may seem, reading the reports on the many exchanges that took place over the years with squadrons from many NATO nations, that the main purpose of them was to decrease stocks held by the brewers at both ends there was indeed a much more serious reason for them, as well described in an exchange in 1977 between 43 and the 496th Tactical Fighter Squadron at Hahn, in Germany. Here 43 soon discovered that the severe restrictions of airspace compared badly with the wide open spaces of the North Sea, and the difficulties were compounded even more by a fog which arrived with a military precision every morning. Most of all they found a bogey entitled by their hosts as 'Interoperability'. Thus, for instance, the compressed air supply adaptors needed to couple the USAF ground equipment to that of the RAF were unavailable. This example, described by a Hahn engineer who like many Americans never used one word if three were

With groundcrew and aircrew, 'Alpha' is being readied for flight

available, was an 'Interoperability man – machine interference'. In English this translates to 'a situation awaiting a solution'.

However, the end report called this '. . . a worthwhile exercise which takes NATO forces a step towards the idea of standardisation on the professional side and breeds individual mutual respect between two national air forces with a common object.' Or put another way, if ever the balloon goes up these peacetime interchanges will have helped to ensure that NATO forces will be conditioned to the attitude that we are all on the same side, that an ally's difficulties will be reason for sympathetic aid and not a reason to gloat at their discomfort as was alas at times evident in past wars. For their part the men of the 496th left Leuchars with the message, 'we're glad you're on our side.'

July 1971 was the occasion also of a notable 'first' for the Royal Air Force and for 43 especially. HRH Prince Charles, then taking a flying training course at Cranwell, expressed a wish to fly supersonic. This request was originally to be met by a flight from Coningsby but subsequently, for reasons undisclosed, a very high level decision moved the action to 43 at Leuchars. Naturally Wing Commander Martin was in the front seat of the two-stick (dual control) Phantom and to what degree or how often the Prince took control is unknown, but it is believed that Balmoral Castle, where the Royal Family were partially in residence, had never before been so close to the underside of a Phantom. The Duke of Edinburgh was especially impressed.

Activity continued to flourish with the summer. Yet another exchange, this time to 441 Squadron of the Royal Canadian Air Force, a quick trip to Valley to 'poop off a few missiles', and a host of replies to demands by the taxpayers asking for an appearance by the RAF's all-star Squadron at Open Days, Field Days, Church Bazaars, etc. So came September 1st and with it the arrival of Wing Commander Jerry Cohu to assume command of the Squadron in place of Hank Martin, who, had he had his way, would have been content to stay with 43 for ever. Such things of course cannot be in the RAF but there were none who did not regret his leaving. In his going he left behind a squadron, that all bias and exaggeration aside, could truly be said, as was equally true of 43 in past years, to be something slightly superior to the rest. In Hank Martin's case he had starting from a base of zero, taken command of men completely new to one another and with all the problems inherent in a new aircraft and weapons systems, produced by the sheer power of his presence and personality a highly-skilled, highly trained and highly motivated Squadron that exhibited in every aspect of life from the heavens through the hangar and crewrooms to the bar and to the Squadron parties the supreme excellence that had for as long as anybody could recall been the hallmark of 43 Squadron. In the years that have elapsed since he left the excellence remains and 43 likewise remain indebted to him for the standards he left behind him.

Let the last words on the subject be his . . . being a modest chap – "I never could understand how No 1 Squadron got a motto like they did with 43 around. Who are they anyhow?"

CHAPTER 30

Cocks O' The North

HANK MARTIN was succeeded by Wing Commander Jerry Cohu whose previous exchange posting flying the Phantom with the US Marine Corps had prepared him well to lead the Fighting Cocks with their new aircraft. Under their new Commanding Officer 43 continued into and through 1972 much as before. The inevitable share of 'Q', training an influx of newcomers in the special requirements of squadron operations, more exchanges with NATO fighter squadrons, flypasts for the Queen's Birthday Parade and one for the town of Goole in Yorkshire. Just who fixed that one up is a mystery. AOC's inspection of course, and a visit from the Chief of the Defence Staff. Three Americans on exchange to the Squadron, (which has always had one pilot and one nav from the USAF at any time), Captains Peter Haynes, Skip Yohe and Tom Carpenter received decorations earned during previous service in South-East Asia. Battle of Britain Day took place in the middle of a massive exercise when half or more of the squadron were operating from Kinloss which gave the chop to any party that night.

Wg Cdr Jerry Cohu

An exchange to Ørland was unusual and from a flying, if not a social, viewpoint was abortive. The Met officers went on strike the day after 43 arrived and went back to work the day after they left. A later exchange with the 525th TFS at Bitburg was more of a success and the last one of 1972 to Grazzanise in Italy provided some light relief on returning to the UK with a fine fighting cock, Roberto, presented by the Italians. The arrival of this bird at Lyneham set all the red lights flashing at the Ministry of Fisheries and Agriculture, in particular with the Veterinary Officers at Tolworth. Instead of coming in glory to Leuchars Roberto was banished into quarantine at Bristol Zoo, or was until the men at the Min decreed that the zoo did not meet the required standard for quarantining fighting cocks and the like. The final outcome of this epic is not known as the relative pages in the diary are fuddled. There was a rumour that Roberto was put to death and cooked and whether or not he finally joined the pen outside the hangar where the squadron keeps its birds, which for some reason never seemed to live very long anyway, is one of the unsolved mysteries of 43 Squadron history.

One last thing recorded in 1972 was a first exercise in refuelling air-to-air with tankers of the USAF. There were no problems with interoperability!

A month's detachment to Malta starting in mid-February should have been 'fun in the sun' but turned out instead to be a wallow in the monsoon since Malta had more rain for the time of year than ever before recorded and the maximum temperature barely exceeded 50°F.

Another visit to Malta and Cyprus near the end of 1973 was more successful although the films that recorded the deeds and misdeeds of the squadron were lost when a nameless pilot opened the can before they were developed. Fortunately, some manuscripts survived which tell how the cry of the black and white chequered clan, 'is there a Fighting Cock in the House?', was heard all over the island. Also that an offer of 20 cents and a one-legged lady of leisure in exchange for Nick Reffold was refused as it was decided that the Coffee Bar could not survive without him. In Cyprus the resident Lightning Squadron, No 56, was shown, so it was said, 'what Air Defence is all about' during a one-day AD exercise, and finally with Christmas rushing towards them the aircraft came home via Malta and Coningsby, just getting into the Lincolnshire base 'by the skin of their teeth' as the weather turned very nasty, and so to Leuchars on 23 December.

In between these two visits to the Mediterranean, there had been a twelve-day visit to Norway which had kept some worthy types out of the RAF Club on the night of the Annual Reunion though Squadron Leader Mike Elsam made a most competent stand-in for the absent Squadron Commander. So life continued at the usual high level of pressure with every demand

Flt Lts John Owen & Nick Thurston stream the 'chute on landing after their aeros display at the 1971 Battle of Britain display at Leuchars

being met as always and no time to wonder what was happening next because it had already arrived. Before August there had been four major detachments and another big one which required eight Phantoms to deploy to St Mawgan in Cornwall in September, followed hot on the heels by Battle of Britain Day where the Squadron led the formation flypast and Flight Lieutenant Brian Clifford had closed the show with solo aerobatics. Hardly had the last hundredweight of litter been disposed of before, next morning, the squadron took the Standard to church in St Andrews and afterwards marched through the streets exercising their Freedom of the Royal Burgh. By 27 September, the squadron had reached peak flying hours, Wing Commander Cohu ordered a Beer Call at 1700 hours and stood down the groundcrew for the weekend.

In August the squadron had bade farewell to the second last of its original 1969 members when Flight Sergeant Harry Webster had left for Germany, leaving only the Adjutant, Warrant Officer Tony Bell to cast an eye over the

Flt Lt Al Winkles, Wg Cdr Keith Beck sip the champers to welcome the new boss

'newcomers' as he was pleased to classify them while averring that if the squadron wasn't what it was, it was still as good if not better than ever. This was in fact a time of much coming and departing with six first tourists coming in from the OCU at Coningsby, and Squadron Leaders Ed Stein and Mike Elsam, and Flight Lieutenant Brian Clifford leaving for pastures new. The Adjutant said that looking around the crewroom now made him feel positively octogenarian! However the major change in personnel came in December when Wing Commander Cohu was posted to Cranwell and the reins of 43 came into the hands of Wing Commander Keith Beck, who like Hank Martin before him was delighted to come to a station within easy reach of the Scottish ski slopes in the Grampians. So with a new Boss the squadron went via the usual Hogmanay revels into 1974.

It appears that not enough happened in January 1974 to be worth recording or perhaps the Squadron Scribe was still stupefied by Hogmanay followed by the run up to Rabbie Burns birthday and the first bit of news surviving is that on 7 February it was "snowing like the devil to be followed by rain – so the man says." Twenty eight days later it was reported that "the Boss is flogging the squadron to the remainder of the Air Defence Force at a symposium but is due home tomorrow for the farewell party of Warrant Officer Jim Murray, retiring at 55, and his replacement is Warrant Officer Jim Laybourne who is coming from The Queen's Flight which suggests that somebody somewhere is trying to raise the tone of the Squadron."

Be that as it may, one aspect in which 43 could go no better was in supplying for 1974 the 11 Group solo aerobatic crew, Flight Lieutenant A 'Sandy' McB Davis and Nick Reffold, the

Flt Lts Sandy Davis and Nick Reffold
keep it low on take-off

latter, it being libellously written, was there only to keep the weight forward and put in the fuel when away from base. These two gave displays at more than twenty air shows in all parts of the country and continued the tradition set in the preceding 3 years by John Owen, Nick Thurston, Roger Beazley, Norman Browne and Brian Clifford. Norman joined Sandy to fill the same slot for 11 Group in 1975 and during the next six years 43 performed this duty in four of them, 1976, 1977, 1978 and 1981, the teams being Squadron Leader Ian Macfadyen and Flight Lieutenant Norman Browne, Flight Lieutenants Mike Bell and Nick Reffold, Flight Lieutenants John Spoor and Andy Moir and finally Squadron Leader Ray Dixon, back on 43 for a second tour, and Flight Lieutenant Colin 'Bonzo' Bond. There may be aeroplanes that can be pulled round in a tighter radius than the Phantom but there are few if any which have a superior shattering effect on the viewing public, which one supposes is what the solo men are all about. Many an engineer, his mind fixed on matters of fatigue, may pale at the sight and sound of a reheated turn but the public love it and after all they paid for the Phantom in the first instance.

1974 being a year of fuel crisis there was some restriction in flying hours though that did not prevent 4 Phantoms, 6 crews and some Hercules going off to the 496th TFS at misty Hahn under Squadron Leader Willis-Fleming. Also, as British Rail was still running, if generally late, an invading force went to the Annual Reunion in London coming back with among other things the top hat from the doorman at the Dorchester Hotel in Park Lane.

The VIPs who seemed to visit the squadron in continuing manner included at this time the Chief of the Defence Staff, Field Marshal Sir Michael Carver, who was taken to Northern Dispersal and shown the latest weapon for the Phantom, the Vulcan gun. Carried on the centreline station this gun, (based on the Gatling used in the American Civil War - nothing new under the sun) was a revolving multi-barrel job throwing out some 6,000 rounds of 20mm ammunition a minute. Had the RAF had it in 1940 the Battle of Britain would have been all over in a week. The reaction of the pilots to this gun was succinct; – 'this is great, let's have more of them'.

The adoption of the Vulcan gun into the squadron's weaponry brought with it the need for APCs (Armament Practice Camps) where proficiency in its use could be gained. The target, at that time towed behind a Canberra, is a banner about 10 metres long and two metres in depth, held in flight in the vertical plane by a spreader bar. This spreader bar being of fairly substantial construction as it must be, is a potential producer of 'foreign objects' in engine intakes if, as can happen, it is damaged by cannon fire and partially or wholly disintegrates, and single engine landings resulting from this cause occurred on more than one occasion. It is also true that some Canberra crews aged prematurely when eager young Phantom men broke away at the end of their firing burst too close for comfort. The results obtained with this cannon improved with the passing of years. In 1978, at APC in Malta, Squadron Leader George Lee and Flight Lieutenant Pete Gray recorded an impossible 92·5%. This is 'impossible' in as much as at the beginning and end of a firing burst a number of unfired rounds are ejected so that theoretically the maximum number of rounds that can be on target is 90%. Not for the first time in recorded history did practice confound the theorists and if further proof be needed in 1983 Flight Lieutenant Fred Grundy provided a hyper impossibility with 101%.

But to return to 1974, for these events were then in the future, an air-to-air refuelling exercise with the USAF was reported as 'reasonably successful, we bent only two probes', and in August the first ever Strike Command Tactical Meet was hosted by Leuchars where there arrived Phantoms from the UK and Germany, Lightnings, Harriers and Hunters all foregathering to exchange news and views and to do all the other things that befall at Tactical Meets. The late Autumn Mediterranean Sunshine Holiday was cancelled this year (fuel crisis again) so the Boss went off to a Senior Officers' course at Cranwell and most of the rest of 43 went under Squadron Leader Pete Desmond to Valley for Missile Firing though in one place it was defined as a 'Leek-eating Detention Course'. By 12 December it was snowing and finally everybody came back and Christmas arrived on time and 1974 ended with

'Harry, stay exactly where you are!'
Refuelling from a USAF KC-135

one famous landmark (or airmark?) being recorded which was that in November 43 had reached 10,000 flying hours in Phantoms since 1969.

1975 with Wing Commander Beck now in his second year in the driving seat, life went on in the usual 43 manner, never dull, generally highly loaded in cockpit, hangar and bar and full of the unusual which stays in the memory long after the days and nights on 'Q' and other routine stuff have been forgotten. A deployment to Kinloss brightened the atmosphere in that Morayshire outpost for a few days after which came an exchange with 323 Squadron of the Royal Netherlands Air Force at Leeuwarden. Squadron Leader Pete Desmond took half the squadron to Holland while the Boss stayed at home with the rest to entertain the visitors, known not unkindly to the hosts as Cloggies. An engine failure at Leeuwarden enlivened the trip for Captain Walt Ford and Nick Reffold though this did not prevent them, as with the rest of the detachment, from enjoying a 'great deal of hard flying, non-stop booze, a visit to a Dutch Submarine and an even better one to the Bokma Distillery. 'We weren't half knackered; it must have been all the hard flying' Here it was that some aircrew had their faith in the Met reports shattered for all time when they were promised 5/8 to 7/8 at 1,800' to 2,200' with tops at 6,000' and better than 10km visibility when what was actually existing was 8/8 at 100 feet, visibility 1000 metres and lots of falling snow!

Then came the annual AOC's Inspection followed by a deployment to the North Pole region. Prior to this, Squadron Leader Desmond had found himself travelling back in time i.e. flying in an open cockpit when his canopy flew off during a Harrier bounce. This novel way of downing a Harrier in the absence of rearward firing armament failed, though there was some talk of a claim from a Northumberland farmer for one dead sheep.

Sandy Davis began his second year as the Group solo aerobatic king having some slight difficulties during the run up such as upsetting the Station Commander at the airfield he visited for vetting by the AOC by including a roll during the climb after take-off. Earlier while practising his routine in the skies around Kinloss he brought down on his head the wrath of the Findhorn Spiritual Community adjacent to the airfield.

A Missile Practice Camp at Valley was followed by Battle of Britain Day at Leuchars in September. It was while rehearsing a 'Canadian Break' to end a 4-ship formation display that 43 lost its first Phantom when Flight Lieutenant Jack Hamill and his nav, Flying Officer Tim Wright ejected from XV580 'Q'. Both aircrew were uninjured but the 'plane crashed in a turnip field two miles south of Kirriemuir, (a town long

1975 aeros team
Sandy Davis and Norman Browne

"TARTAN BUNNETS WILL BE WORN" – The 1976 Fighting Cocks
Standing: Dan Ford, Mel Evans, Ian Macfadyen, Andy Moir, Terry Nash, Bob Fisher, Mike Nethery, Dave Wakefield, Chris Coville, Roger Clements, Dave McNamara, Kevin Harte, Keith Beck, Al Winkles, Sandy Davis, Al Wallace, Norman Browne, Garth Wensley, Dave Pyper, Dave Moss, Ray North, Pete Desmond, Pete Bedwin, Barry Mayner
Kneeling: Nick Reffold, Hugh Geddes, Tim Wright, John Forbes, Ian Pickerell.
(MoD (RAF) Crown Copyright)

famous in RAF balladry as the site of a famous Ball) and was totally destroyed!

The year was rounded off with a squadron detachment to Luqa in Malta, a visit that coincided with the adoption of a new style head-dress, a 'bunnet' in Royal Stewart tartan which did little for sartorial elegance but certainly made 43 so clad stand out in a crowd. The LUQA NEWS for December 1975 had some words to say on the subject:

". . . some may have noticed the recent arrival of a bunch of wild heathen Celtic Phighter Phellows on the Island. It would be impossible to ignore our presence now after a week of high living which invariably produces a wild-eyed look in the faces of our detached (in more ways than one) chaps from Scotland. This appearance has been attributed to the copious quaffing of the local beverages but it is in fact the result of a particularly demanding professional task coupled with the bone-chilling cold winds. We bring with us a touch of the Scottish weather so that we will not be too homesick (2° hotter than at home on 24 November). We hope the other squadrons will not be offended by our brash predilection for flying; it seems that Nimrod flying has gone out of fashion while the Canberra chaps are quietly confident in their ability to photograph the enemy to death in war and bore us to death in the circuit .... "

There was more on a similar vein but that is sufficient to indicate that in spite of local problems the Fighting Cocks were doing the job, for which they had deserted their homesteads in the Kingdom of Fife, of putting lots of holes into lots of towed banners. They came home for Christmas, just before which they sadly said farewell to Keith Beck at the end of his two-year reign in the Boss's seat. His time with 43 had been one of continuing high performance in things serious like flying as well as in the less demanding though equally important occupation of what one might call squadron social life. This had, among many other highlights included the introduction of a 'Cabaret Turn' into the RAF Club at midnight following the Annual Association Reunion Dinner. Although none save 43 members past and present witnessed the show, the star of which was a young and attractive lady whom some of the Leuchars detachment had met during a lunch-hour session, it seemed that some somnambulistic type, obviously a Bomber chap, must have stuck his eye to the keyhole, the result being an admonishment from the Club Secretary, who to do him justice did not seem too aggrieved but was in the position of having to be seen to do something.

The start of 1976 was the usual Hogmanay jollities, hangovers and overdrafts but the cold winds of Leuchars and reality soon dispelled all that. Now commanded by Wing Commander

Roger Palin, and 43 could not have had a better successor to Keith Beck, an exercise on the 7th was followed by Taceval Part I on the 21st. For the unaware, TACEVAL, short for Tactical Evaluation, is part and parcel of RAF life in the modern age, the like of which the RAF pre-war never encountered. In the 30s and before, the annual 'Air Exercises', pre-planned long in advance were a rather jolly game in which as like as not the defending 'Blueland' fighters never, in the total absence of ground aids such as radar, met up with the attacking 'Redland' bombers for all that these were flying somewhat slower than the speed over the threshold of a modern jet. The results did not have a great deal of meaning to any future war on a grand scale. In any case the whole of RAF Policy was subject to the Ten-Year Rule, an assumption made by the politicians that no war in Europe was possible in less than 10 years so there was going to be plenty of time to get ready for it.

Fortunately things are now different and TACEVAL springs from the assumption that War could start with very little notice. Therefore if it is not to be a total waste of the Nation's money and resources the Royal Air Force must be at all times in peace, capable of going onto a war footing at a few hours' notice at any time day or night. Thus Taceval Part I is sprung with no advance notice and the reaction of the station and squadrons must be such that they are in a state of preparedness to meet a full-scale enemy attack.

Taceval Part II is a further development which proceeds to put to the test the performance of the station and the squadrons under simulated wartime conditions. Such in simple terms for the layman are the two stages of Taceval, factors which affect the actions and performance of present day squadrons in every respect.

Since 1976 was the 60th Anniversary of 43 first forming at Stirling the year was an occasion to celebrate these sixty years of Gloria Finis. Following an exchange with 349 Squadron of the Royal Belgian Air Force a larger than usual contingent took the RAF Club by storm, hanging the black and white chequered banner used in parade rehearsals on the pole above the main entrance to the Club where the RAF Ensign was customarily flown. Then they went into the Annual Reunion Dinner, returning the next day to Leuchars in the normal post-dinner state of wishing their heads would go away. Thereafter they started to prepare for a 60th celebration in the form of a three-day event early in June. Old Cocks arrived for this from far and near. Group Captain Phil Champniss arrived from Chivenor in an ex-43 Hunter, Sandy Davis and Dave Terry in a Phantom belonging to the Richthofen JG-71 Wing of the Luftwaffe at Wittmundhaven, their aeroplane marked with the same black crosses as the Fokkers that 43 had flown against 60 years before. When it took off for the return journey on Monday it also carried the marks of 43 Squadron's 60th logo, a tophatted boxing-gloved cock in a '60th Anniversary' circle, as did an F-

F-4F Phantom II "Richthofen" JG-71

104 from Beauvechain, a 23 Squadron Phantom from Wattisham, a Buccaneer, Victor Tanker from 57 Squadron and a Shackleton from No 8, 43's old Hunter mates in Aden. Only the venerable Spitfire, an object of reverence for the young and

Sandy Davis and Dave Terry
and the 60th anniversary logo on the F-4F

of nostalgia for those of more advanced years, was left untouched. A short flying programme after lunch on Saturday included a solo display by Squadron Leader Ian Macfadyen who 'amazed the ignorant, impressed the knowledgeable, and frightened only Norman Browne in the rear seat.' This display should have been the last item in the Flying Programme but was brought forward an hour so that the

The 1976 display Phantom crewed by
Sqn Ldr Ian Macfadyen and Flt Lt Norman Browne

final of the British Amateur Golf Open championship on the Old Course at St Andrews could be played without the flight of golf balls being affected by shock waves emanating from reheated tailpipes.

The remainder of 1976 followed the normal pattern of life. A Tactical Fighter Meet, a visit to Norway described as 'fabulous, alcoholic in the true 43 tradition and zappers placed from Bodø to Maakeroy.

October found 43 involved in Exercise Teamwork providing top cover for a NATO Task Force covering a convoy en-route to Norway. This naval force included the nuclear carrier USS Kennedy which later anchored in the Firth of Forth giving an opportunity for an exchange with 43. Wing Commander Palin, the two Flight Commanders, Squadron Leaders Desmond and Macfadyen and Flight Lieutenants Newman, Reffold, Piper, Nash and Edwards and Lieutenant Batt RN, who at least knew what a carrier looked like, spent 48 hours afloat and being highly impressed came back to report that 'having observed the Tomcat at close quarters the squadron has placed orders with Grumman Aircraft Company Inc. and will re-equip with F-14's next year.

The admiration was however by no means one way as the following signal received on 18 October 1976 proved. The four officers from VF-14 came back with words of praise about the professionalism of the 'Fighting Cocks' in the squadron, in the Mess and on the golf course.

"Up a bit, up a bit, hold it" - Sgt Colin Blevins, Sgt Ken Hargreaves and Cpl Grant Carroll work on a Phantom's landing gear and typify the many without whom all the skill and prowess of those who fly would count for nothing

Prior commitments precluded more of us from attending the affair at Leuchars, which was unfortunate for us as your reputation preceded you. We wish you happy hunting and hope we will have the opportunity to work together next March in the Med'.

October was also farewell for a long serving and faithful member, Flight Sergeant Jock McCandlish, one of those too often unnoticed people to be found in or around the hangar, without whose skill and application there would not have ever been a single Phantom for the budding aces of the Royal Air Force to fly. He retired but did not move too far away so that in years to come he could look in on Open Days and reassure himself that 43 were still the greatest.

So Christmas came and went and 1977 blew in on a gale. The station re-equipped with new bicycles which were soon being belted around the concrete in diamond nines and the like. In February Flight Lieutenants Dave Wildridge and Dave 'Moses' Moss took a Phantom to Wildenrath, ostensibly to help 92 Squadron have a party to mark their replacing the Lightnings with Phantoms. It took in a weekend at Carlsberg after which the two Daves reported they were still standing – just. In July, following the Missile Practice Camp at Aberporth it was announced that 43 had again won the Aberporth Trophy; for the third time in four years as it happened, and in addition had added to the silver on the sideboard with the Dacre Trophy. This double success was reported in the station's newspaper, *'Contact'* as follows:

ABERPORTH TROPHY AND DACRE TROPHY BOTH WON

The triumph of arms makes 43, if not indisputably the very best squadron in the entire RAF, then at least the best fighter squadron for a considerable distance in any direction. The Aberporth Trophy is awarded to the squadron with best results gained during the annual missile firing practice – Sparrow missiles fired against high flying supersonic drones in the area of the Hebrides.

The Dacre Trophy is awarded to the squadron which emerges as the most completely proficient unit in 11 Group after an especially searching examination of every aspect of their operational ability throughout the whole year. And that, written by a non-member of 43 just about says it all, though Wing Commander Palin's message is worth adding. "This is a unique achievement which reflects the dedication of every member of the squadron

Mrs Elizabeth Dacre presenting the trophy and the framed print to Wing Commander Roger Palin
(MoD (RAF) Crown Copyright)

throughout the whole year."

The Dacre Trophy was presented to the Royal Air Force in the first instance by Air Commodore and Mrs Dacre in memory of their

The 12-ship flypast
(MoD (RAF) Crown Copyright)

son, a Flight Lieutenant lost in a Mosquito over Germany during World War II. Presented by Mrs Dacre in person, in 1977 it was handed to 43 Squadron at a parade at Leuchars on 27 August. The parade was timed for 1130 hours but ninety minutes before this, 43 marked the day and the event with a twelve-ship formation flypast, something never before seen since the Phantom age began. With restrictions on flying hours still in force, a problem that had existed ever since

Twelve of the best - after the flypast

XV572 'N' November, complete with underslung gun pod catches the afternoon sun on its return from the Royal Silver Jubilee Display at Finningley
(MoD (RAF) Crown Copyright)

the crisis days of 1973, there was normally no scope for such a luxury as large formation flying. However by skilful planning, four, four, two and two Phantoms were sent off between 0820 and 0910 hours, all on a legitimate training exercise, which was duly carried out. Then surprise, surprise, at 1000 hrs all 12 Phantoms returned to base with time and fuel enough to fly over first in four threes line astern and then back in the opposite direction in three box-fours. It was truly a magnificent sight, the formations were perfect, complete absence of practice notwithstanding and the upturned faces of those below said it all, pride in the squadron just bursting at the seams, good old 43 had done it again; follow THAT, if you can Treble One or 892!!! Indeed it could be said that of all the good things that Roger Palin achieved with 43, and there were many, that Dacre Day Flypast was the master of them all.

Perhaps it was justice in this year of triumph that at the Silver Jubilee Review of the Royal Air Force by HM Queen Elizabeth II the only Squadron that supplied more than one aircraft in the flypast was 43, which had two, besides a third XV572 'N' which, polished to an unbelievable standard of shininess was in the static display, fittingly beside a Victor Tanker of 57 Squadron upon whose service 43 so much relied.

Sqn Ldr George Lee, World Open Class Gliding Champion, between his flying machines

The snow-covered ground shows the track of Alpha's errant path from the runway
(MoD (RAF) Crown Copyright)

So came autumn; October saw an exchange with the 496th TFS of the USAFE at Hahn where as recounted earlier the word 'Interoperability' was added to the language of the English speaking world. In November two events were noted, both happy times as it turned out athough one could have been far from that. Firstly on the 30th, Squadron Leader George Lee received in London the Gold Medal of the Royal Aero Club. Presented by 43's own special supersonic passenger, Prince Charles, the medal was an acknowledgement of the recipient's victory in the 1976 World Open Class Gliding Championship. A Phantom cockpit or that of a glider both came alike to George Lee, he was a master in both. It can be added here that in the following year, 1978, at Chateauroux, he became the first man ever to win the Open Class for a second consecutive time.

The second occurrence in November started with a fault in the nosewheel steering of XV571 which caused it to swing violently off the runway at 90 knots or so. The crew, Flight Lieutenants Steve Gyles and Andy Moir, ejected successfully, sustaining the usual amount of back injury and Andy Moir, in addition, a broken ankle and as some nasty person said,

Canopies gone, seats fired but otherwise intact after repair, Alpha flew again
(MoD (RAF) Crown Copyright)

'more than his normal level of concussion'. Duly taken to the RAF Hospital at Ely for the checks which always follow an ejection the following scene now took place:

Scene I
Enter a young student nurse with notepad for arrival details.
'Flight Lieutenant Moir, RAF Leuchars .... Oh, you're the navigator who ejaculated .... '
Collapse of brave aviator in a heap of laughter, (causing increased pain in the back).
Exit left, Nurse, blushing crimson.

Scene II
Steve Gyles seated centre. Enter same nurse from left.
'Flight Lieutenant Gyles, RAF Leuchars. Oh, you're the pilot who...who...eja...eja...ej'... ;.. baled out.'

The Phantom returned to service within a few weeks. It took a little longer for the crew but fortunately neither suffered from any lasting damage.

So came yet another year and with it what was to be the last visit to RAF Luqa before the British armed services withdrew from the Island. 12 Phantoms, 28 aircrew, 145 groundcrew and a solitary VC10 went off to land there on 16 February. The Station Commander RAF Leuchars, Group Captain Bill Maish set a high target for the squadron pilots with 43% hits but Flight Lieutenant Al Lockwood kept the 43 flag aloft by equalling this fine score the very same day. Later Squadron Leader Lee recorded the 'impossible' 92·5.

Apart from these air-firing sorties, during which one crew survived a wrecked engine and a ruptured fuel tank caused by debris from a shell-shattered spreader bar, normal day to day training continued. An intensive flying phase recorded 43 hours on March 13th. 'All with no

Flt Lt Pete Gray and Sqn Ldr George Lee in front of their record-breaking target banner

Last Call at Malta - March 1978.
In differing states of dress (and undress) Squadron groundcrew assemble during the last APC

aircraft problems, a tribute to a superb performance by our groundcrews'.

This visit to Malta was the last major operation for Wing Commander Palin who left in May, handing over to his successor, Wing Commander Ian McBride, a squadron that would claim in every aspect of the game to be 'Cocks of the North', as they showed for instance in June when two aircraft and five aircrew with a small servicing party spent nine days in Cyprus. Averaging 8 hours flying a day they were 'The first detachment of this type FULLY to complete its task'. All due, said the Detachment Commander, Squadron Leader Andy McHugh, OC 'B' Flight, 'to the servicing crews' skill in keeping our aircraft serviceable'.

An exercise with the 2nd Air Wing of the German Navy in late June was followed by a visit to Gardermoen, Norway in August where 2 v 2 sorties were flown against Norwegian F-5's from bases well inside the Arctic Circle. Exercise Northern Wedding in September, (410 hours flown) was made more difficult by the normal Leuchars Battle of Britain Open Day. The usual evening party was a non-starter as all Phantoms were back on ops at 1800. MPC at Valley followed in November. So ended the first 10 years of Phantom 'Phighting Cocks' as they sometimes spelled it. A decade of achievement equal to all that had gone before, meaning that 43 was still at the top of the league table.

Jimmy Beedle, Hon Secretary of the Fighting Cocks Association, visited the Squadron in June 1978 and presented historical artefacts. The twin throttle butterfly valve from the Merlin engine in Hurricane P3220 (crashed 26 Aug 1940 after Plt Off Lane baled out) and a tailwheel - the sole surviving part of Hurricane P3464 which crashed on 6 July 1940 after Sqn Ldr Lott baled out. The wheel spent many years on a wheel barrow before it was rescued!
These items were gratefully accepted by Sqn Ldr Andy McHugh and Flt Lt Andy Kirk

1979 was a year wholly different from any other in one respect, from April until 18 December, (home just in time for Christmas) 43 were based at Kinloss while the Leuchars runways and taxiways were being extensively repaired and improved. This move, named Operation BOLTHOLE, while sending 43 northwards, gave the other Leuchars squadron, No 111, (Treble One or *Tremblers* depending on which side you are on) a journey in the opposite direction to Coningsby in Lincolnshire. One result was that 43 being nearer the scene of action had more, much more, than their normal share of QRA, a fact wittily expressed in verse at the 1980 Burns Night Supper by the editor of the *St Andrews Citizen*, Malcolm Campbell, who, reciting Holy Willies's prayer added for good measure two verses appropriate to the year that had gone...

Lord, before thy work is done,
Spare a thought for Treble One,
These Bolthole boys were never done,
Admirin' the view.
Ten months sitting on their bums,
But never 'Q'.

But Lord please remember me
And the canny lads of Forty Three,
Ne'er a squadron will there ever be
Wi' sic a grace;
For Lord thou kens as weel as me,
It's Fighting Cocks that own the place.
Amen.

However before the move that inspired this verse came about, several things of note happened at Leuchars. Thus, on 4 January, 'Recovering from seasonal and traditional Scottish illnesses – whisky throat, haggis hangovers and empty wallets, the snow then came out in sympathy with the lorry drivers and council workers, blocking Leuchars for a number of days so that there was no grit on the roads and

'Quick Reaction Alert' interception of a Soviet Bear seen by an accompanying Phantom at 30,000 feet
(MoD (RAF) Crown Copyright)

little food. Things got better towards the end of the month and by February the squadron was flying against USAFE Hercules. F-5 Aggressors were tackled by previously unqualified Cocks to earn the title of 'Fighting' while more DACT (Dissimilar Air Combat Training) was experienced following the arrival of the F-15 Eagles from Bitburg. This latter aircraft is first and foremost an air superiority fighter as 43 discovered so that 'it was hard not to be hypnotised by their performance, although by the end of the week we had developed tactics which reduced the superiority to more manageable proportions – if you can, that is, call running for home at 600 knots a tactic!!'

However if feeling inferior in the air when F-15s were about, on Mother Earth and the football pitch in particular there were no shortcomings and the Squadron soccer team made off with the Station Trophy, not having lost a game all season.

So with March came the trip to Kinloss where the arrival of 43 in a hitherto peaceful maritime station had much the same effect as Tom Morgan and his Hurricanes had had on the Royal Navy at Crail in 1941. Initially the outlook was bleak, – 'the accommodation looked like a Motorway Construction Camp, a home away from home for the Irish on the squadron'. Rapidly escaping from this misery, the squadron went off to Cyprus, sunshine and APC. Their previous year's overall squadron record of 23% having been upped in the meantime by Treble One to 25%, 43, taking umbrage at this insult promptly went better with 28·5%. The move Leuchars-Kinloss-Cyprus in a very short time naturally involved a massive amount of work but even so there was time found to redecorate the Limassol Children's Home as a gesture of goodwill before returning to Kinloss to start in May a round of exercises, one of them, 'Highwood', being with 43's adopted ship, HMS *Fife*. So to Soesterberg in Holland for another round of DACT with the F-15 Eagles of 32nd TFS USAFE. In the Birthday Honours list, Flight Lieutenant John Abell, a squadron stalwart and 2,000 Phantom hours pilot received the Queen's Commendation for Valuable Services in the Air. There is no record to say that this was celebrated in appropriate style but it is hard to believe it wasn't. In August 43 went and came back in due course from another detachment to Norway, Rygge on this occasion being the site for meeting 'Noggy' allies. Squadron Leader Bernie Pierce, SEngO), left for warmer climates (Saudi Arabia, to set up a

'Oscar' peeps out of the Bessonneau canvas hangar - the engineering facility at Kinloss

harem was put forward as one possibility). 'During his term with 43 the high serviceability of the squadron had been the envy of the Phantom Force for which there can be no greater praise'. Those words, written by a flying man are high commendation indeed.

It was while detached to Kinloss that 43 achieved a position in which no other Phantom squadron had previously been. Every pilot and every navigator without exception could claim at least one intercept of a Russian plane. True it could not last very long as it required only one newcomer to be posted in to the Squadron to break the spell but while it lasted 43 could claim, as in other things over the years, to be unique and from this achievement there arose the concept of a very specialised honour in the shape of a Ten Bear Tie. Designed by Mandy Burges, wife of Flight Lieutenant Rodney Burges, it carried on a dark blue background the symbol of a red '10' on the front of a white bear superimposed on a Red Star. Awarded only to those who had made interceptions of ten Russian aeroplanes (for this purpose Bears, Badgers and Coots all counted equally), it became highly prized. Not that Lady Luck did not have some influence in qualifying, for as Squadron Leader John Walmsley, OC 'A' Flight, pointed out he was fortunate to make nine interceptions in one week not long after joining 43, whereas his predecessor, Squadron Leader John Brady, never broke his duck in more than two years.

In September, trade unions at Rolls-Royce went on strike which threatened a possible future shortage in the supply of overhauled engines. Conservation of hours became the order of the day. This was coupled with a low-flying ban, no air combat sorties and no affiliation training. Depression settled in, lightened only by the insistence of the Royal Navy that 43 was the only squadron with which they wished to exercise. 'This meant Treble-One taking over 'Q' which made a nice change'. The strike continued into October but in this month, while adhering strictly to the rules laid down by 11 Group, the Squadron finished only 20 hours short of normal flying hours. By November Rolls-Royce was back at work (well, after all, it was getting near Christmas) and one result of this was a sharp drop in bar hours and a significant increase in night flying hours.

It was indicative of the high morale of 43 during their nine months at Kinloss that its standards and achievements remained as high as ever. A prolonged domestic separation such as this could potentially bring all kinds of troubles in its wake and it says much for Wg Cdr McBride that the arrangements he made to reduce any such troubles were so successful. However all bad, like all good things do not last forever and a date for return to Leuchars was finally fixed. A

Harry MacLean, Ian McBride, Andrea McBride (with flowers), Steve Smyth (with MacDuff) and Martin Barnett (with stuffed Fighting Cock) are seen after the epic supersonic return flight from Kinloss to Leuchars

'Dining Out' night for 43 was arranged by Kinloss, a night to be remembered. An almost endless round of speeches was interrupted when a large chaff-filled balloon resembling the octopus on the 201 Squadron badge was pursued across the ceiling by a model 43 Squadron Phantom with a pin in its nose and burst over the centre table. So seven days before Christmas the Phantoms came in on the renovated runways. Squadron Leader Lee was not among those who did. He was in London receiving again from the Prince of Wales the Britannia Trophy for his second World Gliding Championship success. A fitting reward for an unprecedented double triumph. The return to Leuchars at the end of Bolthole was also a triumph for the Squadron as well as a relief. All 18 deployed aircraft returned on time and in considerable style, paying scant regard to the requirement for pairs of aircraft to carry out a level break into the circuit from 1000 feet and 350 knots.

So on into the 80s with things back at Leuchars and back to normal. Well almost normal for the concrete in front of 43's hangar was incomplete (in contractors language – had not been started). Thus for a time 43 occupied the hangar vacated by 892 RN Squadron now disbanded. It meant small differences to the engineers and groundcrews for whom a hangar was a hangar but it did entail the aircrew having a long walk from the briefing and debriefing still taking place in the usual crewrooms. Still, being back at Leuchars was worth all the aggro.

Taking over 'Q' early in January a marked lack of 'trade' prompted a suggestion that the Russians had all been transferred to Afghanistan. More frustration was added when attempts to use the missile firing range at Benbecula were foiled by a bloody-minded weather god who saw to it that when visibility at Leuchars was nil the sun was shining on the range and likewise sunshine in Fife occurred when the Hebrides were lost in fog.

MacDuff, the Squadron's mascot held aloft by Wg Cdr McBride, safely returned from Kinloss as the third member of Alpha's crew.
A supersonic bird!

Came April, more DACT with the A-5s at Alconbury and also a two day Air Defence exercise coded 'Elder Forest' during which 43 flew more than half the sorties from Leuchars. May and part of June were spent in glorious weather in Cyprus while again expending vast quantities of Vulcan Gun ammunition. From here Flight Lieutenant Pete Ruddock made a home run for 43 by locating a missing fishing boat for which the far better equipped Nimrods had looked without success. Home from Cyprus to more 'Q' and exercises with Hercules of No 47 Squadron of the RAF joined this time with those of the USAFE. And always as ever with the operational demands and the exercises went the task of training and upgrading the less experienced pilots and navigators, those on a first tour from the OCU at Coningsby or in the case of some navs transferred from a different branch, perhaps maritime or transport, who required initiating into the mysteries of fast jets and the job that needed to be done by the occupant of the rear seat of a Phantom.

Half the squadron went in August to Gardermoen in Norway, there to pitch themselves for two weeks against the F-5s and the lately into service F-16s from Rygge and Sola. The food was (libellously?) described as typically Noggy, i.e. whale balls and blubber. The Norwegian press was far more polite giving the visitors extensive coverage even if 'breaking the sound barrier all the time' was a bit wide of the mark.

September had the kind of tempo where all were glad to see October. In the absence of 111 abroad it was a solid month of 'Q' plus Exercise Teamwork. This was another combined NATO exercise which meant multiple Russian recce flights. These were sometimes left to the F-14 Tomcats from the USS Nimitz but it was a cause for satisfaction when the bogeys were met by 43 while far below the Tomcats were unable to launch because of bad weather. Such was the enthusiasm of 43 at being at times the sole defenders of the Northern Approaches that when the rear doors of the 'Q' sheds failed to open Steve Gyles helped with a bit of jet blast and blew them flat, (for those not in the know,

In December 1980 Wing Commander Harry Drew AFC took over as OC 43 Squadron from Wg Cdr Ian McBride. The event was marked with the usual Champers. In this picture are C J Smith, Walter Watts, Harry Maclean, Wg Cdr Harry Drew, Wg Cdr Ian McBride, Jim Henderson (Squadron Warrant Officer), Bertie Southcombe, Ray Dixon and John Brady (MoD (RAF) Crown Copyright)

'Q' sheds described in the previous chapter have doors front and rear. The rear ones are normally shut but should be opened before the Phantom starts up).

Not so popular in 'Teamwork' were the high altitude patrols for defence of the fleet. A lack of targets acting as hostile, and these in most cases were taken by the F-14's, left the Phantom crews with little to do but cruise around high up on what was called TASMO, (Tactical Air Support of Maritime Operations).

A 'no-notice' Royal visit occurred in October. HRH Princess Margaret passing through Leuchars called in, not for the first time, to the crewroom and to sample the coffee bar. It was said, probably by one who wasn't even there, 'she chatted amiably while preferring to drink from a teaspoon rather than a cracked mug proffered by Synders, (Flying Officer Matt Syndercombe)'. This is most likely an example of the truth being embellished in the cause of a good story. Any person acquainted with 43's Coffee Bar could not be unaware that it held the finest selection of drinking mugs in the RAF. Massive porcelain objects, that required a strong, fit aviator to lift, bearing the owner's name and decorated if that be the right word, with what should be the squadron badge if the thing in the centre was more like a Bantam Cock and less like a Dodo. One suspects that the German manufacturers still bear a grudge from one of the World Wars. Nevertheless it is hard to believe that among that collection it was not possible to find one fit for a Princess.

The next visitors of note were not unexpected. Four F-4Fs of 742 Squadron (Zapatas) from the Luftwaffe base at Neuberg. They arrived as four Phantoms of 43 went away in the opposite direction. The weather was poor so there was not a lot of flying at either end of the exchange and the most noteworthy observation recorded was that (in the opinion of the RAF anyway) the better radar in the F-4Ks made them a better aircraft than the German F-4F in spite of the superior slow speed turning ability conferred upon it by the wing slats.

With December came the fifth change in Commanding Officers in the Phantom era. Wing Commander Harry Drew AFC, ex Javelins, Lightnings and a tour in the States, arrived and Wing Commander Ian McBride left, as reluctantly as all his predecessors, for duties elsewhere. His final message was, 'It has been a privilege to command the finest fighter squadron in the world. I hope all Fighting Cocks will continue to work hard at maintaining our reputation and standards'. Somehow, reading those words one heard similar noises of a similar nature from long ago _ _ _ George Lott in 1940 _ _ _ 'The finest Command any man could have or hope to have'. John Langer in 1959 _ _ _ 'two years with the finest has been honour enough for a lifetime'. 'I have always been puzzled how such a tradition could grow up around a number' . . . Lord Douglas of Kirtleside, 'Father of 43 – 1950 or thereabouts.

Meantime 43, with another in the line of superior men whom those responsible

Valley MPC December 1980
Rear: Jon Watts, Jim Giles, Dave Wilson, Ian Malin, Alan Pulfrey - Middle: Dave Shaw, Pat Lawrence, Colin Bond
Front: John Brady (OC 'A'), Roger Newton, Dave Newbury
(MoD (RAF) Crown Copyright)

invariably find to lead them, went off to Valley for MPC. It was described as 'Swift, fierce and very successful. We flew in on Monday and by Wednesday had fired all the available missiles with amazing results. One fired back at us was a rocket from the Station Commander following a party in the bar on Monday night. It missed.'

Coming home it was found that McDuff was dead, he being one of the long line of feathered Fighting Cocks which came into the Mess on squadron 'Dining-In' nights but at other times were to be found in a pen adjacent to the hangar where, in complete disregard of wet start pollution, and multiple decibels, they strutted and crowed and occupied the attention of a number of junior officers who thought they had joined the Air Force to fly. Like the Ravens at the Tower or the Apes at Gibraltar they were a necessary adjunct to a way of life, – 43's way. When they died they were buried with dignity, as was McDuff in Roger Newton's garden, and others came to take their place.

The Fighting Cocks were acclaimed as the RAF's 'Top Guns' in aerial marksmanship when Wg Cdr Harry Drew accepted the Seed Trophy from Yorkshire industrialist Mr Clifford Seed, the Squadron having broken all previous gunnery records on its detachment in Cyprus in the previous year. Also at the presentation were Gp Cpt Jerry Cohu (Stn Cdr) and AVM Peter Latham, AOC No 11 Group, making his last visit to Leuchars before retiring from the RAF
(MoD (RAF) Crown Copyright)

Prior to the MPC at Valley, Harry Drew had had his first official function on 19 November when he received the Seed Trophy on behalf of 43, won as a result of the 1979 Air Gunnery score in Cyprus. This trophy was being awarded for the first time, it having been presented by a Sheffield industrialist, Mr Clifford Seed, and thereafter would be awarded to the squadron in 11 Group which scored the best in Armament Practice Camps. Also present and saying farewell to 43 at the same time was Air Vice-Marshal Peter Latham, AOC 11 Group, who had always had the highest regard for 43.

All festive hangovers disappeared very quickly in 1981 as the squadron moved out of its nice warm hangar to Northern dispersal. Three days out there was equated with a posting to Russia. There were no salt mines but lots of laying of barbed wire, a nasty ploy at any time, building Wendy houses out of sand-bags (which first had to be filled), and generally preparing for Taceval, which came and went with all the upheaval and flap that it entailed. And so to bouts of 'Q', Cyprus for air-to-air firing, overseas trips to Iceland (Keflavik) and Belgium. In July a second Phantom was lost during a night sortie. XT866, 'Oscar', crashed on the final approach: not much above zero feet and outside the safe ejection envelope. Squadron Leader Ray Dixon and Flying Officer Matt Syndercombe both ejected, the nav sustaining slight burns from the rockets on the pilot's seat as he went. Only feet away from the fireball, which seconds before had been an aeroplane, both crewmen, thanks to the engineering genius of Sir James Martin and those who had worked with him, lived to attend the Board of Inquiry, but it had been a dangerously near thing. Matt Syndercombe was some nine months before returning to active service but Ray Dixon, cleared by the medics resumed his performances as the 11 Group solo aerobatic pilot for the 1981 season, his programme unaffected by his narrow escape.

That incident must have been the last in 1981 worth the attention of the squadron's diarist because nothing of any great interest remains to be read. Perhaps he thought it had all happened before and could be summed up in one word, routine. Or that, under the leadership of Wing Commander Drew, an individualist whose methods seemed very suited to the likes of 43 all went according to plan - his plan that is to say - and so the Fighting Cocks prospered, did their 'Q' stints, intercepted enough Russians to necessitate a new order of Ten-Bear ties, visited the Tamdhu Glenlivet Distillery in Morayshire with predictable results, flew more hours every month than planned or expected in spite of a chronic aviation fuel shortage which weighed heavily upon the squadron's shoulders for more than a year and which only lifted when the Falkland Island operations brought a swift change of emphasis. They went to the RAF Club for the annual 'do' and made all the usual noises (an occasion which sadly lacked the presence of the Boss himself he being nobbled for a Court-Martial in Lincolnshire). They fought the Aggressors, fired off missiles and cannon at the specified times and camps, continued to change the colour scheme as the Phantoms went off for majors to the new light grey (Grey Ghosts) overall finish and welcomed with the normal 43 hospitality those visitors who came to inspect the best.

Christmas presumably came and went at the appointed time in 1981 and five months later the squadron diarist, either a new one or the old having been sent on a course in using a pen, was reporting that yet another exchange with the Norwegians had been an equal success in things airbome and things entertaining as had all previous excursions to or from that country. In May it was heard with much sorrow by some present and more past Phantomeers that Lieutenant Commander Gordon Batt had been killed flying a Sea Harrier in the Falklands Campaign. He had been the RN exchange officer with 43 from 1975 to 1977 and had been not only very popular but also a fine pilot.

In August there were trips to the Mediterranean for most of the aircrew but not for a holiday. A new name had come into squadron life, Decimomannu, shortened always to Deci. Here in Sardinia was a NATO facility, ACMI. This was something quite new in training crews in air combat. Without giving away any secrets it can be said that it comprised marine buoys equipped to receive individual flight characteristics from telemetry pods and to transmit the signals to a computer where they could be evaluated, processed and stored. Thereafter the details of a combat could be played back to the participants who could study and leam from their mistakes, if any. At this base, crews of every type of fighter or ground attack aircraft could come and participate in DACT and while in Sardinia on this occasion 43 Squadron crews engaged in combat with F-104s, F-5s, F-15s and F-16s. The value of this type of training is immeasurable, all part of the modern training pattern which ensures that no pilot will in future go into action as woefully lacking in experience and training as was the case in 1940.

Back from Deci it was all systems GO in September - Battle of Britain Day, Exercise Northern Wedding, the two-yearly NATO marine exercise for a transatlantic deployment of a US strike fleet. Though details remain classified it was for 43 an excellent opportunity to practise with ships and all that entails. In between times a dozen or so Russians were intercepted. October, another month when flying was well up on target, involved diversions to bases in Europe and combat against NATO and French squadrons. November and December featured an APC at Akrotiri with Fred Grundy knocking up 101% hits, another 'impossible' score but the holes hadn't been made by seagulls. The results from this APC gave 43 the Seed Trophy yet again and although it wasn't presented until the New Year the 43 Servicing Team, matching the achievements of their airborne partners, won the Skyflash Trophy for the fastest turnround of a Phantom between operational flights. A final 3 days of low-level training just about wrapped up the year, this last exercise not being affected in spite of an American F-111 blocking half the runway at the time.

In August 1983 the Squadron bade farewell to Wing Commander Harry Drew and welcomed Wing Commander Tony Bagnall as the new Boss. The associated farewell and incoming parties tended to spread over several days. Harry Drew had imprinted his own special personality on the squadron and in spite of one of his tenets, 'never believe anything an engineer tells you' he had everybody in every position and job working all-out for 43. He left for a four-month tour with the Phantoms, Harriers and Penguins in the South Atlantic but before doing so he had accepted yet again the Seed Trophy for the best APC results of the previous year, an honour compounded for him by the award also of the Dacre Trophy, though this would not be presented until after his departure due to the Squadron's busy schedule.

CHAPTER 31

Cold War Guardians

THE new Boss arrived just as the Squadron was about to deploy to Cyprus to conduct its annual APC. Squadron Leader Dick Ellis, OC 'B' Flight, led the detachment out to the Mediterranean initially while Tony Bagnall, having previously flown the Lightning but not the Phantom, elected to spend his first week at Leuchars in order to become used to air-to-air refuelling in the F4, an aspect not covered during his OCU syllabus.

The week proved to be a busy one and included a visit from Jimmy Beedle, no doubt to reassure himself that the Fighting Cocks were still in good hands! The CO recalls being led by Flight Lieutenant Fred Grundy on his first trip on the Squadron, a low-level interception sortie. Such sorties on the OCU customarily involved an initial climb to 2,000 feet following take off. The minimum operating height for this trip however, was 250 feet, and that was as high as Fred was prepared to go. Tony Bagnall certainly found things different on 43.

The Squadron was a large one at this time, with 20-22 aircraft, of which around ten had deployed to Cyprus. There was a total of some 50 aircrew, and 250 groundcrew, the latter under the leadership of the SEngO, Squadron Leader Mike Salter. On 11 August, following a gunnery sortie, Squadron Leader John Walmsley and Flight Lieutenant Alastair Inverarity had a nose wheel unlocked indication light prior to landing at Akrotiri. All FRC procedures were followed to no avail until the 'jettison centre-line stores before landing' procedure was carried out. They jettisoned their gun-pod into the sea just off the cliffs and the jolt of the release thankfully locked the nose wheel down!

The otherwise routine detachment was remarkable for the shortest recorded post-APC celebration in the officers' mess at Akrotiri. A 'Tequila Shooter' party lasted only 35 minutes before the somewhat prematurely 'fatigued' aircrew began to seek the sanctuary of the accommodation block. Most achieved their objective but a few ended up in roadside ditches and, in one notable case, in a bath still fully dressed in his DJ! It was a happy detachment, with the ubiquitous Mediterranean sunshine, sporting activities arranged by Squadron Leader Barry Doggett and, for the bachelors, the challenge of attracting the Station Commander's (Air Commodore John Willis) two very pretty daughters.

Early September saw 43 return to Leuchars after five weeks in Cyprus, a time during which they had fired off more rounds than would have been found in the ammunition tanks of a squadron of Hurricanes during a similar period in 1940. The Battle of Britain Open Day followed on the 17th, the yearly opportunity for the Scots to find out how the RAF spends their bawbees. A grand flying display, which in 1983 the CAS, C-in-C Strike Command and his Deputy, and AOC 11 Group all came to view, was added to a funfair atmosphere. This included an A4 Pacific steam engine with whistle, and a hangar full of stalls where 43 and others flogged all kinds of souvenirs and so contributed to various charities. The preparation lasts for days and does little for those whose primary task is servicing or flying in Phantoms but it is something different and is great if the weather stays fine.

The Squadron's return from the Mediterranean was marked by similar warm weather as Scotland enjoyed the latter part of one of its best summers for a while. The pattern of activity centred on aircraft generation and flying exercises, together with a dramatic rise in the number of QRA sorties. It was not unusual for up to six aircraft to be scrambled each day. Indeed, the activity level was such that AAR tankers were deployed forward from Marham to Leuchars to provide more timely support. There were often two such tankers on the ground to cover what almost became a rolling QRA for several weeks, in which various marks of Soviet Bears were intercepted regularly.

The return to Scotland also created the opportunity for the formal presentation by Mrs Elizabeth Dacre of the Dacre Trophy for 1983, won during Harry Drew's tenure. Received by the new CO, it is interesting to note that subsequently, at the request of the Dacre family, Tony Bagnall, when he later became AOC 11 Group, delivered a eulogy at St Clement Danes following Mrs Dacre's passing in 1995.

Of course throughout the year there were the usual stints of 'Q' with generally speaking no shortage of targets to intercept. Plus of course all the things that make up the warp and weft of a year in the life of a Fighter Squadron. Like an exchange of some crews and aircraft with the

'THE DACRE TROPHY'

323rd Squadron of the Royal Netherlands Air Force who came in their F-16s and when not flying went on a weekend visit to Edinburgh followed by a trip to a distillery in the Spey Valley of which it was said, 'those who remembered, enjoyed it very much'. Taceval arrived, both parts of course, which came every year as surely as the sun rises every day, and lots of exercises with ships to ensure that the Royal Navy were kept up to scratch and not too likely to bang off unfriendly Sea Darts at the very friendly Phantoms high above. An exercise also took place with helicopters from 72 Squadron which 43 had not seen since it flew Spitfires in the same Wing in Austria in 1946. Other reportable excitements were a flypast for the US Navy at Edzell to provide a bit of noise for their Fourth of July larks and an interception by the Service Police, at night, of a Fighting Cock (feathered) which had escaped and was a potential piece of Foreign Object liable to cause Damage to compressor blades rotating at high speed. FOD (pronounced fod) is a term burned into the mind of the modem RAF as something potentially damaging and disastrous. Nor does it need to be the result of an ingested bird; a 6mm bolt is just as lethal.

In late November, the Fighting Cocks returned to Cyprus with more operational matters in mind. Operation PULSATOR required fighter escort for RAF Buccaneers operating in conjunction with US forces as the security situation in the Lebanon deteriorated and civil war continued in the wake of the Israeli invasion the previous year. A number of aircrew, including the Boss, deployed to Akrotiri in the support Hercules carrying Skyflash and Sidewinder missile stocks. The journey was enlivened by an onboard fire which resulted in a diversion to Manchester and a delay of some 12 hours. Once in Cyprus, the Boss flew out to the US carrier flagship in a USN COD (Carrier Onboard Delivery) aircraft to attend a briefing on the operation, at which the American admiral made it clear that the USA had decided that Beirut was to be a 'line in the sand' which, if crossed, would elicit a robust US reaction. This was relayed back to Air HQ at Episkopi to make clear the strength of the US commitment as UK plans were developed.

Operation PULSATOR required six Buccaneers of 208 Squadron to fly to Cyprus, where they would provide support for the British contingent of the International Peacekeeping Force in the Lebanon. The Buccaneers were to be escorted by 43's Phantoms. Although the Buccaneers' operational task was to deliver LGBs (Laser Guided Bombs) to whatever target our men on the ground designated if the Embassy came under attack, this mission was designed merely to be a demonstration of force.

For John Walmsley it was the first time he had flown with a loaded pistol but he recalls that no one seemed to be able to tell the crews who they should shoot! Catching the Buccaneers after take-off took a little time as they were not prepared to hang about and the Phantom, armed with a full load of Skyflash, Sidewinder and gun-pod, was hampered by considerable drag. At the same time a US Navy battle group was shelling the Bekaa valley, and its attack aircraft were bombing as well, so tension was pretty high.

While the Phantoms held off the coast, the Buccaneers continued onwards towards Beirut, passing directly over the British base at Hadith before turning to head north for a low level sweep over the Lebanese capital at high speed. Observers on the ground later reported that the desultory shelling from the hills above the British position was joined by bursts of machine gun fire. After their second run, the Buccaneers passed in front of the British base at extremely low level, then dipped down to fly out to sea at minimum altitude. The mission did a great deal for the morale of the British troops and was reported widely in the British Press and on television. However the support rôle played by 43 has largely been unrecorded until now.

Phantoms had been deployed to the Falkland Islands in the wake of the unsuccessful Argentine invasion in 1982, operating from Port

Keepers of the Queen's Peace, 1984
Top: Steve Foote, John Walmsley, Pete Williams, Dick Ellis, Paul Courtnage, Martin Loveridge, Nige Wainwright, Tim Wilkinson, JEngO, Neil Adams, Pete Kelly, Simon Leighton-Porter, Brian Bates, Tony Dewhurst, John Hair   On wing: Dave Cyster, Tony Bagnall, Brett Martin, Pete Humphrys
Front: Dom Riley, Phil Jones, Donny Holland, Jon Watts, Iain Brain, Barry Doggett, Chris Boyd, Rick Suffolk, Evan Evans, Clive Marrison, Steve Green, Johnny Sorrells, Tony Bown, Mike Salter (SEngO)
(MoD (RAF) Crown Copyright)

Stanley once the runway at the modest airfield had been extended to 6,000 feet and equipped with arrester cables. The time soon arrived for the aircraft to be rotated for engineering reasons and 43 undertook the ferrying of the first two replacement aircraft. Tony Bagnall argued with HQ 11 Group, albeit unsuccessfully, that four aircraft should be sent to Ascension Island to ensure that two ultimately arrived at Stanley. In the event he was proved correct. Two more aircraft had to be sent south and the policy of initially despatching four aircraft became the standard routine for these deployments. Group Captain Jock Heron, a Fighting Cock from the Hunter days, recalls an episode during 1984.

"During my tour as Station Commander at RAF West Drayton, fellow Fighting Cock Sir Peter Bairsto was Deputy Commander-in-Chief at Headquarters Strike Command and had endorsed my appointment as Station Commander at RAF Stanley in the Falkland Islands. I flew south in early April 1984 and set about meeting all the personnel under my command, including the Harrier and Phantom crews. Some of them had served previously with the Fighting Cocks either as Hunter or Phantom men and with the 1984 squadron reunion scheduled for early May it seemed timely to have a squadron reunion in the Falklands.

So it was that on Saturday 5 May 1984, some four hours later than the London event, nine members The Fighting Cocks Association, South Atlantic Branch, marked the unique spirit of 43 by holding their annual reunion on the number two 'Coastel' accommodation ship at RAF Stanley and toasting the health of colleagues some six thousand miles away."

Other airborne events of note occurred in 1984. On 16 July John Walmsley led a five-ship formation to overfly Concorde once it had landed at Leuchars with golfers for the British Open golf tournament at St Andrews, while on 19 December, a 12-aircraft formation flew to celebrate the end of the year and conduct 4 v 8 intercepts before making seasonal visits to the radar stations at Saxa Vord and Buchan.

Group Captain Tim Elworthy was Station Commander at Leuchars at this time and knew he had two forceful squadron commanders on 43 and 111. The Tremblers' CO was Chris Coville, himself a former Fighting Cock from the mid-1970s. Their leadership styles very much set the tone during this period, a fact that did not go un-noticed by 43's Flight Lieutenant Ned Kelly, a natural entertainer and comedian, who arranged a competition between the two Wing Commanders during the Christmas all-ranks function. The curtains on the stage drew back to reveal the two men, dressed in lounge suits, each standing beside a Phantom seat pack containing an un-inflated dinghy. The challenge was to see who could get into their dinghy in the shortest time. While history does not record who won, Tony Bagnall certainly recalls that he wrote-off a perfectly good suit due to the stains produced by the packing chalk which two dry cleaning attempts failed to remove.

The size of the Squadron enabled some impressive flying rates to be achieved – on one occasion, 43 sorties in one day. Tony Bagnall remembers a personal best of 43 hours flying in one month that was no mean achievement in a fighter during peacetime. Most importantly, the Squadron made a point of launching a pair every morning at 0830 on the dot, just as the station morning briefing was commencing and as a reminder of which was the pre-eminent squadron.

Air traffic infringements are the bane of all Bosses' lives, particularly when they turn out to be the culprit. An inadvertent infringement of Glasgow airport's zone by the Boss while on a low level sortie to the west coast, although received with equanimity by the airport authority, resulted in him being represented at his dining-out with a picture entitled 'Glasgow's Miles Better', a play on a tourism marketing slogan at the time, 'Glasgow Smiles Better'. The evening was also enlivened by Margie Doggett arranging a 'stripper-gram' and the Boss having the pleasure of a very scantily dressed young lady sitting on his lap after dinner. Margie's gift was all the more considerate in view of Tony's well-known difficulty in remembering wives' names at dining-outs and having to rely on prompt cards held up at the back of the room!

Wing Commander Al Winkles, Tony's successor, arrived at Leuchars railway station on a Sunday in March 1985 to commence his take-over the following day. He was surprised to be met on the platform by Tony with 20 of his Fighting Cocks and a welcoming tray of Fighting Cocktails (Kaluha and Baileys). Tony Bagnall then departed to the Falklands to take command of 23 Squadron at Port Stanley and to supervise its move to the newly built Mount Pleasant airfield. His farewell was honoured by a six-ship formation fly-past on 8 March.

43's new commanding officer quickly slotted into the routine. In October 1985, the squadron departed for RAF Akrotiri in Cyprus taking ten Phantoms on its annual Armament Practice Camp. They arrived on the Monday and occupied the usual dispersal at the south-

Tony Bagnall welcomes the new Boss, Al Winkles

east end of the airfield. Things were not too well organised that first day, and finding accommodation for the airmen and NCOs was problematic. In consequence the Squadron had people spread out all over the base and no one person seemed to know exactly to where everyone had disappeared. Al Winkles certainly didn't!

At least he knew about the aircrew, who had descended into their usual APC barrack block and, as usual, were soon in the process of taking the Mess apart that first night. The CO finally got to bed around 0100 and his next recollection was of being shaken hard by a very tall and very glum-looking RAF policeman. His heart sank as he wondered who had done what to what, but the policeman's first words were: 'Please, Sir, you must move all your aircraft, and you must do this within the hour.' It was 0300!

Quickly locating one of the flight commanders, he ordered him to wake the air and ground crews, and then rushed over to Wing Operations. There he was told that a cruise ship, the *Achille Lauro*, had been hijacked and that Italian Special Forces were due to arrive at Akrotiri, flown in by a C-130 Hercules within the hour, and would occupy the Squadron's dispersal area since it was the most secure one on the base. Al Winkles was instructed by a very harassed Station Commander that he had to move all his aircraft, and all their starting equipment, the whole length of the airfield to the VC10 dispersal site some two miles away in the north-west corner of the airfield. There were to be no protests, no excuses, just move the aircraft – NOW.

The next sixty minutes were lost in frantic attempts by all concerned to find enough groundcrew and pilots to enable a complete vacation of the dispersal, and all this was to be achieved in the dark. The situation was not helped by not knowing where everyone had been billeted nor by the revelation that several pilots and navigators were missing, having gone off base. When heads were counted, it was soon apparent that there were not enough people to man all ten aircraft, so Al set up a rotation of drivers and vehicles to locate and collect people from barrack blocks and then to collect pilots from the VC10 dispersal to bring them back to taxi another aircraft over. What was soon apparent was that there was not going to be enough time to accomplish the move before the Hercules arrived.

What actually happened next that night is lost in a blur of fact and rumour. Navigators became groundcrew and aircraft marshallers, whilst the available groundcrew tackled the move of the ground equipment. There is a distinct possibility, that at least one senior navigator taxied a Phantom the full two miles all by himself. The CO heard of this after the alleged event had taken place and decided not to pursue the matter, but he did find out who was most likely to have done it, if indeed it had been done! The fact remains, however, that the task was achieved. Not in the sixty minutes prescribed, but in time for the arriving Hercules to occupy an empty dispersal area just as dawn broke.

Subsequently, the APC became disrupted for the first three days, and at one stage the Squadron was on stand-by to fly unarmed recce sorties over the hijacked ship with hand-held cameras. Apart from Squadron Leader Barry Mayner, the QWI(N), who was keen to use his brand new video camera, the rest of the aircrew were not over-keen once it was reported that the hijackers had shoulder-launched SAMs, against which the Squadron had no defensive flares. However, the US President, Ronald Reagan, tasked the suitably equipped US Navy F-14s for the job so 43 were, thankfully, stood down.

Once the panic was over, the Squadron was told that it could re-occupy its detachment dispersal area, the Italians having departed. Fortunately the SEngO dispatched a number of armourers with the initial groundcrew party who found quantities of loose ammunition strewn about in a most careless and un-RAF fashion.

On 16 October news was received that Air Vice-Marshal Ken Hayr the new AOC British Forces Cyprus, was arriving by TriStar (1). Al Winkles and his American navigator, Barry Messmer, led a 4-ship to intercept the aircraft. Once they met up he was escorted in with two aircraft on each wing and, after the TriStar had landed, the Phantoms flew past over the top as he stepped on,to the pan at Akrotiri.

Within days, the Air Marshal arrived at 43's dispersal demanding some air-to-air gunnery sorties. Al knew he wasn't current and hadn't seen the front end of a simulator for nearly a year but sent him off anyway, with Barry Mayner in the back seat. Ken Hayr returned with one of the best scores of the APC. What a guy! All in all it had been a most unusual APC detachment.

A busy QRA phase during 1986 saw 43 up near Scapa Flow, protecting the American fleet from 'Orange' forces during one of the many naval exercises the Squadron became involved in. As the squadron was a fleet defence squadron, this of course was a bread and butter assignment. Al Winkles recalls the day he was patrolling to the east of the Shetlands as a singleton, in daylight, when Saxa Vord radar vectored him towards a known high-level target described as a civilian airliner off-track, and not responding to Air Traffic Control instructions. He was ordered to make a cautious interception and to standby to give any assistance that might be required.

A set-piece stern interception brought his Phantom up to what was identified as a Soviet IL-62 Classic, with Aeroflot markings, flying at 35,000 feet, heading west at about ·85 Mach. The Classic was the Russian equivalent of the British VC10 and looked almost exactly like its western brother, with two pairs of jet engines mounted at the rear, just below a high tail-plane which itself was something approaching the 'size of a Spitfire'. As Al remembers, none of these aircraft ever carried military markings, and they were flown by Aeroflot crews and carried civilian passengers.

(1) Ken Hayr CB CBE AFC & Bar, had commanded No.1 Squadron on Harriers, 1970-71. AOC 11 Group 1982. Air Marshal 1988 and Knighted KCB in 1991. Tragically killed in a flying accident at Biggin Hill, flying a Vampire on 2 June 2001.

The Russian machine was heading directly towards the naval exercise area situated to the east of the Shetlands and, in order not to unduly excite the passengers and crew, he maintained his position in line astern until he had closed to about 100 feet directly beneath its engines and in a good spot to see exactly where he was going. He sat there for a couple of minutes deciding the best course of action, but then to his utter surprise he saw ahead, in the underside of the Classic, a large square panel slide open to reveal three large camera lenses. At the same moment he could see ahead, the ships of the American fleet and a carrier group.

It now became obvious that the Russian crew were deliberately ignoring ATC guidance in order to gain intelligence on the NATO fleet, so in order to prevent successful photography Al slid his Phantom forward until he was staring vertically up into the camera bay some 30-40 feet above him. There he sat for the next 6-7 minutes, generally smiling up at the cameras, giving them the thumbs up (amongst other suitable gestures), thereby denying them a view of the sea and the vessels below. Finally the Classic gently swung back onto a south-easterly heading and motored off to its destination, somewhere in Europe. Al doubts if the crew ever knew he was there at the time, and would have loved to have been the proverbial fly on the wall when the Soviet intelligence staff developed the film. Instead of allied ships all they would have seen was a huge RAF Phantom FG1 – McDonnell Douglas rivets, metal and all - and the congenial faces of Al and his navigator.

The move of 43 Squadron to the hardened facility on the north-east side of Leuchars took place in the spring of 1986, beginning with a few engineers and the larger equipment, and taking about a week. The engineers would probably say that it took longer but then they had a lot more to think about and plan for. They had also visited the site a lot earlier than the aircrew. Operations continued throughout the change, initially with a couple of aircraft and finally, after about three days, with all serviceable airframes. Flying Ops moved over early one morning and the engineers moved in stages, leaving the aircraft in deep servicing in the old hangar for some weeks until they were ready to fly. Flying operations continued throughout but at a slower pace.

The crowding in the hardened aircrew ops building was unbelievable and an early edict said that if anyone did not have a good reason for being there, they had to stay in the adjoining Squadron HQ. There were 50 aircrew, two engineering officers and half a dozen engineers in the aircrew Personnel Briefing Facility, but in the engineers' PBF it was worse, with anything up to 200 of the 330 squadron engineers there at any one time. For exercises and for war, all the engineers were on duty and it then became a real bear pit.

Personnel Briefing Facility (PBF) and HQ building just before occupation 1986

There was tolerable space in the aircrew PBF for 40 bunk beds in a room later to become known as the submarine, three briefing rooms, a main briefing room and an ops area. Next to this were two showers and three toilets. The female ops clerks mucked in with good grace and during lock-downs were allocated one of the briefing rooms for their dorm. Lock-downs occurred during Tacevals and Minevals, about three times a year. There was also a changing area for flying kit servicing, and a decontamination area which led to a two-door airlock to the outside world. Under-floor tanks held three months water supply, dry rations, NBC kits and body bags. There was a generator in a room accessible from the engineering section behind the ops desk which gave the Squadron power and decontaminated the air, the amount of which was limited only by the diesel fuel supply, this being enough for several weeks.

Entrance to the Headquarters

There were two problems. Parking more aircraft than there were shelters available, and the lack of sleep. At this time 43 was the largest fighter unit in 11 Group and had 18 aircraft on charge and only 12 shelters. This overcrowding was solved by parking two Phantoms in each of some shelters. However, manning up the rearmost of the two aircraft when the front one was starting up was a choking experience and 'sod's law' always meant that when an aircraft became unserviceable, it was invariably the front one.

Just behind the PBF and HQ building lay an old gamekeepers cottage which was initially hoped to be converted into the aircrew crewroom, sadly this was not possible

Those aircraft that became long-time unserviceable were parked at the rear of two or three shelters that were earmarked as Servicing HASs, and these were the shelters furthest away from the exit gate. All this meant a lot of moving of aircraft around, similar to the problems faced on board an aircraft carrier. The second problem, lack of sleep, was experienced during lock downs when both air and ground crew suffered from sleep deprivation. This was compounded by alerts, extraneous noise and, most of all, by the comings and goings of others reporting for or ending their duty periods.

The hotbed principle was employed during lock-downs especially in the engineers' PBF where there were only about 100 bunks. For the aircrew, the CO was provided with drugs called 'downers' and 'uppers'. The former were allowed to be taken in peacetime exercises but the latter drug was reserved for the real thing. The downer was Temazepam and it was used by some aircrew who suffered sleep deprivation and seemed to work very well. The only rule was that they had to swallow the pill in the duty authorisor's presence to prevent hoarding. The magic bit was that, even if the person was woken prematurely, the drug left no drowsiness and it was safe for him to fly. No drugs were supplied for the engineers who battled on through ice and snow, sometimes for days without proper sleep.

This was also a busy period for other reasons. Al Winkles recalls that the Squadron flew over 200 hours in five days when the Soviets were very active. 43 Squadron reached Q9 at one stage and had at least one fully armed aircraft airborne throughout. The engineers just didn't give up and there was at least one chief armourer who was on duty for all of that period, sleeping where and when he could. He just refused to go home.

Hardened aircraft shelters

Overall, most men on the Squadron felt the move to the 'Hard' was better for operational reasons even though there was a slight loss of squadron integrity as people had to depend more on communications than ever before.

Needless to say, the comms boxes in each HAS, connecting crews to the ops and engineers, regularly failed and runners were often needed. The big loss was the interaction between aircrew and groundcrew as the two PBFs were widely separated. Everyone had to work harder at keeping the ground personnel informed, and not everyone succeeded in this. It just needed a lot of practice and a constant awareness of the need to communicate, however tired one became.

When in Cyprus, Al WInkles and Mike Pugh intercepted a Soviet Il-38 "May" over the Mediterranean. The Phantom, XV581 'E', is armed with a centreline cannon pod

The Squadron celebrated its 70th anniversary in August 1986, delayed from the spring due to operational commitments. Over one weekend it hosted an open day with a barbeque, and a formal dinner. The CO's aircraft (XV571) was painted with a rather gaudy chequered spine and fin which did not go down very well with HQ 11 Group.

The Squadron's oldest surviving member, Lord Balfour of Inchrye, was unable to attend but sent Al Winkles a wonderful letter reminding everyone of his days on Sopwith 1½ Strutters and Camels under the command of Major Sholto Douglas (later MRAF Lord Douglas of Kirtleside). He also suggested that members look again at the surviving propeller, with the names of the earliest squadron pilots and their victories, that adorned the crew room. On the Friday the barbeque was attended by the whole Squadron and some veterans. Even more veterans and their families came along on the Saturday for the open day, which included an air display and a look at the new hardened facility. A Tornado F2, Buccaneer, Hawker Hunter, Lightning, F-16s and Hawks took part in the display, followed by 43's own Phantom aerobatic display, flown by Barry Doggett and Nick Hansen. That evening the Squadron entertained around 60 past members in the officers' mess at a formal dinner.

An alarming incident occurred one dark night around this time. A lone 43 Squadron Phantom became airborne from Leuchars to fly a 'Profit' sortie against a singleton jamming Canberra. 'Profit' was the codename allocated to sorties in which ECM-equipped Canberras from 360 Squadron gave radar and voice jamming practice to 11 Group fighters and other NATO aircraft.

The 43 crew consisted of a junior pilot, Roger Goodrum, and Captain Barry Messmer, an exchange USAF navigator. They got into the stern sector of an ARA (attack/re-attack), where a head-on pass for a simulated front missile firing is continued into a stern attack. The Canberra crew were very good – as usual – and Messmer became suitably confused, but fought through the jamming on his 'tube' and directed his young pilot into a stern position. Finally seeing the target burn-through on his scope Barry gave Roger directions to control the speed overtake according to what he thought was the target's range. Unfortunately, Barry had inadvertently selected the wrong range-scale on his radar scope and, as they completed the stern attack, they were actually at only half the distance from the Canberra than he had thought.

'Alpha' in its 70th Anniversary markings

The result was that they ended up in close line astern on the Canberra with a huge speed overtake.

Barry suddenly realized what was happening and shouted a warning to Roger who was still flying 'heads down' in the radar. Roger then carried out a hard break to starboard at very close range. A slight bump was felt as the Phantom passed through the Canberra's slipstream....or so both aircraft crews believed!

The 70th Anniversary logo embodied the World War Two 'Fighting Cock' emblem.

Landing back at Leuchars, the Canberra crew parked at the Visiting Aircraft Flight area and was aghast to find a scrape mark on their starboard wingtip and fuel tank. Roger, meantime, was doing circuits back at Leuchars when a hurried telephone call to 43 Ops from the Canberra crew was taken by Squadron Leader John Cliffe who immediately instructed 'Get those bloody idiots down now!' Sure enough, when the Phantom was subsequently inspected, a matching scar was revealed running lengthwise along the underside of its fuselage near the centreline tank. Following this incident Roger picked up the nickname of 'Roger Ramjet' after the cartoon character. There but for the grace of God. . .

Another story is related by Al Winkles to show how tough the Phantom was. Wheels-up landings were thankfully very rare and when it did happen the aircraft usually came through the experience well. For 43 this occurred one night in 1986 when a nose wheel failed to extend prior to landing. The pilot was a first tourist on his first night 'solo'. Flight Lieutenant Andy Brown was a tall, lanky officer who looked about 16 years old and was responsible for the Squadron's fighting cock mascots. Indeed, he had recently starred in this role in *The Daily Telegraph's* colour supplement. On this first night sortie in command he was accompanied by the senior navigator, Squadron Leader Martin Barnett, put there to 'watch over him'.

At the end of the intercept sortie, when the wheels were selected 'down' while on the radar approach to land, the indication clearly showed a 'barber's pole' for the nose wheel – an unlocked condition. Emergency 'down' air was selected and the aircraft was subjected to positive and negative 'G' to achieve a down-lock, something not to be undertaken lightly at night on your first solo. Throughout all this the young pilot was quietly encouraged by the back-seater who could only give verbal support and advice from the Flight Reference Cards. Nothing seemed to work so a flypast above the floodlights at the ATC tower was carried out to establish the position of the nose gear visually from the ground. It was seen to be up and with the doors still closed. With fuel running low a landing had to be made sooner rather than later and there was no time to lay a foam carpet.

By this time the CO, having been told of the problem, was up in the tower listening to the chatter. Having had RN carrier experience with the Phantom, Al Winkles knew that an approach-end hook wire engagement would be fatal for the aircraft without a nose wheel. It would pitch down violently and break its back. He also knew that deploying the tail 'chute with the nose off the ground would cause a hard pitch down. Al therefore briefed Andy over the radio on what to do and what to expect. Al relates:

"He followed my instructions to the letter, prompted calmly by his back-seater. Andy landed normally, lowered the nose gently to the ground whilst he still had control of it and immediately stop-cocked both engines. Then, with sparks from the nose lighting up the night, he deployed the tail parachute and kept straight using steady braking. The aircraft quickly came to a halt with no fire and both crew stepped out.' 'On jacking up the aircraft on the runway, it was found that the door operating rod had fractured preventing the extension oleo leg from operating the nose wheel. A fleet-wide inspection followed and the rod was beefed up. Not every Phantom pilot can have had such a memorable first night solo sortie. The lad did well."

In February 1987 the Squadron deployed six aircraft to RAF Valley for an MPC (Missile Practice Camp), run by Squadron Leader Barry Mayner, to conduct Trial Amity. The purpose of the trial, which proved to be a success, was to determine the ability of the Phantom to track and engage small RCS (Radar Cross-Section) targets such as cruise missiles.

Every squadron commander's nightmare is the loss of any of his air or ground personnel. Thus far Al Winkles had been extremely lucky, with just two incidents during his period as 'Boss'. As Al remembered, this was far less than when he had been 43's 'A' Flight Commander nine years earlier. The mid-air collision between the Phantom and Canberra, then the nose wheel failure had fortunately passed off without injury, but the loss of a pilot did occur, although not whilst flying.

Captain Rick Merchant was a newly arrived USAF exchange pilot who was driving his car southwards on the A68 south of Edinburgh. He and a junior pilot travelling with him were both on their way south to attend a training course. Whilst overtaking on this notorious road with its many blind spots, they collided head-on with a young lady driving a Land Rover and the Land Rover won. The lady was not badly hurt, while the junior pilot suffered a broken leg. However Rick was fatally injured.

Al Winkles was woken by the duty officer with the news that Rick had been taken to Newcastle hospital and was unlikely to survive the night. It was essential that his wife Hannah should get to his bedside as quickly as possible. The Station Commander agreed that the Squadron could use the Station SAR Wessex helicopter to get her to the hospital as a road journey would take too long. Al's wife, Meg, agreed to go with her but nobody else could make the trip due to range and payload considerations.

It was a pitch-black night and the weather utterly foul, with strong winds and rain. On the airfield the two ladies struggled into totally unfamiliar immersion suits in 202 Squadron's ops room, followed by a complete and detailed survival briefing by the duty winchman. His audience was comprised of one woman in total shock while the other was thinking apprehensively of the prospect of her first helicopter flight ever, which was to be at night and in terrible weather. Surrounded by total strangers, she had to look after her charge, who was understandably in no condition to think straight. The SAR boys did their bit as usual and they got Hannah to Rick's side just in time. He died soon after she arrived.

In March 1987 the Squadron took part in a detachment to Bodø in Norway, taking four aircraft inside the Arctic Circle for Exercise Cold Winter, a flight that took two hours. There was a good deal of snow on the ground but in the main the runway was kept free of ice. Fortunately the weather was generally good and as far as can be remembered the approach-end arrester wire was not used many times.

The resident squadron had F-16s and the four crews enjoyed some air combat missions with them around the usual intercept work during the week of the detachment. Al Winkles, for example, flew eight sorties in five days. The F-16 pilots comprised half regulars and half reservists, the latter made up of mainly commercial airline pilots. In spite of very low annual flying hours they seemed to make the best use of their aircraft although they had no front aspect missile capability and very poor radar compared to the Phantom. Diversion airfields were few and far between and everyone had to keep a close watch on the fuel states, as the local weather had a tendency to change very quickly. The presence of extremely high ground near the coast was also a hazard that could easily catch out the unwary.

Re-armed with 8 live missiles, a Phantom completes a Operational Turn Round in a HAS - March 1987
(MoD (RAF) Crown Copyright)

The F-16 pilots were those whom the crews often met in the air during intercepts of Russian reconnaissance aircraft. They would intercept the Bears coming out of Murmansk, and then hand them over to 43 halfway down the Norwegian coast. The 43 boys found it interesting to compare logbook entries concerning the many incidents that had happened to them over the years.

One thing the CO remembers was that the bottles of whisky they took with them worked far better than the local currency, and also got them into some famous parties. At £50 a bottle in Kroner terms, these 'gifts' were much appreciated by the hosts.

Roy Macintyre, who was to serve much of his operational flying career with 43, both on the Phantom and Tornado, recalls an incident involving Nobby Clarke and Kevin Poysden:

"During the year the Squadron was on a Capex (Combat Air Patrol Exercise) and was flying an ex-892 Squadron Fleet Air Arm Phantom that had seen more than its fair-share of modifications and patches over the years. While on CAP (and bored) Kev noticed that a particular switch in the rear cockpit, that should

Lady Douglas, widow of Lord Douglas, presented her late husband's first flying log book to Wg Cdr Alan Winkles - a treasured item indeed!
(MoD (RAF) Crown Copyright)

have been wire-locked off, was not. This switch was a legacy from the days when 892 had a tactical nuclear role and illuminated a 'Consent' caption in the front cockpit. This was a fail-safe mechanism to ensure that both crew members agreed to the release of their weapon. Kev began flicking this switch on and off and Nobby called back, 'Hey, Kev, what are you doing?' When Kev explained, Nobby replied, 'Well leave it on, because if I do this, we can drop a nuke.' At this point Nobby rotated the redundant air-to-ground weapon selector round to a gate, pushed the interlock aside and selected 'Special Weapon'. He then pushed the pickle button on his control column. This was shortly followed by a loud thump and a stunned silence from the front cockpit.

"What was that?" asked Kev. 'The centreline tank,' was the reply! "But that's not possible", countered Kev – and he was right, but it had gone none the less. On checking in with Station Ops, Kev reported that their configuration was 'Charlie' (code for wing tanks only). "Don't you mean Delta?" (a three tank fit in an F4) came the response. 'Negative!' was Kev's reply. Nobby didn't bother signing the jet back in but ran towards the squadron PBF and met the Boss who was running the other way – towards him! The subsequent engineering investigation revealed an electrical short-circuit had brought back into play long redundant wires and the impossible had happened. Al Winkles described the whole incident as: "Two 10-year-old boys playing with a box of matches!'"

Another story from Roy Macintyre regarding Nobby partly involved Roy:

"It happened on 16 June 1987 during a NATO squadron exchange with 311 Squadron RNLAF at Volkel in Holland. I was part of the 'away team' but still on Convex (conversion phase on the Squadron prior to full operational status). On this particular day I was flying with Ian Brain as No 2 to Mark 'Phiz' Physic and Kelvin Harris. We were going to conduct two-versus-four low-level overland practice interceptions in one of the German low-flying areas. Our target package was two more 43 Squadron Phantoms, led by Jules Bourne, and two 311 Squadron F-16s.

We started the first run and suddenly I called to Ian that Phiz had an F-16 in his '6'. 'Check our 7!' was Ian's immediate response. There was another F-16 sitting in Fighting Wing. It was a Belgian machine and its pilot was making visual signals. 'Never mind him, he wants us to change frequency,' added Ian, who then signalled back the direction of the impending fight. So it had now become four-versus-four, but Ian seemed happy enough.

The merge occurred and the F-16s quickly turned after the target formation. Phiz and I checked down threat and cross-turned after them. As I rolled out I expected to see six aircraft. 'Ian,' I said, 'there are a lot of aircraft out there.' Ian replied, 'Just stay with Phiz and don't shoot at any Belgians.' Suddenly another Phantom passed down our right-hand side, close enough for me to see 92 Squadron's markings, followed by another in 19 Squadron colours. I could by then see F-15s, F-111s, Harriers and Tornado GR1s all over the place. All the time Ian was urging me to stay with Phiz. I don't know how many times we were 'shot at', I certainly pulled the trigger a lot and then we were out and miraculously still with Phiz.

At the debrief we could account for 22 aircraft in the merge and shortly afterwards we realised that we had run into the TLP [Tactical Leadership Programme] package out of Jever. The postscript is that Nobby Clarke and Kenny Reeves were on that TLP course and in their de-brief that day they received great plaudits for their performance. 'By God, Nobby, you were everywhere in that merge.' Little did the TLP staff realise that there had not been just one 43 Phantom in that fight – but five!"

On Bastille Day 1987 – 14 July – Al Winkles, as Q1, was scrambled to patrol east of the Faeroes to await the expected transit of two Bear Deltas to Cuba – a routine event.

"Sure enough, my trusty navigator made radar contact with them at an astounding range and we motored in behind them. First we closed in on the rear Bear to read its door number,

The Cyprus detachment 1987

Standing at back: Simon Tucker, Dave Calvert, John Jupp

Sitting on top: Paul Willis, Ashley Priddle, Karim Sachedina, Ian Lawrie, John Bowen, Kelvin Harris, Kenny Reeves, Tony Andrew, Roger Wells, Paul Colley, Roger Goodrum, Tony Parker, Pete Humphreys

Standing on wing: John Tyler, Dave Fiddler, Matt Patterson, Mike Tetlow, Keith Crombie, Andy Brown, Chris Weightman, Martin Barnett, Barry Messmer, Chris Longley, Steve Carr, Nigel Wilson

Sitting on wing: Jim Gous (JEngO), Mike Pugh, Jules Bourne, Dick Hanson, Steve Green, Ian Brain, John Cliffe, Andrew Eckersley

Standing in front: Graham Dyson, Barry Doggett, Brett Martin, Chris Lackman, Alan Winkles before edging forward to the leader to read its number. Fully satisfied, we then stayed with the Bears for the next 30 minutes or so, seeing them safely off on their westerly heading over the Atlantic. Turning away to the south-east we headed for home – or so we thought."

As Al and his back-seater coasted in over the north-west coast of Scotland, they were directed by Benbecula radar to a rendezvous with a VC10 tanker. More trade was obviously expected. Having tanked to full they were then, much to their surprise, vectored southwards, down the Irish Sea to a position 100 miles south-west of Cornwall. Portreath radar then explained that their previous trade had, unusually, not continued on towards Cuba, but had turned south down the west coast of Ireland and appeared to be heading for the Bay of Biscay. A further VC10 tanker had been ordered to their location so that they could intercept the Bears and shadow them. Sure enough, the targets appeared out to the west and the Phantom carried out a 120° turn to intercept. Al Winkles takes up the story again:

"We were joined by a VC10, pulled off its training sortie over the North Sea. The tanker fell into line astern as we stationed ourselves on the Bear's port side. By this time the two Russian aircraft had joined together in loose formation. About 150 miles south of Cornwall, my navigator announced in a small voice that we had fallen off his map. However, as we entered the Bay of Biscay we were certain that we would soon be relieved by the French Air Force and we therefore kept a sharp look out for Mirage fighters.

By now we had lost contact with Portreath radar and had just the VC10 for company. The tanker captain then announced that as it was Bastille Day he had been told that we would have to look after the 'trade' alone and that he was trying to find a selection of French airfields that might be open for any possible diversion if we got into difficulties. However, thus far, the airfields he had tried had not even replied to his radio calls! Having given us this good news he then said he was getting short of fuel, that he would give us what he could spare, and then he would leave us as there was another VC10 due to pitch up in around 30 minutes or so. We took on a few thousand pounds of fuel and he left us, having given us a selection of vectors towards the nearest airfields in the St Nazaire/La Rochelle areas – all probably closed.

At this point we felt very vulnerable. We had no maps of France, no specific diversions, no weather information and no radio contact with anyone except for the departing tanker. At this point the Bears seemed quite friendly and, possibly having been monitoring our situation over the radio, they turned towards the north-west. At least now we felt we were heading home. A very long 30 minutes passed and then very faintly we heard what appeared to be a distant conversation between our departing VC10 and the one arriving. Sure enough, the new tanker soon appeared and carried out an immaculate join-up using our air-to-air Tacan. The return route was flown in reverse by the Bears and ourselves, and we finally handed the Soviets over to Norwegian fighters which escorted them on their way back to Murmansk." After that epic 5-hour sortie, Al ordered that in future all 43 Squadron QRA aircraft were to carry maps of Northern France. Better late than never!

The 1987 APC at Akrotiri during July and August was the usual cocktail of success, disappointments and sheer buffoonery. Roy Macintyre won the 'Cup and Spurs' for best academic score by a first tourist. He and his back-seater, Mike Pugh, also got involved in Operation BLUE PENCIL – QRA duties at Akrotiri. On 6 August for instance they intercepted two Russian Badgers north of the island that were westbound for the Aegean.

The APC also saw the last trip on the squadron for one if its favourite navigators, Chris 'CJ' Weightman. When he landed he got his pilot to stop while he changed into a black and white chequered flying suit (run up by a tailor in Limassol). He then sat on the spine while the aircraft taxied back to dispersal. Sadly CJ died with Ian Halden in the Falklands a few years later, their Phantom FGR2 crashing into the sea, cause unknown. (XV421 of 1453 Flight, 30 October 1991.)

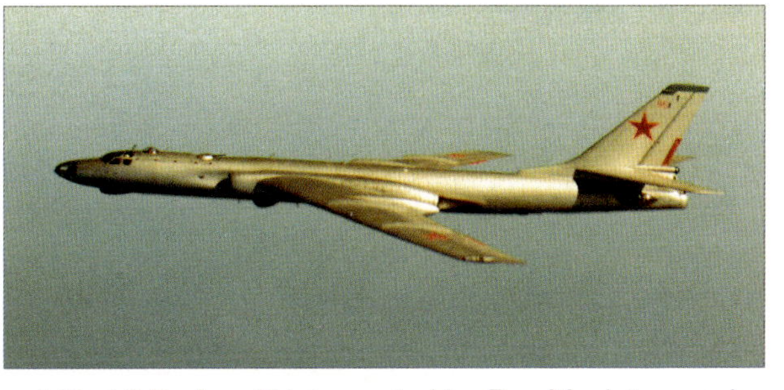

A Tu-16 Badger K intercepted by Roy Macintyre and Mike Pugh over the Mediterranean on 6 August 1987

Wing Commander John Brady took over the reins of 43 on 17 August 1987, following Al Winkles' departure that month. When he arrived the Squadron was in Cyprus on armament practice camp. Indeed, his initial dual check with Squadron Leader John Cliffe, the squadron's QWI(P), continued into an air-firing sortie on the banner.

Having returned from Cyprus on 3 September, the Squadron was deployed to Stornoway as part of Exercise Ocean Safari to test the location as a FOB (Forward Operating Base). Being SACLANT (Supreme Allied Commander Atlantic) assigned, this would be crucial to the Squadron's war role. The deployment went well initially before suspected fuel contamination brought things to a premature end. Something else that came to a similar end occurred with the loss of XT861 'AC' on 7 September, one of the two dual-control aircraft and the last grey-green camouflaged Phantom FG1 in RAF service. Treble One Squadron had borrowed it to use in their display work-up for the 1987 Air Show (its 70th anniversary year), and Battle of Britain Open Day. It was lost in a mid-air collision during formation manoeuvring over the North Sea but Squadron Leader Tom Riddell (111's QFI) and first tourist Flying Officer John 'Herbie' Hancock ejected successfully. They had been front right position in a 'St Andrew's Cross' formation (like the dots on a 5 on a die). The centre aircraft slipped forward and right during a turn and hit 'AC' before anyone realised what was happening. As a consequence, 43 then took over the task and provided a faultless display despite the pre-event publicity crediting the fly-past to 111. This theme was to persist throughout John Brady's tour.

Roy Macintyre recalls another squadron

The Valley Christmas Rocket Show - December 1987
Standing: Keith Conradi, Linton Chilcott, Frank Hall (SEngO), Ash Priddle; Jules Bourne, Tim Twelvetree, Tony Andrew, Martin Owen, John Jupp, Billy Bartle Mason Fenlon, Barry Mayner, Mike Westcott, John Cliffe
Kneeling: Mrs Claus (Helen Scrivener)
Not in photograph: Bill Alexander & John Brady

Now in the 'Grey Ghost' scheme but still with a black radome, XV587 'AG' flies through the Great Glen

exercise:

"Exercise Purple Warrior was held in November 1987 and involved all three Services. The Blue Forces, which included 1 and 43 Squadrons, were tasked with landing on a 'small island' currently held by Orange Forces, and establishing a fixed-wing operating base on it to counter Orange operations from the nearby Orange mainland. The parallels with the Falklands conflict of 1982 were obvious. The 'small island' was in fact south-west Scotland and the airbase was West Freugh.

The weather was appalling for most of the time and everyone was under canvas. There had to be a work party constantly resetting the storm lashings on the tents to prevent them disappearing into adjacent fields. Typically, we 43 Squadron aircrew decided that this was no good, so we commandeered a Motor Club building on the site (which had evidently been condemned) and set up camp-beds in that. At least it was weatherproof. The Harrier boys seemed quite happy to be in tents!

The catering was in the hands of the army and was superb. They managed to feed around 2,000 personnel every day without delay or fuss and I seem to remember the food being pretty good too.

The flying was challenging, not least because the Phantom had to land into the RHAG (Rotary Hydraulic Arrester Gear) cable at West Freugh every time due to its short runway. The last day of the exercise – 17 November – was set up as a show-piece demonstration for a senior Admiral on board HMS *Ark Royal*, which had been involved in the exercise but the weather wrecked the plans again. I managed to lead a flypast of two F-4s and two Sea Harriers in very dubious weather conditions past the *'Ark'* lying in Loch Linnhe."

Weapons training continued during 1987

The Postal Cover produced to commemorate the record flight

with another Missile Practice Camp at RAF Valley in December. This had been preceded in late '87 by affiliation training with other NATO countries, notably Belgium whose air force eventually received a temporary ban from the UK Flight Information region as a result of their habit of using the prohibited 'red' areas on their maps – Balmoral Castle in particular – as turning points.

When John Brady had taken over the Squadron he knew that it was due to disband during his time in command and recognised that this would be more of an issue for the ground personnel who would be concerned at the apparent threat of domestic upheaval should they be posted elsewhere in the UK. This was more customary for the aircrew and therefore less of a concern for them. Thus his emphasis during his time in command was to foster stability and create a measured wind-down period. In this he relied heavily on the support of his SEngO, Squadron Leader Frank Hall who, in the event, was to continue in post with 43 as it re-equipped with the Tornado.

John also inaugurated a policy of having no flying on one Thursday each month, thus ensuring that all groundcrew enjoyed at least one long weekend off in four. By contrast, 111 Squadron continued their policy of scheduling a night shift every Friday, thus continuing maintenance through to the early hours of Saturday every weekend. Equally, the CO adopted a singular approach to the achievement of training statistics, ensuring that the monthly returns reflected what HQ 11 Group wanted to see whilst at the same time ensuring that the flying completed was of maximum benefit to the Squadron.

In February 1988, following an observation from Air Marshal Sir Peter Bairsto, the then chairman of the 43 Squadron Association committee, that the chaps across the runway needed reminding of their place by the more senior squadron, the Boss decided to undertake a notable and newsworthy endeavour. Various options were suggested and considered, including a flight to the North Pole which was quickly rejected. Finally it was decided to combine the milestone of one of the Squadron's aircraft, XV582 'AF', becoming the first RAF Phantom to achieve 5,000 flying hours, with an attempt on the speed record from Land's End to John O'Groats.

There was concern at the Ministry of Defence that the whole enterprise could fall flat from a PR perspective should the record not be beaten. However, John Brady pointed out that, the FAI (Fédération Aéronautique Internationale) allows records to be claimed between any two major geographic features and, as such a record had not previously be attempted, they could not fail!

Phantom 'AF' received a special marking for the 'attempt' – indeed, the design was produced by the artist Dugald Cameron as an aircraft print. This was then used as a template for the actual aircraft, rather than the reverse procedure which was the norm.

The plan was to fly the chosen route with a tanker aircraft positioned at both ends of the country as there was only just enough fuel in the Phantom to complete the mission. When the day arrived, it was discovered that contrary to expectations there was a northerly wind of over 100 mph blowing, which would have made progress from Land's End very slow. A quick check of the aviation record rules by the CO's navigator, Mike Pugh, revealed that a declared airborne course could be flown in either direction, so the chosen route was reversed.

The flight was made on 24 February 1988 at Mach ·95 over land, and Mach 1·3 across the Irish Sea, resulting in an average speed of some 760 mph, which resulted in a time of 46 minutes, 44 seconds, which was duly entered in the Guinness Book of Records. As well as raising funds for Scottish and RAF charities it also resulted in a good spread in the Scottish press, and a half-page photograph in *The Times* newspaper. A job well done and one in the eye for Tremblers!

Early 1988 also witnessed an increase in Russian Bear activity with a consequent increase in QRA scrambles from Leuchars as well as an announcement that The Queen would present the Squadron with a new Standard in June. However, elation was tempered by the tragic loss of two aircrew on 20 April. In unexplained circumstances, Flight Lieutenants 'Nobby' Clarke and Kevin Poysden's aircraft, XT850 'L', flew into the sea 28 miles east of base during a station exercise – Exercise Elder Forest. Sadly, Kevin was engaged to the widow of an officer killed in an earlier Phantom loss.

On 26 May 1988, Her Majesty The Queen arrived at Leuchars in a BAe146 of The Queen's Flight on a day of glorious sunshine and was met by the Air Officer Commanding 11 Group, Air Vice-Marshal Roger Palin, and the Station Commander, Group Captain Tony Bagnall, both former COs of 43. A fly-past by nine Phantoms heralded Her Majesty's arrival, following which the new Standard was formally presented to replace the one held by the Squadron since The Queen's initial presentation back in 1957. While inspecting the first rank of the parade, Her Majesty asked the Boss if these men had been brought in especially for the day. 'No,' replied John Brady, 'yesterday they were servicing our aircraft and tomorrow they shall be doing the same.' The Queen appeared impressed.

A squadron dinner in Dundee was held to enable all personnel to celebrate the new honour

While escorting a southbound Soviet Bear 200 miles west of Shannon, Barry Mayner was taking pictures of the moon with the Bear when a westbound Concorde appeared in the viewfinder "CLICK"!

although some of the NCOs expressed concern that they might be expected to fund the attendance of a number of official guests. They were all much relieved, and extremely pleased, to learn that there would only be one such guest – Jimmy Beedle, the founder of the Squadron Association, a former Flight Sergeant, and the author of this history. Indeed, Jimmy's presence at the event generated renewed interest in the Association from the airmen and NCOs. The following day the Squadron held a Family Open Day, a notable attendee being Lady Douglas, wife of 43's famous first CO, who helped to toast the future of the Squadron under its new Standard. The following month the Squadron was off to sunnier climes for air combat training at the NATO ACMI range at Decimomannu, Sardinia. John Brady:

"One consequence of the presentation of the new Standard was that the old one had to be laid-up. After some deliberation and extensive negotiation with the Church of Scotland, it was agreed that the old Standard could be placed in St Giles' Cathedral, the High Kirk of Edinburgh. So on 18 September our Standard bearer and escort and a great many people from the Squadron brought our old Standard to join the banners of past glory high above the congregation in this impressive house. A sad moment but a fitting resting place for an important emblem of service for 43 Squadron."

October saw a further return to the Mediterranean for the annual APC gunnery training at Akrotiri. John Brady recalls:

"Opportunities were given for groundcrew personnel to have back-seat rides in a Phantom, for which a number of displaced navigators also applied! The extent of the detachment exuberance was such that I had to call my officers together and advise them that they were behaving like Millwall supporters. Undaunted, the whole aircrew complement appeared at

Her Majesty Queen Elizabeth II presents a new Standard to the Squadron on 26 May 1988.
Flt Lt Richard Watts receives the Standard as the Station Commander,
Gp Capt Tony Bagnall, watches anxiously.
The new Standard party comprised WO F T Bone with escorts Chf Tech G Henderson
and Sgt G W Reid.
The old Standard party was Flt Lt Derek Johnston, Standard WO was Flight Sergeant Dave Manley
and escorts Sgt E L Holister and Sgt W A Yates.

BUCKINGHAM PALACE

Officers and Airmen of Number Forty-Three Squadron:

I am delighted to be back at Leuchars, and to be able to present you once again with a new Standard.

Since it was formed at Stirling in 1916, your Squadron has given almost three-quarters of a century of service in the defence of Britain and British interests in many parts of the world. It has always been a Fighter Squadron, and it has led the way in the development both of ground attack and of air defence. Forty-Three Squadron is now the longest serving Phantom Squadron in the Royal Air Force.

Your new Standard, like its predecessors, bears the battle honours won by your predecessors in two World Wars. It is a symbol of their courage, loyalty and sacrifice which we remember with gratitude and which are an inspiration for the future. You who now serve in the Squadron have carried forward this great tradition into the years of peace. The vigilant guarding of our shores plays a significant part not only in our national security but in the British contribution to the North Atlantic Alliance. I know that, if this country were ever to be threatened by aggression, you would be in our first line of defence.

In presenting this new Standard to your charge, I express my full confidence that you will bear it with honour, both as a reminder of the devotion of your predecessors and as a symbol of the great trust which our nation places in you today.

Elizabeth R

26th May, 1988.

morning briefing the following day, dressed in Milwall supporters' T-shirts that had been produced for them overnight by a local supplier!"

In the spring of 1989 the Squadron was directed by HQ 11 Group to disband in July prior to re-forming with the Tornado later in the year. John Brady pointed out the disadvantages of a formal disbandment for such a short period of time, not least the laying-up of the Standard so recently presented by The Queen. His arguments prevailed and the Standard was handed over to the Station Commander for temporary safekeeping, while the silverware

No 43(Fighter) Squadron

BATTLE HONOURS

Western Front 1917 – 1918 Arras Ypres 1917 Cambrai 1917 Somme 1918
Lys Amiens Dunkirk Battle of Britain 1940 Home Defence 1940 – 1942
Fortress Europe 1942 Dieppe North Africa 1942 – 1943 Sicily 1943
Salerno Italy 1943 – 1945 Anzio & Nettuno Gustav Line
France & Germany 1944 Gulf 1991 Iraq 2003

The Squadron Standard was granted by HM King George VI and promulgated on 27 March 1952. It was presented by Her Majesty Queen Elizabeth II at Leuchars on 4 June 1957, the first time that a Royal Air Force Squadron had received its Standard from the hands of the reigning monarch. A new Standard was also presented by Her Majesty Queen Elizabeth II at Leuchars on 26 May 1988. The old Standard was laid up in St Giles' Cathedral, Edinburgh on 18 September 1988.
(MoD (RAF) Crown Copyright)

The Standard, a fringed and tasselled silken banner, mounted on a pike surmounted by a Golden Eagle, was created by His late Majesty King George VI in 1943 to mark the twenty-fifth anniversary of the Royal Air Force.
Squadrons qualify for the award of a Standard after twenty-five years' service or for specially meritorious operations. Eight selected battle honours in scroll surround the Squadron badge. The decorative border is embroidered with the national emblems of the British Isles.

was retained in the officers' mess strong room. Most significantly, the airmen remained at Leuchars under the command of the SEngO, Squadron Leader Frank Hall, from where they detached for various courses to acquire the specialist Tornado knowledge to prepare them for the new challenges ahead.

Jimmy Beedle, who had so recently been a guest at Dundee, died on 6 April 1989. His funeral was held in Harpenden at St Nicholas' Parish Church a week later. Len Telling, Chris Golds and Alan Pollock represented the

XV406 'AV' one of three Phantom FGR2s flown during 1988

Association and John Brady travelled down from Leuchars with a group of squadron personnel.

Later in the year, on 17 September, a memorial service was held for Jimmy at Tangmere Parish Church attended by many former Squadron members including Andy Moir, already designated as the next CO. Jimmy's wife Betty then scattered his ashes on the airfield as he had requested, before joining the congregation for refreshments in the Tangmere Military Aviation Museum, which Jimmy had been instrumental in founding in 1982. His devotion to the RAF, to Tangmere, and to 43 Squadron in particular was unfailing to the end.

Group Captain Jock Heron recalls a visit to the Fighting Cocks during the latter months of the Phantom.

"To mark the occasion of the imminent retirement of the Phantom, a dinner was organised at Leuchars in 1989 to which I was invited and it was intended that, on behalf of my new employers, Rolls Royce, I should present a framed painting of a pair of Phantoms escorting a Bear somewhere over the North Sea. The artist was Chris Golds, a talented Hunter pilot and fellow Fighting Cock who, sadly, had been grounded having been diagnosed with diabetes while commanding one of the Hunter training units at Chivenor, some 20 years earlier. Because he and I had flown together I was particularly pleased to have been invited to perform the brief ceremony after the dinner. The Station Commander, Group Captain Tony Bagnall, presided over the evening which was attended by Sir Peter Bairsto, the Association President. It turned out to be a very robust affair as the

Wing Commander John Brady oversees the Squadron Standard paraded for the last time in front of a Phantom before being held in safekeeping at Leuchars for the new Tornado squadron

One of the new Tornado F3s alongside the trusty flagship "Alpha" just before the last of the Phantoms in 43 Squadron livery disappeared from Leuchars

Phantom fraternity had their tails up and made no secret of their contempt for the Tornado which they regarded as being an inferior mount to their beloved Phantom. Following the meal the Squadron performed a clever playlet which illustrated some improvements to the Tornado which turned it into a Phantom.

The subsequent speeches were interrupted by noisy banter from the floor as the evening wore on and I sensed a difficult few minutes on my feet when it was my turn to speak while presenting Chris Golds' painting. However by confronting, light-heartedly, two of the noisier characters, both of whom had served with me in the Falklands five years earlier, some of the heat was taken out of the situation and I went on to relate some of the significant 1989 anniversaries during the proud history of the Squadron. It was twenty years since the first Phantoms had arrived when the Squadron had reformed at Leuchars. Twenty five years earlier Hunters had been in action in the Aden peninsula and, fifty years before that, the Squadron had received its first Hurricanes and was girding its loins for the Battle of Britain.

I went on to forecast that in the capable hands of the Fighting Cocks the Tornado would become a formidable fighting machine and that the fine reputation of the Squadron would be enhanced. With the passage of another twenty years, further battle honours and the numerous Dacre and Aberporth trophies are proof that my forecast was accurate!"

On 25 May 1989, the new Squadron Commander designate, Wing Commander Andy Moir, had his final trip in a Phantom, flying with John Brady during a station exercise. Andy and John had served together on 43 in 1980 and the sortie provided a gesture of continuity before the final Phantom flight on 27 July. Thus the Fighting Cocks embarked on the next chapter of their history.

A sad end for the Phantom -
Adam's scrapyard in Glasgow 1992

CHAPTER 32

The Tornado Arrives

PLANS had been in place for some time to ensure a gradual return of 43 Squadron to full operational status as the new Tornado F3s began to arrive. The cornerstone of the programme was the retention of the majority of the ex-Phantom groundcrew who remained at Leuchars under the command of the Squadron Engineering Officer, Squadron Leader Frank Hall, as they undertook a comprehensive re-training programme once the Phantoms had departed in the earlier part of 1989. In parallel, a nucleus of aircrew, including the new commanding officer, Wing Commander Andy Moir, commenced training with 229 OCU at Coningsby in June. Andy had experienced a markedly different start to his flying career than most fast jet aircrew, having been on VC10s for his first tour. However his subsequent career had focused entirely on air defence and included two tours on 43 Squadron during its Phantom days as well as air defence staff appointments at the Central Tactics and Trials Organization. He would be the first of a number of 'back-seaters' to command 43.

The Panavia Tornado had initially been conceived as the Multi Role Combat Aircraft (MRCA) for interdiction, strike and reconnaissance. A further variant evolved as the F3 all-weather fighter to replace both the Lightnings and Phantoms in RAF service. Retaining the proven armament of the Phantom with four BAe Skyflash semi-active radar homing missiles and four Sidewinder infra-red missiles, the new aircraft featured an integral Mauser 27mm cannon and the new GEC AI 24 Foxhunter multi-mode track-while-scan radar. Despite the depth of loyalty that the Phantom had earned during its time with 43, the arrival of the Tornado marked a major advance in interception capability, most notably the ability to track multiple targets simultaneously. It was also considerably less thirsty than its predecessor.

By September, the first two aircraft and their crews were ready for their initial appearance at Leuchars and on the 23rd arrived as part of the station's Battle of Britain air display. The new boss arrived, accompanied by Squadron Leader Jim Davidson (Jimmy D), another former Fighting Cock, who had subsequently served with 617 Squadron on the GR1 version of the Tornado before returning to air defence duties as an instructor with 229 OCU. Jim's return to the Fighting Cocks as OC A Flight was to bring a valuable familiarity with the new aircraft as, for the majority of the aircrew, this was to be their first tour on the Tornado. The crew of the other aircraft brought similar levels of experience. Squadron Leader Nick Willey, a former Lightning pilot, was destined to be the new squadron QFI following tours at Valley and on exchange in the USA on the T38 Talon, and his navigator, Squadron Leader Ken Thompson, was an experienced Phantom air defence operator

The two new Tornado F3s at the Leuchars Battle of Britain Airshow

Wg Cdr Andy Moir and Sqn Ldr Jim Davidson

and QWI who had been appointed as OCB Flight.

Andy's other key individuals in his initial cadre of officers included Squadron Leader Steve Cooper, a big lad - known as the "Cooper Twins" - who had served with Andy on 19 Squadron in Germany and who was to become the Squadron's EXO (Executive Officer) and Squadron Leader Clive Marrison, the designated Squadron QWI, who had also previously served on 43. There was a satisfying mix of old and new friends and both aircraft and role experience.

Work-up proper began in November and new crews continued to arrive throughout the early part of 1990. The fleet of aircraft continued to grow too, with both new deliveries from British Aerospace at Warton and transfers from other squadrons. It had been decided at the outset of the F3 re-equipment programme that the aircraft tail letters would be allocated in alphabetical sequence as each squadron formed. Thus as the seventh squadron, 43 was allocated 'G' with its fleet becoming GA, GB, etc. Significantly the sixth aircraft to arrive at Leuchars became GF, thereby bearing the initials of 43's motto, Gloria Finis, so naturally this became the Boss's aircraft.

The new Squadron Standard which had been presented by Her Majesty the Queen in May 1988 had been entrusted to RAF Leuchars as its temporary custodian during the summer interregnum of 1989. An early priority was therefore to return the Standard to its proper owners and this occurred on 14 December in a formal hand-over ceremony at the Northern Dispersal, marking a further milestone in 43's renaissance.

The sad news arrived on New Year's Day that Air Vice-Marshal C G Lott, who had commanded the Squadron in 1939-40, had died the previous day. George Lott had been seriously wounded during the opening phase of the Battle of Britain and had lost his right eye and been forced to bale out of his Hurricane. On 9 January 1990 he was laid to rest in Tangmere churchyard and as the coffin was lowered into the grave a lone Tornado of 43 piloted by Jim Davidson with the Boss in the back flew over in poignant tribute to one of the most distinguished Fighting Cocks.

While the Squadron continued to grow it took part in Exercise Elder Forest in April 1990, the major annual 11 Group air defence exercise. One of the Squadron's former Phantoms was also rescued from the scrapyard and restored, at least in its outward appearance, to become Gate Guardian at the entrance to 43's Northern Dispersal area.

Finally the great day arrived when the Squadron was declared once again to NATO as a fully operational unit on 1 July. The priority task was the resumption of QRA and on 5 July the Squadron launched the first live scramble of a Tornado from RAF Leuchars. Sadly the targets turned back long before they could be intercepted but it was good to see the Fighting Cocks flexing their muscles once more. However this absence of targets became typical of QRA activity in contrast to the levels experienced during the Phantom days when the Cold War had been at its height. The greatest number of intercepts by the Squadron had been achieved in 1979 while it was detached to Kinloss during a runway resurfacing programme at home base. By way of an example, one evening during this period of intense activity Harry MacLean and Al Pulfrey returned to Kinloss after a simulator session at Leuchars. As they approached the bar they were collared by the Boss who invited them to check in with the Squadron as Q9 (the norm was Q1 and Q2 backed up by Q3). After a short rest they duly got airborne early the following morning. A similar level of activity had been experienced in 1987 when at least one aircraft at a time was airborne continuously for five and a half days.
On a rather more harmonious note the Squadron conducted a formation flypast at the opening of

An early three-ship 'Vic' formation - ZE936 'GK', unmarked ZE965 and ZE942 'GH'

the Special Olympics in Glasgow on 24 July, an event for disabled sportsmen and women from around the world. However, such international harmony was soon to be rudely shattered.

In the early hours of 2 August 1990 Iraqi forces crossed into Kuwait and advanced on Kuwait city. International response was swift and within two days Tornado F3s of Coningsby's 5 and 29 Squadrons had deployed to Dhahran in Saudi Arabia from their armament practice camp in Cyprus to oppose any further Iraqi advance. The RAF contingent formed part of the US-led Coalition supporting Operation DESERT SHIELD, the multi-national defensive response within the region pending an Iraqi withdrawal from Kuwait. However, it was soon apparent that resolution of the crisis would take some time and that war was a distinct possibility. Plans were therefore made to rotate the detached F3 squadrons and to modify the aircraft to make them more suitable for Coalition operations in a desert environment. During what ultimately proved to be a transition to war, improved communications, self defence chaff and flares, and engine and weapons system enhancements, combined to produce a significantly more capable aircraft and one in which the aircrew had considerable confidence. A further capability that was less popular, although potentially of equal importance, was the introduction of the AR5 Aircrew Respirator and a chemical protection suit which were to be worn under the flying helmet and suit as an impermeable layer. Although these had been available for some time, the disadvantages of temperature-induced fatigue and reduced mobility viewed against the low level of perceived threat had meant that this equipment was viewed largely as a contingency capability for Cold War operations. However with the prospect of hostilities against an enemy that had already demonstrated its readiness to use chemical weapons the protective equipment was brought into use, with both simulator and live-flying training taking place.

As a now fully operational squadron but one yet to be committed to the Gulf, 43's main activities throughout the autumn were the development of tactics to counter the threat of the Iraqi Air Force and supporting the F3 squadrons already in theatre by ferrying modified aircraft as they became available. Echoes of a previous conflict were to the fore on 15 September as a four-ship from 43 joined 164 other RAF aircraft in a flypast to commemorate the 50th anniversary of the Battle of Britain. This was to be the largest flypast ever mounted by the RAF. As one would expect, such a considerable undertaking required careful planning and co-ordination and this was appropriately vested with the HQ 11 Group staff at Bentley Priory. Five 43 Squadron aircraft and crews were detached to Coningsby and carried out several practices, culminating in a full dress rehearsal on the 13th with RAF Wittering deputising for Buckingham Palace.

The day of the flypast dawned bright and sunny and the Fighting Cocks took to the air to commemorate the proudest moment in RAF history, and one in which their squadron predecessors had played a prominent role. Aircraft were grouped by type, with the majority of formations being of 16 aircraft. Four aircraft from 43, led by Squadron Leader Nick Willey and the Boss, formed a box four on the right wing of the F3 group. The formations grew in size as they prescribed a series of co-ordinated race-tracks to the north of Norfolk and then tucked in behind each other to create an extended stream of aircraft which coasted in by Great Yarmouth and headed for London. A radio call from a Hawk pilot scouting ahead of the main formations confirmed visual contact with Buckingham Palace from the vicinity of St Paul's Cathedral and an air of confidence and expectation seemed to enter every cockpit as the huge assembly of aircraft continued its approach to the capital. It was a moment that few would forget. London seemed to come to a standstill as wave after wave of aircraft passed overhead. Traffic stopped and the bridges over the Thames were crammed with spectators. Perhaps even more surprising was the temporary closure of Heathrow Airport to allow the safe dispersal of the large number of aircraft as they headed west beyond the city. The effects of this must have been felt around the world. It was certainly felt by an errant glider pilot over Northampton, who had clearly not read his Notices to Airmen for the day, as he was suddenly passed by 16 Tornados returning to Coningsby.

By November the Squadron was fully prepared to deploy on Operation GRANBY, the codename for RAF operations in the Gulf, and a full complement of modified F3s had been established at Dhahran. The final aircraft delivery by 43 took place on 17 November and involved a non-stop AAR-supported flight and a return to the UK with 4 unmodified aircraft the following day. At least that was the plan! Four months of desert operations had evidently taken their toll on the engines which had been developing increased rates of oil consumption. The first aircraft to experience a low oil pressure warning and a mandatory engine shutdown made it as far as Nice where the crew needed the entire runway in which to stop having lost their reverse thrust capability. The next to go had an identical problem in the vicinity of Paris and elected to land at Orly airport in view of the lack of cable-equipped airfields nearby and the similar need for a long runway. On landing, the crew, Flight Lieutenants Steve Hayler and Steve Norrie, found themselves taxying past Air Force One. They immediately realised that they had arrived in the middle of the Conference on Security and Co-operation in Europe attended by Presidents Bush and Gorbachev and other world leaders, including Margaret Thatcher, at which the Iraq situation formed the principal item on the agenda! A further aircraft then began to experience similar engine indications but by that time was already approaching Leuchars. In the event, all aircraft recovered to Leuchars within a few days although Flight Lieutenants Al Whyte and Derek Johnston in Nice managed to take two days longer than the others!

The first elements of the Squadron departed from Leuchars towards the end of November and commenced a handover with the Leeming squadrons that had held the fort at Dhahran in the interim. By mid-December the changeover had been completed and a joint F3 unit comprised of 29 and 43 Squadrons, under the overall command of OC 43, and with an enhanced complement of 18 aircraft to permit 24-hour operations, was in place. This proved most timely as it gave a full month to settle in to the local flying environment and to consolidate standard operating procedures and tactics before the expiry, on 16 January 1991, of the UN ultimatum to Iraq.

Training continued throughout this period and constant Combat Air Patrols (CAPs) were maintained by the Tornados alongside Saudi, US and French fighters. An initial French tendency to lapse into their native tongue when operating on common frequencies posed a potential diplomatic challenge. However, they were most gracious when the need for general situation awareness was highlighted and operations continued in English thereafter. National identities were preserved by allocating formation call-signs using sports car prefixes appropriate to each nationality. Thus the F3 missions were enlivened with such dashing identities as Bentley, Morgan and Aston.

Air-to-air refuelling (AAR) from Victor and TriStar tankers, and Airborne Warning and Control from both US and Saudi E-3As, proved to be key elements in operating over the vast areas of barren desert. Crews became totally familiar both with their new environment and with Coalition joint operating procedures. Indeed, it was remarkable to compare the level of airborne preparation on the south side of the border with the negligible amount of Iraqi air activity that was observed to the north and this raised questions over the degree of currency, and thus competence, of the Iraqi pilots in the event of war. Nevertheless, a key air defence responsibility was to ensure the safety of the AWACS from pre-emptive air attacks by high level, high speed aircraft such as the MiG-25 and tactics were devised to ensure the security of this vital asset.

Although the supply of RAF Tornado spares always favoured the units deployed to the Gulf, the extended supply route often meant that keeping the aircraft serviceable was no mean feat. Squadron Leader Frank Hall and his engineers worked tirelessly to maintain optimum levels of aircraft availability. One of the most dynamic characters within the engineering team was Flight Sergeant Bill Reay who, in addition to his primary engineering tasks, took on the key role of positioning the NBC (Nuclear, Biological and Chemical) sentries and detectors around the operating area. Effective NBC defence was vital as the chemical threat was a real possibility given Saddam Hussein's history of using such weapons. Bill was a forceful chap and an accomplished 'fixer', well respected by the airmen and officers alike, and was the ideal choice to take control of this important aspect of the Squadron's preparations at Dhahran.

This, together with the innovative physical hardening of the site using steel shipping containers and prefabricated concrete sections, combined to produce a sense of a high state of readiness and survivability which in turn produced a general feeling of confidence. However this confidence was not shared by the Squadron's local civilian bus drivers who had no protective equipment and yet were prevented from moving from the operating site when Scud ballistic missile alerts occurred. Once again Bill Reay's innovation came to the fore and he issued all drivers with facemasks he had procured from the paint shop. Thereafter these chaps sat contentedly in their vehicles throughout all alerts!

Soon after the Squadron arrived in Saudi during the build-up, all officers were issued with personal weapons. There was a perceived risk to aircrew and key executives, especially whilst off base, such as in, or en route to, the domestic accommodation which was in residential compounds that had been formerly occupied by expatriate workers. On one particular occasion, Frank Hall was warned at morning briefing that there was a heightened risk of insurgent activity against Coalition forces.

Paul Facer, Nick Willey and Paul Lightbody lunching beside an improvised air raid shelter

Tanking from a TriStar

That night Frank was woken by a sound of stealthy movement across the corrugated metal roof above his bedroom. Reaching for his pistol, he cocked it and prepared for an attack but was greatly relieved to hear a 'miaow' rather than anything more sinister.

The Tornado F3's navigation system in 1991 relied heavily on its Inertial Navigation System (INS) which, in common with platforms of that type, had a tendency to drift with time. The system could be updated using radar, visual or other references. However, during prolonged sorties over the featureless Saudi Arabian desert, typically of four or more hours, such external references were not available. Being the senior member of the navigator's union, one would expect Andy Moir to recall the following:

"Accurate navigation was important both for position keeping on CAP and for the avoidance of MEZs (Missile Engagement Zones). The rate of platform drift was such that after only one hour of flight (usually the time taken to transit to the designated CAP position) the system still retained a high degree of accuracy. It therefore became the practice on arrival to select a distinctive feature in the vicinity of the CAP datum, check its position on the INS and then update to this known position whenever the point was overflown during the remainder of the sortie.

The problem, of course, was to find a distinctive feature in the barren sand dunes of the desert. There was generally little to be seen other than the occasional lone camel. It was then discovered that the rate of a camel's wandering, and its random tendency to average out over time, produced a lesser change of position than the drift rate of the INS. So we navigated by camel when we could and it generally worked quite well!"

Christmas 1991 was, of

necessity, a quiet affair given the high level of tasking. However, the Squadron found time to put on a revue for all the personnel at Dhahran, although the non-British members of the contingent became totally bemused at the sight of a group of 43 groundcrew made up as corpses in body bags, and singing: 'Always Look on the Bright Side of Life'!

A visit by the Prince of Wales on 23 December was much appreciated and His Royal Highness met a number of Squadron members, taking great interest in the preparations for the increasing likelihood of combat. Sadly, however, OC 29 Squadron, Wing Commander Roy Trotter, overslept and missed his 'Royal Appointment' much to the mirth of 43. The Boss presented him with a Christmas present of a cockerel alarm clock which crowed at the appropriate time. Roy took the jibe in good heart. A similar visit on 8 January by the Prime Minister, John Major, served to remind everyone of the high level of support at home.

HRH The Prince of Wales at Dhahran

The intensity of flying was providing ample opportunity for the ground personnel to hone their skills, particularly in the speed and frequency of armament turn-rounds. However, the major challenge proved to be the requirement to move early in the New Year from the established operating site set up by the Coningsby and Leeming squadrons in the central part of the airfield. This was to make way for a GR1 unit that was shortly to arrive as part of the build-up for possible war. Despite the added turbulence at an already busy time, the move presented the welcome opportunity to disperse the F3s from the busiest part of the base and a site was chosen that had initially been nominated for an Egyptian F-16 squadron, so henceforth this became known as the Egyptian Dispersal.

Although there was plenty of ramp space and relatively quick access to the runway there were only two 'porta-cabins', which resulted in very cramped conditions for both air and groundcrew personnel. Attention then turned to a disused Royal Saudi Air Force Lightning QRA facility nearby which, although originally designed to operate only two aircraft, was requisitioned and soon adapted to provide an operations room and air raid shelter in the small underground bunker designed to accommodate two pilots. The two parking revetments were no longer suitable for aircraft operations and were therefore allocated respectively as an engineering bay for rectification work and as a site for an improvised chemical warfare shelter. The latter was achieved through the imaginative use of more steel shipping containers and walls of sand-filled gabions concealing the otherwise fragile decontamination tents. Similar ingenuity was displayed by the Royal Engineers in creating air raid shelters around the site with walls of pre-formed concrete road barriers topped with steel plates and covered with sandbags. At least there was no shortage of sand! The aircraft ramp was also protected with sandbags as well as fuel and weapons storage areas. In addition, prefabricated concrete blast walls were placed between the F3 parking bays.

The Tornado operating area at the 'Egyptian Dispersal' received new neighbours in the build-up period, in the shape of a US Patriot surface-to-air missile battery. Initially the US unit had little in the way of infrastructure and was accommodated within an old mosque. Their urgent need for additional accommodation was met by the loan of 43's contingency supply of tents which contributed greatly to fostering good relations with their neighbours and, for example, led to a UK/US volleyball match.

As the imminence of war approached a significant last minute problem arose following an incident many thousands of miles away. A careless RAF staff officer had his laptop computer stolen from his car in London – a not uncommon event. However on this occasion the computer contained an outline of the Coalition's war plan. As a consequence all details such as radio frequencies, code-words and CAP positions had to be changed at extremely short notice in the aircrew information guides that had been painstakingly prepared by the very few personnel on the Squadron cleared to have access to such sensitive information in advance of the outbreak of war.

Nevertheless, by the time of the expiry of UN Resolution 678, which authorised the use of all necessary means to restore international peace and security to the area, the Fighting Cocks were fully prepared and thoroughly familiar with their new theatre of operations. In the early hours of 17 January 1991 the international Coalition of nations embarked on Operation DESERT STORM, the forceful removal of Iraqi forces from Kuwait and the destruction of Iraq's offensive capabilities, by launching the first of many devastating air attacks on key targets in Iraq. The war had started.

The Bunker at Dhahran

By the turn of the year, a 3-flight system inherited from the amalgamated Leeming wing had been replaced by a simpler structure which enabled 43 and 29 Squadrons to operate as distinct units, while sharing a common pool of aircraft and maintaining 24-hour operations on a shift basis that changed every couple of weeks. This pattern continued in the transition to war, with 29 flying the night shift at the time hostilities commenced. As day broke, bringing the prospect of an Iraqi counter-attack, 43 took over.

The initial intensity of flying for the Squadron was remarkable with four sorties an hour being launched continuously throughout the first 24 hours, largely due to the AAR assets at the outset being devoted entirely to the support of the offensive missions. Despite the enlarged fleet of aircraft, the demands on Squadron resources were considerable and the groundcrew became extremely proficient at conducting turn-rounds in increasingly shorter times. Typically two aircraft would be preparing to launch, two would be en-route or returning from CAP, two would be on CAP, two would be on turn-round and two would be at 10-minutes readiness to provide immediate response for reinforcement, or replacement in the event of un-serviceability. Soon the rate of sorties began to reduce as AAR tankers became available for the fighters, although sortie lengths extended correspondingly to ensure a permanent presence on the British-assigned CAPs.

It became rapidly apparent that the enemy, assessed as the third largest air force in the world and possessing some highly capable modern aircraft such as the MiG-29 Fulcrum, was reluctant to confront the Coalition in the air. Indeed, it appeared that the Iraqis were largely stunned and paralysed at the extent and ferocity of the Coalition's offensive air campaign. The closest 43 came to an engagement was on the second day of the war when 'Morgan', comprising the USAF exchange pilot, Captain Brian (Hound) O'Connor and Flight Lieutenant Henry Paul, together with Flight Lieutenant Martin Stephens and the Boss, was ordered off CAP by AWACS to assist friendly aircraft as they headed south out of Kuwait pursued by Iraqi Mirage F1s. Radar contact was achieved with both sets of aircraft and three USAF A-10s were soon passed as the Tornados pressed on towards their targets to the north, who had by this time elected to avoid combat and had turned for home. A fruitless tail chase well out of missile range ensued which was eventually aborted as the Tornados approached the Iraqi surface to air missile (SAM) belts along the border. However, the Fighting Cocks had succeeded in chasing off the attackers and had also extended the speed envelope for jettisoning the 2250 litre under-wing fuel tanks!

On various other occasions the Tornados of both 43 and 29 committed north and came under fire from Iraqi-operated defence systems, most notably, 57 mm and 23 mm AAA guns.' Flight Lieutenant Steve Norrie recalls the type of operations the Squadron was called upon to make:

"There was no such thing as a 'normal day' during Operation DESERT STORM. For 43 Squadron, the vast majority of the flying was dedicated to combat air patrols positioned at and over the Iraqi borders interspersed with numerous tanker joins for vital in-flight refuelling.

For Bentley 01 and 02, 18 February 1991 was one such normal day when the air offensive was in full swing. There had been little or no Iraqi air activity and as Bentley 02 pulled away from the TriStar refuelling drogue and headed back north to CAP in battle formation with 01, the vast featureless desert landscape below gave no hint of the events to come. Reaching the northern extent of CAP, AWACS' authoritative voice crackled over the R/T:

Undercover servicing in a disused revetment

Casualty Reception Area - desert medical centre

'Bentley, vector north, enemy aircraft heading south-east, medium level.' Well-practised procedures ensured that 02 quickly joined up with 01 and both aircraft crossed the border into Iraqi airspace. The vectors given by the AWACS positioned Bentley perilously close to enemy SAM and AAA sites and both crews hawkishly monitored their instruments for the telltale signs of radar lock-on. AWACS continued its instructions: 'Enemy aircraft now 100 nautical miles north, heading east. Bentley vector zero-four-zero.

This would be no quick foray over the border for Bentley. Pre-planned tactics dictated that the F3 should jettison its external tanks to enhance its manoeuvrability as Bentley closed on the enemy aircraft, now within their radar range. The large external tanks, almost full of fuel, were jettisoned and later it was calculated that they were 'dropped' into an area occupied by the republican guard.' Unlike the earlier sortie when tanks were jettisoned in Saudi airspace, this proved to be 43's first 'bombing' sortie of the war!

Bentley was now within 10 nautical miles of the contacts when the enemy aircraft disappeared from AWACS radar. The F3s had radar returns in the area last called by AWACS but these returns looked more like chaff than EA. Coming to the merge, eyes flashed in and out of cockpits as the two crews tried to glimpse where the contacts were. 'Rotate,' ordered Bentley 01 as the lack of a visual sighting confirmed their suspicion of chaff. But as both aircraft turned to reposition, two other aircraft were sighted. Bentley 01 called the 'tally-ho' as the unidentified aircraft were put on the nose but, just as quickly, Bentley 01 identified them as two American F-4s (had they dropped the chaff?). The F-4s acknowledged Bentley's presence by wing-rock and the two formations flew past each other. AWACS now confirmed no further contact with the bogey.

Some 150 nm had to be negotiated back to the Saudi border once Bentley had been ordered south back to CAP. Bentley flew a zig-zag route to avoid overflying the numerous SAM sites, and the RHWR (Radar Homing & Warning Receiver) confirmed that enemy radars were looking for the F3s. The Saudi border seemed a long way away but Bentley eventually crossed back over and returned safely back to Dhahran at the end of a normal day.

A typical night sortie was a practised professional performance. Lights out – using night vision goggles - and including the inevitable air-to-air refuelling. Patrolling on the Iraqi border provided crews with a spectacular, somewhat awe-inspiring view of the bombing campaign in Iraq and Kuwait. Nevertheless the visual display outside was just one of the many distractions. All the returning bombers and escorts were tracked on radar and the occasional suspicious unidentified track would appear.

Bentley formation had just completed the northerly track of the CAP when AWACS vectored them on a heading of 340°. This time there was no mention of enemy aircraft, just simply a command to vector some 60 miles into Iraq. The Bentley crews enquired as to the purpose of the mission, to be told that they were to assist in a search and rescue operation of a downed Allied aircraft. The NVGs worn by the F3 crews were an excellent piece of equipment and it was this facility that AWACS was employing to aid in the rescue operation. Using coded messages, AWACS passed a radio frequency to Bentley with which to try and make contact with the downed aircraft. Despite numerous R/T calls no reply was received. Operating now some 60 to 80 miles inside Iraq, Bentley 01 slipped down to low level to try and catch any glimpse of a distress light while 02 remained at medium level, sanitising the airspace around. For some 40 minutes Bentley remained on station, unable to make contact with anyone on the ground. The eerie light of the moon, allowing good visibility, enhanced the sense of empathy with the downed pilot below.

With fuel reserves dwindling Bentley was forced to retire back to the Saudi border and to leave the remainder of the rescue attempt with AWACS and other Allied aircraft. This time the trip back across the border was less eventful than the previous night when either a SAM 2 or 3 was launched into Bentley's vicinity. At the time, 02 was completing a lights-out join on 01 and had closed visually with NVGs to a matter of a few hundred yards when 01, upon sighting a SAM launch, broke hard and dropped chaff and flares. The chaff proved no problem but the flares exploded very close to 02, ruining the crew's night vision and prompting the R/T enquiry:

'What on earth was that for?' Upon receiving the reason, the reply was, 'Oh, understood.' The remainder of the trip was comparatively uneventful."

Air supremacy was soon achieved by the Coalition forces and the prospect of any similar actions receded rapidly. However Scud attacks became a regular feature, usually at night in an attempt by the Iraqis to conceal their launch sites from satellite surveillance. The first of these attacks occurred on the night of 17 January with a retaliatory attack on Dhahran. This missile was intercepted by a US Patriot SAM but the debris fell perilously close to the 43 and 29 Squadron aircrew off-base accommodation and caused significant damage to an adjacent electricity sub-station, although fortunately without causing any casualties. This was usually the case as missile attacks and interceptions continued on a fairly routine basis throughout the period of hostilities. The Patriot site was quite close to the Egyptian Dispersal and every launch was heralded by an almost simultaneous sonic boom over the flight line. Indeed, confidence in the system became so great that it inclined many personnel to wait to witness the spectacle of Patriot/Scud impacts before masking up and taking to their air raid shelters. Later in the war, however, a Scud did penetrate the Patriot shield and struck a temporary barracks close to the 43 and 29 Squadron airmen's accommodation, killing 28 American servicemen and reminding everyone most forcibly of the fallibility of defensive systems.

Aircraft parked between blast screens

New or previously untried operational capabilities had emerged during the build-up to war. In addition to aircraft self-defence chaff and flare capabilities and an improved emphasis on chemical and biological defensive measures, the increasing use of night vision goggles brought a new dimension to aerial warfare. The goggles were quite heavy and, being mounted on the front of the flying helmet, could create considerable neck ache during the fairly protracted sorties that often lasted more than four hours. The problem was reduced by pilot and navigator alternating in the wearing of goggles and crews soon developed proficiency with this new kit which presented a green monochrome view of the world. Not only did NVGs provide a true lights-out capability, but their use in detecting navigation lights at well beyond normal visual range emphasized the considerable numbers of aircraft engaged in the preparations for war. Once hostilities commenced, and aircraft ceased to display navigation lights, the new capability continued to illustrate vividly the intensity of the conflict. Multiple Launched Rocket Systems (MLRS), SAMs and AAA provided an almost constant display, even at considerable range from CAP positions. Perhaps above all, the ability to conduct silent night tanking completely covertly added a significant advantage to fighter operations.

Not all developments were so sophisticated. Flight Lieutenant Paul Facer, whose secondary duty was as 43 Squadron's Combat Survival and Rescue Officer, recognised that the number of water sachets in the seat pack survival kit was minimal for desert operations. He set about developing a low-tech, but potentially vital, improvement by modifying a commercially available country sports waistcoat that could be worn under the torso harness. The Squadron's safety equipment fitters worked with him to produce a garment that could not only accommodate four extra foil water sachets but could be stored in the crewroom freezer to provide a cooling jacket that was particularly welcome when on cockpit alert during the heat of the day.

It was also essential for safe operations within the US MEZs to change aircraft identification codes to a precise schedule. All flying helmets were therefore modified with digital alarm watches taped inside, programmed to provide the necessary regular reminders. Another innovative solution addressed the need for timely and accurate information on Iraqi SAM dispositions. Launch sites could be moved readily at short notice and current information was vital to ensure the safety of aircrew. Whilst the general level of daily intelligence was good, the Squadron lacked up-to-the-minute information on SAM site movements. Happily this was available from the neighbouring US F-15 squadron which was delighted to provide regular updates to 43's two US exchange officers, thus enabling the squadron intelligence officers to update the tapes for programming the Tornado's onboard computer. By way of thanks, a case of 'compo' rations was delivered daily to the American squadron which had become

"Brolly Ho!"

somewhat tired of its own apparently less appetising MREs (Meals Ready to Eat).

The Falklands War of 1982 is generally considered to have been the first televised conflict although the maritime area of operations and remoteness of the islands were such that TV crews were entirely dependent on the armed forces for access, news transmissions and support facilities. By contrast, much of the Gulf War took place in the full gaze of the international media and it was not unusual for the families at home to be aware, via the US Cable News Network, of missile attacks on Dhahran as they occurred. Frequent telephone calls to the Leuchars switchboard were necessary to reassure families that no casualties had been sustained. Certainly, the TV news coverage of RAF aircrew returning from their missions captured the public imagination and a flood of welfare parcels began to arrive. Flight Lieutenant Paul Lightbody, who seemed to be the only fighter pilot in the Gulf from the Channel Islands, was inundated with gifts from the islanders and he was able to provide his fellow 43 aircrew with a constant supply of everything from socks to fruit cakes!

Typical aircrew rates of flying naturally far exceeded those of peacetime when a good month might yield around 20 flying hours. With sorties being mounted continually and occasionally exceeding four or even five hours in duration, it was not unusual for monthly totals to top twice or even three times this figure. News of the intensity of operations soon got back home and prompted numerous letters of support from the public in addition to the many generous gifts. One letter in particular struck a chord when a resident from the vicinity of the Angus Glens wrote to apologise for her many previous complaints of low flying near her home. She now understood the need to develop airborne skills given the nature of the task that was being undertaken. Such declarations of support were really heartening and it was a pleasure for the Fighting Cocks to invite the lady to visit them at Leuchars upon their return.

On 29 January the Commander in Chief of British Forces in the Gulf, General Sir Peter de la Billière, visited Dhahran and toured the Egyptian Dispersal to view the Tornado F3 operations. By this time the pace of air defence activity had steadied as Iraq's capabilities became more and more eroded. Interceptions of unknown aircraft continued, although all proved in the event to be friendly.

Despite the growing devastation caused by the relentless bombing of Iraq's infrastructure and armed forces, the occupation of Kuwait continued and the prospect of ground war loomed ever closer. On the morning of 24 February Coalition forces crossed the border into Iraq, finally precipitating the collapse of Iraqi

Kuwait's burning oil wells

Oil well inferno

Damaged Iraqi occupied HAS site

resistance. With an allusion to the expression beloved of US sports commentators, the legend 'The fat lady isn't singing yet, but she's started humming the tune' appeared on the intelligence map in the briefing room as a rapidly growing number of symbolic prisoner of war cages began to appear in the areas previously occupied by hostile surface-to-air missile zones. Andy Moir recalled the following anecdote at this time:

"The imminence of victory also prompted a demonstration of a hitherto unknown Scottish military tradition. Chief Technician Ian Hughes, one of the Squadron's engineers, appeared on the Flight Line one morning replete with his bagpipes and began to march up and down playing a selection of stirring airs.

As the leading member of the Leuchars pipe band, of which he subsequently became Pipe Major, Ian was known as an accomplished piper who regularly practised his skills. However, his appearance on this occasion was not merely a practice. Seemingly it is traditional in the Scottish regiments to herald a forthcoming victory with celebratory pipe music and Ian was not about to miss such an opportunity.

By chance, Ian's appearance coincided with an unexpected visit to the Squadron by members of the media news pool which on this occasion happened to include a delighted journalist from *'The Scotsman'*. Yet again, the Fighting Cocks had shown remarkable prescience."

Flight Lieutenant Norrie again:

"With the advent of the ground offensive, F3 air defence operations took on a renewed vigour. On the morning of the start of the Allied ground offensive, Bentley formation again found itself capping on the Iraqi/Saudi border. The intelligence briefing that morning had been sparse in detail as the Allied advance was literally only hours old. Details as to who was where, why, what and when had not been available for Bentley so, on patrol above cloud, the adrenalin was flowing more freely than normal. No sooner had Bentley joined CAP when the AWACS ordered them to vector, yet again, northbound. As Bentley joined in battle formation and headed north-west, AWACS amplified their mission. 'Vector 310° for 50 miles. Locate a downed Allied helicopter.' A quick look at the map revealed we were heading directly towards a heavy concentration of SAM and triple-A sites. Confirming their vector, Bentley was ordered to descend below cloud. There was no time to question this as Bentley descended and broke cloud at about 1,500 feet and what they saw before them nobody had prepared them for. The desert floor was crawling with vehicles. There were track and tyre marks scarring the desert sand everywhere, convoys of trucks heading northwards and heavy armour and guns taking up positions. But whose forces were they? Simple deduction from the fact that nobody had opened fire quickly reassured Bentley that the forces were indeed 'friendly'. Bentley soon arrived at the point to which they had been vectored and were able to report that the position was occupied by friendly forces.

A further vector from AWACS took Bentley over more of the battlefield and again the Tornado crew was able to confirm to AWACS that the downed helicopter was among friendly forces. It was a momentous moment in military history, the cunning and speed of the Allied advance. The crew was also aware that they were witnessing history of world importance in the making."

CAP positions moved progressively further north into Iraq with the advance of Coalition ground forces until finally the F3s moved across to Kuwait following the cessation of offensive action at the beginning of March. Dramatic scenes met the crews as they flew into Kuwaiti airspace. Through the extensive pall of smoke from the numerous burning oil fields, set alight by the retreating Iraqis, the silhouette of a British

43's Gulf Aircrew
On top: Jerry Ward, Mike Oakes, Steve Hayler, Tony 'Pecky' Fullford, Andy Moir, Al Clitherow, John Epsley, Brian 'Hound' O'Connor, John 'Harry' Pilling, Henry Paul, Tony Beresford, Mike Lowry
Leaning on pylon: Sandy Gordon
Standing: Jim Davidson, Paul 'Benny' Facer, Clive 'Noddy' Marrison, Al Whyte, Phil Storey, Derek Johnston, Pete 'Willy' Hackett, Nick Willey, Martin 'Slaps' Stephens, Paul Lightbody, Ken Thompson, Colin McDermott, Joe Lortie, Steve Norrie, Steve Cooper

Airways Boeing 747 tail fin could be seen lurching drunkenly from the bombed-out wreck on the tarmac of Kuwait airport. It was all too evident when flying over the Kuwaiti airbases that every hardened aircraft shelter had been neatly punctured with great precision by a laser-guided bomb (LGB), thus immediately calling into question the wisdom of the major investment in airfield hardening programmes undertaken at home by the NATO nations. The extent of the fighting in Kuwait was also revealed most forcibly by the very real risk of bird strikes from vultures attracted to the battlefields, principally along the Basra Road where hundreds of Iraqi soldiers had been caught out in the open by Coalition aircraft. However, the most dramatic legacy of the war was to be seen in the universal devastation of the oilfields by the retreating Iraqi forces, with hundreds of wellheads burning fiercely and with the surrounding oil-impregnated sand glowing like charcoal. At night it resembled a mediaeval vision of Hell. It was quite literally scorched earth.

Combat Air Patrols continued for about a week after the end of hostilities. Perhaps the most notable event during this period was the interception and escort of a Red Cross aircraft returning from Iraq with Coalition prisoners of war. It was not only terrific to welcome them back but to the immense surprise and delight of all at Dhahran the only RAF aircrew from the base that had been lost, a GR1 crew, were among the returnees, despite having been presumed dead as no parachutes had been seen after their aircraft had been hit by a SAM.

A return visit by the Prime Minister, John Major, on 6 March also emphasised the completion of the Coalition task and, with the comprehensive defeat of Iraq assured, force reductions began to occur rapidly. In-theatre flying ceased for 43 and 29 Squadrons, allowing celebrations both formal (a traditional Saudi banquet seated on carpets in a hangar, at which certificates were presented to all allied forces by our hosts) and informal (a spirited poolside flying suit party where group photographs were taken using the aircrew's latest gadget – an underwater camera!).

Barely a week later the first six Tornado F3s departed on 12 March, using an AAR-supported route that had been established for the return of

43 Squadron in the Gulf

the majority of the considerable number of RAF combat aircraft deployed in the Gulf region. Tanker aircraft operated out of Akrotiri and met their 'chicks' over northern Saudi Arabia, subsequently escorting them to Decimomannu in Sardinia before returning to Cyprus. The final leg to the UK was achieved without AAR support the following day. The night stop in Italy provided an opportunity for the 43 crews to begin to acclimatise to more normal life, notably the ability to enjoy a most welcome beer. However, celebrations were moderated by thoughts of home and the crews in the first four-ship to return departed bright-eyed the following morning.

The weather forecast for Leuchars was encouraging, particularly as it had been hoped to arrive in some style! However, en-route reports began to reveal deteriorating weather at base which precluded a spirited arrival and the formation extended into a gentlemanly trail for a series of individual radar approaches. The Boss's aircraft broke cloud at 200 feet and this was reported to the rest of the formation to a chorus of 'hoorahs'. Soon the initial group of Fighting Cocks was back on the ground enjoying the first of many reunions with families and friends as the remaining personnel returned over the next few days. New acquaintances were also made, notably by OC 'B' Flight, Squadron Leader Ken Thompson, who met his newborn son Mark for the first time. The last of the squadron groundcrew and equipment left Dhahran on Friday 15 March.

Thus the Fighting Cocks returned to their roost in Scotland. Although aircraft had occasionally been fired upon and everyone had experienced the nightly Scud attacks, it was the squadron's constant presence in its defensive counter air role that had proved a key factor in preventing any effective Iraqi incursions into Saudi airspace and generally in keeping the Iraqi Air Force on the ground. It was therefore a proud moment when it was confirmed that 43 had won its first battle honour since 1944.

An added delight upon the return was a visit by the Princess of Wales on 21 March. This had been planned well in advance as a visit to the families, however, to their surprise and evidently also that of the Princess, the speedy end to the war and rapid reduction in force levels, resulted in the chaps returning early and in time to meet Her Royal Highness and to brief her on the Squadron's participation in the campaign. A welcome period of leave followed, preceding the return to normal activities, including the resumption of QRA and the customary schedule of training exercises. Notable among these was an affiliation sortie with 208 (Buccaneer) Squadron under the AEW control of 8 Squadron to mark the last operational sortie of the Shackleton aircraft.

1991 marked the 75th anniversary of the Fighting Cocks although the actual birthday passed without celebration as the squadron was on its period of stand-down on return from active service. However, the occasion was too

Jerry Ward & Joe Lortie in celebratory mood.

A safe homecoming - some of the aircrew celebrate with Leuchars fizz!
Left to right: Flt Lt Paul Facer, Sqn Ldr Nick Willey, Flt Lt Martin Stephens, Fg Off John Espley, Sqn Ldr Steve Cooper, Flt Lt Al Whyte, Wg Cdr Andy Moir, Fg Off Pete Hackett, Flt Lt Colin McDermott, Flt Lt Sandy Gordon and Flt Lt Derek Johnston
(Photograph © and courtesy D.C.Thomson & Co.,Ltd)

important to overlook so on 17 May a formation of four Tornados conducted a commemorative flypast over 43's birthplace, on the fields of Falleninch, and over Stirling Castle where the Squadron Standard was paraded on the battlements.

Training exercises continued throughout June and in the middle of the month four aircraft detached to Coningsby to take part in a flypast to coincide with the Gulf War victory parade through the City of London. On this occasion, Wing Commander Moir was dispatched to mingle with the great and famous at the Mansion House, from which the review of the

The four-ship 75th anniversary flypast over Stirling Castle

To celebrate the 75th Anniversary, all the Tornados were decorated wth 'Cocky' in Middle-Eastern garb on the nose.

parade would take place. Sadly the weather was not so accommodating as during the Battle of Britain anniversary the previous year and the low cloud base and poor visibility prevented the full flypast from taking place. In the event it was a reduced formation of four Tornado GR1s, followed by a similar number of Chinook helicopters, seen cautiously picking their way over the City's skyscrapers. The Boss ended up being the only one to get a view of the parade! On a more local note, the weather dawned similarly uncertain on 27 June for the annual Freedom of St Andrews parade and flypast. This was 43's first opportunity to fly over the town in its Tornados and, although a formation flypast once again proved not to be possible, a solo aircraft flown by Captain 'Hound' O'Connor and the Boss overflew the parade in South Street. This was in marked contrast to the previous year when, in perfect formation, and to the considerable amusement of the Fighting Cocks, a Leuchars Phantom unit (in fact 228 OCU) flew majestically in formation along the parallel Market Street, about 200 yards behind the reviewing platform and assembled onlookers!

The effectiveness of the deterrent role played by the squadron in the Coalition's defensive counter-air strategy in the Gulf had paradoxically denied the Tornados the need to fire their missiles in anger. However, over the first ten days of July the opportunity finally to pull the trigger occurred, as the squadron undertook firings of Skyflash on the Hebrides range during their Missile Practice Camp which embodied Trial Panoramic. The MPC was a great success in exploring and validating the missile's capabilities and resulted in the Aberporth Trophy for 1991 being awarded to 43 Squadron.

A further but quite different trophy arrived later that year. A number of items of Iraqi equipment had been acquired by the RAF as trophies of war to be distributed to selected units. Thus it was with pleasant surprise that a

On a rather misty day 'Golf Foxtrot' leads a four-ship formation north over the Forth Bridges

Chinook landed at Leuchars and disgorged an Iraqi ZU 23-2 anti-aircraft gun in desert camouflage, albeit with its barrels filled with concrete as a crude means of rendering it inoperable. However, a few weeks of enthusiastic attention by the station armourers soon returned it to a more purposeful appearance before it was placed outside the entrance to the squadron headquarters as a proud reminder of recent activities. Indeed, with this and the relatively recently acquired Phantom as a gate guardian, the Northern Dispersal began to take on the appearance of an aviation museum notwithstanding the numerous shiny new Tornados.

August saw 43's first participation in the annual race to London on the 'Glorious Twelfth', strangely, however, without the involvement of any grouse. Andy Moir recalls:

"A local hotelier, with the co-operation of RAF Leuchars and the Parachute Regiment, staged a timed run to London on 12 August in aid of the Airborne Appeal (the Parachute Regiment's charity) and the RAF Benevolent Fund. The event, called the Haggis Handicap Stakes, involved a charity lunch at the Savoy Hotel at which bets would be placed on the time it would take to transport several haggis and bottles of whisky, from a charity clay pigeon shoot at the Sandford Hotel, near Newport on the Tay, to the dining room at the Savoy.

Our Station Commander, Group Captain Lloyd Doble, a Fighting Cock from Phantom days, landed at the Sandford in a Wessex helicopter, allowing me to collect the consignment of haggis and whisky, and then commence the timed run. A quick transit to Leuchars, and a transfer by both of us to a Tornado waiting on the runway with one engine already running, preceded a high-speed dash to Farnborough. Once we had landed the consignment was quickly handed over to the Parachute Regiment's Red Devils team who flew to the centre of London by helicopter, and parachuted into the Thames behind the Savoy, from where they were picked up by the River Police and conveyed to the hotel. Meanwhile, not wishing to miss the fun, Lloyd Doble and I were flown to Battersea heliport and then driven in some style to the Savoy, arriving at the front door in a Daimler at the same time as the Red Devils dripped their way in through the back door. Thanks to the generosity of the many guests a considerable amount was raised for the charities - and the two of us had a pretty good lunch too."

Events now began to assume a more familiar pattern as routine training exercises resumed with deployments to Bitburg in Germany and Andoya in northern Norway during August and September. However, the Battle of Britain open day at Leuchars heralded a major departure from previous such events as Leuchars hosted the Soviet Air Force formation display team in their Su-27 Flanker aircraft. There could hardly have been a more dramatic demonstration of the end of the Cold War than the presence of these latest fighters in the Soviet inventory lined up on the airfield and their pilots being welcomed in the Officers' Mess for the traditional and, as ever, boisterous Friday evening happy hour. The following day's display provided the opportunity for the Soviets to demonstrate the full range of the Flanker's remarkable agility including its unique and unconventional 'Cobra' manoeuvre. This had astonished western spectators when first demonstrated at Farnborough and involved pulling the aircraft to an angle of attack of over 90° to its line of flight causing abrupt deceleration before nosing back down – and all in apparently controlled flight.

October saw the initial phase of a NATO squadron exchange with a detachment of Fighting Cocks departing for Beauvechain to operate with the F-16s of 350 Squadron of the

One of the Soviet Su-27 Flankers

Belgian Air Force. On this occasion the usually simultaneous two-way exchange was split to allow the 43 home team to concentrate on preparing for two other major commitments that month. On the 16th, 43 Squadron led the station parade in the presentation ceremony to RAF Leuchars of the coveted Royal Air Force Wilkinson Sword of Peace for 1990. This award, made annually, is presented to the unit or establishment which is judged to have made the most valuable contribution to enhancing the good name of the air force within the civilian community. Wing Commander Moir accepted the sword on behalf of RAF Leuchars, appropriately receiving it from the reviewing officer, Air Marshal Sir Roger Palin, the Air Member for Personnel, himself a former CO of the Fighting Cocks (1975-78).

The following week saw the first operational evaluation of the squadron since its re-equipment with the Tornado other than, of course, the small matter of the Gulf War! Maxeval was the national, and if anything more rigorous, precursor to the NATO Taceval scheduled for December. An extensive team of evaluators from HQ Strike Command descended on Leuchars to monitor and assess the station's performance over a continuous period of three days, which revealed that all elements of the base were well prepared for the forthcoming NATO evaluation. Once things had returned to normal the squadron was able to host the return element of the NATO squadron exchange during early November and then to send a small detachment to the US Naval Air Station at Keflavik in Iceland later that month to participate in Exercise Hot Springs, a deployment designed to provide experience in joint air defence operations.

The cold of Iceland was soon to be replaced in the New Year 1992, by the milder climate of the Mediterranean as 43 departed for Cyprus in late January on its first Armament Practice Camp with the Tornado. It was great to all be away together again – and in the more relaxed environment of Akrotiri rather than that of the intensive flying undertaken at Dhahran less than a year previously. The high level of proficiency with the aircraft developed over the preceding year had clearly paid dividends and the outstanding scores that were achieved resulted in HQ 11 Group awarding the squadron the 1991-92 Seed Trophy for air-to-air gunnery.

As the detachment drew to a close there remained one further task for the Fighting Cocks to perform. The government of Kuwait had planned a major national celebration to commemorate the first anniversary of the liberation of their country and this was to include a formation flypast of aircraft from the nations that had contributed aircraft to the Coalition during the Gulf War. 43 Squadron had been selected to represent the RAF and on 22 February, a four-ship of Tornado F3s took off from Cyprus for the Gulf once more. Andy Moir relates:

"Whilst the squadron had, of course, spent a considerable amount of time over Kuwait during the war, this was to be the first time that any crews had landed in the country. On arrival I was surprised to be presented with a huge bunch of flowers as I climbed down from the aircraft. Diplomacy was the order of the day in my gracious acceptance of such a generous gift in a desert kingdom. However, I was mightily relieved to be able to present the bouquet that evening to the British Ambassador's wife at an informal reception at the embassy.'

'The following days were spent in briefing and a rehearsal for the multi-national flypast prior to the actual event on the 26th – Kuwait Liberation Day. The opportunity was also taken to explore areas of Kuwait previously only seen from the air. Whilst the oil fires had long since been extinguished, there remained extensive evidence of the devastation cause by the Coalition's precision bombing. Little had we crews realised a year before, whilst flying over the Kuwait military airfields, that within 12 months we would be peering up through the ragged holes in the numerous damaged hardened aircraft shelters. The extent of Kuwaiti resistance was also evident in the city itself – and still not without an element of danger.

One heavily damaged house that had been the site of a fierce battle with the invading Iraqi forces had been preserved as a testimony to the courage of the Kuwaiti resistance. During a squadron visit to the house, in the company of a number of Kuwaiti families with children, a rapid evacuation was ordered as a live rocket-propelled grenade was discovered lodged in the outer wall where it had remained undiscovered since the end of the war. By contrast, the flypast occurred without incident and the Fighting Cocks were soon once again flying westwards over the Arabian desert en route for Scotland and home."

The early spring of 1992 saw a resumption of routine training as well as detachments of varying sizes to Stornoway, Torrejon de Ardoz, near Madrid, and to the German Air Force base at Lechfeld. By late April the squadron was on the move once again as it prepared for its first visit to Alaska to enjoy the freedom of the vast unrestricted training areas there. The Boss was also on the move as he handed over command at the end of an immensely eventful tour in which the Tornado had opened yet another chapter in 43 Squadron's history and which had seen the Fighting Cocks return to battle once more.

The new commanding officer, Wing Commander Malcolm Godfrey, arrived in May 1992. His tour was to see 43 prepare itself for a further operational deployment, for which the Squadron's fleet of aircraft was enhanced to include a number of the improved Stage 1+ Tornados. This would be the standard of aircraft that was ultimately to be deployed for operations over Bosnia, and enabled more effective pre-deployment training to be conducted.

Gulf War medal parade, 1992

Gp Capt Nicholl presents Gulf War campaign medals assisted by
Sqn Ldr Ken Thompson and Fg Off Al Dodds.
(MoD (RAF) Crown Copyright)

Routine training, including Tacevals, continued and no sooner had Mal arrived than short, overnight, exchanges with the French Air Force Mirage F1s at Rheims also commenced. These brief deployments were followed by a longer exchange to Aalborg with the F-16s of the Royal Dutch Air Force's 726 Squadron in June and a NATINADS (NATO Integrated Air Defence System) exercise in September, Northern Banner, which was repeated the following February.

The Squadron's second return to the Gulf, came with Exercise Free Sky in November 1992. This saw six Tornados deploy to Kuwait International Airport having staged through Decimomannu and Akrotiri, supported by VC10 tankers from Operation SOUTHERN WATCH, the operation to monitor and control the airspace south of the 32nd Parallel in Iraq. The exercise was intended to demonstrate the UK's commitment to a defence agreement renewed with Kuwait in the wake of the Gulf War. The squadron operated from Kuwait International Airport as the military airfields were still unusable almost two years after the heavy weight of attacks they had suffered. The tripartite exercise involved Kuwaiti A-4s, Mirage F1s and F-18s, as well as American Navy A-6s, and E-2s from USS Ranger, operating both from their carrier and from Kuwait, together with 43 Squadron. Paul 'Courtney' Courtnage, OC 'A' Flight, relates:

"It was reported in the *Arab Times* on Sunday, 15 November 1992 that: "British and Kuwaiti warplanes began a week of joint manoeuvres in the skies over Kuwait on Saturday. Six British Tornados flew alongside F-18s, Mirage F1s and A-4 Skyhawks of the Kuwait Air force to practise intercepting hostile aircraft." Well, that was us - the Fighting Cocks on tour in the Middle East!

We were invited to go there to offer training and as a show of force, a deterrent to the Iraqis to show them that we still supported the Kuwait government and that any repeat of aggression would be met by force. The plan was to fly in two formations of three F3s each to Decimomannu, refuel and have lunch, then set off for a night hop to Cyprus. I was leading the second formation behind the Boss and made 'Deci', but as I took off and raised the undercarriage, a hydraulic warning light came on in my cockpit, indicating a major leak.

I handed over the lead and turned back for Deci, got down safely, and was met by a very helpful sergeant from 31 Squadron that was currently operating from there, and he immediately got to work on my Tornado, quickly diagnosing the snag and reckoning he could fix it by the next day. Against all odds he did it and the aircraft became serviceable by next lunchtime, which was more than could be said for our outrageous plan we had devised to get us to Kuwait. I phoned the CO who said, "OK Courtney, we'll get airborne from Akrotiri at 1200, meet up with the tanker and then we'll head west and hang around to see if you can join up with us. If you don't, you're on your own." In other words, meet us somewhere over the eastern Med, don't know where, don't know when. No frequencies, no call-signs, no plan of action, no bloody clue really. Not surprisingly we did not meet up.

Now on our own we decided to head for Cairo, fuel willing, and despite it being a weekend, I found someone who thought it would be all right to land there. Upon our arrival the ATC at Cairo International seemed pleased to see us, but my first doubts arose when seeing a collection of old rusting aircraft hulks that were scattered around the airport. When we

During the 1992 visits to Kuwait opportunities were taken to inspect some of the effects of the war.

'Tank commander' Nick Willey

John Espley, Derek Johnston & Sandy Gordon stand in a bombed HAS.

parked we were met by an armed soldier who spoke no English, and a junior member of the British Embassy who seemed genuinely surprised that we had landed here on purpose. I inspected my aircraft and to my dismay the left engine had burned, or lost, an astounding amount of oil and wasn't going to get us across the Arabian Desert.

I managed to get the Egyptians to agree to refuel us while my navigator tried to locate oil for an F3 engine but to no avail. A nice man said we could have all the Boeing 707 oil we wanted, but nothing for a Tornado. By this time the engine had cooled and the oil level had risen somewhat but I was not happy. The Embassy chap, knowing I had an agreed flight plan, said we should get off as quickly as possible. I said I had got in here without a problem but he countered by saying that getting in was not the problem! His tip was for us to get the hell out of here.

We decided to make a run for it, but our armed soldier didn't seem keen to let us go anywhere. However a backhander induced him to see things our way. Then we met a chap with a fuel bowser, so another 'bung' got us fuelled and then we quickly buggered off. For the next three hours we spoke to one or two places I've never heard of and just kept on going, nurturing fuel and engines.

There were a few other problems, especially when we were cutting corners off our flight plan and needing to come up with a plausible excuse for ATC when we eventually showed up on their radar but finally we made Kuwait. After landing I explained to an engineer about the oil problem and he said I should have topped it up. After telling him we couldn't get the right oil one of our groundcrew opened up an obscure panel on the aircraft and - with a grin - pulled out a can of F3 oil."

Colin Malcolm, OC 'B' Flight, recalls:

"Initially the Kuwaitis wished to limit the airspace to a small area approximately 30 nm x 30 nm – a rather limited training area with pre-planned routes and times. However by day two we had access to most of Kuwait for training except the airspace surrounding the airport and the live firing ranges in the country - which were not always notified as danger areas, not even when active!"

The complexity of the training was steadily developed from rather canned 'two versus two' formations to 'free-play' engagements, escorts and bounces. Kuwaiti pilots were keen to learn but were only just starting to find their feet on the F-18, which they tended to operate as they had done with their Mirage F1s, much to the chagrin of their USMC/USN instructors.

"Our crews had opportunities to fly in the F-14, which they enjoyed immensely, A-6s, which they enjoyed a little less, and to spend nights on the carrier – which they probably endured more than enjoyed. COD (Carrier Onboard Delivery) arrival on the USS Ranger, in a Greyhound with no windows, was probably the least welcome event.

The US Navy crews flew in the F3 and the WSOs (Weapon System Operators) were mightily impressed with the plan view offered by the weapons system, but less so by the power of an RB 199. They must have all come from Texas as they found the F3 small after an F-14. All in all there was a good exchange of expertise that no doubt helped to broaden the mind of the Kuwaiti Air Force as it gained experience with more modern aircraft, provided useful experience for UK crews and also contributed significantly to the diplomatic agenda."

On 1 April 1993, the 75th anniversary of the formation of the Royal Air Force, 43 were to be part of a celebration flypast at RAF Marham in Norfolk. Colin Malcolm remembers the event:

"An interesting first rehearsal produced a head-on, co-altitude, very close aboard pass with a formation of heavies (E-3s, Nimrods, etc) holding off the East Anglian coast, which scattered the, by then 12 F3s, into three components – left, right and down. The Leuchars team had a close look at the sea below and an E-3 above! Adrenalin reduced and pulses lowered, as the 12 Tornados rejoined, and entered the stream of aircraft of all types, and large formations, to overfly the dais at Marham. 'Now joined by Tornado GR1s behind to form a single Tornado element in the hold, the lead F3 (not one of ours) elected to fly a fixed ground track/ground speed, to sort out his timing, by adjusting his airspeed on either leg of the hold – the concertina that ensued was not well received by those in the rear of the formation. Finally, the exit route after Marham for the F3s, was north over the Wash, where it was to split, with Coningsby and Leuchars aircraft landing at Coningsby, and Leeming aircraft returning to their base. Here it met the same formation of heavies for yet another close aboard pass and second scatter. As one can imagine, the tele-conference debrief was long – and 'open'.

Subsequent practices ran more smoothly and on the day the weather played its trump card, with Marham being all but washed out in very heavy rain and the flypast being cancelled before we launched."

Chief Technician Jim Campbell, who served on 43 from 1992 until 1997, and then later became Airframe Trade Manager from 1997 to 2006, records his recollections under Wing Commander Godfrey:

"When I arrived on 43 Squadron, Wing Commander Mal Godfrey had recently assumed command. The squadron had not long returned from Gulf Ops and many of the guys were still coming down from the euphoria of a safe return. Others, however, were more subdued, I suspect reflecting on what might have been. The workload was extremely heavy for both air and groundcrew and a lack of spares across the Tornado fleet compounded the problem, with long shifts for the groundcrew and a lack of flying resources for the aircrew being the norm. Workloads increased further when the squadron lost an aircraft in October of the following year. It went down near Barnard Castle following an airborne fire while on a low level sortie in the Pennines but the crew, Flight Lieutenants Stu Walker and Liam Taylor ejected safely. The ensuing investigation determined that a technical failure had been a contributory cause of the accident and the subsequent fleet-wide rectification programme placed an even greater burden on the engineers. Sadly, Stu Walker was to be killed in a subsequent accident in Cyprus the following year."

From April 1994, the main runway at Leuchars was resurfaced and, although work was scheduled to coincide with squadron deployments, and a few operations were conducted from the short cross-runway, 43 was 'Bolt-holed' to Leeming for much of the period. Jim Campbell:

"When the Leuchars runway was being resurfaced, there was limited accommodation available at Leeming so some of the guys were billeted in the Scotch Corner Hotel. This was luxury to which they were not accustomed. The rumour amongst the groundcrew was that the squadron would be bankrupted but nobody cared. Three-star living was definitely the way forward! We had an accomplished pianist amongst us and reverie often lasted until the wee hours with the bar staff relishing the overtime, the lads enjoying a sing-song and the other residents enjoying making complaints to deaf ears.

It was during this period that the squadron was notified that we were to deploy to Italy in support of Operation DENY FLIGHT, the NATO policing of the no-fly zone over Bosnia. 43 was to replace 111 Squadron and would be operating out of Gioia Del Colle with accommodation at Porto Giardino, a coastal holiday complex an hour's drive away. Prior to deployment we would undertake a six week work-up in Cyprus, including an APC and NVG training. We would then have a week at home before deploying for 3-4 months. Morale started to waver as personnel realised the timescales involved."

The ethnic tensions throughout Yugoslavia had built up during 1991 and that June Croatia and Slovenia declared their independence. In Bosnia and Croatia the Serbs formed Serbian Autonomous Regions, renounced by the Bosnian government. This led to armed conflict that escalated after Macedonia declared its independence that September. The UN found itself in the middle of a fight and performing a, supposedly impartial, peacekeeping role. French and British troops did much to patch up local disagreements and UNPROFOR (UN Protection Force) negotiated temporary cease-fires around the protected areas. Part of the UN's mission was to enforce a 'No-fly' zone over Bosnia – Operation DENY FLIGHT. The RAF's F3 squadrons, in rotation, contributed to this multi-national effort, 43's turn coming in 1994. Paul Courtnage:

"We operated out of Gioa and lived in the Hotel Svevo in the town. The normal routine for our three-month tour of duty was to fly the dawn patrol over Bosnia. This involved getting up at 0130 in the morning to take breakfast, have a briefing, launch and transit to the area concerned. We were supported by TriStar tankers and AWACS and our normal time on patrol was about four hours, provided that the formation which was supposed to relieve us turned up.

The operation could not be described as a total success. The UN did not control the region, the security was fragile, supply flights were carried out only when Serbs allowed them and the loss of the Bihac pocket and other protected areas showed that the UN could not guarantee to defend the safe zones. In addition, the no-fly zone was violated daily. I intercepted a Russian-built transport helicopter in southern Bosnia one morning, and my only recourse was to transmit repeated warnings on the international Guard channel that he was in violation of UN resolutions 781 and 786 – which the pilot knew – and that if he didn't clear off – which he didn't – he would be engaged – which he wasn't. It was frustrating. The Serbs would shoot at us regularly and they managed to knock down a US F-16. Not that being shot down was the major concern, it was what sort of reception one would receive if we baled out!

Sqn Ldr Courtnage and Flt Lt Kemsley in UN garb during NATO operations over Bosnia Herzegovina.

Just occasionally the Serbs would go too far and the UN's self-restraint would snap. At such times a mission of some description would be mounted to slap them down again – more often a show of force than direct military action. On the evening of 22 September, I provided top cover for such an operation against a Serb Army tank. In the failing evening light, a Jaguar pilot of our acquaintance dropped his bomb on an un-manned T-55 tank scoring a 'kill'. This was the first bomb to be dropped in anger on the European mainland since 1945."

While preparing for Operation DENY FLIGHT a further challenge was to emerge once the squadron commenced training in Cyprus, when another aircraft crashed on 8 July. While returning from an air-to-air gunnery sortie in conditions of sea fog to the south of Akrotiri, ZH558 crashed into the sea. The deceptive low level visibility was a possible contributory factor. Flight Lieutenants Stu Walker and Nigel Orme were both killed. Jim Campbell continues:

"The effect of this loss on the squadron was devastating. Personnel were flown back to the UK to attend the funerals and came back to Cyprus the next day. A simultaneous service was held at Akrotiri for those unable to get home. On the resumption of flying there was a further serious incident which almost resulted in the loss of an aircraft. However, despite the pilot managing to recover the aircraft successfully, this served to unsettle feelings further.

On the lighter side, the 'Lineys' still used all their initiative to come up with ideas for mayhem. The pinnacle was the construction of a fake snake made from bodge tape and connected to a fishing reel by thin copper wire. The idea was to reel in the snake across the pathway leading to the line hut and give a fright to anyone walking along it. As we were night flying, twilight seemed the best time to spring the surprise on the unwary. Two or three victims later and the guys were revelling in this new found sport. Unfortunately it all fell apart when the last crew of the night headed for their aircraft. As planned, the 'snake' shot across in front of them and a loud scream was heard from the steely-eyed killers and pieces of kit flew into the air. There was then a short period of silence as all present watched the only serviceable pair of NVGs in Cyprus hit the concrete and shatter into small pieces. As the crew looked up, it was with amazement that they realised that every one of the culprits had vanished. Not a soul to be seen and one potentially very irate Boss back at control. You could have heard the bollocking in Limassol!"

In August, as the end of detachment loomed, the Squadron suffered a further blow when it was revealed that Wing Commander Godfrey had been relieved of his command. Most of the groundcrew were shocked by the news, as Mal was generally held in high regard by them. Clearly, the decision had been not taken lightly but it was another blow to a somewhat punch-drunk squadron.

His successor was Wing Commander Pete Legg who arrived with considerable experience of variable geometry (swing-wing) fighters, not only from his prior experience on the F3 OCU but also following an exchange tour with the US Navy flying F-14s. This mirrored similar patterns for two previous commanding officers. In 1959, Squadron Leader Dave Scrimgeour had taken command of the Hunter-equipped Squadron following a posting with the USAF flying the F-86 Sabre and F-100 Super Sabre, while in 1971 Wing Commander Jerry Cohu had similarly taken command after an exchange tour on the Phantom with the USMC.

Pete had begun his refresher training at Coningsby in June with a view to taking charge of 43 in November. This was brought forward abruptly following the fatal accident in Cyprus, so after completing the ground school and less than two weeks of refresher flying he was advised in early August by the AOC 11 Group, Air Vice-Marshal Tony Bagnall, that he was to assume command the following week. Pete Legg's initial brief was to establish whether the squadron was capable of fulfilling its forthcoming commitment as the UK air defence element in Operation DENY FLIGHT.

The squadron returned from its APC in Cyprus a few days later in mid-August and was met at Leuchars by its new Boss. He consulted with the flight commanders, Squadron Leaders Paul Courtnage, Dave Morgan and Colin Malcolm, together with the QWI, Squadron Leader Geoff Booth, all of whom had previously served with Pete. The Boss rapidly confirmed that the majority of sorties in a comprehensive work-up programme had already been completed satisfactorily and that crews were both proficient and current. Indeed, part of this training had been conducted in parallel with the air gunnery whilst in Cyprus. The remainder of work-up sorties were scheduled for the latter part of August, and would include Night Vision Goggle procedures at low level, strafe and helicopter interception and attack techniques. Confident that the Squadron could meet its task, he declared it ready for deployment. Pete started his own DENY FLIGHT work-up at Leuchars and completed it at RAF Leeming with his final tactical sortie from there on 21 September. Three days later he flew his first operational sortie over Bosnia. Geoff Booth recalls the period after the accident and the arrival of the new Boss:

"We saw Cyprus as polishing a team without 'domestic distractions' in terms of getting ready to be away on ops. The accident with Nigel and Stuart hit the boys hard for sure. Sadly the ex-Phantom guys were all too familiar with such events, Courtney and I went through it twice when we were on our first tour on 29 Squadron; it was not something the F3 people had come across very often – lucky them. However, it did focus everyone and we were not going to let the accident affect our preparations and we made a point that on ops you have to put such things behind you and crack-on. So we had a good team with some experienced and very capable crews.

I returned home for the funerals along with the rest of the guys but stayed to pick up Leggy [the Boss] and did his condensed work-up. He hadn't lost his touch but I think he would admit to a pretty steep learning curve. We were THE priority in 11 Group so getting assets seemed a lot easier than the rest of the work-up programme! I was very happy that the guys were prepared based on what was left for them to do back in Cyprus before we took over from *Tremblers*. Courtney had that squared away.

So, were we ready to go? Absolutely. We had followed the mandated work-up syllabus and had followed the advice of our more experienced chaps, some of whom had served in the Gulf, particularly Flight Lieutenant 'Dan' Archer, who was my QWI(P), Flight Lieutenant Ed Moran and the QWI(N), Flight Lieutenant 'Rick' Wakeman, amongst others.

Courtney and I had done the Operation CORPORATE work-up on 29 Squadron back in 1982, getting ready for Ascension and an imminent deployment to the Falklands as soon as a runway was available at Stanley, so we knew the form. We not only did the work-up in constituted crews but as far as we could, flew as constituted pairs, so everyone really knew each other's strengths and weaknesses. As OC Weapons, the work-up was my 'baby' and Cyprus was planned to hone weapons skills, as well as being somewhere we could do some really good NVG work, albeit over the sea."

The squadron then deployed to Gioa Del Colle, Italy, as planned, at the start of September under the command of Paul Courtnage. By the time Pete Legg arrived there towards the end of the month he was delighted to find that 'Courtney' had made an excellent job of getting 43 up and running, and, in the event, Courtney's sound preparations ensured that the deployment continued to run smoothly. Operation DENY FLIGHT then began. Geoff Booth:

"On DENY FLIGHT the chaps had started pretty much exclusively at night but we did get some day slots. The only other NVG-declared folk that I recall, were some USMC F-18Ds and USAF F-15Es. They were swing-role, providing both CAP and on-call CAS (Close Air Support). So we did a mix of day and night sorties and on occasion covered slots where other NATO nations were unable to fly due to poor weather. (Turkish F-16s could not fly if the cloud-base was below 1,500 feet!) So we were the only purely air-to-air NVG-equipped crews.

Fixed wing opposition was Galeb, Jastreb, Orao and the possibility was always there of Serb MiG-29s. The other point perhaps is that you would imagine a no-fly zone has only you in it – quite the opposite. It was a very busy air space with on-call CAS, various recce assets and air tankers going in and out. The same with helicopters – there were plenty around. It made one ask, just who are the bad guys?

At that stage we predominantly saw Mi8 and Mi17 helicopters (Hips) going in and out of places, particularly at night, in the eastern area down by Sebrenica. That said there were also NATO helicopters such as Sea Kings and others, so we were not cleared to engage helicopters at all. As far as we were concerned, we just called in what we saw, where, and when, to the AWACs.

We flew an ambush sortie one day following a hit-and-run raid by some Oraos up in the north-west corner of Bosnia-Herzogovina – what we called the 'Bihac Triangle'. It was a very tight area as there was an SA-2 site over at Banja Luka which we generally aimed to avoid. They had clearly reckoned that because our Rules of Engagement did not allow "hot pursuit" we would only be able to engage while they were in B-H airspace which was the limit of the Operation DENY FLIGHT operating area. We were flying a sort of triangular CAP to stay in the airspace and get some coverage. We did get a couple of contacts, called them in to the AWACs and went through the full pre-attack checks but before we got clearance from 'Magic' (the AWACs call-sign) they turned away and as far as I know they never tried that again."

For the next three months the established pattern of sharing 24-hour CAP with the US, Dutch and French fighters continued. Pairs of aircraft undertook missions of typically four hours' duration with 45 minute transit times and the remainder on CAP or tanking. Area patrols were conducted, most frequently resulting in the visual identification of helicopters using NVGs, particularly during the early stages of the deployment when 43 was mostly tasked at night. Potential targets were also Galeb ground-attack aircraft that had already conducted a number of bombing missions. On one occasion the Boss and Geoff Booth came close to an engagement on two such aircraft, however, at five miles the targets were evidently warned by their ground-based radar that a Tornado was approaching and so turned away and ran south to stay out of missile range. Pete Legg:

"On one memorable occasion I and the leader of a sortie, the American exchange pilot, Captain Pat Moylan, managed to get airborne for a task despite extremely foggy conditions at Gioa. Subsequently, further deterioration prevented the US replacement aircraft getting off to relieve us and, using additional tanker support, our sortie stretched to almost seven hours. This proved challenging, not just by virtue of the extended duration.

When agreeing to extend on task, the AWACS advised us that we would be "tanking with friends from across the channel", which we took to mean that French Mirages would be joining us on the expected RAF TriStar. In the event, our two Tornado crews were surprised to discover on their next tanking bracket that it was the tanker itself that was French – a KC-135. The problem was it was equipped with a modified boom and hose that neither I nor Moylan had used before. Hose position tolerances were extremely fine and required very precise formation flying (see photograph on page 284). However, all went well and the mission was accomplished successfully despite the AWACS' increasing concern at the length of our sortie as we contemplated a second extra refuelling slot.'

Despite our assurances, the controllers insisted that they should check with Gioa in order to seek the approval of 43's CO. I then announced that they were already speaking with 43's Boss and that I approved!"

Geoff Booth also recalls this sortie:

"We taxied as a pair in very poor visibility in the dark (I think we followed a Land Rover out!) and discussed our limits for take-off on this mission. We knew we were on the runway in the middle and pointing exactly down the centre-line and we could see "two lights" in accordance with Group Air Staff Orders, although these were one on each side of the runway! However we were happy to go, so off we launched into the night, popping out of the murk at about 100 feet from an absolute pea-souper.

In the event our relief pair found they could not even safely taxi out in daylight, which meant we would be double-slotted. It was the only time I have heard in a weather report, passed to us by the TriStar, that the visibility was ZERO metres in fog. Apparently it was so thick that they really could not get onto the runway as they could not even see the taxiway or runway lights. So when the TriStar was told that the second pair had been forced to scrub, the tanker pilot went home, leaving us still on task!

The French KC-135 with its modified boom proved entertaining, but we coped. I thought that Leggy had tanked from one previously on the F-4 or F-14, and I had done running commentaries quite a few times on the American KC-135, as the hose extension can be rather unforgiving and can easily rip-off the probe. Anyway, I managed a bit of impromptu technique briefing on the second radio box! Just to round off the sortie, it was still below limits at Gioia when we finished, so we diverted to Brindisi, and managed to get home later in the day."

Jim Campbell: "Apart from the usual operating conditions, such as irregular shift patterns, aircraft unserviceability, poor line accommodation and VIP visits – military and ministerial – it was a fairly uneventful time for the ground personnel. The travelling to and from work was a bind. Coaches were used to transport the bulk of personnel but for many a car journey was inevitable. On more than one occasion coming back from night shift, the driver found himself nodding off at the wheel, waking to the screams of his terrified passengers. Given the constant operational demands, opportunities to let off steam were limited. However, towards the end of the deployment a down-day BBQ was held. The effect of the length of time the groundcrew had been cooped up together, fuelled by a large quantity of beer, resulted in a boisterous occasion frequently reminiscent of a wild-west saloon. The duty SNCO, rather sensibly, generally left well alone. The following day revealed no serious injuries and a much more relaxed atmosphere now that the lid had been removed from the pressure cooker.

Without further incident, the squadron handed over responsibility to the next incumbents and returned to the UK for a spell of well-earned leave and the promise of a highly sought after detachment to Red Flag in the USA. Handing over to XI Squadron, 43 returned to Leuchars having achieved a highly creditable 100% achievement rate of tasked sorties.

Meantime, Pete Legg was rebuilding the squadron and introducing improved communication between air and ground crews, actively encouraging regular briefings and updates for the guys on the squadron's performance in the eyes of 11 Group. A liaison officer was appointed to perform this task and groundcrew made the effort to attend the briefings. In turn, the lads produced the squadron newsletter – Bitter and Twisted – an extremely cynical publication that got the gripes and whinges over in a humorous but pointed fashion. Wing Commander Legg encouraged the newsletter but insisted he was always the first recipient. In this way he controlled the content without stamping authority all over it and in so doing his esteem and respect among his troops was raised further."

Another first for the Fighting Cocks during Pete Legg's tenure was the arrival of the squadron's first woman pilot, Helen Dobbs. As an *ab initio* pilot straight from training and being female, her combat–ready work-up was harder than most, but she outshone her peers in almost every department. A likeable personality, she engaged with the troops immediately and soon had them fighting her corner – not that she needed it. Things did become a trifle obvious though, when an aircraft would be declared unserviceable with a major problem, only to be miraculously fixed and ready when it was needed for a combat work-up mission for Helen.

CHAPTER 33

Back to Iraq

IN February 1995 the Squadron deployed on Exercise Strong Resolve, basing itself at Bergen in Norway. Strong Resolve was a UK reinforcement exercise undertaken alongside Tornado GR4s and Harriers from which 43 returned in early March. An amusing incident occurred when the area radar unit broadcast the codeword for an imminent border incursion into Swedish airspace, requiring all NATO aircraft to immediately turn west as a precaution. The GR4 CO, a navigator, was airborne at the time and furious, vowing to discipline the transgressor – until he discovered it had been his aircraft that had strayed!

June 1995 saw the resumption of NATO Tactical Evaluation (Taceval), an assessment that had been superseded by the more realistic combat operations during the Gulf War and the Bosnian conflict. Nevertheless, the UK national Maxevals had continued. Perhaps as a result of this, and certainly thanks to 43's recent periods of active service, the Squadron recorded the top grading of '1' in all aspects of the evaluation.

On 30 October 1995 the Squadron suffered a mid-air collision between two F3s conducting NVG practice. The rear Tornado collided with the fin of the 'target' aircraft some 60 miles east of Leuchars. The rear aircraft managed to limp back to base, where, after landing, the crew spent an uncomfortable 40 minutes in the cockpit as the ground crew carefully removed the canopy, mindful of the risk of self-initiation of the MDC (miniature detonating cord) or ejector seat. The crew of the other F3 (ZE733), Flight Lieutenants Kev McCarry and John Booth, were forced to eject and spent 40-50 minutes in their dinghies before rescue by a helicopter of 202 Squadron from RAF Boulmer which homed to their emergency beacons. Pete Legg:

"Our recent success was tarnished by a mid-air collision at night. Two of our F3s were conducting mutual NVG practice at 12,000 feet east of Leuchars. As one aircraft closed on the other from astern for a lights-out visual identification (VID) the pilot of the rearmost Tornado was unprepared for the 'bloomed' image from the leader's jet pipes, became temporarily blinded and hit the rear of the target aircraft. While the first crew ejected, the crew of the rear machine then demonstrated remarkable skill in recovering to base despite extensive damage to the forward left fuselage and engine intake area. After landing they spent an uncomfortable 40 minutes in the cockpit as the ground crew removed the canopy."

ZE210 'GD' after the mid-air collision

October 1995 saw 43 conduct Operation CYCLONE CHANGE the ferrying of F3 aircraft to the Falkland Islands as part of the fleet rotation programme. The need for airborne spares required a progressively reducing number of aircraft along the route to ensure that two serviceable Tornados arrived at Mount Pleasant in the Falklands. The procedure remained much as in the Phantom days and involved launching five aircraft from RAF Coningsby, of which four then continued to rendezvous with the tanker. Three of these then continued the 10-hour flight to Ascension Island in company with the tanker and, after an overnight stop, launched once more with two continuing on the nine-hour flight to the Falklands while the final airborne spare headed back to Ascension. The airborne assets for CYCLONE CHANGE comprised two VC10s and a TriStar tanker, a Nimrod MPA for search and rescue cover, and a Hercules ground support aircraft.

Early 1996 saw the Fighting Cocks back in Cyprus for their regular APC and on this occasion they were able to offer a significant number of passenger rides to both squadron and station personnel. The Red Arrows were also at Akrotiri conducting their customary pre-season work-up which culminated in the formal presentation of their distinctive red flying suits and an appropriately boisterous party in the Officers' Mess. One of the team unwisely allowed a nurse to try on his prized new flying suit which the Fighting Cocks managed to spirit away (the flying suit, that is, not the nurse – or perhaps it was the nurse as well?). The suit was then sewn on one of the air-to-air target banners and used for gunnery practice the following day.

The Akrotiri Open Day followed this episode and a further attempt was made to get the flying suit airborne, this time towed behind a Canberra with two Tornados in formation. Sadly the suit, perhaps due to the rigours of its earlier experience, became detached on take off and that was the end of that very flashy red flying suit!

Exercise Cope Thunder took place from 2-27 July 1996. 111 Squadron deployed first to Eielson airbase in Alaska, with 43 later taking over the aircraft when their crews arrived. 43 participated with both the locally based American F-15s from Elmendorf and the deployed F-15s and F-16s, as well as RAF Jaguars of 31 Squadron. A Japanese C-130 also took part although was rarely seen due to 'uncertainties in its position'. Unfortunately a Jaguar GR1A of 41 Squadron was lost when it inadvertently hit trees while the pilot was distracted. However, he ejected successfully after a memorable, if laconic, 'Mayday' call. Pete Legg:

"Arctic survival took on a new dimension for the crews given the presence of bears in Alaska. A Forest Ranger provided a briefing on the local dangers and advised that there were two types – Black Bears and Grizzly Bears. The former, he explained, could climb trees but not run, whereas the latter could run but not climb. His advice was to identify your bear carefully, but if you should get caught, just roll into a ball, let the bear play with you and hope for the best!

One of the Squadron's junior navigators proudly announced that the Tornado crews would be armed when flying and thus had a measure of self-defence. When asked by the Ranger to show him his gun, our young navigator confidently produced his Walther PPK pistol. The Ranger examined it carefully and then recommended that the foresight be filed off. 'Why?' our man enquired. 'So that it won't hurt too much when the bear shoves it up your arse!'"

The detachment returned with their aircraft, routing via Goose Bay. The first sector culminated with extreme weather and Flight Lieutenant Phil Williams declared a Mayday after an apparently major fuel leak occurred following a violent lightning strike. So Phil's aircraft was given priority, vectoring him to Goose Bay for an uneventful landing. As No.2, the Boss's aircraft was vectored behind a slow twin-engined transport aircraft on which it rapidly began to close. Pete was ordered to break off and go round again for another approach. Dusk was becoming night and the airfield wind velocity at Goose Bay was gusting from 50 knots of headwind to 35 knots of crosswind, along with heavy rain. The Boss set himself up for his second PAR (Precision Approach Radar). As his Tornado touched down the airfield was struck by lightning and all the lights went out! A subsequent investigation revealed that the lightning strike on Phil's aircraft had only caused the fuel gauge to fail but it was a pretty tense time nevertheless.

On 17 August, Gregor Townsend led a Scottish XV against the Barbarians in a rugby match in memory of the victims of the Dunblane massacre. A four-ship from 43 conducted a flypast at Murrayfield and later in the same sortie was able to provide a further flypast at the Crail Church where Helen Dobbs was in the process of becoming Mrs Gardiner.

Other events in 43's calendar during 1996 were an APC to Cyprus, a visit to the Squadron by the rugby star Gavin Hastings and then another history-making moment. This was the occasion when the recent bride, Helen Gardiner, became the first female RAF fighter pilot to intercept a Russian aircraft. The target proved to be an Il-38 'May', a maritime patrol aircraft, and she made the interception off the Shetlands from a QRA scramble.

Flt lt Martin Harris and Flt Lt Helen Gardiner after the QRA launch on 10 Sep 1996

November 30 was a significant date for the Scots when the Stone of Destiny returned to Edinburgh after 700 years of English possession. As the foremost Scottish fighter squadron, it fell to 43 to play its part in the welcome and a 'Braveheart' formation of a four-ship crewed entirely by Scottish aircrew, flew over Edinburgh Castle as the Stone entered its precincts. Normally the Boss would have led such a sortie but as he failed to qualify on nationality grounds, the Tornados were led by Group Captain David Hamilton, OC Operations and Deputy Station Commander at Leuchars.

Pete Legg: "It was my practice to walk round the HAS site from time to time for an impromptu inspection. On one occasion I encountered the Squadron Warrant Officer carrying what appeared to be a twisted fin from a 2,250 litre under-wing fuel tank. 'What's that?' I enquired. 'You don't want to know,' came the reply. I insisted – 'What is it?' 'Boss, the tank's fixed and so is the Land Rover. You don't want to know.' I decided to agree, and he went on his way."

As Pete Legg reached the end of his tour as commanding officer, he could look back on his time knowing that he had done a lot of hard work and had given the Squadron a huge push forward. His only disappointment was that he missed the opportunity to take the Squadron out to a Red Flag deployment. His final flight came on 22 January 1997, taking the new CO on a sortie to conduct an airborne handover of command.

His replacement was Wing Commander Simon Bryant, a navigator whom many on the Squadron had not heard of previously but who, like many of his predecessors, would ultimately rise to the highest echelons within the Royal Air Force. Simon took up his appointment very quietly, weighing up the Squadron and its personnel and then began to refine some of the groundwork done by Pete Legg. Although he

Braveheart Formation
painting by Dugald Cameron

Braveheart 1 - ZE342
Pilot - Gp Capt David Hamilton
Navigator - Sqn Ldr Allan Goodison

Braveheart 2 - ZE207
Pilot - Flt Lt Sandy Gordon
Navigator - Flt Lt Gary Dunlop

Braveheart 3 - ZE834
Pilot - Flt Lt Ian 'Jocky' McCombie
Navigator - Sqn Ldr J H F 'Mac' McNeil-Matthews

Braveheart 4 - ZE296
Pilot - Flt Lt Simon Clark
Navigator - Sqn Ldr Keith Cowieson

The formation was airborne from Leuchars at 1130hrs on Saturday, 30 November 1996 and flew to the holding point off St Abbs Head flying a 6-minute racetrack pattern at 2000 ft at 360 kts. From there the formation headed 254°T and descended to 1000 ft to be overhead Edinburgh Castle at 500 ft at 1149 hrs. Thereafter the formation climbed to 2000 ft and overflew Edinburgh Airport, the Forth Bridges and St Andrews before embarking on an training excerise over the North Sea landing back at Leuchars at 1300 hrs.

Wg Cdr Simon Bryant and Wg Cdr Pete Legg

did not take up command until January 1997, he had arrived at Leuchars the previous December. His first move was a small adjustment to the flying programme that eased the burden on the airframes and engineers and this was followed by a period of team-building events. The Roosters Cup golf match between air and ground personnel was expanded to allow more competitors and even some caddies. Various sports events were organised for those with no interest in golf and at the end of the day the Squadron met up for a beer and debrief.

By the mid-90's it had become clear that the end of the Cold War had brought about not only a change in attitude and tactics but a realisation that the hardened base facilities and the austerity of the Squadron's surroundings had become something of an anachronism. The new CO therefore set about adapting the facilities in the Northern Dispersal to better meet the changed requirements 43 faced. Trees were planted, grass cut back and, most significantly, the large bunkroom within the hardened operations area was converted to provide a much-needed mission planning room and an additional briefing room. Networked electronic briefing facilities were installed throughout the 'hard' and adjacent 'soft' areas. The aircrew 'soft' was also extended and a general lick of paint, bought from Squadron funds, was applied by all, including the Boss, to match the older facilities to the new.

An MPC at Valley during June and July 1997 was not only straightforward but also successful, in that 43 was once again awarded the Aberporth Trophy. Roy Macintyre, who was back on the Squadron for another tour, contributes the following to the Squadron's history:

"The 1997 MPC was to be my first event as the new Squadron QWI(P), however, fate – and Kelvin Harris – had other ideas. The task was big and the Squadron had been allocated a total of 19 missiles to fire. Most of the profiles were linked to evaluating the performance of the AIM-9Li, which had just been released into service. The problem for me was that the Falklands plot had been set months prior by Kelvin, and I was only posted in two months before the event. No one noticed that the new QWI(P) was scheduled to be in the South Atlantic during the MPC. Apparently it was too difficult to change and Brian Kemp, the 111 Squadron QWI(P), took over the MPC, much to my disappointment."

Then in September/October came Exercise Dynamic Mix, 43 going to Tanagra in Greece to take part. Just over half the Squadron deployed on this much-enjoyed detachment, and were accommodated in a fantastic hotel across the Bay from the Greek Air Force base near Marathon. The Squadron flew hard all day, returning to party each evening. Flying took the form of missions against F-104s, F-16s, F-4s and Mirage F1s of the Greek Air Force, together with the F-14s of the US Navy. The Greeks proved to be great hosts, arranging trips to Athens to see sights such as the Acropolis. Roy Macintyre recalls this deployment:

"This was hosted by the Greek Air Force and involved several of their bases. 43 Squadron was based at Tanagra, north of Athens, alongside the resident Mirage 2000 squadron. The only other foreign elements I recall being involved were units from the US Sixth Fleet, either off a carrier or based on Crete. We deployed on 23 September and recovered on 10 October. The flying was great and quite quickly ramped up to multi-element missions over a variety of landscapes. I remember missions over the Sparta plains and the mountains to the west near the Adriatic, as well as over the Mediterranean itself. The Greeks were wonderful hosts and we had ample opportunities to do the inevitable 'cultural' visits as well."

In November 1997 there was a full Squadron deployment to utilise the NSACMI (North Sea Air Combat Manoeuvring Instrumentation) Range as well as to strengthen relations with our hosts, the US 493rd Fighter Squadron (The Reapers), at Lakenheath. It took some time for the Squadron members to adjust to operating from 'Little America' in Suffolk! The ATC procedures in particular caught a few of us out. At the end of each week the 493rd held a 'Reaper Call' (their version of one-liners but more focused on flight safety). The person responsible for the biggest gaff of the week got custody of "Spank" the monkey for the next seven days. The Squadron's only 'winner' just happened to be our USAF exchange pilot, John Holdaway! His misdemeanour was running short of fuel and causing chaos in the Lakenheath traffic pattern. Another good story is recalled by Roy Macintyre:

"It was to be a great Friday mission – 7 November 1997. Eight Leuchars F3s were to try and attack a surface HVA [High Value Asset] being defended by eight Leeming F3s. The point was an arbitrary location in the North Sea with a north-south attack axis. I was flying with Andy Bowen (OCW). After the usual feints and bluffs our formation exploded into eight individual aircraft all running for the HVA. A 'kill' was achieved if you reached within one nautical mile of the point without being targeted.

We did that running at Mach 1·1 at 250 feet for the last ten minutes. On our return to base our jubilation was cut short by the authoriser, Squadron Leader Bill Preece, saying that all cockpit tapes were being impounded and an investigation was getting underway. Apparently, Hartlepool nuclear power station had auto-shutdown in response to what was thought to be an earth tremor but was soon established to have been a sonic boom.

Leeming checked their tapes and everyone was clean, so that left us. Andy and I were the only ones to have got anywhere near the south end of the operating area. All eyes shifted to us but I knew that we could not have been the culprits. We checked the map against our position on the tape and the closest we came to the power station was 35 nautical miles, which complied with the approved avoidance distance for supersonic flight even when at altitude. Yet we had been at 250 feet and a boom could not possibly have rolled that far and retained enough energy to cause the shutdown. I knew we were innocent but as we were the only ones to raise our hands, the guns were well and truly aimed at us.

Twenty uncomfortable minutes later a call from Leeming changed everything. In fact one of their aircraft had passed right over the power station at 6,000 feet doing Mach 1·3. That would do it! It was smiles all round when the true culprit became known. He was a former Fighting Cock on Phantoms, who was now Leeming's Station Commander, Group Captain Barry Doggett!"

In January 1998, 43 at last deployed on Exercise Red Flag at Nellis AFB, Las Vegas, famed and much coveted for its tactical training against the USAF in the unrestricted space over the Nevada desert. The Fighting Cocks were selected for this deployment after a long 'drought', thanks in particular to the influence of Wing Commander Ken Thompson, a previous flight commander on 43, by then on the staff at Headquarters 11 Group. In fact for many it was a new experience, although a few old hands had been to Nellis before on Phantoms.

Forty-Three was tasked to be part of Red Air, principally due to the limitations of its weaponry, Skyflash, and took over the aircraft from 111 Squadron. It was also a Night Flag and 43 were not operating with NVGs, although Blue Air was. The Squadron learnt a lot from the exercise both in the air and on the ground, and the delights of Las Vegas were not missed either! It was during this deployment the boys discovered that the Squadron's Italian exchange back-seater, Mario Martorano, was quite a skilled poker player and seemed much at home in the casinos. So much so that he was soon being called 'Don' Martorano out there.

At the end of the exercise, the aircraft were ferried down to Davis Monthan AFB near Tucson, Arizona, where they were handed over to the Leeming Wing for a further US-based exercise.

That June saw Exercise Distant Frontier, again at Eielson AFB, near Fairbanks, Alaska. The Squadron took over the aircraft that had already been deployed and brought them back to the UK after the exercise, via Winnipeg, Bangor Maine and Lajes in the Azores. A particularly successful aspect that emerged during the training was the advantage conferred by the F3's recent introduction of JTIDS (Joint Tactical Information Distribution System) data link. This enabled the Tornados to stay on the ground as long as possible, thereby conserving fuel, while monitoring the air picture being transmitted from the AWACS before choosing the optimum moment to launch against their targets.

Training was conducted against USAF aircraft and RAF Jaguars from Coltishall. Survival training was also carried out in the most realistic of environments, including the rigours of coping with the man-eating mosquitoes of Alaska which proved immune to every type of repellant and quite capable of biting through clothing! Nevertheless, the recreational opportunities in Alaska were enjoyed by all.

Alaska was new territory for most of the boys. They found the terrain around Eielson very different from Nevada but the challenges of countering large target packages were still the same. Although this part of the exercise was RAF-run, Cope Thunder being the USAF-led part, there was a wide variety of units involved, including the F-15 wing at Elmendorf AFB, Anchorage. While it was found that the social life was more 'Northern Exposure' than the Vegas lights, there were plenty of outdoor activities to try including hunting, fishing, white-water rafting, whale watching and all-night golf in the midnight sun. Nearby Fairbanks was also a friendly town. Simon Bryant recalls another incident during the deployment:

"During the exercise a visit by the Leuchars Station Commander, Air Commodore Ray Hodgson, provided further unexpected entertainment. Given his fondness for hot curries, Ray was taken to a nearby steak house in

Fairbanks which prided itself on serving the hottest chilli sauce in the area. Despite being advised to use the sauce sparingly, Ray plunged a chip into the sauce, popped it into his mouth and was literally rendered speechless for ten minutes!

The return trip from Alaska was fraught. We were initially delayed by unserviceability and then suffered extremely bad en-route weather, notably off the east coast of the US where a tanking bracket coincided with the peak of a storm. The intensity of this storm resulted in such violent whiplash during refuelling that I initially thought that my own and my wingman's probes had been snapped off – and at the very edge of our diversion range from a suitable airfield. Happily this proved not to be the case and there was much relief and celebration to mark the subsequent overnight stop in the Azores. There we stayed in the quaintest of hotels, miles from the airfield, displaying a décor evidently unique to the mid-Atlantic! The final leg home was notable for my aircraft's cabin conditioning system becoming stuck on cold and, despite donning all possible clothes in advance, my pilot and I were chilled to the bone when we emerged upon landing!"

Jim Campbell relates:

"Major overseas training detachments were frequent from 1996, with Alaska (Cope Thunder) featuring twice and Canada (Maple Flag) coming later. Adventure training was a constant theme in these detachments to North America, with personnel using their free time to avail themselves of the many opportunities available. The RAF funded various activities but the poor old Physical Training Instructor (PTI) who was on the support staff for Maple Flag had his work cut out trying to sort out the serious applications from the frivolous. Each 'expedition' was given a code name by the applicant, Exercise White Water, for example, is fairly self-explanatory. Exercise Close to the Wind less so. The PTI was given the impression that this was a sailing event whilst in reality those involved allegedly all trotted off to Edmonton for a weekend of drinking and sightseeing. However, the icing on the cake had been the elusive Red Flag at Las Vegas.

Landing in Cyprus

It was an extremely successful time for everyone, the aircrew gaining enormous training value and the groundcrew enjoying enormous partying value. Many personnel took full advantage of the opportunity to visit the nearby Grand Canyon and Hoover Dam, as well as to lose a fortune in the casinos. As the Squadron packed up to come home it was agreed that a postcard should be sent to Pete Legg but, in the midst of all the enjoyment and euphoria, I don't know if it was ever sent."

During September and October 1998, it was off to Cyprus for APC. The aircraft deployed via a fuelling stop and a good Italian breakfast at Pratica di Mare AFB, near Rome. Remarkably, all aircraft launched successfully and no stragglers had been left behind when the Fighting Cocks arrived at Akrotiri.

The Squadron managed to fly a nine-ship formation on 6 October – '. . . just because we could.' Although usually crewed with Flight Lieutenant Helen Gardiner, during this deployment the Boss was flying with Flight Lieutenant Ross Martin who famously forgot that he had one more burst left in his guns and emptied his remaining rounds into the sea, thus considerably reducing his percentage score.

The deployment was the usual cocktail of early starts, banner inspections and afternoons on the beach. This detachment saw the resurrection of the Navigators' Union Dinner, masterminded by Nick Drew and Andy Crumlish, which proved a great success. Even the Akrotiri Station Commander enjoyed it!

Towards the end of the detachment, 43 was joined by Air Chief Marshal Sir John Allison who had come for one last 'hurrah' before retiring from the Service. Roy Macintyre takes up the story of what followed:

"He was with us for a week and wanted to be plain Flying Officer Allison and to be programmed for anything that needed doing. True to his word he resisted the draw of the rest of the station, giving the Station Commander one evening only. He went through an abbreviated gunnery programme, flying with his old ADC from his time as AOC 11 Group, Ray Jones, now the Squadron's EXO. On the last day the Air Chief Marshal went up for an operational shoot and I debriefed his film upon his return. The pictures looked good and I predicted a good score for him.

A relaxed group in front of the Officers' Mess at Leuchars - September 1997.
Standing - Flt Lt Colin Barmby (Int), Fg Off Graham Harvey, Flt Lt Rich Barrow, Flt Lt Mark Pearce, Flt Lt Pete Brombley, Flt Lt Sandy Gordon, Flt Lt John Baldaro (Eng), Flt Lt Martin Jeffries, Flt Lt Ian McCombie, Flt Lt Dave McCallum, Flt Lt Martin Harris, Flt Lt Neil Crawley, Flt Lt Russ Jones, Flt Lt Steve Berg, Flt Lt Helen Gardiner, Flt Lt Matt Thornton
Seated - Flt Lt Phil Jones, Flt Lt Tim Freeman, Flt Lt Roy Macintyre, Sqn Ldr Steve Hayler, Sqn Ldr Phil Luxton, Wg Cdr Simon Bryant, Sqn Ldr Tim Bullement, Sqn Ldr Andy Bowen, Flt Lt Kelvin Harris, Capt John Holdaway USAF, Flt Lt Pete Stopforth

We went outside to mark the banner, where the Boss, EXO and a station photographer were all waiting. When the banner was delivered I unrolled it and started tutting – there were no holes in it. The Boss went white, the EXO nearly fainted, while the photographer put down his camera. The ACM looked surprised too as we both searched the whole length of the banner looking desperately for a purple hole (his colour) – any purple hole! After a few fruitless minutes I pronounced that 'There was no score on the banner, so we had better get the real one out!'

'The ACM clocked immediately what was going on at his expense. Colour returned to the face of the Boss, the EXO started breathing again, and the photographer raised his camera. In fact, the ACM had scored well, but loved having his leg pulled and being back as part of Squadron practical jokes!"

In December 1998 a four-ship formation flypast was flown above London to mark the memorial service for Air Chief Marshal Sir Frederick Rosier GCB CBE DSO, a former Fighting Cock (1936-38), who had died on 10 September. He had flown Hawker Furies with 43, had been a past-president of the 43 Squadron Association, and had also been the last C-in-C of Fighter Command from 1966-68. The Tornados arrived on time and on target, much to the surprise of the (very senior) bomber pilots who were in the congregation at St Clement Danes.

There was a detachment to Coningsby in March 1999, for DACT (Dissimilar Air Combat Training) on the North Sea ACMI Range, versus F-16s of the Royal Netherlands Air Force. In June came a detachment to Marón, near Seville, for training against F-18s of the Spanish Air Force, 43 refuelling en route at St Mawgan.

A detachment to the Czech Republic followed in August, where 43 operated two aircraft out of Prague International Airport. The Tornados flew against the now very aged MiG-21s of the Czech Air Force. Base facilities were rudimentary, complemented by equally basic operating procedures and stereotyped tactics.

Low-level in Scotland

Simon Bryant:

"During this deployment I had the opportunity of a trip in one of the MiGs which meant my career had now gone full circle, from opposing these aircraft during my first tour in Germany on Phantoms, to flying with, and even in, my potential adversaries some 20 years later. 'A hydraulic leak in my Tornado required engineers to be flown out to Prague, albeit with limited success as it turned out, for the problem re-occurred on the return trip home. This caused an unscheduled stop in Germany and more delay for Gavin Parker and me, to add to our already extended stay in Prague."

1999 saw the initial stage of the introduction of AMRAAM to the RAF as a replacement for Skyflash, although this was to continue in service with 43 for some time, and marked a major milestone in the development of the Tornado F3. This achieved a significant improvement in capability, particularly in conjunction with JTIDS which was also continuing to be introduced to the Tornado fleet at this time.

On 2 September 1999, at the end of Simon Bryant's tour, 43 was awarded the Dacre Trophy as the best all-round fighter squadron in 11 Group. However, the parade and lunch were memorable for the absence of the actual trophy. It had been assumed that it would be relinquished by 5 Squadron, the previous holders, and brought to Leuchars by the AOC's ADC! Sadly, this was not the case. However this most prestigious award reflected an immense amount of effort by all in the Squadron and in particular the groundcrew. Ably led by Warrant Officers Jim Dennis and latterly Paul Lofting, they had ensured that the aircrew had the aircraft they needed to achieve the Squadron's tasks. More recollections from Jim Campbell:

"Wing Commander Bryant truly made his mark on the Squadron. He had a rare capacity for remembering people and each member of 43 was known to him by name. Everyone was made to feel that they were playing their part in the overall success and all were given the encouragement needed to go the extra mile. Building on Pete Legg's foundation, he had built a unit that would follow him anywhere and not think twice about it. Under his leadership the Squadron won the Dacre Trophy in September 1999, a prestigious award that certainly enhanced the Fighting Cocks' growing reputation amongst the powers at 11/18 Group, and we were instrumental in introducing and proving an enhanced weapons system for the F3 fleet. We also won the Station Commander's cup and the nicest bit of all was in knowing that we outdid out 'sister' squadron from the other side of the airfield in every respect.

It was a fitting end to his tenure that Wing Commander Bryant was dined out by the Squadron in conjunction with receiving the Dacre Trophy. Rather than having a parade, all personnel, dressed in best blue, attended a formal lunch in the officers' mess. The trophy was (eventually) presented, speeches made and then the Boss was paraded down the road (seated on a flat-top trailer) by his troops to the station rugby club where further festivities lasted until the wee small hours."

Flypasts always generate stories and this one, from Roy Macintyre, is no exception:

"The occasion was a function at the Hydro in Peebles at which the Boss was attending and involved some former WW2 aircrew. I was part of a four-ship flypast being led by Tony Innes and Jon Smith. Tim Bulliment and Martin Harris were deputy lead. All went to plan initially and we arrived at the holding point south of Peebles with about 20 minutes to go. Going round the hold in loose box formation everything was very relaxed, probably too relaxed!

Martin 'Bomber' Harris was a keen caravanner and was busy pointing out to Bully several good caravan sites when, on the final orbit before the push, came the call: 'Lead has a main computer failure, number two – yours!' All of a sudden the formation turned into a wild bucking bronco, left the hold 30° off heading, executed a 60° banked turn back onto track, was now late and the leader was at full power trying to get back on time. I remember making the call: 'Forget the time, hold steady to let us in!' while desperately trying to hold some sort of formation. We arrived on track, a bit late, and not a little flustered, but everyone on the ground thought it was marvellous!"

By August 1999 a new CO designate had already arrived, Wing Commander Paul Colley, 43's third navigator Boss – and he took over the following month. He very soon found that the Squadron was working well and, without any fuss, changed nothing but he did, however, bring his own personality with him. He quickly gained the trust and confidence of the Squadron and engaged equally with all levels of personnel.

Virtually the first task under his leadership was to go to Qatar on Exercise Brave Saker to represent the RAF during 'British Week', which was a high profile flag-waving trip which even HRH Prince Andrew attended, so everyone was on their best behaviour. Air Commodore Ray Dixon, himself a former Fighting Cock, was in

Wg Cdr Paul Colley is welcomed by the Station Commander Air Cdre Raymond Hodgson

overall charge and seemed impressed with the Squadron's behaviour and work ethos.

As the Squadron approached the turn of the century and a new millennium, this deployment to the Middle East on a defence diplomacy mission was serendipity. With operations imminent over southern Iraq, Brave Saker, and then Exercise Desert Thunder to Jordan, allowed both engineers and crews to get an early feel for how the aircraft in its latest weapon and software fit would perform in the desert heat. It also provided crews with invaluable experience in practising dissimilar air combat against Arab pilots flying modern fighters. The Qataris were immensely proud of their new Mirage fighter and the Jordanians proved to be both good hosts and tough opposition in their Mirage F1s and early model F-16s. Overall, it was quite a show, with the concurrent detachment of E-3D Airborne Early Warning aircraft and Hawk trainers, plus several chances to engage socially with both the local and expatriate communities. Prince Andrew took the stand for a multinational flypast led by 43 Squadron to mark the Exercise in Qatar. The CO hosted the Prince, wearing a trademark resplendent black and white waistcoat and had to steadfastly rebuff rude banter from the Prince about it.

Again Jim Campbell records this story:

"It was during the detachment to Qatar that Corporal John Farren, a sooty (engine fitter), laid the foundations of becoming a squadron legend. Also known as 'Johnny Farrino', he was a tall, stocky and bombastic character. He had an opinion on everything and took great umbrage if anyone dared to disagree. He was a keen rugby player who decided he was going to lead the Squadron team against an ex-pat side in Qatar, even before he was selected to go! He cajoled and bullied guys into signing up to play and when the big day arrived he led the lads to the local rugby club ground, ensuring that everyone was in the right frame of mind.

The Squadron had its own kit that travelled everywhere with us, used for a variety of sports. However, Johnny being Johnny had his own. This included scrum cap, shoulder pads, body

A gathering to mark Helen Gardiner's last flight with the Squadron - December 1999
Rear - Russ Martin, Jon Meikle, Matt Nicholas, Nick Stringer, unknown
Middle - Tim Freeman, Pete Stopforth, Doug Cochrane, John Cunningham, Kev McCarry, Dan Constable, Mark Graham, Darren Squires, Jez Poulter, Tim Nolan, John Lyle, Gus MacDonald
Front - Neil Crawley, Wg Cdr Paul Colley, Helen Gardiner

armour, elbow and knee protectors plus shin pads. Fully kitted out, John lined up the team and in full view of all the spectators led them out of the pavilion. With a beaming grin on his face he ran for about four paces before collapsing in agony with a twisted ankle. I don't think there was a dry eye as this man with more body armour than a knight crusader writhed around on the ground clutching his leg.

On completion of the Qatar element of the detachment, the Squadron was sent to Jordan for Exercise Desert Thunder, perhaps to let Saddam Hussein know that the RAF could wander around the world and visit his neighbours at any time. This was another successful visit with the CO demonstrating his diplomatic skills and flair to the hosts. They were impressed by the Squadron's flying and organised trips to the Dead Sea and to the city of Petra, both of which were appreciated greatly."

Paul Colley recalls:

"The mood on the Squadron necessarily became more serious as it worked up to its first deployment on Operation BOLTON, the Iraqi no-fly zone air policing operation which had gained in intensity in the wake of the increased air campaign, notably against Iraqi SAM and triple-A targets, which had commenced in late 1998. Intense training against simulated surface and air-to-air missile threats, much of it at night using the latest generation of night vision equipment, punctuated the early days of the new millennium. After two in-theatre familiarisation sorties with Flight Lieutenant Johnny Miekle in the front seat, I led the Squadron over the border into Iraq on 18 February 2000 on the first of many sorties by 43.

These typically included long and often dull transits to and from the Squadron's Saudi base to Iraq. However, activity became more intense during the air-to-air refuelling and force marshalling phases around Kuwait, before the large packages of US and UK aircraft crossed into Iraq. Missions were usually to protect high value reconnaissance assets as they monitored Iraqi force dispositions. Night missions were particularly sporting, given the need to safely de-conflict the large numbers of aircraft operating in small volumes of airspace with no lights on. The occasional SAM engagement or Iraqi fighter launch spiced up the detachment, but thankfully, enemy engagements were generally sporadic and ineffective.

The Millennium reunion was always set to be a big event in the Squadron's history and the early meetings to discuss it with the Association were a glorious mixture of overwhelming enthusiasm, usually with Willie Marr front and centre, and stoic pragmatism, part Sir Peter Bairsto and part OC 43, who were both keen that the Squadron did not overreach either imagination or finances. Yet the combined effort of Squadron and Association pulled some big rabbits out of the hats, including the money that would allow 43 to celebrate in style at Stirling. In a weekend loaded with great fun, including an impressive flying display at Leuchars topped by Rod Dean's Hunter F6A XF515 'R' in its old 43 Squadron colours (operated by Kennet Aviation as G-KAXF), the dinner in the Great Hall at Stirling Castle stood out above all. As all those attending stepped up onto the Castle ramparts before dinner to watch a Squadron flypast, it was evident that the weather had closed in. Showers were straddling the anticipated approach route and drizzle was falling onto the Castle. Sir Tony Bagnall leaned over and asked the Boss whether the boys would get through. It looked pretty dodgy, but he said that they would. There could not have been a prouder man in Scotland than Paul Colley when Squadron Leader Tony Gent led his four-ship of Tornados out of the gloom, wingmen tucked in as tight as ticks, on track and on time. As everyone walked back in for dinner to the skirl of the pipes, the atmosphere was electric. What a night!"

Rewards for the time spent away on operations came in the form of superb training detachments, first in the spring to Exercise Maple Flag at Cold Lake in Canada, and then to a NATO 'fighter meet' in September at Karup in Denmark. The latter was memorable for its detachment of Polish fighter pilots in their Sukhoi SU-17 fighters. It was a poignant moment for the Fighting Cocks to be flying again alongside the Poles, who had been liberated once more, this time from Soviet rule. Paul Colley:

"The occasion was marked in a short, but wonderful exchange of speeches and dodgy Polish hooch at a post-exercise social gathering. There was a comic moment when, during the exercise, the Poles arrived overhead the airfield from a less-than-conventional direction to join the air traffic pattern. After being lambasted on the airwaves by air traffic control, the leader replied in a heavy Polish accent, 'Repeat please!' This immediately evoked in the minds of all British crews airborne in the pattern at the time, a memory of the very same radio call made in the film The Battle of Britain, in which a frustrated squadron commander had chastised his Polish aircrew with a plea to, 'Stop that Polish chit-chat!' At Karup, several fingers hovered over radio transmit buttons ready to re-

With groundcrew standing behind, 43 Squadron gather for the photographer - late 2001
Rear -Flt Lt G Williams, Flt Lt K Jewitt, Flt Lt D Clarke, Flt Lt R Elworthy, Flt Lt M Lea, Flt Lt S Sutherland, Flt Lt M Higgins, Flt Lt J Poulter, Flt Lt M Pymm, Flt Lt A Bruce, Flt Lt D Cochrane, Flt Lt M Frost, Flt Lt A Lyle, Flt Lt K Harris
Centre - Sqn Ldr K Peet
Front vee - Flt Lt F MacDonald, Flt Lt A Conner, Sqn Ldr P Taylor, Sqn Ldr M Cobb, Gp Capt P Colley, Sqn Ldr C Stevens, Capt P Frigault, Maj T Bouleay, Flt Lt G Hart, Flt Lt M Eliott
(MoD (RAF) Crown Copyright)

live the moment, but admirable restraint probably avoided a diplomatic incident, although not some hearty chuckling inside the cockpits."

On the Canadian detachment, the squadron was accommodated in Bonnyville, a one horse town some 30 miles from the RCAF base at Cold Lake. Johnny Farren starred once again as Jim Campbell remembers:

"Yet again Johnny decided to lead the rugby team to glory but this time he had a secret weapon – a brand new scrum cap, sent to him all the way from New Zealand. If the All Blacks wore them then Johnny was going to be invincible in his. The guys, aware of John's frailties organised a sweepstake to see how long he would last. Everyone had money on him withdrawing before the end but he confounded us all and lasted the full 80 minutes. Even he laughed when he was told about the sweep.

Then he took his scrum cap off and as he did so, most of his scalp came with it, leaving him with a very raw-looking head. What he hadn't realised was that his pride and joy had been rubbing away at the top of his head, amply lubricated by sweat. As the match went on the chafing got worse and the skin blistered and stuck to his cap. It looked extremely painful and a couple of days later one SNCO nearly got thumped for trying to make him wear his beret. Of course, the Lineys found it most entertaining, pretending to slap John's head and seeing what sort of reaction they would get."

The shrinking size of the RAF in the post

Cold War era had already resulted in an amalgamation of 11 Group with 18 Group, the former Maritime Group, in 1996. However the turn of the millennium was to witness the final demise of 11 Group as it was subsumed totally within 1 Group, which effectively became the sole operational command of the RAF. Fighters would no longer have their own distinct Group. Indeed, 43 would ultimately outlive the iconic Bentley Priory - the famous headquarters of Fighter Command during the Battle of Britain - as an operational unit.

The beginning of 2000 saw another operational deployment to Saudi Arabia for the Iraq air-policing missions and yet another rewarding training detachment to Exercise Red Flag at Nellis Air Force Base, in Las Vegas, Nevada. This famous exercise lived up to its expectations with some outstanding flying and a little time to relax. The CO led a group of squadron motorcycle enthusiasts in a six-ship Harley Davidson motorcycle convoy down the Las Vegas strip. He then drummed for the squadron band in the officers' club, where Flight Lieutenant Rob Elworthy, in a typically over-exuberant leap off a table after his virtuoso guitar solo, managed to – quite literally – bring the club roof down when the neck of his guitar momentarily jammed in the ceiling tiles. As Paul Colley reflected: 'How we laughed on the way to the hospital.'

The CO and the Squadron enjoyed another successful year in 2001, Paul Colley leaving in November.

Wing Commander Rich Powell took over from Paul Colley, arriving in early December 2001. His arrival coincided with an emphasis on RAF fast-jet units achieving their annual flying hours task (AFT) as defined in the RAF Management Plan, the pressure coming through the Air Staff from the C-in-C and HQ 1 Group. Meeting this requirement, which was based on a crew flying task (CFT) of 18·5 hours a month per pilot, required a significant increase in the flying hours achieved by 43 Sqn and other Tornado F3 squadrons over previous years. This challenge, especially allowing for periods of poor weather and aircraft availability, required changes to the Squadron's customary methods of operating. Aircrew and groundcrew planning, procedures and processes were reviewed and changed from an average planned daily sortie rate of 10 sorties per day to 16 sorties per day.

January and February 2002 saw fairly routine flying but in March the squadron was sent off on Exercise Cajun Combat to Eglin AFB, Florida on the 18th. Here they flew air combat against the resident USAF F-15Cs and against Canadian F-18s that were also detached there at that time. Jim Campbell:

"At Eglin the idea was to practise scenarios with the Americans, seeing if we could survive going into battle with them on our side. As luck would have it, it was also their spring break while we were there so I am sure you can imagine the excitement of the lads as they were dropped into a seaside resort full of young women. A few had the opportunity to visit New Orleans and the sights and sounds of Bourbon Street will remain with me until dementia kicks in.

The other memorable event was sending two aircraft and a small support party to Chile for the Santiago Airshow. The only blot on an otherwise successful trip was when one of the aircrew managed to drop a pocketful of loose change in the cockpit of his Tornado. Time was tight and the man in question had no idea how much money he had been carrying. The armourers, led by Chief Technician Steve Goodhall, did a splendid job retrieving everything that they could and without any support equipment at their disposal."

Back home again in early April, things were pretty routine until a Staneval was called in late May, and then in mid-June the APC in Cyprus came round again.

The trip out was via Gioa del Colle in Italy, and the Squadron took nine Tornados. The camp lasted until the beginning of June after which the Squadron returned to begin working-up for a deployment to the southern Iraqi no-fly zone as part of Operation RESINATE, the UK component of Operation SOUTHERN WATCH. This consisted of Tornado GR4s based at Ali Al Salem in Kuwait crewed by 12 Squadron, and 43's Tornado F3s, based at Prince Sultan Air Base, south of Riyadh, Saudi Arabia.

The deployment lasted until September, the Squadron flying into the southern no-fly zone with two aircraft at a time as part of the regular F3 tasking. To ensure two aircraft in the no-fly zone, four aircraft would normally be prepared. Three would get airborne and during transit, whilst still on the Saudi side of the border, one aircraft would turn for home while the remaining two would proceed on to the tanker. These were quite long missions, some being 7 to 10 hours in duration. That month, for example, the Boss flew 44 day hours and 37 at night, 82 hours overall.

Altogether there were perhaps 30 fighters in theatre flying these surveillance and containment missions. At this time 43 Squadron had three exchange officers on strength, Captain Laurant Bouchon, a French Mirage 2000 pilot, Captain Paul Frigault, a Canadian F-18 pilot, and Major Tom 'Moses' Bouleay, a USAF F-15 pilot. However, apart from the CO and his senior men, Squadron Leaders Paul Taylor, Mark Cobb, Chris Stevens, Phil Beach and Tony Gent, plus navigators Flight Lieutenant Kelvin Harris and Squadron Leader Colin Wills, virtually everyone else on the squadron was a first tourist, which constituted about 65% dilution, posing some supervisory issues. Squadron Leader Jon Smith, who arrived in May 2002 and would take over as Weapons Leader from Phil Beach, recorded:

"Certainly the emphasis was very much on the routine of flying into the no-fly zone and the entire F3 force was well into the process by then. It became apparent by about November that this would escalate in 2003.

We were asking more of our junior crews than would have traditionally been the case maybe 5-10 years earlier and a number of them were thrust into operational flying ahead of normal time. So we had to take a different approach to supervision to allow these guys to get on with things – take more risks – and gave them responsibility a good deal earlier than would previously have been the case."

In order to help the pressure to improve sortie rates once back at Leuchars, the squadron started introducing 'Hotpit' refuelling, beginning in December 2002, something that was new to the whole F3 fleet. Crews would come back from one sortie to refuel before immediately re-launching with the crew remaining in the aircraft. Initially refuelling was limited to one aircraft, then with more 'hotpit' experience the navigator would change over and later the whole crew would be replaced. Normally the aircraft would have been handed over to the engineers after landing and then taken back by the aircrew. However now it was held onto by the aircrew and then flown again immediately which paid significant dividends in improved sortie rates. Normally there would have been a morning wave and then an afternoon wave, so this new procedure helped speed things up and enabled more flights between these two waves.

Another way of increasing the flying hours, and one that engendered increasingly improved relations with 43's sister squadron, *Tremblers* (often referred to as the 'Girls' School'), across the other side of the airfield, was when the squadrons started to support each other. For instance if 43 couldn't complete various work-ups due to a lack of people or aircraft, the two squadrons would combine resources. As Rich Powell recalls:

"When we deployed on ops over the no-fly zone in Iraq, those personnel left behind would go across to Treble One where the flying was shared between the two squadrons. Equally, when they went away, their remaining crews would come across to 43. This sort of co-operation brought us together, certainly on the aircrew side, and overall things worked well."

During Rich's time in command the squadron got permission to build a Fighting Cocks bar on the domestic part of 43's HAS site and this opened every Thursday evening for all ranks plus the odd party at weekends. Good relationships were also forged by the annual groundcrew versus aircrew golf competitions which were taken very seriously by both sides. The groundcrew always won thanks to some generous handicapping by Corporal 'Hovis' Brown, but then the result was completely forgotten at the subsequent dinner and drinks.

It had become clear late in 2002 that things were going to pick-up in respect of operations in the Gulf. So from December the Squadron began more RESINATE-type flying activities. In January 2003 the Squadron flew to Azraq in Jordan for Exercise Desert Thunder and that was when the word came down that plans were being finalised and that 43 was likely to be involved along with 'Tremblers' in what would become Gulf War 2. It had also become obvious while in Jordan that there were a considerable number of other preparations taking place at Azraq, in that bit of Jordan that sticks out towards Iraq on the eastern side. Preparations were going on for something much bigger, and included the arrival of several other units. Jon Smith:

"Clearly, with half the Squadron, and notably the Executives, out in Jordan on the end of a mobile telephone we were soon talking about many things down an insecure line, including how we were operating and supporting Tremblers on the Operation TELIC push." TELIC was the UK codeword for Gulf War 2 or the Iraq War as it was to become known.

Squadron Leader Bill Preece had joined 43 not long after Rich Powell had taken over, and was the new Executive Officer. Fortunately he had the benefit of about six weeks with his predecessor, Paul Taylor, before he left so had the unique situation of being able to sit back and watch what went on. Not long after Bill finally took over as EXO, the Boss deployed and told Bill that the squadron elements remaining at

Leuchars were all his. It was a great responsibility but a huge opportunity for him. Wing Commander Powell:

"Back at Leuchars, the remaining crews were focused on practising profiles for countering Iraqi aircraft and how to combat surface-to-air missiles. Both received considerable emphasis.

We finally ended up with 18 crews, 12 of which were provided by Treble One and six by 43. We began by deploying by VC10 from 24 February. When we got to Akrotiri, we had to sit on the ground waiting for clearance to cross Saudi airspace for some time, in fact until 1 March when we were finally allowed to depart for Prince Sultan Air Base.

There was a lot of uncertainty, a bit of apprehension, but everyone was trained and comfortable with the aeroplane. The defensive systems we had on the F3 were pretty good and we had JTIDS – the Joint Tactical Information and Distribution System - so we were all pretty well geared up for operations' Jon Smith adds: 'It was all very uncertain, but that which we could control we were absolutely confident with because of our training. In the event, all the analysis of what we thought the enemy was going to do turned out to be very wide of the mark." Rich Powell continues:

"Pre-Operation TELIC missions began for me personally on 4 March. At that stage, we were still flying missions in accordance with Op RESINATE orders and Special Instructions (SPINS) and we hadn't had clearance to transition to Gulf War 2, so we were initially still working to the normal policing ROE (Rules of Engagement), whilst patrolling the no-fly zone.' (Powell's pilot was Martin Higgins, the second aircraft was crewed by Moses Bouleay and Kiwi Sutherland.)

My recollection is that at the time we were gearing up for what became the Shock and Awe Offensive. This was where the air-to-air and air-to-ground engagement was supposed to start. I think that was on Friday 21 March. Prior to that, on the Wednesday, the ROE changed from RESINATE ROE, to full-war ROE. The 37th Parallel line was then removed, which we had to stay south of until then, and it was 43 crews that were the first Coalition aircraft to cross that line and go forward to set up a CAP. It was that night that intelligence indicated that Saddam Hussein and his two sons were in down-town Baghdad, having a meal in a restaurant. Somewhere the decision was made to try to target them.

We were briefed only that some Special

Moving out on Op TELIC the Tornados were refuelled by 216 Squadron TriStars

Forces activity was planned on the ground of the western desert and to expect to see some flashes and explosions. However, there was an air-to-ground attack in Baghdad to target Saddam and his sons, and as it happens, they did not get them. 43's CAP that night, was some way west of Baghdad and we saw a lot of AAA and SAMs being fired. Then on the Friday the Shock and Awe offensive began for real. 43 was up again that night. Among the crews were the two Flight Commanders, Squadron Leader Mark Cobb (OC 'A' Flight) and Squadron Leader, Chris Stevens (OC 'B' Flight), OC Weapons, Squadron Leader Jon Smith, together with Moses Bouleay, Martin Higgins, Richard Powell, Colin Wills, Gavin Littlechild, 'Kiwi' Sutherland, Neil Whitehead, Darren Squires, Gus Hogg and Dave Clark."

The remaining crews at Leuchars from both 43 and 111 Squadrons were earmarked as the

A Tornado deploys flares

Tornado F3 Op TELIC replacement unit under the delegated command of Bill Preece. The additional responsibility at home included the need to maintain two aircraft on QRA every day. Because of the political situation at the time, two of the Squadron's exchange officers, Paul Frigault and Laurant Rouchon, were denied

Refuelling from a USAF KC-135 tanker

involvement in TELIC by their respective governments. Quite naturally they were very frustrated at this decision but that's the way it was. However while most of the Squadron was away the Prime Minister, Tony Blair, visited Leuchars and was delighted to find the squadron's French exchange pilot defending the UK on QRA.

There was naturally a lot of anxiety amongst

Boom man's view

wives, girlfriends and families about their men in theatre, so Bill Preece was also having to cope with this sort of support work too. Again, mobile phones were useful. Bill remembers:

"There was one really awkward situation when *Sky News* broke the story that a Tornado crew had been shot down. As might be imagined the telephone calls I started receiving were from concerned wives, etc, – 'Is it one of ours?' Well, of course, we didn't have any way of knowing so we went through a fairly difficult day until we were finally told it had been a GR4 crew sadly lost to a 'blue-on-blue' error by a US Patriot missile battery.

We also suffered a couple of anti-war demonstrations at Leuchars, one of which

Flt Lt Martin "Higgy" Higgins and Wg Cdr Rich Powell beside ZE161 'UU' "Foghorn Leghorn".

highlighted the fact that we couldn't police everything when we had public footpaths and so on, running down the side of the base. Someone managed to break in and damage one of the aircraft and another incident occurred when peace protesters just sprayed paint over various pieces of ground equipment.

It is also worth recording that there was great co-operation between the amalgamated 43 and 111 at Leuchars. Wing Commander Trevor Field was OC Admin and he and his team

It's getting dark - a Tornado about to get fuel from a USAF KC-10 Extender

ensured everyone knew what was going on."

Wing Commander Rich Powell had one moment of concern as he recalls:

"On 13 March we were out towards the western desert when I had an engine failure and had to divert to Ali Al Salem in Kuwait. When flying these long missions over the Iraq desert we were working the engines pretty hard and we had a couple of engine failures which concentrate the mind somewhat when there is a long transit to the nearest friendly air base.

Squadron Leader Chris Stevens also had to

land at Kuwait on one sortie and had only just touched down when a short range ballistic missile from the Iraqis landed on the airfield. He quickly put on his gas mask but although everything was well it proved to be an unexpected welcome to Kuwait!"

Although the war for 43 was fairly brief it was intense while it lasted. Jon Smith:

"We had a good working relationship between our two squadrons. To single out one guy who gave a lot to the operation, poor old Flight Lieutenant Kelvin Harris worked in the mission planning cell for about 20 hours a day, constantly, while we were in theatre. The mission cycle was so long, for some sorties were up to ten hours in duration, that crews literally did not have enough time in a day to plan their own missions to a large degree. So most of the planning and admin before flying was done by Kelvin and his chaps in the cell, all of whom did an excellent job.

It was an hour or so to transit from Prince Sultan Base into Iraq so, with air-to-air refuelling provided by RAF and USAF tankers, sorties were obviously lengthened. Reporting for duty some three hours prior to take off, then debriefing after landing, resulted in a 15-16 hour day."

Greetings from the pilot!

Chief Tech Jim Campbell was in theatre too and remembers the war period for its very hard work with the professionalism of the ground crews standing out in particular. A couple of his memories from Saudi include guess who? Yep, Johnny Farrino:

"Still keen to impress, John was a regular visitor to the base gym. Wanting to show his prowess to the American ladies, he frequently jumped aboard the jogging machine and ran for miles. Boredom becomes a factor so he decided to buy a Walkman. That night he went to the gym as usual and prepared for his run. After selecting his music he started running, placing the Walkman on the machine's control panel. Unfortunately for him it vibrated loose and fell to the floor. John instinctively bent down to retrieve it and that's where it all went wrong. As he bent forward, his legs went backwards, swiftly followed by the rest of him. The treadmill spat him rearwards into the dumb-bell storage rack. An almighty crash followed as the rack and its contents fell upon the crumpled form at its base. Girls looked on in amazement as an apparition appeared from the pile of debris. They were even more amazed at the cheers of derision that greeted John as he emerged from his metal cocoon. It is one of life's certainties that if you are in an embarrassing situation there will be an audience of Lineys to witness your discomfort.

Unabashed, a couple of days later Johnny visited the pool. Once more he decided to impress the ladies. Speedos pulled up and chest puffed out, he took a dive from the side. Executed perfectly, the only fault with his performance was his lack of perception of the pool's width. There was a splashing sound, bubbles erupted from the surface and the water took on a pinkish tinge. John emerged to a terrific sound of applause, clutching his head and wondering just how he had managed to crack his napper on the far side of the pool. Distance judgement obviously was not a strong point and yes, you guessed it, more ammunition for the Lineys."

The Squadron returned to the UK in dribs and drabs during April and then began a stand-down period, with everyone finally getting back to work on about 19 May. The last of 43 Squadron to leave were Jon Smith and Dave Clark, along with the Boss of 111, Wing Commander Rob Birch, and his navigator Squadron Leader Martin Parker.

On 26 June, 43 Squadron was asked to perform a flypast over Queen Victoria School at

Homeward bound!

Dunblane, and the following month took part in a major air defence exercise (Exercise Nomad) carried out over the North Sea, operating from RAF Waddington from 2 to 24 July. Bill Preece had been the detachment commander, and it was the first time the Squadron had been able to use all the AMRAAM and ASRAAM tactics that Jon Smith had worked up. It was a huge exercise with aircraft from the Dutch, Belgian, Norwegian, French, Swiss and US air forces involved. More routine activities continued in August with missile firings at MPC.

During the previous year the Squadron had started to develop an AMRAAM and later ASRAAM capability but this really kicked in during October 2003. Tactically speaking this was a great step forward for the Tornado and had everyone occupied from then until early 2004.

Jon Smith remembers that aircraft were being modified to take the new weapons at a very slow rate and everyone was mindful that these changes would be needed before the work-up for Maple Flag at Cold Lake, Canada in May. It fundamentally changed the way the crews fought with the aircraft so it was an important period. There were new tactics to develop and Jon was working hard on these, co-operating with all the other F3 squadrons regarding the use of these new weapons. Maple Flag began by crews going out at the end of April and everything was in place by the start on 17 May. The Squadron took over the aircraft that had been used by Treble One, the 43 Squadron crews flying out on commercial airliners, which then flew 111's boys back. While these earlier work-ups were going on, the Boss had a pleasant interlude with the RAF's display team, as he relates:

"On 27 February every year the Red Arrows invite Station Commanders and fast jet Squadron Commanders to go and fly with them. This particular year it ended up with Martin Higgins and myself going with our Station Commander. Higgins was later selected to join the Red Arrows when his tour with 43 ended, so he did well for himself. In all seven flights were made and I flew on four of them."

Armament Practice Camp in Cyprus from 19 September ended with the chance to fly a Diamond Nine. It was the SEngO's 64 thousand dollar bet to get all nine aircraft working at the same time and he achieved it on 1 October. On that date nine Tornados flew in formation over Akrotiri and Episkopi. It was led by Chris Stevens with the Boss in the back seat.

The next day the Squadron conducted a firepower demonstration along the cliffs at Akrotiri and on the 3rd flew back to Leuchars via Italy, all on the same day. Shortly after their return Major Tom Bouleay, the US exchange pilot, returned to the USA and was replaced by Major Ivan Sudac – generally known as the 'Dragon' – a huge fellow, also referred to by brave people as 'Shrek'. A smallish, unassuming sort of chap!! Sadly, Tom was later to be killed in an F-15 crash at Nellis in 2008 while commanding the 65th Aggressor Squadron.

By late September onwards there was a further emphasis on trying to generate more sorties and flying hours. Aircraft were fitted with external fuel tanks, thus limiting the full performance of the aircraft and some crews initially missed out on certain types of sorties. The Squadron had therefore to work in phases and coordinate a mixture of aircraft configurations in order to cover all the training needed. Accordingly, when they were asked to fly a Diamond Nine before Christmas, they only finally managed it on 18 December. It was not publicised in case it couldn't be achieved, but once it had been flown the Boss was able to give the engineers the OK to start their Christmas break. Jon Smith was in one of the Tornados:

"The 'nine' made rendezvous over Bell Rock and then flew to Leuchars, then to the back of St Andrews, and finally came round south to north, over Treble One's dispersal site – just to rub it in a bit – then roared over our own dispersal. Apparently, as we came in low over *Tremblers'* area, their CO, Wing Commander Rob Birch (himself a former Fighting Cock), was just crewing out of his jet, having had a problem on the ground – that rubbed it in even further!"

There was another significant development emerging. Jon Smith further relates:

"At this time we were busy enhancing a relationship with Stirling town (which was soon to achieve city status) where the Squadron had been formed back in 1916. The Provost, Tommy Brooks, had been trying to see if there was any

The Diamond Nine

possibility of getting the Freedom of the Town for 43. The next Provost, Colin O'Brien and his wife Elspeth, were then invited to Leuchars for a dining-in night and towards the end of the evening the Squadron's two fighting cockerels were put on the top table. One of the birds became mesmerised by one of the candelabras and just sat there, rear-end facing directly at Mrs O'Brien, who unknown to us, although that soon became very clear, had a phobia about birds! It was suddenly noticed that she was sitting, seemingly frozen solid, with eyes wide open, staring at the cockerel's behind. Rich Powell:

"Anyway it didn't do the Squadron any lasting harm and later, at the time of the Queen's Golden Jubilee, I went across to Stirling Town Hall, to represent the Squadron during a visit from Her Majesty The Queen. Out of that it was eventually agreed that the Squadron would indeed be given the Freedom of Stirling, although when that happened I had left 43."

Bill Preece also recalls the time the Freedom was announced:

"When it was finally announced, the Boss and the Squadron were away in Canada, so I was asked to represent the Squadron, having only just left on posting to Headquarters 1 Group. I attended the annual Association Dinner at the RAF Club in May, and made the announcement to everyone present."

Mention of the annual Association Dinner at the RAF Club, brings to mind stories by Rich Powell and Jon Smith:

RP - "Each year the 43 Squadron Association appreciated the Squadron being represented at these dinners and also liked to have the Squadron Standard brought too. However, getting this from Leuchars to central London by air, via an EasyJet flight, was never that easy."

JS - "I remember one year arriving at the RAF Club as the taxi drew up outside – with the custodians flying the Squadron Standard out of the cab window."

Another story from Bill Preece recounts a similar episode of self-promotion by 43 back at home:

"At Leuchars there was one particular blast wall on site which just happened to face directly towards Treble One's area. The Station Commander, our former CO Simon Bryant, although hard strapped for cash for maintenance projects, was happy to provide paint and brushes if we wanted to paint this wall. So we decided to promote our identity, and one day we painted the whole wall in big black and white checks. The wall is about 20 feet high and perhaps 30 feet wide. As one is driving back from St Andrews you can see it pretty well. This, of course, was like a red rag to a bull for *Tremblers* and they tried to sneak across to repaint it – in black and yellow squares, but they never really succeeded."

Rich Powell's final sorties with his squadron came when they flew the aircraft to pre-position them at Langley Air Force Base for 11 Squadron on 28 May 2004. He then had to get home in order to hand over to the new CO, Wing Commander Phil Beach. By the time everyone had got back from Maple Flag, Phil had taken over the helm. Soon afterwards the Squadron was again awarded the Dacre Trophy, as the best fighter squadron in the RAF.

In April Bill Preece had also completed his tour and had been posted to 1 Group to take one of the F3 desks. One thing he found once ensconced as a staff officer was that the feedback from all four operational F3 squadrons at that time was that 43 Squadron was streets and streets ahead of the others. Rich Powell's initial task when he took command of the Squadron, had been to increase flying hours. In the financial year 2003-4, the Squadron had flown 4,200 hours, which was probably a record, so when he left the statistics had improved and the crews were certainly getting the hours in. This was quite an achievement given the number of 'young' crews on strength who had all done terrifically well. He had also taken them all through RESINATE, the Iraq War, the introduction of AMRAAM and ASRAAM and had secured the award of the Freedom of the City of Stirling.

The Squadron also played a major part in supporting the other ceremonial and social activities of the Station Commander in his role as Air Officer, Scotland. They flew Sir Fred 'The Shred' Goodwin, then Chief Executive of RBS, just one of a wider group of VIPs that supported the RAF. They also forged close links with the Police College at Kincardine in the same context as well as supporting a number of charities, notably 'Heartstone' which provides funds to educate and develop disadvantaged children.

Wing Commander Powell took his leave of 43 in May 2004 and was subsequently appointed an OBE in recognition of his time as OC 43 Squadron. Squadron Leader Colin 'Wiki' Wills was also appointed an MBE after passing 4,000 flying hours on the F3 and Bill Preece received a C-in-C's Commendation for Meritorious Service, altogether a clear reflection of yet another successful period in the history of the Fighting Cocks.

CHAPTER 34

Gloria Sine Finis

WING COMMANDER Phil Beach took command in June 2004. He was of course no stranger to 43, having been the Squadron's weapons instructor under both Paul Colley and Rich Powell between 2000 and 2002. Soon after, the Squadron headed to Cyprus in late September with a potentially busy few months ahead of it, notably 43's selection as the UK's lead unit for a NATO commitment to provide Air Defence from Lithuania for the newly-joined members of NATO. Britain had not yet made a formal offer but the new OC 'B' Flight, Squadron Leader Dan Storr, had already completed a reconnaissance of the likely bases in Lithuania – choosing a substantial former Soviet Union facility.

As the Cyprus detachment loomed, the Boss made the decision to continue with the APC deployment whilst continuing parallel preparations for the new NATO commitment. He was particularly keen to get to Cyprus as a one week air-to-air combat training exercise had been arranged with the Egyptians. The nine Tornados arrived at Akrotiri without a hitch and prepared for the exercise.

On the other side of the Mediterranean, the Squadron had forward-deployed two officers to liaise with the Egyptian opposition. The first was the equally new EXO, Squadron Leader David Scott, selected for his attention to detail and no-nonsense manner. The second was a first tourist pilot, Flight Lieutenant Adam Rogers, chosen primarily for his appearance – just a fez short of the complete package, as someone observed in the crew room.

The Squadron performed excellently in the exercise, flying from Cyprus to airspace south of Alexandria and recovering back to Akrotiri each day without missing a sortie. This gave the Squadron some excellent AIM-120 training ahead of the more routine air-to-air gunnery practise that is the hallmark of Cyprus detachments. The gunnery progressed smoothly but, as the detachment neared the end, the Boss took a call from Headquarters, informing him that the Squadron was to deploy to Lithuania within days. Leaving Squadron Leader Al Dodds, OC 'A' Flight, to execute recovery of the main party, Phil Beach recovered with a small cadre of crews to oversee the final preparations for the NATO QRA deployment.

On 14 October, nine Tornados of 43 Squadron became airborne simultaneously, as three fully-armed aircraft took off from Leuchars en-route to Lithuania and a six-ship recovery from Akrotiri to the UK took place. The Lithuanian detachment lasted six weeks, following which 43 handed over the UK role to 25 Squadron. During this time, most of the Squadron's aircrew and groundcrew rotated through a detachment that got little press coverage in the UK but Operation SOLSTICE made Squadron Leader Storr a household name, albeit in the suburbs of Riga!

Night servicing under canvas during Op SOLSTICE

Jim Campbell recalls the first few months following Phil's arrival:

"As an old boy, Phil Beach had recent first-hand knowledge of the Squadron and he soon started to make his mark, moulding the outfit the way he wanted it to be. We had proved ourselves to be more than capable of meeting our operational commitments and high on his agenda was raising the profile of the Squadron. He was fortunate in as much as his tenure coincided with some big and notable events.

Providing the UK's QRA presence in Lithuania had to be just about top of the list. We were tasked with taking over this vital protection role and, even though we were heavily committed with other deployments, we rose to the challenge with our customary 'get up and get on with it' attitude. A party was duly assembled and despatched to the wastelands of the Baltic, setting up a suitable operating environment for the aircraft, although the facilities were somewhat limited, and making friends with the locals. Although I wasn't personally there, by all accounts the Squadron achieved both targets – in Spades. Tales filtered back of a truly work hard, play hard ethos from the groundcrew and an exceptionally professional approach from the aircrew.

While this was going on we were also involved with recovering aircraft from an APC in Cyprus and supporting the Tactical Leadership Programme (TLP) deployment in Belgium. As might be imagined, both manpower and airframes were at a premium, the latter being in high demand by 111 Squadron and ourselves because the now aged jets were requiring more and more maintenance, and manpower was being depleted as the RAF redundancy programme progressed.

The Boss had his work cut out trying to meet all the demands that were being placed on us, but manage it he did and although there were a few grumbles, the morale of the troops remained surprisingly high. Amidst any busy periods, the CO always found the time to come to the groundcrew side and chat with the boys. He would then venture into the Trade Manager's office for coffee and sanctuary. It was a nice feeling to be involved in some of the policy making and knowing that, as a TM, you had made a significant contribution to the continuing success of the Squadron. Very much reminiscent of when Simon Bryant had been the CO."

With Christmas then approaching, it would have been understandable for the Boss to reflect with satisfaction on a frenetic but successful first four months and ease into the festive season. However, he had pushed hard to get his squadron the first UK air-to-air slot on the newly formed Advanced Tactical Leadership Course (ATLC) run in the United Arab Emirates. This would provide four crews with outstanding training and would also allow the Squadron to rotate halfway through the detachment, generating two weeks in the Emirates for all Squadron members. Mid-November saw the Squadron deploy six aircraft via Cyprus to Abu Dhabi for a deployment that was as noteworthy on the ground as it was in the air.

From a professional perspective, the flying was first-rate, with 43 operating with a number of Gulf States in complex scenarios. Beyond the immediate ATLC flying, the Squadron participated in some excellent air combat training with French and Gulf State adversaries. On the ground, Abu Dhabi and the immediate surroundings provided plenty of entertainment but on one occasion the Squadron ventured along the motorway to Dubai for the centrepiece of the social calendar. Wing Commander Beach remembers the event well:

"Every year, Dubai hosts an internationally renowned Rugby Sevens tournament. For those not familiar with the event, it is primarily an international tournament with the big names in rugby such as the UK home nations, Australia, New Zealand and South Africa competing for the big prize. Perhaps less well known is the fact that there are three further tournaments at this time in Dubai. These comprise a 'pub' team competition, a semi-professional event, and a full professional 'International Invitation' tournament – open to international players and professional club sides. Normally, entry into the Dubai Sevens is difficult to secure, but the Fighting Cocks had an inside line, having flown Scotland's Rugby ace Andy Nicholl, in celebration of his recent Heineken Cup victory. He promised to assist with the 43 Squadron entry and, sure enough, as the day neared, the fixture list was produced with us on it. The set up at Dubai is something like Wimbledon, with a centre stadium surrounded by a series of outside pitches. Only the top two tournaments were played primarily in the centre stadium, while the lesser competitions were to be fought out in the relative obscurity of the outer grounds. The 43 contingent duly arrived en masse, a sea of black and white checkerboard, and eagerly scanned the notice boards to see who and where we would play first.

It soon became apparent that the Squadron had been entered into the International Invitation event, much to the surprise of the now rather hesitant team. Worse news followed, with a draw that matched the Squadron against St Helens in the first round in the centre stadium. St Helens, a team widely tipped for overall victory, boasted a number of international players including two huge Samoans. A hastily convened tactics conference followed and a game plan devised. This involved piling as many players into a ruck as possible before spinning the ball out to a waiting Jimmy Govern. Little Jimmy, a footballer by background, had a blistering turn of speed that it was hoped would see him to the line.

The team ran out onto the pitch to thunderous applause and quizzical looks at the notice board which, by dint of a lack of available characters, announced the entrance of the Fighting Cock! The whistle blew and the Squadron rolled out its game plan. All went well as, from a bruising mêlée in centre-field, the ball fizzed out to Jimmy on the wing. Jimmy grabbed it and took off, scorching towards the opposition line where glory awaited. The sound of the tackle on Jimmy, performed by an 18-stone Samoan in full flight, could be heard across the Kingdom. One minute gone and the stretcher made an appearance. Poor Jimmy was carted off to a waiting ambulance, returning complete with neck brace some hours later. In his absence, St Helens cantered to an easy win but an unbowed Fighting Cocks team were roundly cheered for a 'game' performance."

The Squadron recovered to the UK in mid-December and enjoyed a relatively peaceful few months save for the steady drumbeat of the ever present QRA duties and Falklands deployment. If the end of 2004 had been busy, there was no sign of a let up in 2005. The year was to be dominated by two events. Participation in NATO Opeval and the Squadron's receipt of the Freedom of Stirling, both events scheduled for the second half of the year, while the first half of the year saw a concerted effort to prepare.

The Squadron's participation in Opeval was a significant challenge. The UK had opted out of formal NATO evaluations some years before in light of the extensive expeditionary warfare experience gained in the Gulf region. However, it had been decided that the time was right to re-enter the NATO system and the Tornado Force was to be assessed at RAF St Mawgan in October. The Tornado Force was to be led by the RAF Marham Station Commander, with OC 43 Squadron commanding the Tornado F3 contingent, of 43 and 111 crews. A sector level training event at RAF Leuchars in January gave an early indication of the work ahead. Although the Squadron was well practised in operations, the specifics of NATO evaluation had to be re-acquired, and this was not just a case of dusting down Opevals from the 1980s. The expeditionary nature of the assessment demanded that a new set of procedures be not only developed but refined. Many lessons were learned in a cold January that would set the Squadron up for formal evaluation. However, it was not all work, work, work, as Phil Beach relates:

"With the first big training event over, a squadron party at my house provided an opportunity to let our hair down. A 'black and white' fancy dress event saw an assortment of some eighty characters descend on Earlshall Road. More notable of these were Flight Lieutenants Kingdom (pantomime cow), Shaw (sheepdog) and Durcan (Michael Jackson). The latter was certainly responsible for leaving a trail of cam-cream handprints throughout the house, and, despite suspicions, no concrete evidence was ever found to link him with dyeing my spaniel in black and white checks.

The party was also eventful for saying farewell to Captain Paul Frigault, the last of the F3 exchange officers, and for the wife of Treble One's CO crashing the event having escaped early from a rather dull formal dinner. The end of the financial year saw 43 take an extended Easter break having completed the annual flying task a week early – the only RAF fighter squadron to meet the target that year."

In early June the Squadron deployed to St Mawgan to conduct a Maxeval, which was the formal dress rehearsal for the NATO evaluation. The Squadron arrived at St Mawgan somewhat in the dark. Preparatory planning had been conducted on behalf of the Leuchars contingent by OC Operations due to the frenetic deployment programme of the previous six months. On arrival it was hard not to detect a degree of Marham bias to the planned Tornado Force bed-down. To the south of the runway, the GR4 squadron and the Marham command team were housed in a HAS complex adjacent to the tented living accommodation. To the north of the runway, the F3 boys were allocated a dank Hesco-Bastion modular shelter as a command node!

Aircraft were to be parked out in the open with engineering housed in adjacent tents, which was not particularly conducive to ground alerts and operational turn rounds. In the event, fate stepped in to level the playing field. The Hesco-Bastion structure was found to be close to the home of an endangered species of bat so the command node had to be re-located – not least to guard against a rabies epidemic!

Simultaneously, the aircraft parking bays were found to be unsuitable, with two jets sinking into the fragile operating surface. The F3 detachment quickly relocated to the south side of the base on the eve of the Maxeval assessment and into a makeshift set-up. The engineering team worked wonders to generate and turn aircraft to meet the task but any hope of a meaningful dress rehearsal was lost. It was obvious that the Squadron was going to undertake Opeval from a standing start.

More immediately, the Squadron's thoughts turned to more ceremonial matters, with events marking the award of the Freedom of the City of Stirling held on the weekend of 3–5 June 2005. The date was selected to coincide with the 43 Squadron Association's 60th Anniversary and represented the culmination of months of rehearsals and preparations. Granting the

Freedom of a City to a squadron, rather than to a station, is extremely rare and the support of the Ministry of Defence for this honour was probably eased by the Vice Chief of the Defence Staff, Sir Anthony Bagnall. It was also Sir Anthony's influence behind the scenes that secured the attendance of the Minister for the Armed Forces, Bill Rammell. Another key individual in supporting the weekend's events was the CEO of the Royal Bank of Scotland, who underwrote the hiring of Stirling Castle for the formal dinner on 3 June. Although fortunes were to turn for Sir Fred Goodwin in later years, his discreet support for the Squadron during this event and many others should be recognised – without him, the Squadron's star would not have shone so brightly during the Tornado years.

The weekend's events started in the afternoon of 3 June with the unveiling of a cairn within sight of the birthplace of 43(F) Squadron. Following speeches by the Boss and Stirling's Provost, Colin O'Brien, the Cairn was unveiled by Sir Anthony. Reconvening in the Council Chambers, the Boss and the Provost attended a reception for local dignitaries before the more formal dinner scheduled for later that evening. At 8pm, some 120 Fighting Cocks, young and old, gathered in Stirling Castle Great Hall for a formal dinner. It was a poignant night, with many former COs gathered together with the Provost of Stirling, Colin O'Brien. Also attending the event was the daughter of Sholto Douglas, Katharine Campbell, who presented a trophy to the Squadron not more than a quarter of a mile from where the great man had formed the Squadron in 1916. The Squadron's Honorary Members and Association were also to the fore and presented a magnificent painting to the Squadron by artist Ronald Wong, depicting that Freedom formation of Tornado F3's overflying Stirling Castle. The Boss wrapped up the evening with a speech recounting the year's events. Perhaps appropriately at such an historic occasion, he revealed that the Squadron had won both the Aberporth weapons trophy and the Dacre Trophy recognising the best fighter squadron that year – the first time that the Squadron had achieved the 'double' in the same year since Roger Palin's days in the 1970's.

Saturday saw the Boss formally receive the Freedom of the City, on behalf of the Squadron, in the Council Chambers before commanding a parade through the centre of the city at which the Fighting Cocks marched, bayonets fixed, with the Central Band of the RAF through the city, the salute being taken by Air Chief Marshal Bagnall and the Provost. Continuing to the nearby King's Park the Squadron formed up as the opening event of the annual Stirling Military Show and as the general salute sounded, a Tornado piloted by Sqn Ldr Al Dodds, with Kelvin Harris navigating, roared overhead with the ramparts of Stirling Castle forming a dramatic backdrop. The celebrations continued through the weekend, concluding on the Sunday with a Service of Remembrance in the Church of the Holy Rude near Stirling Castle where, in a moving service, Squadron members old and new were remembered.

"FREEDOM"
painting by Ronald Wong

Wg Cdr Phil Beach receiving the official Scroll from Provost Colin O'Brien

With bayonets fixed the Squadron marches through Stirling to King's Park

The Scroll conferring the Freedom reads:

"At Stirling on the fourth day of June in the year two thousand and five on which day the Provost and Councillors granted 43 (Fighter) Squadron FREEDOM OF THE CITY OF STIRLING in recognition of the long maintained friendship and links with the Squadron since its establishment near Falleninch Farm, Stirling, in 1916, and to record appreciation of the Squadron's gallantry and loyal service by citizens of the City of Stirling."

In so doing Stirling had officially, and in accordance with tradition, announced:

"Therefore they have conferred and do hereby confer upon You the Freedom of Entry into the city on all ceremonial occasions with bayonets fixed, drums beating and colours flying."

With summer a fading memory, the Squadron preparations for Opeval gathered pace with a number of short set-piece exercises accompanying a concerted statistics-gathering exercise. By the time the Squadron deployed on 14 October, it was in fine pitch. The aircraft departed Leuchars on a Friday to enable essential runway repairs to commence at Leuchars – an unwelcome complication. The deployment was uneventful for the Fighting Cocks but less so for Treble One, which lost an aircraft just after take-off. Thankfully the crew ejected safely.

Arriving at St Mawgan, the Squadron got to work setting up command and control facilities and arranging the purpose-designed aircraft shelters that had been deployed to support the evaluation. For the next few days the Squadron was tested to the limit. Aircrew flew complicated air-to-air missions, together with their GR4 counterparts, and the groundcrew turned the aircraft round in record time, despite weather so atrocious that the NATO examiners even considered cancelling the whole exercise, considering the conditions to be close on unworkable. This was the first time that NATO had seen operational turn-rounds conducted on AMRAAM-equipped aircraft, a missile relatively new to the RAF. 43 Squadron's armourers excelled, evolving new techniques in situ to meet exacting NATO requirements. In the event, the Tornado Force and the Air Defence contingent passed with flying colours and the Squadron visibly relaxed after a punishing but ultimately rewarding nine months. We cannot leave the St Mawgan deployment without a further word from Jim Campbell:

"This exercise was a real-time one that involved deploying to, and operating from, an austere environment, albeit with centralised direction despite the Squadron's considerable experience in detached operations. Tool kits had to be assembled in a certain fashion and spares were to be controlled by a central supply system. The lads groaned because we were all aware that anything that we might require was likely to prove difficult to obtain.

So we did what any self-respecting squadron would do. During the build-up we accumulated what we could and smuggled it down to our austere environment. As the preparation continued and the guys prepared to leave, I went onto my resettlement course but again, stories of the Squadron's achievements quickly filtered back.

The operational flying was a huge success; day and night tasks were all achieved with very few, if any, sorties dropped. The guys managed to annoy the RAF police on a regular basis without, thankfully, any of our lads being arrested. The SEngO banned the use of kettles, seemingly for no better reason than that he could, but the crème-de-la-crème had to be the SNCOs somehow missing the announcement of a booze ban, partying hard whilst off duty and defying the best efforts of anyone to find the source of their merriment!

All who went to the Cornish Baghdad came back very upbeat and again the Squadron's reputation was untarnished. Even though I and some others were not physically there, we felt part of the whole thing."

A slow start to 2006 was anticipated, but a routine sortie in the first week of January was to change that. During air-to-air refuelling over the North Sea, a Squadron programmer struck up conversation with a French Mirage pilot on the tanker's other wing. The French aviator mentioned that the aircraft carrier Charles de

Gaulle was conducting sea trials in two weeks time and air-to-air opposition was needed for the embarked air group. A few hasty telephone calls between Wing Commander Beach and 1 Group HQ followed and on 17 January, six aircraft departed Leuchars for Nimes-Garons NAvy air base in the South of France, for Exercise Lone Bustard. A number of high value sorties were flown in support of the carrier and a bond was formed with the Mirage squadron at Orange air base. 43 also enjoyed the delights of the region, with the detachment split fairly evenly between the pursuit of alpine sports or gastronomy. The end of the financial year arrived and, yet again, the Squadron took a week off having completed the annual flying task early – the only RAF fighter squadron to complete their hours allocation for the second year running. Phil Beach remembers the next exercise:

"April saw the Squadron deploy to Exercise Magic Carpet in Oman. This exercise saw the Squadron fly alongside the RAF Jaguars of 6 Squadron as well as Omani Jaguar and Hawk aircraft. The detachment provided a good mix of flying, not least the introduction of Emergency Close Air Support (E-CAS) to the Squadron's capabilities. The requirement for this came from experiences in the Iraq war, where air-to-air aircraft were often those most advanced into enemy territory. If ground forces required air support, these assets could be – and were – called upon to give emergency assistance ahead of the arrival of more specialised assets.

This initiative was developed by OC Weapons flight, Squadron Leader Mark Barmby. The Squadron formed good links with the SBS boys during the exercise and used the opportunity to share thoughts on tactics, techniques and procedures. The SBS chaps were also keen to show off their kit and a group from 43 enjoyed a day on the firing range employing a variety of weapons. All proved successful save, perhaps, for Flying Officer Jen Smith's employment of a 50-calibre gun; the distance achieved by the round being nearly matched by Jen's rearward recoil!"

May 2006 provided a brief respite for everyone before a deployment to Malbork in Poland. The Squadron flew to Poland in late June for a one week deployment to face the resident Polish MiG-29s. The Poles were fantastic hosts. Thankfully the vodka-fuelled all-ranks welcome party was scheduled for the arrival Friday, with a much-needed weekend of recuperation built into the programme. As anticipated, the Polish pilots suffered from a comparative lack of flying time and the Fighting Cocks used the event to hone some core skills and share techniques with their new NATO allies. There was a certain symmetry to this, given that 43 had served under a Polish commanding officer during WW2, the much decorated Squadron Leader Eugeniusz Horbaczewski, in 1943. In July the Squadron celebrated its 90th year as Phil Beach records:

"July saw the Squadron celebrate its 90th Anniversary in fine style, with an open day followed by a dinner at Leuchars. Once again the Association was extremely well represented and many took the opportunity to visit the Fighting Cock's small history room established within the Squadron headquarters. We also arranged a modest air display, organised by Flight Lieutenant Rich Tuer. Centrepiece of this show was a four-ship of the Squadron's F3s. One of these was an all-black aircraft that represented the '90th anniversary paint scheme', which had been approved at short notice by Headquarters 1 Group. Barbeques, bands and racing cars added to the sense of occasion before the more formal evening events. The dinner that evening provided me with the opportunity to pay tribute to the Squadron's outstanding performance during the preceding year. The event also marked the end of my tenure, handing over the baton to Wing Commander Scott Notman the next day."

The 90th anniversary all-black Tornado ZG757

Jim Campbell also tells a tale about the anniversary day:

"For the flying display we needed a jet in the finest livery and this was provided through the hard work of the station's paint section. ZG757 was a beautiful sight in her distinctive black paint scheme and brought a lump to the throat as she roared overhead in a series of impressive manoeuvres. The Boss strutted about, chest puffed out with justifiable pride, and everyone went away extremely happy and ready for the next stage of proceedings.

Monday morning saw a few with severe hangovers turn up for work but these were soon forgotten as the story filtered through that our pride and joy – GF – had to return to the paint shop ASAP to be restored to its former state. No amount of pleading or reference to common sense was going to persuade anyone to relent, so with quite a lot of swearing, a couple of red faces and a few wry smiles, we complied with their wishes."

As Scott Notman took command in June, the pace of activity continued with yet another long-range deployment for 43's Tornados, this time to India in October, as they participated in the inaugural Exercise Indra Dhanush with the Indian Air Force. This was the first Royal Air Force and Indian Air Force combined exercise in that continent for 43 years and it was a proud and momentous occasion when the Boss introduced his team to their hosts for their forthcoming detachment.

Scotty recalls:

"Number 7 Indian Air Force Squadron was the resident Mirage 2000 outfit, known as the 'Battle Axes', based at Gwalior Air Base near Lashkar, about 80 miles south of Agra – virtually dead centre in the northern half of India. This would be our home for the next two weeks. Seven Squadron was very much an operational unit, having been called into action many times during its history, the most recent occasion being only four years previously. Also taking part were a number of other Indian squadrons, flying a variety of different aircraft types ranging from the venerable MiG-21 to the Sukhoi Su-30, one of the world's most modern and formidable fighter aircraft. It was therefore with much anticipation, not to say trepidation, that we set off into the briefing and subsequent flying exercise.

This exercise drew much media attention in both Britain and India and there was considerable discussion on how the Sukhoi would square up to the Tornado F3. Chief of the Air Staff, Air Chief Marshal Sir Glenn Torpy paid a visit and accepted the opportunity to fly in the SU-30, while our AOC, Air Vice-Marshal Chris Harper, also took time to visit the exercise and see for himself at first hand how we compared against the Indian crews.

The exercise was a tremendous success, forging mutual respect, understanding and re-kindling old alliances that reminded all of us that we had more in common than we might have thought. Thus the Indian Air Force provided us with a great opportunity to fly with, and against, seasoned and experienced pilots and modern aircraft (the MiG-21 excepted). My team was given a unique opportunity and one we would not forget. It also gave the entire Squadron the chance to take in the culture, life and sights of a truly amazing country. This is evidenced by the many photographs brought back by the boys of visits to the Taj Mahal and sitting in Tut-Tuts on the streets of Delhi.

There were obviously the inevitable bouts of 'Delhi-belly' encountered by most of us, with the resultant days spent in bed, but I am confident that the problems we encountered during our time out there have long drifted into our subconscious and the good times stand out. I know they do for me, and Exercise Indra Dhanush sits as the highlight of my fantastic, and proud time, as part of 43 Squadron's history."

In March 2007 two new ab initio crews were welcomed and the flying focus fell largely to training in order to bring 43 back to full combat ready status. There was still time to participate in such multi-national exercises as Neptune Warrior in May, and Wycombe Warrior in July, both proving very useful. The Squadron also provided a crew and an aircraft in support of the RAF Role Demo: an air display involving Tornado F3s, GR4s, Hawks, AWACS, Apaches and Chinooks, touring the country and attending all major air shows. The display was led by 43 Squadron. Scott Notman:

"Away from the regular flying tasks the Squadron took part in a few varied events: a day of golf was enjoyed by all, fighting for the Rooster Cup, the winners, of course, being the aircrew for the third year running. In association with RAF Brize Norton the Squadron launched two aircraft to take part in the charity event 'Cherished Memories' that gave terminally ill children the chance to fly in a VC 10 and watch fast-jets flying in close formation and tanking. On 3 May we hosted a visit by TV chef Gordon Ramsay who spent two days filming and teaching us how to cook."

Further resurfacing work at Leuchars during May and June forced 43 to use only the short runway while the Northern QRA task moved to Leeming to be held by 25 Squadron. In return, 43's crews and engineers went to Coningsby to man Southern QRA for ten days at a time. Once the runway work reached the intersections and halted all flying, 43 deployed to Cyprus for five weeks. There the crews competed in an air-to-air gunnery competition which was won, to everyone's disbelief, by one of the most junior pilots. It was then back to Leeming with periods at Coningsby once more.

Back at Leuchars in September, QRA was reinstated and there followed a spate of Russian interest that seemed keen to test the re-established capability at the station, bringing a renewed sense of purpose to QRA operations. Multiple intercepts were made at all times of the day and night and almost every crew was involved against various Bears and huge Tupolev Tu-160 Blackjacks.

Then in December 43 deployed to Abu Dhabi for four weeks in support of the ATLC, where crews were able to train next to USAF F-16s, RSAF F-15s, FAF Mirage 2000 RD1s, PAF F-16s as well as Mirage 2000-9 and F-16s from the UAE. Typhoons of 3 Squadron also made an appearance. 43 put up good performances, earning special praise from the course staff on more than one occasion. Meantime the 'home team' continued with QRA while giving *Tremblers* a few lessons in how business should be done!

The Squadron passed a January Staneval with flying colours before detaching to Kinloss to take part in Night TLT sorties using NVGs. This preceded Scott Notman's departure in March 2008 when his tour as CO of the Fighting Cocks came to an end.

Back in July 2007 only a few weeks after taking over command of 56 (Reserve) Squadron, the Tornado F3 Operational Conversion Unit, at Leuchars, Wing Commander David Hazell was called to see the Station Commander, Air Commodore Clive Bairsto, the son of Air Marshal Sir Peter Bairsto, the distinguished Fighting Cock from Hunter days. Their discussion that day began the sequence of events that would lead to the end of the Tornado F3 in RAF service with 43 Squadron.

An analysis of the F3 Force had resulted in a need to rationalise its size to ensure that it remained efficient while meeting operational requirements during its last three years of operations. The net result was the need to phase out the training of new crews for the aircraft and to reduce the force from three to two squadrons at Leuchars. This reduction in squadrons would take place in April 2008, once 25(F) Squadron based at Leeming had disbanded, leaving the remainder of the F3 Force based entirely in Scotland. As a result of the geography of the station, the existing locations of the squadrons, and to minimise disruptions when the Typhoon arrived there, the candidates for disbandment were either 56, as its specialist training role would soon come to an end, or 43 Squadron.

It was not certain at this stage which of the two squadrons would be chosen and in the event this was not resolved until January 2008. An initial cost saving measure was suggested in order to preserve the integrity of both units, with both sharing a pool of aircraft and operating from the 56 Squadron line. This would have the advantage of achieving engineering personnel savings by relinquishing the more labour intensive HAS operations. However, it was quickly agreed that competition for aircraft by two squadrons with separate roles, would make this option mostly unworkable. Moreover, Wing Commander David 'Nutty' Hazell had only just begun his command tour with 56, and Scott Notman was approaching the end of his with 43. Thus it was decided that David would take command of the remaining unit from 1 April 2008 (an appropriate date, it being the 90th anniversary of the formation of the RAF) and he was instructed to commence planning the merger in order to produce a unit capable of maintaining the readiness of a fully operational squadron with a dedicated conversion task.

The only question was which squadron number would survive? Subsequently, on the advice of the MoD's Air Historical Branch, the Air Force Board announced that 43(F) Squadron was to remain active because 56 had lost considerable relative seniority as a consequence of having been relegated to reserve status while operating as an OCU.

Planning commenced in August 2007 with the executives of both squadrons taking part in a two-day brainstorming session, reviewing all the functional aspects that the new unit would be required to fulfil. One key issue concerned who would hold the various responsibilities, and in particular those of the flight commanders in the combined unit. Happily, this was largely resolved as a result of planned postings, and in the event the majority of the executive positions came from 56 Squadron. The tasks for the new unit would be to maintain the existing responsibilities of both units, namely to continue producing new crews for 43 and 111 Squadrons, and to meet 43's operational tasks of QRA and deployment for overseas contingencies. While aircrew numbers would remain unchanged at first, aircraft and groundcrew numbers, including station support staff, would be reduced consistent with the combined tasks.

The impact that this would have on station staff as well as Squadron personnel was appreciated from an early stage and, to avoid undue uncertainty and concern, briefings outlining the various options available to groundcrew were held prior to The Fighting Cock's departure for the Advanced Tactical

Leadership Training Course in the United Arab Emirates in November and December 2007. This did much to allay concerns and mirrored closely the approach taken by John Brady back in 1989.

Following minor adjustments to the date of the merger to enable 111 Squadron to return from a detachment to the Gulf and take over QRA duties from 43, Wing Commander Hazell assumed command of 43 Squadron at 1100 hours on 23 April 2008. By his own admission he was somewhat the worse for wear after carrying out his final duties as OC 56 Squadron the night before with the expected gusto! However, a pool drill at 0645 on his first morning as Boss of the Fighting Cocks soon freshened him up. He was not alone in feeling jaded. A new 43 Squadron photograph board was produced that day and those personnel who were ex-56 were readily identified for the remainder of their tours by their ragged, not to say glazed, countenance that April morning.

It had been agreed that no changes to the Squadron headquarters would be made until after 56 Squadron's disbandment parade, also held the previous day. By the time David Hazell returned from the final 56 Squadron lunch three hours later, the existing 43 Squadron aircrew had dutifully transformed the crew room - even to the extent of repainting 56's red and white chequered wall to its new black and white insignia. The Fighting Cocks were still ruling the roost in their typically spirited manner.

After a month of settling in to the new routine, the Squadron set off for Rissala in Finland, on Exercise ADEX 08, an element of the Partnership for Peace programme. The Boss delayed his departure to enable him to make his inaugural appearance as 'Boss Cock' at that year's Association dinner at the RAF Club. Once in Finland the Squadron achieved consistently impressive flying rates, while operating alongside German F-4s and Finnish F-18s, against Danish F-16s and French Mirages.

The detachment was a great success and hugely enjoyable, due in no small measure to the professionalism and wholehearted support provided by the host nation. However, several incidents were particularly memorable for the Boss. One day he had just returned to his accommodation, some 30 minutes drive from the airfield, at the end of a busy day when he received a call informing him that one of the Squadron's junior pilots was about to land, having advised air traffic control that he was going to have to make a landing without a nose wheel which was refusing to come down. A hurried drive back followed by a brisk bicycle ride from the operations room to the runway, revealed a Tornado with its nose resting on the runway, six inches to one side of the centre line. Flight Lieutenant Alex Taylor, assisted by Squadron Leader Colin 'Wiki' Wills in the back, had done a great job of getting down, but expressed to his CO a determination to be more precise next time and get the nose dead on the centre line. The Boss, quite rightly, counselled his junior pilot against future overconfidence!

Further revelations occurred when the Boss and a few of the Squadron were invited to join the Base Commander in a sauna, together with his squadron commander and the German detachment commander. The tiny towel that was provided proved to be for sitting on, and not for a modicum of modesty. It was quickly realised that the view from the upper benches was more appealing than the one at eye-level from the lower decking. The offer of a subsequent skinny dip in a nearby lake was declined in favour of a cooling beer!

Finally, an inadvertent jettisoning of two under-wing fuel tanks rather than the intended unused flares, was rapidly and efficiently remedied by an unflustered response from the Finns, who located the lost tanks in a forest within 400 yards of each other with seemingly little effort and retrieved both by helicopter.

June saw 43 join with *Tremblers* in a diamond nine to provide an element of the Queen's Birthday Flypast at the Trooping of the Colour. The speed adjustments of the preceding C-17 proved challenging, but honour was served and a tight formation maintained as it flew over Buckingham Palace.

Then in October 43 Squadron mounted the 'Gamecock Invitational' in aid of the RAF Benevolent Fund during the week following the Dunhill Golf Tournament at St Andrews. Companies were invited to field a four-ball for a match at the Kingsbarns course, followed by a gala dinner and accommodation at the Fairmont Hotel. The following day a visit to the Squadron to play with 'Big Boys Toys' included a range of activities such as a simulator ride and the opportunity to drive in some Bentley cars acquired for the day. A lucky few participants also experienced passenger rides in the Tornado, undoubtedly for them the highlight of the visit. The event raised an impressive £60,000 for the Benevolent Fund.

The year concluded with the OCU element of 43 Squadron closing in December with the consequent need to reduce the level of manning further to that already undertaken the previous year.

The beginning of 2009 heralded the final months of the Royal Air Force's 90th anniversary year. To mark this auspicious milestone, the Boss decided to exercise the Squadron's right to celebrate its Freedom of Stirling with a parade through the city in February, reviewed by the Provost, and a formal dinner for 150 in the Great Hall of Stirling Castle. In the event this proved to be not only the highlight of his time in command of The Fighting Cocks but also a fitting tribute to another pilot who was soon to leave 43. Flight Lieutenant Roy Macintyre had flown his first operational tour as a fighter pilot back in the Phantom days, 43 being his first posting in 1986. He subsequently completed two more tours on the Squadron with the Tornado, from 1997 to 1999, and from 2008-2009.

Roy was chosen to lead a four-ship formation flypast over Stirling to mark the Freedom parade. Not only was this his final sortie with 43 but it would also be his last flight as an operational pilot before transferring to a training role with the Universities of Glasgow and Strathclyde Air Squadron. Even more fittingly, Stirling was the place of his birth as well as 43's, and the occasion provided a poignant but memorable tribute to both man and squadron. Roy remembers:

"As last trips go, Hollywood could not have written a better script. I was born in Stirling and the only thing I ever wanted to do was to be a pilot in the RAF. Quite soon my focus had narrowed to wanting to be a pilot on Stirling's Squadron - 43 - flying Phantoms. I have enjoyed three, albeit shortish tours on the Squadron, and count myself very lucky.

That my very first tour was with 43 was the perfect start and exceeded my dreams. It was even more fitting that my last trip, and my last flight in the F3, would be over my home town and that of the Squadron.'

In 'Golf-Foxtrot' Roy Macintyre blasts off from Leuchars

'The Squadron was exercising its right to march its colours through the town on 5 February 2009 and was then going to hold a dinner in the castle that night. I was to lead the flypast over the parade. There was extensive TV coverage, so there was 'no pressure' to get it right! Luckily it went off without a hitch and we got back to Leuchars where I was met by OC Ops, Wing Commander Reuter, as everyone else was either at or en-route to Stirling.

'GF' leading the four-ship over a snow-covered Perthshire landscape on the way to Stirling

The dinner in the Great Hall was fantastic and personally the best squadron function I have

The four-ship fly-past and air spare were crewed by Ben Morris and Cody Blake (3), Darren Lownds and Simon Grieve (4), Roy Macintyre and Henry Paul (Lead), Andy Shaw and Andy Miller (2), with Stuart McAdam and James Hunkin (air spare)

Roy signs the '700' after his last Tornado flight with 43 Squadron

ever experienced. It was a good way to sign off. I finished after 21 years on the F3 with 4,557 flying hours, the highest total for a pilot and only surpassed by Colin Wills, a navigator, who eventually finished with over 4,700."

The next event was to deploy to Nevada, as David Hazell recalls:

"The end of February saw 43 depart for Nellis Air Force Base, Nevada, in a joint 'Red Flag' deployment with 111 Squadron. A transit via The Azores, Bermuda and Memphis proved uneventful other than at the last transit stop, where Major Cody 'Burner' Blake, the Squadron's US Air Force exchange officer, led his British colleagues astray during a night of jazz, bourbon and cigars.

Typically realistic training during Red Flag was conducted alongside American F-22s and C-130s of the RAAF, with opposition provided by the US Aggressors in F-15s and F-16s. Being so close to Las Vegas always provided ideal opportunities to relax and on this trip we were able to celebrate Flight Lieutenant Nev Kingdom's stag night. Nev was the QWI(P) with *Tremblers* but had been a former Fighting Cock so the occasion was attended by all the officers on the detachment. The size of the tip alone gave an indication of the scale of the evening - $800!"

Soon after the return from Nellis, the unexpectedly premature disbandment of 43 was announced. It had been anticipated that the Squadron would stand down in March 2010 after the Falklands defence role had been taken over by the new Typhoons in September 2009, leaving only the Northern QRA role for the remaining Tornados.

It was announced in early April that the Tornado crews at Leuchars would be reduced to a total of 12, although this was subsequently adjusted to 16 with a target date of September. The date of 43's disbandment was advanced to reflect this drawdown rate and Monday 13 July 2009 was set in place as the date.

There followed a difficult period of accelerated planning for wind-down, merger and final closure. However, David Hazell's experience barely a year before, during the disbandment of 56 Squadron, had prepared him well and every effort was made to maintain morale and to minimise individual disruption, particularly among the engineering personnel of whom around 200 would need to be posted.

A weekend of events including an open day, all-ranks hangar party and a church service was planned to precede the final parade, flypast and formal lunch on that Monday. However, 43 Squadron was to receive a final and most devastating blow on 2 July. Tornado ZE982 crashed in Glen Kinglas, on the west coast of Scotland while engaged on a training flight. The accident occurred in the late morning near Arrochar by the A83, just west of Loch Lomond, while flying in poor visibility with heavy rain and mist over the hills. The crew, Flight Lieutenants Kenny Thompson and Nige Morton, were killed instantly. Every member of the Squadron was stunned by the accident, particularly as it occurred just 11 days before flying was scheduled to cease and against a background of only two previous fatalities in the 20 years of 43's service with the Tornado.

9 July 2009, the Squadron's final flying day, the Boss unbuckles from his last flight

With two funerals now to take place around the time of the disbandment events, consideration was given to cancelling the planned programme as a mark of respect to lost comrades. It was a difficult decision but the wish to celebrate the Squadron's distinguished service and the recognition that both Kenny and Nige had now joined the roll of honour of those Fighting Cocks who had been lost over the years, inclined the Squadron to do its mourning at a later date.

Air Chief Marshal Sir Roger Palin inspects the Squadron

The final four-ship crews on 13 July
Flt Lt Kelvin Harris, Flt Lt Adam Rogers,
Flt Lt Sam Cowan, Flt Lt Nick Mathew,
Flt Lt Gino Portaluri, Flt Lt Gerry McCormack,
Sqn Ldr Henry Paul, Major Cody Blake USAF
Significantly, Sqn Ldr Henry Paul was back serving with 43 at the end having been part of the early operational work-up in 1990

At the due time on 13 July, Wing Commander Hazell led his Squadron onto the parade ground to the stirring accompaniment of the pipe band of The Royal Scots Dragoon Guards. As he did so he felt 43(F) Squadron rise above its recent tragedy. A flypast by an immaculate box-four marked the Royal salute before the parade was reviewed and addressed by Air Chief Marshal Sir Roger Palin, one of a number of former commanding officers attending the ceremony. As the Standard was marched off for the last time, the poignancy of the moment was heightened by the Tornados returning to fly by in the traditional 'missing man' formation. David Hazell:

"My final duty as OC 43 Squadron was to lay up the Squadron Standard up in the Rotunda at the RAF College, Cranwell. In an emotional ceremony, Flight Lieutenant Rich Bradley handed over the Standard to the College standard party for safekeeping. Although no formal announcement had yet been made as to the future of the Squadron number plate, I made the decision to lay the Standard up in anticipation of the Fighting Cocks returning as a Typhoon squadron.

The Fighting Cocks have continued their distinguished history since the conversion from the mighty F-4 in 1989, with two periods of active service in the Gulf and Iraq Wars and the policing of no-fly zones in the skies over Bosnia and Iraq, while at the same time maintaining the defence of the homeland as part of Northern and Southern QRA, and supporting the continuing defence commitment in the Falkland Islands. The changes and significant personal pressures that military life brings were unrelenting during this period as the RAF transformed from a Cold War posture to the expeditionary doctrine of today.

However the ethos and spirit of the Fighting Cocks did not change one iota. The banter in the crew room may have been tempered slightly in latter days with the introduction of female aircrew, but in the Mess bar the Fighting Cocks still gave the 'Girl's School' from the south side of the airfield a good pasting! On detachments the Squadron performed to the highest standards, both professionally and socially! Being a fighter squadron commander is probably the highlight of most pilots' careers, so having been a 'Ruler of the Roost' – well, life doesn't get any better."

Gloria Finis

Flt Lt Richard Bradley proudly carries the Standard which is paraded for the last time in front of a Tornado

Thruster, on parade for the last time,
at the disbandment lunch!

Postscript

Adapted from Jimmy Beedle's concluding thoughts in 1985

IT is difficult if not impossible to convey to the outsider who has not had the good fortune to meet and to mix with the Fighting Cocks a realistic comprehension of their committed skill and sheer professionalism or to believe that even with their unbounded enthusiasm they could get through such an extraordinary work load without appearing to do anything of the kind, and still possess the energy to indulge in social occasions and parties which have a verve and a liveliness unmatched almost anywhere else. As one might also have gathered from what they have read in these chapters the amount of ale that they can put away is staggering, a fact for which they would no doubt be condemned by some of Robert Burns' *unco guid*. To such the ready answer is that if you have the training and competence to understand and maintain the complex mechanical, electronic and weapons systems that go to make up a fighter aircraft or alternatively can maybe take that same aeroplane off on a dark foul night and rendezvous with a tanker five hundred miles away at thirty thousand feet, or fly faster than the speed of sound at low level in a vibrating multi-decibel environment, or not give way to panic when a major malfunction causes the adrenalin to flow fast and furious, if you can do these things and half a hundred just as complex and maybe as dodgy then in all truth being occasionally awash with beer can't really be such a bad thing.

And above all there is one thing that is sure and certain. If the time should come again when the Fighting Cocks are required to go to war you would find them not wanting in any matters within their control. If past experience is any guide they would almost certainly have more aircraft ready on the line quicker than most and in the air they would put their claims to excellence beyond all doubt.

From Stirling Castle to the 'Q' Sheds at Leuchars is no distance on the map but the Squadron's journey has been long and circuitous, through years of peace and years of war, through days of toil and days of ease. The aeroplanes flown, the science of their construction, the modes of their operation, the uniforms, the Service jargon and habits have all changed beyond recognition. One thing alone remained the same. The men were of the same kind as ever they were, their beginnings lost deep in the far-off history of these islands. Even by the twenty-first century they showed a marked similarity to the men who marched to Agincourt in the fifteenth. A pint of sack, good company in a noisy tavern and a surreptitious nip at a barmaid's bottom have all been the preferred pastimes of the hour yet with all they had the latent power and will to, in various seasons, put down their ale-jugs and go to smite the King of Spain, the Emperor Bonaparte, Adolph Hitler and Saddam Hussein. They were part of the minority who put into practice the dictum of ancient Rome, 'If you would wish for peace, prepare for war'.

'Brave young men' is something they have never claimed to be, just ordinary ones doing an extraordinary job uncommonly well. To quote the first American ever to join 43, 'I can never hope to find myself in better company.' And if those words have been true for nigh on a hundred years so is the spirit that characterised 43 all that time summed up in a question and answer heard at many a noisy gathering from Chile to the Arctic Circle, from the South Atlantic to the Persian Gulf and from India to Alaska.

Solo: 'IS THERE A FIGHTING COCK IN THE HOUSE?'
Chorus: 'YOU BET YOUR SWEET ARSE THERE IS!!'

May the cry of the Cockerel soon return.

Badge
"A gamecock proper"
It was approved by HM King Edward VIII in July 1936
(The official badge was developed from one produced in 1926 when the Squadron was equipped with the Gloster Gamecock).

Motto
Gloria finis – 'Glory is the end'
(the motto of the Brooke family, Sqn Ldr A F Brooke being the CO from July 1925 to January 1928).

Appendix 1

COMMANDING OFFICERS of 43 SQUADRON

Major W Sholto Douglas MC	April 1916 – May 1917
Major A S W Dore	May 1917 – October 1917
Major C C Miles MC	October 1917 – January 1919
Major R S Lucy	January 1919 – June 1919
Major A W C V Parr	June 1919 – August 1919
Major A J Capel DSO	August 1919 – December 1919
Squadron Leader A F Brooke	July 1925 – January 1928
Squadron Leader C N Lowe MC DFC	January 1928 – December 1930
Squadron Leader L H Slatter OBE DSC DFC	December 1930 – January 1932
Squadron Leader R H Hanmer MC	January 1932 – October 1934
Squadron Leader F Wright	October 1934 – April 1935
Squadron Leader A M Wray MC DFC AFC	April 1935 – December 1935
Squadron Leader B V Reynolds	January 1936 – August 1936
Flight Lieutenant R I G Macdougall	August 1936 – February 1937
Squadron Leader R E Bain	February 1937 – November 1939
Squadron Leader C G Lott DSO DFC	November 1939 – July 1940
Squadron Leader J V C Badger DFC	July 1940 – August 1940
Squadron Leader C B Hull DFC	August 1940 – September 1940
Squadron Leader T F D Morgan DFC & Bar	September 1940 – October 1941
Squadron Leader D A R G Le Roy du Vivier DFC & Bar	October 1941 – September 1942
Squadron Leader M Rook DFC	September 1942 – August 1943
Squadron Leader E Horbaczewski DFC	August 1943 – November 1943
Squadron Leader P L Parrott DFC	November 1943 – March 1944
Squadron Leader P B Laing-Meason DFC	March 1944 – June 1944
Squadron Leader A H Jupp DFC	June 1944 – March 1945
Squadron Leader J A Hemingway DFC	March 1945 – December 1945
Squadron Leader L W Seal	December 1945 – March 1946
Squadron Leader C F Ambrose DFC	March 1946 – May 1947
Squadron Leader D L Harvey	February 1949
Squadron Leader P R W Wickham DSO DFC & Bar	February 1949 – December 1949
Squadron Leader H R Allen DFC	December 1949 – February 1952
Squadron Leader E M Higson	Feburary 1952 – December 1952
Squadron Leader R E LeLong DFC & Bar	January 1953 – August 1955
Major R O Roberts (USAF)	August 1955 – June 1957
Squadron Leader J F Langer AFC	June 1957 – July 1959
Squadron Leader D McL Scrimgeour	July 1959 – June 1961
Squadron Leader P G Peacock	June 1961 – October 1963
Squadron Leader P H Champniss	October 1963 – October 1965
Squadron Leader H Davidson	October 1965 – July 1967
Squadron Leader T Thornton	July 1967 – November 1967
Wing Commander I R Martin AFC	July 1969 – July 1971
Wing Commander J J R Cohu	July 1971 – December 1973
Wing Commander K F Beck	December 1973 – December 1975
Wing Commander R H Palin	December 1975 – May 1978
Wing Commander I A D McBride	May 1978 – December 1980
Wing Commander H A W Drew AFC	December 1980 – August 1983
Wing Commander A J C Bagnall OBE	August 1983 – March 1985
Wing Commander A R C Winkles	March 1985 – August 1987
Wing Commander J P Brady	August 1987 – July 1989
Wing Commander A D Moir OBE	August 1989 – April 1992
Wing Commander M Godfrey	May 1992 – August 1994
Wing Commander P D Legg	August 1994 – January 1997
Group Captain S Bryant	January 1997 – September 1999
Group Captain M P Colley	September 1999 – December 2001
Wing Commander R J C Powell	December 2001 – June 2004
Wing Commander P J Beach MBE	June 2004 – August 2006
Wing Commander S R Notman	August 2006 – April 2008
Wing Commander D J Hazell	April 2008 – July 2009

Appendix 2

AIRCRAFT INSIGNIA AND MARKINGS

Initially letters were used to identify aircraft. A white triangle was then painted on the fuselage to the rear of the roundel on 1½ Strutters and Camels. This was replaced from March 1918 by two sloping white bars, one on each side of the roundel and on the centre of the upper wing.

After the war a double row of black and white checks was introduced on Gamecocks in 1926. The chequers were painted across the upper wings and on the fuselage sides. and were used on all subsequent bi-planes until December 1938 when camouflage was hastily introduced. Hurricanes were coded NQ- from December 1938 until a few days after the outbreak of war when they were changed to FT-. Code letters were offcially light grey in colour but in practice were more often white or duck-egg blue according to the colour of available supplies of dope. In North Africa code letters were always white except that sometimes red undercoat was the sole colour available. In November 1943 Flt Lt Laing-Meason introduced into 'A' Flight the two-tone letters used in his previous Squadron (No 145). The letters were red with a white border. After Laing-Meason became Squadron Commander, 'B' Flight introduced blue and white letters. When the first Spitfire Mk IXs arrived in August 1943 they were given code numbers (eg FT-2, FT-6) instead of letters. This custom ceased after a few months when IXs outnumbered Vs. From January 1944 'A' Flight aircraft were lettered from the block A to K, 'B' Flight had the remainder of the alphabet. The black and white chequered strip at the top of the fin dates from August 1945 when, with the smell of victory in the air, an early step was taken to restoring some of 43's peacetime glory! From June 1943 propeller spinners were painted red in accordance with Tactical Air Forces official schemes but glossy pillar-box red was always used instead of the specified dull red undercoat and in addition the spinner base-plate was painted white.

When the unit reformed with Meteors in 1949, the code 'SW' was used until 1951 when squadron codes were dropped and the black and white chequers re-appeared on each side of the fuselage roundel. Individual aircraft letters were carried on the fin and nose wheel door. This was repeated on Meteor 8s, and subsequently on Hunters. A caricature of a 'fighting cock', complete with boxing gloves, was painted on the port side of the Hunter nose. The wing tips, from F4 onwards, carried black and white chequers. When the rear fuselage checks moved to the nose, the cockerel from the Squadron badge on a white disc was displayed between them. When aircraft were 'pooled' in the Aden Strike Wing, No 43's checks were painted on one side of the roundel and No 8 Squadron's markings on the other and the cockerel was deleted.

Reformed with Phantoms, the Squadron painted the chequers on the sides of the engine intakes on each side of the roundel, but it was two years before the 'fighting cock' re-appeared, this time in a white disc on the fin. With the introduction of 'low-visibility' grey camouflage in the 1980s, the markings were toned down, the checks miniaturized and also applied to the top of the fin. The cockerel lost its white background and was toned-down but remained on the fin with the individual aircraft letter. In 1987, two-letter codes were introduced by adding the prefix 'A', to more easily distinguish the Squadron's aircraft from other Phantoms at Leuchars.

The Tornado F3s carried similar markings but the two letter codes were prefixed with 'G' in place of 'A'. The chequers later moved from the nose to the fin cap with variations in display. From time to time the Squadron Commander's aircraft, 'GF' *(Gloria Finis)* carried special markings.

Sopwith 1½ Strutter B2552 'X'
First style markings, white triangle aft of roundel
1917

Sopwith Camel D1785 'Z'
Second style markings, white diagonal stripes astride roundel
July 1918

Sopwith Snipe E8015 'E'
Second style markings, white diagonal stripes astride roundel
December 1918

Gloster Gamecock
First type to carry black and white chequers
Tangmere, 1926 – 1928

Armstrong Whitworth Siskin IIIA J8822 'O'
Tangmere,1929 – 1931

Hawker Fury K1942
Tangmere, 1931 – 1939

Hawker Hurricane Mk I P3784 'FT-U'
Tangmere, July 1940

Supermarine Spitfire Mk Vc (Trop) 'ES352 FT-Y'
In Desert camouflage, July 1943

Supermarine Spitfire Mk LF IX RK855 'FT-C'
Zeltweg, Austria, July 1946 - black and white fin chequers added

Meteor F8 WA756'F'

Silver overall
Leuchars, September 1951

Meteor F8 WH293'Y'

Last F8 to be used by the Squadron
Green and grey camouflage with silver undersides
Leuchars, 1956

Hunter F1 WT587'C'

Fighting Cock caricature emblem on nose
Leuchars, 1955

Hunter FGA9 XG256'G'

Squadron markings now on nose with black and white chequers on wing tips
Khormaksar, Aden, 1963

Phantom FG1 XV579 'R'

In the original grey and green camouflage but with red and blue national markings
Leuchars, 1975

Phantom FG1 XV582 'AF'

In the 'grey ghost' (barley grey) camouflage and toned down markings
carrying the special logo to commemorate the
John O' Groats to Land's End record flight on 24 February 1988

Tornado F3 ZE961 'GA'

carrying the original markings when first delivered
Leuchars, September 1989

Tornado F3 ZE731 'GF'

in special markings to celebrate the Squadron's 80th Anniversary
Leuchars, 1996

These orthographic views or profiles are reproduced from Dugald Cameron's artwork.
In 1977 Dugald published his first aircraft print in this style - a 43 Squadron Phantom - starting, with Alan Carlaw, the 'Squadron Prints' series.

Appendix 3

43 SQUADRON GALLERY

43 Squadron is particularly fortunate to have acquired a fine collection of paintings that record events which, often for obvious reasons, would have otherwise remained only as written memories. A selection of these follow which trace the development of The Fighting Cocks through both World Wars and into the jet age. The artists are Chris Golds, himself a former Hunter pilot with 43 Squadron and Dugald Cameron OBE.

"Six in one day"
by Chris Golds
see pages 21/22

"Gamecocks at play"
by Chris Golds
see Chapter 6

"Furies"
by Dugald Cameron
see Chapter 7

"Two short bursts"
by Chris Golds
page 74

"Air-sea rescue"
by Chris Golds
see page 111

"Once upon a time"
by Chris Golds
see Chapter 28

Appendix 4

SQUADRON BASES

STIRLING, Scotland	Formed 15 April 1916
NETHERAVON, England	30 August 1916
NORTHOLT, England	9 December 1916
ST OMER, France	17 January 1917
TREIZENNES, France	25 January 1917
AUCHEL (Lozinghem), France	30 May 1917
LA GORGUE, France	15 January 1918
AVESNES-LE-COMTE, France	22 March 1918
FOUQUEROLLES (Beauvais), France	3 June 1918
LIETTRES (Aire) , France	21 June 1918
LE TOUQUIN, France	14 July 1918
FIENVILLERS (Amiens), France	2 August 1918
SENLIS-LE-SEC, France	6 October 1918
BOUVINCOURT (Peronne), France	31 October 1918
BISSEGHEM, Belguim	15 November 1918
COGNELÉE, Belgium	26 November 1918
BICKENDORF, Cologne, Germany	19 December 1918
EIL, Germany	12 August 1919
SPITALGATE, England	25 August 1919
	Disbanded 31 December 1919

HENLOW, England	Reformed 1 July 1925
TANGMERE, England	12 December 1926
ACKLINGTON, England	18 November 1939
WICK, Scotland	26 February 1940
TANGMERE, England	31 May 1940
USWORTH, England	8 September 1940
DREM, Scotland	12 December 1940
ACKLINGTON, England	4 October 1941
TANGMERE, England	16 June 1942
KIRTON LINDSEY, England	1 September 1942
GIBRALTAR	5 November 1942
MAISON BLANCHE, Algeria	8 November 1942
JEMAPPES, Algeria	13 March 1943
TINGLEY, Algeria	18 April 1943
DJEBEL ABIOD, Tunisia	29 April 1943
MATEUR I, Tuniaia	26 May 1943
HAL FAR, Malta	9 June 1943
COMISO, Sicily	14 July 1943
PACHINO, Sicily	1 August 1943
PANEBIANCO, Sicily	27 August 1943
CATANIA, Sicily	30 August 1943
CASSALA, Sicily	2 September 1943
FALCONE, Italy	6 September 1943
TUSCIANO, Italy	16 September 1943
CAPODICHINO (Naples), Italy	11 October 1943
LAGO, Italy	15 January 1944
NETTUNO/LA BLANCA (Anzio), Italy	19 May 1944
TRE-CANCELLI, Italy	6 June 1944
TARQUINIA, Italy	14 June 1944
GROSSETTO, Italy	25 June 1944
PIOMBINO, Italy	5 July 1944
CALVI, Corsica	20 July 1944
RAMATUELLE, France	20 August 1944
SISTERON, France	25 August 1944
LYON/BRON, France	7 September 1944
LA JASSE, France	25 September 1944
PERETOLA (Florence), Italy	2 October 1944
RIMINI, Italy	16 November 1944
RAVENNA, Italy	17 February 1945
CAMPOFORDIMO (Rivolto), Italy	5 May 1945
KLAGENFURT, Austria	11 May 1945
ZELTWEG, Austria	10 September 1945
TISSANO, Italy	24 September 1946
TREVISO, Italy	18 January 1947
	Disbanded 16 May 1947

TANGMERE, England	Reformed 11 February 1949
LEUCHARS, Scotland	9 November 1950
NICOSIA, Cyprus	21 June 1961
KHORMAKSAR, Aden	1 March 1963
	Disbanded 7 November 1967

LEUCHARS, Scotland	Reformed 1 September 1969
	Disbanded 13 July 2009

Appendix 5

AIRCRAFT PERFORMANCE DETAILS

Aircraft	Engine	Power	Armament	Max. speed mph	Service Ceiling	Climb Mins to Feet
pwith 1½ Strutter	Clerget	130 hp	1 x ·303 inch Vickers gun 1 x ·303 inch Lewis gun	100 at 6,500 feet	15,500 feet	17·8 to 10,000
pwith Camel	Clerget	130 hp	2 x ·303 inch Vickers guns 4 x 20 lb bombs	113 at 10,000 feet	19,000 feet	10·6 to 10,000
pwith Snipe	Bentley BR2	230 hp	2 x ·303 inch Vickers guns 4 x 20 lb bombs	121 at 10,000 feet	20,500 feet	9·5 to 10,000
amecock	Jupiter VI	425 hp	2 x ·303 inch Vickers guns 4 x 20 lb bombs	155 at 5,000 feet	22,100 feet	7·7 to 10,000
skin IIIA	A-S Jaguar IV	420 hp	2 x ·303 inch Vickers guns 4 x 20 lb bombs	156 at sea level	27,000 feet	7·0 to 10,000
ry I	Kestrel IIS	525 hp	2 x ·303 inch Vickers guns	207 at 14,000 feet	28,000 feet	4·4 to 10,000
urricane I	Merlin II, III	1,030 hp	8 x ·303 inch guns	316 at 17,500 feet	33,200 feet	6·3 to 15,000
urricane II	Merlin XX	1,280 hp	IIa 8 x ·303 inch guns IIb 12 x ·303 inch guns IIc 4 x 20 mm cannons	339 at 22,000 feet (IIc tropical version 20 mph slower)	35,600 feet	9·1 to 20,000
pitfire V	Merlin 45, 46, 47, 50 & 55	1,440 hp	2 x 20 mm cannons 4 x ·303 inch guns	374 at 13,000/ 20,000 feet *	38,000 feet	7·0 to 20,000
pitfire VIII & IX	Merlin 61, 63 66 & 70	1,710 hp	IXc 2 x 20 mm, 4 x ·303 inch IXe 2 x 20 mm, 2 x ·5 inch IXc & IXe 1 x 500 lb bomb	408/416 at 21,000/ 27,000 ft *	43,000 feet	6·4/6·7 to 20,000
leteor F4	2 x Derwent 5	7,000 lbs thrust, SLS	4 x 20 mm cannons	585 at sea level	44,500 feet	11·5 to 40,000
leteor F8	2 x Derwent 8	7,200 lbs thrust, SLS	4 x 20 mm cannons	592 at sea level	44,000 feet	11·6 to 40,000
lunter F1	Avon 104 RA7	7,550 lbs thrust, SLS	4 x 30 mm Aden guns	710/·94M at sea level	(Absolute) 50,800 feet	9·8 to 45,000
lunter F4	Avon 115	7,550 lbs thrust, SLS	4 x 30 mm Aden guns	714/·94M at sea level	52,000 feet	9·85 to 45,000
lunter F6	Avon 203	10,000 lbs thrust, SLS	4 x 30 mm Aden guns 24 x 3 inch RPs or 2 x 1,000 lb bombs	725/·95M at sea level	54,000 feet	10·3 to 50,000
lunter FGA9	Avon 207	10,150 lbs thrust, SLS	4 x 30 mm Aden guns 24 x 3 inch RPs or 2 x 1,000 lb bombs	721/·95M at sea level	53,400 feet	7·5 to 45,000
hantom FG1	2 x Spey 168-25R	Total thrust 24,500 lbs cold 41,000 lbs reheat	4 x Sparrow AAM 4 x Sidewinder AAM 20 mm Vulcan gun	1,386/Mach 2·1 at 40,000 ft	57,200 feet	
ornado F3	2 x RB199 Turbofans	Total thrust 32,820 lbs	AMRAAM, ASRAAM Skyflash, AIM-9 Sidewinder ALARM, 27mm Mauser gun	1,480/Mach 2·2 at 40,000 ft	50,000 feet	Less than 2·0 to 30,000

* Speed and altitude varied depending on rated altitude of supercharger

Appendix 6

SQUADRON AIRCRAFT

No official records exist of aircraft allotted to or used by 43 Squadron prior to equipping with the Fury in 1931 and the records since then are incomplete. The following aircraft are all known to have been, at some time, on Squadron strength. Any numbers of possible but doubtful validity have been excluded. During training, between May 1916 and December 1916, Armstrong Whitworth FK 3, Royal Aircraft Factory BE 2c, AVRO 504 and Bristol Scout D aircraft were used.

SOPWITH 1½ STRUTTER December 1916 – September 1917

A960	Lts Kitto and Ward shot down 1 Hun 16/3/17; ditto 17/3/17
A961	At Northolt 1/17. In use 18/3/17
A962	In use 27/2/17
A970	In use 1/4/17
A971	New from 2 AD St Omer 18/3/17
A982	New from 2 AD St Omer 18/4/17
A1010	
A1040	At Northolt 1/17
A1043	In use 23/9/17
A1052 'L'	In use 8/17
A1079 'B6'	In use 7/17
A1081	At Northolt 19/12/16
A1097	In use 11/3/17
A1100 'C5'	
A1102	At Northolt 24/2/16. Rocker arm broke crossing Channel 26/1/17
A1104	At Northolt 23/12/16
A1105	At Northolt 22/12/16
A1107	Crashed (Ack-Ack) 10/2/17. Lt Edelston wounded
A1108	Shot down by Von Richthofen 4/3/17
A2388	
A2390	At Northolt 18/12/16
A2395	In use 17/3/17
A2398	
A2401	Shot down by Von Richthofen, Givenchy 2/4/17
A2405	
A2406	New from 2 AD 31/3/17. Shot down by Von Richthofen, Farbus 8/4/17
A2407	Collected from Lincoln, 30/1/17. Lt Knox, 1 Hun 6/3/17
A8232	From 2 AD 4/17. Lt O'Brien, 1 Hun 25/4/17
A8235	New from 2 AD 9/4/17
A8339	
A8784 'B2'	In use 7/17
A8785 'B4'	In use 7/17
B2552 'X'	

SOPWITH 1F1 CAMEL September 1917 – October 1918

B2351, B2354, B2392, B2341, B2342

B2510 'A'	
B3839 'W'	Lt Lingham's machine, Auchel, from 12/17

B5620, B5630, B6208, B6210, B7439

C8208 'N'	From 2 A Depot 13/9/17. Crashed 27/10/17
C8209	From 2 A Depot 12/9/17
C8240	
C8247	Lt S H Lewis missing 6/4/18
C8248	Shot down by Lt Weiss, JG 1; 6/4/18
C8263	
C8270	Capt Trollope's machine on 24/3/18 and lost with him on 28/3/18
C8281	
D1785 'Z'	At le Touquin, 7/18

D1848, D6402, D6404, D6452, E1467

SOPWITH 7F1 SNIPE August 1918 – December 1919 (cadre from 28 September 1919)

E6160	Returned to UK from Eil 20/8/19
E8000, E8004	
E8008	Returned to UK from Eil 23/8/19
E8013, E8014	
E8015 'E'	
E8016	
E8021, E8024, E8025, E8029, E8031, E8033, E8037, E8041, E8043	
E8064 'F'	
E8165, F2340, F2387	

SOPWITH 7F1 SNIPE April 1925 – May 1926

E6530, E6612, E6622, E6944, E7538, E7560, E7565, E7724,, F2435

GLOSTER GAMECOCK I April 1926 – June 1928

J7900
J7904 Squadron Leader's aircraft; black and white chequers on spine
J7905, J7906, J7907, J7908, J7909, J7911, J7918, J7919
J7920 All a/c up to J7920 delivered to Henlow and used at the RAF Pageant at Hendon in 1926
J8034, J8035, J8036, J8037, J8038 all delivered at Tangmere during 1927
J8090, J8096, J8414, J8415, J8416, J8417
J8418 Crashed at Eastergate, near Chichester
J8420, J8421

ARMSTRONG WHITWORTH SISKIN IIIA June 1928 – May 1931

J8341, J8363, J8381, J8386, J8394, J8632, J8644, J8653, J8666, J8670, J8822, J8836, J8837, J8844, J8846, J8849, J8851, J8853, J8863, J8866, J8878, J8890, J8893, J8896, J8905, J8906, J8937, J8941, J8944, J8953, J8957, J8958, J8959(a), J8963, J8966, J9304, J9318, J9321, J9326, J9340, J9358, J9359(b), J9365, J9375

(a) Squadron Leader's aircraft; black and white chequered fin.

(b) Destroyed in collision with prototype Hawker Hornet (later re-named Fury) during comparative trials at Tangmere, 1930. The Pilot (Plt Off J Heber-Percy) was unhurt.

ARMSTRONG WHITWORTH SISKIN IIIA (Dual control)

J7003, J7173	On strength August 1928
J7179, J9211	

HAWKER FURY I May 1931 – January 1939

Serial	TOC	Notes
K1928	15/4/31	To HAD 24/8/32
K1929	15/4/31	To Henlow 24/10/32
K1930	15/4/31	To HAD 19/10/35. In use again 9/36
K1931	15/4/31	To HAD 2/10/34
K1932	28/4/31	Still in use 5/37
K1933	28/4/31	Collided with K1936 on 28/2/33. To HAD on 30/3/33
K1934	28/4/31	To ARS 29/5/32
K1935	28/4/31	To Hawkers 12/1/32
K1936	28/4/31	Written off in collision with K1933 on 28/2/33
K1937	28/4/31	To Hawkers 13/3/35
K1938	28/4/31	To Hawkers 6/4/35
K1939	28/4/31	To Hawkers 28/9/31. In use again in 1937
K1940	28/4/31	To Hawkers 23/3/32
K1941	28/4/31	To 5 FTS 4/11/36
K1942	28/4/31	To Eastchurch as 749M 7/1/36
K1943	28/4/31	Crashed 2/6/32. Repaired and still in use in 1937
K1944	28/4/31	To Henlow 9/6/36
K1946		In use 11/36
K2050	28/6/35	To 5 MU early 1938

K2051	1/7/36	To 25 Squadron 28/7/36
K2052	1937	To 9 MU
K2070	11/12/36	
K2074	1936	
K2075	1936	For instructional use (999 M) 20/10/37
K2076	1/7/36	To 25 Squadron 24/7/36
K2080	1936	To 9 MU
K2081	1936	
K2882	11/12/36	To 87 Squadron in 1937
K2883	11/12/36	To 87 Squadron in 1937
K3731	15/2/35	To Brize Norton 30/12/38
K3740	12/6/35	To 9 MU
K5672	19/12/36	To 5 MU Kemble 6/2/39
K5674	2/6/36	To 5 MU Kemble 6/2/39
K5675	1/7/36	To 9 MU
K8250	1937	To CFS
K8251	1937	To 5 FTS
K8252		To 5 MU Kemble 6/2/39
K8253		To 5 MU Kemble 6/2/39
K8254		To 9 FTS
K8256		To Shawbury 30/12/38
K8257		To Station Flight, Northolt 1938
K8299		To 9 MU

HAWKER HURRICANE Mk.I December 1938 – September 1942

Serial	Code	TOC	Notes
L1592	FT-C	18/2/40	Cat 2 (Combat) 1/6/40.
			Now in Science Museum London as KW-R of 615 Squadron
L1608	FT-A	18/2/40	Shot down, (Sgt Ottewill) 7/6/40
L1704		20/4/39	to 111 Squadron 18/5/39
L1722		12/10/39	to 87 Squadron 15/10/39
L1723	NQ-N	6/12/38	
	FT -N	8/6/40	½ He 111, Whitby 3/2/40. To 3 Squadron
L1725		29/11/38	Sgt Arbuthnot baled out 5/12/39. Wreckage dug up in September 1978
L1726	NQ-D	2/12/38	2 e/a dest, 1 dam. (Sgt Ottewill) 1/6/40
	FT-D		
L1727	NQ-R	29/11/38	1 x He 111 dest. (Fg Off Simpson) 3/2/40
	FT-R		1 x He 111 dest. (Fg Off Edmonds) 8/4/40
			Crashed on ferry flight to Usworth 9/9/40
L1728	NQ-B	2/12/38	½ He 111 dest. (Sgt Carey) 30/1/40
	FT-B		Crashed, Cat B at Wick 13/5/40
L1729	NQ-S	3/12/38	Crashed on night take off
	FT-S		(Fg Off Simpson) 21/2/40
L1730		3/12/38	To 111 Squadron 25/8/39
L1731		8/12/38	Taxying accident Tangmere 20/11/39
			To 13 MU for repair 1/12/39
L1732	NQ-E	6/12/38	Flt Lt Hull hit airfield obstruction 29/8/39
	FT-E		To Morris Works at Cowley for repair 18/9/39
L1734	NQ-G	8/12/38	
	FT-G		Collided with L2066 at Acklington 18/1/40. Sgt Mullinger killed.
L1735		10/12/38	Crashed beyond repair (Fg Off Folkes) Tangmere 24/1/39
L1736	FT-H	30/12/38	1 e/a dest. 1 e/a dam. (Fg Off Edmonds) 1/6/40
			Sgt Crisp baled out after combat 16/8/40
L1737		10/12/38	Crashed after battle damage (Sgt Ayling) Rouen (Boos) France 7/6/40
L1738		13/12/38	Crashed night flying (Fg Off Rotheram killed) 22/4/39
L1739	FT-Q	15/12/38	Missing in action (Sgt Montgomery) 14/8/40
L1742		16/10/39	1 x He 111 on drome at Wick (Sgt Hallowes) 8/4/40
			Battle damaged (Plt Off Gorrie) 16/8/40
			Cat 2 To Hawkers for repair 22/8/40
L1744	NQ-A	13/12/38	
	FT-A		Crashed into sea off Coquet Island. (Fg Off Carswell) 9/2/40
L1758		14/4/40	1 x Do 17 off Wick (Sgt Ottewill) 9/5/40
			Missing at Dunkirk (Sgt Gough) 1/6/40

L1824	FT-F	5/9/39	Cat 1 Tangmere 29/9/39. 1 x He 111 dest. (Sqn Ldr Lott) from Wick 28/3/40 Crashed on approach (Plt Off Cruttenden) 9/7/40
L1825	FT-E	29/9/39	Night flying crash (Fg Off Sullivan) 7/10/39 Cat 2 to 4 MU 30/10/39
L1836		Before 27/4/40	Damaged at Wick 27/4/40. Repaired and to Tangmere on 11/6/40 Cat 2 after enemy action and landed at Ford (Plt Off Van den Hove) 4/9/40
L1847	FT-J	16/3/39	1 x He 111, Whitby 3/2/40 (Sgt Hallowes) 1 x He 111, off Acklington 9/2/40 (Sgt Hallowes) Missing (Fg Off Wilkinson killed) over France 7/6/40
L1849	FT-E	3/3/39	1 x He 111 (Sgt Ottewill) off Acklington 3/2/40 Plt Off Cruttenden baled out near Bognor after combat 7/7/40
L1931		4/40	Missing (Fg Off Edmonds killed) over France 7/6/40
L1944		19/9/39	½ He 111 dest. (Fg Off Edmonds) 3/2/40. Crashed (Plt Off Campbell killed) near Hawkinge 29/7/40
L1958		19/5/39	Command Reserve aircraft, to 73 Squadron, France 11/10/39
L1963		27/9/40	Sgt Toogood killed in unexplained dive from high altitude on practice flight. Usworth 27/10/40
L1968		9/9/40	Crashed into sea during Air Firing practice flight. Sgt Stoker killed 4/2/41
L2066		11/39	First squadron aircraft with metal wings and DH 2-pitch propellor. Collided with L1734 at Acklington l8/1/40. Sgt Steeley killed)
L2116		14/1/40	1 x He 111 at Whitby 3/2/40. 1 x He 111 in sea 22/2/40. 1 x He 111 near Wick 8/4/40. All destroyed by Flt Lt Peter Townsend. Lost in action over France (Flt Lt Rowland wounded) 7/6/40
L2143	FT-C	27/10/39	To 13 MU for repair following u/c collapse 17/4/40. Returned to 43 (FT-D) 7/9/40. To 59 OTU 9/2/41
N2321		15/1/40	Crashed at Acklington, Cat 2 22/2/40
N2550		14/4/40	Lost at sea, 40 miles ESE of Wick Fg Off Folkes missing 16/4/40
N2584		6/4/40	Fg Off Carswell baled out after combat, Dunkirk 1/6/40
N2585		5/4/40	Sgt Hallowes destroyed 4 e/a, Dunkirk 1/6/40 Dest 1 x Me 109 and baled out over France 7/6/40
N2615		9/6/40	Crashed in sea (Sgt Pratt killed) 15/6/40
N2618		9/6/40	Crashed on landing (Plt Off James) 16/6/40
N2621		9/6/40	Plt Off Woods-Scawen crash landed on Isle of Wight after combat (2 x Ju 87 claimed as dest.) 16/8/40
N2665		12/4/40	Flt Lt Simpson claimed 2 x Me 109, Dunkirk 1/6/40 and 2 x Me 109 and 1 x Me 110 over France 7/6/40. Cat 2 after night overshoot (Plt Off Lane) 25/7/40. Returned to 43 (FT-Z) on 29/8/40.
P2570			In use at Drem 1/41
P2682		4/9/40	Cat 2 after heavy landing Usworth 14/9/40
P2805	FT-C		Known to be at Drem 12/40 to 2/41
P2826		1/40	To 55 OTU 24/4/41
P3097		29/10/40	In use at Drem 2/41
P3140		11/7/40	Flt Lt Simpson baled out over sea near Worthing 19/7/40
P3142	FT-N		At Drem 1/41
P3179		8/8/40	Sgt Noble, killed in action, Hove 30/8/40
P3202		22/7/40	Plt Off Gray baled out after combat, Bosham 26/8/40
P3214		22/7/40	Battle damage Cat 3. Plt Off Woods-Scawen landed at Tangmere 8/8/40
P3216		22/7/40	Battle damage Cat 2. Plt Off Upton force landed near Selsey 16/8/40
P3220		22/7/40	Plt Off Lane baled out alter combat Near Bosham 26/8/40
P3267		17/6/40	Plt Off Upton force landed, Isle of Wight after combat 8/8/40. Cat 2
P3357		9/40	Forced landing after engine failure at Chirnside, Berwickshire. Sgt Malinowski unhurt. Cat 2 31/10/40
P3386	FT-Y	19/5/40	First Rotol prop on Squadron. Flew throughout the Battle of Britain and was never damaged. Destroyed 12 e/a in the hands of four different pilots. In use until 2/41 when went to 55 OTU. Bumed out in a crash in 1943
P3462	FT-D		In use at Drem 2/41
P3464		9/6/40	Sqn Ldr Lott baled out after combat and aircraft crashed and burned out near Fontwell 9/7/40
P3466	FT-X	9/6/40	Survived until 3/3/41 when undercarriage collapsed on landing at Drem. Cat AC, to 43 Group for repair
P3468		9/6/40	Missing after combat (Plt Off Oelofse) 8/8/40

P3527		9/6/40	Forced landing after engine failure 3 miles S of Usworth. Sgt Siermer (Polish) unhurt. 26/11/40
P3531		9/6/40	Sgt Buck baled out and killed over sea 19/7/40
P3575		19/5/40	At Wick. To 605 Squadron next day 20/5/40
P3665	FT-R	16/9/40	To CRU 20/1/41 Cat B
P3713			In use (non op) at Kirton in Lindsey 9/42
P3717			Heavy landing Cat B Drem 23/4/41
P3775	FT-P	3/2/41	Landing accident (Plt Off Vernon unhurt) 1/5/41
P3776		7/9/40	Forced landing near Aberdeen alter being hit by return fire. (Plt Off Tufnell wounded)
P3781	FT-O	8/6/40	Missing after combat (Plt Off Cruttenden) 8/8/40
P3784	FT-U	8/6/40	Forced landing near Amberley after engine failure. Sgt Hallowes unhurt. Cat 2 20/7/40
P3786		8/6/40	Fg Off Carswell baled out after combat. 2/9/40
P3809		30/10/40	Overshot and overtumed at Drem 11/2/41 (Plt Off Doll unhurt)
P3903		14/8/40	Plt Off du Vivier baled out 2/9/40
P3964		12/7/40	Fg Off Haworth (Missing) baled out over sea 20/7/40
P3971		11/7/40	Battle damage 15/8/40. Lost in bombed hangar 16/8/40
P3972		11/7/40	Flt Lt Morgan baled out Cocking Down 13/8/40
P3973		11/7/40	Missing after combat over sea (Plt Off de Mancha) 21/7/40
P5188		27/8/40	To 145 Squadron 8/12/40
P5191		27/8/40	Wheels up landing 25/9/40. To 83 MU 27/9/40
P5196		27/8/40	Battle damage Cat 2 (Plt Off Van den Hove) 6/9/40. To 13 MU 11/9/40
P5197		10/4/42	Sgt Lewis baled out after Glycol fire 16/5/42
R4102		9/8/40	Destroyed by fire after crash landing following combat 20 miles North of Tangmere (Plt Off Woods-Scawen) 13/8/40
R4107	FT-B	9/8/40	Taken off charge 20/4/41
R4108		9/8/40	Crash landed at Tangmere (Sgt Deller) 12/8/40 Destroyed in bombed hangar while awaiting collection 16/8/40
R4109		9/8/40	Forced landing Pulborough (Flt Lt Carey wounded) Cat 2 18/8/40
R4110		9/8/40	Cat 2 after Combat 12/8/40. Lost in hangar 16/8/40
R4196		21/10/40	Flying accident 21/2/41. To 43 Group for repair
R4225	FT -F	29/8/40	Force landed after fuel failure. Cat 3 10/11/40
R4227		12/40	Plt Off Malarowski (Poland) baled out over Firth of Forth after engine failure on standing patrol 15/2/41
R4231	FT-G	17/8/40	Battle damage Cat 2 26/8/40. Repaired and returned 10/9/40. To 13 MU 9/8/41
V6533		17/8/40	To 19 MU 24/8/40. Believed to be aircraft over-stressed by Sgt Hallowes on 17/8/40, (page 95)
V6537	FT-E	4/2/41	Ferry pilot retracted u/c too early while taking off at Henlow to return aircraft to 43 Sqn at Drem
V6542		17/8/40	Flt Lt Morgan wounded in combat 6/9/40. Aircraft Cat 2 and to 43 Group for repair 8/9/40
V6548		17/8/40	Sqn Ldr Badger baled out wounded over Kent 30/8/40
V6606	FT-X	10/4/42	Cat B night flying accident 30/4/42
V6641		28/8/40	Sqn Ldr Caesar Hull crashed (killed in action) at Purley and aircraft totally destroyed 7/9/40
V6925		28/10/40	Engine failure (Sgt Sika) hit invasion poles near North Berwick. Cat E 9/2/41
V7054			Non op at Kirton in Lindsey 9/42
V7126	FT-F	28/11/40	To 55 OTU 13/5/41
V7206		23/7/40	To 59 OTU 9/2/41
V7221		23/7/40	To 213 Squadron 29/10/40
V7257		19/8/40	Flt Lt Reynell baled out (Killed in Action) 7/9/40
V7259		19/8/40	Plt Off North baled out after combat 26/8/40
V7303		19/8/40	Night Flying accident (Sgt Stoodley killed) 24/10/40
V7308		18/8/40	Plt Off Brunner force landed Tangmere after combat 26/8/40
V7309		18/8/40	Sgt Deller baled out over Kent 7/9/40
V7364		9/8/40	Battle damage. 12/8/40. Inspected by 43 Group 13/8/40. Lost in bombed hangar while awaiting collection 16/8/40
V7366	FT-Q	9/8/40	To 55 OTU 29/4/41
V7420		24/8/40	Plt Off Woods-Scawen baled out (killed) Ivychurch, Kent 2/9/40
V7440	FT-M	24/2/41	To 312 Squadron 3/5/41
V7597	FT-W	16/2/41	To 55 OTU 10/5/41
W9119		16/2/41	To 55 OTU 10/5/41
W9147		16/2/41	To 55 OTU 28/4/41
W9185	FT-K	24/2/41	To 121 Squadron 25/5/41

W9186	FT-A	21/2/41	To 55 OTU 10/5/41
AG236	FT-L	12/7/42	Until 9/42

HAWKER HURRICANE Mk. II April 1941 – August 1942

Serial	Mk.	Code	TOC	Notes
Z2325	IIa	FT-N	30/11/41	To 59 OTU 28/12/41. Returned from 8/3/41 to 1/4/41
Z2385	IIa		2/5/41	To de Havilland 21/12/41
Z2388	IIa	FT-T	3/5/41	To 47 MU 8/10/41
Z2407	IIa	FT-U	2/5/41	To 47 MU 7/11/41
Z2463	IIa	FT-B	27/11/41	To Taylorcraft 1/4/42
Z2464	IIa		23/4/41	Engine failure, forced landing 4/5/41. To 82 MU 25/4/41
Z2520	IIa	FT-S	2/5/41	Crashed in River Tay (Sgt Welling killed) 1/9/41
Z2577	IIa	FT-H	2/5/41	½ Ju 88 (Plt Off Cotton) 7/5/41. To 59 OTU 31/12/41
Z2582	IIa	FT-K	13/10/41	To de Havilland 26/11/41
Z2629	IIa	FT-P	21/4/41	To 245 Squadron 2/2/41
Z2638	IIa	FT-W	2/5/41	½ Ju 88 (Sgt Lister) 7/5/41. Crashed (Plt Off Czajkowski badly injured) 2/6/41. To 43 Group 17/6/41
Z2639	IIa		19/10/41	Crashed on ferry flight. (Sgt Bower killed) 29/11/41
Z2641	IIb		15/4/42	In action at Dieppe. To 245 Squadron 22/9/41
Z2661	IIa			u/c lock failed on landing at Ayr 28/5/41
Z2667	IIa	FT-C	21/4/41	To Civil Rep Org 26/11/41
Z2682	IIa		31/1/42	Crashed 6/3/42. Cat B
Z2684	IIa		19/10/41	Forced landing after engine failure (Plt Off Scuddy) 8/5/41 To 43 Group 17/5/41
Z2685	IIa	FT-K	2/5/41	To 59 OTU 28/12/41
Z2772	IIa	FT-N	21/4/41	Sgt Brady killed on ferry flight 24/11/41
Z2799	IIa	FT-F	2/5/41	To 12 MU 27/10/41
Z2801	IIa		21/4/41	Sgt Haley baled out after getting lost on night ops 7/5/41
Z2807	IIa	FT-D	29/3/41	Collided with Z3270 during practice attacks. Sgt Turner killed 12/10/41
Z2893	IIb	FT-L	7/2/42	Flt Sgt Helbock killed in high-speed stall while testing the Franks G-Suit. Cat E
Z2908	IIb		23/7/41	To 29 MU 30/1/42
Z2915	IIb	FT-P	15/11/41	To 245 Squadron 22/9/42
Z2928	IIb	FT-S	19/10/41	
Z2968	IIb		19/10/41	Flt Sgt Williams force landed in sea 10 miles E of Blyth after engine failure. Pilot saved
Z2971	IIa		2/9/41	Plt Off Bourne hit hill on Ops intercept patrol 5/9/41
Z2985	IIb	FT-W	4/6/41	u/c collapse at night 18/11/41. Repaired and retumed on 17/1/42. To Taylorcraft 1/4/42
Z3029	IIb	FT-Y	17/8/42	Cat B after combat at Dieppe 19/8/42
Z3031	IIb	FT-A	21/4/41	1 x Ju 88 (Flt Lt du Vivier) 28/5/41. Later FT-J
Z3061	IIb			In action at Dieppe 19/8/42
Z3068	IIc		2/4/42	Collided with electricity cables while low-flying (Flt Sgt Reed killed) 17/4/42
Z3072	IIb	FT-R	20/10/41	
Z3078	IIb	FT-S	19/4/41	To CRS Witney 4/12/41
Z3079	IIb	FT-B	19/4/41	1 x Ju 88 dest. (Flt Lt du Vivier) 10/5/41. Plt Off Czajkowski force landed at Longtown after engine failure during chase alter Ju.88. Rtd to 43 Sqn as FT-D 8/42
Z3081	IIb	FT-C	28/6/42	In action Dieppe 19/8/42. To 543 Squadron 4/9/42
Z3143	IIb		19/4/41	Ditched after destroying 1 x Ju 88 (Sqn Ldr Morgan rescued by ship) 24/7/41.
Z3149	IIb		19/4/41	1 x Ju 88 destroyed (Flt Lt du Vivier) 7/5/41
Z3150	IIb	FT-V	19/4/41	3 e/a destroyed in 2 nights 6/5/41 & 7/5/41 Plt Off Mehta (killed) crashed on Peel Fell 3/11/41
Z3169	IIb	FT-W	9/4/42	In action Dieppe. To 245 Squadron 24/9/42
Z3262	IIb	FT-X	8/6/41	Crashed on Ferry Flight (Sgt Lea) Cat B 8/1/42
Z3265	IIb	FT-G	3/6/41	1 x Ju 88 destroyed 8/6/41. 1 x He 111 destroyed 11/7/41 by Sqn Ldr Morgan
Z3270	IIb	FT-B	2/6/41	
Z3310	IIb	FT-E	10/5/41	u/c collapsed l3/6/41. Repaired by 25/9/41. To 47 MU 8/10/41
Z3316	IIb		10/5/41	Forced landing on Ops flight. Cat E 1/5/41 (Flt Sgt le Gal FF)
Z3336	IIb	FT-Y	3/6/41	To Taylorcraft. To Russia 30/1/42

Z3578	IIb	FT-V	1/42	
Z3584	IIb	FT-K	12/12/41	Cat AC 26/6/42. Later to Russia
Z3672	IIb	FT-T	4/8/42	In action Dieppe. To 245 Squadron 22/9/42
Z3687	IIb	FT-E	26/5/42	Cat B after action at Dieppe 19/8/42
Z3684	IIb	FT-L	14/8/42	In action Dieppe 19/8/42
Z3895	IIb	FT-O	17/2/42	In action Dieppe 19/8/42. To 534 Squadron 5/9/42
Z5046	IIb		7/7/41	To 47 MU 10/10/41. Later to Russia
Z5153	IIb	FT-H	6/42	Damaged at Dieppe. To 245 Squadron 22/9/42
Z5324	IIb		31/1/42	
AF961	Mk X	FT-Y	29/4/42	Canadian-built Mark Is redesignated Mark X
AG236	Mk X	FT-L	29/4/42	and used non-operationally 6/42 to 8/42
AM311	IIb			
AM315	IIb	FT-X	4/42	Flew four sorties at Dieppe 19/8/42
BD712	IIc	FT-G	3/12/41	Shot down at Dieppe (Flt Sgt Wik POW) 19/8/42
BD715	IIc	FT-M	3/12/41	½ Ju 88 (Flt Lt May) 9/12/41
BD721	IIb		12/2/42	
BD734	IIc	FT-O	3/12/41	½ Ju 88 (Flt Sgt Pipa) 9/12/41
BD762	IIc	FT-J	3/12/41	
BD954	IIc	FT-D	3/12/41	Crashed on Turbinlite patrol (Flt Lt Hutchison killed) 20/5/42
BE711	IIc	FT-S	1/42	In action Dieppe 19/8/42
BN229	IIc	FT-V	2/1/41	Missing on Intruder Patrol (Sgt Lynds) 5/8/42
BN230	IIc	FT-A	2/1/42	1 x Ju 88 destroyed (Sqn Ldr du Vivier) 25/5/42
BN234	IIc	FT-U	1/42	Crash-landed after return from Dunkirk 19/8/42
BN235	IIc	FT-F	28/1/42	To 532 Sqn
BN372	IIc	FT-J	5/7/42	To 534 Squadron 5/9/42
BP700	IIc	FT-C	19/5/42	To Russia 14/1/43
BP703	IIc	FT-O	20/5/42	Plt Off Snell baled out off Dieppe 19/8/42
BV160	IIa	FT-C	6/42	In action Dieppe 19/8/42
BV162	IIa	FT-H	6/42	
HL560	IIc	FT-N	2/6/42	To 532 Squadron 4/9/42
HL562	IIc	FT-B	3/6/42	To 532 Squadron 4/9/42
HL563	IIc	FT-K	3/6/42	
HL656	IIc	FT-D	6/42	In action Dieppe 19/8/42
HL863	IIc	FT-T	6/42	Missing on Intruder Patrol (Sgt Whitten) 26/7/42

Mk. IIc HURRICANES (Tropicalised) used in North Africa, November 1942 – March 1943

HV356 FT-M HV399 FT-T HV402 FT-V HV403 FT-B HV406 FT-E HV407 FT-S HV408 FT-X
HV409 FT-O HV417 FT-K HV536 FT-J HV541 FT-F HV560 FT-Z HV580 FT- HV674 FT-
HV696 FT-D HV740 FT-A HV817 FT-C

These 17 Hurricanes together with one flown by Wing Commander Pedley took off from Gibraltar on 8 November 1942 without knowing if there would be a secure landing ground at Algiers (page 121). Their subsequent history is not recorded in detail but HV407 crashed on 29/11/42 and HV561 was destroyed in a bombing raid on Maison Blanche on 6/1/43.

Other Hurricanes used before March 1943 were:

HV421, HV424, HV478 FT-S, HV494 FT-P, HV580, HV674, HV696, HV740, HV817, HV876 FT-U, HV953, HV960, HV970, HV973, HW122 FT-W, HW132 FT-N, HW137 FT-R Cat E (Bombed) 15/1/43, HW138 FT-H Flt Sgt Webster baled out 6/1/43, HW139, HW197 FT-Y, HW204 FT-F, HW239 FT-U, HW421 FT-B, HW570 FT-N

SUPERMARINE SPITFIRE Mk. V February 1943 – 3 January 1944

Serial	Mk.	Code	TOC	Notes
AB463	Vb	FT-N	18/2/43	Forced landing en route to Jemappes 13/3/43
BR288	Vc	FT-F	18/2/43	Missing on sweep (Flt Lt Reading) 4/7/43
BR330	Vc	FT-B		In use 9/43
EE782	Vc	FT-D		In use 8/43
EE791	Vc	FT-J	18/2/43	In use 8/43
EF549	Vc	FT-E	7/43	Ditched on Salerno patrol (Flt Sgt Leighton) 10/9/43
EF682	Vc	FT-B	14/11/43	To Bari 3/1/44

ER655	Vc	FT-D	11/43	To Bari 3/1/44
ES112				On loan from 114 MU for standby duty prior to Squadron re-equipping
ES125	Vb		18/2/43	
ES129	Vc		18/2/43	
ES146	Vc			On loan from 114 MU for standby duty prior to Squadron re-equipping
ES183	Vc		18/2/43	Missing after destroying a Ju 88 (Plt Off Wills) 22/2/43
ES246	Vb	FT-W	18/2/43	
ES287	Vc	FT-O	18/2/43	For Major Inspection 23/7/43
ES292	Vc	FT-T	18/2/43	Crashed (Lost air pressure) Hal Far 13/6/43
ES294	Vc	FT-P	18/2/43	With 3203 Servicing Commando for repair 11/43
ES315	Vc	FT-O	30/7/43	
ES352	Vc	FT-Y	18/2/43	To 243 Squadron after engine change 19/8/43
ES355	Vc	FT-S	18/2/43	Missing on sweep (Flt Sgt Brown) 18/6/43
JG724	Vc	FT-H	18/2/43	Flown out to MU, loss of power 17/8/43
JG727	Vc	FT-A	18/2/43	Ditched on convoy patrol after combat (Fg Off Newton) 13/5/43
JG740	Vc	FT-A	16/5/43	Missing on sweep (Fg Off Barker) 4/7/43
JG741	Vc	FT-H	18/2/43	Crashed on take-off (Flt Sgt Lane killed) 11/5/43
JG769	Vb	FT-D	18/2/43	Replaced by Mark IX 8/43
JG869	Vc	FT-S	5/43	Replaced by Mark IX 5/8/43
JG879	Vc	FT-R	18/2/43	Ditched after combat (Plt Off Richards) 12/5/43
JG941	Vc	FT-	7/43	
JK101	Vc	FT-Z	18/2/43	Flown by Sqn Ldr Rook until 8/43. Then out for major insp.
JK188	Vc	FT-D		Battle damage 31/7/43. To Wing RSU for repair
JK191	Vc		11/43	To Bari 3/1/44
JK539	Vc	FT-C	8/43	In use 9/43
JK610	Vc	FT-	7/43	Cat 3. Wrinkled fuselage 12/8/43
JK612	Vc	FT-V	5/43	Cat 3 following enemy action 18/7/43 (Plt Off Leeming)
JK616	Vc	FT-F	14/7/43	
JK721	Vc	FT-B	10/43	Missing on bomber escort (WO M D Smith, POW) 13/11/43
JK872	Vc	FT-		To Bari 3/1/44
JK873	Vc	FT-A	6/8/43	With 3203 Servicing Commando for repair 11/43
JK922	Vc	FT-Y	8/43	To Bari 3/1/44
JK974	Vc	FT -Q	16/5/43	Cat 3. Taxying accident, wrinkled fuselage 25/7/43
JL122	Vc		7/43	
JL133	Vc	FT-T	15/7/43	In use 10/43
JL183	Vc	FT-C	9/43	In use 11/43
LZ945	Vc	FT-W	8/43	Overturned on landing at Roger LG (Salerno) 16/9/43. RTP
LZ982	Vc	FT-P	9/43	To Bari 3/1/44
MA281	Vc		9/43	To Bari 3/1/44
MA345	Vc	FT-G	6/7/43	To Bari 3/1/44
MA682	Vc	FT-J	9/43	To Bari 3/1/44

SUPERMARINE SPITFIRE Mk. VIII August 1944 – November 1944

Serial	Mk.	Code	TOC	Notes
JF571	LF	FT-13	12/9/43	Flown by Sqn Ldr Horbaczewski. 2 x FW 190s destroyed and 1 x FW 190 damaged on 16/9/43. Burst into flames on take-off 17/9/43 Cat 3
JF887	LF	FT-L	19/8/44	Crashed and on fire landing at Florence 1/10/44
MT663	LF	FT-	9/8/44	
MT664	LF	FT-	12/8/44	
MT670	LF	FT-	8/44	
MT677	LF	FT-	18/8/44	
MT680	LF	FT-E	31/7/44	Hit by flak, on fire Fg Off Guest baled out 31/8/44
MT688	LF	FT-C	8/8/44	
MT689	LF	FT-A	26/8/44	
MT714	LF	FT-F	9/8/44	
MT776	LF	FT-H	13/8/44	
MT785	LF	FT-	13/8/44	
MT786	LF	FT-P	15/8/44	
MT929	LF	FT-	12/8/44	
MT930	LF	FT-B	11/8/44	

SUPERMARINE SPITFIRE Mk. IX August1943 – May 1947

All Mk VIIIs were replaced by Mk.IXs during October 1944

(LF = Low altitude fighter role, HF= High altitude fighter role)

Serial	Mk.	Code	TOC	Notes
EN140	F	FT-10	1/8/43	Destroyed 1½ e/a 11/43
EN296	F	FT-	2/45	Shot down (Flak). WO Mathers killed 21/2/45
EN399	F	FT-B	5/1/45	To 110 MU 21/3/45
EN577	LF	FT-O	3/44	Crashed Cat 3 19/4/44
EN630	LF	FT-	1946	In use until 5/47
JG936	F	FT-1	3/10/43	
		FT-C		Shot down, Flak (Flt Sgt Booth killed) 5/2/44
JL351	LF	FT-F	11/44	Flak damage. To 324 Wing RSS 4/45
JL369	LF	FT-		
LZ822	F	FT-	9/43	Destroyed 2 e/a Fg Off Turkington 11/43
LZ923	F	FT-12	9/43	Undercarriage collapsed. To 324 Wing RSS 16/10/43
LZ949	F	FT-J	2/45	To 324 Wing RSS 18/4/45.
				Finished in bare metal overall and called 'the cocoa tin'
MA231	F	FT-	2/45	To 110 MU 5/9/45
MA249	F	FT-	18/8/43	
MA259	F	FT-7	18/8/43	
MA369	F	FT-E	3/45	To 110 MU 5/45
MA398	F	FT-A	3/1/44	Rejected for loss of compression 2/44
MA400	F	FT-4	9/43	
		FT-F		In use until 22/2/44
MA449	F	FT-	3/1/44	In use until 22/2/44
MA451	F	FT-4	18/8/43	
MA462	F	FT-	3/1/44	In use until 22/2/44
MA470	F	FT-8	8/43	Fg Off Craig missing 15/11/43
MA478	F	FT-		1 e/a destroyed 12/11/43 (Flt Sgt Booth)
MA481	F	FT-2	19/8/43	Destroyed 3 e/a during 11/43
MA501	F	FT-3	8/43	2½ e/a destroyed during 11/43.
		FT-E	2/44	Fly out for 240 hour inspection
MA511	F	FT-6	19/8/43	Runaway prop constant speed control. Flt Sgt Webster baled out 19/9/43
MA535	F	FT-8	16/11/43	Mid-air collision with MA627 (Plt Off Brodie killed) 2/1/44
MA546	F	FT-2	9/43	
		FT-V		Still in use 1/44
MA561	F	FT-		In use until 22/2/44
MA572	F	FT-9	18/8/43	Dived into sea from high altitude (Plt Off Snell killed) 31/8/43
MA576	F	FT-5	11/43	In use until 22/2/44
MA589	F	FT-	3/1/44	Missing after combat at Anzio (Fg Off Richards) 22/1/44
MA627	F	FT-9	1943	2½ e/a destroyed 11/43. Collided with MA535 in mid-air 2/1/44
MA690	F	FT-	1946	In use until 5/47
MB973	LF	TBB		Personal machine of OC 324 Wing, Gp Capt T B Beresford.
				In use from late 1944 to 1946
MH426	LF	FT-F	12/5/45	Until 5/47
MH444		FT-A	22/2/44	To 3 Squadron SAAF
MH509	LF	FT-X	22/2/44	Missing on Ops. (WO Saville POW) 13/6/44
MH507	LF	FT-C	22/2/44	
MH530	F	FT-3	10/43	
		FT-A		In use until 22/2/44
MH564	F	FT-	3/1/44	In use until 22/2/44
MH607	F	FT-E	2/44	In use until 22/2/44
MH635	F	FT-	3/1/44	In use until 22/2/44
MH648	F	FT- J	3/1/44	In use until 22/2/44
MH659	F	FT-	3/1/44	Shot down, Flak (WO Luke killed) 5/2/44
MH675	F	FT-	3/1/44	In use until 22/2/44
MH700	F	FT-A	23/4/45	In use until 9/45 then to 110 MU
MH711	F	FT-G	3/1/44	In use until 22/2/44
MH737	LF	FT-O	1/5/45	Crashed, overturned on landing 23/9/46
MH766	LF	FT-B	1/8/44	Replaced by a Mark VIII 12/8/44
MH773	LF	FT-B	28/2/44	Until 18/5/44
MH779	LF	FT-D	8/5/45	In use until 5/47
MH793	LF	FT-F	22/2/44	Missing 5/44
MH807	F	FT-A	2/2/44	Until 22/2/44

MH888	F	FT-B	3/1/44	Until 22/2/44
MH893	F	FT-D	3/1/44	Until 22/2/44
MH896	F	FT-H	21/2/45	Until 8/11/45
MH929	LF	FT-Z	6/44	Disappeared in cloud during sweep from Calvi (Flt Lt Grifhths)
MH954	LF	FT-T	1945	In use until 5/47
MH984	LF	FT-D	22/2/44	Wheels-up landing at Nettuno 4/5/44
MH996	F	FT-H	14/2/45	To 110 MU 10/4/45
MH997	F	FT- J	21/4/45	To 110 MU 4/9/45
MJ134	LF	FT-E	22/2/44	
MJ179	LF	FT-D	6/44	In use until 8/44
MJ234	LF	FT-R	22/2/44	In use until 8/44
MJ236	LF	FT-	22/2/44	In use 5/44
MJ401	LF	FT-	22/2/44	Missing on ops. (Fg Off Cassels) 31/5/44
MJ483	LF	FT- J	22/2/44	Missing en route to Anzio (WO Stevenson) 4/5/44
MJ496	LF	FT-	1/5/45	In use until 5/47
MJ498	LF	FT-P	11/4/45	In use until 5/47
MJ513	LF	FT-	7/44	Replaced by a Mark VIII 8/44
MJ533	LF	FT-O	1/3/44	Until 21/5/44
MJ562	LF	FT-U	18/3/45	Flew last Operational flight of war 2/5/45
MJ577	LF	FT-P	5/5/44	Crashed on landing (Flt Sgt Randall) Calvi 26/7/44
MJ618	LF	FT-G	22/2/44	Engine failure on take-off 31/3/44
MJ624	LF	FT-G	2/4/44	Engine lost power on take-off and overshot 5/44
MJ628	LF	R du V	3/44	Wing Commander du Vivier's aircraft
MJ631	LF	FT-	4/8/44	To 111 Squadron, replaced by a Mark VIII 13/8/44
MJ634	LF	FT-U	20/4/44	
MJ643	LF	FT-	22/2/44	
MJ676	LF	FT- J	4/44	In use until 10/11/44
MJ680	LF	FT-T	5/44	Replaced by Mark VIII 8/44
MJ682	LF	FT-		In use 5/44
MJ725	LF	FT-E	5/44	Replaced by a Mark VIII at Calvi 8/44
MJ736	LF	FT-K	22/2/44	Replaced by a Mark VIII at Calvi 8/44
MJ755	LF	FT-V	22/7/44	Flak damage. Cat C 8/9/44
MJ836	LF	FT-T	3/44	In use until 11/44
MJ955	LF	FT-O	23/10/46	In use until 5/47
MK118	LF	FT-F	5/44	Crashed (Plt Off Simpson killed) on landing Calvi 6/8/44
MK405	LF	FT-		Flak damage. Cat B 18/1/45
MK445	LF	FT-H	11/44	Flak damage. Cat B (Flt Lt Hedderwick) 26/12/44
MK513	LF	FT-X	6/44	In use 8/44
MK528	LF	FT-M	13/4/45	To 113 MU Treviso 6/8/46
MK549	LF	FT-N		Shot down, Flak, (Flt Lt Manson killed) 20/3/45
MK553	LF	FT-A	5/45	Replaced by a Mark VIII at Calvi 26/8/44
MK569	LF	FT-V	10/10/46	In use until 5/47
MK571	LF	FT-B	21/5/44	Replaced by a Mark VIII at Calvi 11/8/44
MK644	LF	FT-	7/44	
MK755	LF	FT-V		Crashed on landing Cat E. (Flt Sgt Webber) 2/10/46
MK769	LF	FT-		SOC 28/4/45
ML139	LF	FT-H	11/4/45	In use until 5/47
ML323	LF	FT-L	13/4/45	To 110 MU 16/4/45
ML410	LF	FT-	16/4/45	
NH184	LF	FT-O	18/4/45	Later FT-R and in use until 5/47
NH252	LF	FT-P	2/8/44	Replaced by a Mark VIII at Calvi 14/8/44
NH371	LF			
PL127	LF	FT-J		In use at Zeltweg 9/45 and until 5/47
PL319	LF	FT-B	16/4/45	Crashed on return from Desert Air Force Flypast 28/5/45
PL355	LF	FT-	11/44	Shot down, Flak (WO Hollis killed) 10/3/45
PL387	HF	FT-	3/9/45	From 93 Squadron on disbanding
PL453	LF	FT-K	10/3/45	To 72 Squadron 16/3/45
PT487	LF	FT-T	10/3/45	Flew on last operational flight of war 2/5/45 Crashed at Klagenfurt 7/6/45
PT526	LF	FT-P	11/44	In use until 3/45
PT530	LF	FT-A	21/11/44	Flak damage Cat B (Sqn Ldr Jupp) 9/1/45
PT534	LF	FT-	11/44	Missing on ops. (Flt Lt Creed POW) 30/1/45
PT542	LF	FT-	11/44	Missing on ops. (Flt Sgt Leigh killed) 4/12/44
PT546	LF	FT -H	11/44	Crashed after Flak damage (Flt Lt Thomas OK) 15/12/44
PT575	LF	FT-	10/44	
PT 585	LF	FT-	7/10/44	Shot down by USAAF Mustangs (Flt Lt Cummings killed) 11/11/44

PT588	LF	FT-	10/44	Flt Lt Thompson baled out after Flak damage led to loss of control 24/10/44
PT667	LF	FT-L	10/44	Shot down by USAAF Mustangs (Flt Lt Creed wounded) 11/11/44
PT700	LF	FT-R	13/11/44	Overturned on landing at Ravenna LG 15/4/45
PT706	LF	FT-	13/11/44	Cat 1 (Flak) 27/1/45
PT712	LF	FT-H	13/11/44	Spun in after Flak damage (Flt Lt Hedderwick killed) 11/2/45
PT757	LF	FT-B	10/44	Crashed near Forli, Flak damage (WO Hollingsworth OK) 4/1/45
PT760	LF	FT-	10/44	In use 12/44
PT773	LF	FT-P	10/44	
PT774	LF	FT-S	10/44	Missing on Ops. (Flt Sgt Hemingway evaded and returned OK) 23/4/45
PT846	LF	FT-D	12/44	Cat 2 (Flak) WO Wilkinson wounded but returned to base) 11/1/45
PV124	LF	FT-D	13/11/44	Cat 2 (Flak) 28/12/44. To Wing RSS and later to 93 Squadron
PV137	LF	FT-C	2/12/44	Shot down by Flak (WO Dauphin killed) 1/1/45
PV193	LF	FT-D	18/4/45	Crashed after Flak damage (Sgt Crookes OK) 30/4/45
PV308	HF	FT-D	16/3/45	Reallocated to 93 Squadron 18/4/45
RK855	LF	FT-C	2/3/45	To 113 MU Treviso for 240 Hour Inspection 9/46
RR246	LF	PT-B	21/3/45	Shot down Flak (Flt Sgt Edwards POW) 14/4/45
SM176	LF	FT-N	21/3/45	Crash landed at Ravenna after Flak damage 11/4/45
SM446	LF	FT-V	9/3/45	
TB539	HF	TBB -BK	3/9/45	Ex 93 Squadron. Personal aircraft of Group Captains Beresford and Kingcombe when Commanding 324 Wing.
TB545	HF	FT-B	3/9/45	Ex 93 Squadron. In use until 5/47
TB546	HF	FT-E	3/9/45	Ex 93 Squadron. In use until 5/47
TB577	HF	FT-Y	3/9/45	Ex 93 Squadron. In use until 5/47
TB909	HF	FT-A	3/9/45	Ex 93 Squadron. In use until 5/47

GLOSTER METEOR F4 February 1949 – September 1950

Serial	Codes	Arr	Dep	To
RA425	SW-S	6/7/48	21/9/50	63 Sqn
RA437	SW-U	8/12/49	25/9/50	63 Sqn
RA489	SW-N	12/1/50	26/9/50	92 Sqn
VT103		20/6/49	24/6/49	1 Sqn
VT104	SW-W	7/4/48	26/9/50	92 Sqn
VT107	SW-Q	15/4/48	13/1/49	Glos
VT132	SW-P, Z	8/4/48	1/10/50	92 Sqn
VT134	SW-M	11/2/49	26/9/50	92 Sqn
VT238	SW-R	24/08/48	25/11/49	Cat 5 Flew into high ground with VT276 at Slindon, Sussex, (Plt II Arthur Venning Lancey killed).
VT242	SW-X	11/12/48	22/9/50	63 Sqn
VT245	SW-Y	23/12/48	26/9/50	92 Sqn
VT256	SW-P	20/9/48	20/09/50	63 Sqn
VT257	SW-T	21/12/48	19/12/49	Cat 5 Crashed on landing at Tangmere.
VT276	SW-N	11/2/49	25/11/49	Cat 5 Flew into high ground with VT238 at Slindon, Sussex, (Plt III Ronald Samuel Jefferies killed).
VT291	SW-R	19/5/50	3/10/50	92 Sqn

GLOSTER METEOR T7 February 1949 – October 1962

Serial	Codes	Arr	Dep	To
VW456	X	14/11/56	30/10/62	29 Sqn
VW488	SW-V	14/7/49	25/5/54	FR
WA733		7/6/61	1/9/61	AFDS
WH224	Z	10/8/62	18/10/62	Akrotiri Stn Flt

GLOSTER METEOR F8 September 1950 – September 1954

Serial	Codes	Arr	Dep	To
VZ440	SW-S, S	29/8/50	2/1/52	66 Sqn
VZ441	SW-T, T	29/8/50	2/9/54	38 MU
VZ451	SW-U, U	29/8/50	5/5/53	Glosters
VZ452	SW-O, O	6/11/50	25/1/54	Cat 4 Avro
VZ455	SW-K	7/9/50	17/5/51	66 Sqn
VZ456	SW-J	5/10/50	26/7/51	609 Sqn

VZ461	SW-W, W	29/08/50	22/10/52	Cat 5 Crashed in sea off Amble (Plt Off Maurice William Prior killed)
VZ463	SW-H	5/10/50	30/4/51	66 Sqn
VZ469	X	29/8/50	19/1/51	Cat 5 Crashed in sea off Leuchars (Fg Off Malcolm Frederick Danton killed)
VZ508		12/12/52	10/2/53	151 Sqn
"		8/5/54	27/9/54	29 MU
VZ513	SW-Y	29/8/50	15/3/54	FRL
VZ514	SW-Z, Z	29/8/50	19/8/54	Avro
VZ550		20/7/51	14/1/52	264 Sqn
WA756	F	12/1/51	30/6/53	32 MU
WA794	X	22/2/51	10/9/54	Avro
WA813	L	192/54	27/9/54	8 MU
WA839	SW-L, L	7/9/50	22/2/53	Cat 5 Crashed at night at Creich, Fife, (Plt Off W Gunnyeon killed)
WA841	SW-M, M	29/8/50	21/9/54	8 MU
WA844	SW-N, N	29/8/50	20/5/54	Cat 4 Avro
WA845	Q	29/8/50	19/4/51	1 Sqn
WA847	SW-P, P	29/8/50	22/6/54	38 MU
WA849	SW-R, R	29/8/50	10/9/54	222 Sqn
WA871	L, E	15/1/51	10/9/54	222 Sqn
WA880		25/1/56	03/2/56	222 Sqn
WA899	G	12/1/51	27/9/54	29 MU
WA907		17/9/52	19/9/52	APS Acklington
WA992	D	13/4/51	20/9/54	38 MU
WE897		6/11/53	24/7/54	Cat 5 M/A/C with WL114 1m NW of Leuchars, (Fg Off Hugh Johnstone Gourley killed)
WE925	H	8/4/54	10/9/54	34 Sqn
WH273		10/11/53	10/9/54	FCCS
WH293	Y	8/5/56	14/10/59	33 MU
WH403		29/12/53	10/9/54	12 Gp Com Flt
WH466	R	4/4/55	19/4/56	Cat 5 Soc
WH504	U	20/11/53	10/9/54	222 Sqn
WK814	PM	12/6/53	6/9/54	Leuchars Stn Flt
WK856		7/1/53	16/9/54	616 Sqn
WK859	J	12/12/52	10/9/54	19 Sqn
WK871	W	18/12/52	10/9/54	72 Sqn
WK873	H	18/12/52	28/9/53	Glosters
WK994	X	4/4/55	10/12/56	12 MU
WL113	L	17/9/59	20/12/60	5 MU
WL114		18/11/53	24/7/54	Cat 5 M/A/C with WE897 and abandoned 1m NW of Leuchars
WL120		6/11/53	10/9/54	72 Sqn

De HAVILLAND VAMPIRE T11 July 1954 – July 1959

Serial	Codes	Arr	Dep	To
WZ428		29/7/54	20/5/55	Marshalls
XD607		8/7/54	29/10/54	Cat 4R
XE888	Z	21/2/58	12/7/59	CAACU
XE897	Z	19/5/55	4/2/58	10MU

HAWKER HUNTER F1 July 1954 – November 1956

Serial	Codes	Arr	Dep	To
WT580	E	16/9/54	8/10/56	229 OCU
WT581	S	7/12/54	12/7/55	Crashed (Fg Off Alan MacKillop Watkinson killed)
WT582	B	11/8/54	18/11/56	FWS
WT583	D	17/9/54	11/9/56	DFLS
WT585	F	23/9/54	19/10/56	DFLS
WT587	N then C	28/9/54	9/10/56	229 OCU
WT588	P	15/7/54	14/9/56	DFLS
WT589		28/9/54	16/11/54	Crashed 7 miles east of Leuchars (Sgt R A Wilding ejected safely)
WT590		17/9/54	22/10/54	Crashed on approach
WT591	N	15/7/54	15/10/54	AFDS
WT592	O	15/7/54	13/8/54	5MU

WT594	U	21/12/54	28/2/56	DFLS
WT595	Q then H	4/10/54	21/8/56	DFLS
WT613	R	7/10/54	20/3/56	DFLS
WT618	O	28/9/54	4/4/56	DFLS
WT622	G	23/9/54	23/10/56	229 OCU
WT623	H	23/9/54	19/1/56	Crashed, Plt Off William Sutherland Carmichael killed
WT641	T	7/12/54	13/3/56	DFLS
WT644	C	8/12/54	14/6/55	Crashed, Plt Off John Stephen Murray killed
WT649	N	16/6/55	13/3/56	DFLS
WW599	A	29/7/54	17/4/56	Engine failure, crashed, (Fg Off J A H Anderson ejected safely)
WW641	Q	9/9/55	10/55	To code DFS
	DFS	10/55	28/2/56	DFLS
WW645	S	9/8/55	26/3/56	DFLS

HAWKER HUNTER F4 February 1956 – July 1958

Serial	Codes	Arr	Dep	To
WV314	N	14/10/57	18/3/58	5 MU
WV315	J	7/5/57	7/3/58	5 MU
WT719	E	19/10/56	14/11/57	Cat 3R
WT773		12/7/55	17/8/55	111 Sqn
WV323	G	1/2/57	5/3/58	5 MU
WV324	U	24/2/56	16/1/57	74 Sqn
WV333	A	24/2/56	15/2/57	Cat 3R
WV366	T	28/2/56	29/4/58	5 MU
WV378	H	19/12/56	5/3/58	5 MU
WV387	Q	24/2/56	10/1/57	67 Sqn
XE663	V	14/5/57	11/10/57	5 MU
XE702	B	12/10/56	16/10/58	5 MU
XE705	P	20/9/56	3/10/56	Multiple bird strike on take-off, ran into River Eden mud flats
XE706	P then A	12/10/56	23/4/58	5 MU
XE709	Q	4/1/57	18/4/58	5 MU
XE712	U	18/12/56	23/4/58	5 MU
XF299	O	6/3/56	6/4/58	5 MU
XF301	R then L	9/3/56	14/1/58	CWP North Weald then Leconfield then 229 OCU
XF302	S	9/3/56	17/3/58	19 MU
XF314	N	28/2/56	19/8/57	CWP North Weald then 229/RS-24
XF982	D	29/8/56	28/1/58	229 OCU
XF992	C	3/9/56	12/2/58	229 OCU
XF993	GAM	14/11/57	25/2/58	CWP North Weald then 229 OCU
XF997	F	3/9/56	28/6/57	Cat 4P/5C
XG341	H	13/8/56	10/12/56	Cat 3R/4R

HAWKER HUNTER F6 (First phase) November 1956 – December 1956

Serial	Codes	Arr	Dep	To
XG129	B	2/11/56	4/12/56	111 Sqn
XG170	C	2/11/56	3/12/56	111 Sqn
XG190	D	2/11/56	29/11/56	111 Sqn
XG194	E	2/11/56		

HAWKER HUNTER F6 (Second phase) January 1958 – July 1960

Serial	Codes	Arr	Dep	To
XE560	G	26/9/58	16/6/60	65 Sqn
XE561	D	24/1/58	9/6/60	19 Sqn
XE581	T	18/3/58	25/2/59	Hawker for FGA9
XE611	Q	8/10/59	29/2/60	CWP for FGA9 (Interim) conversion
XF424	O	15/2/58	25/2/59	Hawker for FGA9
XF434	C	31/1/58	9/4/60	Crashed. (Pilot Fg Off John Cleaver ejected safely)
XF435	P	15/2/58	29/2/60	CWP for FGA9 (Interim) conversion
XF437	F	15/2/58	27/6/60	111 Sqdn
XF439	B	7/3/58	17/6/60	19 Sqn
XF440	U	4/3/58	29/2/60	CWP for FGA9 (Interim) conversion
XF442	G	8/2/58	2/5/58	208 Sqn

XF451	S	7/3/58	17/6/60	65 Sqn
XF454	H	8/2/58	18/3/59	Hawker for FGA9
XF455	N	8/2/58	18/3/59	Hawker for FGA9
XF456	A	28/2/58	29/2/60	CWP for FGA9 (Interim) conversion
XF514	Q	12/3/58	18/9/59	Cat 4 and to Hawker
XF515	R	7/2/58	14/5/60	Cat 3R/103MU
XF526	(56/C)	4/3/60	1/4/60	Probably marked as 56/C
XG205	E	10/1/58	13/6/60	CWP for FGA9 (Interim) conversion

HAWKER HUNTER FGA9 May 1960 – December 1967

Serial	Codes	Arr	Dep	To
XE546	B	28/2/62	12/10/64	8/43 Sqn
XE550	C then X	16/11/61	28/12/67	8/43 not recoded), 19 MU
XE611	Q then J	7/10/63	21/1/66	8/43 Sqn
XE618	U	30/9/67	28/12/67	Kuwait
XE620	R	30/9/67	14/12/67	19 MU
XE623	H	26/6/63	11/8/64	(8/43 not recorded) Crashed, pilot ejected safely
XE655	L	28/12/63	12/10/64	8/43 Sqn
XF431	D then Q	17/6/60	1/12/67	8 Sqn
XF445	R then Q	27/7/60	27/10/64	8/43 Sqn
XF456	A then P	8/4/60	4/3/65	8/43 Sqn
XG136	G	6/5/63	17/4/64	Crashed (Fg Off Martin Stewart Herring killed)
XG154	B	17/6/60	1/12/67	8 Sqn
XG156	F then O	28/6/60	24/11/61	FCMC then 54 Sqn
XG237	C	17/6/60	9/12/61	Coded 'WC' in 9/60, 19 MU
XG255	S	1/7/60	12/1/62	5 MU
XG256	G	1/7/60	1/12/67	208 Sqn
XG261	H	22/7/60	28/11/60	1 Sqn
XG272		15/1/62	1/7/62	20 Sqn
XG292	H	28/2/62	11/8/64	(8/43 not recorded) UK
XG293		16/3/62	1/9/62	20 Sqn
XG296	A then B	16/12/61	10/12/67	8/43 Sqn
XG298	E	5/12/61	28/1/64	208 Sqn
XJ645	N	30/9/67	10/12/67	19 MU
XJ646	P	30/9/67	29/11/67	19 MU
XJ680	E	30/9/67	14/11/67	19 MU
XJ683	L	15/1/62	11/7/63	To UK but Cat 3R 12/7/63 on delivery, to Hawker
XJ684	D	16/12/61	1/11/64	(8/43 not recorded) 19 MU
XJ685		16/3/62	1/7/62	20 Sqn
XJ686		12/62	1/9/62	20 Sqn
XJ692	K then T	1/2/62	1/12/67	8 Sqn
XK137	P	16/11/61	29/63	Cat 4R Hawker

HAWKER HUNTER FGA9 (combined 8 & 43 Squadrons) July 1964 – August 1967

Serial	Codes	Arr	Dep	To
XE530	O	20/2/65	29/1/68	To HSA Cat 4
XE546	B	1/6/64	7/8/67	To 43 Sqn
XE550	C then X	1/6/64	7/8/67	To 43 Sqn
XE552		6/11/64	13/2/67	To 19 MU at St Athan
XE592	F	1/6/64	6/10/64	Crashed - Fg Off Ian Stephens killed
XE609	A	1/6/64	26/06/65	To 19 MU at St Athan
XE611	J	1/6/64	7/8/67	To 8 Sqn
XE618	D	1/6/64	3/11/64	To 19 MU at St Athan
XE620	B	1/6/64	7/8/67	To 43 Sqn
XE623	H	1/6/64	10/8/64	Crashed (pilot Fg Off Ronald Burrows OK)
XE645		25/2/66		
XE649		14/12/64	20/10/66	To 19 MU at St Athan
XE654		28/3/67		
XE655	L	1/6/64	11/6/66	
XF376	K	1/6/64	7/8/67	To 8 Sqn
XF388		8/11/64	18/7/67	To 19 MU at St Athan
XF421	C	1/6/64	17/1/65	From and to 8 Sqn
XF431		25/2/66	7/8/67	To 8 Sqn

XF435	J then H	1/6/64	7/8/67	To 8 Sqn
XF440	L	1/6/64	7/8/67	To 8 Sqn
XF445	Q	1/6/64	7/8/67	To 43 Sqn
XF454		6/8/64	7/8/67	
XF456	P	1/6/64	7/8/67	To 43 Sqn
XG135		6/8/64	6/9/66	To 5 MU at Kemble
XG154	E	1/6/64	7/8/67	To 8 Sqn
XG169	K then B	26/9/66	7/8-67	To 19 MU at St Athan
XG205		31/8/64	26/10/66	To 19 MU at St Athan
XG237	M	1/6/64	8/12/65	To 19 MU at St Athan
XG255		2/2/65	7/8/67	To 43 Sqn
XG256	H	1/6/64	7/8/67	To 8 Sqn
XG261		31/8/64	2/9/66	To 19 MU at St Athan for
XG292	H	1/6/64	6/8/64	To UK
XG296	A then B	1/6/64	7/8/67	To 43 Sqn
XG298		4/6/65	7/8/67	To 43 Sqn
XJ632	C	14/12/64	18/4/67	To 19 MU at St Athan
XJ645		2/2/66	7/8/67	To 43 Sqn
XJ646		13/10/65	7/8/67	To 43 Sqn
XJ680	F then E	1/6/64	7/8/67	To 43 Sqn
XJ684	D	1/6/64	28/7/67	To 19 MU at St Athan
XJ687		23/11/66	7/8/67	To 8 Sqn
XJ688		6/11/65	7/8/67	To 8 Sqn
XJ689	B	9/1/65	7/8/67	To 8 Sqn
XJ692	K	1/6/64	7/8/67	To 8 Sqn
XK150		17/4/67		
XK151		17/4/67	7/8/67	To 8 Sqn

HAWKER HUNTER T7 (including pooled aircraft) March 1959 – November 1967

Serial	Codes	Arr	Dep	Notes
XF321	T then Z	9/8/65	30/9/67	Used by 1417 Flt and 8/43 Sqns
XL565	T then X	26/4/66		8/43 Sqns
XL566	T then W	15/12/59	29/4/67	
XL611	T	12/3/59	9/11/59	Cat 5P/4R to A&AEE
XL612	X then Y	26/8/63	27/9/67	
XL613		29/10/63	28/10/65	
XL623		30/8/60	24/9/60	1 Sqn

McDONNELL DOUGLAS PHANTOM FG1 September 1969 – July 1989

Serial	Code	Arr	Dep	To
XT860	L, AL	8/78	20/4/88	Crashed into North Sea 23m east of Leuchars (Flt Lts Philip Clarke and Kevin Poysden killed)
XT861	C	1/8/72	7/9/87	Crashed near Leuchars
XT863	AS	6/88	2/89	bdr Abingdon
XT866	O	2/79	9/7/81	Crashed on app to Leuchars - both crew ejected safely
XT873	S	3/75	4/78	111 Sqn, rtp 4/92 Adams Scrapyard, Glasgow
XT874	J	6/6/69	3/79	111 Sqn
XT875	K, AK	4/11/69	7/89	111 Sqn
XV571	A	17/6/69	31/7/89	soc, rtp 4/92 Adams Scrapyard, Glasgow
XV572	N, AN	9/72	7/89	111 Sqn, rtp 4/92 Adams Scrapyard, Glasgow
XV573	L	11/70	6/78	111 Sqn, rtp 4/92 Adams Scrapyard, Glasgow
XV574	B	15/9/69	3/82	111 Sqn
XV575	C	26/6/69	9/78	111 Sqn
"	S	8/80	7/88	soc 9/91
XV576	D, AD	28/8/69	31/7/89	soc 9/91
XV577	M, AM	10/75	31/7/89	To 9065M bdr
XV578	O	12/71	9/78	111 Sqn
XV579	R, AR	15/9/73	31/7/89	rtp 4/92 Adams Scrapyard, Glasgow
XV580	Q	3/72	18/9/75	Crashed nr Kirriemuir after loss of control. Both crew ejected.
XV581	E, AE	30/10/69	31/7/89	To 9070M

XV582	F, AF	8/7/69	31/7/89	24 Feb 1988 Land's End/John O'Groats record 46.44 mins Wg Cdr John Brady & Flt Lt Mike Pugh First Phantom to exceed 5000 hours 111 Sqn
XV583	G	8/8/69	11/85	111 Sqn
XV584	I	9/70	12/78	111 Sqn
XV585	H, P, AP	28/8/69	31/7/89	
XV586	J, AJ	9/83	31/7/89	soc 9/91
XV587	G, AG	7/12/78	1/89	111 Sqn
XV590	X, AX	11/12/78	31/7/89	rtp 4/92 Adams Scrapyard, Glasgow

McDONNELL DOUGLAS PHANTOM FGR2 May 1988 – July 1989

XV406	AV	6/88		wfu Carlisle
XV470	AW	6/88	31/7/89	56 Sqn 'BD'
XV489	AU	5/88		First FGR2 to be operated

PANAVIA TORNADO F3 September 1989 – July 2009

The fluid nature of the F3 force makes it difficult to provide exact details of every airframe allocated to the Squadron but the following are known to have been with 43 at some time. Those marked with an asterisk (*) were the initial allocation in 1989/90 and those marked § were with the Squadron in July 2009.

Serial	Code	Arr	Dep	Notes
ZE154	GI	8/95		
ZE156		11/92		
"	UX	14/1/03		
"	GA	7/04		
ZE157	GK	4/99		
ZE159	UV	6/02		
ZE161*	GI	26/7/90		
"	GR	10/00		
"	UU	3/02		
"	GB	1/05		
ZE163§	TW	5/02		
ZE164	UQ	6/03		
"	GD	1/05		
ZE165	UP	5/02		
"	GE	10/04		
ZE199	FL	2/00		
ZE200	UM	5/03		
ZE201	GA	7/97		
ZE203*	GD	13/8/90		
"	GA	1/07		
ZE204*	GJ	7/90		
"	UJ	3/02		
ZE206*	GG	1/90		
"	GL	7/97		
"	UI	1/02		
ZE207	GC	6/91		
"	GC	1/05		
ZE209	AX	1/02		
ZE210*	GL	7/90		25 Sqn
"	GD		7/96	wfu Cat 5
ZE251	GA	2/97	11/98	25 Sqn
ZE254	GE	1/96		
"	AW	5/00		
ZE255	UC	2/02		
"	GC	3/06		
ZE257	UB	2/02		
"	GI	4/05		
ZE258	GA	6/91		
ZE288	GG	8/91		
"	VY	4/03		
ZE289	GB	6/00		
"	VX	3/02		
ZE291	GQ	12/92		
ZE293	GZ	7/04		
ZE294	YX	4/02		
ZE295	YW	6/00		
ZE296	AZ	12/92		
"	GR	3/93		
ZE338	YV	10/03		
" §	GJ	4/05		
ZE341§	GO	1/08		
ZE342		18/6/92		111 Sqn
"		24/4/00		
ZE728		7/97	11/97	111 Sqn
ZE730	GL	9/92		
ZE731	GK	9/92	2/96	
"	GF	2/96		
" §	GP	5/05		
ZE732	GI	9/92		
ZE733	GE	8/91	30/10/95	crashed
ZE734	GB	10/93		
ZE736	AX	5/00		
ZE737	YM	1/04		
"	GK	3/06		
ZE755	GB	6/91	9/93	
"	GJ	1/9/94		
ZE757	GF	6/91	4/93	
"	GA	10/93	9/94	
"	GF	9/94	2/96	
"	GK	2/96		
"		3/97		
ZE758	GO	10/98		
ZE760	AP	8/92		
ZE762	GM	4/93		
"	YD	6/02		
ZE780	GL	4/99		
ZE788	YA	11/03		
"	GL	11/04		
ZE790	GD	2/96		
ZE791	XY	6/01		
ZE792	GJ	3/92	7/94	

ZE793	TE	5/02		
ZE794	A4	6/92		
ZE797	GI	4/99		
"		10/03		
ZE808	GF	9/90	6/91	
ZE810		6/94		111 Sqn
"	XU	8/03		
" §	GG			
ZE812	XR	4/02		
ZE830	GD	6/91	11/95	111 Sqn
ZE831	GG	10/93		
ZE834	GM	2/96		
"	XO	3/03		
ZE837	GH	9/91		
"	GI	7/95		
ZE838	GH	7/92		
"	XL	7/02		
" §	GH	9/04		
ZE858	A5	5/92		
"	GO	9/92	21/10/93 Crashed near A66, Co Durham	
ZE864	GN	2/00		
ZE865	GM	4/00		
ZE887	GE	1/90	12/90	
" §	GF	5/08	7/09	111 Sq,
"			4/3/10 Final flight. To RAF Museum, Hendon	
ZE889	XI	1/02		
ZE907		6/94		25 Sqn
"	GL	5/98		
ZE911	GA	7/95		
ZE936*	GK	4/90		
ZE941	GI	3/97	10/98	25 Sqn
"	KT	5/05		
ZE942*	GH	3/90		
ZE961*	GA	9/89	6/91	
" §	FO		25 Sqn markings	
ZE962*	GB	9/89		
ZE963*	GC	9/89		
"	GE	7/97		

ZE964*	GD	10/89	8/90	111 Sqn
"	GN	3/01		
ZE965		1/90	7/90	111 Sqn
"	GM	4/9/97		
ZE966*	GF	1/90		Gulf
ZE967		1/90		
ZE968	GV	12/97		
"	GN	3/98		
"	DM	5/01		
ZE983	WY	7/02		
ZG751	WP	1/02		
ZG755	GM	11/91		
"	GL	5/06		
ZG757		1/99		
"	WM	11/03		
"	GN	11/04		
ZG772	GS	5/05		
ZG774	GN	4/92		
" §	GV		RAF 90th markings on fin	
ZG778	WG	8/03		
ZG780	GL	1/99		
ZG797	GI	11/98		
"	GF spl c/s	1/06		
ZG798	WA	1/03		
"	GF	6/04		
"	GQ	1/05		
ZH554	GJ	3/93		
ZH556	OT	4/03		
ZH558	GF	5/93	7/7/94	Crashed into sea off Cyprus (Flt Lts Nigel Orme and Stuart John MacDonald Walker killed)
ZH559	MT	9/03		
"	GT	1/05		

The following 18 Tornados were operated by the combined 43 and 29 Squadrons in the Gulf 1990/1991.

ZE158, ZE159, ZE160, ZE168, ZE200, ZE203, ZE764, ZE887, ZE907, ZE908, ZE934, ZE961, ZE962, ZE966, ZE968, ZE969, ZE982, ZE983

AIRCRAFT OTHER THAN NORMAL SQUADRON EQUIPMENT

BE 2c	2771	In use June 1916
BE 2e	7170	In use June 1916
AW FK 3	5526	In use August 1916
BE 12	6648	In use November 1916
Bristol Scout	1745, 4665, 4683, 7041, 7043, 7054	All in use November 1916
Avro 504K	H3105, H5199, H8938	In use 1925
Avro 504N	J8498	In use 1926
Grebe	J7585	In use 1927
Grebe (dual)	J7532	In use 1927
Hart	K6469	In use 1936
Demon	K3774	In use 1937/38 for night-flying training
Demon	K3981	In use 1937/39 for night-flying training
Battle (dual)	L7693	In 2/39. Out on 15/11/39
Magister	P6359, P6360	In use 1939 and early 1940
Magister	P6421	In use late 1940
Magister	P2436	In use at Drem, 1/41
Magister	V1101	In use at Acklington during 1942
Harvard	EZ357	In use at Zeltweg, 1946 and later in Italy in 1947
Bucher 131	Flown from Hungary by two escaping pupil-pilots in April 1945. Taken to Udine when Squadron moved there on 8 May 1945. Crashed in field halfway to Klagenfurt when Squadron moved to that place a few days later.	

Appendix 7

SQUADRON AFFILIATIONS

1. The City of Chichester

Since 1937 No 43 Squadron has been linked with the City of Chichester. This had its beginnings in an Air Ministry scheme for improving relations between RAF Squadrons and Stations and the local population. (No 1 Squadron, also at Tangmere, was linked to Brighton at this time.) The Squadron has benefited on many occasions from the generosity of the City Council and people of Chichester and although 43 have been at Tangmere for only four years since the link began the mutual interest remains.

2. 'China-British' and 'Belgian Congo'

The 'Wings for Victory' campaign, part of the War Savings movement, made it possible from 1941 onwards for individuals or communities to pay for aeroplanes and these machines were then inscribed with the name of the donors. Following a generous contribution from Hong Kong No 43 Squadron was designated 'China-British' in 1941. However in 1942 the Belgian Congo provided sufficient money to equip a squadron. As at this time Sqn Ldr du Vivier was the sole Belgian commanding a Royal Air Force Squadron it was decided to make 43 the Belgian Congo squadron and the 'China-British' title was therefore assigned to No 247 Squadron. Aircraft carrying the names of towns and individual persons in the Belgian Congo were in use at Tangmere in the summer of 1942.

3. 43 (Fighter) Squadron Association

As the Second World War came to a close, 43 Squadron found itself at Klagenfurt in Austria. Before its personnel dispersed, having experienced the Battle of Britain and five invasions together, Flight Sergeant Jimmy Beedle was instrumental in ensuring that the spirit and comradeship that had built up between all its members - officers and non commissioned personnel alike - should not be lost. The 43(F) Squadron (Fighting Cocks) Association he formed remains a thriving example of loyalty to an elite fighter squadron. Membership details and further information may be obtained from the secretary at www.43squadron-association.com

4. The City of Stirling

Stirling was granted city status in 2002 and the Freedom of the City is the greatest civic honour that the City Council can confer. Previously, all such awards had been for the Freedom of the Burgh. In 2005 the Council conferred its first grant of the Freedom of the City to 43 (Fighter) Squadron in recognition of its long friendship and links with Stirling since the Squadron's formation near Falleninch Farm beneath Stirling Castle in April 1916. Granting the Freedom of a City to a squadron, rather than to a station, is an extremely rare honour and one of which 43 Squadron is extremely proud.

Appendix 8

OPERATION QUICKFIRE - CYPRUS 1958

In the first and second editions of this history, nothing of any great detail regarding Operation QUICKFIRE was recorded other than it being a reinforcement exercise. However at the time it was an operation of particular relevance both to 43 Squadron and to Britain's foreign policy. To preserve the original text as far as possible, details provided by the then commanding officer, Air Commodore (then Squadron Leader) J F Langer CBE AFC DL have been added here as an appendix to this third edition of the Squadron's history.

On 1 May 1958 the squadron was put on standby to reinforce Cyprus as part of Operation QUICKFIRE following the American intervention into the Lebanon to prevent Palestinian attacks against Israel. In addition, King Hussein of Jordan, our staunchest ally in the Near East, was under serious threat from Syria and Egypt as well as from within his own Kingdom. Great Britain had a long-standing obligation to support King Hussein and had already despatched a large detachment of the 16th Parachute Regiment to the country and 66(F) Squadron had also been sent out to RAF Nicosia to reinforce 208, the resident Hunter Squadron. Standby required that 43 be prepared to fly out to Cyprus with 12 aircraft within 72 hours notice with a back-up of spares and equipment to last for up to three months. All leave, except compassionate, was cancelled.

May and June passed without the squadron being called and everyone was getting cheesed off because we were due to hand over the standby commitment to 74(F) 'Tiger' Squadron on 17 July. However, two days before that day arrived, HQ Fighter Command telephoned me – in a panic – and asked if we could be ready to fly out on the 16th. My answer was an emphatic 'of course'. Apparently, 74 Squadron had made a complete nonsense of preparing for standby, having only six serviceable aircraft, and had yet to prepare the back-up equipment.

The reason for the panic soon became apparent. Hussein's uncle, King Faisal of Egypt, had just been assassinated, so the threat level had escalated and the British Task Force Commander had requested the standby squadron as a matter of urgency. When I broke the news to the squadron it was greeted with loud cheers.

Thanks to much burning of the midnight oil and the heroic efforts of Captain Al Wegman USAF, our exchange engineering officer and pilot, and of Warrant Officer Simpson and his technicians, the squadron was ready to fly out on 16 July. However, HQ Fighter Command rang to say that the Mistral was blowing up a storm in southern France and that our second refuelling stop, the French Air Force base at Orange Caritat, was out of commission but should clear the following day. Then, unbelievably, they ordered that we were to leave behind two Hunters and two pilots with formation aerobatic experience, to enable 111 Squadron to loop 22 Hunters, in order to beat the record of the Pakistan Air Force which had looped 16 aircraft. What some people would do to get into the Guinness Book of Records!

Aware of the urgency of the reinforcements I studied the possibility of flying out in one day with my flight commanders, John Howe and 'Bodger' Edwards. We decided that by fitting drop tanks it would just be possible to cut out the refuelling stops at Duxford, Gibraltar and El Adem, leaving only two stops – at Orange and Malta, with each leg being approximately two hours. OC Flying Wing vetoed this proposal as we would exceed the daily flying hours limit but, thankfully, the station commander over-ruled him on the grounds that those limits did not apply to transit flights.

The flight to Cyprus went without incident despite the best efforts of the French. Firstly their National Air Traffic Control Service was on strike and refusing to speak English, the ICAO international language. Secondly, the FAF at Orange had swept the runway but not the taxi-ways which were covered with potential FOD, and thirdly they had only one serviceable petrol bowser so refuelling of our aircraft took ages.

After a very late lunch at Malta we arrived overhead Nicosia in impeccable close formation. Upon landing I was climbing down from my aircraft feeling pretty pleased with myself and very proud of my boys, when I was approached by the station commander who greeted me with the immortal words: "I have had enough of you fighter boys and if I have any problems with your lot you will be on the next flight home!" – and promptly stomped off. Not exactly the warmest of welcomes but then Peter Bairsto arrived, with cold beers all round, along with the

OC Flying Wing, P L 'Polly' Parrott DFC & Bar. Peter Parrott had commanded the Fighting Cocks in Italy during WW2.

The squadron was given two days to settle in and I was briefed by Wing Commander Peter Ellis, the Task Force Commander (Air), that our role would be to deploy to Amman airport to provide close air support should the balloon go up. To this end he and I flew to Amman to inspect the facilities which would be available to us at the Royal Jordanian Air Force enclave at the airport. We also liaised with the Parachute Brigade GLO and with an old friend, Wing Commander Jock Dalgleish, who was Air Advisor to the King. In the meantime we would be sharing with 66 and 208 Squadrons the task of keeping armed aircraft on standby to scramble and also to fly on standing patrols to detect and deal with any possible intruders seeking to take advantage of Cyprus's lack of low-looking radar. Any surplus aircraft could be used on army co-operation exercises and for continuation training.

We were briefed to be on readiness from dawn to dusk each day, which, in Cyprus at that time, meant a 14-hour day. Following the arrival of our two missing Hunters we never had less than nine aircraft on line daily thanks to the magnificent efforts of our servicing personnel and before long we were flying more hours than the other two squadrons put together. Thanks to having two engineering officers we were able to use a two shift system of eight hours each. When one shift was on, the other was confined to camp because of the local EOKA terrorist threat but we were able to take advantage of the station's many sports facilities whereas the morning shift was able to deplete the bar stocks of various messes.

About six weeks after our arrival the Syrian army withdrew from its borders with Jordan – obviously they had heard that the Fighting Cocks were spoiling for a fight and had re-thought their position! This resulted in a reduction in the assessment of the threat and of the standby commitments so the RAF squadrons could take it in turn to have the occasional day off. I persuaded Polly Parrott that the pilots badly needed to practise dinghy drill in the sea and he authorised several journeys to Kyrenia on the north coast, in a three-ton truck, plus armed escort provided by the RAF Regiment, to keep everyone safe from terrorists.

We made the most of these trips by visiting Saint Hilarion, a castle built by the Crusaders, Bellapais Abbey and Kyrenia castle. Having done the cultural bit we would then swim in the sea from 'the slab' at the bottom of the castle and re-acquaint ourselves, none too seriously, with our dinghies. This would be followed by lunch at the Harbour Club before visiting Clito's Wine Cellars where, after much tasting, we would buy two large casks of wine, one for the pilots, the other for the ground crews. Soon afterwards, Colonel Grivas, the EOKA leader, fled the country and the curfew was lifted, so I celebrated by treating all the squadron pilots to lunch at the Hotel Berengaria, situated 6,000 feet up near the summit of the Troodos Mountains, from where the views in every direction are marvellous.

Eventually we were told that we would be returning home at the end of September. On the 27th we flew eleven aircraft in close formation over Air HQ at RAF Akrotiri and RAF Nicosia, as well as over Kyrenia, to bid farewell to the Harbour Club. The next day we hosted a drinks party in the Ladies Room to which our many friends were invited but not the station commander or any of his admin staff, who had been unhelpful and inefficient. When all the guests had gone we stayed to finish such drink as was left over and someone invented an A versus B Flight game whereby each pilot in turn would attempt to throw an empty beer can up and down through a ceiling fan without it being hit by the rotating blades. Needless to say most cans were hit and sent flying to the four corners of the room, hitting the walls, landing on the furniture and cracking the glass of one of the pictures and narrowly missing people's heads. It was hilarious but, despite our efforts to clean and tidy up, the following morning I was accosted by a furious PMC with the estimated cost for redecoration and repair which I had to pay before we would be allowed to fly home. Masterfully, I wrote out a cheque without quibbling. When John Howe found out he went round all the pilots and collected slightly more than I had paid out. In fact, it was the only time I made a profit out of an episode of squadron misdemeanour.

The flight home, the easy way with a night stop on Malta, was uneventful and rather boring. On arrival in Scotland we flew a twelve aircraft formation over Leuchars where, on landing, it seemed that the whole station was on the airfield to welcome us back. A fitting end to what had been a very worthwhile reinforcement exercise, albeit that our hopes of seeing some action were not realised.

The lesser assessment of the threat to King Hussein proved somewhat premature. Shortly after we had returned to Leuchars, the King decided to fly to Paris to visit his mother. In due course the flight-plan, which involved flying through Syrian airspace, was filed and approved. So the King, with Jock Dalgleish as co-pilot, set off in the Royal Flight de Havilland Dove, but when well into Syrian skies he was ordered to land at Damascus Airport. When he refused, the aircraft was attacked by two fighter aircraft. Jock, a very experienced fighter pilot, took control and dived to ground level where he managed to evade every subsequent attack until safely back across the Jordanian border. It subsequently transpired that a group of fanatical Muslim Jordanian dissidents had been waiting at Damascus Airport with the intention of lynching the King, who was in his early twenties at that time. He always swore that despite countless further attempts, that was the closest he had ever been to death.

Squadron Leader John Langer briefs his pilots Topping, Scott and Thornton

Appendix 9

GLOSSARY OF TERMS

AA	Anti-aircraft
AAR	Air-to-Air Refuelling
a/c	aircraft
AC2	Aircraftman second class
ACMI	Air Combat Manoeuvring Instrumentation
2AD	2nd Air Depot
ADC	Aide-de-Camp
ADGB	Air Defence of Great Britain
AFDS	Air Fighting Develoment Squadron
AI	Air Intercept
AM	Air Ministry
AM	Air Mechanic
AMRAAM	Advanced Medium Range Air-to-Air Missile (AIM-120)
AOC	Air Officer Commanding
APC	Armament Practice Camp
APS	Armament Practice Station
Archie	Anti-aircraft fire
ARS	Aircraft Repair Station
A-S	Armstrong-Siddeley
ASI	Air speed indicator
ASRAAM	Advanced Short Range Air-to-Air Missile (AIM-132)
ATLC	Advanced Tactical Leadership Course
BAFF	British Air Forces in France
BDR	Battle damage repair
BEF	British Expeditionary Force
CAP	Combat Air Patrol
CCS	Casualty Clearing Station
CFS	Central Flying School
C-in-C	Commander in Chief
CO	Commanding Officer
COD	Carrier Onboard Delivery (a/c rôle)
CofG	Centre of Gravity
comms	communications
CRS	Control and Reporting School
CRU	Civilian Repair Unit
CSM	Company Sergeant Major
CWP	Civilian Working Party
DACT	Dissimilar Air Combat Training
DAF	Desert Air Force
DFC	Distinguished Flying Cross
DFLS	Day Fighter Leaders School
DFM	Distinguished Flying Medal
DH	De Havilland
DSO	Distinguished Service Order
e/a	enemy aircraft
ECM	Electronic Counter Measures
EXO	(Sqn) Executive Officer
FAA	Fleet Air Arm
FC	Fighter Command
FCCS	Fighter Command Communications Sqn
FF	Free French
FOB	Forward Operating Base
FOD	Foreign object damage
FRC	Flight Reference Cards
FTS	Flying Training School
FWS	Fighter Weapons School
GCI	Ground Control Intercept
GLO	Ground Liaison Officer
GOC	General Officer Commanding
HAD	Home Aircraft Depot
HAS	Hardened Aircraft Shelter
HE	High Explosive
hrs	Hours
HQ	Headquarters
IAF	Interceptor Alert Force
IAS	Indicated air speed
INS	Inertial Navigation System
JEngO	Junior Engineering Officer
JG	Jagdgeschwader (Single engine ftr sqn)
KG	Kampfgeschwader (Bomber sqn)
LAC	Leading Aircraftman
LG	Landing Ground
LG	Lehrgeschwader (Trials Unit)
LLOL	Low level over land (practice interception)
LST	Landing Ship Tanks
M/A/C	Mid-air collision
Maxeval	Maximum evaluation
MC	Military Cross
MEZ	Missile Engagment Zone
Mineval	Mini evaluation (Station-run)
MPC	Missile Practice Camp
mph	Miles per hour
MRCA	Multi Role Combat Aircraft
MT	Motor Transport
MTB	Motor Torpedo Boat
MU	Maintenance Unit
NAAFI	Navy, Army and Air Force Institute
NATINADS	NATO Integrated Air Defence System
NBC	Nuclear/Biological/Chemical
NOTAM	Notice to Airmen
NRL	Nav/Radar Leader
OP	Offensive Patrol
Ops	Operations
OTE	Operational Tour Expired
OTU	Operational Training Unit
PAR	Precision Approach Radar
PBF	Personnel Briefing Facility
PI	Practice Interception
POW	Prisoner of war
PRU	Photographic Reconnaissance Unit
PSP	Pierced Steel Planking
OCU	Operational Conversion Unit
QFI	Qualified Flying Instructor
Opeval	Operational evaluation
QRA	Quick Reaction Alert
QWI	Qualified Weapons Instructor
RFC	Royal Flying Corps
RHAG	Rotary Hydraulic Arrester Gear
RNAS	Royal Naval Air Service
RSS/U	Repair and servicing section/unit
rtp	Reduce to produce (scrap and salvage)
SAAF	South African Air Force
SAR	Search and Rescue
SEngO	Senior Engineering Officer
SHQ	Station Headquarters
soc	Struck off charge
Tacan	Tactical Air Navigation System
Taceval	Tactical Evaluation
TM	Trade Manager
TOC	Taken on charge
TLT	Tactical Leadership Training
u/c	Undercarriage
u/s	Unserviceable
UKADR	UK Air Defence Region
VAS	Visiting Aircraft Section
VC	Victoria Cross
WAAF	Women's Auxiliary Air Force
wef	With effect from
wfu	Withdrawn from use
WSO	Weapons Systems Officer
WT	Wireless Telegraphy
ZG	Zerstörergeschwader (Twin engine ftr sqn)

Index – General

Index – People